GUIN

C000053102

SOCCER

WHO'S WHO

Jack Rollin

Cover design: Ad Vantage Studios

©Jack Rollin and Guinness Publishing Ltd, 1984, 1986, 1989, 1990, 1991

First Published in 1984
Second edition 1986
Third edition 1989
Fourth edition 1990

Published in Great Britain by Guinness Publishing Ltd,
33 London Road, Enfield, Middlesex

Typeset in Monotype Times Roman by BPCC Whitefriars
Printed and bound in Great Britain by
BPCC Hazell Books
Aylesbury, Bucks, England
Member of BPCC Ltd

'Guinness' is a registered trade mark of Guinness Publishing Ltd

British Library Cataloguing in Publication Data

Rollin, Jack, 1932–
    Guinness soccer who's who. – 5th ed.
    1. Great Britain. Association Football – biographies.
    Collections
    1. Guinness Who's Who in Soccer
    796.3340922

    ISBN 0-85112-965-x

THE AUTHOR

Jack Rollin was born in London in 1932 and educated at King's, Harrow. There he played soccer, while later at Westcliff-on-Sea High School it was rugby. Within ten days of joining the Royal Air Force he was playing in a Welsh Cup tie for RAF Bridgnorth and in the services he learned shorthand and typing, resuming his career in journalism and covering the 1954 World Cup in Switzerland in a freelance capacity.

In 1958 an ankle injury ended his own career during which, at the age of 14, he had been offered a trial with the United States club Chicago Maroons. He wisely declined a one-off re-appearance in 1971 against the European Cup finalists Panathinaikos of Greece.

For ten years Jack Rollin was Editor of the weekly magazine *Soccer Star* and its companion monthly *World Soccer* before becoming a freelance again in 1970. Since then he has researched football for BBC Television, acted as an assistant to commentators on 'Match of the Day', spoken on radio and appeared on television programmes. He has contributed to *What's on in London* and *Radio Times* and in 1975 he won the Designers and Art Directors Association Silver Award for *Radio Times World Cup Special* for the most outstanding specialist feature of the year.

In 1972 he became one of the compilers of the *Rothmans Football Yearbook* and later became its Editor. He has provided advice on the football sections of the *Encyclopaedia Britannica* and *Guinness Book of Records*. He is a football columnist for the *Sunday Telegraph*.

Jack Rollin contributed to three part-works: *The Game* (8 vols. 1970); *Book of Football* (6 vols. 1972) and *Football Handbook* (1979–80). His articles have appeared in programmes for matches at Wembley Stadium since 1963. He has produced handbooks which include *World Soccer Digest* 1961, 1962 and 1963 and *World Cup Digest* 1966.

In 1978 he carried out the international research for the BBC Television Series 'The Game of the Century' and produced the first edition of *The Guinness Book of Soccer Facts and Feats*.

Other books he has written: *England's World Cup Triumph* (1966), *A Source Book of Football* (1971), *The History of Aldershot Football Club* (1975), *World Cup Guide* (1982), *Soccer at War 1939–45* (1985), *Soccer: The Records* (1985), *Soccer: Records, Facts and Champions* (1988), *Soccer Shorts* (1988) and *More Soccer Shorts* (1991), *The World Cup 1930—1990* (1990), *The Football Fact Book* (1990). In 1974 he contributed the South American section for John Moynihan's *Football Fever*.

The author is married to June and has a daughter Glenda.

FOREWORD

I am delighted to welcome the fifth edition of the *Guinness Soccer Who's Who* by Jack Rollin. It is certainly on a par with all the quality reference books in the Guinness library and will prove an invaluable help to all administrators, managers, soccer writers and supporters of football throughout the United Kingdom.

It is a difficult task to keep abreast of the changing face of personnel at clubs and Jack Rollin is to be congratulated on achieving this task successfully. There are precise details of professional players in England, Wales and Scotland which can be found by quick and easy alphabetical reference and it provides all the information necessary for a football fact-finder.

The book will occupy a prominent place on my desk and I do not hesitate to recommend it.

Gordon Taylor

Gordon Taylor,
Chief Executive, The Professional Footballers' Association

Front cover, from top left:
Paul Gascoigne (Tottenham Hotspur), Peter Reid (Manchester City), Ross McLaren (Swindon Town), Paul Parker (Queen's Park Rangers), Andy Townsend (Chelsea), Mark Hughes (Manchester United), Hans Gillhaus (Aberdeen) and Paul Simpson (Oxford United).

INTRODUCTION

This book features the statistical League careers of all players who made Barclays League appearances during the 1990–91 season as well as those in the Scottish Premier Division and Airdrieonians and Falkirk the promoted teams from the First Division.

Club names in italics indicate temporary transfers where they have not become permanent moves in the same season. Italic figures refer to Lincoln City and Darlington in the GM Vauxhall Conference. All appearances include those as substitute.

The Editor would like to thank Alan Elliott for providing details of Scottish League players and also acknowledge the co-operation and assistance of the Football League in the compilation of this book and in particular Mike Foster, Sheila Murphy and Debbie Birch.

Bibliography: *Rothmans Football Yearbook*

Also published by Guinness:
More Soccer Shorts
The Football Fact Book
The World Cup 1930–1990
Guinness Book of Records

ABBOTT, Greg

Born Coventry 14.12.63.   Ht 5 9
Wt 10 07
Midfield. From Apprentice.

Season	Club	App	Goals
1981–82	Coventry C	—	—
1982–83	Bradford C	11	—
1983–84		35	3
1984–85		42	6
1985–86		39	10
1986–87		33	7
1987–88		32	5
1988–89		28	4
1989–90		35	3
1990–91		26	—

ABEL, Graham

Born Runcorn 17.9.60.   Ht 6 2   Wt 13 00
Defender. From Northwich V and
Runcorn.

Season	Club	App	Goals
1985–86	Chester C	23	2
1986–87		41	1
1987–88		45	2
1988–89		40	3
1989–90		41	7
1990–91		29	4

ABLETT, Gary

Born Liverpool 19.11.65   Ht 6 0
Wt 11 04
Defender. From Apprentice. England B,
Under-21.

Season	Club	App	Goals
1983–84	Liverpool	—	—
1984–85		—	—
1984–85	*Derby Co*	6	—
1985–86	Liverpool	—	—
1986–87	*Hull C*	5	—
1986–87	Liverpool	5	1
1987–88		17	—
1988–89		35	—
1989–90		15	—
1990–91		23	—

ABRAHAM, Gareth

Born Merthyr Tydfil 13.2.69.   Ht 6 4
Wt 12 11
Defender. From Trainee.

Season	Club	App	Goals
1987–88	Cardiff C	2	1
1988–89		31	2
1989–90		37	1
1990–91		2	—

ACHAMPONG, Kenny

Born London 26.6.66.   Ht 5 9   Wt 11 01
Forward. From Apprentice.

Season	Club	App	Goals
1984–85	Fulham	10	3
1985–86		35	3
1986–87		21	6
1987–88		15	3
1988–89		—	—
1988–89	*West Ham U*	—	—
1989–90	Charlton Ath	10	—
1990–91		—	—
1990–91	Leyton Orient	34	4

ADAMS, Mick

Born Sheffield 8.11.61.   Ht 5 6   Wt 10 04
Defender. From Apprentice. England
Youth.

Season	Club	App	Goals
1979–80	Gillingham	4	—
1980–81		13	—
1981–82		31	2
1982–83		44	3
1983–84	Coventry C	17	1
1984–85		31	3
1985–86		31	3
1986–87		11	2
1986–87	Leeds U	17	1
1987–88		40	—
1988–89		16	1
1988–89	Southampton	8	—
1989–90		15	—
1990–91		30	—

ADAMS, Neil

Born Stoke 23.11.65.   Ht 5 7   Wt 10 06
Forward. From Local. England Under-21.

Season	Club	Apps	Goals
1985–86	Stoke C	32	4
1986–87	Everton	12	—
1987–88		8	—
1988–89		—	—
1988–89	*Oldham Ath*	9	—
1989–90	Oldham Ath	27	4
1990–91		31	6

ADAMS, Steve

Born Sheffield 7.5.59. Ht 5 8 Wt 10 12
Forward. From Manawatu U, Rotherham
U, Blackpool, Worksop T.

Season	Club	Apps	Goals
1987–88	Scarborough	28	2
1988–89		20	3
1989–90		—	—
1989–90	Doncaster R	30	1
1990–91		5	1

ADAMS, Tony

Born London 10.10.66. Ht 6 1 Wt 13 3
Defender. From Apprentice. England
Youth, B, Under-21, 19 full caps.

Season	Club	Apps	Goals
1983–84	Arsenal	3	—
1984–85		16	—
1985–86		10	—
1986–87		42	6
1987–88		39	2
1988–89		36	4
1989–90		38	5
1990–91		30	1

ADCOCK, Paul

Born Ilminster 2.5.72. Ht 5 8 Wt 10 02
Forward. From Trainee.

Season	Club	Apps	Goals
1990–91	Plymouth Arg	12	—

ADCOCK, Tony

Born Bethnal Green 27.2.63 Ht 5 11
Wt 11 09
Forward. From Apprentice.

Season	Club	Apps	Goals
1980–81	Colchester U	1	—
1981–82		40	5
1982–83		30	17
1983–84		43	26
1984–85		28	24
1985–86		33	15
1986–87		35	11
1987–88	Manchester C	15	5
1987–88	Northampton T	18	10
1988–89		46	17
1989–90		8	3
1989–90	Bradford C	28	5
1990–91		10	1
1990–91	Northampton T	21	3

ADKINS, Nigel

Born Birkenhead 11.3.65. Ht 5 11
Wt 13 04
Goalkeeper. From Apprentice. England
Schools.

Season	Club	Apps	Goals
1982–83	Tranmere R	10	—
1983–84		4	—
1984–85		38	—
1985–86		34	—
1986–87	Wigan Ath	8	—
1987–88		2	—
1988–89		30	—
1989–90		13	—
1990–91		18	—

AGANA, Tony

Born London 2.10.63. Ht 5 11 Wt 12 02
Forward. From Weymouth.

Season	Club	Apps	Goals
1987–88	Watford	15	1
1987–88	Sheffield U	12	2
1988–89		46	24
1989–90		31	10
1990–91		16	2

AGBOOLA, Reuben

Born London 30.5.62. Ht 5 10 Wt 11 09
Defender. From Apprentice.

Season	Club	Apps	Goals
1979–80	Southampton	—	—
1980–81		6	—
1981–82		5	—
1982–83		37	—

Season	Club	Apps	Goals
1983–84	....	33	—
1984–85	....	9	—
1984–85	Sunderland..............	8	—
1985–86	....	12	—
1986–87	*Charlton Ath*	1	—
1986–87	Sunderland..............	11	—
1987–88	....	38	—
1988–89	....	29	—
1989–90	....	36	—
1990–91	....	5	—
1990–91	*Port Vale*....................	9	—

AGNEW, Paul

Born Lisburn 15.8.65. Ht 5 9 Wt 10 07
Defender. From Cliftonville. Northern
Ireland Schools, Youth, Under-23.

Season	Club	Apps	Goals
1983–84	Grimsby T	1	—
1984–85	....	12	—
1985–86	....	16	—
1986–87	....	29	—
1987–88	....	38	1
1988–89	....	34	—
1989–90	....	24	2
1990–91	....	7	—

AGNEW, Steve

Born Shipley 9.11.65. Ht 5 9 Wt 10 06
Midfield. From Apprentice.

Season	Club	Apps	Goals
1983–84	Barnsley	1	—
1984–85	....	10	1
1985–86	....	2	—
1986–87	....	33	—
1987–88	....	25	6
1988–89	....	39	6
1989–90	....	46	8
1990–91	....	38	8

AITKEN, Roy

Born Irvine 24.11.58 Ht 6 0 Wt 13 00
Midfield. From Celtic BC. Scotland
Schools, Under-21, 56 full caps.

Season	Club	Apps	Goals
1975–76	Celtic............................	12	—
1976–77	....	33	5
1977–78	....	33	2

Season	Club	Apps	Goals
1978–79	....	36	5
1979–80	....	35	3
1980–81	....	33	4
1981–82	....	33	3
1982–83	....	33	6
1983–84	....	31	5
1984–85	....	33	3
1985–86	....	36	—
1986–87	....	42	1
1987–88	....	43	1
1988–89	....	32	—
1989–90	....	18	2
1989–90	Newcastle U..............	22	1
1990–91	....	32	—

AIZLEWOOD, Mark

Born Newport 1.10.59. Ht 6 0 Wt 13 03
Midfield. From Apprentice. Wales Under-
21, 25 full caps.

Season	Club	Apps	Goals
1975–76	Newport Co.................	6	—
1976–77	....	5	—
1977–78	....	27	1
1977–78	Luton T	—	—
1978–79	....	39	—
1979–80	....	10	—
1980–81	....	23	—
1981–82	....	26	3
1982–83	....	—	—
1982–83	Charlton Ath	22	1
1983–84	....	31	1
1984–85	....	38	3
1985–86	....	35	3
1986–87	....	26	1
1986–87	Leeds U	15	—
1987–88	....	17	—
1988–89	....	38	3
1989–90	Bradford C	39	1
1990–91	Bristol C	42	2

ALBISTON, Arthur

Born Edinburgh 14.7.57. Ht 5 7
Wt 11 03
Defender. From Apprentice. Scotland
Schoolboy, Under-21, 14 full caps.

Season	Club	Apps	Goals
1974–75	Manchester U.............	2	—
1975–76	....	3	—

Season	Club	Apps	Goals
1976–77		17	—
1977–78		28	—
1978–79		33	—
1979–80		25	—
1980–81		42	1
1981–82		42	1
1982–83		38	1
1983–84		40	2
1984–85		39	—
1985–86		37	1
1986–87		22	—
1987–88		11	—
1988–89	WBA	43	2
1989–90	Dundee	10	—
1990–91		—	—
1990–91	Chesterfield	3	1

ALDRIDGE, John

Born Liverpool 18.9.58 Ht 5 11
Wt 11 10
Forward. From South Liverpool. Eire. 39
caps.

Season	Club	Apps	Goals
1978–79	Newport Co	—	—
1979–80		38	14
1980–81		27	7
1981–82		36	11
1982–83		41	17
1983–84		28	20
1983–84	Oxford U	8	4
1984–85		42	30
1985–86		39	23
1986–87		25	15
1986–87	Liverpool	10	2
1987–88		36	26
1988–89		35	21
1989–90		2	1

To Real Sociedad

ALEXANDER, Graham

Born Coventry 10.10.71. Ht 5 10
Wt 11 00
Defender. From Trainee.

Season	Club	Apps	Goals
1989–90	Scunthorpe U	—	—
1990–91		1	—

ALEXANDER, Ian

Born Glasgow 26.1.63. Ht 5 8 Wt 10 07
Defender. From Leicester J.

Season	Club	Apps	Goals
1981–82	Rotherham U	8	—
1982–83		3	—
1983–84	Motherwell	16	1
1984–85		8	1
1984–85	Morton	7	1
From Pezoporikos			
1986–87	Bristol R	22	1
1987–88		45	1
1988–89		42	—
1989–90		43	1
1990–91		39	1

ALEXANDER, Keith

Born Nottingham 14.11.58. Ht 6 4
Wt 13 06
Forward. From Barnet.

Season	Club	Apps	Goals
1988–89	Grimsby T	44	14
1989–90		38	12
1990–91		1	—
1990–91	Stockport Co	11	—
1990–91	Lincoln C	23	3

ALLEN, Bradley

Born Harold Wood 13.9.71. Ht 5 7
Wt 10 00
Forward. From schoolboys. England
Youth.

Season	Club	Apps	Goals
1988–89	QPR	1	—
1989–90		—	—
1990–91		10	2

ALLEN, Clive

Born London 20.5.61. Ht 5 10 Wt 12 03
Forward. From Apprentice. England
Schools, Youth, Under-21, 3 full caps.
Football League.

Season	Club	Apps	Goals
1978–79	QPR	10	4
1979–80		39	28
1980–81	Arsenal	—	—
1980–81	Crystal Palace	25	9

Season	Club	League Appearances/Goals	
1981–82	QPR	37	13
1982–83		25	13
1983–84		25	14
1984–85	Tottenham H	13	7
1985–86		19	9
1986–87		39	33
1987–88		34	11
From Bordeaux			
1989–90	Manchester C	30	10
1990–91		20	4

ALLEN, Malcolm

Born Dioniolen 21.3.67. Ht 5 8 Wt 11 02
Forward. From Apprentice. Wales Youth,
B, 11 full caps.

Season	Club	App	Goals
1984–85	Watford	—	—
1985–86		13	2
1986–87		4	—
1987–88		22	3
1987–88	*Aston Villa*	4	—
1988–89	Norwich C	23	5
1989–90		12	3
1989–90	Millwall	8	2
1990–91		21	7

ALLEN, Martin

Born Reading 14.8.65 Ht 5 10 Wt 11 00
Midfield. From school. England Youth,
Under-21.

Season	Club	App	Goals
1983–84	QPR	—	—
1984–85		5	—
1985–86		31	3
1986–87		32	5
1987–88		38	4
1988–89		28	4
1989–90		2	—
1989–90	West Ham U	39	9
1990–91		40	3

ALLEN, Paul

Born Aveley 28.8.62. Ht 5 7 Wt 10 10
Midfield. From Apprentice. England
Youth, Under-21.

Season	Club	App	Goals
1979–80	West Ham U	31	2

Season	Club	League Appearances/Goals	
1980–81		3	1
1981–82		28	—
1982–83		33	—
1983–84		19	—
1984–85		38	3
1985–86	Tottenham H	33	1
1986–87		37	3
1987–88		39	3
1988–89		37	1
1989–90		32	6
1990–91		36	3

ALLISON, Michael

Born Elderslie 17.3.66. Ht 5 11 Wt 11 08
Goalkeeper. From Horwich RMI

Season	Club	App	Goals
1989–90	Chesterfield	—	—
1990–91		16	—

ALLISON, Neil

Born Hull 20.10.73.
Defender. From Trainee.

Season	Club	App	Goals
1990–91	Hull C	1	—

ALLISON, Wayne

Born Huddersfield 16.10.68. Ht 6 1
Wt 12 06
Forward.

Season	Club	App	Goals
1986–87	Halifax T	8	4
1987–88		35	4
1988–89		41	15
1989–90	Watford	7	—
1990–91	Bristol C	37	6

ALLON, Joe

Born Gateshead 12.11.66. Ht 5 10
Wt 11 12
Forward. From Trainee. England Youth.

Season	Club	App	Goals
1984–85	Newcastle U	1	—
1985–86		3	1
1986–87		5	1
1987–88	Swansea C	32	11
1988–89		2	—

Season	Club		App	Goals
1988–89	Hartlepool U		21	4
1989–90			45	18
1990–91			46	28

ALLPRESS, Tim

Born Hitchin 27.1.71. Ht 6 0 Wt 12 00
Defender. From Trainee.

Season	Club	App	Goals
1989–90	Luton T	1	—
1990–91		—	—

AMPADU, Kwame

Born Bradford 20.12.70. Ht 5 10
Wt 10 13
Forward. From Trainee. Eire Youth, Under-21.

Season	Club	App	Goals
1988–89	Arsenal	—	—
1989–90		2	—
1990–91		—	—
1990–91	*Plymouth Arg*	6	1
1990–91	*WBA*	7	1

ANDERS, Jason

Born Rochdale 13.3.74. Ht 5 10
Wt 10 06
Forward. From Trainee.

Season	Club	App	Goals
1990–91	Rochdale	2	—

ANDERSON, Colin

Born Newcastle 26.4.62. Ht 5 8
Wt 10 08
Midfield. From Apprentice.

Season	Club	App	Goals
1979–80	Burnley	—	—
1980–81		2	—
1981–82		4	—
1982–83	Torquay U	42	5
1983–84		39	4
1984–85		28	2
1984–85	*QPR*	—	—
1984–85	WBA	—	—
1985–86		11	—
1986–87		28	1
1987–88		23	1

Season	Club	App	Goals
1988–89		42	6
1989–90		13	—
1990–91		23	2

ANDERSON, John

Born Dublin 7.11.59. Ht 5 11 Wt 11 06
Defender. From Apprentice. Eire, Youth Under-21. 16 full caps.

Season	Club	App	Goals
1977–78	WBA	—	—
1978–79		—	—
1979–80	Preston	5	—
1980–81		8	—
1981–82		38	—
1982–83	Newcastle U	33	1
1983–84		41	1
1984–85		35	1
1985–86		38	3
1986–87		32	1
1987–88		35	1
1988–89		21	1
1989–90		37	4
1990–91		27	1

ANDERSON, Viv

Born Nottingham 29.8.56. Ht 6 0
Wt 11 08
Defender. From Apprentice. England Under-21 B, 30 full caps, Football League.

Season	Club	App	Goals
1974–75	Nottingham F	16	—
1975–76		21	—
1976–77		38	1
1977–78		37	3
1978–79		40	1
1979–80		41	3
1980–81		31	—
1981–82		39	—
1982–83		25	1
1983–84		40	6
1984–85	Arsenal	41	3
1985–86		39	2
1986–87		40	4
1987–88	Manchester U	31	2
1988–89		6	—
1989–90		16	—
1990–91		1	—
1990–91	Sheffield W	22	2

ANDERTON, Darren

Born Southampton 3.3.72. Ht 6 0
Wt 11 07
Forward. From Trainee. England Youth.

| 1989–90 | Portsmouth | — | — |
| 1990–91 | | 20 | — |

ANDERTON, Steven

Born Lancaster 2.10.69
Midfield. From Trainee.

| 1989–90 | Preston NE | 1 | — |
| 1990–91 | | — | — |

ANDREWS, Ian

Born Nottingham 1.12.64. Ht 6 2
Wt 12 02
Goalkeeper. From Apprentice. England Youth.

1982–83	Leicester C	—	—
1983–84		2	—
1983–84	*Swindon T*	1	—
1984–85	Leicester C	31	—
1985–86		39	—
1986–87		42	—
1987–88		12	—
1988–89	Celtic	5	—
1988–89	*Leeds U*	1	—
1989–90	Celtic	—	—
1989–90	Southampton	3	—
1990–91		1	—

ANGELL, Brett

Born Marlborough 20.8.68   Ht 6 1
Wt 12 03
Forward. From Portsmouth and Cheltenham T.

1987–88	Derby Co	—	—
1988–89	Stockport Co	26	5
1989–90		44	23
1990–91	Southend U	42	15

ANGUS, Ian

Born Glasgow 19.11.61. Ht 5 10
Wt 10 03
Midfield. From Eastercraigs.

1979–80	Aberdeen	—	—
1980–81		19	1
1981–82		1	1
1982–83		5	3
1983–84		12	—
1984–85		28	2
1985–86		17	2
1986–87		2	1
1986–87	Dundee	29	4
1987–88		40	6
1988–89		15	—
1989–90		4	—
1989–90	*Plymouth Arg*	—	—
1990–91	Motherwell	20	2

ANGUS, Terry

Born Coventry 14.1.66.
Defender. From VS Rugby.

| 1990–91 | Northampton T | 42 | 2 |

ANSAH, Andy

Born Lewisham 19.3.69. Ht 5 10
Wt 11 01
Forward. From Crystal Palace.

1988–89	Brentford	7	2
1989–90		1	—
1989–90	Southend U	7	1
1990–91		40	9

ANTHROBUS, Steve

Born Lewisham 10.11.68. Ht 6 2
Wt 12 13
Forward.

1986–87	Millwall	—	—
1987–88		3	—
1988–89		3	—
1989–90		15	4
1989–90	*Southend U*	—	—
1989–90	Wimbledon	10	—

1990–91	....	3	—

APPLEBY, Matthew

Born Middlesbrough 16.4.72.   Ht 5 10
Wt 11 02
Defender. From Trainee.

1989–90	Newcastle U................	—	—
1990–91	....	1	—

APPLETON, Steve

Born Liverpool 27.7.73.
Defender. From Trainee.

1990–91	Wigan Ath..................	10	—

ARCHDEACON, Owen

Born Greenock 4.3.66.   Ht 5 9   Wt 10 08
Forward. From Gourock United. Scotland
Youth, Under-21.

1982–83	Celtic............................	—	—
1983–84	....	1	—
1984–85	....	3	1
1985–86	....	23	3
1986–87	....	29	2
1987–88	....	10	1
1988–89	....	10	—
1989–90	Barnsley	21	3
1990–91	....	45	2

ARCHIBALD, Steve

Born Glasgow 27.9.56.   Ht 5 10   Wt 11 02
Forward. From Fernhill Ath. Scotland
Under-21, 27 full caps.

1974–75	Clyde............................	4	—
1975–76	....	16	2
1976–77	....	31	3
1977–78	....	14	2
1977–78	Aberdeen......................	10	4
1978–79	....	32	13
1979–80	....	34	12
1980–81	Tottenham H..............	41	20
1981–82	....	27	6
1982–83	....	31	11

1983–84	....	32	21
From Barcelona			
1987–88	Blackburn R..............	20	6
1988–89	Hibernian....................	31	13
1989–90	....	13	2
1990–91	St Mirren	16	2

ARDLEY, Neil

Born Epsom 1.9.72.
Midfield. From Trainee.

1990–91	Wimbledon	1	—

ARMSTRONG, Chris

Born Newcastle 19.6.71.   Ht 6 0
Wt 11 00
Forward.

1988–89	Wrexham	—	—
1989–90	....	22	3
1990–91	....	38	10

ARMSTRONG, Gordon

Born Newcastle 15.7.67.   Ht 6 0
Wt 11 10
Midfield. From Apprentice.

1984–85	Sunderland................	4	—
1985–86	....	14	2
1986–87	....	41	5
1987–88	....	37	5
1988–89	....	45	8
1989–90	....	46	8
1990–91	....	35	6

ARMSTRONG, Lee

Born Workington 19.10.72.
Defender. From Trainee.

1990–91	Carlisle U....................	6	—

ARNOLD, Ian

Born Durham City 4.7.72.
Forward. From Trainee.

1989–90	Middlesbrough............	—	—

1990–91		2 —

ARNOTT, Doug

Born Lanark 5.8.64. Ht 5 7   Wt 10 07
Forward. From Pollok Juniors.

1986–87	Motherwell	1	—
1987–88		2	—
1988–89		14	1
1989–90		30	5
1990–91		29	14

ASH, Mark

Born Sheffield 22.1.68.   Ht 5 9   Wt 11 04
Defender. From Apprentice.

1985–86	Rotherham U	—	—
1986–87		17	—
1987–88		2	—
1988–89		1	—
1989–90	Scarborough	11	—
1990–91		9	—

ASHBY, Barry

Born London 21.11.70.   Ht 6 2   Wt 12 03
Defender. From Trainee.

1988–89	Watford	—	—
1989–90		18	1
1990–91		23	—

ASHCROFT, Lee

Born Preston 7.9.72.
Forward. From Trainee.

1990–91	Preston NE	14	1

ASHLEY, Kevin

Born Birmingham 31.12.68.   Ht 5 7
Wt 10 04
Defender. From Apprentice.

1986–87	Birmingham C	7	—
1987–88		1	—
1988–89		15	—

1989–90		31	1
1990–91		3	—
1990–91	Wolverhampton W	16	—

ASHURST, Jack

Born Coatbridge 12.10.54   Ht 6 0
Wt 12 04
Defender. From Apprentice.

1971–72	Sunderland	—	—
1972–73		11	—
1973–74		19	1
1974–75		6	—
1975–76		21	—
1976–77		31	—
1977–78		38	2
1978–79		11	1
1979–80		3	—
1979–80	Blackpool	25	—
1980–81		28	3
1981–82	Carlisle U	46	1
1982–83		30	—
1983–84		41	1
1984–85		42	—
1985–86		35	—
1986–87	Leeds U	41	1
1987–88		41	—
1988–89		7	—
1988–89	Doncaster R	30	1
1989–90		43	—
From Bridlington			
1990–91	Doncaster R	29	1

ASKEW, Billy

Born Lumley 2.10.59.   Ht 5 5   Wt 10 07
Midfield. From Apprentice.

1977–78	Middlesbrough	—	—
1978–79		—	—
1979–80		1	—
1980–81		5	—
1981–82		6	—
1981–82	*Blackburn R*	—	—
1982–83	Hull C	36	6
1983–84		33	1
1984–85		46	6
1985–86		33	2
1986–87		27	—

Season	Club	App	Goals
1987–88		30	3
1988–89		16	—
1989–90		32	1
1989–90	Newcastle U	4	—
1990–91		2	—
1990–91	*Shrewsbury T*	5	—

ASPIN, Neil

Born Gateshead 12.4.65. Ht 6 0 Wt 12 3
Defender. From Apprentice.

Season	Club	App	Goals
1981–82	Leeds U	1	—
1982–83		15	—
1983–84		21	1
1984–85		32	1
1985–86		38	2
1986–87		41	1
1987–88		26	—
1988–89		33	—
1989–90	Port Vale	42	—
1990–91		41	1

ASPINALL, Warren

Born Wigan 13.9.67. Ht 5 8 Wt 10 6
Forward. From Apprentice. England
Youth.

Season	Club	App	Goals
1984–85	Wigan Ath	10	1
1985–86		—	—
1985–86	Everton	1	—
1985–86	*Wigan Ath*	41	21
1986–87	Everton	6	—
1986–87	Aston Villa	12	3
1987–88		32	11
1988–89	Portsmouth	40	11
1989–90		3	—
1990–91		33	4

ATHERTON, Peter

Born Orrell 6.4.70. Ht 5 11 Wt 12 03
Defender. From Trainee.

Season	Club	App	Goals
1987–88	Wigan Ath	16	—
1988–89		40	1
1989–90		46	—
1990–91		46	—

ATKIN, Paul

Born Nottingham 3.9.69. Ht 6 0
Wt 12 04
Defender. From Trainee. England Youth.

Season	Club	App	Goals
1987–88	Notts Co	—	—
1988–89		—	—
1988–89	Bury	1	—
1989–90		9	1
1990–91		11	—

ATKINS, Bob

Born Leicester 16.10.62. Ht 6 0
Wt 12 02
Defender. Local.

Season	Club	App	Goals
1982–83	Sheffield U	8	—
1983–84		16	3
1984–85		16	—
1984–85	Preston NE	13	—
1985–86		34	2
1986–87		41	1
1987–88		45	1
1988–89		39	—
1989–90		28	1
1990–91		—	—

ATKINS, Mark

Born Doncaster 14.8.68. Ht 6 1
Wt 12 00
Defender.

Season	Club	App	Goals
1986–87	Scunthorpe U	26	—
1987–88		22	2
1988–89	Blackburn R	46	6
1989–90		41	7
1990–91		42	4

ATKINSON , Brian

Born Darlington 19.1.71. Ht 5 10
Wt 12 00
Midfield. From Trainee. England
Under-21.

Season	Club	App	Goals
1988–89	Sunderland	3	—
1989–90		13	—
1990–91		6	—

ATKINSON, Dalian

Born Shrewsbury 21.3.68. Ht 6 1
Wt 12 10
Forward. England B.

Season	Club	App	Goals
1985–86	Ipswich T	1	—
1986–87		8	—
1987–88		17	8
1988–89		34	10
1989–90	Sheffield W	38	10

To Real Sociedad

ATKINSON, Graeme

Born Hull 11.11.71.
Midfield. From Trainee.

Season	Club	App	Goals
1989–90	Hull C	13	1
1990–91		16	—

ATTEVELD, Ray

Born Amsterdam 8.9.66. Ht 5 10
Wt 12 00
Midfield. From Haarlem.

Season	Club	App	Goals
1989–90	Everton	18	1
1990–91		20	—

AUSTIN, Dean

Born Hemel Hempstead 26.4.70.
Defender. From St. Albans C.

Season	Club	App	Goals
1989–90	Southend U	7	—
1990–91		44	—

AWFORD, Andy

Born Worcester 14.7.72. Ht 5 9
Wt 11 09
Defender. From Worcester C, Portsmouth
Trainee. England Youth.

Season	Club	App	Goals
1988–89	Portsmouth	4	—
1989–90		—	—
1990–91		14	—

AYLOTT, Trevor

Born London 26.11.57. Ht 6 1 Wt 14 00
Forward. From Apprentice.

Season	Club	App	Goals
1976–77	Chelsea	—	—
1976–77	*QPR*	—	—
1977–78	Chelsea	11	2
1978–79		15	—
1979–80		3	—
1979–80	Barnsley	18	4
1980–81		37	11
1981–82		41	11
1982–83	Millwall	32	5
1982–83	Luton T	12	2
1983–84		20	8
1984–85	Crystal Palace	35	8
1985–86		18	4
1985–86	*Barnsley*	9	—
1986–87	Bournemouth	37	10
1987–88		43	9
1988–89		40	6
1989–90		18	2
1990–91		9	—
1990–91	Birmingham C	25	—

1990–91	*Bristol R*		6	1

BABB, Phil

Born Lambeth 30.11.70.   Ht 6 0
Wt 12 03
Defender.

Season	Club	App	Goals
1988–89	Millwall	—	—
1989–90			
1990–91	Bradford C	34	10

BACON, Paul

Born London 20.12.70.   Ht 5 9   Wt 10 04
Defender. From Trainee.

Season	Club	App	Goals
1988–89	Charlton Ath	—	—
1989–90		—	—
1990–91		1	—

BADDELEY, Lee

Born Cardiff 12.7.74.
Defender. From Trainee.

Season	Club	App	Goals
1990–91	Cardiff C	2	—

BAILEY, Danny

Born Leyton 21.5.64.   Ht 5 7   Wt 12 07
Midfield. From Apprentice.

Season	Club	App	Goals
1980–81	Bournemouth	2	—
From Local			
1983–84	Torquay U	1	—
From Wealdstone			
1989–90	Exeter C	46	1
1990–91		18	1
1990–91	Reading	26	2

BAILEY, Dennis

Born Lambeth 13.11.65.   Ht 5 10
Wt 11 06
Forward. From Fulham, Farnborough T.

Season	Club	App	Goals
1987–88	Crystal Palace	5	1
1988–89		—	—
1988–89	*Bristol R*	17	9
1989–90	Birmingham C	43	18
1990–91		32	5

BAILEY, John

Born Liverpool 1.4.57.   Ht 5 8   Wt 11 03
Defender. From Apprentice.

Season	Club	App	Goals
1975–76	Blackburn R	6	—
1976–77		34	—
1977–78		41	1
1978–79		39	—
1979–80	Everton	42	2
1980–81		31	—
1981–82		12	—
1982–83		37	1
1983–84		33	—
1984–85		15	—
1985–86		1	—
1985–86	Newcastle U	28	—
1986–87		8	—
1987–88		4	—
1988–89	Bristol C	35	—
1989–90		38	1
1990–91		7	—

BAILIE, Colin

Born Belfast 31.3.64.   Ht 5 11   Wt 10 11
Defender. From Apprentice.

Season	Club	App	Goals
1981–82	Swindon T	1	—
1982–83		26	1
1983–84		38	3
1984–85		42	—
1985–86	Reading	26	—
1986–87		37	1
1987–88		21	—
1988–89	Cambridge U	23	1
1989–90		36	—
1990–91		32	2

BAILLIE, Lex

Born Hamilton 6.7.66   Ht 6 2   Wt 12 0
Defender. From Burnbank BC

Season	Club	App	Goals
1987–88	Celtic	13	—
1988–89		9	—
1989–90		—	—
1990–91		9	1

BAINES, Paul

Born Tamworth 15.1.72.
Midfield. From Trainee.

| 1990–91 | Stoke C | 2 | — |

BAIRD, Ian

Born Rotherham 1.4.64. Ht 6 0
Wt 12 10
Forward. From Apprentice. England
Schools.

1981–82	Southampton	—	—
1982–83		11	2
1983–84		6	1
1983–84	*Cardiff C*	12	6
1984–85	Southampton	5	2
1984–85	*Newcastle U*	5	1
1984–85	Leeds U	10	6
1985–86		35	12
1986–87		40	15
1987–88	Portsmouth	20	1
1987–88	Leeds U	10	3
1988–89		43	10
1989–90		24	4
1989–90	Middlesbrough	19	5
1990–91		44	14

BAKER, Clive

Born N. Walsham 14.3.59. Ht 5 9
Wt 11 00
Goalkeeper. From Amateur.

1977–78	Norwich C	2	—
1978–79		2	—
1979–80		—	—
1980–81		10	—
1981–82		—	—
1982–83		—	—
1983–84		—	—
1984–85	Barnsley	37	—
1985–86		42	—
1986–87		39	—
1987–88		44	—
1988–89		46	—
1989–90		37	—
1990–91		46	—

BAKER, Graham

Born Southampton 3.12.58. Ht 5 9
Wt 10 08
Midfield. From Apprentice. England
Under-21.

1977–78	Southampton	3	1
1978–79		22	5
1979–80		23	4
1980–81		39	8
1981–82		26	4
1982–83	Manchester C	27	4
1983–84		36	8
1984–85		29	4
1985–86		10	—
1986–87		15	3
1987–88	Southampton	36	5
1988–89		21	4
1989–90		3	—
1989–90	*Aldershot*	7	2
1990–91	Fulham	6	1

BAKER, Paul

Born Newcastle 5.1.63. Ht 6 1 Wt 12 10
Midfield. From Bishop Auckland.

1984–85	Southampton	—	—
1985–86	Carlisle U	35	2
1986–87		36	9
1987–88	Hartlepool U	39	19
1988–89		40	7
1989–90		43	16
1990–91		46	12

BAKER, Steve

Born Newcastle 2.12.61. Ht 5 5
Wt 10 08
Midfield. From Apprentice.

1979–80	Southampton	—	—
1980–81		1	—
1981–82		5	—
1982–83		7	—
1983–84		8	—
1983–84	*Burnley*	10	—
1984–85	Southampton	9	—
1985–86		13	—
1986–87		26	—

1987–88		4	—		1987–88	Arsenal	—	—
1987–88	Leyton Orient	9	3		1988–89		—	—
1988–89		46	3		1989–90	Colchester U	4	—
1989–90		32	—		1990–91	Norwich C	—	—
1990–91		25	—					

BALAVAGE, John

Born Bellshill 15.10.60. Ht 6 2 Wt 12 00
Goalkeeper. From Albion Rovers BC.

1978–79	Albion R	27	—
1979–80		33	—
1980–81		33	—
1981–82		31	—
1982–83		22	—
1983–84		20	—
1984–85	St Johnstone	5	—
1985–86		38	—
1986–87		26	—
1987–88		37	—
1988–89		39	—
1989–90		38	—
1990–91		2	—

BALFOUR, Evan

Born Edinburgh 9.9.65 Ht 5 11 Wt 12 6
Midfield. From Whitburn J

| 1989–90 | Airdrieonians | 36 | 5 |
| 1990–91 | | 33 | 6 |

BALL, Kevin

Born Hastings 12.11.64. Ht 5 9 Wt 12 00
Defender. From Apprentice.

1983–84	Portsmouth	1	—
1984–85		—	—
1985–86		9	—
1986–87		16	—
1987–88		29	1
1988–89		14	1
1989–90		36	2
1990–91	Sunderland	33	3

BALL, Steve

Born Colchester 2.9.69 Ht 6 0 Wt 12 01
Midfield. From Trainee.

BALMER, Stuart

Born Falkirk 20.6.69. Ht 6 1 Wt 12 04
Defender. From Celtic BC.

1987–88	Celtic	—	—
1988–89		—	—
1989–90		—	—
1990–91	Charlton Ath	24	—

BALTACHA, Sergei

Born Ukraine 17.2.58 Ht 6 0 Wt 12 00
Midfield. From Dynamo Kiev. USSR full caps.

1988–89	Ipswich T	20	1
1989–90		8	—
1990–91	St Johnstone	34	—

BAMBER, Dave

Born St. Helens 1.2.59 Ht 6 3 Wt 13 10
Forward. From Manchester Univ.

1979–80	Blackpool	7	1
1980–81		15	3
1981–82		38	15
1982–83		26	10
1983–84	Coventry C	19	3
1983–84	Walsall	10	3
1984–85		10	4
1984–85	Portsmouth	4	1
1985–86		—	—
1985–86	Swindon T	23	9
1986–87		42	9
1987–88		41	13
1988–89	Watford	18	3
1988–89	Stoke C	23	6
1989–90		20	2
1989–90	Hull C	19	3
1990–91		9	2
1990–91	Blackpool	23	17

BANGER, Nicky

Born Southampton 25.2.71. Ht 5 8
Wt 10 06
Forward. From Trainee.

Season	Club		
1988–89	Southampton	—	—
1989–90		—	—
1990–91		6	—

BANKS, Ian

Born Mexborough 9.1.61. Ht 5 9
Wt 13 00
Midfield. From Apprentice.

Season	Club		
1978–79	Barnsley	2	—
1979–80		38	3
1980–81		45	14
1981–82		42	15
1982–83		37	5
1983–84	Leicester C	26	3
1984–85		33	9
1985–86		31	2
1986–87		3	—
1986–87	Huddersfield T	37	8
1987–88		41	9
1988–89	Bradford C	30	3
1988–89	WBA	4	—
1989–90	Barnsley	37	3
1990–91		33	2

BANNISTER, Gary

Born Warrington 22.7.60. Ht 5 8
Wt 11 05
Forward. From Apprentice. England
Under-21.

Season	Club		
1978–79	Coventry C	4	1
1979–80		7	—
1980–81		11	2
1981–82	Sheffield W	42	21
1982–83		39	20
1983–84		37	14
1984–85	QPR	42	17
1985–86		36	16
1986–87		34	15
1987–88		24	8
1987–88	Coventry C	8	1
1988–89		24	8

Season	Club		
1989–90		11	2
1989–90	WBA	13	2
1990–91		44	13

BANNON, Eamonn

Born Edinburgh 18.4.58. Ht 5 9
Wt 11 11
Midfield. From Links BC. Scotland
Schools, Under-21, 9 full caps.

Season	Club		
1976–77	Hearts	13	1
1977–78		39	12
1978–79		19	5
1978–79	Chelsea	19	1
1979–80		6	—
1979–80	Dundee U	24	4
1980–81		34	8
1981–82		36	12
1982–83		32	10
1983–84		33	7
1984–85		35	10
1985–86		31	11
1986–87		39	9
1987–88		26	1
1988–89	Hearts	30	2
1989–90		33	2
1990–91		19	2

BANTON, Dale

Born Kensington 15.5.61. Ht 5 10
Wt 11 05
Forward. From Apprentice.

Season	Club		
1979–80	West Ham U	4	—
1980–81		—	—
1981–82		1	—
1982–83	Aldershot	45	24
1983–84		46	19
1984–85		15	4
1984–85	York C	30	12
1985–86		35	10
1986–87		29	6
1987–88		33	16
1988–89		11	4
1988–89	Walsall	10	—
1988–89	*Grimsby T*	8	1
1989–90	Aldershot	23	1
1990–91		21	2

BAPTIE, Crawford

Born Glasgow 24.2.59   Ht 6 1   Wt 11 7
Midfield. From Baillieston

Season	Club	App	Goals
1984–85	Falkirk	26	4
1985–86		19	2
1985–86	Motherwell	16	3
1986–87		17	—
1986–87	Falkirk	8	—
1987–88		35	9
1988–89		28	2
1989–90		34	8
1990–91		26	3

BARACLOUGH, Ian

Born Leicester 4.12.70.
Forward. From Trainee.

Season	Club	App	Goals
1988–89	Leicester C	—	—
1989–90		—	—
1989–90	Wigan Ath	9	2
1990–91	Leicester C	—	—
1990–91	Grimsby T	4	—

BARBER, Fred

Born Ferryhill 26.8.63.   Ht 5 10   Wt 12 00
Goalkeeper. From Apprentice.

Season	Club	App	Goals
1981–82	Darlington	—	—
1982–83		12	—
1983–84		46	—
1984–85		45	—
1985–86		32	—
1985–86	Everton	—	—
1986–87		—	—
1986–87	Walsall	36	—
1987–88		46	—
1988–89		44	—
1989–90		25	—
1989–90	Peterborough U	6	—
1990–91	Walsall	2	—
1990–91	Chester C	8	—
1990–91	Blackpool	2	—

BARBER, Philip

Born Tring 10.6.65.   Ht 5 11   Wt 12 05
Forward. From Aylesbury.

Season	Club	App	Goals
1983–84	Crystal Palace	9	2
1984–85		23	4
1985–86		39	9
1986–87		31	5
1987–88		37	7
1988–89		46	6
1989–90		30	1
1990–91		19	1

BARDSLEY, David

Born Manchester 11.9.64.   Ht 5 10
Wt 11 00
Defender. From Apprentice. England
Youth.

Season	Club	App	Goals
1981–82	Blackpool	1	—
1982–83		28	—
1983–84		16	—
1983–84	Watford	25	—
1984–85		17	—
1985–86		13	2
1986–87		41	5
1987–88		4	—
1987–88	Oxford U	34	1
1988–89		37	6
1989–90		3	—
1989–90	QPR	31	1
1990–91		38	—

BARHAM, Mark

Born Folkestone 12.7.62.   Ht 5 7
Wt 11 00
Midfield. From Apprentice. England
Youth, 2 full caps.

Season	Club	App	Goals
1979–80	Norwich C	4	—
1980–81		35	1
1981–82		27	4
1982–83		38	4
1983–84		11	2
1984–85		14	1
1985–86		35	9
1986–87		13	2
1987–88	Huddersfield T	26	1
1988–89		1	—
1988–89	Middlesbrough	4	—
1989–90	WBA	4	—
1989–90	Brighton	17	2

1990–91		32	4

BARKER, Simon

Born Farnworth 4.11.64. Ht 5 9
Wt 11 00
Midfield. From Apprentice. England
Under-21.

1982–83	Blackburn R	—	—
1983–84		28	3
1984–85		38	2
1985–86		41	10
1986–87		42	11
1987–88		33	9
1988–89	QPR	25	1
1989–90		28	3
1990–91		35	1

BARLOW, Andy

Born Oldham 24.11.65. Ht 5 9 Wt 11 01
Defender.

1984–85	Oldham Ath	33	—
1985–86		26	—
1986–87		29	2
1987–88		26	—
1988–89		15	—
1989–90		44	1
1990–91		46	—

BARLOW, Martin

Born Barnstable 25.6.71
Midfield. From Trainee.

1988–89	Plymouth Arg	1	—
1989–90		1	—
1990–91		30	1

BARLOW, Stuart

Born Liverpool 16.7.68.
Forward.

1990–91	Everton	2	—

BARNARD, Leigh

Born Worsley 29.10.58. Ht 5 8 Wt 11 07
Midfield. From Apprentice.

1977–78	Portsmouth	11	—
1978–79		28	7
1979–80		5	—
1980–81		18	1
1981–82		17	—
1981–82	*Peterborough U*	4	—
1982–83	Swindon T	46	4
1983–84		36	7
1984–85		32	2
1984–85	*Exeter C*	6	2
1985–86	Swindon T	38	3
1986–87		41	3
1987–88		17	2
1988–89		2	—
1989–90		5	—
1989–90	Cardiff C	35	8
1990–91		28	1

BARNES, Bobby

Born Kingston 17.12.62. Ht 5 7
Wt 10 09
Forward. From Apprentice.

1980–81	West Ham	6	1
1981–82		3	—
1982–83		—	—
1983–84		13	2
1984–85		20	2
1985–86		1	—
1985–86	*Scunthorpe U*	6	—
1985–86	Aldershot	14	8
1986–87		25	11
1987–88		10	7
1987–88	Swindon T	28	10
1988–89		17	3
1988–89	Bournemouth	10	—
1989–90		4	—
1989–90	Northampton T	37	18
1990–91		43	13

BARNES, David

Born London 16.11.61. Ht 5 10
Wt 11 01
Defender. From Apprentice. England
Youth.

1979–80	Coventry C	3	—
1980–81		—	—

Season	Club	Appearances	Goals
1981–82		6	—
1981–82	Ipswich T	—	—
1982–83		6	—
1983–84		11	—
1984–85		—	—
1984–85	Wolves	23	1
1985–86		38	1
1986–87		26	2
1987–88		1	—
1987–88	Aldershot	30	—
1988–89		39	1
1989–90	Sheffield U	24	—
1990–91		28	1

BARNES, John

Born Jamaica 7.11.63   Ht 5 11   Wt 12 00
Forward. From Sudbury Court. England
Under-21, 65 full caps.

Season	Club	Appearances	Goals
1981–82	Watford	36	13
1982–83		42	10
1983–84		39	11
1984–85		40	12
1985–86		39	9
1986–87		37	10
1987–88	Liverpool	38	15
1988–89		33	8
1989–90		34	22
1990–91		35	16

BARNES, Paul

Born Leicester 16.11.67.   Ht 5 10
Wt 10 06
Forward. From Apprentice.

Season	Club	Appearances	Goals
1985–86	Notts Co	14	4
1986–87		—	—
1987–88		11	2
1988–89		15	7
1989–90		13	1
1989–90	Stoke C	5	—
1990–91		6	—
1990–91	Chesterfield	1	—

BARNES, Robert

Born Stoke 26.11.69   Ht 5 8   Wt 10 08
Defender. From Trainee.

Season	Club	Appearances	Goals
1988–89	Manchester C	—	—
1989–90	Wrexham	8	—
1990–91		1	—

BARNETT, Dave

Born London 16.4.67.   Ht 6 1   Wt 12 08
Midfield. From Windsor & Eton.

Season	Club	Appearances	Goals
1988–89	Colchester U	20	—
1989–90	WBA	—	—
1990–91	Walsall	5	—

BARNETT, Gary

Born Stratford 11.3.63.   Ht 5 6   Wt 9 13
Forward. From Apprentice.

Season	Club	Appearances	Goals
1980–81	Coventry C	—	—
1990–91	Huddersfield T	22	1
1981–82		—	—
1982–83	Oxford U	22	2
1982–83	Wimbledon	5	1
1983–84	Oxford U	19	7
1984–85		2	—
1984–85	Fulham	2	1
1985–86	Oxford U	2	—
1985–86	Fulham	36	6
1986–87		42	9
1987–88		42	9
1988–89		28	5
1989–90		32	1
1990–91	Huddersfield T	22	1

BARNSLEY, Andy

Born Sheffield 9.6.62.   Ht 6 0   Wt 11 07
Defender. From Denaby U.

Season	Club	Appearances	Goals
1984–85	Rotherham U	—	—
1985–86		28	—
1986–87	Sheffield U	42	1
1987–88		32	—
1988–89		3	—
1988–89	Rotherham U	27	—
1989–90		37	3
1990–91		19	—

BARR, Billy

Born Halifax 21.1.69.   Ht 5 11   Wt 11 07
Defender. From Trainee.

Season	Club	Apps	Goals
1987–88	Halifax T	30	—
1988–89		43	4
1989–90		23	2
1990–91		37	1

BARRAS, Tony

Born Teesside 29.3.71 Ht   Wt
Forward. From Trainee.

Season	Club	Apps	Goals
1988–89	Hartlepool U	3	—
1989–90		9	—
1990–91	Stockport Co	40	—

BARRATT, Tony

Born Salford 18.10.65.   Ht 5 7   Wt 10 03
Defender. From Billingham T.

Season	Club	Apps	Goals
1985–86	Grimsby T	22	—
From Billingham T			
1986–87	Hartlepool U	23	—
1987–88		43	3
1988–89		32	1
1988–89	York C	12	—
1989–90		46	4
1990–91		29	1

BARRETT, Earl

Born Rochdale 28.4.67   Ht 5 10
Wt 11 00
Defender. From Apprentice. England B,
Under-21, 1 full cap.

Season	Club	Apps	Goals
1984–85	Manchester C	—	—
1985–86		1	—
1985–86	Chester C	12	—
1986–87	Manchester C	2	—
1987–88		—	—
1987–88	Oldham Ath	18	—
1988–89		44	—
1989–90		46	2
1990–91		46	3

BARRICK, Dean

Born Hemsworth 30.9.69.   Ht 5 9
Wt 11 04
Midfield. From Trainee.

Season	Club	Apps	Goals
1987–88	Sheffield W	—	—
1988–89		8	2
1989–90		3	—
1990–91		—	—
1990–91	Rotherham U	19	2

BARRON, Dougie

Born Edinburgh 25.10.61   Ht 5 11
Wt 11 00
Defender. From Bainsford F.

Season	Club	Apps	Goals
1980–81	St Johnstone	1	—
1981–82		17	—
1982–83		5	1
1983–84		20	2
1984–85		37	1
1985–86		37	2
1986–87		35	—
1987–88		38	1
1988–89		38	—
1989–90		17	—
1990–91		11	—

BARROW, Graham

Born Chorley 13.6.54.   Ht 6 2   Wt 13 07
Midfield. From Altrincham.

Season	Club	Apps	Goals
1981–82	Wigan Ath	41	12
1982–83		28	3
1983–84		42	5
1984–85		38	9
1985–86		30	7
1986–87	Chester C	41	5
1987–88		38	4
1988–89		35	3
1989–90		28	1
1990–91		20	—

BARTLETT, Kevin

Born Portsmouth 12.10.62.   Ht 5 9
Wt 10 12
Forward. From Apprentice.

Season	Club	Apps	Goals
1980–81	Portsmouth	2	—
1981–82		1	—
From Fareham			
1986–87	Cardiff C	23	4

Season	Club	League Appearances/Goals	
1987–88	....	37	12
1988–89	....	22	9
1988–89	WBA	17	3
1989–90	....	20	7
1989–90	Notts Co	14	8
1990–91	....	40	13

BARTON, Warren

Born London 19.3.69. Ht 6 0 Wt 11 00
Defender. From Leytonstone/Ilford.
England B.

| 1989–90 | Maidstone U .... | 42 | — |
| 1990–91 | Wimbledon .... | 37 | 3 |

BARTRAM, Vince

Born Birmingham 7.8.68. Ht 6 2
Wt 13 04
Goalkeeper. From Local.

1985–86	Wolverhampton W	—	—
1986–87	....	1	—
1987–88	....	—	—
1988–89	....	—	—
1989–90	....	—	—
1989–90	*Blackpool*	9	—
1990–91	Wolverhampton W	4	—
1990–91	*WBA*	—	—

BART-WILLIAMS, Chris

Born Freetown 16.6.74.
Midfield. From Trainee. England Youth.

| 1990–91 | Leyton Orient .... | 21 | 2 |

BATES, Jamie

Born London 24.2.68. Ht 6 1 Wt 12 12
Defender. From Trainee.

1986–87	Brentford	24	1
1987–88	....	23	1
1988–89	....	36	1
1989–90	....	15	—
1990–91	....	32	2

BATTY, David

Born Leeds 2.12.68. Ht 5 7 Wt 10 07
Midfield. From Trainee. England B,
Under-21, 5 full caps.

1987–88	Leeds U	23	1
1988–89	....	30	—
1989–90	....	42	—
1990–91	....	37	—

BATTY, Lawrence

Born London 15.2.64 Ht 6 0 Wt 13 07
Goalkeeper. From Farense.

1984–85	Fulham	—	—
1985–86	....	2	—
1986–87	....	2	—
1987–88	....	—	—
1987–88	*Crystal Palace*	—	—
1988–89	Fulham	1	—
1989–90	....	2	—
1990–91	....	2	—
1990–91	Brentford	—	—

BATTY, Paul

Born Edington 9.1.64. Ht 5 7 Wt 10 07
Midfield. From Apprentice.

1981–82	Swindon T	—	—
1982–83	....	39	1
1983–84	....	41	4
1984–85	....	28	2
1985–86	Chesterfield	26	—
1986–87	Exeter C	33	2
1987–88	....	32	6
1988–89	....	15	1
1989–90	....	20	2
1989–90	*Cambridge U*	—	—
1990–91	Exeter C	11	—

BAZELEY, Darren

Born Northampton 5.10.72.
Forward. From Trainee.

| 1989–90 | Watford .... | 1 | — |
| 1990–91 | .... | 7 | — |

BEADLE, Peter

Born London 13.5.72. Ht   Wt
Midfield. From Trainee.

| 1988–89 | Gillingham .... | 2 | — |

26

1989–90	....	10	2
1990–91	....	22	7

BEAGRIE, Peter

Born Middlesbrough 28.11.65. Ht 5 9
Wt 10 08
Midfield. From Local. England B,
Under-21.

1983–84	Middlesbrough............	—	—
1984–85	....	7	1
1985–86	....	26	1
1986–87	Sheffield U	41	9
1987–88	....	43	2
1988–89	Stoke C	41	7
1989–90	....	13	—
1989–90	Everton	19	—
1990–91	....	17	2

BEARDSLEY, Peter

Born Newcastle 18.1.61. Ht 5 8
Wt 12 00
Forward. From Wallsend BC. England B,
49 full caps. Football League.

1979–80	Carlisle U	37	8
1980–81	....	43	10
1981–82	....	22	4
From Vancouver Whitecaps			
1982–83	Manchester U	—	—
From Vancouver Whitecaps			
1983–84	Newcastle U	35	20
1984–85	....	38	17
1985–86	....	42	19
1986–87	....	32	5
1987–88	Liverpool	38	15
1988–89	....	37	10
1989–90	....	29	10
1990–91	....	27	11

BEARDSMORE, Russell

Born Wigan 28.9.68. Ht 5 6 Wt 8 10
Midfield. From Apprentice. England
Under-21.

1986–87	Manchester U	—	—
1987–88	....	—	—

1988–89	....	23	2
1989–90	....	21	2
1990–91	....	12	—

BEASANT, Dave

Born Willesden 20.3.59. Ht 6 4 Wt 13 00
Goalkeeper. From Edgware T. England B,
2 full caps.

1979–80	Wimbledon	2	—
1980–81	....	34	—
1981–82	....	46	—
1982–83	....	46	—
1983–84	....	46	—
1984–85	....	42	—
1985–86	....	42	—
1986–87	....	42	—
1987–88	....	40	—
1988–89	Newcastle U	20	—
1988–89	Chelsea	22	—
1989–90	....	38	—
1990–91	....	35	—

BEASLEY, Andy

Born Sedgley 5.2.64. Ht 6 1 Wt 12 02
Goalkeeper. From Apprentice.

1981–82	Luton T.	—	—
1982–83	....	—	—
1983–84	....	—	—
1983–84	*Mansfield T*	—	—
1983–84	*Gillingham*	—	—
1984–85	Mansfield T	3	—
1985–86	....	—	—
1986–87	....	—	—
1986–87	*Peterborough U*	7	—
1987–88	Mansfield T	8	—
1987–88	*Scarborough*	4	—
1988–89	Mansfield T	6	—
1989–90	....	26	—
1990–91	....	42	—

BEATON, David

Born Bridge of Allan 8.8.67. Ht 5 11
Wt 11 4
Defender. From Bothkennar YM

1985–86	Stenhousemuir	2	—

Season	Club	Apps	Goals
1986–87		10	—
1987–88		39	7
1988–89		36	6
1989–90	Falkirk	23	2
1990–91		9	1
1990–91	East Fife	13	3

BEAUCHAMP, Joe

Born Oxford 13.3.71   Ht 5 11   Wt 11 10
Forward. From Trainee.

Season	Club	Apps	Goals
1988–89	Oxford U	1	—
1989–90		3	—
1990–91		4	—

BEAUMONT, Chris

Born Sheffield 5.12.65   Ht 5 11   Wt 11 07
Forward. From Denaby.

Season	Club	Apps	Goals
1988–89	Rochdale	34	7
1989–90	Stockport Co	22	5
1990–91		45	15

BEAUMONT, David

Born Edinburgh 10.12.63.   Ht 5 10
Wt 11 05
Midfield. 'S' Form. Scotland Youth,
Under-21.

Season	Club	Apps	Goals
1980–81	Dundee U	—	—
1981–82		—	—
1982–83		—	—
1983–84		2	—
1984–85		18	1
1985–86		13	—
1986–87		28	—
1987–88		10	1
1988–89		18	1
1988–89	Luton T	15	—
1989–90		19	—
1990–91		33	—

BEAUMONT, Nigel

Born Pontefract 11.2.67.   Ht 6 1
Wt 12 07
Defender.

Season	Club	Apps	Goals
1984–85	Bradford C	—	—
1985–86		2	—
1986–87		—	—
1987–88		—	—
1988–89	Wrexham	21	—
1989–90		43	3
1990–91		37	1

BEAVON, Stuart

Born Wolverhampton 30.11.58.   Ht 5 6
Wt 10 04
Midfield. From Apprentice.

Season	Club	Apps	Goals
1976–77	Tottenham H	—	—
1977–78		—	—
1978–79		1	—
1979–80		3	—
1979–80	Notts Co	6	—
1980–81	Reading	37	6
1981–82		40	5
1982–83		46	4
1983–84		36	7
1984–85		46	2
1985–86		44	3
1986–87		42	3
1987–88		34	2
1988–89		39	9
1989–90		32	3
1990–91	Northampton T	41	10

BECKFORD, Darren

Born Manchester 12.5.67.   Ht 6 1
Wt 11 01
Forward. From Apprentice. England
Youth.

Season	Club	Apps	Goals
1984–85	Manchester C	4	—
1985–86		3	—
1985–86	Bury	12	5
1986–87	Manchester C	4	—
1986–87	Port Vale	11	4
1987–88	Port Vale	40	9
1988–89		42	20
1989–90		42	17
1990–91		43	22

BECKFORD, Jason

Born Manchester 14.2.70. Ht 5 9
Wt 12 04
Forward. From Trainee. England Youth.

1987–88	Manchester C	5	—
1988–89		8	1
1989–90		5	—
1990–91		2	—
1990–91	*Blackburn R*	4	—

BEEKS, Steve

Born Ashford 10.4.71. Ht 5 10 Wt 11 05
Midfield. From Trainee.

| 1989–90 | Aldershot | 1 | — |
| 1990–91 | | 2 | — |

BEENEY, Mark

Born Pembury 30.12.67. Ht 6 4
Wt 14 07
Goalkeeper.

1986–87	Gillingham	2	—
1987–88	Maidstone U	—	—
1988–89		—	—
1989–90		33	—
1989–90	*Aldershot*	7	—
1990–91	Maidstone U	17	—
1990–91	Brighton & HA	2	—

BEESLEY, Paul

Born Wigan 21.7.65. Ht 6 1 Wt 11 11
Defender. From Marine.

1984–85	Wigan Ath	2	—
1985–86		17	—
1986–87		39	—
1987–88		42	1
1988–89		44	2
1989–90		11	—
1989–90	Leyton Orient	32	1
1990–91	Sheffield U	37	1

BEESTON, Carl

Born Stoke 30.6.67. Ht 5 9 Wt 11 13
Midfield. From Apprentice. England
Under-21.

1984–85	Stoke C	1	—
1985–86		5	—
1986–87		—	—
1987–88		12	—
1988–89		23	2
1989–90		38	2
1990–91		37	2

BEGLIN, Jim

Born Waterford 29.7.63. Ht 5 11
Wt 11 00
Defender. From Shamrock R. Eire B, 15
full caps.

1982–83	Liverpool	—	—
1983–84		—	—
1984–85		10	1
1985–86		34	1
1986–87		20	—
1987–88		—	—
1988–89		—	—
1989–90	Leeds U	19	—
1989–90	*Plymouth Arg*	5	—
1990–91	Leeds U	—	—
1990–91	*Blackburn R*	6	—

BELL, Doug

Born Paisley 5.9.59. Ht 5 11 Wt 12 01
Midfield. From Cumbernauld. Scotland
Under-21.

1977–78	St Mirren	2	1
1978–79		—	—
1979–80	Aberdeen	9	—
1980–81		17	1
1981–82		13	1
1982–83		23	1
1983–84		24	3
1984–85		22	—
1985–86	Rangers	23	—
1986–87		12	1
1986–87	*St Mirren*	4	—
1986–87	Hibernian	16	2
1987–88		16	1
1987–88	Shrewsbury T	15	2
1988–89		26	1
1988–89	*Hull C*	4	—
1989–90	Shrewsbury T	9	3

| 1989–90 | Birmingham C | 15 | — |
| 1990–91 | | 1 | — |

BELL, Michael

Born Newcastle 15.11.71.
Midfield. From Trainee.

| 1989–90 | Northampton T | 6 | — |
| 1990–91 | | 28 | — |

BELLAMY, Gary

Born Worksop 4.7.62.   Ht 6 2   Wt 11 05
Defender. From Apprentice.

1980–81	Chesterfield	3	—
1981–82		25	—
1982–83		42	—
1983–84		38	1
1984–85		22	2
1985–86		12	2
1986–87		42	2
1987–88	Wolverhampton W	24	2
1988–89		43	1
1989–90		39	3
1990–91		26	3

BENALI, Francis

Born Southampton 30.12.68.   Ht 5 9
Wt 11 01
Forward. From Apprentice.

1986–87	Southampton	—	—
1987–88		—	—
1988–89		7	—
1989–90		27	—
1990–91		12	—

BENBOW, Ian

Born Hereford 9.1.69.   Ht 5 10   Wt 11 00
Midfield. From Trainee.

1987–88	Hereford U	21	2
1988–89		34	1
1989–90		27	1
1990–91		1	—

BENJAMIN, Chris

Born Sheffield 5.12.72.   Ht 5 11   Wt 13 00
Forward. From Trainee.

| 1990–91 | Chesterfield | 11 | 1 |

BENJAMIN, Ian

Born Nottingham 11.12.61.   Ht 5 11
Wt 12 00
Midfield. From Apprentice. England
Youth.

1978–79	Sheffield U	2	2
1979–80		3	1
1979–80	WBA	—	—
1980–81		2	—
1981–82	Notts Co	—	—
1982–83	Peterborough U	46	6
1983–84		34	8
1984–85	Northampton T	44	18
1985–86		46	22
1986–87		46	18
1987–88		14	1
1987–88	Cambridge U	25	2
1988–89	Chester C	22	2
1988–89	Exeter C	20	3
1989–90		12	1
1989–90	Southend U	15	4
1990–91		46	13

BENNETT, Craig

Born Doncaster 29.8.73.
Forward. From Trainee.

| 1990–91 | Doncaster R | 2 | — |

BENNETT, Dave

Born Manchester 11.7.59.   Ht 5 9
Wt 10 07
Forward. From Amateur.

1978–79	Manchester C	1	—
1979–80		25	2
1980–81		26	7
1981–82		—	—
1981–82	Cardiff C	36	6
1982–83		41	12
1983–84	Coventry C	34	6
1984–85		34	2
1985–86		38	6
1986–87		31	7

Season	Club	League Appearances/Goals
1987–88	....	28 4
1988–89	....	7 —
1988–89	Sheffield W..................	10 —
1989–90	....	18 —
1990–91	Swindon T	1 —

BENNETT, Gary

Born Liverpool 20.9.63.   Ht 6 1   Wt 12 06
Forward. Local.

1984–85	Wigan Ath	20 3
1985–86	Chester C.....................	43 13
1986–87	....	33 13
1987–88	....	43 10
1988–89	....	7 —
1988–89	Southend U.................	17 2
1989–90	....	25 4
1989–90	Chester C.....................	8 1
1990–91	....	30 3

BENNETT, Gary

Born Manchester 4.12.61.   Ht 6 1
Wt 12 01
Defender. From Amateur.

1979–80	Manchester C	— —
1980–81	....	— —
1981–82	Cardiff C.....................	19 1
1982–83	....	36 8
1983–84	....	32 2
1984–85	Sunderland..................	37 3
1985–86	....	28 3
1986–87	....	41 4
1987–88	....	38 2
1988–89	....	40 3
1989–90	....	36 3
1990–91	....	37 2

BENNETT, Michael

Born London 27.7.69.   Ht 5 10   Wt 11 11
Midfield. From Apprentice. England
Youth.

1986–87	Charlton Ath	2 —
1987–88	....	16 1
1988–89	....	11 —
1989–90	....	6 1

Season	Club	League Appearances/Goals
1989–90	Wimbledon	7 1
1990–91	....	6 —

BENNETT, Mike

Born Bolton 24.12.62.   Ht 5 8   Wt 10 07
Defender. From Apprentice.England
Youth.

1979–80	Bolton W	8 —
1980–81	....	6 1
1981–82	....	35 —
1982–83	....	16 —
1983–84	Wolverhampton W	6 —
1983–84	Cambridge U	11 —
1984–85	....	34 —
1985–86	....	31 —
1986–87	Bradford C	— —
1986–87	Preston NE.................	42 1
1987–88	....	34 —
1988–89	....	— —
1989–90	....	10 —
1990–91	Carlisle U...................	17 —

BENNETT, Tom

Born Falkirk 12.12.69   Ht 5 11   Wt 11 08
Defender. From Trainee.

1987–88	Aston Villa.................	— —
1988–89	Wolverhampton W	2 —
1989–90	....	30 —
1990–91	....	26 —

BENNYWORTH, Ian

Born Hull 15.1.62.   Ht 6 0   Wt 12 07
Defender. From Apprentice.

1979–80	Hull C........................	1 —
From Gainsborough T, Nuneaton		
1987–88	Scarborough...............	39 1
1988–89	....	35 2
1989–90	....	15 —
1989–90	Hartlepool U	27 2
1990–91	....	43 —

BENSTEAD, Graham

Born Aldershot 20.8.63.   Ht 6 2   Wt 12 04
Goalkeeper. From Apprentice. England
Youth.

Season	Club	App	Goals
1981–82	QPR	—	—
1982–83		—	—
1983–84		—	—
1984–85		—	—
1984–85	*Norwich C*	1	—
1985–86	Norwich C	—	—
1986–87		13	—
1987–88		2	—
1987–88	*Colchester U*	18	—
1987–88	*Sheffield U*	8	—
1988–89	Sheffield U	39	—
1989–90		—	—
1990–91	Brentford	45	—

BENT, Junior

Born Huddersfield 1.3.70. Ht 5 5
Wt 10 06
Forward. From Trainee.

Season	Club	App	Goals
1987–88	Huddersfield T	7	—
1988–89		22	5
1989–90		7	1
1989–90	*Burnley*	9	3
1989–90	Bristol C	1	—
1990–91		20	2

BERESFORD, John

Born Sheffield 4.9.66. Ht 5 5 Wt 10 08
Midfield. From Apprentice. England
Schools, Youth.

Season	Club	App	Goals
1983–84	Manchester C	—	—
1984–85		—	—
1985–86		—	—
1986–87	Barnsley	27	1
1987–88		34	3
1988–89		27	1
1988–89	Portsmouth	2	—
1989–90		28	—
1990–91		42	2

BERESFORD, Marlon

Born Lincoln 2.9.69. Ht 6 1 Wt 12 06
Goalkeeper. From Trainee.

Season	Club	App	Goals
1987–88	Sheffield W	—	—
1988–89		—	—

Season	Club	App	Goals
1989–90		—	—
1989–90	*Bury*	1	—
1989–90	*Ipswich T*	—	—
1990–91	Sheffield W	—	—
1990–91	*Northampton T*	13	—
1990–91	*Crewe Alex*	3	—

BERGSSON, Gudni

Born Iceland 21.7.65 Ht 5 10 Wt 10 07
Defender. From Valur. Iceland Youth,
Under-21, full caps.

Season	Club	App	Goals
1988–89	Tottenham H	8	—
1989–90		18	—
1990–91		12	1

BERNARD, Paul

Born Edinburgh 30.12.72. Ht 5 11
Wt 11 08
Midfield. From Trainee.

Season	Club	App	Goals
1990–91	Oldham Ath	2	1

BERRY, George

Born West Germany 19.11.57. Ht 6 0
Wt 13 02
Defender. From Apprentice. Wales 5 full
caps.

Season	Club	App	Goals
1975–76	Wolverhampton W	—	—
1976–77		1	—
1977–78		7	—
1978–79		30	3
1979–80		41	—
1980–81		25	1
1981–82		20	—
1982–83	Stoke C	31	5
1983–84		8	—
1984–85		32	1
1984–85	*Doncaster R*	1	—
1985–86	Stoke C	41	3
1986–87		40	8
1987–88		36	5
1988–89		33	4
1989–90		16	1
1990–91	Peterborough U	32	6

BERRY, Greg

Born Essex 5.3.71   Ht 5 11   Wt 12 00
Forward. From East Thurrock.

Season	Club	App	Goals
1989–90	Leyton Orient	9	1
1990–91		35	5

BERRY, Les

Born Plumstead 4.5.56.   Ht 6 2   Wt 11 13
Defender. From Apprentice.

Season	Club	App	Goals
1973–74	Charlton Ath	—	—
1974–75		—	—
1975–76		15	1
1976–77		39	2
1977–78		41	2
1978–79		38	1
1979–80		42	2
1980–81		44	2
1981–82		25	—
1982–83		39	1
1983–84		42	—
1984–85		26	—
1985–86		7	—
1986–87	Brighton	23	—
1986–87	*Gillingham*	11	—
1987–88	Gillingham	20	—
1988–89		—	—
1989–90	Maidstone U	38	—
1990–91		25	2

BERRY, Neil

Born Edinburgh 6.4.63.   Ht 6 0   Wt 12 00
Defender. From Apprentice. Scotland
Youth.

Season	Club	App	Goals
1980–81	Bolton W	—	—
1981–82		3	—
1982–83		9	—
1983–84		14	—
1984–85		6	—
1984–85	Hearts	3	—
1985–86		32	2
1986–87		30	3
1987–88		35	—
1988–89		32	1
1989–90		10	1
1990–91		19	1

BERRY, Steve

Born Gosport 4.4.63.   Ht 5 7   Wt 11 06
Midfield. From Apprentice.

Season	Club	App	Goals
1980–81	Portsmouth	—	—
1981–82		27	2
1982–83		1	—
1983–84		—	—
1983–84	*Aldershot*	7	—
1984–85	Sunderland	34	2
1985–86		1	—
1985–86	Newport Co	26	3
1986–87		34	3
1986–87	Swindon T	1	—
1987–88		3	—
1987–88	Aldershot	36	6
1988–89		12	—
1988–89	Northampton T	34	3
1989–90		41	2
1990–91		27	2

BERRYMAN, Stephen

Born Blackburn 26.12.66
Goalkeeper.

Season	Club	App	Goals
1989–90	Hartlepool U	1	—
1990–91	Exeter C	—	—
1990–91	Cambridge U	1	—

BERTSCHIN, Keith

Born Enfield 25.8.56.   Ht 6 1   Wt 11 08
Forward. From Barnet. England Youth,
Under-21.

Season	Club	App	Goals
1973–74	Ipswich T	—	—
1974–75		—	—
1975–76		3	2
1976–77		29	6
1977–78	Birmingham C	42	11
1978–79		9	2
1979–80		37	12
1980–81		30	4
1981–82	Norwich C	36	12
1982–83		40	8
1983–84		33	7
1984–85		5	2
1984–85	Stoke C	25	2
1985–86		42	19

Season	Club		
1986–87		21	8
1986–87	Sunderland	11	2
1987–88		25	5
1988–89	Walsall	20	—
1989–90		35	9
1990–91		—	—
1990–91	Chester C	19	—

BETT, Jim

Born Hamilton 25.11.59.   Ht 5 11
Wt 12 03
Midfield. From school. Scotland Schools,
Under-21, 25 full caps.

Season	Club		
1976–77	Airdrieonians	1	—
1977–78		7	—
From Iceland and Lokeren			
1980–81	Rangers	34	4
1981–82		35	11
1982–83		35	6
From Lokeren			
1985–86	Aberdeen	24	3
1986–87		38	4
1987–88		38	10
1988–89		31	5
1989–90		30	3
1990–91		36	7

BIGGINS, Wayne

Born Sheffield 20.11.61.   Ht 5 11
Wt 11 00
Forward. From Apprentice.

Season	Club		
1979–80	Lincoln C	—	—
1980–81		8	1
From Matlock Town and King's Lynn			
1983–84	Burnley	20	8
1984–85		46	18
1985–86		12	3
1985–86	Norwich C	28	7
1986–87		31	4
1987–88		20	5
1988–89	Manchester C	32	9
1989–90	Stoke C	35	10
1990–91		38	12

BILLING, Peter

Born Liverpool 24.10.64.   Ht 6 2
Wt 13 00
Defender. From South Liverpool.

Season	Club		
1985–86	Everton	1	—
1986–87		—	—
1986–87	Crewe Alex	19	—
1987–88		32	—
1988–89		37	1
1989–90	Coventry C	18	—
1990–91		15	—

BINGHAM, David

Born Dunfermline 3.9.70.   Ht 5 10
Wt 10 11
Forward. From Inverkeithing U.

Season	Club		
1989–90	St Johnstone	1	—
1990–91		7	2

BIRCH, Paul

Born West Bromwich 20.11.62   Ht 5 6
Wt 10 04
Midfield. From Apprentice.

Season	Club		
1980–81	Aston Villa	—	—
1981–82		—	—
1982–83		—	—
1983–84		22	2
1984–85		25	3
1985–86		27	2
1986–87		29	3
1987–88		38	6
1988–89		12	—
1989–90		12	—
1990–91		8	—
1990–91	Wolverhampton W	20	2

BIRTLES, Garry

Born Nottingham 27.7.56.   Ht 6 0
Wt 12 03
Forward. From Long Eaton U. England
Under-21, B, 3 full caps.

Season	Club		
1976–77	Nottingham F	1	—
1977–78		—	—

Season	Club	App	Goals
1978–79	....	35	14
1979–80	....	42	12
1980–81	....	9	6
1980–81	Manchester U	25	—
1981–82	....	33	11
1982–83	....	—	—
1982–83	Nottingham F.............	25	7
1983–84	....	34	15
1984–85	....	13	2
1985–86	....	25	—
1986–87	....	28	14
1987–88	Notts Co.....................	43	7
1988–89	....	20	2
1989–90	Grimsby T	38	8
1990–91	....	23	1

BISHOP, Charlie

Born Nottingham 16.2.68.   Ht 6 0
Wt 12 01
Defender. From Stoke C Apprentice.

Season	Club	App	Goals
1986–87	Watford	—	—
1987–88	Bury	17	—
1988–89	....	38	3
1989–90	....	30	1
1990–91	....	29	2

BISHOP, Eddie

Born Liverpool 28.11.62   Ht 5 8
Wt 11 07
Midfield. From Winsford U, Northwich
Vic, Altrincham, Runcorn.

Season	Club	App	Goals
1987–88	Tranmere R	5	1
1988–89	....	35	8
1989–90	....	28	7
1990–91	....	8	3
1990–91	Chester C....................	19	7

BISHOP, Ian

Born Liverpool 29.5.65.   Ht 5 9   Wt 10 12
Midfield. From Apprentice. England B.

Season	Club	App	Goals
1983–84	Everton	1	—
1983–84	*Crewe Alex*................	4	—
1984–85	Everton	—	—
1984–85	Carlisle U...................	30	2

Season	Club	App	Goals
1985–86	....	36	6
1986–87	....	42	3
1987–88	....	24	3
1988–89	Bournemouth..............	44	2
1989–90	Manchester C	19	2
1989–90	West Ham U	17	2
1990–91	....	40	4

BISSETT, Nicky

Born Fulham 5.4.64   Ht 6 2   Wt 12 10
Defender. From Barnet.

Season	Club	App	Goals
1988–89	Brighton......................	16	—
1989–90	....	29	6
1990–91	....	3	—

BLACK, Eric

Born Bellshill 1.10.63.   Ht 5 8   Wt 10 04
Forward. Unattached. Scotland Schools,
Youth, B, Under-21, 2 full caps.

Season	Club	App	Goals
1981–82	Aberdeen....................	13	3
1982–83	....	31	12
1983–84	....	18	6
1984–85	....	27	17
1985–86	....	26	8
To Metz			

BLACK, Kenny

Born Stenhousemuir 29.11.63.   Ht 5 8
Wt 10 11
Defender. From Linlithgow Rose.
Scotland Schools, Youth.

Season	Club	App	Goals
1980–81	Rangers......................	—	—
1981–82	....	8	—
1982–83	....	14	1
1983–84	Motherwell.................	17	—
1984–85	Hearts	32	7
1985–86	....	29	2
1986–87	....	42	1
1987–88	....	42	4
1988–89	....	33	1
1989–90	Portsmouth	41	2
1990–91	....	21	1

BLACK, Kingsley

Born Luton 22.6.68.   Ht 5 8   Wt 10 11
Midfield. From school. Northern Ireland,
16 full caps.

1986–87	Luton T	—	—
1987–88		13	—
1988–89		37	8
1989–90		36	11
1990–91		37	7

BLACK, Tom

Born Lanark 11.10.62.   Ht 5 8   Wt 10 12
Defender. From Bellshill YM.

1980–81	Airdrieonians	—	—
1981–82		—	—
1982–83		5	—
1983–84		32	4
1984–85		37	1
1985–86		12	—
1986–87		24	1
1987–88		29	1
1988–89		37	4
1989–90	St Mirren	31	1
1990–91		34	2

BLACKMORE, Clayton

Born Neath 23.9.64.   Ht 5 9   Wt 11 06
Midfield. From Apprentice. Wales Schools,
Youth, Under-21, 27 full caps.

1982–83	Manchester U	—	—
1983–84		1	—
1984–85		1	—
1985–86		12	3
1986–87		12	1
1987–88		22	3
1988–89		28	3
1989–90		28	2
1990–91		35	4

BLACKSTONE, Ian

Born Harrogate 7.8.64.   Ht 6 0   Wt 13 02
Forward. From Harrogate T.

| 1990–91 | York C | 28 | 6 |

BLACKWELL, Dean

Born London 5.12.69   Ht 6 1   Wt 12 10
Defender. From Trainee. England
Under-21.

1988–89	Wimbledon	—	—
1989–90		3	—
1989–90	*Plymouth Arg*	7	—
1990–91	Wimbledon	35	—

BLADES, Paul

Born Peterborough 5.1.65.   Ht 6 0
Wt 10 12
Defender. From Apprentice. England
Youth.

1982–83	Derby Co	6	—
1983–84		4	—
1984–85		22	—
1985–86		30	—
1986–87		16	—
1987–88		31	—
1988–89		38	1
1989–90		19	—
1990–91	Norwich C	21	—

BLAKE, Mark

Born Portsmouth 19.12.67.   Ht 6 1
Wt 12 08
Defender. From Apprentice. England
Youth.

1985–86	Southampton	1	—
1986–87		8	1
1987–88		6	1
1988–89		3	—
1989–90		—	—
1989–90	*Colchester U*	4	1
1989–90	*Shrewsbury T*	10	—
1990–91	Shrewsbury T	46	2

BLAKE, Mark

Born Nottingham 16.12.70   Ht 5 11
Wt 12 03
Midfield. From Trainee. England Schools,
Youth, Under-21.

| 1989–90 | Aston Villa | 9 | — |

| 1990–91 | .... | 7 | — |
| 1990–91 | *Wolverhampton W* .... | 2 | — |

BLAKE, Nathan

Born Cardiff 27.1.72   Ht 5 10   Wt 12 00
Defender. From Chelsea Trainee and
Cardiff C Trainee. Wales B, Under-21.

| 1989–90 | Cardiff C .... | 6 | — |
| 1990–91 | .... | 40 | 4 |

BLAKE, Noel

Born Jamaica 12.1.62.   Ht 6 0   Wt 13 11
Defender. From Walsall Amateur and
Sutton Coldfield T.

1979–80	Aston Villa	3	—
1980–81	....	—	—
1981–82	....	1	—
1981–82	*Shrewsbury T*	6	—
1982–83	Aston Villa	—	—
1982–83	Birmingham C	37	3
1983–84	....	39	2
1984–85	Portsmouth	42	3
1985–86	....	42	4
1986–87	....	41	3
1987–88	....	19	—
1988–89	Leeds U	44	4
1989–90	....	7	—
1989–90	Stoke C	18	—
1990–91	....	44	3

BLISSETT, Gary

Born Manchester 29.6.64.   Ht 6 1
Wt 11 13
Forward. From Manchester C, Manchester
U. Amateur, and Altrincham.

1983–84	Crewe Alex	22	3
1984–85	....	29	9
1985–86	....	38	11
1986–87	....	33	16
1986–87	Brentford	10	5
1987–88	....	41	9
1988–89	....	36	6
1989–90	....	37	11
1990–91	....	26	10

BLISSETT, Luther

Born W. Indies 1.2.58.   Ht 5 10   Wt 12 03
Forward. From Juniors. England Under-
21, B, 14 full caps.

1975–76	Watford	3	1
1976–77	....	4	—
1977–78	....	33	6
1978–79	....	41	21
1979–80	....	42	10
1980–81	....	42	11
1981–82	....	40	19
1982–83	....	41	27
1983–84	AC Milan	30	5
1984–85	Watford	41	21
1985–86	....	23	7
1986–87	....	35	11
1987–88	....	25	4
1988–89	....	3	1
1988–89	Bournemouth	30	19
1989–90	....	46	18
1990–91	....	45	19

BLOOMER, Bob

Born Sheffield 21.6.66.   Ht 5 10   Wt 11 06
Midfield.

1985–86	Chesterfield	6	—
1986–87	....	31	3
1987–88	....	38	1
1988–89	....	44	10
1989–90	....	22	1
1989–90	Bristol R	—	—
1990–91	....	13	—

BLUNDELL, Chris

Born Billinge 7.12.69   Ht 5 10   Wt 10 09
Defender. From Trainee.

1987–88	Oldham Ath	1	—
1988–89	....	2	—
1989–90	....	—	—
1990–91	....	—	—
1990–91	Rochdale	14	—

BODAK, Peter

Born Birmingham 12.8.61. Ht 5 8
Wt 11 07
Midfield. From Apprentice.

Season	Club		
1979–80	Coventry C	—	—
1980–81		23	3
1981–82		9	2
1982–83	Manchester U	—	—
1982–83	Manchester C	14	1
From Hong Kong, Belgium, Walsall			
1986–87	Crewe Alex	26	7
1987–88		27	—
1987–88	Swansea C	9	—
1988–89		22	4
From Hong Kong			
1990–91	Walsall	4	1

BODIN, Paul

Born Cardiff 13.9.64. Ht 6 0 Wt 13 01
Midfield. From Chelsea Amateur. Wales
Youth, Under-21, 9 full caps.

Season	Club		
1981–82	Newport Co	—	—
1982–83	Cardiff C	31	—
1983–84		26	3
From Bath C			
1987–88	Newport Co	6	1
1987–88	Swindon T	5	1
1988–89		16	1
1989–90		41	5
1990–91		31	2
1990–91	Crystal Palace	5	—

BOGIE, Ian

Born Newcastle 6.12.67. Ht 5 7
Wt 10 02
Midfield. From Apprentice. England
Schools.

Season	Club		
1985–86	Newcastle U	—	—
1986–87		1	—
1987–88		7	—
1988–89		6	—
1988–89	Preston NE	13	1
1989–90		35	3
1990–91		31	8

BOLDER, Bob

Born Dover 2.10.58. Ht 6 3 Wt 14 06
Goalkeeper. From Dover.

Season	Club		
1976–77	Sheffield W	—	—
1977–78		23	—
1978–79		19	—
1979–80		31	—
1980–81		39	—
1981–82		42	—
1982–83		42	—
1983–84	Liverpool	—	—
1984–85		—	—
1985–86		—	—
1985–86	Sunderland	22	—
1985–86	*Luton T*	—	—
1986–87	Charlton Ath	26	—
1987–88		35	—
1988–89		38	—
1989–90		38	—
1990–91		39	—

BOLLAN, Gary

Born Dundee 24.3.73 Ht 5 11 Wt 12 4
Midfield. From Celtic BC. Scotland
Youth.

Season	Club		
1987–88	Celtic	—	—
1988–89		—	—
1989–90		—	—
1990–91	Dundee U	2	—

BOND, Kevin

Born London 22.6.57. Ht 6 2 Wt 13 10
Defender. From Bournemouth.
Apprentice. England B.

Season	Club		
1974–75	Norwich C	—	—
1975–76		1	—
1976–77		3	—
1977–78		28	—
1978–79		42	2
1979–80		40	9
1980–81		28	1
From Seattle S			
1981–82	Manchester C	33	3
1982–83		40	3
1983–84		34	4

Season	Club	Apps	Goals
1984–85	....	3	1
1984–85	Southampton	33	1
1985–86	....	34	1
1986–87	....	34	1
1987–88	....	39	3
1988–89	Bournemouth	27	1
1989–90	....	31	—
1990–91	....	30	2

BONNER, Pat

Born Donegal 25.5.60.   Ht 6 2   Wt 13 01
Goalkeeper. From Keadie Rovers. Eire 50
full caps.

Season	Club	Apps	Goals
1978–79	Celtic............................	2	—
1979–80	....	—	—
1980–81	....	36	—
1981–82	....	36	—
1982–83	....	36	—
1983–84	....	33	—
1984–85	....	34	—
1985–86	....	30	—
1986–87	....	43	—
1987–88	....	32	—
1988–89	....	26	—
1989–90	....	36	—
1990–91	....	36	—

BOOKER, Bob

Born Watford 25.1.58.   Ht 6 3   Wt 13 03
Midfield. From Bedmond Sports.

Season	Club	Apps	Goals
1978–79	Brentford	3	—
1979–80	....	12	6
1980–81	....	26	7
1981–82	....	38	4
1982–83	....	39	6
1983–84	....	29	4
1984–85	....	38	7
1985–86	....	44	7
1986–87	....	2	—
1987–88	....	12	—
1988–89	....	8	—
1988–89	Sheffield U	26	2
1989–90	....	42	8
1990–91	....	29	3

BOOTH, Scott

Born Aberdeen 16.12.71   Ht 5 7
Wt 10 03
Forward. From Schools. Scotland Youth,
Under-21.

Season	Club	Apps	Goals
1988–89	Aberdeen.....................	—	—
1989–90	....	2	—
1990–91	....	19	6

BOOTHROYD, Adrian

Born Bradford 8.2.71.   Ht 5 8   Wt 10 12
Defender. From Trainee.

Season	Club	Apps	Goals
1989–90	Huddersfield T	10	—
1990–91	Bristol R	3	—

BORROWS, Brian

Born Liverpool 20.12.60   Ht 5 10
Wt 10 12
Defender. From Amateur. England B.

Season	Club	Apps	Goals
1979–80	Everton	—	—
1980–81	....	—	—
1981–82	....	15	—
1982–83	....	12	—
1982–83	Bolton W	9	—
1983–84	....	44	—
1984–85	....	42	—
1985–86	Coventry C	41	—
1986–87	....	41	1
1987–88	....	33	—
1988–89	....	38	1
1989–90	....	37	1
1990–91	....	38	6

BORTHWICK, John

Born Hartlepool 24.3.64.   Ht 6 0
Wt 10 12
Forward. From Local.

Season	Club	Apps	Goals
1982–83	Hartlepool U	2	—
1983–84	....	10	—
1984–85	....	6	1
1985–86	....	32	8
1986–87	....	14	—
1987–88	....	34	5

Season	Club	Appearances	Goals
1988–89		19	1
1989–90	Darlington	*42*	*19*
1990–91		46	10

BOSNICH, Mark

Born Sydney (Australia) 13.1.72.
Goalkeeper.

Season	Club	Appearances	Goals
1989–90	Manchester U	1	—
1990–91		2	—

BOUGHEY, Darren

Born Stoke 30.11.70.   Ht 5 9   Wt 10 13
Forward. From Trainee.

Season	Club	Appearances	Goals
1989–90	Stoke C	7	—
1990–91		—	—
1990–91	*Wigan Ath*	2	2
1990–91	*Exeter C*	8	1

BOULD, Stephen

Born Stoke 16.11.62.   Ht 6 3   Wt 13 04
Defender. From Apprentice.

Season	Club	Appearances	Goals
1980–81	Stoke C	—	—
1981–82		2	—
1982–83		14	—
1982–83	*Torquay U*	9	—
1983–84	Stoke C	38	2
1984–85		38	3
1985–86		33	—
1986–87		28	1
1987–88		30	—
1988–89	Arsenal	30	2
1989–90		19	—
1990–91		38	—

BOWDEN, Jon

Born Stockport 21.1.63.   Ht 6 1   Wt 12 07
Midfield. From Local.

Season	Club	Appearances	Goals
1979–80	Oldham Ath	—	—
1980–81		—	—
1981–82		5	2
1982–83		31	2
1983–84		31	1

Season	Club	Appearances	Goals
1984–85		15	—
1985–86		—	—
1985–86	Port Vale	36	3
1986–87		34	4
1987–88	Wrexham	26	1
1988–89		42	10
1989–90		33	1
1990–91		40	5

BOWEN, Jason

Born Merthyr 24.8.72.
Midfield. From Trainee.

Season	Club	Appearances	Goals
1990–91	Swansea C	3	—

BOWEN, Mark

Born Neath 7.12.63.   Ht 5 8   Wt 11 13
Defender. From Apprentice. Wales
Schools, Youth, Under-21, 11 full caps.

Season	Club	Appearances	Goals
1981–82	Tottenham H	—	—
1982–83		—	—
1983–84		7	—
1984–85		6	—
1985–86		2	1
1986–87		2	1
1987–88	Norwich C	24	1
1988–89		35	2
1989–90		38	7
1990–91		37	1

BOWLING, Ian

Born Sheffield 27.7.65   Ht 6 3   Wt 14 08
Goalkeeper. From Gainsborough T.

Season	Club	Appearances	Goals
1988–89	Lincoln C	8	—
1989–90		—	—
1989–90	*Hartlepool U*	1	—
1990–91	Lincoln C	16	—

BOWMAN, David

Born Tunbridge Wells 10.3.60.   Ht 5 10
Wt 11 02
Midfield. From Salvesen BC. Scotland
Under-21.

Season	Club	Appearances	Goals
1980–81	Hearts	17	1

Season	Club	App	Goals
1981–82		16	1
1982–83		39	5
1983–84		33	—
1984–85		11	1
1984–85	Coventry C	10	—
1985–86		30	2
1986–87	Dundee U	29	
1987–88		39	1
1988–89		29	1
1989–90		24	1
1990–91		20	1

BOWYER, Gary

Born Manchester 22.6.71   Ht 6 0
Wt 12 13
Defender.

Season	Club	App	Goals
1989–90	Hereford U	14	2
1990–91	Nottingham F	—	—

BOYD, Charlie

Born Liverpool 20.9.69.   Ht 5 6   Wt 9 04
Forward. From Trainee.

Season	Club	App	Goals
1987–88	Liverpool	—	—
1988–89		—	—
1989–90		—	—
1990–91	Chesterfield	1	—

BOYD, Tom

Born Glasgow 24.11.65.   Ht 5 11
Wt 11 04
Defender. 'S' Form. Scotland Youth, B,
Under-21, 4 full caps.

Season	Club	App	Goals
1983–84	Motherwell	13	—
1984–85		36	—
1985–86		31	—
1986–87		31	—
1987–88		42	2
1988–89		36	1
1989–90		33	1
1990–91		30	2

BOYLE, Jimmy

Born Glasgow 19.2.67   Ht 5 6   Wt 11 2
Defender. From Celtic BC

Season	Club	App	Goals
1985–86	Queen's Park	30	1
1986–87		39	3
1987–88		39	8
1988–89		39	4
1989–90	Airdrieonians	31	1
1990–91		11	—

BRABIN, Gary

Born Liverpool 9.12.70
Midfield. From Trainee.

Season	Club	App	Goals
1989–90	Stockport Co	1	—
1990–91		1	—

BRACEWELL, Paul

Born Stoke 19.7.62.   Ht 5 8   Wt 10 09
Midfield. From Apprentice. England
Under-21, 3 full caps.

Season	Club	App	Goals
1979–80	Stoke C	6	—
1980–81		40	2
1981–82		42	1
1982–83		41	2
1983–84	Sunderland	38	4
1984–85	Everton	37	2
1985–86		38	3
1986–87		—	—
1987–88		—	—
1988–89		20	2
1989–90		—	—
1989–90	Sunderland	37	2
1990–91		37	—

BRACEY, Lee

Born Ashford 11.9.68   Ht 6 1   Wt 12 08
Goalkeeper. From Trainee.

Season	Club	App	Goals
1987–88	West Ham U	—	—
1988–89	Swansea C	30	—
1989–90		31	—
1990–91		35	—

BRADLEY, Darren

Born Birmingham 24.11.65.   Ht 5 7
Wt 11 12
Defender. From Apprentice. England
Youth.

Season	Club			
1983–84	Aston Villa	—	—	
1984–85		2	—	
1985–86		18	—	
1985–86	WBA	10	—	
1986–87		14	1	
1987–88		19	—	
1988–89		26	—	
1989–90		27	2	
1990–91		39	1	

BRADLEY, Pat

Born Sydney 27.4.72. Ht 5 10 Wt 12 03
Midfield. From Trainee.

Season	Club		
1990–91	Bury	1	—

BRADLEY, Russell

Born Birmingham 28.3.66. Ht 6 0
Wt 12 05
Midfield. From Dudley T.

Season	Club		
1987–88	Nottingham F	—	—
1988–89		—	—
1988–89	*Hereford U*	12	1
1989–90	Hereford U	33	1
1990–91		41	2

BRADSHAW, Carl

Born Sheffield 2.10.68. Ht 6 0 Wt 11 00
Forward. From Apprentice. England
Youth.

Season	Club		
1986–87	Sheffield W	9	2
1986–87	*Barnsley*	6	1
1987–88	Sheffield W	20	2
1988–89		3	—
1988–89	Manchester C	5	—
1989–90		—	—
1989–90	Sheffield U	30	3
1990–91		27	1

BRADSHAW, Darren

Born Sheffield 19.3.67. Ht 5 11 Wt 11 04
Midfield. From Matlock T.

Season	Club		
1987–88	Chesterfield	18	—

Season	Club		
1987–88	York C	25	1
1988–89		34	2
1989–90		—	—
1989–90	Newcastle U	12	—
1990–91		7	—

BRADSHAW, Mark

Born Ashton 7.6.69. Ht 5 10 Wt 11 05
Defender. From Trainee.

Season	Club		
1986–87	Blackpool	4	—
1987–88		16	—
1988–89		—	—
1989–90		21	1
1990–91		1	—
1990–91	*York C*	1	—

BRADSHAW, Paul

Born Altrincham 28.4.56. Ht 6 3
Wt 13 04
Goalkeeper. From Apprentice. England
Youth, Under-21.

Season	Club		
1973–74	Blackburn R	18	—
1974–75		—	—
1975–76		12	—
1976–77		41	—
1977–78		7	—
1977–78	Wolverhampton W	34	—
1978–79		39	—
1979–80		37	—
1980–81		38	—
1981–82		42	—
1982–83		—	—
1983–84		10	—
From Vancouver W			
1984–85	WBA	—	—
1985–86		8	—
1986–87	Bristol R	5	—
1987–88	Newport Co	23	—
1988–89	WBA	2	—
1989–90		4	—
1990–91	Peterborough U	39	—

BRADY, Kieron

Born Glasgow 17.9.71 Ht 5 9 Wt 11 13
Midfield. From Trainee.

Season	Club		
1989–90	Sunderland	11	2
1990–91		14	2

BRAIN, Simon

Born Evesham 31.3.66.   Ht 5 6   Wt 10 08
Forward. From Cheltenham T.

1990–91	Hereford U	22	8

BRAMHALL, John

Born Warrington 20.11.56.   Ht 6 2
Wt 13 06
Defender. From Amateur.

1976–77	Tranmere R	8	—
1977–78		10	—
1978–79		35	2
1979–80		45	1
1980–81		37	1
1981–82		35	3
1981–82	Bury	9	—
1982–83		46	6
1983–84		45	6
1984–85		42	4
1985–86		25	1
1985–86	*Chester C*	4	—
1986–87	Rochdale	46	9
1987–88		40	4
1988–89	Halifax T	39	3
1989–90		23	2
1989–90	Scunthorpe U	21	—
1990–91		11	—

BRANAGAN, Keith

Born Fulham 10.7.66.   Ht 6 1   Wt 13 00
Goalkeeper.

1983–84	Cambridge U	1	—
1984–85		19	—
1985–86		9	—
1986–87		46	—
1987–88		35	—
1987–88	Millwall	—	—
1988–89		—	—
1989–90		16	—
1989–90	*Brentford*	2	—
1990–91	Millwall	18	—

BRANNAN, Ged

Born Liverpool 15.1.72.   Ht 6 0   Wt 13 03
Defender. From Trainee.

1990–91	Tranmere R	18	1

BRAY, Ian

Born Neath 6.12.62.   Ht 5 8   Wt 11 06
Defender. From Apprentice.

1980–81	Hereford U	—	—
1981–82		16	2
1982–83		27	—
1983–84		23	1
1984–85		42	1
1985–86	Huddersfield T	32	1
1986–87		13	—
1987–88		30	—
1988–89		—	—
1989–90		14	—
1990–91	Burnley	11	—

BRAZIL, Derek

Born Dublin 14.12.68.   Ht 5 11   Wt 10 05
Defender. From Rivermount BC. Eire
Youth, B, Under-21, Under-23.

1985–86	Manchester U	—	—
1986–87		—	—
1987–88		—	—
1988–89		1	—
1989–90		1	—
1990–91		—	—
1990–91	*Oldham Ath*	1	—

BRAZIL, Gary

Born Tunbridge Wells 19.9.62.   Ht 5 11
Wt 9 13
Forward. From Crystal Palace Apprentice.

1980–81	Sheffield U	3	—
1981–82		1	—
1982–83		33	5
1983–84		19	2
1984–85		6	2
1984–85	*Port Vale*	6	3
1984–85	Preston NE	17	3

Season	Club	App	Goals
1985–86		43	14
1986–87		45	18
1987–88		36	14
1988–89		25	9
1988–89	Newcastle U	7	—
1989–90		16	2
1990–91	Fulham	42	4

BREACKER, Tim

Born Bicester 2.7.65. Ht 5 11 Wt 13 00
Defender. England Under-21.

Season	Club	App	Goals
1983–84	Luton T	2	—
1984–85		35	—
1985–86		36	—
1986–87		29	1
1987–88		40	1
1988–89		22	—
1989–90		38	1
1990–91		8	—
1990–91	West Ham U	24	1

BREMNER, Kevin

Born Banff 7.10.57. Ht 5 9 Wt 12 05
Forward. From Keith.

Season	Club	App	Goals
1980–81	Colchester U	34	8
1981–82		46	21
1982–83		15	2
1982–83	*Birmingham C*	4	1
1982–83	*Wrexham*	4	1
1982–83	*Plymouth Arg*	5	1
1982–83	Millwall	17	6
1983–84		42	16
1984–85		37	11
1985–86	Reading	22	7
1986–87		42	15
1987–88	Brighton	44	8
1988–89		41	15
1989–90		43	13
1990–91	Peterborough U	17	3

BRENNAN, Mark

Born Rossendale 4.10.65. Ht 5 10
Wt 10 13
Midfield. From Apprentice. England
Youth, Under-21.

Season	Club	App	Goals
1982–83	Ipswich T	—	—
1983–84		19	1
1984–85		36	2
1985–86		40	3
1986–87		37	7
1987–88		36	6
1988–89	Middlesbrough	25	3
1989–90		40	3
1990–91	Manchester C	16	3

BRESSINGTON, Graham

Born Eton 8.7.66. Ht 6 0
Defender. From Wycombe W.

Season	Club	App	Goals
1987–88	Lincoln C	*12*	—
1988–89		30	1
1989–90		43	2
1990–91		37	—

BREVETT, Rufus

Born Derby 24.9.69. Ht 5 8 Wt 11 00
Defender. From Trainee.

Season	Club	App	Goals
1987–88	Doncaster R	17	—
1988–89		23	—
1989–90		42	—
1990–91		27	3
1990–91	QPR	10	—

BRIEN, Tony

Born Dublin 10.2.69. Ht 5 11 Wt 11 09
Defender. From Apprentice.

Season	Club	App	Goals
1986–87	Leicester C	—	—
1987–88		15	1
1988–89		1	—
1988–89	Chesterfield	29	1
1989–90		43	3
1990–91		43	3

BRIGGS, Gary

Born Leeds 8.5.58. Ht 6 3 Wt 12 10
Defender. From Apprentice

Season	Club	App	Goals
1977–78	Middlesbrough	—	—
1977–78	Oxford U	20	2

Season	Club	Apps	Goals
1978–79		39	—
1979–80		46	1
1980–81		42	1
1981–82		45	1
1982–83		37	1
1983–84		38	3
1984–85		42	4
1985–86		38	—
1986–87		40	3
1987–88		18	1
1988–89		15	1
1989–90	Blackpool	17	2
1990–91		30	—

BRIGHT, David

Born Bathavon 5.9.72.
Midfield. From school.

Season	Club	Apps	Goals
1990–91	Stoke C	1	—

BRIGHT, Mark

Born Stoke 6.6.62.   Ht 6 0   Wt 13 00
Forward. From Leek T.

Season	Club	Apps	Goals
1981–82	Port Vale	2	—
1982–83		1	1
1983–84		26	9
1984–85	Leicester C	16	—
1985–86		24	6
1986–87		2	—
1986–87	Crystal Palace	28	8
1987–88		38	25
1988–89		46	20
1989–90		36	12
1990–91		32	9

BRIGHTWELL, David

Born Lutterworth 7.1.71.   Ht 6 1
Wt 13 05
Midfield. From Trainee.

Season	Club	Apps	Goals
1987–88	Manchester C	—	—
1988–89		—	—
1989–90		—	—
1990–91		—	—
1990–91	*Chester C*	6	—

BRIGHTWELL, Ian

Born Lutterworth 9.4.68.   Ht 5 10
Wt 11 07
Midfield. From Congleton T. England
Schools, Youth, Under-21.

Season	Club	Apps	Goals
1986–87	Manchester C	16	1
1987–88		33	5
1988–89		26	6
1989–90		28	2
1990–91		33	—

BRILEY, Les

Born Lambeth 2.10.56.   Ht 5 7   Wt 11 00
Midfield. From Apprentice.

Season	Club	Apps	Goals
1974–75	Chelsea	—	—
1975–76		—	—
1976–77	Hereford U	34	1
1977–78		27	1
1977–78	Wimbledon	14	1
1978–79		26	1
1979–80		21	—
1979–80	Aldershot	12	—
1980–81		44	—
1981–82		37	2
1982–83		28	—
1983–84		36	1
1984–85	Millwall	33	—
1985–86		39	1
1986–87		33	3
1987–88		44	4
1988–89		31	2
1989–90		26	2
1990–91		21	1

BRISCOE, Robert

Born Derby 4.9.69.   Ht 5 8   Wt 10 13
Defender. From Trainee.

Season	Club	Apps	Goals
1987–88	Derby Co	—	—
1988–89		—	—
1989–90		10	1
1990–91		3	—

BRITTON, Gerard

Born Glasgow 20.10.70   Ht 6 1   Wt 11 0
Forward. From Celtic BC

Season	Club	App	Goals
1987–88	Celtic	—	—
1988–89		—	—
1989–90		—	—
1990–91		2	—

BROADBENT, Graham

Born Halifax 20.12.58   Ht 6 0   Wt 12 07
Forward. From Emley.

Season	Club	App	Goals
1988–89	Halifax T	12	2
1989–90		13	—
1990–91		7	1

BROCK, Kevin

Born Middleton Stoney 9.9.62.   Ht 5 9
Wt 10 12
Midfield. From Apprentice. England
Schools, Under-21.

Season	Club	App	Goals
1979–80	Oxford U	19	2
1980–81		26	5
1981–82		28	5
1982–83		37	4
1983–84		45	3
1984–85		37	6
1985–86		23	—
1986–87		31	1
1987–88	QPR	26	2
1988–89		14	—
1988–89	Newcastle U	21	2
1989–90		44	2
1990–91		38	5

BROCKIE, Vincent

Born Greenock 2.2.69.   Ht 5 8   Wt 10 10
Defender. From Trainee.

Season	Club	App	Goals
1987–88	Leeds U	2	—
1988–89		—	—
1988–89	Doncaster R	23	2
1989–90		24	3
1990–91		7	2

BRODDLE, Julian

Born Laughton 1.11.64.   Ht 5 9   Wt 11 07
Midfield. From Apprentice.

Season	Club	App	Goals
1981–82	Sheffield U	1	—
1982–83		—	—
1983–84	Scunthorpe U	13	1
1984–85		45	14
1985–86		41	7
1986–87		38	10
1987–88		7	—
1987–88	Barnsley	19	1
1988–89		38	3
1989–90		20	—
1989–90	Plymouth Arg	9	—
1990–91		—	—
1990–91	*Bradford C*	—	—
1990–91	St Mirren	10	—

BROMAGE, Russel

Born Stoke 9.11.59.   Ht 5 11   Wt 11 05
Defender. From Apprentice.

Season	Club	App	Goals
1977–78	Port Vale	6	—
1978–79		20	2
1979–80		29	1
1980–81		45	4
1981–82		45	—
1982–83		46	2
1983–84		38	1
1983–84	*Oldham Ath*	2	—
1984–85	Port Vale	37	1
1985–86		40	1
1986–87		41	1
1987–88	Bristol C	30	—
1988–89		13	1
1989–90		3	—
1990–91	Brighton	1	—
1990–91	*Maidstone U*	3	—

BROOK, Gary

Born Dewsbury 9.5.64.   Ht 5 10
Wt 12 04
Forward. From Frickley Ath.

Season	Club	App	Goals
1987–88	Newport Co	14	2
1987–88	Scarborough	5	—
1988–89		44	12
1989–90		15	3
1989–90	Blackpool	25	6
1990–91		4	—
1990–91	*Notts Co*	1	—

Season	Club	Apps	Goals
1990–91	*Scarborough*	8	—

BROOKE, Gary

Born Bethnal Green 24.11.60. Ht 5 6
Wt 10 5
Midfield. From Apprentice.

Season	Club	Apps	Goals
1978–79	Tottenham H	—	—
1979–80		—	—
1980–81		18	3
1981–82		16	4
1982–83		23	7
1983–84		12	—
1984–85		4	1
1985–86	Norwich C	13	2
1986–87		1	—
From Gröningen			
1988–89	Wimbledon	10	—
1989–90		2	—
1989–90	*Stoke C*	8	—
1990–91	Brentford	11	1
1990–91	Reading	4	—

BROOKS, Shaun

Born London 9.10.62. Ht 5 7 Wt 11 00
Midfield. From Apprentice. England
Schools, Youth.

Season	Club	Apps	Goals
1979–80	Crystal Palace	1	—
1980–81		17	—
1981–82		25	2
1982–83		7	2
1983–84		4	—
1983–84	Orient	36	9
1984–85		29	5
1985–86		38	7
1986–87		45	5
1987–88	Bournemouth	37	6
1988–89		36	3
1989–90		35	4
1990–91		13	—

BROWN, David

Born Hartlepool 28.1.57. Ht 6 1
Wt 12 08
Goalkeeper. From Horden C.W.

Season	Club	Apps	Goals
1976–77	Middlesbrough	—	—

Season	Club	Apps	Goals
1977–78		10	—
1978–79		—	—
1979–80		—	—
1979–80	*Plymouth Arg*	5	—
1979–80	Oxford U	18	—
1980–81		3	—
1981–82		—	—
1981–82	Bury	27	—
1982–83		45	—
1983–84		28	—
1984–85		46	—
1985–86		—	—
1986–87	Preston NE	24	—
1987–88		27	—
1988–89		23	—
1988–89	*Scunthorpe U*	5	—
1989–90	Halifax T	27	—
1990–91		11	—

BROWN, Grant

Born Sunderland 19.11.69. Ht 6 0
Wt 11 12
Defender. From Trainee.

Season	Club	Apps	Goals
1987–88	Leicester C	2	—
1988–89		12	—
1989–90	Lincoln C	34	2
1990–91		32	1

BROWN, John

Born Stirling 26.1.62. Ht 5 11 Wt 10 02
Midfield. From Blantyre Welfare.

Season	Club	Apps	Goals
1979–80	Hamilton A	19	—
1980–81		38	6
1981–82		28	5
1982–83		9	—
1983–84		39	—
1984–85	Dundee	34	7
1985–86		29	11
1986–87		31	10
1987–88		20	3
1987–88	Rangers	9	2
1988–89		29	1
1989–90		27	1
1990–91		27	1

BROWN, Jon

Born Barnsley 8.9.66. Ht 5 10 Wt 11 03
Defender. From Denaby U

1990–91	Exeter C	29	—

BROWN, Kenny

Born Barking 11.7.67. Ht 5 8 Wt 11 06
Defender. From Apprentice.

1984–85	Norwich C	—	—
1985–86		—	—
1986–87		18	—
1987–88		7	—
1988–89	Plymouth Arg	39	1
1989–90		44	—
1990–91		43	3

BROWN, Kevan

Born Andover 2.1.66 Ht 5 9 Wt 11 08
Defender.

1983–84	Southampton	—	—
1984–85		—	—
1985–86		—	—
1986–87		—	—
1986–87	Brighton	15	—
1987–88		35	—
1988–89		3	—
1988–89	Aldershot	28	—
1989–90		42	2
1990–91		40	—

BROWN, Malcolm

Born Salford 13.12.56. Ht 6 2 Wt 13 01
Defender. From Apprentice.

1973–74	Bury	1	—
1974–75		—	—
1975–76		5	—
1976–77		5	—
1977–78	Huddersfield T	30	1
1978–79		42	—
1979–80		46	2
1980–81		46	3
1981–82		46	1
1982–83		46	9

1983–84	Newcastle U	—	—
1984–85		39	—
1985–86	Huddersfield T	37	—
1986–87		33	1
1987–88		25	—
1988–89		1	—
1988–89	Rochdale	11	—
1989–90	Stockport Co	37	2
1990–91		34	1

BROWN, Mike

Born Birmingham 8.2.68. Ht 5 9
Wt 10 12
Forward. From Apprentice.

1985–86	Shrewsbury T	—	—
1986–87		22	2
1987–88		41	5
1988–89		41	—
1989–90		43	1
1990–91		43	1

BROWN, Nicky

Born Hull 16.10.66. Ht 6 0 Wt 12 07
Forward. From Local.

1984–85	Hull C	—	—
1985–86		1	—
1986–87		—	—
1987–88		10	—
1988–89		13	—
1989–90		34	2
1990–91		3	—

BROWN, Phil

Born South Shields 30.5.59 Ht 5 11
Wt 11 06
Defender. Local.

1978–79	Hartlepool U	—	—
1979–80		10	—
1980–81		46	1
1981–82		44	4
1982–83		44	2
1983–84		31	—
1984–85		42	1
1985–86	Halifax T	45	2

Season	Club	League Appearances/Goals
1986–87	....	46 12
1987–88	....	44 5
1988–89	Bolton W	46 4
1989–90	....	46 1
1990–91	....	45 —

BROWN, Richard

Born Nottingham 13.1.67.
Defender. From Derby Co, Ilkeston T.

1984–85	Sheffield W.....................	— —
1985–86	....	— —
From Kettering T		
1990–91	Blackburn R	— —
1990–91	*Maidstone U*	3 —

BROWN, Steve

Born Northampton 6.7.66. Ht 5 9
Wt 10 12
Forward.

1985–86	Northampton T	— —
From Irthlingborough D		
1989–90	Northampton T	21 1
1990–91	....	40 2

BROWN, Tony

Born Bradford 17.9.58. Ht 6 2   Wt 12 07
Defender. From Thackley.

1982–83	Leeds U	1 —
1983–84	....	22 1
1984–85	....	1 —
1984–85	*Doncaster R*	14 —
1985–86	Doncaster R...............	38 2
1986–87	....	35 —
1986–87	Scunthorpe U	22 —
1988–89	....	32 2
1989–90	Rochdale....................	43 —
1990–91	....	26 —

BRUCE, Steve

Born Newcastle 31.12.60. Ht 6 0   Wt 12 6
Defender. From Apprentice. England
Youth.

1978–79	Gillingham	— —

Season	Club	League Appearances/Goals
1979–80	....	40 6
1980–81	....	41 4
1981–82	....	45 6
1982–83	....	39 7
1983–84	....	40 6
1984–85	Norwich C	39 1
1985–86	....	42 8
1986–87	....	41 3
1987–88	....	19 2
1987–88	Manchester U	21 2
1988–89	....	38 2
1989–90	....	34 3
1990–91	....	31 13

BRYANT, Matthew

Born Bristol 21.9.70. Ht 6 1   Wt 12 11
Defender. From Trainee.

1989–90	Bristol C	— —
1990–91	....	22 1
1990–91	*Walsall*	13 —

BRYCE, Steven

Born Shotts 30.6.69. Ht 5 8   Wt 10 07
Forward. From Motherwell BC.

1987–88	Motherwell.................	— —
1988–89	....	9 —
1989–90	....	3 —
1990–91	....	4 1

BRYSON, Ian

Born Kilmarnock 26.11.62. Ht 5 11
Wt 11 11
Midfield.

1981–82	Kilmarnock.................	14 3
1982–83	....	28 1
1983–84	....	25 4
1984–85	....	36 3
1985–86	....	38 14
1986–87	....	32 10
1987–88	....	42 5
1988–89	Sheffield U	37 8
1989–90	....	39 9
1990–91	....	29 7

BUCKLE, Paul

Born Hatfield 16.12.70. Ht 5 8   Wt 10 08
Midfield. From Trainee.

1987–88	Brentford	1	—
1988–89		—	—
1989–90		10	—
1990–91		26	—

BUCKLEY, John

Born Glasgow 10.5.62. Ht 5 9   Wt 10 13
Forward. From Queen's Park and Celtic.

1982–83	Partick T	8	1
1983–84		37	4
1984–85	Doncaster R	39	6
1985–86		45	5
1986–87	Leeds U	9	1
1986–87	*Leicester C*	5	—
1987–88	Leeds U	1	—
1987–88	*Doncaster R*	6	—
1987–88	Rotherham U	26	—
1988–89		36	5
1989–90		40	7
1990–91		3	1
1990–91	Partick Th	26	5

BUCKLEY, Neil

Born Hull 25.9.68. Ht 6 2   Wt 13 06
Defender. From Trainee.

1986–87	Hull C	1	—
1987–88		—	—
1988–89		13	—
1989–90		10	1
1989–90	*Burnley*	5	—
1990–91	Hull C	31	2

BULL, Steve

Born Tipton 28.3.65. Ht 5 11   Wt 11 04
Forward. From Apprentice. England
Under-21, B, 13 full caps.

1985–86	WBA	1	—
1986–87		3	2
1986–87	Wolverhampton W	30	14
1987–88		44	34

1988–89		45	37
1989–90		42	24
1990–91		43	26

BULLIMORE, Wayne

Born Sutton-in-Ashfield 12.9.70 Ht 5 9
Wt 10 06
Midfield. From Trainee. FA Schools.

1988–89	Manchester U	—	—
1989–90		—	—
1990–91		—	—
1990–91	Barnsley	—	—

BULLOCK, Steven

Born Stockport 5.10.66. Ht 5 9   Wt 11 08
Midfield. From school.

1983–84	Oldham Ath	1	—
1984–85		9	—
1985–86		8	—
1986–87	Tranmere R	30	1
1987–88	Stockport Co	41	—
1988–89		22	—
1989–90		27	—
1990–91		30	—

BUMSTEAD, John

Born Rotherhithe 27.11.58. Ht 5 7
Wt 10 05
Midfield. From Apprentice.

1977–78	Chelsea	—	—
1978–79		8	1
1979–80		28	3
1980–81		41	1
1981–82		21	4
1982–83		36	4
1983–84		31	7
1984–85		25	3
1985–86		32	1
1986–87		29	8
1987–88		17	1
1988–89		29	2
1989–90		29	2
1990–91		13	1

BUNN, Frankie

Born Birmingham 6.11.62.   Ht 6 0
Wt 11 00
Forward. From Apprentice.

1980–81	Luton T	3	1
1981–82		2	—
1982–83		4	—
1983–84		30	3
1984–85		20	5
1985–86	Hull C	42	14
1986–87		35	4
1987–88		18	5
1987–88	Oldham Ath	21	9
1988–89		28	12
1989–90		29	5
1990–91		—	—

BURGESS, Daryl

Born Birmingham 20.4.71.   Ht 5 11
Wt 12 03
Defender. From Trainee.

| 1989–90 | WBA | 34 | — |
| 1990–91 | | 25 | — |

BURGESS, Dave

Born Liverpool. 20.1.60   Ht 5 10
Wt 11 04
Defender. Local.

1981–82	Tranmere R	46	1
1982–83		46	—
1983–84		44	—
1984–85		41	—
1985–86		41	—
1986–87	Grimsby T	31	—
1987–88		38	—
1988–89	Blackpool	46	—
1989–90		19	1
1990–91		—	—

BURKE, David

Born Liverpool 6.8.60.   Ht 5 10   Wt 11 00
Defender. From Apprentice. England
Youth.

| 1977–78 | Bolton W | — | — |

1978–79		20	1
1979–80		27	—
1980–81		22	—
1981–82	Huddersfield T	41	1
1982–83		44	1
1983–84		42	—
1984–85		31	1
1985–86		—	—
1986–87		21	—
1987–88		10	—
1987–88	Crystal Palace	31	—
1988–89		39	—
1989–90		11	—
1990–91	Bolton W	14	—

BURKE, Mark

Born Solihull 12.2.69.   Ht 5 10   Wt 11 08
Forward. From Apprentice. England
Youth.

1986–87	Aston Villa	1	—
1987–88		6	—
1987–88	Middlesbrough	16	—
1988–89		29	5
1989–90		12	1
1990–91		—	—
1990–91	*Darlington*	5	1
1990–91	*Ipswich T*	—	—
1990–91	Wolverhampton W	6	—

BURLEY, Craig

Born Ayr 24.9.71.   Ht 6 1   Wt 11 07
Midfield. From Trainee.

| 1989–90 | Chelsea | — | — |
| 1990–91 | | 1 | — |

BURLEY, George

Born Cumnock 3.6.56.   Ht 5 9   Wt 11 02
Defender. From Apprentice. Scotland
Schools, Youth, Under-21, Under-23, 11
full caps.

1973–74	Ipswich T	20	—
1974–75		31	—
1975–76		42	—
1976–77		40	2

Season	Club	Appearances	Goals
1977–78		31	1
1978–79		38	1
1979–80		38	—
1980–81		23	—
1981–82		29	—
1982–83		31	1
1983–84		28	1
1984–85		37	—
1985–86		6	—
1985–86	Sunderland	27	—
1986–87		27	—
1987–88		—	—
1988–89	Gillingham	46	2
1989–90	Motherwell	34	—
1990–91		20	—

BURNS, Phil

Born Stockport 18.12.66   Ht 6 0
Wt 12 00
Goalkeeper. From Huddersfield T,
Trainee, Army.

Season	Club	Appearances	Goals
1988–89	Reading	—	—
1989–90		—	—
1990–91		12	—

BURNS, Willie

Born Motherwell 10.12.69.   Ht 5 11
Wt 10 10
Defender. From Trainee. Scottish Youth.

Season	Club	Appearances	Goals
1987–88	Manchester C	—	—
1988–89		—	—
1989–90	Rochdale	44	1
1990–91		28	1

BURRIDGE, John

Born Workington 3.12.51.   Ht 5 11
Wt 13 03
Goalkeeper. From Apprentice.

Season	Club	Appearances	Goals
1968–69	Workington	1	—
1969–70		—	—
1970–71		26	—
1970–71	Blackpool	3	—
1971–72		34	—
1972–73		22	—

Season	Club	Appearances	Goals
1973–74		30	—
1974–75		38	—
1975–76		7	—
1975–76	Aston Villa	30	—
1976–77		35	—
1977–78		—	—
1977–78	*Southend U*	6	—
1977–78	Crystal Palace	10	—
1978–79		42	—
1979–80		36	—
1980–81		—	—
1980–81	QPR	19	—
1981–82		20	—
1982–83	Wolverhampton W	42	—
1983–84		32	—
1984–85		—	—
1984–85	*Derby Co*	6	—
1984–85	Sheffield U	30	—
1985–86		42	—
1986–87		37	—
1987–88	Southampton	31	—
1988–89		31	—
1989–90		—	—
1989–90	Newcastle U	28	—
1990–91		39	—

BURROWS, Adrian

Born Sutton 16.1.59.   Ht 5 11   Wt 11 12
Defender. Local.

Season	Club	Appearances	Goals
1979–80	Mansfield T	17	—
1980–81		20	3
1981–82		41	2
1982–83	Northampton T	43	4
1983–84		45	—
1984–85	Plymouth Arg	39	—
1985–86		7	2
1986–87		17	1
1987–88		23	1
1987–88	*Southend U*	6	—
1988–89	Plymouth Arg	43	1
1989–90		46	1
1990–91		45	4

BURROWS, David

Born Dudley 25.10.68.   Ht 5 9   Wt 11 07
Defender. From Apprentice. England B,
Under-21.

Season	Club	App	Goals
1985–86	WBA	1	—
1986–87		15	1
1987–88		21	—
1988–89		9	—
1988–89	Liverpool	21	—
1989–90		26	—
1990–91		35	—

BURTON, Mike

Born Birmingham 5.11.69 Ht 5 8
Wt 11 00
Forward. From Trainee.

Season	Club	App	Goals
1988–89	Birmingham C	4	—
1989–90		—	—
1990–91		—	—
1990–91	Sheffield W	—	—
1990–91	Shrewsbury T	6	—

BURTON, Paul

Born Hereford 6.8.73 Ht 5 9 Wt 10 01
Midfield.

Season	Club	App	Goals
1989–90	Hereford U	2	—
1990–91		2	—

BURVILL, Glen

Born Canning Town 26.10.62. Ht 5 9
Wt 10 10
Midfield. From Apprentice.

Season	Club	App	Goals
1980–81	West Ham U	—	—
1981–82		—	—
1982–83		—	—
1983–84	Aldershot	38	12
1984–85		27	3
1984–85	Reading	14	—
1985–86		16	—
1985–86	*Fulham*	9	2
1986–87	Aldershot	36	2
1987–88		43	9
1988–89		42	7
1989–90		33	3
1990–91		41	2

BUSHELL, Steve

Born Manchester 28.12.72. Ht 5 7
Wt 10 05
Midfield. From Trainee.

Season	Club	App	Goals
1990–91	York C	15	—

BUTCHER, Terry

Born Singapore 28.12.58. Ht 6 4
Wt 14 0
Defender. From Amateur. England Under-21 B, 77 full caps

Season	Club	App	Goals
1976–77	Ipswich T	—	—
1977–78		3	—
1978–79		21	2
1979–80		36	2
1980–81		40	4
1981–82		27	1
1982–83		42	—
1983–84		34	1
1984–85		41	2
1985–86		27	4
1986–87	Rangers	43	3
1987–88		11	1
1988–89		34	2
1989–90		34	3
1990–91		5	—
1990–91	Coventry C	6	—

BUTLER, Barry

Born Farnworth 4.6.62. Ht 6 2 Wt 13 0
Defender. From Atherton T.

Season	Club	App	Goals
1985–86	Chester C	14	—
1986–87		44	—
1987–88		16	—
1988–89		35	—
1989–90		44	4
1990–91		43	5

BUTLER, Brian

Born Salford 4.7.66. Ht 5 7 Wt 10 05
Defender. From Apprentice.

Season	Club	App	Goals
1984–85	Blackpool	—	—
1985–86		19	1
1986–87		37	3
1987–88		18	1
1988–89	Stockport Co	32	2
1989–90	Halifax T	30	3
1990–91		26	1

BUTLER, John

Born Liverpool 7.2.62.   Ht 5 11   Wt 11 10
Defender. From Prescot Cables.

1981–82	Wigan Ath	1	—
1982–83		40	5
1983–84		41	3
1984–85		45	3
1985–86		36	—
1986–87		36	—
1987–88		26	1
1988–89		20	3
1988–89	Stoke C	25	1
1989–90		44	—
1990–91		31	2

BUTLER, John

Born Bellshill 25.1.69   Ht 5 10   Wt 12 4
Midfield. From Orbiston BC

1985–86	St Mirren	—	—
1986–87		3	—
1987–88		8	—
1988–89	Airdrieonians	17	—
1989–90		19	2
1990–91		10	3

BUTLER, Lee

Born Sheffield 30.5.66.   Ht 6 2   Wt 14 02
Goalkeeper. From Haworth Colliery.

1986–87	Lincoln C	30	—
1987–88	Aston Villa	—	—
1988–89		4	—
1989–90		—	—
1990–91		4	—
1990–91	*Hull C*	4	—

BUTLER, Paul

Born Bradford 2.11.72.   Ht 6 2   Wt 13 00
Defender. From Trainee.

1990–91	Rochdale	2	—

BUTLER, Peter

Born Halifax 27.8.66.   Ht 5 9   Wt 11 02
Midfield. From Apprentice.

1984–85	Huddersfield T	4	—
1985–86		1	—
1985–86	*Cambridge U*	14	1
1986–87	Bury	11	—
1986–87	Cambridge U	29	4
1987–88		26	5
1987–88	Southend U	15	3
1988–89		35	2
1989–90		41	2
1990–91		42	2

BUTLER, Steve

Born Birmingham 27.1.62.   Ht 6 2
Wt 13 00
Forward. From Windsor and Eton,
Wokingham.

1984–85	Brentford	3	1
1985–86		18	2
To Maidstone U (1986)			
1989–90		44	21
1990–91		32	20
1990–91	Watford	10	1

BUTLER, Tony

Born Stockport 28.9.72.   Ht 6 1   Wt 11 07
Defender. From Trainee.

1990–91	Gillingham	6	—

BUTTERS, Guy

Born Hillingdon 30.10.69   Ht 6 3
Wt 13 00
Defender. From Trainee. England
Under-21.

1988–89	Tottenham H	28	1
1989–90		7	—
1989–90	*Southend U*	16	3
1990–91	Portsmouth	23	—

BUTTERWORTH, Garry

Born Peterborough 8.9.69   Ht 5 8
Wt 10 11
Midfield. From Trainee.

1986–87	Peterborough U	1	—

1987–88	....	11	—
1988–89	....	8	—
1989–90	....	39	3
1990–91	....	46	—

BUTTERWORTH, Ian

Born Crewe 25.1.65.   Ht 6 1   Wt 12 10
Defender. From Apprentice. England
Under-21.

1981–82	Coventry C	14	—
1982–83	....	30	—
1983–84	....	24	—
1984–85	....	22	—
1985–86	Nottingham F.............	23	—
1986–87	....	4	—
1986–87	Norwich C	28	—
1987–88	....	35	—
1988–89	....	37	2
1989–90	....	22	—
1990–91	....	31	—

BUTTIGIEG, John

Born Sliema 5.10.63   Ht 6 0   Wt 11 13
Defender. From Sliema W. Malta full
caps.

1988–89	Brentford	18	—
1989–90	....	22	—
1990–91	....	—	—
1990–91	*Swindon T*	3	—

BYRNE, David

Born London 5.3.61.   Ht 5 8   Wt 10 09
Forward. From Kingstonian.

1985–86	Gillingham	23	3
1986–87	Millwall.......................	40	4
1987–88	....	23	2
1988–89	....	—	—
1988–89	*Cambridge U*	4	—
1988–89	*Blackburn R*	4	—
1988–89	Plymouth Arg.............	13	1
1989–90	....	32	1
1989–90	*Bristol R*......................	2	—
1990–91	Plymouth Arg.............	14	—
1990–91	Watford	17	2

BYRNE, John

Born Manchester 1.2.61.   Ht 6 0
Wt 12 04
Forward. From Apprentice. Eire 20 full
caps.

1978–79	York C........................	—	—
1979–80	....	9	2
1980–81	....	38	6
1981–82	....	29	6
1982–83	....	43	12
1983–84	....	46	27
1984–85	....	10	2
1984–85	QPR	23	3
1985–86	....	36	12
1986–87	....	40	11
1987–88	....	27	4
From Le Havre			
1990–91	Brighton......................	38	9

BYRNE, Mick

Born Dublin 14.1.60   Ht 5 11   Wt 12 03
Forward. From Shamrock R.

1988–89	Huddersfield T...........	37	7
1989–90	....	19	4
1989–90	*Shelbourne*....................	—	—
1990–91	Huddersfield T...........	—	—
To Shamrock R			

BYRNE, Paul

Born Dublin 30.6.72.   Ht 5 9   Wt 11 6
Midfield. From Trainee.

1989–90	Oxford U	3	—
1990–91	....	2	—

CADETTE, Richard

Born Hammersmith 21.3.65.   Ht 5 8
Wt 11 07
Forward. From Wembley.

Season	Club		
1984–85	Orient	21	4
1985–86	Southend U	44	24
1986–87		46	24
1987–88	Sheffield U	28	7
1988–89	Brentford	32	12
1989–90		16	1
1989–90	*Bournemouth*	8	1
1990–91	Brentford	28	6

CAESAR, Gus

Born London 5.3.66.   Ht 6 0   Wt 12 00
Defender. From Apprentice. England
Under-21.

Season	Club		
1983–84	Arsenal	—	—
1984–85		—	—
1985–86		2	—
1986–87		15	—
1987–88		22	—
1988–89		2	—
1989–90		3	—
1990–91		—	—
1990–91	*QPR*	5	—

CALDERWOOD, Colin

Born Stranraer 20.1.65.   Ht 6 0   Wt 12 00
Defender. From Amateur.

Season	Club		
1981–82	Mansfield T	1	—
1982–83		28	—
1983–84		30	1
1984–85		41	—
1985–86	Swindon T	46	2
1986–87		46	1
1987–88		34	1
1988–89		43	4
1989–90		46	3
1990–91		23	2

CALDWELL, Dave

Born Aberdeen 31.7.60.   Ht 5 10
Wt 12 02
Forward. From Inverness Caley.

Season	Club		
1979–80	Mansfield T	3	—
1980–81		28	8
1981–82		33	9
1982–83		35	10
1983–84		38	21
1984–85		20	9
1984–85	*Carlisle U*	4	—
1984–85	*Swindon T*	5	—
1985–86	Chesterfield	22	3
1986–87		36	14
1987–88		10	—
1987–88	Torquay U	24	4
From KV Overpelt			
1989–90	Torquay U	17	6
From KV Overpelt			
1990–91	Chesterfield	23	4

CALLAGHAN, Aaron

Born Dublin 8.10.66.   Ht 5 11   Wt 11 2
Defender. From Apprentice. Eire Youth,
Under-21.

Season	Club		
1984–85	Stoke C	5	—
1985–86		—	—
1985–86	*Crewe Alex*	8	—
1986–87	Stoke C	2	—
1986–87	Oldham Ath	5	—
1987–88		11	2
1988–89	Crewe Alex	41	4
1989–90		41	2
1990–91		39	—

CALLAGHAN, Nigel

Born Singapore 12.9.62.   Ht 5 9
Wt 10 00
Midfield. From Apprentice. England
Under-21.

Season	Club		
1979–80	Watford	1	—
1980–81		21	2
1981–82		37	5
1982–83		41	9
1983–84		41	10

Season	Club		
1984–85	....	38	8
1985–86	....	23	4
1986–87	....	20	3
1986–87	Derby Co	18	4
1987–88	....	40	4
1988–89	....	18	2
1988–89	Aston Villa	16	1
1989–90	....	8	—
1990–91	....	2	—
1990–91	*Derby Co*	12	1
1990–91	*Watford*	12	1

CALVERT, Mark

Born Consett 11.9.70 Ht 5 9 Wt 11 05
Forward. From Trainee.

1988–89	Hull C	5	—
1989–90	....	—	—
1990–91	....	7	—

CAME, Mark

Born Exeter 14.9.61. Ht 6 0 Wt 12 13
Defender. From Winsford U.

1983–84	Bolton W	—	—
1984–85	....	23	1
1985–86	....	35	1
1986–87	....	43	—
1987–88	....	43	5
1988–89	....	2	—
1989–90	....	19	—
1990–91	....	8	—

CAMERON, Ian

Born Glasgow 24.8.66. Ht 5 9 Wt 10 04
Midfield. 'S' Form. Scotland Schools,
Youth.

1983–84	St Mirren	8	—
1984–85	....	9	1
1985–86	....	12	—
1986–87	....	31	6
1987–88	....	41	8
1988–89	....	26	2
1989–90	Aberdeen	11	—
1990–91	....	10	1

CAMPBELL, David

Born Eglinton 2.6.65. Ht 5 10 Wt 11 02
Midfield. From Oxford BC(NI). Northern
Ireland, 10 full caps.

1983–84	Nottingham F	—	—
1984–85	....	1	—
1985–86	....	18	3
1986–87	....	14	—
1986–87	*Notts Co*	18	2
1987–88	Nottingham F	8	—
1987–88	Charlton Ath	21	1
1988–89	....	9	—
1988–89	*Plymouth Arg*	1	—
1988–89	Bradford C	12	1
1989–90	....	23	3
1990–91	....	—	—
1990–91	*Shamrock R*	—	—

CAMPBELL, David

Born Dublin 13.9.69.
Defender. From Bohemians.

1990–91	Huddersfield T	1	—

CAMPBELL, Greg

Born Portsmouth 13.7.65. Ht 5 11
Wt 11 05
Forward. From Manchester U. Amateur
and West Ham U. Apprentice.

1982–83	West Ham U	—	—
1983–84	....	—	—
1984–85	....	2	—
1985–86	....	3	—
1986–87	....	—	—
1986–87	*Brighton*	2	—
1987–88	West Ham U	—	—
From Sparta			
1988–89	Plymouth Arg	13	3
1989–90	....	22	3
1990–91	Northampton T	25	4

CAMPBELL, Kevin

Born Lambeth 4.2.70. Ht 6 0 Wt 13 01
Forward. From Trainee.

1987–88	Arsenal	1	—
1988–89		—	—
1988–89	*Leyton Orient*	16	9
1989–90	Arsenal	15	2
1989–90	*Leicester C*	11	5
1990–91	Arsenal	22	9

CANHAM, Tony

Born Leeds 8.6.60. Ht 5 9 Wt 11 07
Midfield. From Harrogate Railway.

1984–85	York C	3	1
1985–86		41	13
1986–87		38	9
1987–88		18	2
1988–89		41	9
1989–90		34	4
1990–91		41	5

CARBERRY, Jimmy

Born Liverpool 13.10.69 Ht 5 7
Wt 10 06
Midfield. From Trainee.

1988–89	Everton	—	—
1989–90	Wigan Ath	32	3
1990–91		28	3

CAREY, Brian

Born Cork 31.5.68.
Defender. From Cork C

1989–90	Manchester U	—	—
1990–91		—	—
1990–91	*Wrexham*	3	—

CARMICHAEL, Matt

Born Singapore 13.5.64. Ht 6 2
Wt 11 07
Forward. From Army.

| 1989–90 | Lincoln C | 26 | 5 |
| 1990–91 | | 26 | 2 |

CARPENTER, Richard

Born Sheppey 30.9.72. Ht 5 11 Wt 12 00
Midfield. From Trainee.

| 1990–91 | Gillingham | 9 | 1 |

CARR, Cliff

Born London 19.6.64. Ht 5 5 Wt 10 04
Midfield. From Apprentice. England
Under-21.

1982–83	Fulham	6	1
1983–84		41	4
1984–85		38	4
1985–86		35	4
1986–87		25	1
1987–88	Stoke C	41	—
1988–89		41	1
1989–90		22	—
1990–91		20	—

CARR, Darren

Born Bristol 4.9.68. Ht 6 2 Wt 13 00
Defender.

1985–86	Bristol R	1	—
1986–87		20	—
1987–88		9	—
1987–88	Newport Co	9	—
1987–88	Sheffield U	3	—
1988–89		10	1
1989–90		—	—
1990–91		—	—
1990–91	Crewe Alex	36	—

CARR, Franz

Born Preston 24.9.66. Ht 5 7 Wt 10 12
Midfield. From Apprentice. England
Schools, Youth, Under-21.

1984–85	Blackburn R	—	—
1985–86	Nottingham F	23	3
1986–87		36	4
1987–88		22	4
1988–89		23	3
1989–90		14	1
1989–90	*Sheffield W*	12	—
1990–91	Nottingham F	13	2
1990–91	*West Ham U*	3	—

CARSTAIRS, Jim

Born St. Andrews 29.1.71 Ht 6 0
Wt 12 05
Defender. From Trainee.

Season	Club	App	Goals
1988–89	Arsenal	—	—
1989–90		—	—
1990–91		—	—
1990–91	*Brentford*	8	—

CARTER, Danny

Born Hackney 29.6.69 Ht 5 11 Wt 11 12
Forward. From Billericay.

Season	Club	App	Goals
1988–89	Leyton Orient	1	—
1989–90		31	5
1990–91		42	5

CARTER, Jimmy

Born London 9.11.65. Ht 5 10 Wt 10 08
Midfield. From Apprentice.

Season	Club	App	Goals
1983–84	Crystal Palace	—	—
1984–85		—	—
1985–86	QPR	—	—
1986–87	Millwall	12	1
1987–88		26	—
1988–89		20	5
1989–90		28	2
1990–91		24	3
1990–91	Liverpool	5	—

CARTER, Steve

Born Sunderland 13.4.72. Ht 5 8
Wt 12 00
Forward. From Manchester U Trainee.

Season	Club	App	Goals
1990–91	Scarborough	34	3

CARTER, Tim

Born Bristol 5.10.67. Ht 6 2 Wt 13 11
Goalkeeper. From Apprentice. England
Youth.

Season	Club	App	Goals
1985–86	Bristol R	2	—
1986–87		38	—
1987–88		7	—
1987–88	*Newport Co*	1	—
1987–88	*Carlisle U*	4	—
1987–88	Sunderland	1	—
1988–89		2	—
1988–89	*Bristol C*	3	—
1989–90	Sunderland	18	—
1990–91		1	—

CARTWRIGHT, Lee

Born Rawtenstall 19.9.72.
Midfield. From Trainee.

Season	Club	App	Goals
1990–91	Preston NE	14	1

CARTWRIGHT, Neil

Born Stourbridge 20.2.71 Ht 5 9
Wt 10 13
Forward. From Trainee.

Season	Club	App	Goals
1988–89	WBA	1	—
1989–90		7	—
1990–91		—	—

CASCARINO, Tony

Born St Paul's Cray 1.9.62. Ht 6 2
Wt 13 12
Forward. From Crockenhill. Eire 33 full
caps.

Season	Club	App	Goals
1981–82	Gillingham	24	5
1982–83		38	15
1983–84		37	12
1984–85		43	16
1985–86		34	14
1986–87		43	16
1987–88	Millwall	39	20
1988–89		38	13
1989–90		28	9
1989–90	Aston Villa	10	2
1990–91		36	9

CASE, Jimmy

Born Liverpool 18.5.54. Ht 5 9 Wt 12 08
Midfield. From Sth Liverpool. England
Under-23.

Season	Club	League Appearances/Goals	
1973–74	Liverpool	—	—
1974–75		1	—
1975–76		27	6
1976–77		27	1
1977–78		33	5
1978–79		37	7
1979–80		37	3
1980–81		24	1
1981–82	Brighton	33	3
1982–83		35	3
1983–84		35	4
1984–85		24	—
1984–85	Southampton	10	1
1985–86		36	2
1986–87		39	3
1987–88		38	—
1988–89		34	—
1989–90		33	3
1990–91		25	1

CASEY, Paul

Born Rinteln 6.10.61 Ht 5 8 Wt 10 06
Defender. From Apprentice.

Season	Club	App	Goals
1979–80	Sheffield U	8	1
1980–81		5	—
1981–82		12	—
From Boston			
1987–88	Lincoln C	*10*	—
1988–89		8	—
1989–90		12	—
1990–91		29	4

CASH, Stuart

Born Tipton 5.9.65. Ht 5 11 Wt 11 10
Defender. From Halesowen.

Season	Club	App	Goals
1989–90	Nottingham F	—	—
1989–90	*Rotherham U*	8	1
1990–91	Nottingham F	—	—
1990–91	*Brentford*	11	—

CASTLE, Steve

Born Barkingside 17.5.66. Ht 5 11
Wt 12 05
Midfield. From Apprentice.

Season	Club	App	Goals
1984–85	Orient	21	1

Season	App	Goals
1985–86	23	4
1986–87	24	5
1987–88	42	10
1988–89	24	6
1989–90	27	7
1990–91	45	12

CATON, Tommy

Born Liverpool 6.10.62. Ht 6 2 Wt 13 00
Defender. From Apprentice. England
Schools, Youth, Under-21.

Season	Club	App	Goals
1979–80	Manchester C	42	—
1980–81		30	—
1981–82		39	1
1982–83		38	5
1983–84		16	2
1983–84	Arsenal	26	—
1984–85		35	1
1985–86		20	1
1986–87		—	—
1986–87	Oxford U	17	2
1987–88		36	1
1988–89		—	—
1988–89	Charlton Ath	13	1
1989–90		24	1
1990–91		20	3

CAWLEY, Peter

Born London 15.9.65. Ht 6 4 Wt 13 00
Defender. From Chertsey.

Season	Club	App	Goals
1986–87	Wimbledon	—	—
1986–87	*Bristol R*	10	—
1987–88	Wimbledon	—	—
1988–89		1	—
1988–89	*Fulham*	5	—
1989–90	Bristol R	3	—
1990–91	Southend U	7	1
1990–91	Exeter C	7	—

CECERE, Michele

Born Chester 4.1.68. Ht 6 0 Wt 11 04
Forward. From Apprentice.

Season	Club	App	Goals
1985–86	Oldham Ath	—	—
1986–87		14	4

Season	Club	Appearances	Goals
1987–88	....	25	2
1988–89	....	13	2
1988–89	Huddersfield T............	31	4
1989–90	....	23	4
1989–90	*Stockport Co*	1	—
1990–91	Huddersfield T............	—	—
1990–91	Walsall	32	6

CHALMERS, Paul

Born Glasgow 31.10.63. Ht 5 10
Wt 10 03
Forward. From Eastercraigs. Scotland
Youth.

Season	Club	Appearances	Goals
1980–81	Celtic...........................	—	—
1981–82	....	—	—
1982–83	....	—	—
1983–84	....	—	—
1984–85	....	1	1
1985–86	....	3	—
1985–86	*Bradford C*	2	—
1986–87	St Mirren	23	2
1987–88	....	36	10
1988–89	....	33	11
1989–90	....	9	—
1989–90	Swansea C..................	16	4
1990–91	....	21	2

CHAMBERLAIN, Alec

Born March 20.6.64. Ht 6 2 Wt 13 00
Goalkeeper. From Ramsey T.

Season	Club	Appearances	Goals
1981–82	Ipswich T.....................	—	—
1982–83	Colchester U	—	—
1983–84	....	46	—
1984–85	....	46	—
1985–86	....	46	—
1986–87	....	46	—
1987–88	Everton	—	—
1987–88	*Tranmere R*	15	—
1988–89	Luton T	6	—
1989–90	....	38	—
1990–91	....	38	—

CHAMBERLAIN, Mark

Born Stoke 19.11.61. Ht 5 9 Wt 10 07
Forward. From Apprentice. England
Schools, Under-21, 8 full caps.

Season	Club	Appearances	Goals
1978–79	Port Vale....................	8	—
1979–80	....	11	—
1980–81	....	31	9
1981–82	....	46	8
1982–83	Stoke C	37	6
1983–84	....	40	7
1984–85	....	28	1
1985–86	....	7	3
1985–86	Sheffield W..................	21	2
1986–87	....	24	5
1987–88	....	21	1
1988–89	Portsmouth	28	6
1989–90	....	38	6
1990–91	....	25	2

CHAMBERS, Steve

Born Worksop 20.7.68 Ht 5 10 Wt 10 10
Defender. From Apprentice.

Season	Club	Appearances	Goals
1985–86	Sheffield W..................	—	—
1986–87	Mansfield T.................	5	—
1987–88	....	8	—
1988–89	....	5	—
1989–90	....	7	—
1990–91	....	32	—

CHANDLER, Jeff

Born Hammersmith 19.6.59. Ht 5 7
Wt 10 01
Midfield. From Apprentice. Eire Under-21,
2 full caps.

Season	Club	Appearances	Goals
1976–77	Blackpool....................	—	—
1977–78	....	13	2
1978–79	....	24	5
1979–80	....	—	—
1979–80	Leeds U	17	2
1980–81	....	9	—
1981–82	....	—	—
1981–82	Bolton W	33	2
1982–83	....	37	4
1983–84	....	46	14
1984–85	....	41	16
1985–86	Derby Co	37	10
1986–87	....	9	—
1986–87	*Mansfield T*	6	—
1987–88	Bolton W	3	2
1988–89	....	20	2

1989–90		1	—
1989–90	Cardiff C	24	—
1990–91		1	—

CHANNING, Justin

Born Reading 19.11.68. Ht 5 10
Wt 10 02
Defender. From Apprentice. England
Youth.

1986–87	QPR	2	—
1987–88		14	1
1988–89		9	1
1989–90		23	2
1990–91		5	—

CHAPMAN, Gary

Born Leeds 1.5.64   Ht 5 10   Wt 12 00
Forward. Local.

1988–89	Bradford C	2	—
1989–90		3	—
1989–90	Notts Co	19	4
1990–91		6	—
1990–91	*Mansfield T*	6	—

CHAPMAN, Ian

Born Brighton 31.5.70.   Ht 5 8   Wt 11 05
Defender. FA Schools.

1986–87	Brighton	5	—
1987–88		—	—
1988–89		19	—
1989–90		42	—
1990–91		23	—

CHAPMAN, Lee

Born Lincoln 5.12.59.   Ht 6 1   Wt 13 00
Forward. From Amateur. England B,
Under-21.

1978–79	Stoke C	—	—
1978–79	*Plymouth Arg*	4	—
1979–80	Stoke C	17	3
1980–81		41	15
1981–82		41	16

1982–83	Arsenal	19	3
1983–84		4	1
1983–84	Sunderland	15	3
1984–85	Sheffield W	40	15
1985–86		31	10
1986–87		41	19
1987–88		37	19
From Niort			
1988–89	Nottingham F	30	8
1989–90		18	7
1989–90	Leeds U	21	12
1990–91		38	21

CHAPMAN, Vincent

Born Newcastle 5.12.67.   Ht 5 9
Wt 11 00
Defender. From Tow Law T.

1987–88	Huddersfield T	6	—
1988–89		—	—
1988–89	*York C*	—	—
1989–90	Rochdale	4	—
1990–91		20	1

CHAPPLE, Phil

Born Norwich 26.11.66.   Ht 6 2   Wt 12 07
Defender. From Apprentice.

1984–85	Norwich C	—	—
1985–86		—	—
1986–87		—	—
1987–88		—	—
1987–88	Cambridge U	6	1
1988–89		46	3
1989–90		45	5
1990–91		43	5

CHARD, Phil

Born Corby 16.10.60.   Ht 5 8   Wt 11 03
Midfield. From Nottingham F. Amateur.

1978–79	Peterborough U	6	1
1979–80		20	2
1980–81		—	—
1981–82		39	3
1982–83		44	4
1983–84		38	7

1984–85	....	25	1
1985–86	Northampton T	41	7
1986–87	....	40	12
1987–88	....	34	8
1987–88	Wolverhampton W	9	2
1988–89	....	19	3
1989–90	....	6	—
1989–90	Northampton T	29	2
1990–91	....	43	7

CHARLERY, Ken

Born Stepney 28.11.64. Ht 6 1 Wt 12 07
Forward. From Fisher Ath, Basildon U,
Beckton U (1989).

1989–90	Maidstone U	30	2
1990–91	....	29	9
1990–91	Peterborough U	4	—

CHARLES, Gary

Born London 13.4.70. Ht 5 9 Wt 10 13
Defender. England Under-21, 2 full caps.

1987–88	Nottingham F	—	—
1988–89	....	1	—
1988–89	*Leicester C*	8	—
1989–90	Nottingham F	1	—
1990–91	....	10	—

CHARLES, Steve

Born Sheffield 10.5.60. Ht 5 9 Wt 10 07
Midfield. From Sheffield University.
England Schools.

1979–80	Sheffield U	14	1
1980–81	....	31	6
1981–82	....	30	1
1982–83	....	35	—
1983–84	....	11	1
1984–85	....	2	1
1984–85	Wrexham	32	7
1985–86	....	40	20
1986–87	....	41	10
1987–88	Mansfield T	46	12
1988–89	....	46	7
1989–90	....	43	7
1990–91	....	39	4

CHARLTON, Simon

Born Huddersfield 25.10.71. Ht 5 7
Wt 10 11
Defender. From Trainee. FA Schools.

| 1989–90 | Huddersfield T .... | 3 | — |
| 1990–91 | .... | 30 | — |

CHEETHAM, Michael

Born Amsterdam 30.6.67 Ht 5 11
Wt 11 05
Midfield. From Army.

1988–89	Ipswich T	3	—
1989–90	....	1	—
1989–90	Cambridge U	36	10
1990–91	....	44	7

CHEREDNIK, Aleksey

Born USSR 12.12.60. Ht 5 9 Wt 11 07
Defender. From Dnepr.

| 1989–90 | Southampton .... | 8 | — |
| 1990–91 | .... | 15 | — |

CHERRY, Paul

Born Derby 14.10.64. Ht 6 0 Wt 11 07
Defender. From Salvesen BC.

1984–85	Hearts	3	—
1985–86	....	5	—
1986–87	Cowdenbeath	35	5
1987–88	....	35	8
1988–89	St Johnstone	39	2
1989–90	....	39	4
1990–91	....	20	—

CHERRY, Steve

Born Nottingham 5.8.60. Ht 5 11
Wt 11 00
Goalkeeper. From Apprentice. England
Youth.

1977–78	Derby Co	—	—
1978–79	....	—	—
1979–80	....	4	—

Season	Club	League Appearances/Goals	
1980–81	*Port Vale*	4	—
1981–82	Derby Co	4	—
1982–83		31	—
1983–84		38	—
1984–85	Walsall	41	—
1985–86		30	—
1986–87		—	—
1986–87	Plymouth Arg	21	—
1987–88		37	—
1988–89		15	—
1988–89	*Chesterfield*	10	—
1988–89	Notts Co	18	—
1989–90		46	—
1990–91		46	—

CHETTLE, Steve

Born Nottingham 27.9.68.   Ht 6 1
Wt 12 00
Defender. From Apprentice. England
Under-21.

Season	Club	League Appearances/Goals	
1986–87	Nottingham F	—	—
1987–88		30	—
1988–89		28	2
1989–90		22	1
1990–91		37	2

CHILDS, Gary

Born Birmingham 19.4.64.   Ht 5 7
Wt 10 08
Midfield. From Apprentice. England
Youth.

Season	Club	League Appearances/Goals	
1981–82	WBA	2	—
1982–83		—	—
1983–84		1	—
1983–84	Walsall	30	2
1984–85		40	2
1985–86		33	5
1986–87		28	8
1987–88	Birmingham C	32	1
1988–89		23	1
1989–90	Grimsby T	44	5
1990–91		25	4

CHIVERS, Gary

Born Stockwell 15.5.60.   Ht 5 11
Wt 11 05
Defender. From Apprentice.

Season	Club	League Appearances/Goals	
1978–79	Chelsea	5	—
1979–80		29	2
1980–81		40	2
1981–82		29	—
1982–83		30	—
1983–84	Swansea C	10	—
1983–84	QPR	—	—
1984–85		23	—
1985–86		14	—
1986–87		23	—
1987–88	Watford	14	—
1987–88	Brighton	10	—
1988–89		46	6
1989–90		41	3
1990–91		39	3

CHRISTIE, Trevor

Born Newcastle 28.2.59.   Ht 6 2
Wt 12 00
Forward. From Apprentice.

Season	Club	League Appearances/Goals	
1976–77	Leicester C	—	—
1977–78		5	—
1978–79		26	8
1979–80	Notts Co	41	9
1980–81		39	14
1981–82		35	13
1982–83		33	9
1983–84		39	19
1984–85	Nottingham F	14	5
1984–85	Derby Co	20	7
1985–86		45	15
1986–87	Manchester C	9	3
1986–87	Walsall	35	13
1987–88		36	7
1988–89		28	2
1988–89	Mansfield T	12	1
1989–90		45	13
1990–91		35	10

CLAESEN, Nico

Born Leut 1.10.62.   Ht 5 8   Wt 10 00
Forward. From Standard Liege. Belgium
full caps.

Season	Club	Apps	Goals
1986–87	Tottenham H	26	8
1987–88		24	10

To Antwerp

CLARIDGE, Steve

Born Portsmouth 10.4.66.   Ht 5 11
Wt 11 08
Forward. From Portsmouth, Fareham.

Season	Club	Apps	Goals
1984–85	Bournemouth	6	1
1985–86		1	—
From Weymouth			
1988–89	Crystal Palace	—	—
1988–89	Aldershot	37	9
1989–90		25	10
1989–90	Cambridge U	20	4
1990–91		30	12

CLARK, Billy

Born Christchurch 19.5.67.   Ht 6 0
Wt 12 03
Defender. From Local.

Season	Club	Apps	Goals
1984–85	Bournemouth	1	—
1985–86		1	—
1986–87		—	—
1987–88		2	—
1987–88	Bristol R	31	1
1988–89		11	—
1989–90		—	—
1990–91		14	1

CLARK, Howard

Born Coventry 19.9.68.   Ht 5 11
Wt 11 01
Defender. From Apprentice.

Season	Club	Apps	Goals
1986–87	Coventry C	—	—
1987–88		—	—
1988–89		9	1
1989–90		9	—
1990–91		2	—

CLARK, John

Born Edinburgh 22.9.64.   Ht 6 0
Wt 13 01
Defender. 'S' Form. Scotland Youth.

Season	Club	Apps	Goals
1981–82	Dundee U	—	—
1982–83		1	—
1983–84		9	1
1984–85		10	3
1985–86		11	1
1986–87		30	3
1987–88		28	3
1988–89		20	2
1989–90		29	1
1990–91		18	2

CLARK, Lee

Born Wallsend 27.10.72.   Ht 5 7
Wt 11 07
Midfield. From Trainee. England Youth.

Season	Club	Apps	Goals
1989–90	Newcastle U	—	—
1990–91		19	2

CLARK, Martin

Born Uddington 13.10.68   Ht 5 9
Wt 10 11
Midfield. From Hamilton A.

Season	Club	Apps	Goals
1987–88	Clyde	26	—
1988–89		25	2
1988–89	Nottingham F	—	—
1989–90		—	—
1989–90	*Falkirk*	3	1
1989–90	*Mansfield T*	14	1
1990–91	Mansfield T	24	—

CLARK, Paul

Born Benfleet 14.9.58.   Ht 5 9   Wt 13 13
Midfield. From Apprentice. England
Schools, Youth.

Season	Club	Apps	Goals
1976–77	Southend U	25	—
1977–78		8	1
1977–78	Brighton	26	3
1978–79		33	4
1979–80		11	2

Season	Club	App	Goals
1980–81		9	—
1981–82	*Reading*	2	—
1982–83	Southend U	31	1
1983–84		20	—
1984–85		29	1
1985–86		39	1
1986–87		46	—
1987–88		30	—
1988–89		16	—
1989–90		25	—
1990–91		40	—

CLARKE, Andy

Born London 22.7.67. Ht 5 10   Wt 11 07
Forward. From Barnet.

Season	Club	App	Goals
1990–91	Wimbledon	12	3

CLARKE, Brian

Born Eastbourne 10.10.68. Ht 6 3
Wt 13 08
Defender.

Season	Club	App	Goals
1987–88	Gillingham	—	—
1988–89		10	—
1989–90		3	—
1990–91		20	—

CLARKE, Colin

Born Newry 30.10.62. Ht 6 0   Wt 13 06
Forward. From Apprentice. Northern
Ireland, 30 full caps.

Season	Club	App	Goals
1980–81	Ipswich T	—	—
1981–82	Peterborough	27	4
1982–83		37	9
1983–84		18	5
1983–84	*Gillingham*	8	1
1984–85	Tranmere R	45	22
1985–86	Bournemouth	46	26
1986–87	Southampton	33	20
1987–88		40	16
1988–89		9	—
1988–89	*Bournemouth*	4	2
1988–89	QPR	12	5
1989–90		34	6
1990–91	Portsmouth	42	13

CLARKE, David

Born Nottingham 3.12.64. Ht 5 10
Wt 11 00
Midfield. From Apprentice. England
Youth.

Season	Club	App	Goals
1982–83	Notts Co	16	—
1983–84		20	—
1984–85		22	—
1985–86		42	1
1986–87		23	6
1987–88	Lincoln C	*30*	5
1988–89		36	4
1989–90		30	2
1990–91		15	—

CLARKE, Mick

Born Birmingham 22.12.67. Ht 5 11
Wt 11 05
Forward. From Birmingham C
Apprentice.

Season	Club	App	Goals
1986–87	Barnsley	23	3
1987–88		14	—
1988–89		3	—
1989–90	Scarborough	36	1
1990–91		1	—

CLARKE, Nicky

Born Walsall 20.8.67. Ht 5 11   Wt 12 00
Defender. From Apprentice.

Season	Club	App	Goals
1984–85	Wolverhampton W	—	—
1985–86		23	1
1986–87		24	—
1987–88		8	—
1988–89		8	—
1989–90		3	—
1990–91		14	—

CLARKE, Simon

Born Chelmsford 23.9.71. Ht 5 11
Wt 11 02
Forward. From Trainee.

Season	Club	App	Goals
1990–91	West Ham U	1	—

CLARKE, Stephen

Born Saltcoats 29.8.63. Ht 5 10
Wt 10 02
Defender. From Beith Juniors. Scotland
Youth, Under-21, B. Football League.

Season	Club	Apps	Goals
1981–82	St Mirren	—	—
1982–83		31	—
1983–84		33	2
1984–85		33	—
1985–86		31	3
1986–87		23	1
1986–87	Chelsea	16	—
1987–88		38	1
1988–89		36	—
1989–90		24	3
1990–91		18	1

CLARKE, Wayne

Born Wolverhampton 28.2.61. Ht 6 0
Wt 11 08
Forward. From Apprentice. England
Schools, Youth.

Season	Club	Apps	Goals
1977–78	Wolverhampton W	1	—
1978–79		8	1
1979–80		16	2
1980–81		24	3
1981–82		29	6
1982–83		39	12
1983–84		31	6
1984–85	Birmingham C	40	17
1985–86		28	5
1986–87		24	16
1986–87	Everton	10	5
1987–88		27	10
1988–89		20	3
1989–90	Leicester C	11	1
1989–90	Manchester C	9	—
1990–91		7	1
1990–91	*Shrewsbury T*	7	6
1990–91	*Stoke C*	9	3

CLARKSON, Ian

Born Birmingham 4.12.70 Ht 5 11
Wt 11 08
Defender. From Trainee.

Season	Club	Apps	Goals
1988–89	Birmingham C	9	—
1989–90		20	—
1990–91		37	—

CLAYTON, Gary

Born Sheffield 2.2.63. Ht 5 11 Wt 12 08
Midfield. From Rotherham U Apprentice,
Burton Alb.

Season	Club	Apps	Goals
1986–87	Doncaster R	35	5
1987–88	Cambridge U	45	5
1988–89		46	1
1989–90		10	1
1990–91		6	—
1990–91	*Peterborough U*	4	—

CLAYTON, John

Born Elgin 20.8.61. Ht 5 11 Wt 11 07
Forward. From Apprentice.

Season	Club	Apps	Goals
1978–79	Derby C	1	—
1979–80		—	—
1980–81		9	1
1981–82		14	3
From Bulova, Hong Kong			
1983–84	Chesterfield	33	5
1984–85	Tranmere R	44	31
1985–86		3	4
1985–86	Plymouth Arg	36	12
1986–87		21	3
1987–88		20	6
To Fortuna Sittard			

CLAYTON, Paul

Born Dunstable 4.1.65. Ht 5 11
Wt 11 03
Forward. From Apprentice.

Season	Club	Apps	Goals
1982–83	Norwich C	—	—
1983–84		7	—
1984–85		5	—
1985–86		1	—
1986–87		—	—
1987–88		—	—
1987–88	Darlington	12	3
1988–89		10	—
1988–89	Crewe Alex	20	6

| 1989–90 | .... | 18 | 4 |
| 1990–91 | .... | 22 | 2 |

CLELAND, Alec

Born Glasgow 10.12.70. Ht 5 8 Wt 10 00
Defender. From S Form. Scotland
Under-21.

1987–88	Dundee U	1	—
1988–89	....	9	—
1989–90	....	15	—
1990–91	....	20	2

CLEMENT, Andy

Born Cardiff 12.11.67. Ht 5 8 Wt 11 00
Defender. From Apprentice. Wales Youth.

1985–86	Wimbledon	—	—
1986–87	....	4	—
1986–87	*Bristol R*.....................	6	—
1987–88	Wimbledon	11	—
1987–88	*Newport Co*................	5	1
1988–89	Wimbledon	11	—
1989–90	....	—	—
From Woking
1990–91	Plymouth Arg.............	16	—

CLEMENTS, Kenny

Born Manchester 9.4.55 Ht 6 1 Wt 12 06
Defender. From Amateur.

1975–76	Manchester C	27	—
1976–77	....	35	—
1977–78	....	42	—
1978–79	....	15	—
1979–80	....	—	—
1979–80	Oldham Ath.................	36	1
1980–81	....	40	—
1981–82	....	27	1
1982–83	....	38	—
1983–84	....	41	—
1984–85	....	24	—
1984–85	*Manchester C*.............	12	1
1985–86	Manchester C	30	—
1986–87	....	39	—
1987–88	....	25	—
1987–88	Bury	9	1

1988–89	....	44	—
1989–90	....	28	—
1990–91	Shrewsbury T.............	20	—

CLOSE, Shaun

Born Islington 8.9.66. Ht 5 8 Wt 10 01
Forward. From Trainee.

1984–85	Tottenham H	—	—
1985–86	....	—	—
1986–87	....	2	—
1987–88	....	7	—
1987–88	Bournemouth.............	16	6
1988–89	....	23	2
1989–90	....	—	—
1989–90	Swindon T..................	11	—
1990–91	....	14	—

CLOUGH, Nigel

Born Sunderland 19.3.66. Ht 5 9
Wt 11 05
Forward. From AC Hunters, England B,
Under-21, 4 full caps.

1984–85	Nottingham F.............	9	1
1985–86	....	39	15
1986–87	....	42	14
1987–88	....	34	19
1988–89	....	36	14
1989–90	....	38	9
1990–91	....	37	14

COATSWORTH, Gary

Born Sunderland 7.10.68. Ht 6 1
Wt 11 06
Defender.

1986–87	Barnsley	—	—
1987–88	....	6	—
1988–89	....	—	—
1989–90	Darlington	*3*	*1*
1990–91	....	12	1

COBB, Gary

Born Luton 6.8.68. Ht 5 8 Wt 11 05
Midfield. From Apprentice.

Season	Club	App	Goals
1986–87	Luton T	2	—
1987–88		7	—
1988–89		—	—
1988–89	*Northampton T*	1	—
1989–90	Luton T	—	—
1989–90	*Swansea C*	5	—
1990–91	Fulham	11	—

COBB, Paul

Born Thurrock 13.12.72.
Forward.

Season	Club	App	Goals
1990–91	Leyton Orient	4	—

COCKERILL, Glenn

Born Grimsby 25.8.59.   Ht 6 0   Wt 12 06
Midfield. From Louth U.

Season	Club	App	Goals
1976–77	Lincoln C	4	—
1977–78		13	1
1978–79		35	6
1979–80		19	3
1979–80	Swindon T	10	1
1980–81		16	—
1981–82	Lincoln C	44	11
1982–83		38	8
1983–84		33	6
1983–84	Sheffield U	10	1
1984–85		40	7
1985–86		12	2
1985–86	Southampton	30	7
1986–87		42	7
1987–88		39	2
1988–89		34	6
1989–90		36	4
1990–91		32	2

COCKERILL, John

Born Cleethorpes 12.7.61   Ht 6 0
Wt 12 07
Midfield. From Stafford R.

Season	Club	App	Goals
1988–89	Grimsby T	29	6
1989–90		33	5
1990–91		35	7

COCKRAM, Allan

Born Kensington 8.10.63.   Ht 5 8
Wt 10 08
Midfield. Local.

Season	Club	App	Goals
1980–81	Tottenham H	—	—
1981–82		—	—
1982–83		—	—
1983–84		2	—
1984–85		—	—
1985–86	Bristol R	1	—
From St Albans			
1987–88	Brentford	7	2
1988–89		37	7
1989–90		26	2
1990–91		20	3

CODDINGTON, Matt

Born Lytham St Annes 17.9.69   Ht 6 0
Wt 11 10
Goalkeeper. From Trainee.

Season	Club	App	Goals
1988–89	Middlesbrough	—	—
1989–90		—	—
1989–90	*Bury*	—	—
1989–90	*Halifax T*	—	—
1990–91	Darlington	—	—

CODNER, Robert

Born Walthamstow 23.1.65   Ht 5 11
Wt 11 05
Midfield. From Leicester C, Barnet.

Season	Club	App	Goals
1988–89	Brighton	28	1
1989–90		45	9
1990–91		42	8

CODY, Stephen

Born Calderbank 1.6.69   Ht 5 9   Wt 11 6
Midfield. From Bargeddie U

Season	Club	App	Goals
1989–90	Kilmarnock	20	—
1990–91	Falkirk	17	1

COLE, Andrew

Born Nottingham 15.10.71.   Ht 5 11
Wt 11 02
Forward. From Trainee. England Youth.

Season	Club	Apps	Goals
1989–90	Arsenal	—	—
1990–91		1	—

COLE, David

Born Barnsley 28.9.62. Ht 6 0 Wt 11 10
Defender. From Sunderland.

Season	Club	Apps	Goals
1984–85	Swansea C	8	—
1984–85	Swindon T	20	—
1985–86		44	3
1986–87		5	—
1986–87	Torquay U	29	—
1987–88		46	5
1988–89		35	1
1989–90	Rochdale	43	5
1990–91		41	2

COLE, Michael

Born Stepney 3.9.66. Ht 6 0 Wt 12 05
Forward. From Amateur.

Season	Club	Apps	Goals
1983–84	Ipswich T	—	—
1984–85		2	—
1985–86		18	1
1986–87		16	2
1987–88		2	—
1987–88	Port Vale	4	1
1987–88	Fulham	9	1
1988–89		36	3
1989–90		1	—
1990–91		2	—

COLEMAN, Chris

Born Swansea 10.6.70. Ht 6 2 Wt 12 10
Defender. From Apprentice. Wales
Under-21.

Season	Club	Apps	Goals
1987–88	Swansea C	30	—
1988–89		43	—
1989–90		46	2
1990–91		41	—

COLEMAN, David

Born Salisbury 8.4.67. Ht 5 7 Wt 10 08
Defender.

Season	Club	Apps	Goals
1985–86	Bournemouth	1	—

Season	Club	Apps	Goals
1986–87		1	—
1987–88		5	—
1987–88	Colchester U	6	1
1988–89	Bournemouth	9	1
1989–90		27	1
1990–91		7	—

COLEMAN, Nicky

Born Crayford 6.5.66. Ht 5 10 Wt 11 12
Defender. From Apprentice.

Season	Club	Apps	Goals
1983–84	Millwall	—	—
1984–85		1	—
1985–86		6	—
1985–86	Swindon T	13	4
1986–87	Millwall	42	—
1987–88		36	—
1988–89		—	—
1989–90		3	—
1990–91		—	—

COLEMAN, Simon

Born Worksop 13.3.68. Ht 6 0 Wt 10 08
Midfield.

Season	Club	Apps	Goals
1985–86	Mansfield T	—	—
1986–87		2	—
1987–88		44	2
1988–89		45	5
1989–90		5	—
1989–90	Middlesbrough	36	1
1990–91		19	1

COLES, David

Born Wandsworth 15.6.64 Ht 6 0
Wt 11 00
Goalkeeper. From Apprentice.

Season	Club	Apps	Goals
1981–82	Birmingham C	—	—
1982–83		—	—
1982–83	Mansfield T	3	—
1983–84	Aldershot	45	—
1984–85		34	—
1985–86		29	—
1986–87		1	—
1987–88		11	—
1987–88	Newport Co	14	—

From HJK Helsinki

Season	Club	Apps	Goals
1988–89	Colchester U	—	—
1988–89	Crystal Palace	—	—
1988–89	Brighton	1	—
1989–90	Aldershot	28	—
1990–91		2	—

COLLETON, Antony

Born Manchester 17.1.74. Ht 5 8
Wt 10 06
Forward. From Trainee.

1990–91	Rochdale	1	—

COLLIER, Darren

Born Stockton 1.12.67 Ht 5 11 Wt 11 09
Goalkeeper. From Middlesbrough.

1988–89	Blackburn R	1	—
1989–90		16	—
1990–91		10	—

COLLINGS, Paul

Born Liverpool 30.9.68 Ht 6 2 Wt 12 00
Goalkeeper.

1988–89	Tranmere R	1	—
1989–90		—	—
1990–91		3	—

COLLINS, Darren

Born Winchester 24.5.67
Forward. From Liphook, Petersfield U.

1988–89	Northampton T	8	—
1989–90		35	8
1990–91		8	1

COLLINS, John

Born Galashiels 31.1.68. Ht 5 7 Wt 9 10
Midfield. From Hutchison Vale BC.
Scotland Youth, Under-21, 6 full caps.

1984–85	Hibernian	—	—
1985–86		19	1

1986–87		30	1
1987–88		44	6
1988–89		35	2
1989–90		35	6
1990–91	Celtic	35	1

COLLYMORE, Stan

Born Stone 22.1.71.
Forward. From Stafford R.

1990–91	Crystal Palace	6	—

COLQUHOUN, John

Born Stirling 14.7.63. Ht 5 7 Wt 10 0
Forward. From Grangemouth Inter.

1980–81	Stirling Albion	13	—
1981–82		37	13
1982–83		39	21
1983–84		15	11
1983–84	Celtic	12	2
1984–85		20	2
1985–86	Hearts	36	8
1986–87		43	13
1987–88		44	15
1988–89		36	5
1989–90		36	6
1990–91		36	7

COLVILLE, Bob

Born Nuneaton 27.4.63. Ht 5 10
Wt 11 11
Forward. From Rhos.

1983–84	Oldham Ath	4	1
1984–85		7	1
1985–86		17	2
1986–87		4	—
1986–87	Bury	8	1
1987–88		3	—
1987–88	Stockport Co	40	14
1988–89		31	6
1989–90	York C	24	—
1990–91	Crewe Alex	—	—

COMSTIVE, Paul

Born Southport 25.11.61. Ht 6 1
Wt 12 07
Midfield. From Amateur.

Season	Club	Apps	Goals
1979–80	Blackburn R	—	—
1980–81		3	—
1981–82		2	—
1982–83		1	—
1982–83	*Rochdale*	9	2
1983–84	Wigan Ath	29	2
1984–85		6	—
1984–85	Wrexham	28	3
1985–86		35	3
1986–87		36	2
1987–88	Burnley	44	8
1988–89		38	9
1989–90		—	—
1989–90	Bolton W	31	1
1990–91		18	2

COMYN, Andy

Born Manchester 2.6.68. Ht 6 1
Wt 12 00
Defender. From Alvechurch.

Season	Club	Apps	Goals
1989–90	Aston Villa	4	—
1990–91		11	—

CONN, Samuel

Born Lanark 26.10.61   Ht 5 11   Wt 12 0
Midfield. From Polkemmet J

Season	Club	Apps	Goals
1980–81	Falkirk	17	1
1981–82		9	2
1982–83	Albion R	34	6
1983–84		30	5
1984–85		31	2
1985–86		33	6
1986–87		17	4
1986–87	Clydebank	19	1
1987–88	Falkirk	36	2
1988–89	Airdrieonians	31	8
1989–90		31	2
1990–91		21	1

CONNELLY, Dino

Born Glasgow 6.1.70.   Ht 5 9   Wt 10 08
Midfield. From Celtic BC, Arsenal
Trainee. Scotland Schools, Youth.

Season	Club	Apps	Goals
1987–88	Arsenal	—	—

Season	Club	Apps	Goals
1988–89		—	—
1989–90		—	—
1990–91	Barnsley	9	—

CONNOLLY, Patrick

Born Glasgow 25.6.70.   Ht 5 8   Wt 9 04
Midfield. From S Form. Scotland
Under-21.

Season	Club	Apps	Goals
1986–87	Dundee U	—	—
1987–88		—	—
1988–89		2	—
1989–90		15	5
1990–91		10	2

CONNOR, Robert

Born Kilmarnock 4.8.60.   Ht 5 11
Wt 11 04
Midfield. From Ayr U BC. Scotland
Youth, B, Under-21, 4 full caps.

Season	Club	Apps	Goals
1977–78	Ayr U	9	—
1978–79		29	—
1979–80		38	9
1980–81		39	8
1981–82		30	—
1982–83		39	4
1983–84		39	7
1984–85	Dundee	34	7
1985–86		35	2
1986–87		2	—
1986–87	Aberdeen	32	4
1987–88		34	1
1988–89		36	4
1989–90		34	1
1990–91		29	6

CONNOR, Terry

Born Leeds 9.11.62.   Ht 5 9   Wt 11 08
Forward. From Apprentice. England
Youth, Under-21.

Season	Club	Apps	Goals
1979–80	Leeds U	23	6
1980–81		27	4
1981–82		27	4
1982–83		19	5
1982–83	Brighton	7	1

Season	Club	App	Goals
1983–84	....	40	13
1984–85		38	14
1985–86		33	14
1986–87		38	9
1987–88	Portsmouth	19	4
1988–89		14	5
1989–90		15	3
1990–91	Swansea C....................	33	5

CONROY, Mike

Born Glasgow 31.12.65. Ht 6 0 Wt 11 00
Forward. From Apprentice.

Season	Club	App	Goals
1983–84	Coventry C	—	—
1983–84	Clydebank....................	2	—
1984–85		26	11
1985–86		28	7
1986–87		36	9
1987–88		22	11
1987–88	St Mirren	10	1
1988–89	Reading.......................	13	4
1989–90		34	2
1990–91		33	1

COOK, Andy

Born Romsey 10.8.69. Ht 5 9 Wt 10 12
Defender. From Apprentice.

Season	Club	App	Goals
1987–88	Southampton	2	—
1988–89		3	—
1989–90		4	1
1990–91		7	—

COOK, Jason

Born Edmonton 29.12.69 Ht 5 7
Wt 10 06
Midfield. From Trainee.

Season	Club	App	Goals
1988–89	Tottenham H	—	—
1989–90	Southend U.................	29	1
1990–91		1	—

COOK, Mike

Born Coventry 18.10.68 Ht 5 9 Wt 10 12
Midfield. From Trainee.

Season	Club	App	Goals
1986–87	Coventry C	—	—

Season	Club	App	Goals
1987–88	....	—	—
1987–88	York C	6	1
1988–89	Coventry C	—	—
1989–90	Cambridge U	15	1
1990–91		2	—
1990–91	York C	6	—

COOK, Mitch

Born Scarborough 15.10.61. Ht 6 0
Wt 12 0
Midfield. From Scarborough.

Season	Club	App	Goals
1984–85	Darlington	31	3
1985–86		3	1
1985–86	Middlesbrough.............	6	—
1986–87	Scarborough...............	—	—
1987–88		38	5
1988–89		43	5
1989–90	Halifax T	37	2
1990–91		17	—
1990–91	Scarborough	9	1
1990–91	Darlington	9	1

COOK, Paul

Born Liverpool 22.2.67. Ht 5 11
Wt 10 10
Midfield.

Season	Club	App	Goals
1984–85	Wigan Ath	2	—
1985–86		13	2
1986–87		27	4
1987–88		41	8
1988–89	Norwich C	4	—
1989–90		2	—
1989–90	Wolverhampton W	28	2
1990–91		42	6

COOKE, John

Born Salford 25.4.62. Ht 5 8 Wt 11 00
Forward. From Apprentice. England
Youth.

Season	Club	App	Goals
1979–80	Sunderland.................	4	1
1980–81		17	1
1981–82		10	1
1982–83		14	1
1983–84		4	—

Season	Club	App	Goals
1984–85	....	6	—
1984–85	*Carlisle U*	6	2
1985–86	Sheffield W	—	—
1985–86	Carlisle U	33	4
1986–87	....	36	2
1987–88	....	37	5
1988–89	Stockport Co	34	6
1989–90	....	24	1
1990–91	Chesterfield	20	1

COOKE, Richard

Born Islington 4.9.65. Ht 5 6 Wt 9 00
Forward. From Apprentice. England
Youth, Under-21.

Season	Club	App	Goals
1982–83	Tottenham H	—	—
1983–84	....	9	1
1984–85	....	—	—
1985–86	....	2	1
1986–87	....	—	—
1986–87	*Birmingham C*	5	—
1986–87	Bournemouth	23	8
1987–88	....	34	5
1988–89	....	15	3
1988–89	Luton T	6	—
1989–90	....	11	1
1990–91	....	—	—
1990–91	Bournemouth	10	2

COOKSON, Steve

Born Wolverhampton 19.2.72. Ht 6 1
Wt 10 10
Forward. From Trainee.

Season	Club	App	Goals
1989–90	Torquay U	10	1
1990–91	....	2	—

COOMBS, Paul

Born Bristol 4.9.70 Ht 5 11 Wt 12 05
Forward. From QPR schoolboy, Aldershot
trainee.

Season	Club	App	Goals
1988–89	Aldershot	1	—
1989–90	....	12	1
1990–91	....	3	—

COOPER, Colin

Born Durham 28.2.67. Ht 5 10 Wt 11 01
Defender. England Under-21.

Season	Club	App	Goals
1984–85	Middlesbrough	—	—
1985–86	....	11	—
1986–87	....	46	—
1987–88	....	43	2
1988–89	....	35	2
1989–90	....	21	2
1990–91	....	32	—

COOPER, David

Born London 23.6.71. Ht 5 10 Wt 11 10
Forward. From Trainee.

Season	Club	App	Goals
1989–90	Wimbledon	—	—
1990–91	Plymouth Arg	3	—

COOPER, Davie

Born Hamilton 25.2.56. Ht 5 8 Wt 12 05
Forward. From Hamilton Avondale.
Scotland Under-21. 22 full caps.

Season	Club	App	Goals
1974–75	Clydebank	26	4
1975–76	....	26	13
1976–77	....	38	11
1977–78	Rangers	35	6
1978–79	....	30	5
1979–80	....	30	2
1980–81	....	25	3
1981–82	....	30	3
1982–83	....	31	5
1983–84	....	34	6
1984–85	....	32	5
1985–86	....	32	4
1986–87	....	42	8
1987–88	....	33	1
1988–89	....	23	1
1989–90	Motherwell	31	6
1990–91	....	34	6

COOPER, Gary

Born Edgware 20.11.65. Ht 5 8 Wt 11 03
Defender. From Brentford, QPR and
Fisher Ath (1989)

Season	Club	App	Goals
1989–90	Maidstone U	33	4
1990–91	....	27	3
1990–91	Peterborough U	6	1

COOPER, Graham

Born Bolton 18.11.65. Ht 5 10   Wt 10 11
Midfield. From Amateur.

1983–84	Huddersfield T	3	1
1984–85		34	5
1985–86		—	—
1986–87		12	2
1987–88		25	5
1988–89	Wrexham	36	11
1989–90		18	3
1990–91		9	2
1990–91	*York C*	2	—
1990–91	Halifax T	17	1

COOPER, Leigh

Born Reading 7.5.61. Ht 5 8   Wt 10 09
Defender. From Apprentice.

1979–80	Plymouth Arg	14	—
1980–81		28	3
1981–82		43	5
1982–83		45	4
1983–84		43	2
1984–85		21	—
1985–86		40	1
1986–87		35	—
1987–88		37	—
1988–89		15	—
1989–90		2	—
1990–91	Aldershot	33	2

COOPER, Mark

Born Wakefield 18.12.68. Ht 5 8
Wt 11 04
Midfield. From Trainee.

1987–88	Bristol C	—	—
1988–89		—	—
1989–90	Exeter C	5	—
1989–90	*Southend U*	5	—
1990–91	Exeter C	42	11

COOPER, Mark

Born Cambridge 5.4.67. Ht 6 2   Wt 13 04
Forward. From Apprentice.

1983–84	Cambridge U	2	—
1984–85		18	3
1985–86		19	1
1986–87		32	13
1986–87	Tottenham H	—	—
1987–88		—	—
1987–88	Shrewsbury T	6	2
1987–88	Gillingham	31	8
1988–89		18	3
1988–89	Leyton Orient	14	4
1989–90		39	11
1990–91		22	9

COOPER, Neale

Born India 24.11.63. Ht 6 1   Wt 12 07
Defender. From King St. Scotland
Schools, Youth, Under-21.

1979–80	Aberdeen	—	—
1980–81		5	—
1981–82		27	3
1982–83		31	2
1983–84		26	—
1984–85		20	1
1985–86		23	—
1986–87	Aston Villa	13	—
1987–88		7	—
1988–89		—	—
1988–89	Rangers	14	1
1989–90		3	—
1990–91		—	—

COOPER, Neil

Born Aberdeen 12.8.59. Ht 5 11
Wt 12 07
Defender. From Hilton Academy.
Scotland Schools, Youth.

1974–75	Aberdeen	1	—
1975–76		2	—
1976–77		—	—
1977–78		1	—
1978–79		7	1
1979–80		1	—
1979–80	Barnsley	20	3
1980–81		30	2
1981–82		10	1
1981–82	Grimsby T	16	1

Season	Club	League Appearances/Goals	
1982–83	....	24	1
1983–84	....	7	—
1983–84	St Mirren	25	—
1984–85	....	10	—
1985–86	....	30	—
1986–87	....	39	1
1987–88	....	27	1
1988–89	....	30	—
1989–90	Hibernian..................	27	—
1990–91	....	11	—

COOPER, Paul

Born Brierley Hill 21.12.53.   Ht 5 10
Wt 12 12
Goalkeeper. From Apprentice.

Season	Club	League Appearances/Goals	
1971–72	Birmingham C	12	—
1972–73	....	3	—
1973–74	....	2	—
1973–74	Ipswich T	1	—
1974–75	....	2	—
1975–76	....	40	—
1976–77	....	34	—
1977–78	....	40	—
1978–79	....	41	—
1979–80	....	40	—
1980–81	....	38	—
1981–82	....	32	—
1982–83	....	35	—
1983–84	....	36	—
1984–85	....	36	—
1985–86	....	36	—
1986–87	....	36	—
1987–88	Leicester C	32	—
1988–89	....	24	—
1988–89	Manchester C	8	—
1989–90	....	7	—
1990–91	Stockport Co	22	—

COOPER, Steve

Born Birmingham 22.6.64.   Ht 5 11
Wt 10 12
Forward.

Season	Club	League Appearances/Goals	
1983–84	Birmingham C	—	—
1983–84	*Halifax T*	7	1
1984–85	*Mansfield T*..............	—	—
1984–85	Newport Co	38	11

Season	Club	League Appearances/Goals	
1985–86	Plymouth Arg.............	38	8
1986–87	....	12	4
1987–88	....	23	3
1988–89	Barnsley	35	6
1989–90	....	30	5
1990–91	....	12	2
1990–91	Tranmere	17	2

CORDNER, Scott

Born Grimsby 3.8.72.   Ht 6 1   Wt 12 04
Forward. From Trainee

Season	Club	League Appearances/Goals	
1990–91	Chesterfield	4	1

CORK, Alan

Born Derby 4.3.59.   Ht 6 0   Wt 12 00
Forward. From Amateur.

Season	Club	League Appearances/Goals	
1977–78	Derby C	—	—
1977–78	*Lincoln C*	5	—
1977–78	Wimbledon	17	4
1978–79	....	45	22
1979–80	....	42	12
1980–81	....	41	23
1981–82	....	6	—
1982–83	....	7	5
1983–84	....	42	29
1984–85	....	28	11
1985–86	....	38	11
1986–87	....	30	5
1987–88	....	34	9
1988–89	....	25	2
1989–90	....	31	5
1990–91	....	25	5

CORK, David

Born Doncaster 28.10.62.   Ht 5 9
Wt 11 08
Midfield. From Apprentice.

Season	Club	League Appearances/Goals	
1980–81	Arsenal.......................	—	—
1981–82	....	—	—
1982–83	....	—	—
1983–84	....	7	1
1984–85	....	—	—
1985–86	Huddersfield T............	38	8
1986–87	....	36	9

Season	Club	League Appearances/Goals	
1987–88	....	36	8
1988–89	....	—	—
1988–89	*WBA*	4	—
1988–89	Scunthorpe U	15	—
1989–90	Darlington	*41*	*12*
1990–91	....	34	8

CORNER, David

Born Sunderland 15.5.66. Ht 6 2
Wt 12 13
Defender. From Apprentice. England
Youth.

Season	Club	League Appearances/Goals	
1983–84	Sunderland.................	—	—
1984–85	....	3	—
1985–86	....	9	—
1985–86	*Cardiff C*	6	—
1986–87	Sunderland.................	17	1
1987–88	....	4	—
1987–88	*Peterborough U*	9	—
1988–89	Leyton Orient	4	—
1989–90	Darlington	*41*	*9*
1990–91	....	15	—

CORNER, Stuart

Born Glasgow 16.9.71   Ht 5 6   Wt 10 0
Forward. From Musselburgh Ath

Season	Club	League Appearances/Goals	
1990–91	Falkirk	1	—

CORNFORTH, John

Born Whitley Bay 7.10.67. Ht 6 1
Wt 12 08
Defender. From Apprentice.

Season	Club	League Appearances/Goals	
1984–85	Sunderland.................	1	—
1985–86	....	—	—
1986–87	....	—	—
1986–87	*Doncaster R*	7	3
1987–88	Sunderland.................	12	2
1988–89	....	15	—
1989–90	....	2	—
1989–90	*Shrewsbury T*	3	—
1989–90	*Lincoln C*	9	1
1990–91	Sunderland.................	2	—

CORNISH, Ricky

Born Lewisham 1.12.70.
Defender. From Ipswich T Schoolboy and
Cambridge U Trainee.

Season	Club	League Appearances/Goals	
1990–91	Aldershot	9	—

CORNWELL, John

Born Bethnal Green 13.10.64. Ht 6 0
Wt 12 00
Defender. From Apprentice.

Season	Club	League Appearances/Goals	
1981–82	Orient..........................	3	—
1982–83	....	31	3
1983–84	....	42	7
1984–85	....	36	10
1985–86	....	44	8
1986–87	....	46	7
1987–88	Newcastle U................	24	1
1988–89	....	9	—
1988–89	Swindon T	6	—
1989–90	....	19	—
1990–91	Southend U................	19	2

COSTELLO, Peter

Born Halifax 31.10.69 Ht 6 0   Wt 11 07
Forward. From Trainee.

Season	Club	League Appearances/Goals	
1988–89	Bradford C	8	2
1989–90	....	12	—
1990–91	Rochdale.....................	34	10
1990–91	Peterborough U	5	—

COTON, Tony

Born Tamworth 19.5.61. Ht 6 2
Wt 13 07
Goalkeeper. From Mile Oak.

Season	Club	League Appearances/Goals	
1978–79	Birmingham C	—	—
1979–80	....	—	—
1979–80	*Hereford U*...................	—	—
1980–81	Birmingham C	3	—
1981–82	....	15	—
1982–83	....	28	—
1983–84	....	41	—
1984–85	....	7	—
1984–85	Watford	33	—

Season	Club	League Appearances/Goals	
1985–86		40	—
1986–87		31	—
1987–88		37	—
1988–89		46	—
1989–90		46	—
1990–91	Manchester C	33	—

COTTEE, Tony

Born West Ham 11.7.65. Ht 5 8
Wt 11 11
Forward. From Apprentice. England
Youth, Under-21, 7 full caps.

Season	Club	League Appearances/Goals	
1982–83	West Ham U	8	5
1983–84		39	15
1984–85		41	17
1985–86		42	20
1986–87		42	22
1987–88		40	13
1988–89	Everton	36	13
1989–90		27	13
1990–91		29	10

COTTERILL, Steve

Born Cheltenham 20.7.64 Ht 6 1
Wt 12 05
Forward. From Burton A.

Season	Club	League Appearances/Goals	
1988–89	Wimbledon	4	1
1989–90		2	1
1990–91		4	1

COTTON, Perry

Born Chislehurst 11.11.65
Midfield. From New Zealand.

Season	Club	League Appearances/Goals	
1988–89	Scunthorpe U	1	—
1989–90		17	1
1990–91		15	1

COUGHLIN, Russell

Born Swansea 15.2.60. Ht 5 8 Wt 11 12
Midfield. From Apprentice.

Season	Club	League Appearances/Goals	
1977–78	Manchester C	—	—
1978–79		—	—

Season	Club	League Appearances/Goals	
1978–79	Blackburn R	11	—
1979–80		10	—
1980–81		3	—
1980–81	Carlisle U	25	3
1981–82		37	5
1982–83		38	2
1983–84		30	3
1984–85	Plymouth Arg	38	3
1985–86		45	10
1986–87		40	5
1987–88		8	—
1987–88	Blackpool	24	2
1988–89		43	5
1989–90		35	1
1990–91		—	—
1990–91	*Shrewsbury T*	5	—
1990–91	Swansea C	29	—

COUSINS, Jason

Born Hayes 14.10.70. Ht 6 0 Wt 12 07
Defender. From Trainee.

Season	Club	League Appearances/Goals	
1989–90	Brentford	13	—
1990–91		8	—

COVERDALE, Drew

Born Teeside 20.9.69. Ht 5 10 Wt 11 02
Defender. From Trainee.

Season	Club	League Appearances/Goals	
1988–89	Middlesbrough	—	—
1989–90	Darlington	*19*	*1*
1990–91		16	3

COWAN, Tom

Born Bellshill 28.8.69. Ht 5 8 Wt 10 08
Defender. From Netherdale BC.

Season	Club	League Appearances/Goals	
1988–89	Clyde	16	2
1988–89	Rangers	4	—
1989–90		3	—
1990–91		5	—

COWANS, Gordon

Born Durham 27.10.58. Ht 5 7 Wt 9 8
Midfield. From Apprentice. England
Youth, Under-21, B, 10 full caps.

Season	Club	Apps	Goals
1975–76	Aston Villa	1	—
1976–77		18	3
1977–78		35	7
1978–79		34	4
1979–80		42	6
1980–81		42	5
1981–82		42	6
1982–83		42	10
1983–84		—	—
1984–85		30	1
1985–86	Bari	20	—
1986–87		38	3
1987–88		36	—
1988–89	Aston Villa	33	2
1989–90		34	4
1990–91		38	1

COWDRILL, Barry

Born Birmingham 3.1.57.   Ht 5 11
Wt 11 04
Defender. From Sutton Coldfield T.

Season	Club	Apps	Goals
1979–80	WBA	9	—
1980–81		10	—
1981–82		8	—
1982–83		2	—
1983–84		22	—
1984–85		9	—
1985–86		10	—
1985–86	*Rotherham U.*	2	—
1986–87	WBA	29	—
1987–88		32	—
1988–89	Bolton W	38	—
1989–90		44	3
1990–s91		36	1

COWELL, Jim

Born Bellshill 28.7.61   Ht 6 0   Wt 11 9
Forward. From Shettleston J

Season	Club	Apps	Goals
1984–85	Hearts	1	—
1985–86	Ayr U	23	2
1986–87		28	4
1987–88		39	6
1988–89		30	2
1989–90		5	—
1989–90	Falkirk	9	—
1990–91		3	—

Season	Club	Apps	Goals
1990–91	East Fife	18	—

COWLING, David

Born Doncaster 27.11.58.   Ht 5 7
Wt 11 04
Forward. From Mansfield T. Apprentice.

Season	Club	Apps	Goals
1977–78	Huddersfield T	—	—
1978–79		26	1
1979–80		40	10
1980–81		43	4
1981–82		38	8
1982–83		41	7
1983–84		41	3
1984–85		32	4
1985–86		39	6
1986–87		34	—
1987–88		6	—
1987–88	*Scunthorpe U*	1	—
1987–88	Reading	10	1
1988–89	Scunthorpe U	39	2
1989–90		32	—
1990–91		18	3

COX, Brian

Born Sheffield 7.5.61.   Ht 6 0   Wt 13 05
Goalkeeper. From Apprentice.

Season	Club	Apps	Goals
1978–79	Sheffield Wed	4	—
1979–80		15	—
1980–81		3	—
1981–82	Huddersfield T	14	—
1982–83		45	—
1983–84		23	—
1984–85		37	—
1985–86		37	—
1986–87		37	—
1987–88		20	—
1988–89	Mansfield T	39	—
1989–90		15	—
1990–91	Hartlepool U	34	—

COX, Neil

Born Scunthorpe 8.10.71.   Ht 5 11
Wt 12 10
Midfield. From Trainee.

Season	Club	Apps	Goals
1989–90	Scunthorpe U	—	—

Season	Club	App	Goals
1990–91	....	17	1
1990–91	Aston Villa..................	—	—

COYLE, Owen

Born Glasgow 14.7.66   Ht 5 11   Wt 10 5
Forward. From Renfrew YM

Season	Club	App	Goals
1984–85	Dumbarton	—	—
1985–86	....	16	5
1986–87	....	43	17
1987–88	....	41	14
1988–89	....	3	—
1988–89	Clydebank..................	36	16
1989–90	....	27	17
1989–90	Airdrieonians	10	10
1990–91	....	28	20

COYNE, Tommy

Born Glasgow 14.11.62.   Ht 6 0   Wt 10 07
Forward. From Hillwood BC.

Season	Club	App	Goals
1981–82	Clydebank..................	31	9
1982–83	....	38	18
1983–84	....	11	10
1983–84	Dundee U	18	3
1984–85	....	21	3
1985–86	....	13	2
1986–87	Dundee....................	20	9
1987–88	....	43	33
1988–89	....	26	9
1988–89	Celtic....................	7	—
1989–90	....	23	7
1990–91	....	26	18

CRABBE, Scott

Born Edinburgh 12.8.68.   Ht 5 7
Wt 10 00
Midfield. From Tynecastle BC. Scotland
Under-21.

Season	Club	App	Goals
1986–87	Hearts	5	—
1987–88	....	5	—
1988–89	....	1	—
1989–90	....	35	12
1990–91	....	21	3

CRAINIE, Danny

Born Kilsyth 24.5.62   Ht 5 8   Wt 10 11
Forward. From Celtic BC

Season	Club	App	Goals
1979–80	Celtic............................	—	—
1980–81	....	—	—
1981–82	....	16	7
1982–83	....	7	—
1983–84	....	1	—
1983–84	Wolverhampton W	28	3
1984–85	....	13	—
1984–85	*Blackpool*	6	—
1985–86	Wolverhampton W	23	1
1985–86	Dundee......................	3	—
From Cork C, Wollongong C			
1990–91	Airdrieonians	28	1

CRANSON, Ian

Born Easington 2.7.64.   Ht 5 11
Wt 11 07
Defender. From Apprentice. England
Under-21.

Season	Club	App	Goals
1982–83	Ipswich T....................	—	—
1983–84	....	8	—
1984–85	....	20	1
1985–86	....	42	1
1986–87	....	32	2
1987–88	....	29	1
1987–88	Sheffield W..................	4	—
1988–89	....	26	—
1989–90	Stoke C....................	17	2
1990–91	....	9	—

CREANEY, Gerard

Born Coatbridge 13.4.70.   Ht 5 10
Wt 10 07
Forward. From Celtic BC. Scotland
Under-21.

Season	Club	App	Goals
1987–88	Celtic............................	—	—
1988–89	....	—	—
1989–90	....	6	1
1990–91	....	31	7

CRICHTON, Paul

Born Pontefract 3.10.68.   Ht 6 1
Wt 12 05
Goalkeeper. From Apprentice.

Season	Club	App	Goals
1986–87	Nottingham F.............	—	—

Season	Club	League Appearances/Goals	
1986–87	Notts Co	5	—
1986–87	Darlington	5	—
1986–87	Peterborough U	4	—
1987–88	Nottingham F	—	—
1987–88	Darlington	3	—
1987–88	Swindon T	4	—
1987–88	Rotherham U	6	—
1988–89	Nottingham F	—	—
1988–89	Torquay U	13	—
1988–89	Peterborough U	31	—
1989–90		16	—
1990–91	Doncaster R	20	—

CROFT, Brian

Born Chester 27.9.67. Ht 5 9 Wt 11 06
Midfield.

Season	Club	League Appearances/Goals	
1984–85	Chester C	—	—
1985–86		1	—
1986–87		21	1
1987–88		37	2
1988–89	Cambridge U	17	2
1989–90	Chester C	44	3
1990–91		38	—

CROFT, Gary

Born Burton-on-Trent 17.2.74.
Midfield. From Trainee.

Season	Club	League Appearances/Goals	
1990–91	Grimsby T	1	—

CROMBIE, Dean

Born Lincoln 9.8.57. Ht 6 0 Wt 11 12
Defender. From Ruston Sports.

Season	Club	League Appearances/Goals	
1976–77	Lincoln C	13	—
1977–78		20	—
1978–79	Grimsby T	46	1
1979–80		39	—
1980–81		33	—
1981–82		38	—
1982–83		32	1
1983–84		40	—
1984–85		39	—
1985–86		34	1
1986–87		19	—
1986–87	Reading	4	—

Season	Club	League Appearances/Goals	
1987–88	Bolton W	24	—
1988–89		31	—
1989–90		38	1
1990–91		2	—
1990–91	Lincoln C	1	—

CROOK, Ian

Born Romford 18.1.63. Ht 5 8 Wt 10 06
Midfield. From Apprentice. England B.

Season	Club	League Appearances/Goals	
1980–81	Tottenham H	—	—
1981–82		4	—
1982–83		4	—
1983–84		3	—
1984–85		5	1
1985–86		4	—
1986–87	Norwich C	33	5
1987–88		23	1
1988–89		26	1
1989–90		35	—
1990–91		32	3

CROOKS, Garth

Born Stoke 10.3.58. Ht 5 8 Wt 12 01
Forward. From Apprentice. England
Under-21.

Season	Club	League Appearances/Goals	
1975–76	Stoke C	2	—
1976–77		23	6
1977–78		42	18
1978–79		40	12
1979–80		40	12
1980–81	Tottenham H	40	16
1981–82		27	13
1982–83		26	8
1983–84		10	1
1983–84	Manchester U	7	2
1984–85	Tottenham H	22	10
1985–86	WBA	19	5
1986–87		21	11
1986–87	Charlton Ath	7	2
1987–88		28	10
1988–89		14	2
1989–90		—	—
1990–91		7	1

CROSBY, Gary

Born Sleaford 8.5.64. Ht 5 7 Wt 9 11
Midfield. From Lincoln U.

Season	Club	Apps	Goals
1986–87	Lincoln C	7	—
From Grantham			
1987–88	Nottingham F	14	1
1988–89		13	—
1989–90		34	5
1990–91		29	2

CROSBY, Phil

Born Leeds 9.11.62. Ht 5 9 Wt 11 04
Defender. From Apprentice. England
Youth.

Season	Club	Apps	Goals
1979–80	Grimsby T	4	—
1980–81		10	—
1981–82		15	1
1982–83		10	—
1983–84	Rotherham U	39	—
1984–85		33	—
1985–86		12	—
1986–87		34	—
1987–88		28	—
1988–89		37	2
1989–90	Peterborough U	42	—
1990–91		45	—

CROSS, Nicky

Born Birmingham 7.2.61. Ht 5 9
Wt 11 12
Forward. From Apprentice.

Season	Club	Apps	Goals
1978–79	WBA	—	—
1979–80		—	—
1980–81		2	1
1981–82		22	2
1982–83		32	4
1983–84		25	3
1984–85		24	5
1985–86	Walsall	44	21
1986–87		39	16
1987–88		26	8
1987–88	Leicester C	17	6
1988–89		41	9
1989–90	Port Vale	42	13
1990–91		19	2

CROSS, Paul

Born Barnsley 31.10.65. Ht 5 7 Wt 9 06
Midfield. From Apprentice.

Season	Club	Apps	Goals
1983–84	Barnsley	—	—
1984–85		1	—
1985–86		20	—
1986–87		18	—
1987–88		38	—
1988–89		—	—
1989–90		36	—
1990–91		2	—

CROSS, Ryan

Born Plymouth 11.10.72. Ht 5 11
Wt 11 00
Defender. From Trainee.

Season	Club	Apps	Goals
1990–91	Plymouth Arg	7	—

CROSS, Steve

Born Wolverhampton 22.12.59. Ht 5 10
Wt 11 05
Defender. From Apprentice.

Season	Club	Apps	Goals
1976–77	Shrewsbury T	5	—
1977–78		1	—
1978–79		19	2
1979–80		19	—
1980–81		35	2
1981–82		34	3
1982–83		33	5
1983–84		41	9
1984–85		40	5
1985–86		35	8
1986–87	Derby Co	6	—
1987–88		15	3
1988–89		19	—
1989–90		8	—
1990–91		21	—

CROSSLEY, Mark

Born Barnsley 16.6.69. Ht 6 0 Wt 13 09
Goalkeeper. England Under-21.

Season	Club	Apps	Goals
1987–88	Nottingham F	—	—
1988–89		2	—

1989–90	....	8	—
1989–90	*Manchester U*.............	—	—
1990–91	Nottingham F............	38	—

CROSSLEY, Richard

Born Huddersfield 5.9.70
Defender. From Huddersfield T Trainee.

| 1989–90 | York C........................ | 1 | — |
| 1990–91 | .... | 5 | — |

CROWN, David

Born Enfield 16.2.58. Ht 5 10 Wt 12 01
Forward. From Walthamstow Ave.

1980–81	Brentford	38	6
1981–82	....	8	2
1981–82	Portsmouth	27	2
1982–83	....	1	—
1982–83	*Exeter C*.....................	7	3
1983–84	Reading.......................	45	7
1984–85	....	43	8
1985–86	Cambridge U	43	24
1986–87	....	46	12
1987–88	....	17	9
1987–88	Southend U.................	28	17
1988–89	....	44	25
1989–90	....	41	19
1990–91	Gillingham	30	11

CRUMPLIN, John

Born Bath 26.5.67. Ht 5 8 Wt 11 10
Midfield. From Bognor Regis.

1986–87	Brighton......................	5	—
1987–88	....	26	2
1988–89	....	12	—
1989–90	....	25	2
1990–91	....	46	—

CULLEN, David

Born Durham 10.1.73.
Defender. From Trainee.

| 1990–91 | Doncaster R................ | 1 | — |

CULLEN, Tony

Born Newcastle 30.9.69 Ht 5 6 Wt 11 07
Forward. Local.

1988–89	Sunderland..................	7	—
1989–90	....	16	—
1989–90	*Carlisle U*...................	2	1
1990–91	Sunderland..................	5	—
1990–91	*Rotherham U*..............	3	1

CULPIN, Paul

Born Kirby Muxloe 8.2.62. Ht 5 10
Wt 10 08
Forward.

| 1981–82 | Leicester C................. | — | — |
| From Nuneaton |
1985–86	Coventry C	7	1
1986–87	....	2	1
1987–88	....	—	—
1987–88	Northampton T	20	10
1988–89	....	39	13
1989–90	....	4	—
1989–90	Peterborough U	12	2
1990–91	....	28	10

CULVERHOUSE, Ian

Born Bishop's Stortford 22.9.64.
Ht 5 10 Wt 11 02
Defender. From Apprentice. England
Youth.

1982–83	Tottenham H	—	—
1983–84	....	2	—
1984–85	....	—	—
1985–86	....	—	—
1985–86	Norwich C	30	—
1986–87	....	25	—
1987–88	....	33	—
1988–89	....	38	—
1989–90	....	32	—
1990–91	....	34	—

CUNDY, Jason

Born Wimbledon 12.11.69 Ht 6 1
Wt 13 07
Defender. From Trainee. England
Under-21.

| 1988–89 | Chelsea........................ | — | — |
| 1989–90 | .... | — | — |

Season	Club	App	Goals
1990–91	....	29	1

CUNNINGHAM, Ken

Born Dublin 28.6.71
Defender. Eire Under-21.

Season	Club	App	Goals
1989–90	Millwall......................	5	—
1990–91	....	23	—

CUNNINGHAM, Tony

Born Jamaica 12.11.57.   Ht 6 1   Wt 13 02
Forward. From Stourbridge.

Season	Club	App	Goals
1979–80	Lincoln C....................	38	12
1980–81	....	34	6
1981–82	....	46	11
1982–83	....	5	3
1982–83	Barnsley	29	7
1983–84	....	13	4
1983–84	Sheffield W..................	28	5
1984–85	Manchester C	18	1
1984–85	Newcastle U................	13	1
1985–86	....	17	1
1986–87	....	17	2
1987–88	Blackpool....................	40	10
1988–89	....	31	7
1989–90	Bury	25	8
1990–91	....	33	9
1990–91	Bolton W	9	4

CUNNINGTON, Edward

Born Bellshill 12.11.69   Ht 6 3   Wt 13 5
Forward. From Chelsea app.

Season	Club	App	Goals
1990–91	Dunfermline Ath	7	—

CUNNINGTON, Shaun

Born Bourne 4.1.66.   Ht 5 9   Wt 11 00
Defender. From Bourne T.

Season	Club	App	Goals
1982–83	Wrexham	4	—
1983–84	....	42	—
1984–85	....	41	6
1985–86	....	42	2
1986–87	....	46	1
1987–88	....	24	3

Season	Club	App	Goals
1987–88	Grimsby T	15	2
1988–89	....	44	1
1989–90	....	44	3
1990–91	....	46	2

CURBISHLEY, Alan

Born Forest Gate 8.11.57.   Ht 5 10
Wt 11 07
Midfield. From Apprentice. England
Schools, Youth, Under-21.

Season	Club	App	Goals
1974–75	West Ham U	2	—
1975–76	....	14	2
1976–77	....	10	1
1977–78	....	32	1
1978–79	....	27	1
1979–80	Birmingham C	42	3
1980–81	....	29	6
1981–82	....	29	1
1982–83	....	30	1
1982–83	Aston Villa.................	7	—
1983–84	....	26	1
1984–85	....	3	—
1984–85	Charlton Ath	23	2
1985–86	....	30	4
1986–87	....	10	—
1987–88	Brighton.....................	34	6
1988–89	....	37	6
1989–90	....	45	1
1990–91	Charlton Ath	25	—

CURLE, Keith

Born Bristol 14.11.63.   Ht 6 0   Wt 12 07
Defender. From Apprentice. England B.

Season	Club	App	Goals
1981–82	Bristol R	20	2
1982–83	....	12	2
1983–84	Bristol R	—	—
1983–84	Torquay U	16	5
1983–84	Bristol C	6	—
1984–85	....	40	—
1985–86	....	44	1
1986–87	....	28	—
1987–88	....	3	—
1987–88	Reading.......................	30	—
1988–89	....	10	—
1988–89	Wimbledon	18	—
1989–90	....	38	2

1990–91	....	37	1

CURRAN, Chris

Born Manchester 6.1.71   Ht 6 1   Wt 12 06
Defender. From Trainee.

1989–90	Crewe Alex	1	—
1990–91	....	4	—

CURRAN, Chris

Born Birmingham 17.9.71   Ht 5 11
Wt 11 09
Defender. From Trainee.

1989–90	Torquay U	1	—
1990–91	....	13	—

CURRAN, Henry

Born Glasgow 9.10.66.   Ht 5 8   Wt 11 04
Midfield. From Eastercraigs.

1984–85	Dumbarton	2	—
1985–86	....	6	—
1986–87	....	8	—
1986–87	Dundee U	3	—
1987–88	....	6	—
1988–89	....	6	—
1989–90	St Johnstone	31	3
1990–91	....	35	9

CURRIE, David

Born Stockton 27.11.62.   Ht 5 11
Wt 12 09
Forward. Local.

1981–82	Middlesbrough............	1	—
1982–83	....	8	—
1983–84	....	39	15
1984–85	....	39	12
1985–86	....	26	4
1986–87	Darlington	45	12
1987–88	....	31	21
1987–88	Barnsley	15	7
1988–89	....	41	16
1989–90	....	24	7
1989–90	Nottingham F.............	8	1

1990–91	Oldham Ath...............	27	2

CURTIS, Andy

Born Doncaster 2.12.72.   Ht 5 10
Wt 11 07
Midfield. From Trainee.

1990–91	York C........................	5	—

CUSACK, Nicky

Born Rotherham 24.12.65.   Ht 6 0
Wt 11 13
Forward. From Alvechurch.

1987–88	Leicester C.................	16	1
1988–89	Peterborough U..........	44	10
1989–90	Motherwell.................	31	11
1990–91	....	29	4

CUTLER, Chris

Born Manchester 7.4.64.   Ht 5 11
Wt 11 09
Forward. From Amateur.

1981–82	Bury	2	—
1982–83	....	5	—
1983–84	....	12	2
1984–85	....	4	1
1985–86	Crewe Alex	28	6
1986–87	....	35	5
1987–88	....	36	6
1988–89	....	3	2
1989–90	....	38	5
1990–91	....	—	—

DAILLY, Christian

Born Dundee 23.10.73   Ht 5 10   Wt 10 11
Forward. S Form. Scotland Youth,
Under-21.

1990–91	Dundee U	18	5

DAISH, Liam

Born Portsmouth 23.9.68   Ht 6 2
Wt 13 05
Defender. From Apprentice. Eire
Under-21.

1986–87	Portsmouth	1	—
1987–88		—	—
1988–89	Cambridge U	28	—
1989–90		42	1
1990–91		13	1

DALE, Carl

Born Colwyn Bay 29.4.66.   Ht 6 0
Wt 12 00
Forward. From Bangor C.

1987–88	Chester C	—	—
1988–89		41	22
1989–90		31	9
1990–91		44	10

DALEY, Philip

Born Walton 12.4.67   Ht 6 2   Wt 12 09
Forward. From Newton.

1989–90	Wigan Ath	33	6
1990–91		41	10

DALEY, Tony

Born Birmingham 18.10.67.   Ht 5 7
Wt 10 11
Forward. From Apprentice. England
Youth.

1984–85	Aston Villa	5	—
1985–86		23	2
1986–87		33	3

1987–88		14	3
1988–89		29	5
1989–90		32	6
1990–91		23	2

DALTON, Paul

Born Middlesbrough 25.4.67   Ht 5 11
Wt 12 00
Midfield. From Brandon.

1987–88	Manchester U	—	—
1988–89		—	—
1988–89	Hartlepool U	17	2
1989–90		45	11
1990–91		46	11

DALZIEL, Ian

Born South Shields 24.10.62.   Ht 5 8
Wt 11 10
Defender. From Apprentice.

1979–80	Derby Co	—	—
1980–81		—	—
1981–82		4	—
1982–83		18	4
1983–84	Hereford U	30	4
1984–85		26	—
1985–86		41	3
1986–87		28	—
1987–88		25	1
1988–89	Carlisle U	42	1
1989–90		24	1
1990–91		13	—

DAMERELL, Mark

Born Plymouth 31.7.65.   Ht 5 9   Wt 11 00
Forward. From St. Blazey.

1989–90	Plymouth Arg	1	—
1990–91		4	—

DANIEL, Ray

Born Luton 10.12.64.   Ht 5 8   Wt 11 09
Midfield. From Apprentice.

1982–83	Luton T	3	—

Season	Club	App	Goals
1983–84	....	7	2
1983–84	*Gillingham*	5	—
1984–85	Luton T	7	1
1985–86	....	5	1
1986–87	Hull C	9	—
1987–88	....	26	2
1988–89	....	23	1
1989–90	Cardiff C	43	1
1990–91	....	13	—
1990–91	Portsmouth	14	—

DANZEY, Michael

Born Widnes 8.2.71. Ht 6 1 Wt 12 12
Forward. From Trainee

Season	Club	App	Goals
1988–89	Nottingham F	—	—
1989–90	....	—	—
1989–90	*Chester C*	2	—
1990–91	Peterborough U	1	—

DARBY, Julian

Born Bolton 3.10.67. Ht 6 0 Wt 11 04
Defender. England Schools.

Season	Club	App	Goals
1984–85	Bolton W	—	—
1985–86	....	2	—
1986–87	....	28	—
1987–88	....	35	2
1988–89	....	44	5
1989–90	....	46	10
1990–91	....	45	9

D'AURIA, David

Born Swansea 26.3.70. Ht 5 8 Wt 11 00
Midfield. From Trainee.

Season	Club	App	Goals
1987–88	Swansea C	4	—
1988–89	....	14	2
1989–90	....	7	—
1990–91	....	20	4

DAVENPORT, Peter

Born Birkenhead 24.3.61. Ht 5 10
Wt 11 06
Forward. From Everton Amateur,
Cammell Laird. England B, 1 full cap.

Season	Club	App	Goals
1981–82	Nottingham F	5	4
1982–83	....	18	6
1983–84	....	33	15
1984–85	....	35	16
1985–86	....	27	13
1985–86	Manchester U	11	1
1986–87	....	39	14
1987–88	....	34	5
1988–89	....	8	2
1988–89	Middlesbrough	24	4
1989–90	....	35	3
1990–91	Sunderland	29	7

DAVEY, Simon

Born Swansea 1.10.70.
Forward. From Trainee.

Season	Club	App	Goals
1986–87	Swansea C	1	—
1987–88	....	4	—
1988–89	....	3	—
1989–90	....	18	2
1990–91	....	18	2

DAVIDSON, Jonathan

Born Cheadle 1.3.70 Ht 5 8 Wt 11 11
Defender. From Trainee.

Season	Club	App	Goals
1988–89	Derby Co	—	—
1989–90	....	6	—
1990–91	....	5	—

DAVIES, Alan

Born Manchester 5.12.61. Ht 5 8
Wt 11 4
Midfield. From Apprentice. Wales Under-
21, 11 full caps.

Season	Club	App	Goals
1981–82	Manchester U	1	—
1982–83	....	3	—
1983–84	....	3	—
1984–85	....	—	—
1985–86	Newcastle U	14	1
1985–86	*Charlton Ath*	1	—
1986–87	Newcastle U	7	—
1986–87	*Carlisle U*	4	1
1987–88	Swansea C	42	3
1988–89	....	42	5

| 1989–90 | Bradford C | 26 | 1 |
| 1990–91 | Swansea C | 35 | 3 |

DAVIES, Andy

Born Wolverhampton 6.6.72
Defender. From Trainee.

1988–89	Torquay U	3	—
1989–90		10	—
1990–91	Hartlepool U	4	—

DAVIES, Billy

Born Glasgow 31.5.64. Ht 5 5 Wt 9 08
Midfield. From Pollok U BC.

1980–81	Rangers	—	—
1981–82		4	—
1982–83		4	—
1983–84		3	1
1984–85		—	—
1985–86		—	—
From Elfsborg			
1987–88	St Mirren	18	—
1988–89		27	4
1989–90		29	1
1990–91	Leicester C	6	—
1990–91	Dunfermline Ath	26	—

DAVIES, Gordon

Born Merthyr 3.8.55. Ht 5 9 Wt 11 05
Forward. From Merthyr T. Wales 18 full
caps.

1977–78	Fulham	5	1
1978–79		32	9
1979–80		39	15
1980–81		45	18
1981–82		41	24
1982–83		38	19
1983–84		36	22
1984–85		11	5
1984–85	Chelsea	12	6
1985–86		1	—
1985–86	Manchester C	26	9
1986–87		5	—
1986–87	Fulham	21	6
1987–88		39	13

1988–89		34	14
1989–90		23	6
1990–91		30	6

DAVIES, John

Born Glasgow 25.9.66 Ht 5 7 Wt 10 0
Midfield. From Anniesland U

1985–86	Clydebank	3	—
1986–87		14	—
From Jonkoping			
1987–88	Clydebank	22	3
1988–89		38	3
1989–90		31	5
1990–91		14	1
1990–91	St Johnstone	21	1

DAVIES, Kenneth

Born Stockton 22.12.70. Ht 6 0
Wt 11 00
Midfield. From Trainee.

| 1989–90 | Hartlepool U | 3 | — |
| 1990–91 | | 3 | — |

DAVIES, Michael

Born Stretford 19.1.66. Ht 5 8 Wt 10 07
Midfield. From Apprentice.

1983–84	Blackpool	3	—
1984–85		17	—
1985–86		36	5
1986–87		42	6
1987–88		38	—
1988–89		30	2
1989–90		23	—
1990–91		37	1

DAVIS, Darren

Born Sutton-in-Ashfield 5.2.67. Ht 6 0
Wt 11 00
Defender. From Apprentice. England
Youth.

| 1983–84 | Notts Co | 1 | — |
| 1984–85 | | 4 | — |

1985–86	....	22	1
1986–87	....	45	—
1987–88	....	20	—
1988–89	Lincoln C....................	38	2
1989–90	....	34	—
1990–91	....	30	2
1990–91	Maidstone U..............	11	—

DAVIS, Paul

Born London 9.12.61.   Ht 5 10   Wt 10 10
Midfield. From Apprentice. England B,
Under-21.

1979–80	Arsenal........................	2	—
1980–81	....	10	1
1981–82	....	38	4
1982–83	....	41	4
1983–84	....	35	1
1984–85	....	24	1
1985–86	....	29	4
1986–87	....	39	4
1987–88	....	29	5
1988–89	....	12	1
1989–90	....	11	1
1990–91	....	37	3

DAVIS, Steve

Born Birmingham 26.7.65.   Ht 6 0
Wt 12 07
Defender. From Stoke C. Apprentice.
England Youth.

1983–84	Crewe Alex	24	—
1984–85	....	40	—
1985–86	....	45	1
1986–87	....	33	—
1987–88	....	3	—
1987–88	Burnley	33	5
1988–89	....	37	—
1989–90	....	31	1
1990–91	....	46	5

DAVIS, Steve

Born Hexham 30.10.68.   Ht 6 2   Wt 12 08
Defender. From Trainee.

| 1987–88 | Southampton .... | — | — |

1988–89	....	—	—
1989–90	....	4	—
1989–90	Burnley.....................	9	—
1990–91	Southampton	2	—
1990–91	Notts Co......................	2	—

DAVISON, Aidan

Born Sedgefield 11.5.68.   Ht 6 1
Wt 13 02
Goalkeeper. From Billingham Syn.

1987–88	Notts Co	—	—
1988–89	....	1	—
1989–90	....	—	—
1989–90	Leyton Orient..............	—	—
1989–90	Bury	—	—
1989–90	Chester C	—	—
1990–91	Bury	—	—
1990–91	Blackpool	—	—

DAVISON, Bobby

Born S. Shields 17.7.59.   Ht 5 8   Wt 11 08
Forward. From Seaham C.W.

1980–81	Huddersfield T............	2	—
1981–82	Halifax T	46	20
1982–83	....	17	9
1982–83	Derby Co.....................	26	8
1983–84	....	40	14
1984–85	....	46	24
1985–86	....	41	17
1986–87	....	40	19
1987–88	....	13	1
1987–88	Leeds U	16	5
1988–89	....	39	14
1989–90	....	29	11
1990–91	....	5	1

D'AVRAY, Mich

Born Johannesburg 19.2.62.   Ht 6 2
Wt 12 11
Forward. From Apprentice. England
Under-21.

1979–80	Ipswich T	2	—
1980–81	....	5	1
1981–82	....	13	2

Season	Club	League Appearances/Goals	
1982–83		17	2
1983–84		23	6
1984–85		33	6
1985–86		26	5
1986–87		19	4
1986–87	Leicester C	3	—
1987–88	Ipswich T	29	7
1988–89		32	3
1989–90		12	1

To NEC Nijmegen

DAWES, Ian

Born Croydon 22.2.63. Ht 5 8 Wt 10 02
Defender. From Apprentice. England
Schools.

Season	Club		
1980–81	QPR	—	—
1981–82		5	—
1982–83		42	—
1983–84		42	2
1984–85		42	—
1985–86		42	1
1986–87		23	—
1987–88		33	—
1988–89	Millwall	30	1
1989–90		38	4
1990–91		40	—

DAWS, Tony

Born Sheffield 10.9.66. Ht 5 9 Wt 10 12
Forward. From Apprentice. England
Youth.

Season	Club		
1984–85	Notts Co	7	1
1985–86		1	—
1986–87	Sheffield U	11	3
1987–88	Scunthorpe U	10	3
1988–89		46	24
1989–90		33	11
1990–91		34	14

DAWSON, Ally

Born Glasgow 25.2.58   Ht 5 10
Wt 12 00
Defender. From School. Scotland Youth,
Under-21, 5 full caps.

Season	Club		
1975–76	Rangers	3	—

Season	Club		
1976–77		1	—
1977–78		2	—
1978–79		23	1
1979–80		32	—
1980–81		22	2
1981–82		25	1
1982–83		25	—
1983–84		28	—
1984–85		26	1
1985–86		24	1
1986–87		7	—
1987–88	Blackburn R	22	—
1988–89		6	—
1989–90		12	—
1990–91	Airdrieonians	10	1

DAWSON, Jason

Born Burslem 9.2.71
Forward. From Stoke C Schoolboy, Port
Vale Trainee.

Season	Club		
1989–90	Port Vale	—	—
1989–90	Rochdale	27	2
1990–91		28	5

DAWSON, Robert

Born Stirling 1.8.63 Ht 5 9 Wt 10 10
Defender. From Fallin Violet.

Season	Club		
1981–82	Stirling A	18	—
1982–83		36	—
1983–84		33	2
1984–85		34	—
1985–86		39	—
1986–87		39	—
1987–88	St Mirren	24	—
1988–89		9	—
1989–90		1	—
1990–91		14	—

DAY, Keith

Born Grays 29.11.62. Ht 6 1 Wt 11 00
Defender. From Aveley.

Season	Club		
1984–85	Colchester U	45	4
1985–86		30	5
1986–87		38	3

Season	Club	Appearances	Goals
1987–88	Orient	41	3
1988–89		45	2
1989–90		39	1
1990–91		24	1

DAY, Mervyn

Born Chelmsford 26.6.55. Ht 6 2
Wt 15 01
Goalkeeper. From Apprentice. England Youth, Under-23.

Season	Club	Appearances	Goals
1972–73	West Ham U	—	—
1973–74		33	—
1974–75		42	—
1975–76		41	—
1976–77		42	—
1977–78		23	—
1978–79		13	—
1979–80	Orient	42	—
1980–81		40	—
1981–82		42	—
1982–83		46	—
1983–84	Aston Villa	14	—
1984–85		16	—
1984–85	Leeds U	18	—
1985–86		40	—
1986–87		34	—
1987–88		44	—
1988–89		45	—
1989–90		44	—
1990–91		—	—
1990–91	Coventry C	—	—

DE MANGE, Ken

Born Dublin 3.9.64. Ht 5 10 Wt 11 12
Midfield. From Home Farm. Eire Youth, B. Under-21, 2 full caps.

Season	Club	Appearances	Goals
1983–84	Liverpool	—	—
1984–85		—	—
1985–86		—	—
1986–87		—	—
1986–87	Scunthorpe U	3	2
1987–88	Liverpool	—	—
1987–88	Leeds U	15	1
1987–88	Hull C	9	1
1988–89		32	1
1989–90		21	—

Season	Club	Appearances	Goals
1990–91		6	—
1990–91	Cardiff C	15	—

DEAKIN, Ray

Born Liverpool 19.6.59. Ht 5 8 Wt 12 04
Defender. From Apprentice.

Season	Club	Appearances	Goals
1977–78	Everton	—	—
1978–79		—	—
1979–80		—	—
1980–81		—	—
1981–82	Port Vale	23	6
1982–83	Bolton W	30	1
1983–84		41	1
1984–85		34	—
1985–86	Burnley	46	3
1986–87		46	—
1987–88		37	3
1988–89		14	—
1989–90		33	—
1990–91		37	—

DEANE, Brian

Born Leeds 7.2.68. Ht 6 3 Wt 12 07
Forward. From Apprentice. England B, 2 full caps.

Season	Club	Appearances	Goals
1985–86	Doncaster R	3	—
1986–87		20	2
1987–88		43	10
1988–89	Sheffield U	43	22
1989–90		45	21
1990–91		38	13

DEARDEN, Kevin

Born Luton 8.3.70 Ht 5 11 Wt 12 08
Goalkeeper. From Trainee.

Season	Club	Appearances	Goals
1988–89	Tottenham H	—	—
1988–89	Cambridge U	15	—
1989–90	Tottenham H	—	—
1989–90	Hartlepool U	10	—
1989–90	Oxford U	—	—
1989–90	Swindon T	1	—
1990–91	Tottenham H	—	—
1990–91	Peterborough U	7	—
1990–91	Hull C	3	—

DEARY, John

Born Ormskirk 18.10.62.   Ht 5 10
Wt 12 04
Midfield. From Apprentice.

Season	Club	App	Goals
1979–80	Blackpool	—	—
1980–81		10	—
1981–82		27	—
1982–83		45	6
1983–84		31	6
1984–85		32	13
1985–86		40	7
1986–87		44	3
1987–88		37	3
1988–89		37	5
1989–90	Burnley	41	2
1990–91		43	7

DEAS, Paul

Born Perth 22.2.72   Ht 5 11   Wt 11 0
Midfield. From Kinnoull J

Season	Club	App	Goals
1990–91	St Johnstone	1	—

DEEHAN, John

Born Solihull 6.8.57.   Ht 6 0   Wt 11 03
Forward. From Apprentice. England
Youth, Under-21.

Season	Club	App	Goals
1974–75	Aston Villa	—	—
1975–76		15	7
1976–77		27	13
1977–78		36	12
1978–79		26	10
1979–80		6	—
1979–80	WBA	28	3
1980–81		15	2
1981–82		4	—
1981–82	Norwich C	22	10
1982–83		40	20
1983–84		34	15
1984–85		40	13
1985–86		26	4
1986–87	Ipswich T	29	10
1987–88		20	1
1988–89	Manchester C	—	—
1989–90		—	—
1989–90	Barnsley	—	—

Season	Club	App	Goals
1990–91		11	2

DEMPSEY, Mark

Born Manchester 14.1.64.   Ht 5 8
Wt 9 12
Midfield. From Apprentice.

Season	Club	App	Goals
1981–82	Manchester U	—	—
1982–83		—	—
1983–84		—	—
1984–85		—	—
1984–85	*Swindon T*	5	—
1985–86	Manchester U	1	—
1986–87	Sheffield U	30	5
1987–88		33	4
1988–89		—	—
1988–89	*Chesterfield*	3	—
1988–89	Rotherham U	27	1
1989–90		22	3
1990–91		26	3

DEMPSEY, Mark

Born Dublin 10.12.72.   Ht 5 7   Wt 10 09
Midfield. From Trainee.

Season	Club	App	Goals
1990–91	Gillingham	2	—

DENNIS, Mark

Born Streatham 2.5.61.   Ht 5 9   Wt 11 02
Defender. From Apprentice. England
Youth, Under-21.

Season	Club	App	Goals
1978–79	Birmingham C	31	—
1979–80		40	—
1980–81		19	—
1981–82		17	—
1982–83		23	1
1983–84		—	—
1983–84	Southampton	20	—
1984–85		31	—
1985–86		24	—
1986–87		20	2
1986–87	QPR	—	—
1987–88		11	—
1988–89		17	—
1989–90	Crystal Palace	8	—
1990–91		1	—

DENNIS, Tony

Born Eton 1.12.63. Ht 5 7   Wt 10 02
Midfield. From Plymouth Arg, Bideford,
Taunton, Slough.

Season	Club	App	Goals
1988–89	Cambridge U	18	3
1989–90		17	2
1990–91		20	2

DENNISON, Robert

Born Banbridge 30.4.63.   Ht 5 7
Wt 11 00
Forward. From Glenavon. Northern
Ireland 12 full caps.

Season	Club	App	Goals
1985–86	WBA	12	1
1986–87		4	—
1986–87	Wolverhampton W	10	3
1987–88		43	3
1988–89		43	8
1989–90		46	8
1990–91		42	5

DENTON, Eddie

Born Oxford 18.5.70.   Ht 5 10   Wt 11 03
Midfield. From Oxford U.

Season	Club	App	Goals
1990–91	Watford	2	—

DEVINE, Steve

Born Strabane 11.12.64.   Ht 5 9
Wt 11 00
Midfield. From Apprentice. Northern
Ireland Youth.

Season	Club	App	Goals
1982–83	Wolverhampton W	—	—
1983–84	Derby Co	10	—
1984–85		1	—
1985–86	Stockport Co	2	—
1985–86	Hereford U	11	1
1986–87		41	1
1987–88		43	—
1988–89		41	—
1989–90		34	1
1990–91		38	—

DEVLIN, Mark

Born Irvine 18.1.73.   Ht 5 9   Wt 11 03
Midfield. From Trainee.

Season	Club	App	Goals
1990–91	Stoke C	21	2

DEVONSHIRE, Alan

Born London 13.4.56.   Ht 5 11   Wt 11 07
Midfield. From Southall & Ealing Bor.
England B, 8 full caps.

Season	Club	App	Goals
1976–77	West Ham U	28	—
1977–78		34	3
1978–79		41	5
1979–80		34	5
1980–81		39	6
1981–82		35	1
1982–83		39	3
1983–84		22	1
1984–85		—	—
1985–86		38	3
1986–87		20	2
1987–88		1	—
1988–89		20	—
1989–90		7	—
1990–91	Watford	24	1

DEWHURST, Robert

Born Keighley 10.9.71.   Ht 6 3   Wt 13 01
Defender. From Trainee.

Season	Club	App	Goals
1990–91	Blackburn R	13	—

DIBBLE, Andy

Born Cwmbran 8.5.65.   Ht 6 2   Wt 13 07
Goalkeeper. From Apprentice. Wales
Schools, Youth, Under-21, 3 full caps.

Season	Club	App	Goals
1981–82	Cardiff C	1	—
1982–83		20	—
1983–84		41	—
1984–85	Luton T	13	—
1985–86		7	—
1985–86	*Sunderland*	12	—
1986–87	Luton T	1	—
1986–87	*Huddersfield T*	5	—
1987–88	Luton T	9	—

Season	Club	App	Goals
1988–89	Manchester C	38	—
1989–90		31	—
1990–91		3	—
1990–91	*Aberdeen*	5	—
1990–91	*Middlesborough*	19	—

DICK, James

Born Bellshill 21.6.72
Midfield. From Royal Albert J

Season	Club	App	Goals
1990–91	Airdrieonians	3	—

DICKENS, Alan

Born Plaistow 3.9.64. Ht 5 11 Wt 12 05
Midfield. From Apprentice. England
Youth, Under-21.

Season	Club	App	Goals
1982–83	West Ham U	15	6
1983–84		10	—
1984–85		25	2
1985–86		41	4
1986–87		36	3
1987–88		28	3
1988–89		37	5
1989–90	Chelsea	22	1
1990–91		16	—

DICKENSON, Kevin

Born London 24.11.62. Ht 5 6 Wt 10 06
Defender. From Tottenham H Apprentice.

Season	Club	App	Goals
1979–80	Charlton Ath	1	—
1980–81		—	—
1981–82		7	—
1982–83		12	—
1983–84		42	1
1984–85		13	—
1985–86	Orient	46	1
1986–87		39	—
1987–88		22	1
1988–89		39	1
1989–90		31	—
1990–91		7	—

DICKINS, Matt

Born Sheffield 3.9.70. Ht 6 4 Wt 14 00
Goalkeeper. From Trainee.

Season	Club	App	Goals
1989–90	Sheffield U	—	—
1989–90	*Leyton Orient*	—	—
1990–91	Lincoln C	7	—

DICKS, Julian

Born Bristol 8.8.68. Ht 5 7 Wt 11 07
Defender. From Apprentice. England
Under-21.

Season	Club	App	Goals
1985–86	Birmingham C	23	—
1986–87		34	—
1987–88		32	1
1987–88	West Ham U	8	—
1988–89		34	2
1989–90		40	9
1990–91		13	4

DIGBY, Fraser

Born Sheffield 23.4.67. Ht 6 1 Wt 12 12
Goalkeeper. From Apprentice. England
Youth, Under-21.

Season	Club	App	Goals
1984–85	Manchester U	—	—
1985–86		—	—
1985–86	*Oldham Ath*	—	—
1985–86	*Swindon T*	—	—
1986–87	Manchester U	—	—
1986–87	Swindon T	39	—
1987–88		31	—
1988–89		46	—
1989–90		45	—
1990–91		41	—

DIGWEED, Perry

Born London 26.10.59. Ht 6 0 Wt 11 04
Goalkeeper. From Apprentice.

Season	Club	App	Goals
1976–77	Fulham	1	—
1977–78		—	—
1978–79		2	—
1979–80		11	—
1980–81		1	—
1980–81	Brighton	15	—
1981–82		12	—
1982–83		15	—
1983–84		4	—
1983–84	*WBA*	—	—

Season	Club	Apps	Goals
1984–85	Brighton	—	—
1984–85	*Charlton Ath*	—	—
1985–86	Brighton	33	—
1986–87		22	—
1987–88	*Newcastle U*	—	—
1987–88	*Chelsea*	3	—
1988–89	Brighton	1	—
1989–90		11	—
1990–91		42	—

DILLON, Kevin

Born Sunderland 18.12.59. Ht 6 0
Wt 12 07
Midfield. From Apprentice. England
Youth, Under-21.

Season	Club	Apps	Goals
1977–78	Birmingham C	17	1
1978–79		36	2
1979–80		31	6
1980–81		39	2
1981–82		36	1
1982–83		27	3
1982–83	Portsmouth	11	5
1983–84		36	9
1984–85		37	9
1985–86		31	5
1986–87		39	8
1987–88		32	9
1988–89		29	—
1989–90	Newcastle U	43	—
1990–91		19	—

DIXON, Kerry

Born Luton 24.7.61. Ht 6 0 Wt 13 00
Forward. From Tottenham H Apprentice
and Dunstable. England Under-21, 8 full
caps.

Season	Club	Apps	Goals
1980–81	Reading	39	13
1981–82		42	12
1982–83		35	26
1983–84	Chelsea	42	28
1984–85		41	24
1985–86		38	14
1986–87		36	10
1987–88		33	11
1988–89		39	25
1989–90		38	20

Season	Club	Apps	Goals
1990–91		33	10

DIXON, Lee

Born Manchester 17.3.64. Ht 5 9
Wt 11 03
Defender. Local. England B, 8 full caps.

Season	Club	Apps	Goals
1982–83	Burnley	3	—
1983–84		1	—
1983–84	Chester	16	1
1984–85		41	—
1985–86	Bury	45	5
1986–87	Stoke C	42	3
1987–88		29	2
1987–88	Arsenal	6	—
1988–89		33	1
1989–90		38	5
1990–91		38	5

DOBBIN, Jim

Born Dunfermline 17.9.61. Ht 5 10
Wt 10 06
Midfield. From Whitburn BC. Scotland
Youth.

Season	Club	Apps	Goals
1980–81	Celtic	—	—
1981–82		—	—
1982–83		—	—
1983–84		2	—
1983–84	*Motherwell*	2	—
1983–84	Doncaster R	11	2
1984–85		17	1
1985–86		31	6
1986–87		5	4
1986–87	Barnsley	30	4
1987–88		16	2
1988–89		41	5
1989–90		28	1
1990–91		14	—

DOBBINS, Wayne

Born Bromsgrove 30.8.68. Ht 5 7
Wt 10 08
Midfield. From Apprentice.

Season	Club	Apps	Goals
1986–87	WBA	6	—
1987–88		10	—

1988–89	....	16	—
1989–90	....	5	—
1990–91	....	8	—

DOBSON, Paul

Born Hartlepool 17.12.62.   Ht 5 11
Wt 10 02
Forward. From Newcastle U Amateur.

1981–82	Hartlepool U	5	—
1982–83	....	26	8
From Horden			
1983–84	....	27	12
1984–85	....	38	10
1985–86	....	15	2
1986–87	Torquay U	39	16
1987–88	....	38	22
1988–89	Doncaster R................	24	10
1988–89	Scarborough................	18	5
1989–90	....	37	15
1990–91	....	6	2
1990–91	*Halifax T*	1	1
1990–91	*Hereford U*.................	6	1
1990–91	Lincoln C....................	10	1

DOBSON, Tony

Born Coventry 5.2.69.   Ht 6 1   Wt 12 10
Defender. From Apprentice. England
Under-21.

1986–87	Coventry C	1	—
1987–88	....	1	—
1988–89	....	16	—
1989–90	....	30	—
1990–91	....	6	1
1990–91	Blackburn R	17	—

DOCKER, Ian

Born Gravesend 12.9.69.   Ht 5 8
Wt 11 02
Defender. From Trainee.

1987–88	Gillingham	1	—
1988–89	....	35	—
1989–90	....	20	—
1990–91	....	31	3

DODD, Jason

Born Bath 2.11.70.   Ht 5 10   Wt 11 10
Defender. England Under-21.

1988–89	Southampton	—	—
1989–90	....	22	—
1990–91	....	19	—

DODDS, Davie

Born Dundee 23.9.58.   Ht 5 11   Wt 11 05
Forward. 'S' Form. Scotland Schools,
Youth, Under-21, 2 full caps.

1975–76	Dundee U	—	—
1976–77	....	—	—
1977–78	....	1	—
1977–78	*Arbroath*....................	6	1
1977–78	Dundee U	9	1
1978–79	....	27	10
1979–80	....	21	6
1980–81	....	24	14
1981–82	....	35	14
1982–83	....	36	22
1983–84	....	33	15
1984–85	....	26	8
1985–86	....	31	12
From Neuchatel			
1986–87	Aberdeen.....................	26	4
1987–88	....	23	9
1988–89	....	23	4
1989–90	....	1	—
1989–90	Rangers......................	14	4
1990–91	....	3	—

DOLAN, Eamonn

Born Dagenham 20.9.67.   Ht 5 10
Wt 12 01
Forward. From Apprentice. Eire Youth,
Under 21.

1984–85	West Ham U	—	—
1985–86	....	—	—
1986–87	....	1	—
1987–88	....	4	—
1988–89	....	—	—
1988–89	*Bristol C*....................	3	—
1989–90	West Ham U	10	3
1990–91	....	—	—

1990–91 Birmingham C 10   1

DOLAN, Jim

Born Salsburgh 22.2.69. Ht 5 10
Wt 10 07
Forward. From Motherwell BC.

Season	Club		
1987–88	Motherwell..................	—	—
1988–89	....	5	—
1989–90	....	12	—
1990–91	....	8	1

DONACHIE, Willie

Born Glasgow 5.10.51 Ht 5 9 Wt 11 05
Defender. From Juniors. Scotland Under-23, 35 full caps.

Season	Club		
1968–69	Manchester C	—	—
1969–70	....	3	—
1970–71	....	11	—
1971–72	....	37	—
1972–73	....	40	1
1973–74	....	42	—
1974–75	....	40	1
1975–76	....	40	—
1976–77	....	42	—
1977–78	....	39	—
1978–79	....	38	—
1979–80	....	19	—
From Portland Timbers			
1981–82	Norwich C	11	—
From Portland Timbers			
1982–83	Burnley	23	—
1983–84	....	37	3
1984–85	Oldham Ath...............	39	—
1985–86	....	33	—
1986–87	....	33	—
1987–88	....	31	3
1988–89	....	9	—
1989–90	....	7	—
1990–91	....	17	—

DONAGHY, Mal

Born Belfast 13.9.57. Ht 5 11 Wt 12 02
Defender. From Larne. Northern Ireland Under-21, 70 full caps.

Season	Club		
1978–79	Luton T	40	—
1979–80	....	42	1
1980–81	....	42	—
1981–82	....	42	9
1982–83	....	40	3
1983–84	....	40	1
1984–85	....	42	1
1985–86	....	42	—
1986–87	....	42	—
1987–88	....	32	1
1988–89	....	6	—
1988–89	Manchester U	30	—
1989–90	....	14	—
1989–90	*Luton T*	5	—
1990–91	Manchester U	25	—

DONNELLY, Darren

Born Liverpool 28.12.71. Ht 5 10
Wt 11 06
Forward. From Trainee.

Season	Club		
1990–91	Blackburn R	2	—

DONNELLY, Paul

Born Liverpool 23.12.71 Ht 5 8
Wt 10 00
Defender. From Trainee.

Season	Club		
1988–89	Halifax T	1	—
1989–90	....	1	—
1990–91	....	11	—

DONOVAN, Kevin

Born Halifax 17.12.71. Ht 5 7 Wt 10 10
Forward. From Trainee.

Season	Club		
1989–90	Huddersfield T...........	1	—
1990–91	....	6	1

DONOWA, Lou

Born Ipswich 24.9.64 Ht 5 9 Wt 11 00
Forward. From Apprentice. England Under-21.

Season	Club		
1982–83	Norwich C	1	—
1983–84	....	25	4
1984–85	....	34	7

1985–86	....	2	—
1985–86	*Stoke C*	4	1

From Coruna, Willem II Tilburg

1989–90	Ipswich T	23	1
1990–91	Bristol C	24	3

DORIGO, Tony

Born Australia 31.12.65. Ht 5 10
Wt 10 09
Defender. From Apprentice. England B,
Under-21, 6 full caps.

1983–84	Aston Villa..................	1	—
1984–85	....	31	—
1985–86	....	38	1
1986–87	....	41	—
1987–88	Chelsea........................	40	—
1988–89	....	40	6
1989–90	....	35	3
1990–91	....	31	2

DOUGLAS, Colin

Born Hurlford 9.9.62. Ht 6 1 Wt 11 07
Defender. From Celtic.

1981–82	Doncaster R................	42	3
1982–83	....	38	7
1983–84	....	44	15
1984–85	....	46	10
1985–86	....	42	13
1986–87	Rotherham U	43	3
1987–88	....	40	1
1988–89	Doncaster R................	46	2
1989–90	....	45	2
1990–91	....	46	—

DOWIE, Iain

Born Hatfield 9.1.65 Ht 6 1 Wt 12 12
Forward. From Hendon. Northern Ireland
Under-23, 7 full caps.

1988–89	Luton T	8	—
1989–90	....	29	9
1989–90	*Fulham*	5	1
1990–91	Luton T	29	7
1990–91	West Ham U	12	4

DOWNING, Keith

Born Oldbury 23.7.65. Ht 5 8 Wt 11 00
Midfield. From Mile Oak R.

1984–85	Notts Co	12	—
1985–86	....	3	—
1986–87	....	8	1
1987–88	Wolverhampton W	34	1
1988–89	....	32	1
1989–90	....	31	3
1990–91	....	31	1

DOWNS, Greg

Born Carlton 13.12.58. Ht 5 9 Wt 10 07
Defender. From Apprentice.

1976–77	Norwich C	—	—
1977–78	....	1	—
1977–78	*Torquay U*..................	1	1
1978–79	Norwich C	3	—
1979–80	....	18	—
1980–81	....	29	2
1981–82	....	28	1
1982–83	....	28	—
1983–84	....	42	4
1984–85	....	20	—
1985–86	Coventry C	41	—
1986–87	....	39	2
1987–88	....	27	2
1988–89	....	22	—
1989–90	....	17	—
1990–91	Birmingham C	17	—

DOWSON, Alan

Born Gateshead 17.6.70 Ht 5 8 Wt 10 06
Defender. From Trainee.

1988–89	Millwall......................	—	—
1989–90	....	—	—
1989–90	*Fulham*	4	—
1990–91	Millwall......................	1	—

DOYLE, Maurice

Born Ellesmere Port 17.10.69 Ht 5 8
Wt 10 07
Forward. From Trainee.

1987–88	Crewe Alex	4	—
1988–89		4	2
1989–90	QPR	—	—
1990–91		—	—
1990–91	*Crewe Alex*	7	2
1990–91	*Wolverhampton W*	—	—

DOYLE, Steve

Born Neath 2.6.58. Ht 5 9   Wt 11 01
Midfield. From Apprentice. Wales
Under-21.

1974–75	Preston NE	13	—
1975–76		24	1
1976–77		22	—
1977–78		32	1
1978–79		29	2
1979–80		14	—
1980–81		27	1
1981–82		36	3
1982–83	Huddersfield T	42	2
1983–84		36	2
1984–85		36	2
1985–86		42	—
1986–87		5	—
1986–87	Sunderland	33	—
1987–88		32	1
1988–89		35	1
1989–90	Hull C	36	2
1990–91		11	—
1990–91	Rochdale	31	—

DOZZELL, Jason

Born Ipswich 9.12.67   Ht 6 2   Wt 12 04
Forward. From school. England Youth,
Under-21.

1983–84	Ipswich T	5	1
1984–85		14	2
1985–86		41	3
1986–87		42	2
1987–88		39	1
1988–89		29	11
1989–90		46	8
1990–91		30	6

DRAPER, Mark

Born Derby 11.11.70   Ht 5 10   Wt 11 04
Midfield. From Trainee. England
Under-21.

1988–89	Notts Co	20	3
1989–90		34	3
1990–91		45	9

DREYER, John

Born Alnwick 11.6.63   Ht 6 0   Wt 11 06
Defender. From Wallingford T

1984–85	Oxford U	—	—
1985–86		—	—
1985–86	*Torquay U*	5	—
1985–86	*Fulham*	12	2
1986–87	Oxford U	25	2
1987–88		35	—
1988–89	Luton T	18	1
1989–90		38	2
1990–91		38	3

DRINKELL, Kevin

Born Grimsby 18.6.60.   Ht 5 11   Wt 12 06
Forward. From Apprentice.

1976–77	Grimsby T	4	2
1977–78		26	5
1978–79		28	7
1979–80		33	16
1980–81		41	7
1981–82		28	6
1982–83		39	17
1983–84		36	15
1984–85		35	14
1985–86	Norwich C	41	22
1986–87		42	16
1987–88		38	12
1988–89	Rangers	32	12
1989–90		4	—
1989–90	Coventry C	22	5
1990–91		15	—

DRISCOLL, Andy

Born Staines 21.10.71   Ht 5 7   Wt 10 13
Midfield. From West Ham schoolboy,
Brentford trainee.

1988–89	Brentford	1	—
1989–90		12	2
1990–91		—	—

DRIZIC, Milos

Born Nis (Yugoslavia) 31.12.60 Ht 6 5
Wt 14 10
Defender. From Red Star Belgrade

| 1990–91 | Dunfermline Ath | 5 | 1 |

DRYDEN, Richard

Born Stroud 14.6.69. Ht 6 0 Wt 11 02
Defender.

1986–87	Bristol R	6	—
1987–88		6	—
1988–89		1	—
1988–89	Exeter C	21	—
1989–90		30	7
1990–91		41	6
1990–91	*Manchester C*	—	—

DRYSDALE, Jason

Born Bristol 17.11.70. Ht 5 10 Wt 10 07
Defender. From Trainee. England Youth

1988–89	Watford	—	—
1989–90		20	—
1990–91		30	—

DUBLIN, Dion

Born Leicester 22.4.69. Ht 6 0 Wt 12 04
Forward.

1987–88	Norwich C	—	—
1988–89	Cambridge U	21	6
1989–90		46	15
1990–91		46	16

DUBLIN, Keith

Born Wycombe 29.1.66. Ht 5 11
Wt 12 07
Defender. From Apprentice. England
Youth.

1983–84	Chelsea	1	—
1984–85		11	—
1985–86		11	—
1986–87		28	—
1987–88	Brighton	46	5
1988–89		43	—
1989–90		43	—
1990–91	Watford	43	—

DUFFIELD, Peter

Born Middlesbrough 4.2.69. Ht 5 6
Wt 10 07
Forward.

1986–87	Middlesbrough	—	—
1987–88	Sheffield U	11	1
1987–88	*Halifax T*	12	6
1988–89	Sheffield U	38	11
1989–90		5	2
1990–91		2	—
1990–91	*Rotherham U*	17	4

DUFFY, Darrell

Born Birmingham 18.1.71 Ht 5 11
Wt 11 00
Defender. From Trainee. FA Schools,
England Youth.

1988–89	Aston Villa	1	—
1989–90		—	—
1990–91		—	—

DUFFY, Neil (Cornelius)

Born Glasgow 5.6.67 Ht 6 1 Wt 11 13
Defender. From Shamrock (SA)

| 1989–90 | Dundee U | — | — |
| 1990–91 | Falkirk | 25 | 2 |

DUGGAN, Andy

Born Bradford 19.9.67. Ht 6 3 Wt 13 00
Defender.

1984–85	Barnsley	—	—
1985–86		—	—
1986–87		2	1

Season	Club	App	Goals
1987–88	....	—	—
1987–88	*Rochdale*	3	—
1988–89	Barnsley	—	—
1988–89	Huddersfield T	14	2
1989–90	....	15	1
1990–91	....	—	—
1990–91	*Hartlepool U*	2	—
1990–91	Rochdale	1	—

DUNBAR, Ian

Born Newcastle 6.6.71   Ht 5 9   Wt 10 03
Forward.

1989–90	Hartlepool U	1	—
1990–91	....	2	—

DUNN, Iain

Born Derwent 1.4.72.   Ht 5 10   Wt 11 07
Forward. From school. England Youth

1988–89	York C	26	6
1989–90	....	18	2
1990–91	....	33	3

DUNNE, Joe

Born Dublin 25.5.73.   Ht 5 9   Wt 11 00
Midfield. From Trainee.

1990–91	Gillingham	26	—

DUNPHY, Sean

Born Rotherham 5.11.70   Ht 6 3
Wt 13 05
Defender. From Trainee.

1989–90	Barnsley	6	—
1990–91	Lincoln C	—	—

DUNWELL, Richard

Born Islington 17.6.71.
Forward. From Millwall.

1990–91	Aldershot	1	—

DURIE, Gordon

Born Paisley 6.12.65.   Ht 6 0   Wt 11 06
Forward. From Hill of Beath Hawthorn.
Scotland B, Under-21, 12 full caps.

1981–82	East Fife	13	1
1982–83	....	25	2
1983–84	....	34	16
1984–85	....	9	7
1984–85	Hibernian	22	8
1985–86	....	25	6
1985–86	Chelsea	1	—
1986–87	....	25	5
1987–88	....	26	12
1988–89	....	32	17
1989–90	....	15	5
1990–91	....	24	12

DURNIN, John

Born Bootle 18.8.65.   Ht 5 10   Wt 11 04
Forward. From Waterloo Dock.

1985–86	Liverpool	—	—
1986–87	....	—	—
1987–88	....	—	—
1988–89	....	—	—
1988–89	*WBA*	5	2
1988–89	Oxford U	19	3
1989–90	....	42	13
1990–91	....	26	9

DURRANT, Iain

Born Glasgow 29.10.66.   Ht 5 8   Wt 9 07
Midfield. From Glasgow United. Scotland
Youth, Under-21, 5 full caps.

1984–85	Rangers	5	—
1985–86	....	30	2
1986–87	....	39	4
1987–88	....	40	10
1988–89	....	8	2
1989–90	....	—	—
1990–91	....	4	1

DUXBURY, Lee

Born Skipton 7.10.69   Ht 5 10   Wt 11 07
Midfield. From Trainee.

1988–89	Bradford C	1	—
1989–90	....	12	1
1989–90	*Rochdale*	10	—
1990–91	Bradford C	45	5

DUXBURY, Mike

Born Accrington 1.9.59. Ht 5 9
Wt 11 02
Defender. From Apprentice. England
Under-21, 10 full caps.

Season	Club	Apps	Goals
1976–77	Manchester U	—	—
1977–78		—	—
1978–79		—	—
1979–80		—	—
1980–81		33	2
1981–82		24	—
1982–83		42	1
1983–84		39	—
1984–85		30	1
1985–86		23	1
1986–87		32	1
1987–88		39	—
1988–89		18	—
1989–90		19	—
1990–91	Blackburn R	22	—

DYCHE, Sean

Born Kettering 28.6.71   Ht 6 0   Wt 11 07
Midfield. From Trainee.

Season	Club	Apps	Goals
1988–89	Nottingham F	—	—
1989–90		—	—
1989–90	Chesterfield	22	2
1990–91		28	2

DYER, Alex

Born West Ham 14.11.65. Ht 5 11
Wt 12 04
Midfield. From Watford Apprentice.

Season	Club	Apps	Goals
1983–84	Blackpool	9	—
1984–85		36	8
1985–86		39	8
1986–87		24	3
1986–87	Hull C	17	4
1987–88		28	8
1988–89		15	2
1988–89	Crystal Palace	7	2
1989–90		10	—
1990–91	Charlton Ath	35	7

DZIEKANOWSKI, Dariusz

Born Warsaw 30.9.62   Ht 6 1   Wt 12 13
Forward. From Legia Warsaw. Poland full
caps.

Season	Club	Apps	Goals
1989–90	Celtic	33	8
1990–91		15	2

EARLE, Robbie

Born Newcastle, Staffs. 27.1.65.   Ht 5 9
Wt 10 10
Forward. From Stoke C.

Season	Club		
1981–82	Port Vale	—	—
1982–83		8	1
1983–84		12	—
1984–85		46	15
1985–86		46	15
1986–87		35	6
1987–88		25	4
1988–89		44	13
1989–90		43	12
1990–91		35	11

EASTER, Graham

Born Epsom 26.9.69   Ht 5 7   Wt 10 07
Midfield. From Trainee.

Season	Club		
1988–89	WBA	—	—
1988–89	Huddersfield T	—	—
1989–90	Crewe Alex	3	—
1990–91	Preston NE	1	—

EAVES, David

Born Blackpool 13.2.73.
Forward. From Trainee.

Season	Club		
1990–91	Preston NE	3	—

EBBRELL, John

Born Bromborough 1.10.69.   Ht 5 7
Wt 9 12
Midfield. FA Schools, England Youth, B,
Under-21.

Season	Club		
1986–87	Everton	—	—
1987–88		—	—
1988–89		4	—
1989–90		17	—
1990–91		36	3

ECKHARDT, Jeff

Born Sheffield 7.10.65.   Ht 6 0   Wt 11 07
Defender.

Season	Club		
1984–85	Sheffield U	7	—
1985–86		33	2
1986–87		22	—
1987–88		12	—
1987–88	Fulham	29	1
1988–89		43	2
1989–90		40	2
1990–91		29	2

EDINBURGH, Justin

Born Brentwood 18.12.69   Ht 5 9
Wt 11 06
Defender. From Trainee.

Season	Club		
1988–89	Southend U	15	—
1989–90		22	—
1989–90	*Tottenham H*	—	—
1990–91	Tottenham H	16	1

EDMONDSON, Darren

Born Coniston 4.11.71.   Ht 6 0   Wt 12 02
Defender. From Trainee.

Season	Club		
1990–91	Carlisle U	31	—

EDWARDS, Andy

Born Epping 17.9.71   Ht 6 2   Wt 12 07
Midfield. From Trainee.

Season	Club		
1988–89	Southend U	1	—
1989–90		8	—
1990–91		2	1

EDWARDS, Dean

Born Wolverhampton 25.2.62.   Ht 5 10
Wt 10 07
Forward. From Apprentice.

Season	Club		
1979–80	Shrewsbury	4	—
1980–81		6	1
1981–82		3	—
From Palloseura and Telford U			
1985–86	Wolverhampton W	23	7
1986–87		8	2
1986–87	Exeter C	11	5
1987–88		43	12

Season	Club	Appearances	Goals
1988–89	Torquay U	40	8
1989–90		30	3
1990–91		39	15

EDWARDS, Keith

Born Stockton 16.7.57.   Ht 5 11
Wt 11 07
Forward.

Season	Club	Appearances	Goals
1975–76	Sheffield U	3	—
1976–77		31	18
1977–78		36	11
1978–79	Hull C	46	24
1979–80		41	19
1980–81		40	13
1981–82		5	1
1981–82	Sheffield U	41	35
1982–83		42	13
1983–84		44	33
1984–85		29	13
1985–86		35	20
1986–87	Leeds U	30	6
1987–88		8	—
1987–88	Aberdeen	9	2
1987–88	Hull C	9	3
1988–89		44	26
1989–90		2	—
1989–90	Stockport Co	27	10
1989–90	*Huddersfield T*	10	4
1990–91	Huddersfield T	18	4
1990–91	*Plymouth Arg*	3	1

EDWARDS, Matthew

Born Hammersmith 15.6.71.   Ht 5 10
Wt 9 08
Midfield. From Trainee.

Season	Club	Appearances	Goals
1989–90	Tottenham H	—	—
1990–91		—	—
1990–91	*Reading*	8	—

EDWARDS, Neil

Born Aberdare 5.12.70.   Ht 5 8   Wt 11 02
Goalkeeper. From Trainee.

Season	Club	Appearances	Goals
1988–89	Leeds U	—	—
1989–90		—	—

Season	Club	Appearances	Goals
1990–91		—	—
1990–91	*Huddersfield T*	—	—

EDWARDS, Paul

Born Liverpool 22.2.65   Ht 5 11
Wt 11 05
Goalkeeper. From St. Helens T.

Season	Club	Appearances	Goals
1988–89	Crewe Alex	10	—
1989–90		8	—
1990–91		9	—

EDWARDS, Paul R

Born Birkenhead 25.12.63.   Ht 5 11
Wt 11 00
Defender. From Altrincham.

Season	Club	Appearances	Goals
1987–88	Crewe Alex	13	1
1988–89		45	4
1989–90		28	1
1989–90	Coventry C	8	—
1990–91		23	—

EDWARDS, Robert

Born Manchester 23.2.70   Ht 5 8
Wt 11 07
Forward. From Trainee.

Season	Club	Appearances	Goals
1987–88	Crewe Alex	6	1
1988–89		4	—
1989–90		4	—
1990–91		29	11

EDWARDS, Robert

Born Kendal 1.7.73.   Ht 6 0   Wt 11 06
Defender. Wales Under-21.

Season	Club	Appearances	Goals
1989–90	Carlisle U	12	—
1990–91		36	5
1990–91	Bristol C	—	—

EELES, Tony

Born Chatham 15.11.70   Ht 5 7   Wt 9 12
Midfield. From Trainee.

Season	Club	Appearances	Goals
1988–89	Gillingham	3	—

Season	Club		Apps	Goals
1989–90	....		33	2
1990–91	....		6	—

EHIOGU, Ugo

Born London 3.11.72. Ht 6 1 Wt 12 00
Defender. From Trainee.

1990–91	WBA	2	—

EKOKU, Efan

Born Manchester 8.6.67. Ht 6 1
Wt 12 00
Forward. From Sutton U.

1990–91	Bournemouth	20	3

ELI, Roger

Born Bradford 11.9.65. Ht 5 11
Wt 11 03
Defender. From Apprentice.

1983–84	Leeds U	—	—
1984–85	....	1	—
1985–86	....	1	—
1985–86	Wolverhampton W	14	—
1986–87	....	4	—
1987–88	Cambridge U	—	—
1987–88	Crewe Alex	27	1
1988–89	York C	4	1
1988–89	Bury	2	—
From Northwich Vic.			
1989–90	Burnley	29	—
1990–91	....	26	10

ELKINS, Gary

Born Wallingford 4.5.66. Ht 5 09
Wt 11 12
Midfield. From Apprentice. England
Youth.

1983–84	Fulham	—	—
1984–85	....	21	—
1985–86	....	13	—
1986–87	....	9	—
1987–88	....	29	—
1988–89	....	22	1

1989–90	....	10	1
1989–90	*Exeter C*	5	—
1990–91	Wimbledon	10	—

ELLIOT, Eamon

Born Belfast 27.8.71. Ht 5 5 Wt 9 09
Defender. From Trainee. Northern Ireland
Youth.

1990–91	Carlisle U	4	—

ELLIOTT, Matthew

Born Surrey 1.11.68 Ht 6 3 Wt 13 06
Defender. From Epsom & Ewell.

1988–89	Charlton Ath	—	—
1988–89	Torquay U	13	2
1989–90	....	33	2
1990–91	....	45	6

ELLIOTT, Robbie

Born Newcastle 25.12.73. Ht 5 10
Wt 10 13
Defender. From Trainee.

1990–91	Newcastle U	6	—

ELLIOTT, Tony

Born Nuneaton 30.11.69. Ht 6 0
Wt 12 12
Goalkeeper. England Youth.

1986–87	Birmingham C	—	—
1987–88	....	—	—
1988–89	....	—	—
1988–89	Hereford U	23	—
1989–90	....	29	—
1990–91	....	5	—

ELLIOTT, Paul

Born London 18.3.64. Ht 6 2 Wt 11 11
Defender. From Apprentice. England
Youth, Under-21.

1980–81	Charlton Ath	—	—

Season	Club	League Appearances/Goals		
1981–82		....	38	1
1982–83		....	25	—
1982–83	Luton T	....	13	1
1983–84		....	38	2
1984–85		....	9	1
1985–86		....	6	—
1985–86	Aston Villa	....	23	2
1986–87		....	34	5

From Bari.

Season	Club	League Appearances/Goals		
1989–90	Celtic	....	27	—
1990–91		....	27	2

ELLIOTT, Steve

Born Haltwistle 15.9.58.   Ht 5 11
Wt 12 00
Forward. From Apprentice.

Season	Club	League Appearances/Goals		
1977–78	Nottingham F	....	—	—
1978–79		....	4	—
1978–79	Preston NE	....	7	—
1979–80		....	42	16
1980–81		....	35	9
1981–82		....	35	10
1982–83		....	45	19
1983–84		....	44	16
1984–85	Luton T	....	12	3
1984–85	Walsall	....	28	5
1985–86		....	41	16
1986–87	Bolton W	....	38	9
1987–88		....	19	2
1988–89		....	3	—
1988–89	Bury	....	31	11
1989–90		....	—	—
1989–90	Rochdale	....	22	6
1990–91		....	30	3

ELLIS, Mark

Born Bradford 6.1.62.   Ht 5 9   Wt 10 12
Forward. Local.

Season	Club	League Appearances/Goals		
1980–81	Bradford C	....	4	1
1981–82		....	18	—
1982–83		....	25	3
1983–84		....	37	8
1984–85		....	45	7
1985–86		....	25	3
1986–87		....	31	5
1987–88		....	22	2

Season	Club	League Appearances/Goals		
1988–89		....	5	1
1989–90		....	6	—
1990–91		....	—	—
1990–91	Halifax T	....	30	4

ELLIS, Neil

Born Bebington 30.4.69.   Ht 6 0
Wt 12 00
Forward. From Bangor City

Season	Club	League Appearances/Goals		
1990–91	Chester C	....	21	1

ELLIS, Tony

Born Salford 20.10.64.   Ht 5 11   Wt 11 00
Forward. From Horwich RMI, Northwich Vic.

Season	Club	League Appearances/Goals		
1986–87	Oldham Ath	....	5	—
1987–88		....	3	—
1987–88	Preston NE	....	24	4
1988–89		....	45	19
1989–90		....	17	3
1989–90	Stoke C	....	24	6
1990–91		....	38	9

ELLISON, Tony

Born Bishop Auckland 13.1.73.
Forward. From Trainee

Season	Club	League Appearances/Goals		
1990–91	Darlington	....	13	3

ELSEY, Karl

Born Swansea 20.11.58.   Ht 5 11
Wt 12 07
Midfield. From Pembroke Boro.

Season	Club	League Appearances/Goals		
1978–79	QPR	....	3	—
1979–80		....	4	—
1980–81	Newport C	....	34	2
1981–82		....	40	7
1982–83		....	42	5
1983–84		....	7	1
1983–84	Cardiff C	....	29	1
1984–85		....	30	4
1985–86	Gillingham	....	46	5
1986–87		....	43	2

Season	Club	League Appearances/Goals	
1987–88	....	39	6
1988–89	Reading........................	44	3
1989–90	Maidstone U..............	44	4
1990–91	....	28	1

ELSTRUP, Lars

Born Roby, Denmark 24.3.63. Ht 5 11
Wt 11 11
Forward. From OB Odense. Denmark full
caps.

1989–90	Luton T	23	4
1990–91	....	37	15

EMERSON, Dean

Born Salford 27.12.62. Ht 5 10 Wt 11 07
Midfield. From Local.

1981–82	Stockport Co	23	1
1982–83	....	45	3
1983–84	....	44	1
1984–85	....	44	2
1985–86	Rotherham U	45	7
1986–87	....	10	1
1986–87	Coventry C	19	—
1987–88	....	20	—
1988–89	....	18	—
1989–90	....	12	—
1990–91	....	24	—

EMSON, Paul

Born Lincoln 22.10.58. Ht 5 10
Wt 11 00
Forward. From Brigg T.

1978–79	Derby Co	6	—
1979–80	....	26	4
1980–81	....	38	4
1981–82	....	41	5
1982–83	....	16	—
1983–84	Grimsby T	39	6
1984–85	....	35	4
1985–86	....	23	5
1986–87	Wrexham	35	3
1987–88	....	14	2
1988–89	Darlington	34	5
1989–90	....	*34*	*7*

ESHELBY, Paul

Born Sheffield 29.5.70. Ht 5 9 Wt 11 00
Midfield.

1989–90	Exeter C......................	1	—
1990–91	....	18	1
1990–91	Scarborough................	3	—

EVANS, Allan

Born Dunfermline 12.10.56. Ht 6 1
Wt 12 13
Defender. From Dunfermline U. Scotland
Youth, 4 full caps.

1973–74	Dunfermline Ath	9	—
1974–75	....	26	—
1975–76	....	26	1
1976–77	....	37	13
1977–78	Aston Villa..................	9	1
1978–79	....	37	6
1979–80	....	35	8
1980–81	....	39	7
1981–82	....	38	2
1982–83	....	40	4
1983–84	....	36	7
1984–85	....	38	6
1985–86	....	35	3
1986–87	....	26	6
1987–88	....	20	1
1988–89	....	27	—
1989–90	Leicester C..................	14	—
1990–91	....	—	—
1990–91	Darlington	1	—

EVANS, Ceri

Born Christchurch 2.10.63. Ht 6 1
Wt 14 02
Defender. From Otaga Univ, Worcester
Coll. (Oxford). New Zealand full caps.

1988–89	Oxford U......................	4	—
1989–90	....	24	2
1990–91	....	18	1

EVANS, David

Born W. Bromwich 20.5.58.   Ht 5 11
Wt 12 04
Defender. From Apprentice.

Season	Club		
1975–76	Aston Villa	—	—
1976–77		—	—
1977–78		—	—
1978–79		2	—
1979–80	Halifax T	45	3
1980–81		39	1
1981–82		46	2
1982–83		42	1
1983–84		46	2
1984–85	Bradford C	45	1
1985–86		35	—
1986–87		42	1
1987–88		43	1
1988–89		34	—
1989–90		24	—
1990–91	Halifax T	42	1

EVANS, Gareth

Born Coventry 14.1.67   Ht 5 8   Wt 10 06
Forward. From Apprentice.

Season	Club		
1984–85	Coventry C	—	—
1985–86		6	—
1986–87		1	—
1986–87	Rotherham U	34	9
1987–88		29	4
1987–88	Hibernian	12	2
1988–89		35	5
1989–90		28	3
1990–91		15	2
1990–91	*Northampton T*	2	—
1990–91	*Stoke C*	5	1

EVANS, Mark

Born Leeds 24.8.70   Ht 6 0   Wt 11 08
Goalkeeper. From Trainee.

Season	Club		
1988–89	Bradford C	3	—
1989–90		5	—
1990–91		3	—

EVANS, Mike

Born Plymouth 1.1.73.   Ht 6 0   Wt 11 02
Forward. From Trainee.

Season	Club		
1990–91	Plymouth Arg	4	—

EVANS, Stewart

Born Maltby 15.11.60   Ht 6 4   Wt 11 05
Forward. From Rotherham U Apprentice.

Season	Club		
1978–79	Rotherham U	—	—
1979–80		—	—
From Gainsborough TH			
1980–81	Sheffield U	—	—
1981–82	Wimbledon	18	4
1982–83		42	14
1983–84		45	12
1984–85		40	14
1985–86		30	6
1986–87	WBA	14	1
1986–87	Plymouth Arg	5	—
1987–88		37	10L
1988–89		3	—
1988–89	Rotherham U	25	6
1989–90		20	4
1990–91		20	4
1990–91	*Torquay U*	15	5

EVANS, Terry

Born London 12.4.65.   Ht 6 5   Wt 15 01
Defender. From Hillingdon B.

Season	Club		
1985–86	Brentford	19	1
1986–87		1	—
1987–88		29	4
1988–89		45	5
1989–90		44	3
1990–91		36	2

EYRES, David

Born Liverpool 26.2.64.   Ht 5 10
Wt 11 00
Forward. From Rhyl.

Season	Club		
1989–90	Blackpool	35	7
1990–91		36	6

FAIRCLOUGH, Chris

Born Nottingham 12.4.64.   Ht 5 11
Wt 11 02
Defender. From Apprentice. England
Under-21.

Season	Club	App	Goals
1981–82	Nottingham F	—	—
1982–83		15	—
1983–84		31	—
1984–85		35	—
1985–86		—	—
1986–87		26	1
1987–88	Tottenham H	40	4
1988–89		20	1
1988–89	Leeds U	11	—
1989–90		42	8
1990–91		34	4

FAIRCLOUGH, David

Born Liverpool 5.1.57.   Ht 5 10   Wt 11 00
Forward. From Apprentice. England
Under-21.

Season	Club	App	Goals
1973–74	Liverpool	—	—
1974–75		—	—
1975–76		14	7
1976–77		20	3
1977–78		29	10
1978–79		4	2
1979–80		14	5
1980–81		9	4
1981–82		—	—
1982–83		8	3
From Lucerne			
1984–85	Norwich C	2	—
1985–86	Oldham Ath	17	1
1986–87	Rochdale	—	—
From Beveren.			
1989–90	Tranmere R	14	1
1990–91	Wigan Ath	7	1

FAIRCLOUGH, Wayne

Born Nottingham 27.4.68.   Ht 5 10
Wt 9 12
Defender. From Apprentice.

Season	Club	App	Goals
1985–86	Notts Co	5	—

Season	Club	App	Goals
1986–87		9	—
1987–88		29	—
1988–89		20	—
1989–90		8	—
1989–90	Mansfield T	13	—
1990–91		41	6

FAIRWEATHER, Carlton

Born London 22.9.61.   Ht 5 11   Wt 11 00
Forward. From Tooting & Mitcham.

Season	Club	App	Goals
1984–85	Wimbledon	13	2
1985–86		20	7
1986–87		26	8
1987–88		21	4
1988–89		26	3
1989–90		21	1
1990–91		5	1

FALCO, Mark

Born Hackney 22.10.60.   Ht 6 0
Wt 12 00
Forward. From Apprentice. England
Youth.

Season	Club	App	Goals
1978–79	Tottenham H	1	1
1979–80		9	2
1980–81		3	1
1981–82		21	5
1982–83		16	5
1982–83	*Chelsea*	3	—
1983–84	Tottenham H	36	13
1984–85		42	22
1985–86		40	18
1986–87		6	—
1986–87	Watford	33	14
1987–88	Rangers	14	5
1987–88	QPR	19	5
1988–89		27	12
1989–90		21	5
1990–91		20	5

FALCONER, Willie

Born Aberdeen 5.4.66.   Ht 6 1   Wt 11 09
Midfield. From Lewis United. Scotland
Schools, Youth.

Season	Club	App	Goals
1982–83	Aberdeen	1	—

Season	Club	App	Goals
1983–84		8	1
1984–85		16	4
1985–86		8	—
1986–87		8	—
1987–88		36	8
1988–89	Watford	33	5
1989–90		30	3
1990–91		35	4

FARNINGHAM, Ray

Born Dundee 10.4.61. Ht 5 8 Wt 10 07
Forward. From Celtic BC.

Season	Club	App	Goals
1978–79	Forfar Ath	1	—
1979–80		38	5
1980–81		34	4
1981–82		39	5
1982–83		21	3
1983–84		37	6
1984–85		31	4
1985–86		37	2
1986–87		2	—
1986–87	Motherwell	29	3
1987–88		29	6
1988–89		18	3
1989–90	Dunfermline Ath	17	—
1990–91		10	—

FARNWORTH, Simon

Born Chorley 28.10.63. Ht 6 0 Wt 11 13
Goalkeeper. From Apprentice. England
Schools.

Season	Club	App	Goals
1981–82	Bolton W	—	—
1982–83		—	—
1983–84		36	—
1984–85		46	—
1985–86		31	—
1986–87		—	—
1986–87	*Stockport Co*	10	—
1986–87	*Tranmere R*	7	—
1986–87	Bury	14	—
1987–88		39	—
1988–89		45	—
1989–90		7	—
1990–91	Preston NE	23	—

FARRELL, Andy

Born Colchester 7.10.65. Ht 6 0
Wt 11 00
Defender. From school.

Season	Club	App	Goals
1983–84	Colchester U	15	—
1984–85		38	—
1985–86		24	1
1986–87		28	4
1987–88	Burnley	45	3
1988–89		36	4
1989–90		36	2
1990–91		37	2

FARRELL, David

Born Glasgow 29.10.69 Ht 5 9 Wt 10 12
Midfield. From Oxford U app.

Season	Club	App	Goals
1988–89	Hibernian	—	—
1989–90		—	—
1990–91		2	—

FARRELL, Sean

Born Watford 28.2.69 Ht 6 1 Wt 12 08
Midfield. From Apprentice

Season	Club	App	Goals
1986–87	Luton T	—	—
1987–88		—	—
1987–88	*Colchester U*	9	1
1988–89	Luton T	—	—
1989–90		1	—
1990–91		20	1

FASHANU, John

Born Kensington 18.9.62. Ht 6 1
Wt 11 12
Forward. From Cambridge U. Amateur.
England 2 full caps.

Season	Club	App	Goals
1979–80	Norwich C	—	—
1980–81		—	—
1981–82		5	1
1982–83		2	—
1983–84		—	—
1983–84	*Crystal Palace*	1	—
1983–84	Lincoln C	26	6
1984–85		10	4

Season	Club	App	Goals
1984–85	Millwall	25	4
1985–86		25	8
1985–86	Wimbledon	9	4
1986–87		37	11
1987–88		38	14
1988–89		30	12
1989–90		24	11
1990–91		35	20

FEE, Greg

Born Halifax 24.6.64.   Ht 6 1   Wt 12 00
Defender.

Season	Club	App	Goals
1982–83	Bradford C	3	—
1983–84		4	—
From Boston UH			
1987–88	Sheffield W	16	—
1988–89		8	—
1989–90		2	—
1990–91		—	—
1990–91	Preston NE	15	—
1990–91	Northampton T	1	—
1990–91	Leyton Orient	5	—
1990–91	Mansfield T	10	—

FEELEY, Andy

Born Hereford 30.9.61.   Ht 5 10
Wt 12 00
Midfield. From Apprentice.

Season	Club	App	Goals
1978–79	Hereford U	26	—
1979–80		25	3
1979–80	Chelsea	—	—
1980–81	Hereford	—	—
From Trowbridge T			
1983–84	Leicester C	3	—
1984–85		35	—
1985–86		26	—
1986–87		12	—
1987–88	Brentford	34	—
1988–89		33	—
1989–90	Bury	30	2
1990–91		27	—

FELGATE, David

Born Blaenau Ffestiniog 4.3.60.   Ht 6 2
Wt 13 06
Goalkeeper. From Blaenau Ffestiniog.
Wales Schools, Under-21, 1 full cap.

Season	Club	App	Goals
1978–79	Bolton W	—	—
1978–79	Rochdale	35	—
1979–80	Bolton W	—	—
1979–80	Bradford C	—	—
1979–80	Crewe Alex	14	—
1979–80	Rochdale	12	—
1980–81	Bolton W	—	—
1980–81	Lincoln C	42	—
1981–82		43	—
1982–83		46	—
1983–84		46	—
1984–85		21	—
1984–85	Cardiff C	4	—
1984–85	Grimsby T	12	—
1985–86	Grimsby T	12	—
1985–86	Bolton W	15	—
1986–87		20	—
1986–87	Rotherham U	—	—
1987–88	Bolton W	46	—
1988–89		46	—
1989–90		40	—
1990–91		46	—

FELLENGER, David

Born Edinburgh 6.6.69.   Ht 5 8   Wt 10 02
Midfield. From Hutchinson Vale BC.

Season	Club	App	Goals
1987–88	Hibernian	—	—
1988–89		2	—
1989–90		12	1
1990–91		12	1

FENSOME, Andy

Born Northampton 18.2.69.   Ht 5 8
Wt 11 02
Midfield. From Trainee.

Season	Club	App	Goals
1986–87	Norwich C	—	—
1987–88		—	—
1988–89		—	—
1988–89	Newcastle U	—	—
1989–90	Cambridge U	24	—

1990–91		36	—

FENWICK, Terry

Born Camden, Co. Durham 17.11.59.
Ht 5 11 Wt 11 01
Defender. From Apprentice. England
Youth, Under-21, 20 full caps.

1976–77	Crystal Palace	—	—
1977–78		10	—
1978–79		24	—
1979–80		15	—
1980–81		21	—
1980–81	QPR	19	2
1981–82		36	5
1982–83		39	3
1983–84		41	10
1984–85		41	2
1985–86		37	7
1986–87		21	1
1987–88		22	3
1987–88	Tottenham H	17	—
1988–89		34	8
1989–90		10	—
1990–91		4	—
1990–91	*Leicester C*	8	1

FERDINAND, Les

Born London 18.12.66. Ht 5 11
Wt 13 05
Forward. From Hayes.

1986–87	QPR	2	—
1987–88		1	—
1987–88	*Brentford*	3	—
1988–89	QPR	—	—
1988–89	*Besiktas*	—	—
1989–90	QPR	9	2
1990–91		18	8

FEREDAY, Wayne

Born Warley 16.6.63. Ht 5 9 Wt 11 08
Midfield. From Apprentice. England
Under-21.

1980–81	QPR	6	2
1981–82		4	—

1982–83		5	—
1983–84		17	4
1984–85		26	7
1985–86		34	2
1986–87		37	2
1987–88		37	4
1988–89		31	—
1989–90	Newcastle U	25	—
1990–91		8	—
1990–91	Bournemouth	18	—

FERGUSON, Darren

Born Glasgow 9.2.72.
Midfield. From Trainee.

1990–91	Manchester U	5	—

FERGUSON, Derek

Born Glasgow 31.7.67. Ht 5 8 Wt 10 11
Midfield. From Gartcosh United. Scotland
Schools, Youth, Under-21, 2 full caps.

1983–84	Rangers	1	—
1984–85		8	—
1985–86		19	—
1986–87		30	1
1987–88		32	4
1988–89		16	2
1989–90		5	—
1989–90	*Dundee*	4	—
1990–91	Hearts	28	2

FERGUSON, Duncan

Born Stirling 27.12.71 Ht 6 3 Wt 13 5
Forward. From Carse Thistle

1990–91	Dundee U	9	1

FERGUSON, Iain

Born Newarthill 4.8.62. Ht 5 7 Wt 10 07
Forward. From Fir Park BC. Scotland
Youth, Under-21.

1979–80	Dundee	13	5
1980–81		11	1
1981–82		34	12

Season	Club	Apps	Goals		Season	Club	Apps	Goals
1982–83	....	29	9		1983–84	QPR	30	1
1983–84	....	33	12		1984–85	....	32	6
1984–85	Rangers	28	6		1985–86	....	17	—
1985–86	....	4	—		1986–87	....	18	2
1986–87	*Dundee*	3	2		1987–88	Portsmouth	18	—
1986–87	Dundee U	36	16		1988–89	....	17	2
1987–88	....	39	11		1989–90	....	29	4
1988–89	Hearts	29	5		1990–91	....	3	—
1989–90	....	11	1		1990–91	Oldham Ath	2	—
1989–90	*Charlton Ath*	1	—		1990–91	*Millwall*	1	—
1989–90	*Bristol C*	11	2					
1990–91	Hearts	12	2					
1990–91	Motherwell	15	8					

FINCH, John

Born Lambeth 5.7.66. Ht 6 1 Wt 11 12
Defender. From Dorking.

1990–91	Fulham	1	—

FERGUSON, Ian

Born Glasgow 15.3.67. Ht 5 10 Wt 10 11
Midfield. From Clyde BC. Scotland B,
Under-21, 3 full caps.

1984–85	Clyde	2	—
1985–86	....	19	4
1986–87	....	5	—
1986–87	St Mirren	35	4
1987–88	....	22	6
1987–88	Rangers	8	1
1988–89	....	30	6
1989–90	....	24	—
1990–91	....	11	1

FINDLAY, William

Born Kilmarnock 29.8.70. Ht 5 10
Wt 10 13
Midfield. From Kilmarnock BC. Scotland
Under-21.

1987–88	Hibernian	—	—
1988–89	....	3	1
1989–90	....	10	—
1990–91	....	26	2

FERNEY, Martin

Born Lambeth 8.11.71. Ht 5 11
Wt 12 04
Defender. From Trainee.

1990–91	Fulham	14	—

FINLEY, Alan

Born Liverpool 10.12.67 Ht 6 3
Wt 14 03
Defender. From Marine.

1988–89	Shrewsbury T	34	1
1989–90	....	29	1
1990–91	Stockport Co	19	3

FILLERY, Mike

Born Mitcham 17.9.60. Ht 5 11
Wt 13 00
Midfield. From Apprentice. England
Schools, Youth.

1978–79	Chelsea	7	—
1979–80	....	41	11
1980–81	....	36	6
1981–82	....	40	6
1982–83	....	37	9

FINNIGAN, Tony

Born Wimbledon 17.10.62. Ht 5 10
Wt 11 09
Defender. Crystal Palace Apprentice.

1980–81	Fulham	—	—
1981–82	....	—	—
1982–83	....	—	—
1983–84	....	—	—

Season	Club	Appearances	Goals
1984–85	Crystal Palace	11	1
1985–86		36	3
1986–87		41	6
1987–88		17	—
1988–89	Blackburn R	17	—
1989–90		19	—
1990–91	Hull C	18	1
1990–91	Swindon T	3	—

FIORE, Mark

Born Southwark 18.11.69   Ht 5 10
Wt 11 10
Midfield. From Trainee.

Season	Club	Appearances	Goals
1988–89	Wimbledon	1	—
1989–90		—	—
1989–90	Plymouth Arg	12	1
1990–91		38	3

FISHER, Alex

Born Southampton 30.1.73.
Defender. From Trainee.

Season	Club	Appearances	Goals
1990–91	Aldershot	2	—

FITZPATRICK, Paul

Born Liverpool 5.10.65.   Ht 6 4   Wt 12 00
Midfield.

Season	Club	Appearances	Goals
1984–85	Tranmere R	—	—
1985–86	Liverpool	—	—
1984–85	Preston NE	—	—
1984–85	Bolton W	3	—
1985–86		11	—
1986–87	Bristol C	19	2
1987–88		24	5
1988–89		1	—
1988–89	Carlisle U	32	—
1988–89	*Preston NE*	2	—
1989–90	Carlisle U	45	4
1990–91		32	—

FLECK, Robert

Born Glasgow 11.8.65.   Ht 5 7   Wt 10 8
Forward. From Possil YM. Scotland
Youth, Under-21, 4 full caps.

Season	Club	Appearances	Goals
1983–84	Partick T	2	1
1983–84	Rangers	1	—
1984–85		8	—
1985–86		15	3
1986–87		40	19
1987–88		21	7
1987–88	Norwich C	18	7
1988–89		33	10
1989–90		27	7
1990–91		29	5

FLEMING, Craig

Born Calder 6.10.71   Ht 6 0   Wt 11 07
Defender. From Trainee.

Season	Club	Appearances	Goals
1988–89	Halifax T	1	—
1989–90		10	—
1990–91		46	—

FLEMING, Gary

Born Londonderry 17.2.67.   Ht 5 9
Wt 11 03
Defender. From Apprentice. Northern
Ireland 12 full caps.

Season	Club	Appearances	Goals
1984–85	Nottingham F	2	—
1985–86		16	—
1986–87		34	—
1987–88		22	—
1988–89		—	—
1989–90	Manchester C	14	—
1989–90	*Notts Co*	3	—
1989–90	Barnsley	12	—
1990–91		44	—

FLEMING, Mark

Born Hammersmith 11.8.69.   Ht 5 8
Wt 11 02
Defender. From Trainee.

Season	Club	Appearances	Goals
1987–88	QPR	2	—
1988–89		1	—
1989–90	Brentford	17	—
1990–91		18	1

FLEMING, Paul

Born Halifax 6.9.67.   Ht 5 7   Wt 10 00
Defender.

1985–86	Halifax T	13	—
1986–87		15	—
1987–88		9	—
1988–89		23	—
1989–90		40	1
1990–91		39	—

FLEMING, Terry

Born Marston Green 5.1.73.
Midfield. From Trainee.

1990–91	Coventry C	2	—

FLETCHER, Andrew

Born Saltburn 12.8.71. Ht 6 0 Wt 13 00
Forward. From Trainee.

1989–90	Middlesbrough	—	—
1990–91	Scarborough	6	1

FLETCHER, Steve

Born Hartlepool 26.6.72.
Forward. From Trainee.

1990–91	Hartlepool U	14	2

FLOUNDERS, Andy

Born Hull 13.12.63. Ht 5 11 Wt 11 06
Forward. From Apprentice.

1980–81	Hull C	5	—
1981–82		13	5
1982–83		23	13
1983–84		30	9
1984–85		39	14
1985–86		25	10
1986–87		24	3
1986–87	Scunthorpe U	15	6
1987–88		45	24
1988–89		46	16
1989–90		44	18
1990–91		46	23

FLOWER, John

Born Northampton 9.12.64. Ht 6 4
Wt 15 04
Defender. From Corby T.

1989–90	Sheffield U	—	—
1990–91		—	—
1990–91	Aldershot	32	2

FLOWERS, Tim

Born Kenilworth 3.2.67. Ht 6 2
Wt 13 09
Goalkeeper. From Apprentice. England
Youth, Under-21.

1984–85	Wolverhampton W	38	—
1985–86		25	—
1985–86	*Southampton*	—	—
1986–87	Southampton	9	—
1986–87	*Swindon T*	2	—
1987–88	Southampton	9	—
1987–88	*Swindon T*	5	—
1988–89	Southampton	7	—
1989–90		35	—
1990–91		37	—

FLYNN, Brian

Born Port Talbot 12.10.55. Ht 5 4
Wt 10 00
Midfield. From Apprentice. Wales Schools,
Under-23, 66 full caps.

1972–73	Burnley	—	—
1973–74		2	—
1974–75		26	—
1975–76		39	4
1976–77		41	2
1977–78		12	2
1977–78	Leeds U	29	1
1978–79		41	3
1979–80		24	3
1980–81		41	3
1981–82		17	1
1981–82	*Burnley*	2	—
1982–83	Leeds U	2	—
1982–83	Burnley	28	1
1983–84		43	9
1984–85		9	1
1984–85	Cardiff C	22	—
1985–86		10	—
1985–86	Doncaster R	27	—
1986–87	Bury	19	—

From Limerick

Season	Club	League Appearances/Goals	
1987–88	Doncaster R	24	1
1987–88	Wrexham	17	1
1988–89		41	1
1989–90		23	2
1990–91		11	1

FLYNN, Mike

Born Oldham 23.2.69.   Ht 6 0   Wt 11 00
Defender. From Trainee.

Season	Club	App	Goals
1986–87	Oldham Ath	—	—
1987–88		31	1
1988–89		9	—
1988–89	Norwich C	—	—
1989–90		—	—
1989–90	Preston NE	23	1
1990–91		35	1

FOLEY, Steve

Born Liverpool 4.10.62.   Ht 5 8   Wt 11 09
Forward. From Apprentice.

Season	Club	App	Goals
1980–81	Liverpool	—	—
1981–82		—	—
1982–83		—	—
1983–84		—	—
1983–84	*Fulham*	3	—
1984–85	Grimsby T	31	2
1985–86	Sheffield U	28	5
1986–87		38	9
1987–88	Swindon T	35	4
1988–89		40	8
1989–90		23	4
1990–91		44	7

FORD, Gary

Born York 8.2.61.   Ht 5 8   Wt 11 10
Midfield. From Apprentice.

Season	Club	App	Goals
1978–79	York C	33	4
1979–80		29	2
1980–81		43	4
1981–82		41	8
1982–83		45	11
1983–84		46	11
1984–85		44	5
1985–86		40	3

Season	Club	App	Goals
1986–87		45	4
1987–88	Leicester C	16	2
1987–88	Port Vale	23	3
1988–89		22	7
1989–90		—	—
1989–90	*Walsall*	13	2
1990–91	Port Vale	30	2
1990–91	Mansfield T	12	1

FORD, Mike

Born Bristol 9.2.66.   Ht 6 0   Wt 11 02
Defender. From Apprentice.

Season	Club	App	Goals
1983–84	Leicester C	—	—
From Devizes			
1984–85	Cardiff C	20	1
1985–86		44	4
1986–87		36	1
1987–88		45	7
1988–89	Oxford U	10	1
1989–90		31	2
1990–91		28	1

FORD, Tony

Born Grimsby 14.5.59.   Ht 5 8   Wt 12 13
Forward. From Apprentice. England B.

Season	Club	App	Goals
1975–76	Grimsby T	14	—
1976–77		6	—
1977–78		34	2
1978–79		45	15
1979–80		37	5
1980–81		28	4
1981–82		35	7
1982–83		37	4
1983–84		42	8
1984–85		42	6
1985–86		34	3
1985–86	*Sunderland*	9	1
1986–87	Stoke C	41	6
1987–88		44	7
1988–89		27	—
1988–89	WBA	11	1
1989–90		42	8
1990–91		46	5

FOREMAN, Darren

Born Southampton 12.2.68.   Ht 5 10
Wt 10 08
Forward. England Schools.

1986–87	Barnsley	16	1
1987–88		9	4
1988–89		5	—
1989–90		17	3
1989–90	Crewe Alex	14	3
1990–91		9	1
1990–91	Scarborough	14	5

FORREST, Craig

Born Vancouver 20.9.67.   Ht 6 5
Wt 14 01
Goalkeeper. From Apprentice. Canada full caps.

1985–86	Ipswich T	—	—
1986–87		—	—
1987–88		—	—
1987–88	*Colchester U*	11	—
1988–89	Ipswich T	28	—
1989–90		45	—
1990–91		43	—

FORREST, Gerry

Born Stockton 21.1.57.   Ht 5 9   Wt 10 11
Defender. From South Bank.

1976–77	Rotherham U	—	—
1977–78		44	—
1978–79		46	—
1979–80		43	4
1980–81		44	2
1981–82		35	1
1982–83		39	—
1983–84		45	—
1984–85		44	—
1985–86		17	—
1985–86	Southampton	22	—
1986–87		38	—
1987–88		37	—
1988–89		17	—
1989–90		1	—
1990–91	Rotherham U	34	—

FORSYTH, Mike

Born Liverpool 20.3.66.   Ht 5 11
Wt 12 02
Defender. From Apprentice. England Youth, B, Under-21

1983–84	WBA	8	—
1984–85		10	—
1985–86		11	—
1985–86	*Northampton T*	—	—
1985–86	Derby Co	—	—
1986–87		41	1
1987–88		39	3
1988–89		38	—
1989–90		38	—
1990–91		35	—

FOSTER, Adrian

Born Kidderminster 20.7.71   Ht 5 9
Wt 11 00
Forward. From Trainee.

| 1989–90 | WBA | 14 | 1 |
| 1990–91 | | 5 | — |

FOSTER, Colin

Born Chislehurst 16.7.64.   Ht 6 4
Wt 14 01
Defender. From Apprentice

1981–82	Orient	23	2
1982–83		43	2
1983–84		11	1
1984–85		42	1
1985–86		36	2
1986–87		19	2
1986–87	Nottingham F	9	1
1987–88		39	2
1988–89		18	2
1989–90		6	—
1989–90	West Ham U	22	1
1990–91		36	3

FOSTER, George

Born Plymouth 26.9.56.   Ht 5 10
Wt 11 02
Defender. From Apprentice.

Season	Club	Apps	Goals
1973–74	Plymouth Arg	5	—
1974–75		—	—
1975–76		16	1
1976–77		15	2
1976–77	*Torquay U*	6	3
1977–78	Plymouth Arg	46	3
1978–79		28	—
1979–80		46	—
1980–81		46	—
1981–82		10	—
1981–82	*Exeter C*	28	—
1982–83	Derby Co	30	—
1983–84	Mansfield T	42	—
1984–85		44	—
1985–86		46	—
1986–87		45	—
1987–88		44	—
1988–89		42	—
1989–90		42	—
1990–91		34	—

FOSTER, Steve

Born Portsmouth 24.9.57.   Ht 6 1
Wt 13 13
Defender. From Apprentice. England
Under-21, 3 full caps.

Season	Club	Apps	Goals
1975–76	Portsmouth	11	—
1976–77		31	1
1977–78		31	3
1978–79		36	2
1979–80	Brighton	38	1
1980–81		42	1
1981–82		40	2
1982–83		36	1
1983–84		16	1
1983–84	Aston Villa	7	1
1984–85		8	2
1984–85	Luton T	25	1
1985–86		35	3
1986–87		28	2
1987–88		39	2
1988–89		36	3
1989–90	Oxford U	35	4
1990–91		38	3

FOSTER, Wayne

Born Leigh 11.9.63.   Ht 5 8   Wt 11 00
Forward. From Apprentice. England
Youth.

Season	Club	Apps	Goals
1981–82	Bolton W	23	2
1982–83		24	4
1983–84		30	3
1984–85		28	4
1985–86	Preston NE	31	3
1986–87	Hearts	31	4
1987–88		39	4
1988–89		9	1
1989–90		17	1
1990–91		28	1

FOWLER, Lee

Born Nottingham 26.1.69   Ht 5 8
Wt 11 07
Forward. From Trainee.

Season	Club	Apps	Goals
1987–88	Stoke C	1	—
1988–89		—	—
1989–90		15	—
1990–91		17	—

FOX, Matthew

Born Birmingham 13.7.71   Ht 6 0
Wt 13 00
Defender. From Trainee.

Season	Club	Apps	Goals
1988–89	Birmingham C	3	—
1989–90		—	—
1990–91		11	—

FOX, Peter

Born Scunthorpe 5.7.57.   Ht 5 11
Wt 13 08
Goalkeeper. From Apprentice.

Season	Club	Apps	Goals
1972–73	Sheffield W	1	—
1973–74		—	—
1974–75		20	—
1975–76		27	—
1976–77		1	—
1976–77	*West Ham U*	—	—
1977–78	Sheffield W	—	—

Season	Club		
1977–78	*Barnsley*	1	—
1977–78	Stoke C	—	—
1978–79		1	—
1979–80		23	—
1980–81		42	—
1981–82		38	—
1982–83		35	—
1983–84		42	—
1984–85		14	—
1985–86		37	—
1986–87		39	—
1987–88		17	—
1988–89		29	—
1989–90		38	—
1990–91		44	—

FOX, Ruel

Born Ipswich 14.1.68.   Ht 5 6   Wt 10 00
Midfield. From Apprentice.

1985–86	Norwich C	—	—
1986–87		3	—
1987–88		34	2
1988–89		4	—
1989–90		7	3
1990–91		28	4

FOYLE, Martin

Born Salisbury 2.5.63.   Ht 5 10   Wt 11 02
Forward. From Amateur.

1980–81	Southampton	—	—
1981–82		—	—
1982–83		7	1
1983–84		5	—
1983–84	*Blackburn R*	—	—
1984–85	Aldershot	44	15
1985–86		20	9
1986–87		34	11
1986–87	Oxford U	4	—
1987–88		33	10
1988–89		40	14
1989–90		13	2
1990–91		36	10

FRAIN, David

Born Sheffield 11.10.62.   Ht 5 8   Wt 10 05
Forward. From Rowlinson YC.

1985–86	Sheffield U	7	1
1986–87		19	3
1987–88		18	1
1988–89	Rochdale	42	12
1989–90	Stockport Co	29	2
1990–91		43	3

FRAIN, John

Born Birmingham 8.10.68.   Ht 5 7
Wt 11 10
Midfield. From Apprentice.

1985–86	Birmingham C	3	—
1986–87		3	1
1987–88		14	2
1988–89		28	3
1989–90		38	1
1990–91		42	3

FRANCE, Paul

Born Huddersfield 10.9.68.   Ht 6 1
Wt 11 08
Midfield. From Trainee.

1987–88	Huddersfield T	8	—
1988–89		3	—
1988–89	*Cobh Ramblers*	—	—
1989–90	Bristol C	—	—
1990–91	Burnley	2	—

FRANCIS, John

Born Dewsbury 21.11.63   Ht 5 8
Wt 11 02
Forward. From Emley.

1988–89	Sheffield U	22	1
1989–90		20	5
1989–90	Burnley	19	4
1990–91		45	14

FRANCIS, Kevin

Born Moseley 6.12.67   Ht 6 7   Wt 15 08
Forward. From Mile Oak R.

1988–89	Derby Co	—	—
1989–90		8	—

| 1990–91 | .... | 2 | — |
| 1990–91 | Stockport Co .... | 13 | 5 |

FRANCIS, Lee

Born London 24.10.69.   Ht 5 10
Wt 10 11
Defender. From Trainee.

1987–88	Arsenal......................	—	—
1988–89	....	—	—
1989–90	....	—	—
1989–90	*Chesterfield*	2	—
1990–91	Chesterfield	29	1

FRANCIS, Sean

Born Birmingham 1.8.72.   Ht 5 10
Wt 11 09
Forward. From Trainee.

| 1989–90 | Birmingham C .... | — | — |
| 1990–91 | .... | 3 | — |

FRANCIS, Steve

Born Billericay 29.5.64.   Ht 5 11
Wt 11 05
Goalkeeper. From Apprentice. England
Youth.

1981–82	Chelsea......................	29	—
1982–83	....	37	—
1983–84	....	—	—
1984–85	....	2	—
1985–86	....	3	—
1986–87	....	—	—
1986–87	Reading......................	14	—
1987–88	....	34	—
1988–89	....	22	—
1989–90	....	46	—
1990–91	....	34	—

FRANCIS, Trevor

Born Plymouth 19.4.54.   Ht 5 10
Wt 11 07
Forward. From Apprentice. England
Youth, Under-23, 52 full caps.

| 1970–71 | Birmingham C .... | 22 | 15 |

1971–72	....	39	12
1972–73	....	31	6
1973–74	....	37	6
1974–75	....	23	13
1975–76	....	35	17
1976–77	....	42	21
1977–78	....	42	25
From Detroit E			
1978–79	Birmingham C	9	3
1978–79	Nottingham F.............	20	6
From Detroit E			
1979–80	Nottingham F.............	30	14
1980–81	....	18	6
1981–82	....	2	2
1981–82	Manchester C	26	12
1982–83	Sampdoria...................	14	7
1983–84	....	15	3
1984–85	....	24	6
1985–86	....	15	1
1986–87	Atalanta......................	21	1
1987–88	Rangers......................	18	—
1987–88	QPR............................	9	—
1988–89	....	19	7
1989–90	....	4	5
1989–90	Sheffield W.................	12	—
1990–91	....	38	4

FRANKLAND, Tony

Born Greenwich 11.10.72.   Ht 6 1
Wt 10 07
Midfield. From School.

| 1989–90 | Exeter C...................... | 4 | — |
| 1990–91 | .... | 3 | — |

FREEMAN, Clive

Born Leeds 12.9.62.
Defender.

1987–88	Doncaster R................	—	—
From Bridlington T			
1990–91	Swansea C..................	2	—

FREESTONE, Roger

Born Newport 19.8.68.   Ht 6 2   Wt 12 03
Goalkeeper. Wales Under-21.

| 1986–87 | Newport Co................. | 13 | — |

Season	Club	Apps	Goals
1986–87	Chelsea	6	—
1987–88		15	—
1988–89		21	—
1989–90		—	—
1989–90	*Swansea C*	14	—
1989–90	*Hereford U*	8	—
1990–91	Chelsea	—	—

FRENCH, Hamish

Born Aberdeen 7.2.64.   Ht 5 10   Wt 11 04
Midfield. From Keith.

Season	Club	Apps	Goals
1987–88	Dundee U	20	2
1988–89		18	3
1989–90		12	2
1990–91		19	3

FRIDGE, Les

Born Inverness 27.8.68.   Ht 5 11
Wt 11 12
Goalkeeper. From Apprentice. Scotland
Youth, Under-21.

Season	Club	Apps	Goals
1985–86	Chelsea	1	—
1986–87		—	—
1986–87	St Mirren	1	—
1987–88		3	—
1988–89		15	—
1989–90		8	—
1990–91		11	—

FRIEL, George

Born Reading 11.10.70.   Ht 5 8   Wt 10 11
Forward. From Trainee.

Season	Club	Apps	Goals
1989–90	Reading	3	—
1990–91		13	1

FRY, Chris

Born Cardiff 23.10.69   Ht 5 9   Wt 9 06
Forward. From Trainee.

Season	Club	Apps	Goals
1988–89	Cardiff C	9	—
1989–90		23	1
1990–91		23	—

FULTON, Stephen

Born Greenock 10.8.70.   Ht 5 10
Wt 11 00
Midfield. From Celtic BC. Scotland
Under-21.

Season	Club	Apps	Goals
1986–87	Celtic	—	—
1987–88		—	—
1988–89		3	—
1989–90		16	—
1990–91		21	—

FUTCHER, Paul

Born Chester 25.9.56.   Ht 6 0   Wt 12 03
Defender. From Apprentice. England
Under-21.

Season	Club	Apps	Goals
1972–73	Chester	2	—
1973–74		18	—
1974–75	Luton T	19	—
1975–76		41	—
1976–77		40	1
1977–78		31	—
1978–79	Manchester C	24	—
1979–80		13	—
1980–81	Oldham Ath	36	1
1981–82		37	—
1982–83		25	—
1982–83	Derby Co	17	—
1983–84		18	—
1983–84	Barnsley	10	—
1984–85		36	—
1985–86		37	—
1986–87		36	—
1987–88		41	—
1988–89		41	—
1989–90		29	—
1990–91	Halifax T	15	—
1990–91	Grimsby T	22	—

FUTCHER, Ron

Born Chester 25.9.56.   Ht 6 0   Wt 12 10
Forward. From Apprentice.

Season	Club	Apps	Goals
1973–74	Chester	4	—
1974–75	Luton	17	7
1975–76		31	10
1976–77		33	13

Season	Club		
1977–78	....	39	10
1978–79	Manchester C	17	7

From Minnesota K, Portland T, Tulsa R and NAC Breda

Season	Club		
1984–85	Barnsley	19	6
1985–86	....	40	17
1986–87	....	25	13
1986–87	Bradford C	10	4
1987–88	....	32	14
1988–89	Port Vale	41	17
1989–90	....	11	3
1989–90	Burnley	23	7
1990–91	....	34	18

FYFE, Tony

Born Carlisle 23.2.62.   Ht 6 2   Wt 12 00
Forward.

Season	Club		
1987–88	Carlisle U....................	10	4
1988–89	....	25	4
1989–90	....	13	4
1989–90	*Scarborough*	6	1
1989–90	Halifax T	12	—
1990–91	....	4	—
1990–91	Carlisle U....................	16	3

GABBIADINI, Marco

Born Nottingham 20.1.68.   Ht 5 10 Wt 12 04
Forward. From Apprentice. England B, Under-21.

Season	Club		
1984–85	York C.....................	1	—
1985–86	....	22	4
1986–87	....	29	9
1987–88	....	8	1
1987–88	Sunderland.................	35	21
1988–89	....	36	18
1989–90	....	46	21
1990–91	....	31	9

GABBIADINI, Ricardo

Born Newport 11.3.70   Ht 6 0   Wt 13 00
Forward. From Trainee.

Season	Club		
1987–88	York C.....................	1	—
1988–89	Sunderland.................	—	—
1989–90	....	1	—
1989–90	*Blackpool*	5	3
1989–90	*Brighton*	1	—
1989–90	*Grimsby T*	3	1
1990–91	Sunderland.................	—	—
1990–91	*Crewe Alex*.................	2	—
1990–91	Hartlepool U	5	—

GAGE, Kevin

Born Chiswick 21.4.64.   Ht 5 10 Wt 12 11
Defender. From Apprentice. England Youth.

Season	Club		
1980–81	Wimbledon	1	—
1981–82	....	21	1
1982–83	....	26	4
1983–84	....	24	4
1984–85	....	37	2
1985–86	....	29	1
1986–87	....	30	3
1987–88	Aston Villa.................	44	2
1988–89	....	28	3
1989–90	....	22	3
1990–91	....	21	—

GAHAGAN, John

Born Glasgow 24.8.58.   Ht 5 9   Wt 10 07
Forward. From Shettleston Juniors.

Season	Club	App	Goals
1977–78	Clydebank	5	—
1978–79		—	—
1979–80	Motherwell	17	3
1980–81		34	1
1981–82		39	7
1982–83		28	4
1983–84		30	7
1984–85		31	5
1985–86		21	3
1986–87		19	—
1987–88		23	—
1988–89		14	2
1989–90		26	3
1990–91		1	—

GALE, Shaun

Born Reading 8.10.69.   Ht 6 0   Wt 11 06
Defender. From Trainee.

Season	Club	App	Goals
1989–90	Portsmouth	—	—
1990–91		3	—

GALE, Tony

Born London 19.11.59.   Ht 6 1   Wt 13 07
Defender. From Apprentice. England
Youth, Under-21.

Season	Club	App	Goals
1977–78	Fulham	38	8
1978–79		36	2
1979–80		42	4
1980–81		40	1
1981–82		44	1
1982–83		42	2
1983–84		35	1
1984–85	West Ham U	37	—
1985–86		42	—
1986–87		32	2
1987–88		18	—
1988–89		31	—
1989–90		36	1
1990–91		24	1

GALL, Mark

Born London 14.5.63.   Ht 5 10   Wt 12 00
Forward. From Wandsworth and
Greenwich Borough (1988).

Season	Club	App	Goals
1989–90	Maidstone U	41	18
1990–91		34	11

GALLACHER, Bernard

Born Johnstone 22.3.67.   Ht 5 9
Wt 11 00
Defender. From Apprentice.

Season	Club	App	Goals
1984–85	Aston Villa	—	—
1985–86		—	—
1986–87		1	—
1987–88		43	—
1988–89		4	—
1989–90		7	—
1990–91		2	—
1990–91	*Blackburn R*	4	—

GALLACHER, John

Born Glasgow 26.1.69.   Ht 5 10   Wt 10 08
Forward.

Season	Club	App	Goals
1987–88	Falkirk	2	—
1988–89		16	5
1989–90	Newcastle U	28	6
1990–91		1	—

GALLACHER, Kevin

Born Clydebank 23.11.66.   Ht 5 6
Wt 10 00
Forward. From Duntocher BC. Scotland
Youth, B, Under-21, 5 full caps.

Season	Club	App	Goals
1983–84	Dundee U	—	—
1984–85		—	—
1985–86		20	3
1986–87		37	10
1987–88		26	4
1988–89		31	9
1989–90		17	1
1989–90	Coventry C	15	3
1990–91		32	11

GALLACHER, Stuart

Born Bangour 25.2.72   Ht 5 7   Wt 10 7
Midfield. From Hamilton Thistle

1990–91	Dunfermline Ath	1	—

GALLAGHER, Eddie

Born Glasgow 21.11.64.   Ht 5 9   Wt 10 06
Forward. From Campsie BW.

1985–86	Partick T	23	4
1986–87		30	5
1987–88		34	13
1988–89		3	2
1988–89	Hamilton A	14	3
1988–89	Dunfermline Ath	7	1
1989–90		14	1
1990–91		3	—

GALLIMORE, Tony

Born Crewe 21.2.72.   Ht 5 10   Wt 11 10
Midfield. From Trainee.

1989–90	Stoke C	1	—
1990–91		7	—

GALLOWAY, Mick

Born Oswestry 30.5 65.   Ht 5 11   Wt 11 7
Defender. From Amateur. Scotland
Youth, Under-21.

1983–84	Mansfield T	17	—
1984–85		31	3
1985–86		6	—
1985–86	Halifax T	19	—
1986–87		43	3
1987–88		17	2
1987–88	Hearts	25	6
1988–89		31	2
1989–90	Celtic	33	2
1990–91		6	1

GANNON, Jim

Born London 7.9.68.   Ht 6 2   Wt 13 00
Defender. From Dundalk.

1988–89	Sheffield U	—	—
1989–90		—	—
1989–90	*Halifax T*	2	—
1989–90	Stockport Co	7	1
1990–91		41	6

GANNON, John

Born Wimbledon 18.12.66.   Ht 5 8
Wt 10 10
Midfield. From Apprentice.

1984–85	Wimbledon	—	—
1985–86		1	1
1986–87		2	—
1986–87	*Crewe Alex*	15	—
1987–88	Wimbledon	13	1
1988–89		—	—
1988–89	*Sheffield U*	16	1
1989–90	Sheffield U	39	3
1990–91		22	—

GARDINER, Mark

Born Cirencester 25.12.66.   Ht 5 10
Wt 10 07
Forward. From Apprentice.

1983–84	Swindon T	1	—
1984–85		4	—
1985–86		1	—
1986–87		4	—
1986–87	Torquay U	22	3
1987–88		27	1
1988–89	Crewe Alex	38	10
1989–90		26	6
1990–91		33	10

GARDNER, James

Born Dunfermline 27.9.67.   Ht 5 10
Wt 10 02
Midfield. From Ayresome North AFC

1986–87	Queen's Park	1	—
1987–88		1	—
1988–89	Motherwell	—	—
1989–90		1	—
1990–91		—	—

GARDNER, Lee

Born Ayr 11.7.70. Ht 5 5 Wt 9 05
Midfield. From Aberdeen Lads.

1987–88	Aberdeen	1	—
1988–89		—	—
1989–90		—	—
1990–91		—	—
1990–91	*Oxford U*	7	—

GARLAND, Peter

Born Croydon 20.1.71. Ht 5 9 Wt 12 00
Midfield. From Trainee. England Youth.

| 1989–90 | Tottenham H | — | — |
| 1990–91 | | 1 | — |

GARNER, Andy

Born Chesterfield 8.3.66. Ht 6 0
Wt 12 01
Forward. From Apprentice.

1983–84	Derby Co	13	5
1984–85		16	3
1985–86		16	5
1986–87		2	—
1987–88		24	4
1988–89	Blackpool	42	11
1989–90		46	8
1990–91		36	13

GARNER, Darren

Born Plymouth 10.12.71 Ht 5 6
Wt 10 01
Midfield. From Trainee.

1988–89	Plymouth Arg	1	—
1989–90		1	—
1990–91		5	1

GARNER, Simon

Born Boston 23.11.59. Ht 5 9 Wt 11 12
Forward. From Apprentice.

| 1978–79 | Blackburn R | 25 | 8 |
| 1979–80 | | 28 | 6 |

1980–81		33	7
1981–82		36	14
1982–83		41	22
1983–84		42	19
1984–85		37	12
1985–86		38	12
1986–87		40	10
1987–88		40	14
1988–89		44	20
1989–90		43	18
1990–91		12	1

GARNETT, Shaun

Born Wallasey 22.11.69 Ht 6 2 Wt 11 00
Midfield. From Trainee.

1987–88	Tranmere R	1	—
1988–89		—	—
1989–90		4	—
1990–91		16	1

GARVEY, Steve

Born Tameside 22.11.73.
Forward. From Trainee

| 1990–91 | Crewe Alex | 1 | — |

GASCOIGNE, Paul

Born Gateshead 27.5.67. Ht 5 10
Wt 11 07
Midfield. From Apprentice. England B,
Under-21, 20 full caps.

1984–85	Newcastle U	2	—
1985–86		31	9
1986–87		24	5
1987–88		35	7
1988–89	Tottenham H	32	6
1989–90		34	6
1990–91		26	7

GATES, Eric

Born Ferryhill 28.6.55. Ht 5 6 Wt 10 06
Forward. From Apprentice. England H2
full caps.

| 1972–73 | Ipswich T | — | — |

Season	Club	Apps	Goals
1973–74		6	—
1974–75		6	—
1975–76		13	1
1976–77		12	1
1977–78		24	2
1978–79		22	7
1979–80		36	13
1980–81		37	11
1981–82		38	9
1982–83		24	3
1983–84		37	13
1984–85		41	13
1985–86	Sunderland	39	9
1986–87		27	5
1987–88		42	19
1988–89		37	4
1989–90		36	6
1990–91	Carlisle U	38	8

GATTING, Steve

Born Park Royal 29.5.59. Ht 5 11
Wt 12 08
Defender. From Apprentice.

Season	Club	Apps	Goals
1976–77	Arsenal	—	—
1977–78			
1978–79		21	1
1979–80		14	1
1980–81		23	3
1981–82		—	—
1981–82	Brighton	39	3
1982–83		40	4
1983–84		35	4
1984–85		8	—
1985–86		17	—
1986–87		40	1
1987–88		46	3
1988–89		29	3
1989–90		19	—
1990–91		43	1

GAUGHAN, Steve

Born Doncaster 14.4.70 Ht 5 11
Wt 11 02
Midfield.

Season	Club	Apps	Goals
1987–88	Doncaster R	4	—
1988–89		34	2

Season	Club	Apps	Goals
1989–90		29	1
1990–91	Sunderland	—	—

GAVIN, Mark

Born Bailleston 10.12.63. Ht 5 8
Wt 10 07
Midfield. From Apprentice.

Season	Club	Apps	Goals
1981–82	Leeds U	—	—
1982–83		7	1
1983–84		12	1
1984–85		11	1
1984–85	*Hartlepool U*	7	—
1985–86	Carlisle U	13	1
1985–86	Bolton W	8	1
1986–87		41	2
1987–88	Rochdale	23	6
1987–88	Hearts	7	—
1988–89		2	—
1988–89	Bristol C	29	3
1989–90		40	3
1990–91	Watford	13	—

GAVIN, Pat

Born Hammersmith 5.6.67 Ht 6 0
Wt 12 00
Forward. From Hanwell T.

Season	Club	Apps	Goals
1988–89	Gillingham	13	7
1989–90	Leicester C	—	—
1989–90	*Gillingham*	34	1
1990–91	Leicester C	3	—
1990–91	Peterborough U	11	5

GAYLE, Brian

Born London 6.3.65. Ht 6 1 Wt 12 07
Defender.

Season	Club	Apps	Goals
1984–85	Wimbledon	12	1
1985–86		13	—
1986–87		32	1
1987–88		26	1
1988–89	Manchester C	41	3
1989–90		14	—
1989–90	Ipswich T	20	—
1990–91		33	4

GAYLE, Howard

Born Liverpool 18.5.58.   Ht 5 10
Wt 10 09
Midfield. Local. England Under-21.

Season	Club	App	Goals
1977–78	Liverpool	—	—
1978–79		—	—
1979–80		—	—
1979–80	*Fulham*	14	—
1980–81	Liverpool	4	1
1981–82		—	—
1982–83	Liverpool	—	—
1982–83	*Birmingham C*	13	1
1982–83	*Newcastle U*	8	2
1983–84	Birmingham C	33	8
1984–85	Sunderland	25	2
1985–86		23	2
1986–87	Stoke C	6	2
1987–88	Blackburn R	13	1
1988–89		45	19
1989–90		30	5
1990–91		24	4

GAYLE, John

Born Birmingham 30.7.64   Ht 6 4
Wt 13 01
Forward. From Burton Alb.

Season	Club	App	Goals
1988–89	Wimbledon	2	—
1989–90		11	1
1990–91		7	1
1990–91	Birmingham C	22	6

GAYLE, Marcus

Born Hammersmith 27.9.70
Midfield. From Trainee. England Youth.

Season	Club	App	Goals
1988–89	Brentford	3	—
1989–90		9	—
1990–91		33	6

GAYNOR, Tommy

Born Limerick 29.1.63.   Ht 6 1   Wt 13 02
Forward. From Limerick.

Season	Club	App	Goals
1986–87	Doncaster R	23	4
1987–88		10	3
1987–88	Nottingham F	12	3
1988–89		19	4
1989–90		11	—
1990–91		11	3
1990–91	*Newcastle U*	4	1

GEDDIS, David

Born Carlisle 12.3.58.   Ht 6 0   Wt 11 08
Forward. From Apprentice. England
Youth, B.

Season	Club	App	Goals
1975–76	Ipswich T	—	—
1976–77		2	—
1976–77	*Luton T*	13	4
1977–78	Ipswich T	26	4
1978–79		15	1
1979–80		—	—
1979–80	Aston Villa	20	2
1980–81		9	4
1981–82		14	6
1982–83		4	—
1982–83	*Luton T*	4	—
1983–84	Aston Villa	—	—
1983–84	Barnsley	31	14
1984–85		14	10
1984–85	Birmingham C	18	12
1985–86		26	6
1986–87		2	—
1986–87	*Brentford*	4	—
1986–87	Shrewsbury T	15	5
1987–88		15	5
1988–89		9	1
1988–89	Swindon T	10	3
1989–90		—	—
1989–90	*Darlington*	9	3
1990–91		13	—

GEE, Phil

Born Pelsall 19.12.64.   Ht 5 9   Wt 10 04
Forward. From Riley Sports and Gresley
R.

Season	Club	App	Goals
1985–86	Derby Co	4	2
1986–87		41	15
1987–88		38	6
1988–89		12	1
1989–90		8	1
1990–91		2	—

GEMMILL, Scot

Born Paisley 2.1.71.   Ht 5 10   Wt 10 01
Midfield. From School.

Season	Club		
1989–90	Nottingham F	—	—
1990–91		4	—

GENNOE, Terry

Born Shrewsbury 16.3.53.   Ht 6 2
Wt 13 00
Goalkeeper. From Bricklayers Sports.

Season	Club		
1972–73	Bury	1	—
1973–74		2	—
1973–74	*Blackburn R*	—	—
1974–75	Bury	—	—
1974–75	*Leeds U*	—	—
1975–76	Halifax T	26	—
1976–77		26	—
1977–78		26	—
1977–78	Southampton	—	—
1978–79		23	—
1979–80		13	—
1980–81	*Everton*	—	—
1980–81	*Crystal Palace*	3	—
1981–82	Blackburn R	35	—
1982–83		33	—
1983–84		30	—
1984–85		37	—
1985–86		32	—
1986–87		11	—
1987–88		39	—
1988–89		43	—
1989–90		28	—
1990–91		1	—

GERMAN, David

Born Sheffield 16.10.73.
Midfield. From Sheffield W Schoolboy.

Season	Club		
1990–91	Halifax T	1	—

GERNON, Irvin

Born Birmingham 30.12.62.   Ht 6 1
Wt 12 08
Defender. From Apprentice. England
Youth, Under-21.

Season	Club		
1979–80	Ipswich T	—	—
1980–81		—	—
1981–82		4	—
1982–83		26	—
1983–84		19	—
1984–85		13	—
1985–86		11	—
1986–87		3	—
1986–87	*Northampton T*	9	—
1986–87	Gillingham	14	—
1987–88		21	1
1988–89		—	—
1988–89	Reading	22	—
1989–90		3	—
1989–90	Northampton T	12	1
1990–91		8	—

GIBBINS, Roger

Born Enfield 6.9.55   Ht 5 10   Wt 11 09
Forward. From Apprentice. England
Schools.

Season	Club		
1972–73	Tottenham H	—	—
1973–74		—	—
1974–75		—	—
1975–76	Oxford U	19	2
1976–77	Norwich C	20	5
1977–78		28	7
From New England Tea Men			
1979–80	Cambridge U	35	4
1980–81		30	4
1981–82		35	4
1981–82	Cardiff C	46	8
1982–83		42	4
1983–84		40	5
1984–85		11	—
1985–86	Swansea C	35	6
1986–87	Newport Co	46	8
1987–88		33	1
1987–88	Torquay U	12	2
1988–89		21	3
From Newport Co.			
1988–89	Cardiff C	12	—
1989–90		38	1
1990–91		43	5

GIBBS, Nigel

Born St Albans 20.11.65.   Ht 5 6
Wt 10 10
Defender. From Apprentice. England
Youth, Under-21.

Season	Club	App	Goals
1983–84	Watford	3	—
1984–85		12	—
1985–86		40	1
1986–87		15	—
1987–88		30	—
1988–89		46	1
1989–90		41	—
1990–91		34	—

GIBSON, Colin

Born Bridport 6.4.60   Ht 5 8   Wt 10 11
Defender. From Apprentice. England
Under-21, B.

Season	Club	App	Goals
1977–78	Aston Villa	—	—
1978–79		12	—
1979–80		31	2
1980–81		21	—
1981–82		23	—
1982–83		23	1
1983–84		28	1
1984–85		40	4
1985–86		7	2
1985–86	Manchester U	18	5
1986–87		24	1
1987–88		29	2
1988–89		2	—
1989–90		6	1
1990–91		—	—
1990–91	*Port Vale*	6	2
1990–91	Leicester C	18	1

GIBSON, Terry

Born Walthamstow 23.12.62.   Ht 5 5
Wt 10 00
Forward. From Apprentice. England
Schools, Youth.

Season	Club	App	Goals
1979–80	Tottenham H	1	—
1980–81		—	—
1981–82		1	—
1982–83		16	4

Season	Club	App	Goals
1983–84	Coventry C	36	17
1984–85		38	15
1985–86		24	11
1985–86	Manchester U	7	—
1986–87		16	1
1987–88		—	—
1987–88	Wimbledon	17	6
1988–89		17	5
1989–90		18	5
1990–91		19	5

GIGGS, Ryan

Born Cardiff 29.11.73.
Forward. From School. Wales Youth,
Under-21.

Season	Club	App	Goals
1990–91	Manchester U	2	1

GILBERT, Billy

Born Lewisham 10.11.59.   Ht 5 11
Wt 12 00
Defender. From Apprentice   England
Schools, Youth, Under-21.

Season	Club	App	Goals
1976–77	Crystal Palace	—	—
1977–78		18	—
1978–79		41	1
1979–80		40	1
1980–81		39	—
1981–82		31	—
1982–83		34	—
1983–84		34	1
1984–85	Portsmouth	35	—
1985–86		36	—
1986–87		36	—
1987–88		21	—
1988–89		12	—
1989–90	Colchester U	27	—
1990–91		—	—
1990–91	Maidstone U	4	—

GILBERT, David

Born Lincoln 22.6.63.   Ht 5 4   Wt 10 04
Midfield. From Apprentice.

Season	Club	App	Goals
1980–81	Lincoln C	1	—
1981–82		29	1

1982–83	Scunthorpe U	1	—	

From Boston U

1986–87	Northampton T	45	8
1987–88		41	6
1988–89		34	7
1988–89	Grimsby T	11	3
1989–90		45	10
1990–91		44	12

GILKES, Michael

Born Hackney 20.7.65. Ht 5 8 Wt 10 02
Forward.

1984–85	Reading	16	2
1985–86		9	2
1986–87		7	—
1987–88		39	4
1988–89		46	9
1989–90		42	2
1990–91		21	1

GILL, Gary

Born Middlesbrough 28.11.64. Ht 5 11
Wt 12 04
Defender. From Apprentice.

1982–83	Middlesbrough	—	—
1983–84		6	—
1983–84	*Hull C*	1	—
1984–85	Middlesbrough	14	—
1985–86		9	—
1986–87		36	2
1987–88		3	—
1988–89		8	—
1989–90		1	—
1990–91	Darlington	36	8

GILLESPIE, Gary

Born Stirling 5.7.60. Ht 6 2 Wt 12 07
Defender. From school. Scotland Under-
21, 13 full caps.

1977–78	Falkirk	22	—
1978–79	Coventry C	15	—
1979–80		38	1
1980–81		37	1
1981–82		40	2

1982–83		42	2
1983–84	Liverpool	—	—
1984–85		12	1
1985–86		14	3
1986–87		37	—
1987–88		35	4
1988–89		15	1
1989–90		13	4
1990–91		30	1

GILLHAUS, Hans

Born Helmond 5.11.63. Ht 5 9 Wt 12 04
Forward. From PSV Eindhoven. Holland
full caps.

1989–90	Aberdeen	20	8
1990–91		35	14

GILLIGAN, Jimmy

Born London 24.1.64. Ht 6 0 Wt 12 06
Forward. From Apprentice. England
Youth.

1981–82	Watford	1	—
1982–83		4	2
1982–83	*Lincoln C*	3	—
1983–84	Watford	12	4
1984–85		10	—
1985–86	Grimsby T	25	4
1986–87	Swindon T	17	5
1986–87	*Newport Co*	5	1
1986–87	Lincoln C	11	1
1987–88	Cardiff C	46	19
1988–89		46	15
1989–90		7	1
1989–90	Portsmouth	32	5
1990–91	Swansea C	37	16

GILZEAN, Ian

Born Enfield 10.12.69. Ht 6 1 Wt 12 08
Forward. From Trainee. Scotland Youth.

1988–89	Tottenham H	—	—
1989–90		—	—
1990–91		—	—

GITTENS, Jon

Born Moseley 22.1.64. Ht 6 0 Wt 12 06
Defender. From Paget R.

Season	Club	Appearances	Goals
1985–86	Southampton	4	—
1986–87		14	—
1987–88	Swindon T	29	—
1988–89		29	1
1989–90		40	4
1990–91		28	1
1990–91	Southampton	8	—

GLEASURE, Peter

Born Luton 8.10.60.　Ht 5 11　Wt 12 13
Goalkeeper. From Apprentice.

Season	Club	Appearances	Goals
1978–79	Millwall	—	—
1979–80		—	—
1980–81		13	—
1981–82		38	—
1982–83		4	—
1982–83	*Northampton T*	11	—
1983–84	Northampton T	46	—
1984–85		43	—
1985–86		44	—
1986–87		46	—
1987–88		46	—
1988–89		46	—
1989–90		46	—
1990–91		16	—
1990–91	*Gillingham*	3	—

GLEGHORN, Nigel

Born Seaham 12.8.62.　Ht 6.0　Wt 12 13
Midfield. From Seaham Red Star.

Season	Club	Appearances	Goals
1985–86	Ipswich T	21	2
1986–87		29	7
1987–88		16	2
1988–89	Manchester C	32	6
1989–90		2	1
1989–90	Birmingham C	43	9
1990–91		42	6

GLOVER, Dean

Born West Bromwich 29.12.63.　Ht 5 10
Wt 11 13
Defender. From Apprentice.

Season	Club	Appearances	Goals
1981–82	Aston Villa	—	—
1982–83		—	—
1983–84		—	—
1984–85		5	—
1985–86		18	—
1986–87		—	—
1986–87	*Sheffield U*	5	—
1987–88	Aston Villa	5	—
1987–88	Middlesbrough	38	4
1988–89		12	1
1988–89	Port Vale	22	—
1989–90		44	4
1990–91		41	1

GLOVER, Lee

Born Kettering 24.4.70.　Ht 5 10
Wt 12 01
Forward. From Trainee. Scotland
Under-21.

Season	Club	Appearances	Goals
1986–87	Nottingham F	—	—
1987–88		20	3
1988–89		—	—
1989–90		—	—
1989–90	*Leicester C*	5	1
1989–90	*Barnsley*	8	—
1990–91	Nottingham F	8	1

GOATER, Shaun

Born Bermuda 25.2.70.　Ht 5 11
Wt 11 04
Forward.

Season	Club	Appearances	Goals
1988–89	Manchester U	—	—
1989–90		—	—
1989–90	Rotherham U	12	2
1990–91		22	2

GODDARD, Karl

Born Leeds 29.12.67.　Ht 5 9　Wt 10 10
Defender. From Apprentice. England
Schools.

Season	Club	Appearances	Goals
1985–86	Manchester U	—	—
1986–87	Bradford C	20	—
1987–88		29	—
1988–89		23	—
1989–90		1	—
1989–90	*Exeter C*	1	—

Season	Club	League Appearances/Goals	
1989–90	*Colchester U*	16	1
1990–91	Bradford C	—	—
1990–91	Hereford C	8	1

GODDARD, Paul

Born Harlington 12.10.59.   Ht 5 8
Wt 11 13
Forward. From Apprentice. England
Under-21, 1 full cap.

Season	Club		
1977–78	QPR	7	1
1978–79		23	6
1979–80		40	16
1980–81	West Ham U	37	17
1981–82		39	15
1982–83		39	10
1983–84		5	1
1984–85		40	9
1985–86		6	1
1986–87		4	1
1986–87	Newcastle U	26	11
1987–88		35	8
1988–89	Derby Co	31	7
1989–90		18	8
1989–90	Millwall	14	1
1990–91		6	—
1990–91	Ipswich T	19	6

GODFREY, Kevin

Born Kennington 24.2.60.   Ht 5 10
Wt 10 11
Forward. From Apprentice.

Season	Club		
1976–77	Orient	—	—
1977–78		11	—
1978–79		6	—
1979–80		5	1
1980–81		9	2
1981–82		42	8
1982–83		45	11
1983–84		41	10
1984–85		40	10
1985–86		16	4
1985–86	*Plymouth Arg*	7	1
1986–87	Orient	36	10
1987–88		34	7
1988–89	Brentford	29	8
1989–90		27	2

Season	Club		
1990–91		32	4

GODFREY, Paul

Born Derby 27.9.72.   Ht 5 7   Wt 10 03
Forward. From Trainee

Season	Club		
1990–91	Chesterfield	2	—

GODFREY, Peter

Born Falkirk 12.10.57.   Ht 6 0   Wt 11 07
Defender. From Linlithgow Rose.

Season	Club		
1979–80	Stenhousemuir	2	—
1980–81	Meadowbank T	2	—
1981–82		30	6
1982–83		38	3
1983–84		37	3
1984–85		19	—
1984–85	St Mirren	15	1
1985–86		34	3
1986–87		38	1
1987–88		24	—
1988–89		27	1
1989–90		22	2
1990–91		14	—

GOLDSMITH, Craig

Born Peterborough 27.8.63   Ht 5 7
Wt 11 03
Forward. From Blackstones.

Season	Club		
1988–89	Peterborough U	40	6
1989–90		6	—
1989–90	Carlisle U	26	1
1990–91		4	—

GOLDSMITH, Martin

Born Walsall 4.11.69   Ht 6 0   Wt 11 11
Forward. From Trainee.

Season	Club		
1988–89	Walsall	2	—
1989–90		1	—
1989–90	*Larne*	—	—
1990–91	Walsall	4	2

GOLLEY, Mark

Born Beckenham 28.10.62.   Ht 6 1
Wt 13 00
Midfield. From Crystal Palace, Sutton U
(1988)

Season	Club		
1989–90	Maidstone U	45	3
1990–91		36	—

GOODING, Mick

Born Newcastle 12.4.59   Ht 5 7   Wt 10 13
Forward. From Bishop Auckland.

Season	Club		
1979–80	Rotherham U	34	3
1980–81		37	4
1981–82		22	2
1982–83		9	1
1982–83	Chesterfield	12	—
1983–84		—	—
1983–84	Rotherham U	26	7
1984–85		44	10
1985–86		40	8
1986–87		46	8
1987–88	Peterborough U	44	18
1988–89		3	3
1988–89	Wolverhampton W	31	4
1989–90		13	—
1989–90	Reading	27	3
1990–91		44	7

GOODISON, Wayne

Born Wakefield 23.9.64.   Ht 5 8
Wt 11 07
Defender. From Apprentice.

Season	Club		
1982–83	Barnsley	3	—
1983–84		—	—
1984–85		12	—
1985–86		21	—
1986–87		—	—
1986–87	Crewe Alex	35	—
1987–88		34	—
1988–89		25	1
1989–90	Rochdale	45	4
1990–91		34	—

GOODMAN, Don

Born Leeds 9.5.66.   Ht 5 10   Wt 11 10
Forward. From school.

Season	Club		
1983–84	Bradford C	2	—
1984–85		25	5
1985–86		20	4
1986–87		23	5
1986–87	WBA	10	2
1987–88		40	7
1988–89		36	15
1989–90		39	21
1990–91		22	8

GOODMAN, Jon

Born Walthamstow 2.6.71.
Forward. From Bromley.

Season	Club		
1990–91	Millwall	23	5

GOODWIN, Shaun

Born Rotherham 14.6.69.   Ht 5 7
Wt 8 10
Midfield. From Trainee.

Season	Club		
1987–88	Rotherham U	3	—
1988–89		41	4
1989–90		38	6
1990–91		34	3

GOODYEAR, Clive

Born Lincoln 15.1.61.   Ht 6 0   Wt 11 04
Defender. Local.

Season	Club		
1978–79	Luton T	—	—
1979–80		1	—
1980–81		5	1
1981–82		32	1
1982–83		35	2
1983–84		17	—
1984–85	Plymouth Arg	33	2
1985–86		41	2
1986–87		32	1
1987–88	Wimbledon	22	—
1988–89		—	—
1989–90		4	—
1990–91		—	—

| 1990–91 | Brentford .... | 10 | — |

GORAM, Andy

Born Bury 13.4.64.   Ht 5 11   Wt 11 06
Goalkeeper. From West Bromwich
Apprentice. Scotland Under-21, 15 full
caps.

1981–82	Oldham Ath...............	3	—
1982–83	....	38	—
1983–84	....	22	—
1984–85	....	41	—
1985–86	....	41	—
1986–87	....	41	—
1987–88	....	9	—
1987–88	Hibernian...................	33	1
1988–89	....	36	—
1989–90	....	34	—
1990–91	....	35	—

GORDON, Colin

Born Stourbridge 17.1.63.   Ht 6 1
Wt 12 12
Forward. From Oldbury U.

1984–85	Swindon T	33	17
1985–86	....	39	16
1986–87	Wimbledon	3	—
1986–87	*Gillingham*..................	4	2
1987–88	Reading......................	20	8
1987–88	*Bristol C*.....................	8	4
1988–89	Reading......................	4	1
1988–89	Fulham	17	2
1989–90	Birmingham C	21	3
1990–91	....	5	—
1990–91	*Hereford U*.................	6	—
1990–91	*Walsall*	6	1
1990–91	*Bristol R*....................	4	—

GORDON, Dale

Born Gt Yarmouth 9.1.67.   Ht 5 10
Wt 11 08
Forward. From Apprentice. England
Schools, Youth B, Under-21.

| 1983–84 | Norwich C .... | — | — |
| 1984–85 | .... | 23 | 3 |

1985–86	....	6	1
1986–87	....	41	5
1987–88	....	21	3
1988–89	....	38	5
1989–90	....	26	3
1990–91	....	36	7

GORE, Ian

Born Liverpool 10.1.68.   Ht 5 11
Wt 12 04
Midfield.

1986–87	Birmingham C	—	—
From Southport			
1987–88	Blackpool...................	—	—
1988–89	....	21	—
1989–90	....	34	—
1990–91	....	41	—

GORE, Shaun

Born London 21.9.68.   Ht 6 3   Wt 14 05
Defender.

1985–86	Fulham	5	—
1986–87	....	7	—
1987–88	....	8	—
1988–89	....	6	—
1989–90	....	—	—
1990–91	....	—	—
1990–91	*Halifax T*	15	—

GORMAN, Paul

Born Dublin 6.8.63   Ht 5 10   Wt 12 00
Defender. From Apprentice. Eire Youth,
Under-21.

1980–81	Arsenal......................	—	—
1981–82	....	4	—
1982–83	....	—	—
1983–84	....	2	—
1984–85	Birmingham C	6	—
1984–85	Carlisle U..................	7	1
1985–86	....	24	—
1986–87	....	35	—
1987–88	....	37	—
1988–89	....	43	6
1989–90	....	2	—

1989–90	*Shelbourne*	—	—
1989–90	Shrewsbury T	19	1
1990–91		30	—

GORMAN, Paul

Born Macclesfield 18.9.68.   Ht 5 10
Wt 12 05
Forward.

1987–88	Doncaster R	7	1
1988–89		9	1
From Fisher Ath			
1990–91	Charlton Ath	8	2

GORMLEY, Eddie

Born Dublin 23.10.68.   Ht 5 7   Wt 10 07
Midfield. From Bray W. Eire U-21.

1987–88	Tottenham H	—	—
1988–89		—	—
1988–89	*Chesterfield*	4	—
1988–89	*Motherwell*	—	—
1989–90	Tottenham H	—	—
1989–90	*Shrewsbury T*	—	—
1990–91	Doncaster R	40	5

GORTON, Andy

Born Salford 23.9.66.   Ht 5 11   Wt 11 04
Goalkeeper.

1984–85	Oldham Ath	—	—
1985–86		1	—
1986–87		1	—
1986–87	*Stockport Co*	14	—
1987–88	Oldham Ath	24	—
1987–88	*Tranmere R*	1	—
1988–89	Stockport Co	34	—
1989–90	Lincoln C	20	—
From Glossop			
1990–91	Oldham Ath	—	—
1990–91	Crewe Alex	3	—

GOSNEY, Andy

Born Southampton 8.11.63.   Ht 6 4
Wt 13 02
Goalkeeper. From Apprentice. England
Youth.

1981–82	Portsmouth	1	—
1982–83		—	—
1983–84		—	—
1984–85		—	—
1985–86		4	—
1986–87		—	—
1987–88		4	—
1988–89		14	—
1989–90		—	—
1990–91		24	—

GOSS, Jeremy

Born Cyprus 11.5.65.   Ht 5 9   Wt 10 09
Midfield. Amateur. England Youth, Wales
2 full caps.

1982–83	Norwich C	—	—
1983–84		1	—
1984–85		5	—
1985–86		—	—
1986–87		1	—
1987–88		22	2
1988–89		—	—
1989–90		7	—
1990–91		19	1

GOTSMANOV, Sergei

Born USSR 17.3.59.   Ht 5 9   Wt 11 04
Midfield. From Dynamo Minsk. USSR
full caps.

1989–90	Brighton	16	4
1990–91	Southampton	8	—

GOUCK, Andy

Born Blackpool 8.6.72.   Ht 5 9   Wt 11 02
Midfield. From Trainee.

1989–90		8	1
1990–91		5	—

GOUGH, Richard

Born Stockholm 5.4.62.   Ht 6 0   Wt 12 00
Defender. From Witz University. Scotland
Under-21, 52 full caps.

1980–81	Dundee U	4	—

Season	Club	App	Goals
1981–82	....	30	1
1982–83	....	34	8
1983–84	....	33	3
1984–85	....	33	6
1985–86	....	31	5
1986–87	Tottenham H.............	40	2
1987–88	....	9	—
1987–88	Rangers......................	31	5
1988–89	....	35	4
1989–90	....	26	—
1990–91	....	26	—

GOULD, Jonathan

Born London 18.7.68.
Goalkeeper.

Season	Club	App	Goals
1990–91	Halifax T	23	—

GOURLAY, Archie

Born Greenock 29.6.69. Ht 5 8 Wt 10 00
Midfield.

Season	Club	App	Goals
1987–88	Morton	2	—
1987–88	Newcastle U...............	—	—
1988–89	....	1	—
1989–90	....	—	—
1989–90	*Morton*	4	—
1990–91	Newcastle U...............	2	—

GRAHAM, Deniol

Born Cannock 4.10.69. Ht 5 10
Wt 10 05
Forward. From Trainee. Wales Under-21.

Season	Club	App	Goals
1987–88	Manchester U.............	1	—
1988–89	....	—	—
1989–90	....	1	—
1990–91	....	—	—

GRAHAM, Jimmy

Born Glasgow 15.11.69. Ht 5 11
Wt 11 00
Defender. From Trainee.

Season	Club	App	Goals
1988–89	Bradford C	1	—
1989–90	....	6	—

Season	Club	App	Goals
1989–90	*Rochdale*	11	—
1990–91	Rochdale....................	28	1

GRAHAM, Mike

Born Lancaster 24.2.59. Ht 5 9 Wt 11 07
Defender. From Apprentice.

Season	Club	App	Goals
1976–77	Bolton W	—	—
1977–78	....	1	—
1978–79	....	9	—
1979–80	....	9	—
1980–81	....	27	—
1981–82	Swindon T	30	1
1982–83	....	46	—
1983–84	....	36	—
1984–85	....	29	—
1985–86	Mansfield T...............	45	—
1986–87	....	41	—
1987–88	....	46	1
1988–89	....	1	—
1988–89	Carlisle U..................	44	2
1989–90	....	43	—
1990–91	....	13	—

GRAHAM, Tommy

Born Glasgow 31.3.58. Ht 5 10 Wt 11 10
Forward. From Arthurlie.

Season	Club	App	Goals
1977–78	Aston Villa.................	—	—
1978–79	....	—	—
1978–79	Barnsley	27	12
1979–80	....	11	1
1980–81	....	—	—
1980–81	Halifax T	34	9
1981–82	....	37	8
1982–83	Doncaster R...............	11	2
1982–83	Scunthorpe U	13	3
1983–84	....	27	4
1984–85	....	38	9
1985–86	....	31	5
1986–87	Scarborough..............	—	—
1987–88	....	44	7
1988–89	....	43	4
1989–90	....	24	—
1989–90	Halifax T	21	1
1990–91	....	23	3

GRANT, Brian

Born Bannockburn 19.6.64. Ht 5 9
Wt 10 07
Midfield. From Fallin Violet.

Season	Club	App	Goals
1981–82	Stirling Alb	1	—
1982–83		1	—
1983–84		24	3
1984–85	Aberdeen	—	—
1985–86		—	—
1986–87		15	4
1987–88		7	1
1988–89		26	1
1989–90		31	6
1990–91		32	2

GRANT, Kim

Born Ghana 25.9.72. Ht 5 10   Wt 10 12
Forward. From Trainee.

Season	Club	App	Goals
1990–91	Charlton Ath	12	2

GRANT, Peter

Born Bellshill 30.8.65. Ht 5 9   Wt 10 03
Midfield. From Celtic BC. Scotland
Schools, Youth, B, Under-21, 2 full caps.

Season	Club	App	Goals
1982–83	Celtic	—	—
1983–84		3	—
1984–85		20	4
1985–86		30	1
1986–87		37	1
1987–88		37	2
1988–89		21	—
1989–90		26	—
1990–91		27	—

GRANT, Roddy

Born Bloucester 16.9.66. Ht 5 11
Wt 11 00
Forward. From Strathbrock Jun.

Season	Club	App	Goals
1986–87	Cowdenbeath	24	14
1987–88		32	11
1988–89		8	2
1988–89	St Johnstone	28	5
1989–90		37	19

Season	Club	App	Goals
1990–91		30	7

GRAY, Andy

Born Lambeth 22.2.64. Ht 5 11
Wt 13 03
Midfield. From Corinthian C. and
Dulwich H. England Under-21.

Season	Club	App	Goals
1984–85	Crystal Palace	21	5
1985–86		30	10
1986–87		30	6
1987–88		17	6
1987–88	Aston Villa	19	1
1988–89		18	3
1988–89	QPR	11	2
1989–90	Crystal Palace	35	6
1990–91		30	4

GRAY, Frank

Born Glasgow 27.10.54. Ht 5 11
Wt 12 05
Defender. From Apprentice. Scotland
Schools, Under-23, 32 full caps.

Season	Club	App	Goals
1971–72	Leeds U	—	—
1972–73		4	1
1973–74		6	—
1974–75		18	2
1975–76		42	2
1976–77		41	3
1977–78		41	3
1978–79		41	6
1979–80	Nottingham F	41	2
1980–81		40	3
1981–82	Leeds U	37	—
1982–83		42	5
1983–84		24	4
1984–85		39	1
1985–86	Sunderland	34	4
1986–87		38	4
1987–88		34	—
1988–89		40	—
1989–90	Darlington	*36*	*1*
1990–91		43	7

GRAY, Gareth

Born Longridge 24.2.70   Ht 6 2   Wt 11 02
Goalkeeper. From Darwen.

137

1988–89	Bolton W	— —
1989–90		— —
1990–91	Rochdale	— —

GRAY, Kevin

Born Sheffield 7.1.72   Ht 6 0   Wt 13 00
Midfield. From Trainee.

1988–89	Mansfield T	1	—
1989–90		16	—
1990–91		31	1

GRAY, Martin

Born Stockton 17.8.71.   Ht 5 9   Wt 10 11
Midfield. From Trainee.

1989–90	Sunderland	— —
1990–91		— —
1990–91	*Aldershot*	5 —

GRAY, Philip

Born Belfast 2.10.68.   Ht 5 10   Wt 11 07
Forward. From Apprentice. Northern
Ireland Schools, Youth, Under-23.

1986–87	Tottenham H	1	—
1987–88		1	—
1988–89		1	—
1989–90		—	—
1989–90	*Barnsley*	3	—
1990–91	Tottenham H	6	—
1990–91	*Fulham*	3	—

GRAY, Steven

Born Irvine 7.2.67.   Ht 5 6   Wt 10 02
Midfield. From Kilmarnock BC. Scotland
Youth, Under-21.

1984–85	Aberdeen	—	—
1985–86		13	1
1986–87		13	1
1987–88		7	—
1988–89		4	—
1989–90	Airdrieonians	31	8
1990–91		15	1

GRAY, Stuart

Born Withernsea 19.4.60.   Ht 5 10
Wt 11 05
Defender. Local.

1980–81	Nottingham F	14	1
1981–82		33	2
1982–83		2	—
1982–83	*Bolton W*	10	—
1983–84	Barnsley	17	8
1984–85		7	—
1985–86		36	2
1986–87		40	11
1987–88		20	2
1987–88	Aston Villa	20	5
1988–89		35	4
1989–90		29	—
1990–91		22	—

GRAYSON, Neil

Born York 1.1.64.
Defender. From Rowntree Mackintosh.

1989–90	Doncaster R	6	1
1990–91		23	5
1990–91	York C	1	—

GRAYSON, Simon

Born Ripon 16.12.69   Ht 5 11   Wt 10 11
Midfield. From Trainee.

1987–88	Leeds U	2	—
1988–89		— —
1989–90		— —
1990–91		— —

GREALISH, Tony

Born Paddington 21.9.56.   Ht 5 7
Wt 12 00
Midfield. From Apprentice. Eire Youth, 44
full caps.

1974–75	Orient	25	2
1975–76		38	1
1976–77		33	2
1977–78		36	—
1978–79		39	5

Season	Club	League Appearances/Goals	
1979–80	Luton T	41	2
1980–81		37	—
1981–82	Brighton	37	1
1982–83		38	2
1983–84		25	3
1983–84	WBA	11	—
1984–85		38	4
1985–86		16	1
1986–87		—	—
1986–87	Manchester C	11	—
1987–88	Rotherham U	38	3
1988–89		39	3
1989–90		33	—
1990–91	Walsall	31	1

GREAVES, Steve

Born London 17.1.70   Ht 5 9   Wt 11 03
Midfield. From Trainee.

Season	Club	League Appearances/Goals	
1987–88	Fulham	1	—
1988–89		—	—
1988–89	*Waterford*	—	—
1989–90	Fulham	—	—
1989–90	*Brighton*	—	—
1990–91	Preston NE	2	—

GREEN, Richard

Born Wolverhampton 22.11.67.   Ht 6 0
Wt 11 08
Defender.

Season	Club	League Appearances/Goals	
1986–87	Shrewsbury T	15	—
1987–88		31	2
1988–89		39	3
1989–90		40	—
1990–91		—	—
1990–91	Swindon T	—	—

GREEN, Ron

Born Birmingham 3.10.56.   Ht 6 2
Wt 14 00
Goalkeeper. From Alvechurch.

Season	Club	League Appearances/Goals	
1977–78	Walsall	1	—
1978–79		1	—
1979–80		39	—
1980–81		24	—
1981–82		46	—
1982–83		35	—
1983–84		17	—
1983–84	*WBA*	—	—
1984–85	Shrewsbury T	19	—
1984–85	*Bristol R*	18	—
1985–86	Bristol R	38	—
1986–87	Scunthorpe U	43	—
1987–88		35	—
1988–89	Wimbledon	4	—
1988–89	*Shrewsbury T*	17	—
1988–89	*Manchester C*	—	—
1988–89	Walsall	2	—
1989–90		21	—
1990–91		44	—

GREEN, Scott

Born Walsall 15.1.70   Ht 6 0   Wt 11 12
Forward. From Trainee.

Season	Club	League Appearances/Goals	
1988–89	Derby Co	—	—
1989–90		—	—
1989–90	Bolton W	5	2
1990–91		41	6

GREENALL, Colin

Born Billinge 30.12.63.   Ht 5 10   Wt 11 06
Defender. From Apprentice.

Season	Club	League Appearances/Goals	
1980–81	Blackpool	12	—
1981–82		18	—
1982–83		24	1
1983–84		39	4
1984–85		44	3
1985–86		43	1
1986–87		3	—
1986–87	Gillingham	37	2
1987–88		25	2
1987–88	Oxford U	12	—
1988–89		40	2
1989–90		15	—
1989–90	*Bury*	3	—
1990–91	Bury	31	—

GREENMAN, Chris

Born Bristol 22.12.68   Ht 5 10   Wt 11 06
Defender. From school.

1988–89	Coventry C	—	—
1989–90		—	—
1990–91		—	—

GREENWOOD, Nigel

Born Preston 27.11.66. Ht 5 11 Wt 12 00
Forward. From Apprentice.

1984–85	Preston NE	15	5
1985–86		30	9
1986–87	Bury	37	15
1987–88		30	4
1988–89		23	1
1989–90		20	5
1989–90	Preston NE	5	—
1990–91		5	1

GREGORY, David

Born Sudbury 23.1.70. Ht 5 11 Wt 11 06
Midfield. From Trainee.

1987–88	Ipswich T	—	—
1988–89		2	—
1989–90		4	—
1990–91		21	1

GREGORY, Tony

Born Doncaster 21.3.68. Ht 5 8
Wt 11 09
Midfield. From Apprentice. England
Schools, Youth.

1985–86	Sheffield W	5	—
1986–87		10	1
1987–88		—	—
1988–89		3	—
1989–90		—	—
1990–91	Halifax T	12	1

GREW, Mark

Born Bilston 15.2.58. Ht 5 11 Wt 12 08
Goalkeeper. From Amateur.

1976–77	WBA	—	—
1977–78		—	—
1978–79		—	—

1978–79	*Wigan Ath*	4	—
1978–79	*Notts Co*	—	—
1979–80	WBA	—	—
1980–81		—	—
1981–82		23	—
1982–83		10	—
1983–84	Leicester C	5	—
1983–84	*Oldham Ath*	5	—
1983–84	Ipswich T	—	—
1984–85		6	—
1985–86		—	—
1985–86	*Fulham*	4	—
1985–86	*WBA*	1	—
1985–86	*Derby Co*	—	—
1986–87	Port Vale	3	—
1987–88		41	—
1988–89		37	—
1989–90		43	—
1990–91		14	—
1990–91	*Blackburn R*	13	—

GREWCOCK, Neil

Born Leicester 26.4.62. Ht 5 6 Wt 11 09
Forward. From Apprentice.

1979–80	Leicester C	1	1
1980–81		7	—
1981–82		—	—
1981–82	*Gillingham*	13	1
1982–83	Gillingham	21	3
From Shepshed C			
1984–85	Burnley	46	6
1985–86		38	7
1986–87		36	9
1987–88		32	—
1988–89		13	1
1989–90		7	2
1990–91		30	2

GREYGOOSE, Dean

Born Thetford 18.12.64. Ht 5 11
Wt 11 05
Goalkeeper. From Apprentice. England
Youth.

1982–83	Cambridge U	—	—
1983–84		16	—
1984–85		10	—

Season	Club		
1984–85	*Orient*	—	—
1985–86	Cambridge U	—	—
1985–86	*Lincoln C*	6	—
1985–86	Orient	1	—
1986–87		—	—
1986–87	C. Palace	—	—
1987–88		—	—
1987–88	Crewe Alex	43	—
1988–89		36	—
1989–90		32	—
1990–91		31	—

GRIDELET, Phil

Born Edgware 30.4.67. Ht 5 11 Wt 12 00
Midfield. From Watford, Hendon, Barnet.

1990–91	Barnsley	4	—

GRIFFIN, James

Born Hamilton 1.1.67 Ht 5 8 Wt 11 04
Defender. From Fir Park BC.

1985–86	Motherwell	1	—
1986–87		—	—
1987–88		6	—
1988–89		1	—
1989–90		11	—
1990–91		23	4

GRIFFITH, Cohen

Born Georgetown 26.12.62. Ht 5 10
Wt 11 07
Forward. From Kettering T.

1989–90	Cardiff C	38	9
1990–91		45	9

GRIFFITHS, Brian

Born Prescot 26.1.65 Ht 5 9 Wt 11 00
Forward. From St Helens T.

1988–89	Wigan Ath	29	8
1989–90		45	7
1990–91		43	12

GRIFFITHS, Carl

Born Coventry 15.7.71 Ht 5 9 Wt 10 06
Forward. From Trainee. Wales Youth,
Under-21.

1988–89	Shrewsbury T	28	6
1989–90		18	4
1990–91		19	4

GRIFFITHS, Ian

Born Birkenhead 17.4.60. Ht 5 6
Wt 10 02
Midfield. From Amateur.

1978–79	Tranmere R	3	—
1979–80		2	—
1980–81		30	—
1981–82		38	—
1982–83		43	4
1983–84	Rochdale	41	5
1984–85		1	—
1984–85	Port Vale	12	—
1985–86	Wigan Ath	38	3
1986–87		31	3
1987–88		13	1
From Bolton W			
1990–91	Wigan Ath	11	—
1990–91	Wrexham	11	—

GRIFFITHS, Neil

Born Halifax 4.9.72.
Defender. From Trainee.

1990–91	Halifax T	1	—

GRITT, Steve

Born Bournemouth 31.10.57. Ht 5 10
Wt 11 04
Midfield. From Apprentice.

1976–77	Bournemouth	6	3
1977–78	Charlton Ath	34	3
1978–79		39	3
1979–80		31	7
1980–81		40	—
1981–82		34	3
1982–83		27	1
1983–84		33	1
1984–85		35	1
1985–86		11	2
1986–87		14	1
1987–88		27	—

Season	Club	League Appearances/Goals
1988–89	....	22	2
1989–90	Walsall	20	1
1989–90	Charlton Ath	2	—
1990–91	....	10	—

GROBBELAAR, Bruce

Born Durban 6.10.57. Ht 6 1   Wt 13 00
Goalkeeper. From Vancouver Whitecaps.
Zimbabwe full caps.

1979–80	Crewe Alex	24	1
From Vancouver Whitecaps			
1980–81	Liverpool	—	—
1981–82	....	42	—
1982–83	....	42	—
1983–84	....	42	—
1984–85	....	42	—
1985–86	....	42	—
1986–87	....	31	—
1987–88	....	38	—
1988–89	....	21	—
1989–90	....	38	—
1990–91	....	31	—

GROVES, Paul

Born Derby 28.2.66. Ht 5 11   Wt 11 05
Midfield. From Burton Alb.

1987–88	Leicester C	1	1
1988–89	....	15	—
1989–90	....	—	—
1989–90	*Lincoln C*	8	1
1989–90	Blackpool	19	1
1990–91	....	46	11

GROVES, Perry

Born London 19.4.65. Ht 5 11   Wt 12 01
Forward. From Apprentice.

1981–82	Colchester U	9	—
1982–83	....	17	2
1983–84	....	42	2
1984–85	....	44	10
1985–86	....	43	12
1986–87	....	1	—
1986–87	Arsenal	25	3
1987–88	....	34	6

1988–89	....	21	4
1989–90	....	30	4
1990–91	....	32	3

GUNN, Andy

Born Barking 2.2.71. Ht 6 0   Wt 12 01
Forward. From Trainee.

1988–89	Watford	—	—
1989–90	....	—	—
1989–90	Crewe Alex	1	—
1990–91	....	3	—

GUNN, Bryan

Born Thurso 22.12.63. Ht 6 2   Wt 13 13
Goalkeeper. From Invergordon BC.
Scotland Schools, Youth, Under-21, B, 1
full cap.

1980–81	Aberdeen	—	—
1981–82	....	—	—
1982–83	....	1	—
1983–84	....	—	—
1984–85	....	2	—
1985–86	....	10	—
1986–87	....	2	—
1986–87	Norwich C	29	—
1987–88	....	38	—
1988–89	....	37	—
1989–90	....	37	—
1990–91	....	34	—

GUNN, Bryn

Born Kettering 21.8.58. Ht 6 2   Wt 13 7
Defender. From Apprentice.

1975–76	Nottingham F	11	—
1976–77	....	—	—
1977–78	....	—	—
1978–79	....	1	—
1979–80	....	2	—
1980–81	....	26	—
1981–82	....	37	—
1982–83	....	33	1
1983–84	....	4	—
1984–85	....	17	—
1985–86	....	—	—

1985–86	*Shrewsbury T*	9	—
1985–86	*Walsall*	6	—
1985–86	*Mansfield T*	5	—
1986–87	Peterborough U	39	7
1987–88		46	—
1988–89		46	7
1989–90	Chesterfield	46	8
1990–91		36	2

GURINOVICH, Igor

Born Minsk 5.3.60.
Midfield. From Dynamo Minsk. USSR
full caps.

| 1990–91 | Brighton | 4 | 1 |

GUTHRIE, Peter

Born Newcastle 10.10.61.   Ht 6 1
Wt 12 13
Goalkeeper. From Blyth S, Weymouth

1987–88	Tottenham H	—	—
1987–88	*Swansea C*	14	—
1988–89	Tottenham H	—	—
1988–89	*Charlton Ath*	—	—
1989–90	Tottenham H	—	—
From Barnet			
1990–91	Bournemouth	10	—

GYNN, Mick

Born Peterborough 19.8.61.   Ht 5 5
Wt 10 10
Midfield. From Apprentice.

1978–79	Peterborough U	11	2
1979–80		27	1
1980–81		29	7
1981–82		46	6
1982–83		43	17
1983–84	Coventry C	23	2
1984–85		39	4
1985–86		12	1
1986–87		22	5
1987–88		25	3
1988–89		8	1
1989–90		34	3
1990–91		35	8

HAAG, Kelly

Born Enfield 6.10.70.
Forward. From Trainee.

| 1989–90 | Brentford | 5 | — |
| 1990–91 | Fulham | 23 | 3 |

HACKETT, Gary

Born Stourbridge 11.10.62.   Ht 5 7
Wt 11 03
Forward. From Bromsgrove R.

1983–84	Shrewsbury T	31	3
1984–85		38	5
1985–86		42	6
1986–87		39	3
1987–88	Aberdeen	15	—
1987–88	Stoke C	1	—
1988–89		46	5
1989–90		26	2
1989–90	WBA	14	2
1990–91		5	—

HACKETT, Warren

Born Newham 16.12.71.
Defender. From Tottenham H Trainee.

| 1990–91 | Leyton Orient | 4 | — |

HADDOCK, Peter

Born Newcastle 9.12.61.   Ht 5 11
Wt 11 05
Defender. From Apprentice.

1979–80	Newcastle U	—	—
1980–81		—	—
1981–82		30	—
1982–83		17	—
1983–84		3	—
1984–85		1	—
1985–86		6	—
1985–86	*Burnley*	7	—
1986–87	Leeds U	11	—
1987–88		40	1
1988–89		12	—

| 1989–90 | | 40 | — |
| 1990–91 | | 15 | — |

HAGUE, Paul

Born Durham 16.9.72.   Ht 6 2   Wt 12 06
Defender. From Trainee.

| 1990 91 | Gillingham | 7 | — |

HAINES, Ivan

Born Chatham 14.9.68.   Ht 5 9   Wt 10 12
Midfield.

1987–88	Gillingham	1	—
1988–89		12	—
1989–90		26	—
1990–91		12	—

HALBERT, Paul

Born St Albans 28.10.73.
Midfield. From Trainee.

| 1990–91 | Aldershot | 3 | — |

HALES, Kevin

Born Dartford 13.1.61.   Ht 5 7   Wt 10 04
Defender. From Apprentice.

1978–79	Chelsea	—	—
1979–80		7	—
1980–81		—	—
1981–82		10	2
1982–83		3	—
1983–84	Orient	43	2
1984–85		33	—
1985–86		31	2
1986–87		33	1
1987–88		42	6
1988–89		35	9
1989–90		39	2
1990–91		5	—

HALL, Derek

Born Manchester 5.1.65.   Ht 5 8
Wt 12 03
Midfield. From Apprentice.

1982–83	Coventry C	1	—
1983–84		—	—
1983–84	*Torquay U*	10	2
1984–85	Torquay U	45	4
1985–86	Swindon T	10	—
1986–87	Southend U	43	9
1987–88		40	3
1988–89		40	3
1989–90	Halifax T	41	4
1990–91		8	—

HALL, Gareth

Born Croydon 20.3.69   Ht 5 8   Wt 10 07
Defender. Wales Under-21, 8 full caps.

1986–87	Chelsea	1	—
1987–88		13	—
1988–89		22	—
1989–90		13	1
1990–91		24	—

HALL, Paul

Born Manchester 3.7.72.   Ht 5 9
Wt 10 02
Forward. From Trainee.

| 1989–90 | Torquay U | 10 | — |
| 1990–91 | | 17 | — |

HALL, Richard

Born Ipswich 14.3.72.   Ht 6 1   Wt 13 00
Defender. From Trainee.

1989–90	Scunthorpe U	1	—
1990–91		21	3
1990–91	Southampton	1	—

HALL, Wayne

Born Rotherham 25.10.68   Ht 5 8
Wt 10 04
Midfield. From Darlington.

1988–89	York C	2	—
1989–90		27	3
1990–91		46	1

HALLE, Gunnar

Born Oslo 11.8.65. Ht 5 11 Wt 11 02
Defender. From Lillestrom. Norway full
caps.

1990–91	Oldham Ath	17	—

HALLWORTH, Jon

Born Stockport 26.10.65. Ht 6 1
Wt 14 03
Goalkeeper. From school.

1983–84	Ipswich T	—	—
1984–85		—	—
1984–85	*Swindon T*	—	—
1984–85	*Fulham*	—	—
1984–85	*Bristol R*	2	—
1985–86	Ipswich T	6	—
1986–87		6	—
1987–88		33	—
1988–89		—	—
1988–89	Oldham Ath	16	—
1989–90		15	—
1990–91		46	—

HALPIN, John

Born Broxburn 15.11.61. Ht 5 10
Wt 11 05
Midfield. From Celtic BC. Scotland
Youth.

1981–82	Celtic	3	—
1982–83		—	—
1983–84		4	—
1984–85	*Sunderland*	—	—
1984–85	Carlisle U	19	1
1985–86		33	5
1986–87		7	—
1987–88		23	3
1988–89		33	7
1989–90		17	—
1990–91		21	1

HALSALL, Mick

Born Bootle 21.7.61. Ht 5 10 Wt 11 04
Midfield. From Apprentice.

1979–80	Liverpool	—	—
1980–81		—	—
1981–82		—	—
1982–83		—	—
1982–83	Birmingham C	12	1
1983–84		21	2
1984–85		3	—
1984–85	Carlisle U	26	5
1985–86		41	4
1986–87		25	2
1986–87	Grimsby T	12	—
1987–88	Peterborough U	45	4
1988–89		42	1
1989–90		46	10
1990–91		45	6

HAMILTON, Brian

Born Paisley 5.8.67. Ht 6 0 Wt 11 07
Defender. From Pollok United BC.
Scotland Schools, Under-21.

1985–86	St Mirren	8	—
1986–87		28	3
1987–88		27	—
1988–89		23	1
1989–90	Hibernian	28	1
1990–91		26	2

HAMILTON, David

Born South Shields 7.11.60. Ht 5 6
Wt 10 06
Defender. From Apprentice. England
Youth.

1978–79	Sunderland	—	—
1979–80		—	—
1980–81		—	—
1980–81	Blackburn R	3	—
1981–82		17	—
1982–83		32	2
1983–84		26	2
1984–85		3	—
1984–85	*Cardiff C*	10	—
1985–86	Blackburn R	33	3
1986–87	Wigan Ath	41	3
1987–88		45	2
1988–89		17	2
1989–90	Chester C	28	—

Season	Club	League Appearances/Goals
1990–91	Burnley	11 —

HAMILTON, Ian

Born Stevenage 14.12.67.   Ht 5 9
Wt 11 03
Forward. From Apprentice.

1985–86	Southampton	— —
1986–87		— —
1987–88		— —
1987–88	Cambridge U	9 1
1988–89		15 —
1988–89	Scunthorpe U	27 1
1989–90		43 6
1990–91		34 2

HAMILTON, Lindsay

Born Bellshill 11.8.62.   Ht 6 2   Wt 13 07
Goalkeeper. From Thorniewood.

1982–83	Stenhousemuir	4 —
1983–84		38 —
1984–85		39 —
1985–86		29 —
1986–87		13 —
1986–87	Rangers	— —
1987–88		— —
1988–89		— —
1988–89	Charlton Ath	— —
1989–90	Rangers	— —
1989–90	Leeds U	— —
1989–90	Clydebank	1 —
1989–90	Stirling Albion	1 —
1990–91	Rangers	— —
1990–91	St Johnstone	34 —

HAMMOND, Nicky

Born Hornchurch 7.9.67.   Ht 6 0
Wt 11 13
Goalkeeper. From Apprentice.

1985–86	Arsenal	— —
1986–87		— —
1986–87	Bristol R	3 —
1986–87	Peterborough U	— —
1986–87	Aberdeen	— —
1987–88	Swindon T	4 —

1988–89		— —
1989–90		— —
1990–91		5 —

HANCOCK, Tony

Born Manchester 31.1.67   Ht 6 1
Wt 12 12
Forward. From Stockport Georgians

1988–89	Stockport Co	22 5
1989–90	Burnley	17 —
1989–90	Preston NE	— —
1990–91		— —

HANSBURY, Roger

Born Barnsley 26.1.55.   Ht 5 11   Wt 12 0
Goalkeeper. From Apprentice.

1972–73	Norwich C	— —
1973–74		— —
1974–75		4 —
1975–76		— —
1976–77		4 —
1976–77	Bolton W	— —
1977–78	Norwich C	14 —
1977–78	Cambridge U	11 —
1978–79	Norwich C	18 —
1978–79	Orient	— —
1979–80	Norwich C	16 —
1980–81		22 —
1981–82		— —
From Eastern, Hong Kong.		
1983–84	Burnley	46 —
1984–85		37 —
1985–86	Cambridge U	37 —
1985–86	Birmingham C	— —
1986–87		31 —
1987–88		22 —
1987–88	Sheffield U	5 —
1988–89	Birmingham C	3 —
1988–89	Wolverhampton W	3 —
1989–90	Birmingham C	1 —
1989–90	Colchester U	4 —
1989–90	Cardiff C	35 —
1990–91		46 —

HARBEY, Graham

Born Chesterfield 29.8.64.   Ht 5 8
Wt 10 8
Defender. From Apprentice.

1982–83	Derby Co	—	—
1983–84		19	—
1984–85		4	1
1985–86		3	—
1986–87		14	—
1987–88	Ipswich T	35	1
1988–89		23	—
1989–90		1	—
1989–90	WBA	30	—
1990–91		21	1

HARDING, Paul

Born Mitcham 6.3.64.   Ht 5 10   Wt 12 05
Midfield. From Barnet.

| 1990–91 | Notts Co | 24 | — |

HARDWICK, Steve

Born Mansfield 6.9.56.   Ht 5 11   Wt 13 00
Goalkeeper. From Amateur. England
Youth.

1974–75	Chesterfield	5	—
1975–76		12	—
1976–77		21	—
1976–77	Newcastle U	—	—
1977–78		9	—
1978–79		31	—
1979–80		41	—
1980–81		4	—
1981–82		—	—
1982–83		7	—
1982–83	Oxford U	18	—
1983–84		46	—
1984–85		42	—
1985–86		23	—
1985–86	C. Palace	3	—
1986–87	Oxford U	23	—
1987–88		4	—
1987–88	Sunderland	6	—
1988–89	Huddersfield T	46	—
1989–90		21	—
1990–91		42	—

HARDY, Jason

Born Burnley 14.12.69   Ht 5 10   Wt 11 04
Midfield. From Trainee.

1986–87	Burnley	1	—
1987–88		—	—
1988–89		17	1
1989–90		22	—
1990–91		—	—

HARDY, Phil

Born Chester 9.4.73.
Defender.

| 1989–90 | Wrexham | 1 | — |
| 1990–91 | | 32 | — |

HARDYMAN, Paul

Born Portsmouth 11.3.64.   Ht 5 8
Wt 11 07
Defender. Local. England Under-21.

1983–84	Portsmouth	3	—
1984–85		15	—
1985–86		21	1
1986–87		33	—
1987–88		20	1
1988–89		25	1
1989–90	Sunderland	42	7
1990–91		32	—

HARFORD, Mick

Born Sunderland 12.2.59   Ht 6 2
Wt 13 09
Forward. From Lambton St BC. England
B, 2 full caps.

1977–78	Lincoln C	27	9
1978–79		31	6
1979–80		36	16
1980–81		21	10
1980–81	Newcastle U	19	4
1981–82	Bristol C	30	11
1981–82	Birmingham C	12	9
1982–83		29	6
1983–84		39	8
1984–85		12	2

Season	Club	League Appearances/Goals	
1984–85	Luton T	22	15
1985–86	....	37	22
1986–87	....	18	4
1987–88	....	25	9
1988–89	....	33	7
1989–90	....	4	—
1989–90	Derby Co	16	4
1990–91	....	36	8

HARGREAVES, Christian

Born Cleethorpes 12.5.72.   Ht 5 10
Wt 10 13
Forward. From Trainee.

1989–90	Grimsby T	19	2
1990–91	....	18	3

HARKES, John

Born New Jersey 8.3.67.   Ht 5 10
Wt 11 10
Midfield. From United States Soccer
Federation. USA full caps.

1990–91	Sheffield W	23	2

HARKNESS, Steven

Born Carlisle 27.8.71   Ht 5 9   Wt 10 11
Midfield. From Trainee. England Youth.

1988–89	Carlisle U	13	—
1989–90	Liverpool	—	—
1990–91	....	—	—

HARLE, David

Born Denaby 15.8.63.   Ht 5 9   Wt 11 02
Midfield. From Apprentice. England
Youth.

1979–80	Doncaster R	1	—
1980–81	....	34	1
1981–82	....	26	2
1982–83	Exeter C	37	6
1983–84	....	6	—
1983–84	Doncaster R	29	6
1984–85	....	37	9
1985–86	....	17	2

Season	Club	League Appearances/Goals	
1985–86	Leeds U	3	—
1985–86	*Bristol C*	8	—
1986–87	Bristol C	15	2
1986–87	Scunthorpe U	26	2
1987–88	....	45	6
1988–89	....	18	2
1988–89	Peterborough U	7	—
1989–90	....	15	2
1989–90	Doncaster R	10	—
1990–91	....	22	2

HARLE, Michael

Born Lewisham 31.10.72.   Ht 6 0
Wt 12 00
Midfield. From Trainee.

1990–91	Gillingham	2	—

HARO, Mark

Born Irvine 21.10.71   Ht 6 2   Wt 11 7
Defender. From Glenrothes Strollers

1990–91	Dunfermline Ath	8	—

HARPER, Alan

Born Liverpool 1.11.60.   Ht 5 9   Wt 10 10
Defender. From Apprentice. England
Youth.

1977–78	Liverpool	—	—
1978–79	....	—	—
1979–80	....	—	—
1980–81	....	—	—
1981–82	....	—	—
1982–83	....	—	—
1983–84	Everton	29	1
1984–85	....	13	—
1985–86	....	21	—
1986–87	....	36	3
1987–88	....	28	—
1988–89	Sheffield W	24	—
1989–90	....	11	—
1989–90	Manchester C	21	—
1990–91	....	29	1

HARPER, Steve

Born Stoke 3.2.69.   Ht 5 10   Wt 11 05
Forward. From Trainee.

1987–88	Port Vale	21	2
1988–89		7	—
1988–89	Preston NE	5	—
1989–90		36	10
1990–91		36	—

HARRIS, Mark

Born Reading 15.7.63.   Ht 6 1   Wt 12 05
Defender. From Wokingham.

1987–88	Crystal Palace	—	—
1988–89		2	—
1989–90		—	—
1989–90	*Burnley*	4	—
1989–90	Swansea C	41	2
1990–91		41	1

HARRISON, Gerry

Born Lambeth 15.4.72.   Ht 5 10
Wt 12 12
Midfield. From Trainee.

| 1989–90 | Watford | 3 | — |
| 1990–91 | | 6 | — |

HARRISON, Tom

Born Edinburgh 22.1.74   Ht 5 9   Wt 10 7
Forward. From Salvesen BC. Scotland
Youth.

| 1990–91 | Hearts | 3 | — |

HARRISON, Wayne

Born Stockport 15.11.67.   Ht 5 8
Wt 10 07
Forward. From Apprentice.

1984–85	Oldham Ath	5	1
1984–85	Liverpool	—	—
1984–85	*Oldham Ath*	1	—
1985–86	Liverpool	—	—
1986–87		—	—
1987–88		—	—
1988–89		—	—
1988–89	*Crewe Alex*	3	1
1989–90	Liverpool	—	—

| 1990–91 | | — | — |

HART, Nigel

Born Golborne 1.10.58.   Ht 6 0   Wt 12 03
Defender. Local.

1978–79	Wigan Ath	—	—
1979–80		1	—
1979–80	Leicester C	—	—
1980–81		—	—
1981–82	Blackpool	28	—
1982–83		9	—
1982–83	Crewe Alex	28	—
1983–84		37	3
1984–85		44	6
1985–86		23	—
1986–87		10	1
1986–87	Bury	11	—
1987–88		34	2
1988–89	Stockport Co	38	2
1989–90		1	—
1989–90	Chesterfield	27	2
1990–91		19	—
1990–91	York C	1	—

HARTFORD, Asa

Born Clydebank 24.10.50.   Ht 5 7
Wt 11 04
Midfield. From Amateur. Scotland Under-
21, Under-23, 50 full caps.

1967–68	WBA	6	1
1968–69		26	7
1969–70		34	1
1970–71		34	2
1971–72		39	1
1972–73		41	3
1973–74		33	3
1974–75	Manchester C	30	2
1975–76		39	9
1976–77		40	4
1977–78		37	4
1978–79		39	3
1979–80	Nottingham F	3	—
1979–80	Everton	35	1
1980–81		39	5
1981–82		7	—
1981–82	Manchester C	30	3

Season	Club	App	Goals
1982–83	....	38	3
1983–84	....	7	1
From Ft Lauderdale			
1984–85	Norwich C	28	2
1985–86	Bolton W	46	5
1986–87	....	35	3
1987–88	Stockport Co	31	—
1988–89	....	14	—
1988–89	Oldham Ath..................	7	—
1989–90	Shrewsbury T..............	17	—
1990–91	....	8	—
1990–91	Bury	—	—

HARVEY, Graham

Born Musselburgh 23.4.61. Ht 5 11
Wt 11 04
Forward. From Ormiston Primrose.

Season	Club	App	Goals
1982–83	Hibernian......................	14	1
1983–84	....	16	2
1984–85	....	3	—
1984–85	Dundee..........................	7	2
1985–86	....	30	5
1986–87	....	33	12
1987–88	....	29	4
1988–89	....	20	4
1989–90	....	6	1
1990–91	Airdrieonians	27	11

HARVEY, Jimmy

Born Lurgan 2.5.58. Ht 5 9 Wt 11 04
Midfield. From Glenavon. Northern
Ireland, Under-23.

Season	Club	App	Goals
1977–78	Arsenal........................	1	—
1978–79	....	2	—
1979–80	....	—	—
1979–80	*Hereford U*..................	11	—
1980–81	Hereford U	30	1
1981–82	....	42	5
1982–83	....	41	5
1983–84	....	44	9
1984–85	....	34	5
1985–86	....	42	9
1986–87	....	34	5
1986–87	Bristol C	2	—
1987–88	....	1	—
1987–88	*Wrexham*......................	6	—

Season	Club	App	Goals
1987–88	Tranmere R	33	3
1988–89	....	42	4
1989–90	....	46	7
1990–91	....	39	3

HARVEY, Lee

Born Harlow 21.12.66. Ht 5 11   Wt 11 07
Midfield. From Local. England Youth.

Season	Club	App	Goals
1983–84	Orient..........................	4	—
1984–85	....	4	—
1985–86	....	12	2
1986–87	....	15	1
1987–88	....	23	1
1988–89	....	29	6
1989–90	....	37	6
1990–91	....	26	3

HARVEY, Richard

Born Letchworth 17.4.69. Ht 5 9
Wt 11 10
Defender. From Apprentice. England
Schools, Youth.

Season	Club	App	Goals
1986–87	Luton T	5	—
1987–88	....	—	—
1988–89	....	12	—
1989–90	....	26	—
1990–91	....	29	—

HATELEY, Mark

Born Liverpool 7.11.61. Ht 6 1   Wt 11 07
Forward. From Apprentice. England
Youth, Under-21, 31 full caps.

Season	Club	App	Goals
1978–79	Coventry C	1	—
1979–80	....	4	—
1980–81	....	19	3
1981–82	....	34	13
1982–83	....	35	9
1983–84	Portsmouth	38	22
1984–85	AC Milan....................	21	7
1985–86	....	22	8
1986–87	....	23	2
To Monaco and Rangers.			
1990–91	Rangers........................	33	10

HATHAWAY, Ian

Born Worsley 22.8.68   Ht 5 8   Wt 10 06
Forward. From WBA Apprentice.
Bedworth U.

Season	Club		
1988–89	Mansfield T	12	1
1989–90		22	1
1990–91		10	—
1990–91	Rotherham U	5	1

HAUSER, Thomas

Born West Germany 10.4.65   Ht 6 3
Wt 12 06
Forward. From Berne OB.

Season	Club		
1988–89	Sunderland	13	2
1989–90		18	6
1990–91		10	1

HAWKE, Warren

Born Durham 20.9.70   Ht 5 10   Wt 10 11
Midfield. From Trainee.

Season	Club		
1988–89	Sunderland	4	—
1989–90		8	1
1990–91		7	—

HAWKER, Phil

Born Solihull 7.12.62.   Ht 6 1   Wt 11 06
Defender. From Apprentice. England
Youth.

Season	Club		
1980–81	Birmingham C	11	—
1981–82		20	1
1982–83		4	—
1982–83	Walsall	5	—
1983–84		11	—
1984–85		20	—
1985–86		33	4
1986–87		23	1
1987–88		29	2
1988–89		26	2
1989–90		30	1
1990–91	WBA	1	—

HAY, Alan

Born Dunfermline 28.11.58   Ht 5 11
Wt 11 03
Defender. From Bolton W. Amateur.

Season	Club		
1978–79	Bristol C	—	—
1979–80		4	—
1980–81		36	1
1981–82		34	—
1981–82	St Mirren	—	—
1982–83	York C	42	1
1983–84		42	1
1984–85		45	—
1985–86		21	1
1986–87	Tranmere R	28	—
From Scotland			
1988–89	York C	1	—
1988–89	Sunderland	1	—
1989–90	Torquay U	8	—
1990–91		2	—

HAYES, Martin

Born Walthamstow 21.3.66.   Ht 5 10
Wt 11 12
Forward. From Apprentice. England B,
Under-21.

Season	Club		
1983–84	Arsenal	—	—
1984–85		—	—
1985–86		11	2
1986–87		35	19
1987–88		27	1
1988–89		17	1
1989–90		12	3
1990–91	Celtic	7	—

HAYLOCK, Garry

Born Bradford 31.12.70.   Ht 5 11
Wt 12 00
Midfield. From Trainee.

Season	Club		
1989–90	Huddersfield T	—	—
1989–90	Shelbourne	—	—
1990–91	Huddersfield T	12	4
1990–91	Shelbourne	—	—

HAYLOCK, Paul

Born Lowestoft 24.3.63.   Ht 5 9
Wt 11 10
Defender. From Apprentice.

Season	Club	App	Goals
1980–81	Norwich C	—	—
1981–82		21	—
1982–83		42	1
1983–84		39	—
1984–85		41	1
1985–86		12	1
1986–87	Gillingham	45	—
1987–88		32	—
1988–89		31	—
1989–90		44	—
1990–91		—	—
1990–91	Maidstone U	16	—

HAYWARD, Steve

Born Walsall 8.9.71   Ht 5 10   Wt 11 07
Midfield. From Trainee. England Youth.

Season	Club	App	Goals
1988–89	Derby Co	—	—
1989–90		3	—
1990–91		1	—

HAZARD, Mike

Born Sunderland 5.2.60   Ht 5 7   Wt 10 05
Midfield. From Apprentice.

Season	Club	App	Goals
1977–78	Tottenham H	—	—
1978–79		—	—
1979–80		3	—
1980–81		4	—
1981–82		28	5
1982–83		18	1
1983–84		11	2
1984–85		23	4
1985–86		4	1
1985–86	Chelsea	18	1
1986–87		18	6
1987–88		28	2
1988–89		4	—
1989–90		13	—
1989–90	Portsmouth	8	1
1990–91		—	—
1990–91	Swindon T	34	8

HAZEL, Desmond

Born Bradford 15.7.67.   Ht 5 10
Wt 10 10
Forward. From Apprentice.

Season	Club	App	Goals
1985–86	Sheffield W	—	—
1986–87		—	—
1986–87	*Grimsby T*	9	2
1987–88	Sheffield W	6	—
1988–89	Rotherham U	42	6
1989–90		33	2
1990–91		39	3

HAZEL, Ian

Born London 1.12.67.   Ht 5 10   Wt 10 04
Midfield. From Apprentice.

Season	Club	App	Goals
1985–86	Wimbledon	—	—
1986–87		—	—
1987–88		6	—
1988–89		1	—
1988–89	*Bristol R*	3	—
1989–90	Bristol R	8	—
1990–91		6	—

HEALD, Paul

Born Wath-on-Dearne 20.8.68.   Ht 6 2
Wt 12 05
Goalkeeper. From Trainee.

Season	Club	App	Goals
1987–88	Sheffield U	—	—
1988–89		—	—
1988–89	Leyton Orient	28	—
1989–90		37	—
1990–91		38	—

HEANEY, Neil

Born Middlesbrough 3.11.71.   Ht 5 9
Wt 11 01
Forward. From Trainee. England Youth.

Season	Club	App	Goals
1989–90	Arsenal	—	—
1990–91		—	—
1990–91	*Hartlepool U*	3	—

HEARD, Pat

Born Hull 17.3.60. Ht 5 9 Wt 11 05
Defender. From Apprentice. England
Youth.

Season	Club		
1977–78	Everton	—	—
1978–79		10	—
1979–80		1	—
1979–80	Aston Villa	9	—
1980–81		—	—
1981–82		8	2
1982–83		7	—
1982–83	Sheffield W	19	2
1983–84		5	1
1984–85		1	—
1984–85	Newcastle U	34	2
1985–86		—	—
1985–86	Middlesbrough	25	2
1985–86	Hull C	8	—
1986–87		37	1
1987–88		35	4
1988–89	Rotherham U	30	4
1989–90		14	3
1990–91	Cardiff C	38	3

HEATH, Adrian

Born Stoke 11.1.61. Ht 5 6 Wt 10 01
Forward. From Apprentice. England
Under-21, B.

Season	Club		
1978–79	Stoke C	2	—
1979–80		38	5
1980–81		38	6
1981–82		17	5
1981–82	Everton	22	6
1982–83		38	10
1983–84		36	12
1984–85		17	11
1985–86		36	10
1986–87		41	11
1987–88		29	9
1988–89		7	2
From Espanol			
1989–90	Aston Villa	9	—
1989–90	Manchester C	12	2
1990–91		35	1

HEATH, Philip

Born Stoke 24.11.64. Ht 5 10 Wt 12 01
Forward. From Apprentice.

Season	Club		
1982–83		1	—
1983–84		4	1
1984–85		36	2
1985–86		38	5
1986–87		38	1
1987–88		39	8
1988–89	Oxford U	16	1
1989–90		21	—
1990–91		—	—
1990–91	Cardiff C	11	1

HEATHCOTE, Mike

Born Durham 10.9.65. Ht 6 2 Wt 12 05
Defender. From Middlesbrough,
Spennymoor U.

Season	Club		
1987–88	Sunderland	1	—
1987–88	*Halifax T*	7	1
1988–89	Sunderland	—	—
1989–90		8	—
1989–90	*York C*	3	—
1990–91	Shrewsbury T	39	6

HEBBERD, Trevor

Born Winchester 19.6.58. Ht 6 0
Wt 11 04
Midfield. From Apprentice.

Season	Club		
1976–77	Southampton	12	2
1977–78		12	1
1978–79		22	2
1979–80		36	2
1980–81		11	—
1981–82		4	—
1981–82	*Bolton W*	6	—
1981–82	*Leicester C*	4	1
1981–82	Oxford U	15	2
1982–83		39	10
1983–84		46	11
1984–85		42	6
1985–86		41	3
1986–87		38	2
1987–88		39	3
1988–89	Derby Co	37	5

| 1989–90 | .... | 23 | 4 |
| 1990–91 | .... | 21 | 1 |

HEDDLE, Ian

Born Dunfermline 2.3.63. Ht 5 10
Wt 11 00
Midfield. From Dunfermline Railway.

1983–84	Dunfermline Ath	1	—
1984–85	....	3	1
1985–86	....	25	3
1986–87	....	10	2
1986–87	St Johnstone	19	2
1987–88	....	36	9
1988–89	....	36	2
1989–90	....	39	5
1990–91	....	7	—

HEDMAN, Rudi

Born London 16.11.64. Ht 6 3 Wt 12 02
Defender. Local.

1983–84	Colchester U	4	—
1984–85	....	30	2
1985–86	....	39	3
1986–87	....	44	4
1987–88	....	42	—
1988–89	....	17	1
1988–89	Crystal Palace	5	—
1989–90	....	12	—
1989–90	*Leyton Orient*	5	—
1990–91	Crystal Palace	1	—

HEDWORTH, Chris

Born Newcastle 5.1.64. Ht 6 1 Wt 10 11
Defender. From Apprentice.

1981–82	Newcastle U	—	—
1982–83	....	4	—
1983–84	....	—	—
1984–85	....	1	—
1985–86	....	4	—
1986–87	Barnsley	20	—
1987–88	....	5	—
1988–89	Halifax T	11	—
1989–90	....	27	—
1990–91	Blackpool	20	—

HELLIWELL, Ian

Born Rotherham 7.12.62. Ht 6 3
Wt 13 12
Forward. From Matlock T.

1987–88	York C	32	8
1988–89	....	41	11
1989–90	....	46	14
1990–91	....	41	7

HEMMING, Chris

Born Newcastle 13.4.66. Ht 5 10
Wt 12 10
Defender. From school.

1983–84	Stoke C	3	—
1984–85	....	16	1
1985–86	....	24	—
1986–87	....	22	—
1987–88	....	24	1
1988–89	....	4	—
1988–89	*Wigan Ath*	4	—
1989–90	Hereford U	35	2
1990–91	....	6	1

HENDON, Ian

Born Ilford 5.12.71. Ht 6 0 Wt 12 10
Defender. From Trainee. England Youth.

| 1989–90 | Tottenham H .... | — | — |
| 1990–91 | .... | 2 | — |

HENDRIE, John

Born Lennoxtown 24.10.63. Ht 5 7
Wt 11 07
Forward. From Apprentice. Scotland
Youth.

1981–82	Coventry C	6	—
1982–83	....	12	2
1983–84	....	3	—
1983–84	*Hereford U*	6	—
1984–85	Bradford C	46	9
1985–86	....	42	10
1986–87	....	42	14
1987–88	....	43	13
1988–89	Newcastle U	34	4

Season	Club	App	Goals
1989–90	Leeds U	27	5
1990–91	Middlesbrough	41	3

HENDRY, Alan

Born Paisley 14.12.70. Ht 5 8   Wt 10 0
Midfield. From Shettleston J

1990–91	Airdrieonians	2	—

HENDRY, Colin

Born Keith 7.12.65.   Ht 6 1   Wt 12 00
Defender. From Islavale. Scotland B.

1983–84	Dundee	4	—
1984–85		4	—
1985–86		20	—
1986–87		13	2
1986–87	Blackburn R	13	3
1987–88		44	12
1988–89		38	7
1989–90		7	—
1989–90	Manchester C	25	3
1990–91		32	1

HENDRY, John

Born Glasgow 6.1.70.   Ht 5 11   Wt 10 00
Forward. From Hillington YC.

1988–89	Dundee	2	—
1989–90		—	—
1989–90	*Forfar Ath*	10	6
1990–91	Tottenham H	4	2

HENRY, Charlie

Born Acton 13.2.62.   Ht 5 11   Wt 12 08
Forward. From Apprentice.

1980–81	Swindon T	32	—
1981–82		42	3
1982–83		19	—
1983–84		29	—
1984–85		16	—
1985–86		38	18
1986–87		10	1
1987–88		15	1
1986–87	*Torquay U*	6	1

1986–87	*Northampton T*	4	1
1988–89	Swindon T	22	3
1989–90	Aldershot	40	5
1990–91		41	13

HENRY, Liburd

Born Dominica 29.8.67.   Ht 5 11
Wt 11 00
Forward. From Colchester U, Rainham T,
Millwall, Leytonstone/Ilford.

1987–88	Watford	—	—
1988–89		1	—
1988–89	*Halifax T*	5	—
1989–90	Watford	9	1
1990–91	Maidstone U	30	2

HENRY, Nick

Born Liverpool 21.2.69.   Ht 5 6   Wt 9 08
Midfield. From Trainee.

1987–88	Oldham Ath	5	—
1988–89		18	—
1989–90		41	—
1990–91		43	4

HENSHAW, Gary

Born Leeds 18.2.65.   Ht 5 8   Wt 11 08
Midfield. From Apprentice.

1982–83	Grimsby T	—	—
1983–84		4	—
1984–85		7	1
1985–86		10	4
1986–87		29	4
1987–88	Bolton W	31	2
1988–89		21	2
1989–90		14	—
1989–90	*Rochdale*	9	1
1990–91	Bolton W	4	—

HERITAGE, Peter

Born Bexhill 8.11.60.   Ht 6 1   Wt 13 00
Forward. From Hythe Town.

1989–90	Gillingham	42	9
1990–91		15	2

1990–91	Hereford U	18	1

HERRERA, Roberto

Born Torbay 12.6.70 Ht 5 7 Wt 10 06
Defender. From Trainee.

1987–88	QPR	—	—
1988–89		2	—
1989–90		1	—
1990–91		3	—

HERRING, Paul

Born Hyde 1.7.73. Ht 5 11 Wt 11 03
Midfield. From Trainee.

1990–91	Rochdale	1	—

HESELTINE, Wayne

Born Bradford 3.12.69. Ht 5 9 Wt 11 06
Defender. From Trainee.

1987–88	Manchester U	—	—
1988–89		—	—
1989–90		—	—
1989–90	Oldham Ath	1	—
1990–91		—	—

HESFORD, Iain

Born Zambia 4.3.60. Ht 6 2 Wt 14 10
Goalkeeper. From Apprentice. England
Youth, Under-21.

1977–78	Blackpool	14	—
1978–79		33	—
1979–80		30	—
1980–81		42	—
1981–82		39	—
1982–83		44	—
1983–84	Sheffield W	—	—
1984–85		—	—
1984–85	*Fulham*	3	—
1985–86	Sheffield W	—	—
1985–86	*Notts Co*	10	—
1986–87	Sunderland	38	—
1987–88		39	—
1988–89		20	—

1988–89	Hull C	22	—
1989–90		38	—
1990–91		31	—

HETHERSTON, Peter

Born Bellshill 6.11.64 Ht 5 9 Wt 10 7
Midfield. From Bargeddie Am

1984–85	Falkirk	12	2
1985–86		22	2
1986–87		36	3
1987–88	Watford	5	—
1987–88	Sheffield U	11	—
1988–89	Falkirk	31	3
1989–90		22	2
1990–91		26	4

HEWITSON, Mark

Born Oxford 27.2.71. Ht 5 8 Wt 10 10
Midfield. From Trainee.

1988–89	Oxford U	—	—
1989–90		—	—
1990–91	Bristol R	—	—

HEWITT, Jamie

Born Chesterfield 17.5.68. Ht 5 10
Wt 10 08
Defender. From school.

1984–85	Chesterfield	—	—
1985–86		17	—
1986–87		42	2
1987–88		28	2
1988–89		40	1
1989–90		42	6
1990–91		43	—

HEWITT, John

Born Aberdeen 9.2.63. Ht 5 8 Wt 10 08
Forward. From Middlefield Wasps.
Scotland Schools, Youth, Under-21.

1979–80	Aberdeen	4	—
1980–81		21	2
1981–82		25	11

Season	Club	League Appearances/Goals	
1982–83	....	16	4
1983–84	....	32	12
1984–85	....	21	3
1985–86	....	23	6
1986–87	....	34	11
1987–88	....	37	1
1988–89	....	27	3
1989–90	Celtic..................	12	—
1990–91	....	4	—

HICKS, Martin

Born Stratford-on-Avon 27.2.57 Ht 6 3
Wt 13 06
Defender. From Stratford T.

Season	Club	League Appearances/Goals	
1976–77	Charlton Ath	—	—
1977–78	....	—	—
1977–78	Reading..................	19	1
1978–79	....	46	1
1979–80	....	1	1
1980–81	....	27	2
1981–82	....	44	3
1982–83	....	32	1
1983–84	....	46	1
1984–85	....	40	2
1985–86	....	34	2
1986–87	....	34	3
1987–88	....	44	1
1988–89	....	45	3
1989–90	....	44	2
1990–91	....	44	—

HICKS, Stuart

Born Peterborough 30.5.67. Ht 6 1
Wt 12 06
Defender. From Peterborough U
Apprentice, Wisbech.

Season	Club	League Appearances/Goals	
1987–88	Colchester U	7	—
1988–89	....	37	—
1989–90	....	20	—
1990–91	Scunthorpe U	46	1

HIGGINS, Dave

Born Liverpool 19.8.61 Ht 6 0 Wt 11 00
Defender. From Eagle.

Season	Club	League Appearances/Goals	
1983–84	Tranmere R	20	—

Season	Club	League Appearances/Goals	
1984–85	....	8	—
From S. Liverpool, Caernarforn			
1987–88	Tranmere R	33	1
1988–89	....	43	1
1989–90	....	45	1
1990–91	....	33	2

HIGNETT, Craig

Born Whiston 12.1.70. Ht 5 10 Wt 11 00
Midfield.

Season	Club	League Appearances/Goals	
1987–88	Crewe Alex	—	—
1988–89	....	1	—
1989–90	....	35	8
1990–91	....	38	13

HILAIRE, Vince

Born Forest Hill 10.10.59. Ht 5 6
Wt 10 07
Forward. From Apprentice. England
Youth, Under-21, B.

Season	Club	League Appearances/Goals	
1976–77	Crystal Palace..............	3	—
1977–78	....	30	2
1978–79	....	31	6
1979–80	....	42	5
1980–81	....	31	4
1981–82	....	36	5
1982–83	....	42	5
1983–84	....	40	2
1984–85	Luton T	6	—
1984–85	Portsmouth	26	7
1985–86	....	41	8
1986–87	....	41	8
1987–88	....	38	2
1988–89	Leeds U	42	6
1989–90	....	2	—
1989–90	*Stoke C*..................	5	1
1989–90	*Charlton Ath*	—	—
1990–91	Leeds U	—	—
1990–91	Stoke C..................	10	2

HILDERSLEY, Ron

Born Fife 6.4.65. Ht 5 4 Wt 9 2
Forward. From Apprentice. Scotland
Schools.

Season	Club	League Appearances/Goals	
1982–83	Manchester C	1	—

Season	Club	Apps	Goals
1983–84	....	—	—
1983–84	*Chester C*	9	—
1984–85	Chester C	9	—
1985–86	Rochdale	16	—
1986–87	Preston NE	33	2
1987–88	....	25	1
1987–88	*Cambridge U*	9	3
1988–89	Blackburn R	25	4
1989–90	....	5	—
1990–91	Wigan Ath	4	—

HILDITCH, Mark

Born Royton 20.8.60. Ht 6 0 Wt 12 01
Forward. From Amateur.

Season	Club	Apps	Goals
1977–78	Rochdale	3	1
1978–79	....	27	3
1979–80	....	44	3
1980–81	....	44	12
1981–82	....	40	14
1982–83	....	39	7
1983–84	Tranmere R	39	8
1984–85	....	3	1
1985–86	....	7	3
1986–87	Wigan Ath	28	8
1987–88	....	29	8
1988–89	....	25	3
1989–90	....	21	7
1990–91	Rochdale	14	2

HILEY, Scott

Born Plymouth 27.9.68. Ht 5 9 Wt 10 07
Midfield. From Trainee.

Season	Club	Apps	Goals
1986–87	Exeter C	—	—
1987–88	....	15	1
1988–89	....	37	5
1989–90	....	46	—
1990–91	....	46	2

HILL, Andy

Born Maltby 20.1.65. Ht 5 10 Wt 12 00
Defender. From Apprentice. England Youth.

Season	Club	Apps	Goals
1982–83	Manchester U	—	—
1983–84	....	—	—
1984–85	Bury	43	3
1985–86	....	35	2
1986–87	....	42	1
1987–88	....	43	2
1988–89	....	43	—
1989–90	....	46	2
1990–91	....	12	—
1990–91	Manchester C	8	1

HILL, Colin

Born Hillingdon 12.11.63. Ht 5 11
Wt 12 02
Defender. From Apprentice. Northern Ireland 4 full caps.

Season	Club	Apps	Goals
1981–82	Arsenal	—	—
1982–83	....	7	—
1983–84	....	37	1
1984–85	....	2	—
1985–86	....	—	—
1985–86	*Brighton*	—	—
From Maritimo.			
1987–88	Colchester U	25	—
1988–89	....	44	—
1989–90	Sheffield U	43	—
1990–91	....	24	—

HILL, David

Born Nottingham 6.6.66. Ht 5 10
Wt 11 03
Midfield. Local.

Season	Club	Apps	Goals
1983–84	Scunthorpe U	2	—
1984–85	....	29	2
1985–86	....	42	2
1986–87	....	41	3
1987–88	....	26	3
1988–89	Ipswich T	36	—
1989–90	....	2	—
1990–91	....	23	—
1990–91	Scunthorpe U	9	1

HILL, Jonathan

Born Wigan 20.8.70. Ht 5 10 Wt 11 10
Midfield. From Crewe Alex Trainee.

Season	Club	Apps	Goals
1989–90	Rochdale	25	—

1990–91	11	1

HILL, Keith

Born Bolton 17.5.69. Ht 6 0 Wt 11 03
Defender. From Apprentice.

1986–87	Blackburn R	—	—
1987–88		1	—
1988–89		15	1
1989–90		25	—
1990–91		22	2

HILL, Paul

Born Nottingham 28.1.73.
Defender. From Trainee.

1990–91	Peterborough U	1	—

HILL, Ricky

Born London 5.3.59. Ht 5 10 Wt 13 10
Midfield. From Apprentice. England
Youth, 3 full caps.

1975–76	Luton T	2	1
1976–77		11	4
1977–78		40	5
1978–79		38	3
1979–80		40	6
1980–81		42	7
1981–82		38	5
1982–83		42	9
1983–84		26	2
1984–85		39	2
1985–86		38	3
1986–87		30	2
1987–88		17	2
1988–89		33	3

From Le Havre.

1990–91	Leicester C	26	—

HILLIER, David

Born Blackheath 19.12.69 Ht 5 10
Wt 11 06
Midfield. From Trainee. England
Under-21.

1987–88	Arsenal	—	—

1988–89		—	—
1989–90		—	—
1990–91		16	—

HILLYARD, Ron

Born Rotherham 31.3.53.   Ht 5 11
Wt 11 07
Goalkeeper. From Amateur.

1969–70	York C	3	—
1970–71		34	—
1971–72		17	—
1971–72	*Hartlepool U*	23	—
1972–73	York C	4	—
1973–74		3	—
1973–74	*Bury*	—	—
1973–74	*Brighton*	—	—
1974–75	Gillingham	46	—
1975–76		44	—
1976–77		25	—
1977–78		44	—
1978–79		46	—
1979–80		46	—
1980–81		37	—
1981–82		44	—
1982–83		42	—
1983–84		8	—
1984–85		25	—
1985–86		46	—
1986–87		27	—
1987–88		18	—
1988–89		19	—
1989–90		42	—
1990–91		4	—

HIMSWORTH, Gary

Born Appleton 19.12.69   Ht 5 7   Wt 9 08
Forward. From Trainee.

1987–88	York C	31	2
1988–89		32	2
1989–90		23	4
1990–91		2	—
1990–91	Scarborough	23	1

HINCHCLIFFE, Andy

Born Manchester 5.2.69 Ht 5 10
Wt 12 10
Defender. From Apprentice. England
Youth, Under-21.

1986–87	Manchester C	—	—
1987–88		42	1
1988–89		39	5
1989–90		31	2
1990–91	Everton	21	1

HINDMARCH, Rob

Born Stannington 27.4.61. Ht 6 1
Wt 13 04
Defender. From Apprentice. England
Youth.

1977–78	Sunderland	2	—
1978–79		—	—
1979–80		21	—
1980–81		29	—
1981–82		36	2
1982–83		14	—
1983–84		13	—
1983–84	*Portsmouth*	2	—
1984–85	Derby Co	22	1
1985–86		39	6
1986–87		33	2
1987–88		19	—
1988–89		25	—
1989–90		26	—
1990–91	Wolverhampton W	40	2

HINE, Mark

Born Middlesbrough 18.5.64. Ht 5 8
Wt 9 11
Midfield. Local.

1983–84	Grimsby T	—	—
1984–85		9	—
1985–86		13	1
1986–87	Darlington	43	2
1987–88		45	4
1988–89		40	2
1989–90		—	—
1989–90	Peterborough U	22	4
1990–91		33	4

1990–91	Scunthorpe U	12	2

HIRST, David

Born Barnsley 7.12.67. Ht 5 11 Wt 13 01
Forward. From Apprentice. England
Youth, B, Under-21, 2 full caps.

1985–86	Barnsley	28	9
1986–87	Sheffield W	21	6
1987–88		24	3
1988–89		32	7
1989–90		38	14
1990–91		41	24

HIRST, Lee

Born Sheffield 26.1.69. Ht 6 2 Wt 12 07
Defender.

1989–90	Scarborough	10	—
1990–91		32	2

HITCHCOCK, Kevin

Born Custom House 5.10.62. Ht 6 1
Wt 12 02
Goalkeeper. From Barking.

1983–84	Nottingham F	—	—
1983–84	*Mansfield T*	14	—
1984–85	Mansfield T	43	—
1985–86		46	—
1986–87		46	—
1987–88		33	—
1987–88	Chelsea	8	—
1988–89		3	—
1989–90		—	—
1990–91		3	—
1990–91	*Northampton T*	17	—

HOBSON, Gary

Born North Ferriby 12.11.72.
Defender. From Trainee.

1990–91	Hull C	4	—

HOBSON, Gordon

Born Sheffield 27.11.57. Ht 5 9 Wt 10 11
Forward. From Sheffield RGRS.

Season	Club		
1977–78	Lincoln C	5	2
1978–79		33	6
1979–80		43	10
1980–81		44	21
1981–82		32	7
1982–83		41	14
1983–84		36	6
1984–85		38	7
1985–86	Grimsby T	41	15
1986–87		11	3
1986–87	Southampton	20	7
1987–88		13	1
1988–89		—	—
1988–89	Lincoln C	32	14
1989–90		29	8
1990–91	Exeter C	37	7

HOCKADAY, David

Born Billingham 9.11.57. Ht 5 10
Wt 10 09
Defender. From Amateur.

Season	Club		
1975–76	Blackpool	—	—
1976–77		5	—
1977–78		—	—
1978–79		18	4
1979–80		7	1
1980–81		36	4
1981–82		41	7
1982–83		40	8
1983–84	Swindon T	36	3
1984–85		22	1
1985–86		37	1
1986–87		40	1
1987–88		43	—
1988–89		44	—
1989–90		20	—
1990–91		3	—
1990–91	Hull C	35	1

HODDLE, Carl

Born Harlow 8.3.67. Ht 6 0 Wt 11 00
Midfield. From Bishop's Stortford.

Season	Club		
1989–90	Leyton Orient	26	2
1990–91		2	—

HODGE, Martin

Born Southport 4.2.59. Ht 6 1 Wt 14 06
Goalkeeper. From Apprentice.

Season	Club		
1976–77	Plymouth Arg	—	—
1977–78		5	—
1978–79		38	—
1979–80	Everton	23	—
1980–81		2	—
1981–82	*Preston NE*	28	—
1982–83	*Oldham Ath*	4	—
1982–83	*Gillingham*	4	—
1982–83	*Preston NE*	16	—
1983–84	Sheffield W	42	—
1984–85		42	—
1985–86		42	—
1986–87		42	—
1987–88		29	—
1988–89	Leicester C	19	—
1989–90		46	—
1990–91		10	—

HODGE, Steve

Born Nottingham 25.10.62. Ht 5 8
Wt 9 11
Midfield. From Apprentice. England
Under-21, B, 24 full caps.

Season	Club		
1980–81	Nottingham F	—	—
1981–82		1	—
1982–83		39	8
1983–84		39	10
1984–85		42	12
1985–86		2	—
1985–86	Aston Villa	36	8
1986–87		17	4
1986–87	Tottenham H	19	4
1987–88		26	3
1988–89	Nottingham F	34	7
1989–90		34	10
1990–91		14	3

HODGES, David

Born Hereford 17.1.70 Ht 5 9 Wt 10 02
Midfield.

Season	Club		
1986–87	Mansfield T	3	—
1987–88		22	2

1988–89	....	39	4
1989–90	....	19	1
1990–91	....	2	—
1990–91	Torquay U	10	—

HODGES, Glyn

Born Streatham 30.4.63.   Ht 6 0
Wt 12 03
Forward. From Apprentice. Wales Youth,
B, Under-21, 13 full caps.

1980–81	Wimbledon	30	5
1981–82	....	34	2
1982–83	....	37	9
1983–84	....	42	15
1984–85	....	22	3
1985–86	....	30	6
1986–87	....	37	9
1987–88	Newcastle U................	7	—
1987–88	Watford	24	3
1988–89	....	27	5
1989–90	....	35	7
1990–91	Crystal Palace.............	7	—
1990–91	Sheffield U	12	4

HODGES, Kevin

Born Bridport 12.6.60   Ht 5 8   Wt 10 00
Midfield. From Apprentice.

1977–78	Plymouth Arg.............	—	—
1978–79	....	12	—
1979–80	....	44	5
1980–81	....	41	5
1981–82	....	46	11
1982–83	....	46	11
1983–84	....	43	4
1984–85	....	45	10
1985–86	....	46	16
1986–87	....	35	5
1987–88	....	37	6
1988–89	....	31	1
1989–90	....	44	4
1990–91	....	42	3

HODGES, Mark

Born Sheffield 24.10.71.   Ht 6 0   Wt 11 00
Defender. From Trainee.

| 1990–91 | Rotherham U .... | 4 | — |

HODSON, Simeon

Born Lincoln 5.3.66.   Ht 5 10   Wt 11 06
Defender. From Apprentice.

1983–84	Notts Co.....................	13	—
1984–85	....	14	—
1984–85	Charlton Ath	5	—
1985–86	....	15	—
1985–86	Lincoln C....................	15	—
1986–87	....	41	—
1987–88	Newport Co................	34	1
1987–88	WBA...........................	7	—
1988–89	....	9	—
1989–90	....	10	—
1990–91	....	30	—

HOGG, Graeme

Born Aberdeen 17.6.64.   Ht 6 1   Wt 13 01
Defender. From Apprentice. Scotland
Under-21.

1982–83	Manchester U.............	—	—
1983–84	....	16	1
1984–85	....	29	—
1985–86	....	17	—
1986–87	....	11	—
1987–88	....	10	—
1987–88	*WBA*	7	—
1988–89	Portsmouth	41	1
1989–90	....	39	1
1990–91	....	20	—

HOLDEN, Andy

Born Flint 14.9.62.   Ht 6 1   Wt 13 10
Defender. From Rhyl. Wales Under-21, 1
full cap.

1983–84	Chester......................	44	7
1984–85	....	38	6
1985–86	....	10	2
1986–87	....	8	2
1986–87	Wigan Ath	11	1
1987–88	....	15	2
1988–89	....	23	1
1988–89	Oldham Ath................	13	4

1989–90	....	6	—
1990–91	....	2	—

HOLDEN, Rick

Born Skipton 9.9.64. Ht 5 11 Wt 12 07
Midfield.

1985–86	Burnley	1	—
1986–87	Halifax T	32	2
1987–88	....	35	10
1987–88	Watford	10	2
1988–89	....	32	6
1989–90	Oldham Ath................	45	9
1990–91	....	42	5

HOLDSWORTH, David

Born London 8.11.68. Ht 5 11 Wt 11 04
Defender. From Trainee. England Youth,
Under-21.

1986–87	Watford	—	—
1987–88	....	—	—
1988–89	....	33	1
1989–90	....	44	3
1990–91	....	15	2

HOLDSWORTH, Dean

Born London 8.11.68. Ht 5 11 Wt 11 13
Forward. From Trainee.

1986–87	Watford	2	—
1987–88	*Carlisle U*...................	4	1
1987–88	*Port Vale*....................	6	2
1988–89	Watford	10	2
1988–89	*Swansea C*...................	5	1
1988–89	*Brentford*....................	7	1
1989–90	Watford	4	1
1989–90	Brentford	39	24
1990–91	....	30	5

HOLLAND, Paul

Born Lincoln 8.7.73.
Midfield. From School.

1990–91	Mansfield T................	1	—

HOLLAND, Simon

Born Sunderland 26.3.73.
Forward. From Trainee.

1990–91	Doncaster R................	1	—

HOLLIDAY, John

Born Penrith 13.3.70. Ht 6 4 Wt 11 00
Defender.

1989–90	Carlisle U...................	—	—
1990–91	....	1	—

HOLLOWAY, Ian

Born Kingswood 12.3.63. Ht 5 8
Wt 10 10
Midfield. From Apprentice.

1980–81	Bristol R	1	—
1981–82	....	1	—
1982–83	....	31	7
1983–84	....	36	1
1984–85	....	42	6
1985–86	Wimbledon	19	2
1985–86	*Brentford*....................	13	2
1986–87	Brentford	16	—
1986–87	*Torquay U*..................	5	—
1987–88	....	1	—
1987–88	Bristol R	43	5
1988–89	....	44	6
1989–90	....	46	8
1990–91	....	46	7

HOLMES, Andy

Born Stoke 7.1.69. Ht 6 1 Wt 12 12
Defender. From Apprentice.

1986–87	Stoke C	—	—
1987–88	....	2	—
1988–89	....	—	—
1989–90	....	6	—
1990–91	Doncaster R................	11	—

HOLMES, Matt

Born Luton 1.8.69 Ht 5 7 Wt 10 07
Forward. From Trainee.

1988–89	Bournemouth..............	4	1
1988–89	*Cardiff C*.....................	1	—
1989–90	Bournemouth..............	22	2

| 1990–91 | .... | 42 | 2 |

HOLMES, Micky

Born Blackpool 9.9.65. Ht 5 8 Wt 10 12
Midfield.

1984–85	Bradford C	5	—
1985–86	Burnley	—	—
1985–86	Wolverhampton W	26	3
1986–87	....	37	8
1987–88	....	20	2
1988–89	Huddersfield T	7	—
1988–89	Cambridge U	11	—
1989–90	Rochdale	38	2
1990–91	....	16	5
1990–91	Torquay U	22	2

HOLMES, Paul

Born Wortley 18.2.68. Ht 5 10 Wt 11 00
Defender. From Apprentice.

1985–86	Doncaster R	5	1
1986–87	....	16	—
1987–88	....	26	—
1988–89	Torquay U	25	—
1989–90	....	44	2
1990–91	....	33	1

HOLSGROVE, Paul

Born Wellington 26.8.69. Ht 6 1
Wt 12 00
Forward. From Trainee.

1986–87	Aldershot	—	—
1987–88	....	2	—
1988–89	....	1	—
1988–89	*Wimbledon*	—	—
1989–90	Aldershot	—	—
1989–90	*WBA*	—	—
From Wokingham
1990–91	Luton T	1	—

HONOR, Chris

Born Bristol 5.6.68. Ht 5 9 Wt 10 09
Defender. From Apprentice.

| 1985–86 | Bristol C .... | 1 | — |

1986–87	....	2	—
1986–87	*Torquay U*	3	—
1987–88	Bristol C	17	—
1988–89	....	26	—
1989–90	....	14	1
1989–90	*Hereford U*	3	—
1990–91	Bristol C	—	—
1990–91	*Swansea C*	2	—

HONOUR, Brian

Born Horden 16.2.64. Ht 5 7 Wt 12 05
Midfield. From Apprentice.

1981–82	Darlington	1	—
1982–83	....	32	3
1983–84	....	41	1
From Peterlee
1984–85	Hartlepool U	17	—
1985–86	....	46	8
1986–87	....	32	2
1987–88	....	44	—
1988–89	....	34	1
1989–90	....	9	—
1990–91	....	42	4

HOOPER, Michael

Born Bristol 10.2.64. Ht 6 2 Wt 13 05
Goalkeeper.

1983–84	Bristol C	—	—
1984–85	....	1	—
1984–85	*Wrexham*	20	—
1985–86	Wrexham	14	—
1985–86	Liverpool	—	—
1986–87	....	11	—
1987–88	....	2	—
1988–89	....	17	—
1989–90	....	—	—
1990–91	....	7	—
1990–91	*Leicester C*	14	—

HOPKINS, Jeff

Born Swansea 14.4.64. Ht 6 0 Wt 12 12
Defender. From Apprentice. Wales Youth,
Under-21, 16 full caps.

| 1980–81 | Fulham .... | 1 | — |

Season	Club	League Appearances/Goals	
1981–82	....	35	—
1982–83	....	41	1
1983–84	....	33	—
1984–85	....	40	2
1985–86	....	23	—
1986–87	....	20	1
1987–88	....	26	—
1988–89	Crystal Palace............	43	—
1989–90	....	27	2
1990–91	....	—	—

HOPKINS, Robert

Born Birmingham 25.10.61.　Ht 5 7
Wt 10 07
Midfield. From Apprentice.

Season	Club	League Appearances/Goals	
1979–80	Aston Villa.................	2	1
1980–81	....	—	—
1981–82	....	—	—
1982–83	....	1	—
1982–83	Birmingham C............	11	2
1983–84	....	32	5
1984–85	....	39	9
1985–86	....	38	4
1986–87	....	3	1
1986–87	Manchester C	7	1
1986–87	WBA........................	25	4
1987–88	....	29	2
1988–89	....	29	5
1988–89	Birmingham C............	9	—
1989–90	....	18	6
1990–91	....	23	3

HOPKINS, Tony

Born Pontypool 17.2.71.
Defender. From Newport Co, Chelsea and
Bristol C Trainee.

Season	Club	League Appearances/Goals	
1990–91	Aldershot	10	—

HORNE, Barry

Born St. Asaph 18.5.62.　Ht 5 10
Wt 12 02
Midfield. From Rhyl. Wales 22 full caps.

Season	Club	League Appearances/Goals	
1984–85	Wrexham	44	6
1985–86	....	46	3

Season	Club	League Appearances/Goals	
1986–87	....	46	8
1987–88	Portsmouth	39	3
1988–89	....	31	4
1988–89	Southampton	11	—
1989–90	....	29	4
1990–91	....	38	1

HORNE, Brian

Born Billericay 5.10.67.　Ht 5 11
Wt 13 13
Goalkeeper. From Apprentice. England
Youth, Under-21.

Season	Club	League Appearances/Goals	
1985–86	Millwall......................	—	—
1986–87	....	32	—
1987–88	....	43	—
1988–89	....	38	—
1989–90	....	22	—
1990–91	....	28	—

HORNER, Philip

Born Leeds 10.11.66.　Ht 6 1　Wt 12 07
Forward. From Lincoln C Schoolboy.

Season	Club	League Appearances/Goals	
1984–85	Leicester C..................	—	—
1985–86	....	—	—
1985–86	*Rotherham U*..............	4	—
1986–87	Leicester C..................	3	—
1987–88	....	7	—
1988–89	Halifax T	38	3
1989–90	....	34	1
1990–91	Blackpool...................	39	7

HOUCHEN, Keith

Born Middlesbrough 25.7.60.　Ht 6 2
Wt 12 08
Forward. From Chesterfield Amateur.

Season	Club	League Appearances/Goals	
1977–78	Hartlepool U	13	4
1978–79	....	39	12
1979–80	....	41	14
1980–81	....	45	17
1981–82	....	32	18
1981–82	Orient........................	14	1
1982–83	....	32	10
1983–84	....	30	9
1983–84	York C.......................	7	1

Season	Club	League Appearances/Goals	
1984–85	....	35	12
1985–86	....	25	6
1985–86	Scunthorpe U	9	3
1986–87	Coventry C	20	2
1987–88	....	21	3
1988–89	....	13	2
1988–89	Hibernian....................	7	2
1989–90	....	29	8
1990–91	....	21	1

HOUGH, David

Born Crewe 20.2.66. Ht 5 11 Wt 11 10
Defender. From Apprentice. Wales Youth.

Season	Club	League Appearances/Goals	
1983–84	Swansea C...................	2	—
1984–85	....	25	2
1985–86	....	31	3
1986–87	....	31	3
1987–88	....	20	—
1988–89	....	40	—
1989–90	....	32	1
1990–91	....	41	—

HOUGHTON, Ray

Born Glasgow 9.1.62. Ht 5 8 Wt 11 04
Midfield. Amateur. Eire 41 full caps.

Season	Club	League Appearances/Goals	
1979–80	West Ham U	—	—
1980–81	....	—	—
1981–82	....	1	—
1982–83	Fulham	42	5
1983–84	....	40	3
1984–85	....	42	8
1985–86	....	5	—
1985–86	Oxford U	35	4
1986–87	....	37	5
1987–88	....	11	1
1987–88	Liverpool	28	5
1988–89	....	38	7
1989–90	....	19	1
1990–91	....	32	7

HOUGHTON, Scott

Born Hitchin 22.10.71. Ht 5 5 Wt 11 06
Midfield. From Trainee. England Schools,
Youth.

Season	Club	League Appearances/Goals	
1990–91	Tottenham H	—	—

Season	Club	League Appearances/Goals	
1990–91	*Ipswich T*....................	8	1

HOUSTON, Peter

Born Baillieston 19.7.58. Ht 5 10 Wt 11 0
Midfield. From Livingston U

Season	Club	League Appearances/Goals	
1979–80	Albion R....................	32	18
1980–81	....	38	4
1981–82	....	38	9
1982–83	....	15	1
1982–83	Falkirk	21	8
1983–84	....	37	10
1984–85	....	39	10
1985–86	....	38	5
1986–87	Dumbarton	38	5
1987–88	....	42	3
1988–89	Falkirk	33	3
1989–90	....	31	—
1990–91	....	13	2

HOWARD, Jonathan

Born Sheffield 7.10.71. Ht 5 10 Wt 11 07
Forward. From Trainee.

Season	Club	League Appearances/Goals	
1990–91	Rotherham U	1	—

HOWARD, Terence

Born Stepney 26.2.66. Ht 6 1 Wt 11 07
Defender. From Apprentice. England
Youth.

Season	Club	League Appearances/Goals	
1983–84	Chelsea.......................	—	—
1984–85	....	4	—
1985–86	....	1	—
1985–86	*C Palace*....................	4	—
1986–87	Chelsea.......................	1	—
1986–87	*Chester C*	2	—
1986–87	Orient........................	12	2
1987–88	....	41	2
1988–89	....	46	5
1989–90	....	45	7
1990–91	....	46	3

HOWELLS, David

Born Guildford 15.12.67. Ht 5 11
Wt 11 01
Forward. From Trainee. England Youth.

Season	Club	Appearances	Goals
1984–85	Tottenham H	—	—
1985–86		1	1
1986–87		1	—
1987–88		11	—
1988–89		27	3
1989–90		34	5
1990–91		29	4

HOWELLS, Gareth

Born Guildford 13.6.70. Ht 6 1
Wt 12 08
Goalkeeper. From Trainee.

Season	Club	Appearances	Goals
1988–89	Tottenham H	—	—
1989–90		—	—
1989–90	*Swindon T*	—	—
1989–90	*Leyton Orient*	—	—
1990–91	Torquay U	45	—

HOWEY, Steve

Born Sunderland 26.10.71   Ht 6 1
Wt 10 05
Midfield. From Trainee.

Season	Club	Appearances	Goals
1988–89	Newcastle U	1	—
1989–90		—	—
1990–91		11	—

HOWLETT, Gary

Born Dublin 2.4.63.   Ht 5 8   Wt 10 11
Midfield. From Home Farm. Eire Youth,
1 full cap.

Season	Club	Appearances	Goals
1980–81	Coventry C	—	—
1981–82		—	—
1982–83	Brighton	9	1
1983–84		17	—
1984–85		6	1
1984–85	Bournemouth	17	2
1985–86		20	2
1986–87		23	3
1987–88		—	—
1987–88	*Aldershot*	1	—
1987–88	*Chester C*	6	1
1987–88	York C	18	2
1988–89		23	4
1989–90		43	4

Season	Club	Appearances	Goals
1990–91		17	3

HOYLAND, Jamie

Born Sheffield 23.1.66.   Ht 6 0   Wt 12 08
Midfield. From Apprentice. England
Youth.

Season	Club	Appearances	Goals
1983–84	Manchester C	1	—
1984–85		1	—
1985–86		—	—
1986–87	Bury	36	2
1987–88		44	8
1988–89		46	9
1989–90		46	16
1990–91	Sheffield U	21	—

HOYLE, Colin

Born Derby 15.1.72.   Ht 5 11   Wt 12 03
Forward. From Trainee.

Season	Club	Appearances	Goals
1989–90	Arsenal	—	—
1989–90	*Chesterfield*	3	—
1990–91	Barnsley	—	—

HUCKER, Peter

Born London 28.10.59.   Ht 6 2   Wt 12 12
Goalkeeper. From Apprentice. England
Under-21.

Season	Club	Appearances	Goals
1977–78	QPR	—	—
1977–78	*Cambridge U*	—	—
1978–79	QPR	—	—
1979–80		—	—
1980–81		1	—
1981–82		22	—
1982–83		42	—
1983–84		42	—
1984–85		42	—
1985–86		11	—
1986–87		—	—
1986–87	Oxford U	5	—
1987–88		27	—
1987–88	*WBA*	7	—
1988–89	Oxford U	26	—
1988–89	*Manchester U*	—	—
1989–90	Oxford U	8	—
1989–90	Millwall	—	—

Season	Club	League Appearances/Goals
1990–91	....	— —
1990–91	Aldershot	27 —

HUGHES, Adrian

Born Billinge 19.12.70 Ht 6 2 Wt 12 12
Defender. From Everton schoolboy,
Preston NE Trainee.

1987–88	Preston NE	1 —
1988–89	....	23 1
1989–90	....	35 1
1990–91	....	26 1

HUGHES, Ceri

Born Pontypridd 26.2.71. Ht 5 9
Wt 11 06
Midfield. From Trainee. Wales Youth,
Under-21.

1989–90	Luton T	1 —
1990–91	....	17 1

HUGHES, Darren

Born Prescot 6.10.65. Ht 5 11 Wt 10 11
Defender. From Apprentice.

1983–84	Everton	1 —
1984–85	....	2 —
1985–86	Shrewsbury T.............	31 1
1986–87	....	6 —
1986–87	Brighton.....................	26 2
1987–88	....	— —
1987–88	Port Vale....................	43 1
1988–89	....	44 —
1989–90	....	38 1
1990–91	....	17 —

HUGHES, John

Born Edinburgh 9.9.64. Ht 6 0 Wt 13 07
Forward. From Newtongrange Star

1988–89	Berwick R...................	27 10
1989–90	....	14 4
1989–90	Swansea C...................	24 4
1990–91	Falkirk	32 2

HUGHES, Ken

Born Barmouth 9.1.66. Ht 6 0 Wt 11 06
Goalkeeper.

1985–86	Crystal Palace.............	— —
1986–87	Shrewsbury T.............	6 —
1987–88	....	2 —
1988–89	....	7 —
1989–90	....	— —
1990–91	....	36 —

HUGHES, Mark

Born Port Talbot 3.2.62. Ht 6 0
Wt 12 08
Defender. From Apprentice. Wales Youth.

1979–80	Bristol R	1 —
1980–81	....	38 1
1981–82	....	22 2
1982–83	....	4 —
1982–83	*Torquay U*..................	9 1
1983–84	Bristol R	9 —
1984–85	Swansea C...................	12 —
1984–85	Bristol C	20 —
1985–86	....	2 —
1985–86	Tranmere R	32 —
1986–87	....	38 1
1987–88	....	20 —
1988–89	....	37 1
1989–90	....	45 4
1990–91	....	42 2

HUGHES, Mark

Born Wrexham 1.11.63. Ht 5 9 Wt 11 12
Forward. From Apprentice. Wales Youth,
Under-21, 35 full caps.

1980–81	Manchester U.............	— —
1981–82	....	— —
1982–83	....	— —
1983–84	....	11 4
1984–85	....	38 16
1985–86	....	40 17
From Barcelona, *Bayern Munich*		
1988–89	Manchester U.............	38 14
1989–90	....	37 13
1990–91	....	31 10

HUGHES, Michael

Born Larne 2.8.71 Ht 5 6 Wt 10 08
Forward. From Carrick R. Northern
Ireland Under-23.

Season	Club		
1988–89	Manchester C	1	—
1989–90		—	—
1990–91		1	—

HUGHES, Philip

Born Manchester 19.11.64. Ht 5 11
Wt 13 08
Goalkeeper. From Manchester U.
Apprentice. Northern Ireland Youth, 3 full
caps.

1982–83	Leeds U	—	—
1983–84		2	—
1984–85		4	—
1985–86	Bury	41	—
1986–87		32	—
1987–88		7	—
1987–88	Wigan Ath	31	—
1988–89		16	—
1989–90		33	—
1990–91		19	—

HUGHES, Zac

Born Bentley 6.6.71 Ht 5 11 Wt 11 12
Defender. From Trainee.

1987–88	Rochdale	2	—
1988–89		—	—
1989–90		—	—
1990–91		—	—

HUGHTON, Chris

Born West Ham 11.12.58. Ht 5 7
Wt 11 05
Defender. From Amateur. Eire Under-21,
52 full caps.

1977–78	Tottenham H	—	—
1978–79		—	—
1979–80		39	1
1980–81		34	1
1981–82		37	2
1982–83		38	3
1983–84		34	3
1984–85		31	1
1985–86		33	1
1986–87		9	—

1987–88		13	—
1988–89		21	—
1989–90		8	—
1990–91		—	—
1990–91	West Ham U	32	—

HUISTRA, Pieter

Born Goenga 18.1.67 Ht 5 7 Wt 11 4
Forward. From FC Twente Enschede

1990–91	Rangers	27	4

HULL, Alan

Born Rochford 4.9.62. Ht 5 9 Wt 11 00
Forward. From Southend U, Basildon,
Barking.

1987–88	Leyton Orient	36	5
1988–89		17	5
1989–90		24	6
1990–91		2	—

HULME, Kevin

Born Farnworth 2.12.67 Ht 5 10
Wt 11 09
Forward. From Radcliffe Borough.

1988–89	Bury	5	—
1989–90		19	1
1989–90	*Chester C*	4	—
1990–91	Bury	24	7

HUMES, Tony

Born Blyth 19.3.66. Ht 6 1 Wt 11 03
Defender. From Apprentice.

1983–84	Ipswich T	—	—
1984–85		—	—
1985–86		—	—
1986–87		22	2
1987–88		27	—
1988–89		26	3
1989–90		24	3
1990–91		16	2

HUMPHREY, John

Born Paddington 31.1.61. Ht 5 10
Wt 11 03
Defender. From Apprentice.

Season	Club	Apps	Goals
1978–79	Wolverhampton W	—	—
1979–80		2	—
1980–81		12	—
1981–82		23	—
1982–83		42	3
1983–84		28	—
1984–85		42	—
1985–86	Charlton Ath	39	2
1986–87		39	—
1987–88		40	—
1988–89		38	1
1989–90		38	—
1990–91	Crystal Palace	38	1

HUMPHRIES, Glenn

Born Hull 11.8.64. Ht 6 0 Wt 12 00
Defender. From Apprentice. England
Youth

Season	Club	Apps	Goals
1980–81	Doncaster R	1	—
1981–82		14	—
1982–83		40	5
1983–84		44	2
1984–85		27	—
1985–86		29	—
1986–87		17	1
1986–87	*Lincoln C*	9	—
1987–88	Doncaster R	8	—
1987–88	Bristol C	24	—
1988–89		22	—
1989–90		37	—
1990–91		2	—
1990–91	Scunthorpe U	10	1

HUNT, Andy

Born Thurrock 9.6.70. Ht 6 0 Wt 11 07
Forward. From Kettering T.

Season	Club	Apps	Goals
1990–91	Newcastle U	16	2

HUNT, Paul

Born Swindon 8.10.71. Ht 5 5 Wt 10 02
Forward. From Trainee.

Season	Club	Apps	Goals
1989–90	Swindon T	4	—
1990–91		2	—

HUNTER, Geoff

Born Hull 27.10.59. Ht 5 10 Wt 10 10
Defender. From Apprentice.

Season	Club	Apps	Goals
1976–77	Manchester U	—	—
1977–78		—	—
1978–79		—	—
1979–80	Crewe Alex	41	4
1980–81		46	4
1981–82	Port Vale	41	3
1982–83		46	4
1983–84		42	1
1984–85		42	2
1985–86		45	5
1986–87		5	—
1987–88	Wrexham	39	4
1988–89		38	4
1989–90		21	3
1990–91		24	3

HUNTER, Gordon

Born Wallyford 3.5.67. Ht 5 10
Wt 10 05
Midfield. From Musselburgh Windsor.
Scotland Youth, Under-21.

Season	Club	Apps	Goals
1983–84	Hibernian	1	—
1984–85		6	—
1985–86		25	—
1986–87		29	—
1987–88		35	—
1988–89		33	1
1989–90		34	—
1990–91		20	1

HUNTER, Paul

Born Kirkcaldy 30.8.68. Ht 6 0
Wt 12 09
Forward. From Leven Royal Colts.

Season	Club	Apps	Goals
1984–85	East Fife	5	1
1985–86		20	7
1986–87		38	8
1987–88		39	17
1988–89		33	9
1989–90		29	14
1989–90	Hull C	9	3
1990–91		18	2

HURLOCK, Terry

Born Hackney 22.9.58. Ht 5 9 Wt 13 04
Midfield. From Leytonstone and Ilford.
England B.

Season	Club	Apps	Goals
1980–81	Brentford	42	4
1981–82		40	2
1982–83		39	3
1983–84		32	4
1984–85		40	3
1985–86		27	2
1985–86	Reading	16	—
1986–87		13	—
1986–87	Millwall	13	1
1987–88		28	4
1988–89		34	3
1989–90		29	—
1990–91	Rangers	29	2

HURST, Lee

Born Nuneaton 21.9.70. Ht 6 0
Wt 11 09
Midfield. From Trainee.

Season	Club	Apps	Goals
1989–90	Coventry C	—	—
1990–91		4	—

HUTCHINGS, Chris

Born Winchester 5.7.57. Ht 5 10
Wt 11 00
Defender. From Harrow Bor.

Season	Club	Apps	Goals
1980–81	Chelsea	12	1
1981–82		35	1
1982–83		36	—
1983–84		4	1
1983–84	Brighton	26	1
1984–85		42	1
1985–86		29	1
1986–87		36	—
1987–88		20	1
1987–88	Huddersfield T	23	—
1988–89		41	5
1989–90		46	5
1990–91	Walsall	40	—

HUTCHINSON, Ian

Born Teeside 7.11.72.
Defender. From Trainee.

Season	Club	Apps	Goals
1990–91	Halifax T	3	—

HUTCHINSON, Thomas

Born Glasgow 15.5.71. Ht 5 11 Wt 11 00
Midfield. From Tullibody Hearts.

Season	Club	Apps	Goals
1989–90	St Mirren	1	—
1990–91		2	—

HUTCHISON, Donald

Born Gateshead 9.5.71. Ht 6 2 Wt 11 04
Forward. From Trainee.

Season	Club	Apps	Goals
1989–90	Hartlepool U	13	2
1990–91		11	—
1990–91	Liverpool	—	—

HUTCHISON, Tommy

Born Cardenden 22.9.47. Ht 6 0
Wt 12 06
Midfield. From Dundonald Bluebell.
Scotland Under-23, 17 full caps.

Season	Club	Apps	Goals
1965–66	Alloa	16	1
1966–67		29	2
1967–68		23	1
1967–68	Blackpool	9	—
1968–69		32	2
1969–70		41	2
1970–71		38	1
1971–72		35	2
1972–73		10	3
1972–73	Coventry C	30	2
1973–74		41	3
1974–75		42	4
1975–76		42	1
1976–77		33	3
1977–78		40	3
1978–79		42	6
1979–80		40	1
1980–81		4	1
1981–82	Manchester C	24	3
1982–83		22	1

From Bulova, Hong Kong.

Season	Club	App	Goals
1983–84	Burnley	46	4
1984–85		46	—
1985–86	Swansea C	41	3
1986–87		41	1
1987–88		7	—
1988–89		44	3
1989–90		36	2
1990–91		9	—

HYSEN, Glenn

Born Gothenburg 30.10.59   Ht 6 1
Wt 12 08
Defender. From IFK Gothenburg, PSV
Eindhoven, Fiorentina. Sweden full caps.

Season	Club	App	Goals
1989–90	Liverpool	35	1
1990–91		32	—

HYSLOP, Christian

Born Watford 14.6.72.   Ht 5 10   Wt 11 13
Defender. From Trainee.

Season	Club	App	Goals
1989–90	Southend U	—	—
1990–91		11	—

INCE, Paul

Born Ilford 21.10.67.   Ht 5 10   Wt 11 07
Midfield. From Trainee. England Youth,
Under-21.

Season	Club	App	Goals
1985–86	West Ham U	—	—
1986–87		10	1
1987–88		28	3
1988–89		33	3
1989–90		1	—
1989–90	Manchester U	26	—
1990–91		31	3

INGLETHORPE, Alex

Born Epsom 14.11.71.   Ht 5 10   Wt 11 07
Forward. From School.

Season	Club	App	Goals
1990–91	Watford	1	—

INGLIS, John

Born Edinburgh 16.10.66   Ht 6 0
Wt 13 0
Defender. From Hutchison Vale

Season	Club	App	Goals
1983–84	East Fife	4	1
1984–85		9	—
1985–86		30	—
1986–87		13	—
1986–87	Brechin C	15	—
1987–88		26	3
1988–89		12	1
1988–89	Meadowbank T	12	1
1989–90		38	3
1990–91	St Johnstone	31	1

IORFA, Dominic

Born Lagos 1.10.68.   Ht 6 1   Wt 12 12
Forward. From Antwerp. Nigeria full
caps.

Season	Club	App	Goals
1989–90	QPR	1	—
1990–91		6	—

IOVAN, Stefan

Born Rumania 23.8.60.
Defender. From Steaua Bucharest.
Rumania full caps.

1990–91 Brighton...................... 2 —

IRELAND, Simon

Born Barnstaple 23.11.71.
Forward. From School.

1990–91 Huddersfield T........... 6 —

IRONS, David

Born Glasgow 18.7.61. Ht 6 0 Wt 11 04
Midfield. From Kello Rovers.

1984–85 Ayr U 34 6
1985–86 .... 37 6
1986–87 .... 4 1
1986–87 Clydebank.................. 23 1
1987–88 .... 31 6
1987–88 Dunfermline Ath 11 1
1988–89 .... 36 2
1989–90 .... 23 2
1990–91 .... 34 4

IRONS, Kenny

Born Liverpool 4.11.70. Ht 5 9 Wt 11 00
Forward. From Trainee.

1989–90 Tranmere R .... 3 —
1990–91 .... 32 6

IRONSIDE, Ian

Born Sheffield 8.3.64. Ht 6 2 Wt 13 00
Goalkeeper. From Barnsley Apprentice, N.
Ferriby U.

1987–88 Scarborough.............. 6 —
1988–89 .... 28 —
1989–90 .... 14 —
1990–91 .... 40 —

IRVINE, Alan

Born Glasgow 12.7.58. Ht 5 9 Wt 11 03
Forward. From Glasgow BC.

1977–78 Queen's Park.............. 4 —
1978–79 .... 8 —

1979–80 .... 38 5
1980–81 .... 38 4
1981–82 Everton 25 3
1982–83 .... 14 1
1983–84 .... 21 —
1984–85 Crystal Palace............ 35 5
1985–86 .... 41 3
1986–87 .... 33 4
1987–88 Dundee U 16 2
1988–89 .... 7 1
1989–90 .... 1 —
1989–90 Blackburn R 25 1
1990–91 .... 27 2

IRVINE, Alan J

Born Broxburn 29.11.62 Ht 6 2 Wt 11 6
Forward. From Hibernian

1982–83 Falkirk .... 1 —
1983–84 .... 23 2
1984–85 .... 34 5
1985–86 .... 34 6
1986–87 .... 18 4
1986–87 Liverpool .... 2 —
1987–88 Dundee U .... 7 —
1987–88 Shrewsbury T............. 6 1
1988–89 .... 31 5
1989–90 .... — —
1990–91 St Mirren .... 11 —

IRVINE, Brian

Born Bellshill 24.5.65. Ht 6 2 Wt 13 0
Defender. From Victoria Park. Scotland 1
full cap.

1983–84 Falkirk .... 3 —
1984–85 .... 35 —
1985–86 Aberdeen.................... 1 —
1986–87 .... 20 1
1987–88 .... 16 1
1988–89 .... 27 2
1989–90 .... 31 1
1990–91 .... 29 2

IRWIN, Denis

Born Cork 31.70.65. Ht 5 8 Wt 11 00
Defender. From Apprentice. Eire Schools,
Youth, B, Under-21, 6 full caps.

Season	Club	App	Goals
1983–84	Leeds U	12	—
1984–85		41	1
1985–86		19	—
1986–87	Oldham Ath	41	1
1987–88		43	—
1988–89		41	2
1989–90		42	1
1990–91	Manchester U	34	—

JACK, Paul

Born Malaya 15.5.65 Ht 5 10 Wt 11 7
Midfield. fm Fallin Miners Welfare

Season	Club	App	Goals
1985–86	Arbroath	14	—
1986–87		35	1
1987–88		31	—
1988–89		25	5
1989–90	Airdrieonians	26	2
1990–91		35	—

JACK, Ross

Born Inverness 21.3.59. Ht 5 11
Wt 12 00
Forward. From Apprentice.

Season	Club	App	Goals
1976–77	Everton	—	—
1977–78		—	—
1978–79		1	1
1979–80		—	—
1979–80	*Cardiff C*	—	—
1979–80	Norwich C	—	—
1980–81		11	—
1981–82		35	10
1982–83		10	—
1983–84	Lincoln C	36	9
1984–85		24	7
1985–86	Dundee	6	—
1986–87		28	4
1987–88		4	—
1987–88	Dunfermline Ath	25	4
1988–89		36	18
1989–90		36	16
1990–91		33	8

JACKSON, Darren

Born Edinburgh 25.7.66. Ht 5 10
Wt 10 10
Forward. From Broxburn Am.

Season	Club	App	Goals
1985–86	Meadowbank T	39	17
1986–87		9	5
1986–87	Newcastle U	23	3
1987–88		31	2
1988–89		15	2
1988–89	Dundee U	1	—

| 1989–90 | .... | 25 | 7 |
| 1990–91 | .... | 33 | 12 |

JACKSON, Darren

Born Bristol 24.9.71. Ht 6 1 Wt 12 08
Defender. From Trainee.

| 1989–90 | Oxford U .... | 1 | — |
| 1990–91 | .... | 5 | — |

JACKSON, Matthew

Born Leeds 19.10.71. Ht 6 1 Wt 12 12
Defender. From School. England Schools.

| 1990–91 | Luton T .... | — | — |
| 1990–91 | *Preston NE* .... | 4 | — |

JACKSON, Peter

Born Bradford 6.4.61. Ht 6 0 Wt 12 07
Defender. From Apprentice.

1978–79	Bradford C	9	1
1979–80	....	12	—
1980–81	....	45	1
1981–82	....	32	8
1982–83	....	41	3
1983–84	....	42	3
1984–85	....	45	8
1985–86	....	42	—
1986–87	....	10	—
1986–87	Newcastle U	31	1
1987–88	....	28	2
1988–89	....	1	—
1988–89	Bradford C	32	3
1989–90	....	26	2
1990–91	Huddersfield T	38	1

JACKSON, Robbie

Born Altrincham 9.2.73.
Forward. From Manchester C Trainee.

| 1990–91 | Walsall .... | 1 | 2 |

JACOBS, Wayne

Born Sheffield 3.2.69. Ht 5 9 Wt 10 02
Defender. From Apprentice.

1986–87	Sheffield W	—	—
1987–88	....	6	—
1987–88	Hull C	6	—
1988–89	....	33	—
1989–90	....	46	3
1990–91	....	19	1

JAKUB, Joe

Born Falkirk 7.12.56. Ht 5 6 Wt 9 06
Midfield. From Apprentice.

1973–74	Burnley	—	—
1974–75	....	—	—
1975–76	....	1	—
1976–77	....	5	—
1977–78	....	—	—
1978–79	....	13	—
1979–80	....	23	—
1980–81	....	—	—
1981–82	Bury	33	1
1982–83	....	46	2
1983–84	....	46	3
1984–85	....	46	11
1985–86	....	40	3
1986–87	....	44	6
1987–88	....	10	1
From AZ Alkmaar			
1988–89	Chester C	42	1
1989–90	Burnley	46	5
1990–91	....	46	3

JAMES, David

Born Welwyn 1.8.70 Ht 6 4 Wt 14 13
Goalkeeper. From Trainee. England
Youth, Under-21.

1988–89	Watford	—	—
1989–90	....	—	—
1990–91	....	46	—

JAMES, Julian

Born Tring 22.3.70. Ht 5 10 Wt 11 11
Midfield. From Trainee. England
Under-21.

| 1987–88 | Luton T .... | 3 | — |
| 1988–89 | .... | 1 | — |

| 1989–90 | | 20 | 1 |
| 1990–91 | | 17 | 1 |

JAMES, Martin

Born Formby 18.5.71. Ht 5 10 Wt 11 07
Midfield. From Trainee.

| 1989–90 | Preston NE | — | — |
| 1990–91 | | 37 | 2 |

JAMES, Robbie

Born Swansea 23.3.57. Ht 5 11 Wt 13 0
Forward. From Apprentice. Wales Under-21, 47 full caps.

1972–73	Swansea C	1	—
1973–74		29	2
1974–75		42	8
1975–76		45	8
1976–77		46	14
1977–78		42	16
1978–79		43	14
1979–80		29	6
1980–81		35	8
1981–82		42	14
1982–83		40	9
1983–84	Stoke C	40	6
1984–85		8	—
1984–85	QPR	20	2
1985–86		28	1
1986–87		39	1
1987–88	Leicester C	23	—
1987–88	Swansea C	19	3
1988–89		41	9
1989–90		30	4
1990–91	Bradford C	46	3

JAMES, Tony

Born Sheffield 27.6.67 Ht 6 3 Wt 13 08
Defender. From Gainsborough T.

1988–89	Lincoln C	28	—
1989–90		1	—
1989–90	Leicester C	31	2
1990–91		38	8

JASPER, Dale

Born Croydon 14.1.64. Ht 6 0 Wt 12 00
Defender. From Amateur.

1981–82	Chelsea	—	—
1982–83		—	—
1983–84		3	—
1984–85		7	—
1985–86		—	—
1986–87	Brighton	35	2
1987–88		14	4
1988–89	Crewe Alex	39	1
1989–90		40	1
1990–91		25	1

JEFFELS, Simon

Born Darton 18.1.66. Ht 6 1 Wt 11 08
Defender. From Apprentice. England Youth.

1983–84	Barnsley	3	—
1984–85		18	—
1985–86		11	—
1986–87		3	—
1987–88		7	—
1987–88	*Preston NE*	1	—
1988–89	Carlisle U	29	—
1989–90		—	—
1990–91		21	3

JEFFERS, John

Born Liverpool 5.10.68. Ht 5 10
Wt 11 10
Forward. From Trainee. England Schools.

1986–87	Liverpool	—	—
1987–88		—	—
1988–89		—	—
1988–89	Port Vale	15	—
1989–90		40	1
1990–91		31	2

JEMSON, Nigel

Born Preston 10.8.69. Ht 5 10 Wt 11 10
Forward. From Trainee. England Under-21.

1985–86	Preston NE	1	—
1986–87		4	3
1987–88		27	5
1987–88	Nottingham F	—	—

Season	Club	Appearances	Goals
1988–89		—	—
1988–89	*Bolton W*	5	—
1988–89	*Preston NE*	9	2
1989–90	Nottingham F	18	4
1990–91		23	8

JENKINS, Iain

Born Prescot 24.11.72.
Defender. From Trainee.

Season	Club	Appearances	Goals
1990–91	Everton	1	—

JENKINS, Steve

Born Merthyr 16.7.72.
Forward. From Trainee.

Season	Club	Appearances	Goals
1990–91	Swansea C	1	—

JENKINSON, Leigh

Born Thorne 9.7.69. Ht 6 0 Wt 12 02
Forward. From Trainee.

Season	Club	Appearances	Goals
1987–88	Hull C	3	1
1988–89		11	—
1989–90		22	—
1990–91		26	—
1990–91	*Rotherham U*	7	—

JEPSON, Ron

Born Stoke 12.5.63. Ht 6 1 Wt 13 02
Forward. From Nantwich.

Season	Club	Appearances	Goals
1988–89	Port Vale	2	—
1989–90		5	—
1989–90	*Peterborough U*	18	5
1990–91	Port Vale	15	—
1990–91	Preston NE	14	3

JESS, Eoin

Born Aberdeen 13.12.70. Ht 5 7
Wt 10 10
Forward. From Rangers S Form. Scotland
Under-21.

Season	Club	Appearances	Goals
1987–88	Aberdeen	—	—

Season	Club	Appearances	Goals
1988–89		2	—
1989–90		11	3
1990–91		27	13

JEWELL, Paul

Born Liverpool 28.9.64. Ht 5 8 Wt 11 10
Forward. From Apprentice.

Season	Club	Appearances	Goals
1982–83	Liverpool	—	—
1983–84		—	—
1984–85	Wigan Ath	26	9
1985–86		29	6
1986–87		39	9
1987–88		43	11
1988–89	Bradford C	39	4
1989–90		30	4
1990–91		38	4

JOBLING, Kevin

Born Sunderland 1.1.68. Ht 5 9
Wt 10 11
Midfield. From Apprentice.

Season	Club	Appearances	Goals
1985–86	Leicester C	—	—
1986–87		3	—
1987–88		6	—
1987–88	Grimsby T	15	1
1988–89		32	4
1989–90		33	1
1990–91		45	—

JOBSON, Richard

Born Hull 9.5.63. Ht 6 1 Wt 13 05
Defender. From Burton Alb.

Season	Club	Appearances	Goals
1982–83	Watford	13	1
1983–84		13	2
1984–85		2	1
1984–85	Hull C	8	—
1985–86		36	7
1986–87		40	5
1987–88		44	2
1988–89		46	1
1989–90		45	2
1990–91		2	—
1990–91	Oldham Ath	44	1

JOHNROSE, Lenny

Born Preston 29.11.69. Ht 5 11 Wt 12 00
Forward. From Trainee.

Season	Club		
1987–88	Blackburn R	1	—
1988–89		—	—
1989–90		8	3
1990–91		26	7

JOHNS, Nicky

Born Bristol 8.6.57. Ht 6 2 Wt 11 08
Goalkeeper. From Minehead.

Season	Club		
1975–76	Millwall	—	—
1976–77		16	—
1977–78		34	—
From Tampa Bay R			
1978–79	*Sheffield U*	1	—
1978–79	Charlton Ath	10	—
1979–80		34	—
1980–81		37	—
1981–82		40	—
1982–83		42	—
1983–84		36	—
1984–85		30	—
1985–86		38	—
1986–87		16	—
1987–88		5	—
1987–88	QPR	7	—
1988–89		3	—
1989–90		—	—
1989–90	Maidstone U	13	—
1990–91		29	—

JOHNSEN, Erland

Born Frederikstad (Norway) 5.4.67.
Ht 6 0 Wt 12 10
Defender. From Bayern Munich. Norway
full caps.

Season	Club		
1989–90	Chelsea	18	—
1990–91		6	—

JOHNSON, Alan

Born Ince 19.2.71 Ht 5 11 Wt 11 12
Defender. From Trainee.

Season	Club		
1988–89	Wigan Ath	8	1
1989–90		33	1
1990–91		43	5

JOHNSON, David

Born Northampton 10.3.67. Ht 5 10
Wt 11 02
Defender. From Irthlingborough D.

Season	Club		
1989–90	Northampton T	7	—
1990–91		25	—

JOHNSON, Gavin

Born Eye 10.10.70 Ht 6 0 Wt 10 07
Defender. From Trainee.

Season	Club		
1988–89	Ipswich T	4	—
1989–90		6	—
1990–91		7	—

JOHNSON, Marvin

Born Wembley 29.10.68. Ht 5 11
Wt 11 06
Defender. From Apprentice.

Season	Club		
1986–87	Luton T	—	—
1987–88		9	—
1988–89		16	—
1989–90		12	—
1990–91		26	—

JOHNSON, Nigel

Born Rotherham 23.6.64. Ht 6 2
Wt 13 04
Defender. From Apprentice.

Season	Club		
1982–83	Rotherham U	11	—
1983–84		43	1
1983–84	*Nottingham F*	—	—
1984–85	Rotherham U	35	—
1985–86	Manchester C	4	—
1986–87		—	—
1987–88	Rotherham U	23	—
1988–89		26	2
1989–90		43	2
1990–91		17	1

JOHNSON, Peter

Born Harrogate 5.10.58.   Ht 5 9
Wt 11 06
Defender. From Apprentice.

Season	Club		
1976–77	Middlesbrough	—	—
1977–78		4	—
1978–79		21	—
1979–80		18	—
1980–81	Newcastle U	16	—
1981–82		—	—
1982–83		—	—
1982–83	*Bristol C*	20	—
1982–83	Doncaster R	12	—
1983–84	Darlington	44	1
1984–85		45	1
1985–86	Crewe Alex	8	—
1985–86	Exeter C	5	—
1986–87	Southend U	44	2
1987–88		39	1
1988–89		43	—
1989–90	Gillingham	45	2
1990–91		24	—

JOHNSON, Rob

Born Bedford 22.2.62.   Ht 5 7   Wt 11 03
Midfield. From Apprentice.

Season	Club		
1979–80	Luton T	—	—
1980–81		—	—
1981–82		—	—
1982–83		—	—
1983–84		2	—
1983–84	*Lincoln C*	4	—
1984–85	Luton T	—	—
1985–86		15	—
1986–87		34	—
1987–88		25	—
1988–89		21	—
1989–90	Leicester C	13	—
1990–91		12	—

JOHNSON, Tommy

Born Newcastle 15.1.71.   Ht 5 10
Wt 11 02
Forward. From Trainee. England
Under-21.

Season	Club		
1988–89	Notts Co	10	4
1989–90		40	18
1990–91		37	16

JOHNSTON, Craig

Born S. Africa 8.12.60.   Ht 5 8   Wt 10 13
Midfield. From Lake McQuarrie, Sydney
C and Apprentice. England Under-21.

Season	Club		
1977–78	Middlesbrough	5	1
1978–79		2	—
1979–80		30	5
1980–81		27	10
1980–81	Liverpool	—	—
1981–82		18	6
1982–83		33	7
1983–84		29	2
1984–85		11	—
1985–86		41	7
1986–87		28	3
1987–88		30	5
1988–89		—	—
1989–90		—	—
1990–91		—	—

JOHNSTON, Mo

Born Glasgow 30.4.63.   Ht 5 9   Wt 10 06
Forward. From Milton Battlefield.
Scotland Under-21, 36 full caps.

Season	Club		
1980–81	Partick T	—	—
1981–82		32	9
1982–83		39	22
1983–84		14	10
1983–84	Watford	29	20
1984–85		9	3
1984–85	Celtic	27	14
1985–86		32	15
1986–87		40	23
From Nantes			
1989–90	Rangers	36	15
1990–91		29	11

JOHNSTON, Sammy

Born Glasgow 13.4.67.   Ht 5 9   Wt 10 07
Midfield. From Bishopbriggs BC

Season	Club		
1984–85	St Johnstone	3	—

1985–86	....	27	2
1986–87	....	39	6
1987–88	....	39	11
1988–89	....	30	3
1989–90	....	37	7
1990–91	....	1	—

JONES, Alex

Born Blackburn 27.11.64.   Ht 6 2
Wt 12 08
Defender. From Apprentice.

1982–83	Oldham Ath................	2	—
1983–84	....	2	—
1984–85	....	5	—
1984–85	*Stockport Co*..............	3	—
1985–86	Oldham Ath................	—	—
1986–87	Preston NE................	46	1
1987–88	....	22	2
1988–89	....	30	—
1989–90	....	3	—
1989–90	Carlisle U...................	36	4
1990–91	....	26	—

JONES, Andy

Born Wrexham 9.1.63.   Ht 5 11   Wt 13 06
Forward. From Rhyl. Wales 6 full caps.

1985–86	Port Vale...................	41	12
1986–87	....	43	31
1987–88	....	6	6
1987–88	Charlton Ath	25	6
1988–89	....	9	4
1988–89	*Port Vale*..................	17	3
1989–90	Charlton Ath	25	5
1989–90	*Bristol C*.....................	4	1
1990–91	Charlton Ath	7	—
1990–91	Bournemouth..............	33	8

JONES, David

Born Wrexham 6.5.71.   Ht 5 9   Wt 11 04
Forward. From Trainee. Wales Schools.

| 1989–90 | Aston Villa................ | — | — |
| 1990–91 | .... | — | — |

JONES, David

Born Harrow 3.7.64   Ht 6 3   Wt 14 04
Forward.

1987–88	Chelsea.......................	—	—
1988–89	Bury...........................	1	—
1988–89	Leyton Orient	2	—
1988–89	Burnley	4	—
1989–90	Ipswich T	—	—
1989–90	Doncaster R................	27	12
1990–91	....	13	2

JONES, Joey

Born Llandudno 4.3.55.   Ht 5 10
Wt 11 09
Defender. From Amateur. Wales Under-
23, 72 full caps.

1972–73	Wrexham	17	—
1973–74	....	41	—
1974–75	....	40	2
1975–76	Liverpool	13	—
1976–77	....	39	3
1977–78	....	20	—
1978–79	....	—	—
1979–80	Wrexham	30	2
1980–81	....	36	3
1981–82	....	37	1
1982–83	....	36	—
1983–84	....	7	—
1982–83	Chelsea.......................	28	1
1983–84	....	34	1
1984–85	....	16	—
1985–86	Huddersfield T............	38	1
1986–87	....	30	2
1987–88	Wrexham	35	—
1988–89	....	41	8
1989–90	....	24	1
1990–91	....	21	2

JONES, Keith

Born Dulwich 14.10.64.   Ht 5 8   Wt 11 03
Midfield. From Apprentice. England
Schools, Youth.

1982–83	Chelsea.......................	2	—
1983–84	....	—	—
1984–85	....	19	2
1985–86	....	14	2
1986–87	....	17	3
1987–88	....	—	—
1987–88	Brentford	36	1

1988–89	....	40	3
1989–90	....	42	2
1990–91	....	45	6

JONES, Lee

Born Wrexham 29.5.73. Ht 5 7 Wt 9 11
Forward. From Trainee.

| 1990–91 | Wrexham .... | 18 | 5 |

JONES, Linden

Born Tredegar 5.3.61. Ht 5 6 Wt 10 08
Defender. From Apprentice. Wales
Under-21.

1978–79	Cardiff C	14	—
1979–80	....	17	1
1980–81	....	29	1
1981–82	....	36	—
1982–83	....	43	—
1983–84	....	6	—
1983–84	Newport Co	32	—
1984–85	....	44	4
1985–86	....	31	1
1986–87	....	35	—
1987–88	Reading	28	3
1988–89	....	29	3
1989–90	....	39	—
1990–91	....	27	2

JONES, Mark

Born Berinsfield 26.9.61. Ht 5 6
Wt 10 03
Midfield. From Apprentice.

1979–80	Oxford U	2	—
1980–81	....	36	1
1981–82	....	21	3
1982–83	....	26	1
1983–84	....	20	2
1984–85	....	18	—
1985–86	....	6	—
1986–87	....	—	—
1986–87	Swindon T	40	9
1987–88	....	—	—
1988–89	....	—	—
1989–90	....	—	—

| 1990–91 | Cardiff C .... | 22 | 1 |

JONES, Mark

Born Warley 22.10.61. Ht 5 8 Wt 10 08
Defender. From Apprentice.

1979–80	Aston Villa	—	—
1980–81	....	—	—
1981–82	....	2	—
1982–83	....	17	—
1983–84	....	5	—
1983–84	Brighton	6	—
1984–85	....	3	—
1984–85	Birmingham C	10	—
1985–86	....	19	—
1986–87	....	5	—
1986–87	Shrewsbury T	—	—
1987–88	Hereford U	28	—
1988–89	....	41	—
1989–90	....	41	1
1990–91	....	46	1

JONES, Murray

Born Bexley 7.10.64 Ht 6 4 Wt 14 00
Forward. From Carshalton.

1989–90	Crystal Palace	—	—
1990–91	Bristol C	—	—
1990–91	*Doncaster R*	5	—
1990–91	Exeter C	20	3

JONES, Paul

Born Walsall 6.9.65. Ht 6 1 Wt 11 04
Forward. From Apprentice.

1982–83	Walsall	2	—
1983–84	....	4	—
1984–85	....	22	—
1985–86	....	26	1
1986–87	....	27	3
1987–88	....	43	11
1988–89	....	16	—
1988–89	*Wrexham*	5	—
1989–90	Walsall	3	—
1989–90	Wolverhampton W	13	—
1990–91	....	1	—

JONES, Philip

Born Liverpool 1.12.69.   Ht 5 8   Wt 10 09
Midfield. From Trainee.

Season	Club	Apps	Goals
1987–88	Everton	1	—
1988–89		—	—
1989–90		—	—
1989–90	*Blackpool*	6	—
1990–91	Everton	—	—
1990–91	Wigan Ath	20	1

JONES, Richard

Born Pontypool 26.4.69   Ht 5 11
Wt 11 01
Defender.

Season	Club	Apps	Goals
1986–87	Newport Co	10	—
1987–88		31	1
1988–89	Hereford U	38	1
1989–90		19	3
1990–91		40	1

JONES, Rob

Born Wrexham 5.11.71.   Ht 5 11
Wt 11 00
Defender. From Schoolboy, Trainee.

Season	Club	Apps	Goals
1987–88	Crewe Alex	5	—
1988–89		19	1
1989–90		11	—
1990–91		32	1

JONES, Robert

Born Liverpool 12.11.71.
Midfield. From Crewe Alex Schoolboy.

Season	Club	Apps	Goals
1989–90	Wrexham	1	—
1990–91		6	1

JONES, Shane

Born Tredegar 8.11.72.
Midfield. From Trainee.

Season	Club	Apps	Goals
1989–90	Hereford U	15	—
1990–91		18	1

JONES, Tommy

Born Aldershot 7.10.64   Ht 5 10
Wt 11 07
Midfield. From Chelsea apprentice,
Farnborough, Weymouth.

Season	Club	Apps	Goals
1987–88	Aberdeen	28	3
1988–89		—	—
1988–89	Swindon T	40	6
1989–90		44	2
1990–91		43	—

JONES, Vaughan

Born Tonyrefail 2.9.59.   Ht 5 8   Wt 11 11
Defender. From Apprentice. Wales
Under-21.

Season	Club	Apps	Goals
1976–77	Bristol R	1	—
1977–78		—	—
1978–79		22	1
1979–80		23	1
1980–81		21	1
1981–82		34	—
1982–83	Newport Co	43	—
1983–84		25	4
1984–85	Cardiff C	11	—
1984–85	Bristol R	20	—
1985–86		32	—
1986–87		34	1
1987–88		46	3
1988–89		45	2
1989–90		46	2
1990–91		44	1

JONES, Vinny

Born Watford 5.1.65.   Ht 5 11   Wt 11 10
Midfield. From Wealdstone.

Season	Club	Apps	Goals
1986–87	Wimbledon	22	4
1987–88		24	2
1988–89		31	3
1989–90	Leeds U	45	5
1990–91		1	—
1990–91	Sheffield U	31	2

JONSSON, Siggi

Born Akranes 27.9.66. Ht 5 11 Wt 12 06
Midfield. From I A Akranes. Iceland full
caps.

Season	Club		
1984–85	Sheffield W	3	—
1985–86		10	2
1985–86	*Barnsley*	5	—
1986–87	Sheffield W	13	—
1987–88		13	1
1988–89		28	1
1989–90	Arsenal	6	—
1990–91		2	—

JORDAN, David

Born Gillingham 26.10.71. Ht 6 0
Wt 11 07
Forward. From Trainee.

Season	Club		
1989–90	Gillingham	—	—
1990–91		2	—

JOSEPH, Francis

Born Kilburn 6.3.60. Ht 5 10 Wt 12 12
Forward. From Hillingdon Bor.

Season	Club		
1980–81	Wimbledon	11	1
1981–82		40	13
1982–83	Brentford	43	24
1983–84		43	18
1984–85		3	—
1985–86		8	1
1986–87		13	1
1986–87	*Wimbledon*	5	1
1987–88	Reading	11	2
1987–88	*Bristol R*	3	—
1987–88	*Aldershot*	10	2
1988–89	Sheffield U	13	3
1988–89	Gillingham	15	1
1989–90		3	—
1989–90	Crewe Alex	16	2
1990–91	Fulham	4	—

JOSEPH, Roger

Born Paddington 24.12.65 Ht 5 11
Wt 11 10
Defender. From Juniors. England B.

Season	Club		
1984–85	Brentford	1	—
1985–86		28	1
1986–87		32	1
1987–88		43	—
1988–89	Wimbledon	31	—
1989–90		19	—
1990–91		38	—

JOYCE, Joe

Born Consett 18.3.61. Ht 5 9 Wt 10 05
Defender. From school.

Season	Club		
1979–80	Barnsley	8	—
1980–81		33	—
1981–82		20	—
1982–83		32	1
1983–84		40	1
1984–85		41	—
1985–86		40	—
1986–87		34	—
1987–88		38	2
1988–89		45	—
1989–90		—	—
1990–91		3	—
1990–91	Scunthorpe U	21	—

JOYCE, Sean

Born Doncaster 15.2.67. Ht 5 8
Wt 10 05
Midfield.

Season	Club		
1985–86	Doncaster R	15	—
1986–87		14	—
1986–87	*Exeter C*	1	—
1987–88	Doncaster R	12	1
1988–89	Torquay U	30	3
1989–90		41	5
1990–91		25	3

JOYCE, Tony

Born Wembley 24.9.71.
Defender. From Trainee.

Season	Club		
1989–90	QPR	—	—
1990–91	Aldershot	3	—

JOYCE, Warren

Born Oldham 20.1.65. Ht 5 8 Wt 11 5
Midfield. Local.

Season	Club	League Appearances/Goals		Season	Club	League Appearances/Goals	
1982–83	Bolton W	8	—				
1983–84		45	3	1986–87		13	2
1984–85		45	5	1987–88		23	16
1985–86		31	4	1988–89		29	9
1986–87		44	5	1988–89	*Ipswich T*	2	—
1987–88		11	—	1989–90	Halifax T	17	7
1987–88	Preston NE	22	—	1989–90	Hereford U	25	3
1988–89		40	9	1990–91		3	1
1989–90		44	11	1990–91	Halifax T	34	9
1990–91		42	9				

JUDGE, Alan

Born Kingsbury 14.5.60. Ht 5 11
Wt 11 06
Goalkeeper. From Amateur.

Season	Club	Apps	Goals
1977–78	Luton T	—	—
1978–79		—	—
1979–80		1	—
1980–81		2	—
1981–82		4	—
1982–83		4	—
1982–83	*Reading*	33	—
1983–84	Reading	41	—
1984–85		3	—
1984–85	Oxford U	—	—
1985–86		19	—
1985–86	*Lincoln C*	2	—
1986–87	Oxford U	9	—
1987–88		9	—
1987–88	*Cardiff C*	8	—
1988–89	Oxford U	20	—
1989–90		17	—
1990–91		6	—

JURYEFF, Ian

Born Gosport 24.11.62. Ht 5 11 Wt 12 0
Forward. From Apprentice.

Season	Club	Apps	Goals
1980–81	Southampton	—	—
1981–82		—	—
1982–83		—	—
From Sweden			
1983–84	Southampton	2	—
1983–84	*Mansfield T*	12	5
1984–85	Southampton	—	—
1984–85	*Reading*	7	1
1984–85	Orient	19	7
1985–86		27	10

KAMARA, Alan

Born Sheffield 15.7.58.   Ht 5 9   Wt 10 12
Defender. From Kiveton Park.

1979–80	York C	10	—
1980–81	Darlington	45	—
1981–82		43	—
1982–83		46	1
From York RI, Retford, Burton Alb			
1987–88	Scarborough	29	—
1988–89		44	1
1989–90		45	1
1990–91		41	—

KAMARA, Chris

Born Middlesbrough 25.12.57.   Ht 6 1
Wt 12 00
Midfield. From Apprentice.

1975–76	Portsmouth	24	4
1976–77		39	3
1977–78	Swindon T	40	10
1978–79		28	2
1979–80		34	5
1980–81		45	4
1981–82	Portsmouth	11	—
1981–82	Brentford	31	5
1982–83		44	11
1983–84		38	6
1984–85		39	6
1985–86	Swindon T	20	1
1986–87		42	3
1987–88		25	2
1988–89	Stoke C	38	4
1989–90		22	1
1989–90	Leeds U	11	1
1990–91		7	—

KANE, Paul

Born Edinburgh 20.6.65.   Ht 5 8   Wt 9 09
Midfield. From Salvesen BC. Scotland
Youth.

1982–83	Hibernian	—	—
1983–84		13	1
1984–85		34	8

1985–86		32	5
1986–87		37	1
1987–88		44	10
1988–89		35	5
1989–90		31	3
1990–91		21	—
1990–91	Oldham Ath	17	—

KAVANAGH, Jason

Born Birmingham 23.11.71   Ht 5 9
Wt 11 00
Midfield. From Birmingham C schoolboys.
FA Schools. England Youth

1988–89	Derby Co	—	—
1989–90		—	—
1990–91		11	—

KAY, John

Born Sunderland 29.1.64.   Ht 5 10
Wt 11 06
Defender. From Apprentice.

1981–82	Arsenal	—	—
1982–83		7	—
1983–84		7	—
1984–85	Wimbledon	21	1
1984–85	*Middlesbrough*	8	—
1985–86	Wimbledon	26	1
1986–87		16	—
1987–88	Sunderland	46	—
1988–89		11	—
1989–90		32	—
1990–91		30	—

KEANE, Roy

Born Cork 10.8.71.   Ht 5 10   Wt 11 03
Midfield. From Cobh Ramblers. Eire
Youth, Under-21, 1 full cap.

1990–91	Nottingham F	35	8

KEARNEY, Mark

Born Ormskirk 12.6.62.   Ht 5 10
Wt 11 00
Defender. From Marine.

Season	Club	Apps	Goals
1981–82	Everton	—	—
1982–83		—	—
1982–83	Mansfield T	11	1
1983–84		17	2
1984–85		38	4
1985–86		31	7
1986–87		43	10
1987–88		4	—
1988–89		45	2
1989–90		41	3
1990–91		20	—
1990–91	*Bury*	13	1
1990–91	Bury	9	—

KEARNS, Jamie

Born Hammersmith 28.10.71.
Defender. From Trainee.

Season	Club	Apps	Goals
1990–91	Cambridge U	1	—

KEARTON, Jason

Born Ipswich (Australia) 9.7.69.   Ht 6 1
Wt 11 10
Goalkeeper. From Brisbane Lions.

Season	Club	Apps	Goals
1988–89	Everton	—	—
1989–90		—	—
1990–91		—	—

KEE, Paul

Born Belfast 8.11.69   Ht 6 3   Wt 12 05
Goalkeeper. From Ards. Northern Ireland
7 full caps.

Season	Club	Apps	Goals
1988–89	Oxford U	—	—
1989–90		21	—
1990–91		13	—

KEELEY, John

Born Plaistow 27.7.61.   Ht 6 1   Wt 14 02
Goalkeeper. From Apprentice.

Season	Club	Apps	Goals
1979–80	Southend U	4	—
1980–81		—	—
1981–82		27	—
1982–83		7	—

Season	Club	Apps	Goals
1983–84		16	—
From Chelmsford C			
1986–87	Brighton	20	—
1987–88		46	—
1988–89		37	—
1989–90		35	—
1990–91	Oldham Ath	—	—

KEEN, Kevin

Born Amersham 25.2.67.   Ht 5 6
Wt 10 03
Midfield. From Wycombe W and
Apprentice. England Schools, Youth.

Season	Club	Apps	Goals
1983–84	West Ham U	—	—
1984–85		—	—
1985–86		—	—
1986–87		13	—
1987–88		23	1
1988–89		24	3
1989–90		44	10
1990–91		40	—

KELLY, Alan

Born Preston 11.8.68.   Ht 6 2   Wt 12 05
Goalkeeper. Eire Youth, Under-21,
Under-23.

Season	Club	Apps	Goals
1985–86	Preston NE	13	—
1986–87		22	—
1987–88		19	—
1988–89		—	—
1989–90		42	—
1990–91		23	—

KELLY, David

Born Birmingham 25.11.65.   Ht 5 11
Wt 11 03
Forward. From Alvechurch. Eire B,
Under-21, Under-23, 10 full caps.

Season	Club	Apps	Goals
1983–84	Walsall	6	3
1984–85		32	7
1985–86		28	10
1986–87		42	23
1987–88		39	20
1988–89	West Ham U	25	6

1989–90	....	16	1
1989–90	Leicester C..................	10	7
1990–91	....	44	14

KELLY, Gary

Born Fulwood 3.8.66. Ht 5 10 Wt 12 03
Goalkeeper. From Apprentice. Eire B,
Under-21.

1984–85	Newcastle U................	—	—
1985–86	....	—	—
1986–87	....	3	—
1987–88	....	37	—
1988–89	....	9	—
1988–89	*Blackpool*	5	—
1989–90	Newcastle U................	4	—
1989–90	Bury...........................	38	—
1990–91	....	46	—

KELLY, Gavin

Born Beverley 29.9.68. Ht 6 0 Wt 12 13
Goalkeeper.

1987–88	Hull C........................	—	—
1988–89	....	3	—
1989–90	....	8	—
1989–90	*Bristol R*......................	—	—
1990–91	Bristol R	7	—

KELLY, James

Born Liverpool 14.2.73. Ht 5 7 Wt 11 10
Midfield. From Trainee.

| 1990–91 | Wrexham .... | 12 | — |

KELLY, James

Born Stirling 4.9.71 Ht 5 11 Wt 11 4
Midfield. From Garioch Juv

| 1989–90 | Airdrieonians .... | 1 | — |
| 1990–91 | .... | 1 | — |

KELLY, John

Born Bebbington 20.10.60. Ht 5 10
Wt 10 09
Forward. From Cammell Laird.

1979–80	Tranmere R	28	4
1980–81	....	29	5
1981–82	....	7	—
1981–82	Preston NE.................	30	5
1982–83	....	29	2
1983–84	....	34	13
1984–85	....	37	7
1985–86	Chester C...................	43	8
1986–87	....	42	9
1987–88	Swindon T	7	1
1987–88	Oldham Ath...............	10	—
1988–89	....	42	6
1989–90	Walsall.......................	26	1
1989–90	*Huddersfield T*............	10	—
1990–91	Walsall.......................	13	—
1990–91	Huddersfield T...........	4	—

KELLY, Mark

Born Sutton 27.11.69. Ht 5 8 Wt 9 10
Forward. England Youth, Eire, B, Under-
21, Under-23, 4 full caps.

1986–87	Portsmouth	—	—
1987–88	....	3	—
1988–89	....	28	1
1989–90	....	13	—
1990–91	....	5	1
1990–91	*Tottenham H*...............	—	—

KELLY, Mark

Born Blackpool 7.10.66. Ht 5 9
Wt 10 05
Midfield.

1985–86	Shrewsbury T..............	—	—
1986–87	....	—	—
1987–88	Cardiff C....................	36	1
1988–89	....	28	—
1989–90	....	41	1
1990–91	Fulham	18	—

KELLY, Norman

Born Belfast 10.10.70 Ht 5 8 Wt 11 00
Midfield. From Trainee. Northern Ireland
Youth.

| 1987–88 | Oldham Ath................ | 1 | — |

1988–89	....	1	—
1989–90	....	—	—
1989–90	*Wigan Ath*....................	4	—
1990–91	Oldham Ath...............	—	—
1990–91	Dunfermline Ath	2	—

KELLY, Tom

Born Bellshill 28.3.64. Ht 5 10   Wt 11 10
Defender. From Hibs.

1985–86	Hartlepool U	15	—
1986–87	Torquay U.................	38	—
1987–88	....	38	—
1988–89	....	44	—
1989–90	York C.......................	35	2
1989–90	Exeter C.....................	12	2
1990–91	....	22	1

KELLY, Tony

Born Meridan 14.2.66.
Midfield. From St. Albans C.

1989–90	Stoke C......................	9	—
1990–91	....	29	3

KELLY, Tony

Born Prescot 1.10.64. Ht 5 1   Wt 11 09
Midfield. From Liverpool Apprentice.

1983–84	Derby Co....................	—	—
1983–84	Wigan Ath	29	2
1984–85	....	40	4
1985–86	....	32	9
1985–86	Stoke C......................	1	—
1986–87	....	35	4
1987–88	WBA.........................	26	1
1988–89	....	—	—
1988–89	*Chester C*....................	5	—
1988–89	*Colchester U*...............	13	2
1988–89	Shrewsbury T..............	20	5
1989–90	....	43	5
1990–91	....	38	5

KENDALL, Mark

Born Blackwood 20.9.58.   Ht 6 0
Wt 12 04
Goalkeeper. From Apprentice. Wales
Schools, Under-21.

1976–77	Tottenham H	—	—
1977–78	....	—	—
1978–79	....	23	—
1979–80	....	2	—
1979–80	*Chesterfield*	9	—
1980–81	Tottenham H	4	—
1980–81	Newport Co................	28	—
1981–82	....	46	—
1982–83	....	44	—
1983–84	....	43	—
1984–85	....	44	—
1985–86	....	46	—
1986–87	....	21	—
1986–87	Wolverhampton W	24	—
1987–88	....	46	—
1988–89	....	36	—
1989–90	....	41	—
1990–91	Swansea C..................	11	—

KENNA, Jeff

Born Dublin 27.8.70. Ht 5 11   Wt 11 07
Defender. From Trainee.

1988–89	Southampton	—	—
1989–90	....	—	—
1990–91	....	2	—

KENNEDY, Alan

Born Sunderland 31.8.54.   Ht 5 9
Wt 10 07
Defender. From Apprentice. England
Under-23, B, 2 full caps.

1972–73	....	2	—
1973–74	Newcastle U...............	18	—
1974–75	....	28	3
1975–76	....	42	1
1976–77	....	42	2
1977–78	....	26	3
1978–79	Liverpool	37	3
1979–80	....	37	1
1980–81	....	19	2
1981–82	....	34	3
1982–83	....	42	3
1983–84	....	42	2
1984–85	....	32	1
1985–86	....	8	—
1985–86	Sunderland.................	32	2

1986–87	....	22	—
1987–88	Hartlepool U	5	—
1987–88	Wigan Ath	22	—
From Colne Dynamoes			
1989–90	Wrexham	7	—
1990–91	....	9	—

KENNEDY, Andy

Born Stirling 8.10.64.   Ht 6 1   Wt 11 10
Forward. From Sauchie Ath.

1983–84	Rangers......................	13	3
1984–85	....	2	—
1984–85	Birmingham C	7	4
1985–86	....	32	6
1986–87	....	9	1
1986–87	*Sheffield U*..................	9	1
1987–88	Birmingham C	28	7
1988–89	Blackburn R	25	10
1989–90	....	34	13
1990–91	Watford	18	3

KENNEDY, Mick

Born Salford 9.4.61.   Ht 5 10   Wt 11 08
Midfield. From Apprentice. Eire Under-21,
2 caps.

1978–79	Halifax T	30	—
1979–80	....	46	4
1980–81	Huddersfield T	42	2
1981–82	....	39	7
1982–83	Middlesbrough............	38	5
1983–84	....	30	—
1984–85	Portsmouth	37	—
1985–86	....	39	2
1986–87	....	35	2
1987–88	....	18	—
1987–88	Bradford C	15	1
1988–89	....	30	1
1988–89	Leicester C................	9	—
1989–90	Luton T	32	—
1990–91	Stoke C	32	3

KENT, Kevin

Born Stoke 19.3.65.   Ht 5 11   Wt 11 00
Forward. From Apprentice.

| 1982–83 | WBA .... | — | — |

1983–84	....	2	—
1984–85	Newport Co................	33	1
1985–86	Mansfield T................	34	8
1986–87	....	46	6
1987–88	....	45	10
1988–89	....	39	5
1989–90	....	38	3
1990–91	....	27	4
1990–91	Port Vale...................	11	—

KEOWN, Martin

Born Oxford 24.7.66.   Ht 6 1   Wt 13 04
Defender. From Apprentice. England
Youth, Under-21.

1983–84	Arsenal........................	—	—
1984–85	....	—	—
1984–85	*Brighton*	16	—
1985–86	Arsenal.......................	22	—
1985–86	*Brighton*	7	1
1986–87	Aston Villa.................	36	—
1987–88	....	42	3
1988–89	....	34	—
1989–90	Everton	20	—
1990–91	....	24	—

KERFOOT, Jason

Born Preston 17.4.73.
Defender. From Trainee.

| 1990–91 | Preston NE................ | 1 | — |

KERNAGHAN, Alan

Born Otley 25.4.67.   Ht 6 2   Wt 13 00
Forward. From Apprentice.

1984–85	Middlesbrough............	8	1
1985–86	....	6	—
1986–87	....	13	—
1987–88	....	35	6
1988–89	....	23	—
1989–90	....	37	4
1990–91	....	24	—
1990–91	*Charlton Ath*	13	—

KERR, Dylan

Born Valetta 14.1.67   Ht 5 11   Wt 12 05
Defender. From Arcadia Shepherds.

Season	Club	League Appearances/Goals	
1988–89	Leeds U	3	—
1989–90		5	—
1990–91		—	—

KERR, Paul

Born Portsmouth 9.6.64.   Ht 5 8
Wt 11 03
Forward. From Apprentice.

Season	Club	League Appearances/Goals	
1982–83	Aston Villa	—	—
1983–84		2	—
1984–85		10	—
1985–86		6	1
1986–87		6	2
1986–87	Middlesbrough	20	—
1987–88		44	5
1988–89		20	1
1989–90		17	1
1990–91		24	6
1990–91	Millwall	10	2

KERSLAKE, David

Born London 19.6.66.   Ht 5 8   Wt 11 00
Midfield. From Apprentice. England
Schools, Youth, Under-21.

Season	Club	League Appearances/Goals	
1983–84	QPR	—	—
1984–85		1	—
1985–86		14	1
1986–87		3	—
1987–88		18	5
1988–89		21	—
1989–90		1	—
1989–90	Swindon T	28	—
1990–91		37	—

KEVAN, David

Born Wigtown 31.8.68.   Ht 5 8   Wt 9 10
Midfield. From Apprentice.

Season	Club	League Appearances/Goals	
1985–86	Notts Co	3	—
1986–87		33	1
1987–88		32	—
1988–89		18	2
1989–90		3	—
1989–90	*Cardiff C*	7	—
1989–90	Stoke C	17	—

Season	Club	League Appearances/Goals	
1990–91		5	—
1990–91	*Maidstone U*	3	—

KIDD, Walter

Born Edinburgh 10.3.58.   Ht 5 11
Wt 12 03
Defender. From Newtongrange Star.

Season	Club	League Appearances/Goals	
1977–78	Hearts	23	—
1978–79		30	—
1979–80		34	2
1980–81		25	1
1981–82		30	—
1982–83		37	—
1983–84		31	1
1984–85		33	1
1985–86		28	—
1986–87		35	—
1987–88		18	—
1988–89		20	—
1989–90		17	1
1990–91		4	—

KIELY, Dean

Born Manchester 10.10.70   Ht 6 1
Wt 11 08
Goalkeeper. From WBA schoolboy. FA
Schools. England Youth.

Season	Club	League Appearances/Goals	
1987–88	Coventry C	—	—
1988–89		—	—
1989–90		—	—
1989–90	*Ipswich T*	—	—
1989–90	*York C*	—	—
1990–91	York C	17	—

KILCLINE, Brian

Born Nottingham 7.5.62.   Ht 6 2
Wt 12 00
Defender. From Apprentice. England
Under-21.

Season	Club	League Appearances/Goals	
1979–80	Notts Co	16	1
1980–81		42	1
1981–82		36	3
1982–83		40	3
1983–84		24	1

Season	Club	App	Goals
1984–85	Coventry C	26	2
1985–86		32	7
1986–87		29	3
1987–88		28	8
1988–89		33	4
1989–90		11	1
1990–91		14	3

KILNER, Andy

Born Bolton 11.10.66.
Forward. From Apprentice.

Season	Club	App	Goals
1985–86	Burnley	5	—

From Sweden

Season	Club	App	Goals
1990–91	Stockport Co	24	11

KIMBLE, Alan

Born Poole 6.8.66. Ht 5 9 Wt 11 07
Defender.

Season	Club	App	Goals
1984–85	Charlton Ath	6	—
1985–86		—	—
1985–86	*Exeter C*	1	—
1986–87	Cambridge U	35	—
1987–88		41	2
1988–89		45	6
1989–90		44	8
1990–91		43	4

KIMBLE, Garry

Born Poole 6.8.66. Ht 5 8 Wt 11 00
Forward.

Season	Club	App	Goals
1984–85	Charlton Ath	9	1
1985–86		—	—
1985–86	*Exeter C*	1	—
1986–87	Cambridge U	29	2
1987–88		12	—
1987–88	Doncaster R	34	1
1988–89		31	—
1989–90	Fulham	3	—
1989–90	Maidstone U	—	—
1989–90	Gillingham	14	—
1990–91		34	1

KING, Adam

Born Hillingdon 4.10.69 Ht 5 11
Wt 12 12
Forward. From Trainee. English Youth.

Season	Club	App	Goals
1988–89	West Ham U	—	—
1989–90		—	—
1989–90	Plymouth Arg	8	—
1990–91		8	—
1990–91	*Bristol R*	—	—

KING, Phil

Born Bristol 28.12.67. Ht 5 8 Wt 11 09
Defender. From Apprentice. England B.

Season	Club	App	Goals
1984–85	Exeter C	16	—
1985–86		11	—
1986–87	Torquay U	24	3
1986–87	Swindon T	21	—
1987–88		44	1
1988–89		37	2
1989–90		14	1
1989–90	Sheffield W	25	—
1990–91		43	—

KINNAIRD, Paul

Born Glasgow 11.11.66. Ht 5 8 Wt 10 10
Forward. From Apprentice.

Season	Club	App	Goals
1984–85	Norwich C	—	—
1985–86	Dundee U	—	—
1986–87		7	—
1987–88		11	—
1987–88	Motherwell	10	—
1988–89		24	—
1988–89	St Mirren	6	—
1989–90		25	—
1990–91		23	4

KIRK, Steve

Born Kirkcaldy 3.1.63. Ht 5 11
Wt 11 04
Midfield. From Buckhaven Hibs.

Season	Club	App	Goals
1979–80	East Fife	25	2
1980–81	Stoke C	—	—
1981–82		12	—
1982–83	Partick T	—	—
1982–83	East Fife	25	8
1983–84		33	5
1984–85		38	8
1985–86		39	14

1986–87	Motherwell	35	10
1987–88		38	4
1988–89		33	14
1989–90		34	8
1990–91		29	2

KIRKWOOD, David

Born St Andrews 27.8.67   Ht 5 10
Wt 11 07
Midfield. From Leven Royal Colts.
Scotland Under-21.

1983–84	East Fife	14	2
1984–85		17	4
1985–86		34	2
1986–87		35	2
1987–88	Rangers	4	—
1988–89		2	—
1989–90	Hearts	19	—
1990–91		9	1
1990–91	Airdrieonians	16	—

KITE, Phil

Born Bristol 26.10.62.   Ht 6 3   Wt 13 03
Goalkeeper. From Apprentice. England
Youth.

1980–81	Bristol R	4	—
1981–82		27	—
1982–83		46	—
1983–84		19	—
1983–84	*Tottenham H*	—	—
1984–85	Southampton	1	—
1985–86		3	—
1985–86	*Middlesbrough*	2	—
1986–87	Gillingham	17	—
1987–88		26	—
1988–89		27	—
1989–90	Bournemouth	7	—
1990–91	Sheffield U	7	—

KITSON, Paul

Born Co Durham 9.1.71.   Ht 5 11
Wt 10 12
Forward. From Trainee. England
Under-21.

| 1988–89 | Leicester C | — | — |

| 1989–90 | | 13 | — |
| 1990–91 | | 7 | — |

KIWOMYA, Chris

Born Huddersfield 2.12.69.   Ht 5 9
Wt 10 07
Forward.

1986–87	Ipswich T	—	—
1987–88		—	—
1988–89		26	2
1989–90		29	5
1990–91		37	10

KNIGHT, Alan

Born Balham 3.6.61.   Ht 6 0   Wt 13 00
Goalkeeper. From Apprentice. England
Youth, Under-21.

1977–78	Portsmouth	1	—
1978–79		—	—
1979–80		8	—
1980–81		1	—
1981–82		45	—
1982–83		46	—
1983–84		42	—
1984–85		42	—
1985–86		38	—
1986–87		42	—
1987–88		36	—
1988–89		32	—
1989–90		46	—
1990–91		22	—

KNIGHT, Ian

Born Hartlepool 26.10.66.   Ht 6 2
Wt 13 11
Defender. From Apprentice. England
Under-21.

1984–85	Barnsley	—	—
1985–86	Sheffield W	4	—
1986–87		15	—
1987–88		—	—
1988–89		2	—
1989–90		—	—
1989–90	*Scunthorpe U*	2	—

1989–90	Grimsby T	9	1
1990–91		8	1

KNIGHT, Keith

Born Cheltenham 16.2.69 Ht 5 8
Wt 10 09
Forward. From Cheltenham T.

1988–89	Reading	29	7
1989–90		13	1
1990–91		1	—

KNILL, Alan

Born Slough 8.10.64. Ht 6 4 Wt 11 10
Defender. From Apprentice. Wales Youth,
1 full cap.

1982–83	Southampton	—	—
1983–84		—	—
1984–85	Halifax T	44	1
1985–86		33	2
1986–87		41	3
1987–88	Swansea C	46	1
1988–89		43	2
1989–90	Bury	43	1
1990–91		20	1

KNOWLES, Darren

Born Sheffield 8.10.70. Ht 5 6 Wt 10 01
Midfield. From Trainee.

1989–90	Sheffield U	—	—
1989–90	Stockport Co	9	—
1990–91		12	—

KONTCHELSKIS, Andrej

Born Kirowgrad 23.1.69.
Midfield. From Dyhamo Kiev. USSR full
caps.

1990–91	Manchester U	1	—

KOZMA, Istvan

Born Paszto, Hungary 3.12.64. Ht 6 00
Wt 11 13
Midfield. From Ujpest Dozsa, Bordeaux.
Hungary full caps.

1989–90	Dunfermline Ath	33	6
1990–91		34	2

KRISTENSEN, Bjorn

Born Malling 10.10.63 Ht 6 1 Wt 12 05
Defender. From Aarhus. Denmark full
caps.

1988–89	Newcastle U	5	—
1989–90		33	3
1990–91		40	1

KRIVOKAPIC, Miodrag

Born Niksic 6.9.59 Ht 6 1 Wt 12 12
Defender. From Red Star Belgrade.
Yugoslavia full caps.

1988–89	Dundee U	24	1
1989–90		26	—
1990–91		24	—

KRUSZYNSKI, Detsi

Born Divschav 14.10.61 Ht 6 0 Wt 12 12
Midfield. From Homburg.

1988–89	Wimbledon	16	—
1989–90		27	2
1990–91		27	2

KUHL, Martin

Born Frimley 10.1.65. Ht 5 11 Wt 11 13
Midfield. From Apprentice.

1982–83	Birmingham C	2	—
1983–84		22	1
1984–85		27	2
1985–86		37	1
1986–87		23	1
1986–87	Sheffield U	10	1
1987–88		28	3
1987–88	Watford	4	—
1988–89		—	—
1988–89	Portsmouth	32	1
1989–90		40	9
1990–91		41	13

KUZNETSOV, Oleg

Born Kiev 2.3.63
Defender. From Dinamo Kiev

1990–91 Rangers...................... 2 —

LAKE, Michael

Born Manchester 6.11.66.   Ht 6 1
Wt 13 07
Midfield. From Macclesfield T.

| 1989–90 | Sheffield U | 4 | — |
| 1990–91 | | 7 | — |

LAKE, Paul

Born Manchester 28.10.68.   Ht 6 0
Wt 12 02
Midfield. From Trainee. England
Under-21.

1986–87	Manchester C	3	1
1987–88		33	3
1988–89		38	3
1989–90		31	—
1990–91		3	—

LAMB, Alan

Born Gateshead 30.10.70.   Ht 5 10
Wt 11 12
Forward.

1987–88	Nottingham F	—	—
1988–89		—	—
1988–89	*Hereford U*	10	2
1989–90	Nottingham F	—	—
1989–90	Hartlepool U	10	—
1990–91		4	—

LAMBERT, Matthew

Born Morecambe 28.9.71.
Defender. From Trainee.

| 1990–91 | Preston NE | 5 | — |

LAMBERT, Paul

Born Glasgow 7.8.69.   Ht 5 8   Wt 9 08
Midfield. From Linwood Rangers BC.
Scotland Under-21

| 1985–86 | St Mirren | 1 | — |
| 1986–87 | | 36 | 2 |

Season	Club	Apps	Goals
1987–88		36	2
1988–89		16	2
1989–90		25	3
1990–91		31	2

LANCASHIRE, Graham

Born Blackpool 19.10.72.
Forward. From Trainee.

Season	Club	Apps	Goals
1990–91	Burnley	1	—

LANCASTER, Dave

Born Preston 8.9.61. Ht 6 3 Wt 14 00
Forward. From Colne Dynamoes.

Season	Club	Apps	Goals
1990–91	Blackpool	8	1
1990–91	*Chesterfield*	12	4

LANE, Martin

Born Altrincham 12.4.61. Ht 5 9
Wt 11 04
Defender. From Amateur.

Season	Club	Apps	Goals
1979–80	Manchester U	—	—
1980–81		—	—
1981–82		—	—
1982–83	Chester	41	2
1983–84		38	—
1984–85		31	—
1985–86		44	1
1986–87		21	—
1986–87	Coventry C	1	—
1987–88		2	—
1988–89		—	—
1988–89	*Wrexham*	6	—
1988–89	Chester C	23	—
1989–90		36	—
1990–91		40	—

LANGE, Tony

Born London 10.12.64. Ht 6 0 Wt 12 09
Goalkeeper. From Apprentice.

Season	Club	Apps	Goals
1982–83	Charlton Ath	—	—
1983–84		6	—
1984–85		2	—
1985–86		4	—
1985–86	*Aldershot*	7	—
1986–87	Aldershot	45	—
1987–88		35	—
1988–89		45	—
1989–90	Wolverhampton W	5	—
1990–91		3	—
1990–91	*Aldershot*	2	—

LANGLEY, Kevin

Born St. Helens 24.5.64. Ht 6 1
Wt 10 03
Midfield. From Apprentice.

Season	Club	Apps	Goals
1981–82	Wigan Ath	2	—
1982–83		28	2
1983–84		44	1
1984–85		43	1
1985–86		43	2
1986–87	Everton	16	2
1986–87	*Manchester C*	9	—
1987–88	Manchester C	—	—
1987–88	*Chester C*	9	—
1987–88	Birmingham C	7	—
1988–89		36	2,
1989–90		33	—
1990–91		—	—
1990–91	Wigan Ath	39	2

LANGLEY, Richard

Born London 20.3.65. Ht 5 7 Wt 11 05
Defender. From Corinthian C.

Season	Club	Apps	Goals
1986–87	Fulham	1	—
1987–88		15	—
1988–89		19	—
1989–90		11	—
1990–91		4	—

LAW, Brian

Born Merthyr 1.1.70. Ht 6 2 Wt 11 12
Defender. From Apprentice. Wales Under-21, 1 full cap.

Season	Club	Apps	Goals
1987–88	QPR	1	—
1988–89		6	—
1989–90		10	—

1990–91		3	—

LAW, Nicky

Born London 8.9.61. Ht 6 0 Wt 13 05
Defender. From Apprentice.

1979–80	Arsenal	—	—
1980–81		—	—
1981–82	Barnsley	19	—
1982–83		28	—
1983–84		31	1
1984–85		35	—
1985–86		1	—
1985–86	Blackpool	39	1
1986–87		27	—
1986–87	Plymouth Arg	12	2
1987–88		26	3
1988–89	Notts Co	44	4
1989–90		3	—
1989–90	*Scarborough*	12	—
1990–91	Rotherham U	32	2

LAWFORD, Craig

Born Dewsbury 25.11.72. Ht 5 10
Wt 11 10
Defender. From Trainee.

1989–90	Bradford C	1	—
1990–91		—	—

LAWRENCE, Alan

Born Edinburgh 19.8.62 Ht 5 7 Wt 10 6
Forward. From Easthouses BC

1984–85	Meadowbank T	35	—
1985–86		38	17
1986–87		29	6
1986–87	Dundee	4	1
1987–88		22	1
1988–89		10	—
1988–89	Airdrieonians	7	2
1989–90		34	9
1990–91		38	13

LAWRENCE, George

Born London 14.9.62. Ht 5 10 Wt 13 05
Forward. From Apprentice.

1980–81	Southampton	—	—
1981–82		4	—
1981–82	*Oxford U*	15	4
1982–83	Southampton	6	1
1982–83	Oxford U	22	9
1983–84		34	9
1984–85		7	3
1984–85	Southampton	11	1
1985–86		21	2
1986–87		36	8
1987–88	Millwall	17	4
1988–89		11	—
1989–90	Bournemouth	33	3
1990–91		34	2

LAWS, Brian

Born Wallsend 14.10.61. Ht 5 9
Wt 11 00
Defender. From Apprentice. England B.

1979–80	Burnley	1	—
1980–81		42	2
1981–82		44	6
1982–83		38	4
1983–84	Huddersfield T	31	—
1984–85		25	1
1984–85	Middlesbrough	11	1
1985–86		42	2
1986–87		26	8
1987–88		28	1
1988–89	Nottingham F	22	1
1989–90		38	3
1990–91		32	—

LE SAUX, Graeme

Born Jersey 17.10.68. Ht 6 0 Wt 12 00
Defender. England B, Under-21.

1987–88	Chelsea	—	—
1988–89		1	—
1989–90		7	1
1990–91		28	4

LE TISSIER, Matthew

Born Guernsey 14.10.68. Ht 6 0
Wt 11 06
Forward. From Vale Recreation, Trainee.
England Youth, B.

1986–87	Southampton	24	6
1987–88		19	—
1988–89		28	9
1989–90		35	20
1990–91		35	19

LEABURN, Carl

Born Lewisham 30.3.69.   Ht 6 3
Wt 11 03
Forward. From Apprentice. England Youth.

1986–87	Charlton Ath	3	1
1987–88		12	—
1988–89		32	2
1989–90		13	—
1989–90	*Northampton T.*	9	—
1990–91	Charlton Ath	20	1

LEADBITTER, Chris

Born Middlesbrough 17.10.67.   Ht 5 9
Wt 10 07
Forward. From Apprentice.

1985–86	Grimsby T	—	—
1986–87	Hereford U	6	—
1987–88		30	1
1988–89	Cambridge U	31	6
1989–90		43	4
1990–91		39	1

LEANING, Andy

Born York 18.5.63.   Ht 6 1   Wt 14 07
Goalkeeper. From Rowntree Mackintosh.

1984–85	York C	—	—
1985–86		30	—
1986–87		39	—
1987–88	Sheffield U	21	—
1988–89		—	—
1988–89	Bristol C	6	—
1989–90		19	—
1990–91		29	—

LEE, Chris

Born Halifax 18.6.71.   Ht 5 10   Wt 11 07
Midfield. From Trainee.

1989–90	Bradford C	—	—
1990–91	Rochdale	26	2
1990–91	Scarborough	9	—

LEE, Dave

Born Manchester 5.11.67.   Ht 5 8
Wt 10 02
Midfield. From Blackburn schools.

1984–85	Bury	—	—
1985–86		1	—
1986–87		30	4
1987–88		40	3
1988–89		45	4
1989–90		45	8
1990–91		45	15

LEE, David

Born Kingswood 26.11.69   Ht 6 3
Wt 13 12
Defender. From Trainee. England Youth, Under-21.

1988–89	Chelsea	20	4
1989–90		30	1
1990–91		21	1

LEE, Iain

Born Hamilton 7.7.67   Ht 5 10   Wt 10 7
Forward. From Darvel J

1988–89	Alloa	30	2
1989–90		36	4
1990–91	St Johnstone	5	—

LEE, Jason

Born Newham 9.5.71.   Ht 6 3   Wt 13 08
Forward. From Trainee.

1989–90	Charlton Ath	1	—
1990–91		—	—
1990–91	*Stockport Co*	2	—
1990–91	Lincoln C	17	3

LEE, Raymond

Born Bristol 19.9.70   Ht 5 8   Wt 11 12
Midfield. From Trainee.

Season	Club	App	Goals
1988–89	Arsenal	—	—
1989–90		—	—
1990–91	Scarborough	10	—

LEE, Robert

Born West Ham 1.2.66. Ht 5 10
Wt 11 13
Forward. From Hornchurch. England
Under-21.

Season	Club	App	Goals
1983–84	Charlton Ath	11	4
1984–85		39	10
1985–86		35	8
1986–87		33	3
1987–88		23	2
1988–89		31	5
1989–90		37	1
1990–91		43	13

LEE, Sammy

Born Liverpool 7.2.59. Ht 5 7 Wt 10 01
Midfield. From Apprentice. England
Youth, Under-21, 14 full caps.

Season	Club	App	Goals
1976–77	Liverpool	—	—
1977–78		2	1
1978–79		2	—
1979–80		7	—
1980–81		37	—
1981–82		35	3
1982–83		40	3
1983–84		42	2
1984–85		17	—
1985–86		15	—
1986–87	QPR	30	—
From Osasuna			
1989–90	Southampton	2	—
1990–91		—	—
1990–91	Bolton W	4	—

LEGG, Andy

Born Neath 28.7.66. Ht 5 8 Wt 10 07
Midfield. From Briton Ferry

Season	Club	App	Goals
1988–89	Swansea C	6	—
1989–90		26	3
1990–91		39	5

LEIGHTON, Jim

Born Johnstone 24.7.58. Ht 6 1
Wt 12 09
Goalkeeper. From Dalry Thistle. Scotland
Under-21, 58 full caps.

Season	Club	App	Goals
1978–79	Aberdeen	11	—
1979–80		1	—
1980–81		35	—
1981–82		36	—
1982–83		35	—
1983–84		36	—
1984–85		34	—
1985–86		26	—
1986–87		42	—
1987–88		44	—
1988–89	Manchester U	38	—
1989–90		35	—
1990–91		—	—
1990–91	*Arsenal*	—	—

LEISHMAN, Graham

Born Manchester 6.4.68 Ht 5 9 Wt 10 07
Forward. From Irlam T.

Season	Club	App	Goals
1988–89	Mansfield T	12	1
1989–90		4	1
1990–91		11	1

LEITCH, Scott

Born Motherwell 6.10.69 Ht 5 9 Wt 11 4
Forward. From Shettleston J

Season	Club	App	Goals
1990–91	Dunfermline Ath	13	3

LEMON, Paul

Born Middlesbrough 3.6.66. Ht 5 10
Wt 11 06
Forward. From Apprentice.

Season	Club	App	Goals
1984–85	Sunderland	11	—
1984–85	*Carlisle U*	2	—
1985–86	Sunderland	5	—
1986–87		32	5
1987–88		41	9
1988–89		18	1
1989–90		—	—

Season	Club		App	Goals
1989–90	*Walsall*		2	—
1989–90	*Reading*		3	—
1990–91	Sunderland		—	—
1990–91	Chesterfield		39	2

LENNON, Daniel

Born Whitburn 6.4.69   Ht 5 5   Wt 9 5
Midfield. From Hutchison Vale BC

Season	Club		App	Goals
1987–88	Hibernian		1	—
1988–89			1	—
1989–90			—	—
1990–91			6	—

LENNON, Neil

Born Lurgan 25.6.71.   Ht 5 9   Wt 11 06
Defender. From Trainee. Northern Ireland
Under-23.

Season	Club		App	Goals
1987–88	Manchester C		1	—
1988–89			—	—
1989–90			—	—
1990–91	Crewe Alex		34	3

LEONARD, Mark

Born St Helens 27.9.62.   Ht 5 11
Wt 11 10
Forward. From Witton Albion.

Season	Club		App	Goals
1981–82	Everton		—	—
1982–83			—	—
1982–83	*Tranmere R*		7	—
1983–84	Crewe Alex		38	10
1984–85			16	5
1984–85	Stockport Co		23	4
1985–86			44	20
1986–87			6	—
1986–87	Bradford C		24	3
1987–88			28	10
1988–89			44	7
1989–90			24	5
1990–91			18	4

LEONARD, Mick

Born Carshalton 9.5.59.   Ht 5 11
Wt 11 00
Goalkeeper. From Epsom & Ewell

Season	Club		App	Goals
1976–77	Halifax T		19	—
1977–78			20	—
1978–79			25	—
1979–80			5	—
1979–80	Notts Co		9	—
1980–81			4	—
1981–82			—	—
1982–83			6	—
1983–84			18	—
1984–85			31	—
1985–86			23	—
1986–87			41	—
1987–88			45	—
1988–89			27	—
1988–89	Chesterfield		16	—
1989–90			46	—
1990–91			30	—
1990–91	*Halifax T*		3	—

LEVEIN, Craig

Born Dunfermline 22.10.64.   Ht 6 0
Wt 11 04
Defender. From Lochore Welfare.
Scotland Youth, Under-21, 6 full caps.

Season	Club		App	Goals
1981–82	Cowdenbeath		15	—
1982–83			30	—
1983–84			15	—
1983–84	Hearts		22	—
1984–85			36	1
1985–86			33	2
1986–87			12	—
1987–88			21	—
1988–89			9	—
1989–90			35	—
1990–91			33	4

LEVER, Mark

Born Beverley 29.3.70   Ht 6 3   Wt 12 08
Defender. From Trainee.

Season	Club		App	Goals
1987–88	Grimsby T		1	—
1988–89			37	2
1989–90			38	2
1990–91			40	2

LEWIS, Allan

Born Pontypridd 31.5.71.   Ht 6 2
Wt 13 00
Defender. From Trainee.

| 1989–90 | Cardiff C | 11 | — |
| 1990–91 | | 27 | — |

LEWIS, Dudley

Born Swansea 17.11.62.   Ht 5 11
Wt 10 10
Defender. From Apprentice. Wales
Schools, Under-21, 1 full cap.

1979–80	Swansea C	—	—
1980–81		12	—
1981–82		1	—
1982–83		23	1
1983–84		37	—
1984–85		43	1
1985–86		24	—
1986–87		32	—
1987–88		18	—
1988–89		40	—
1989–90	Huddersfield T	28	—
1990–91		6	—

LEWIS, Mickey

Born Birmingham 15.2.65.   Ht 5 6
Wt 10 10
Midfield. From school. England Youth.

1981–82	WBA	4	—
1982–83		5	—
1983–84		14	—
1984–85		1	—
1984–85	Derby Co	22	—
1985–86		5	1
1986–87		—	—
1987–88		16	—
1988–89	Oxford U	36	—
1989–90		45	1
1990–91		34	1

LEWORTHY, David

Born Portsmouth 22.10.62.   Ht 5 9
Wt 12 00
Forward. From Apprentice.

1980–81	Portsmouth	—	—
1981–82		1	—
From Fareham TH			
1984–85	Tottenham H	6	3
1985–86		5	—
1985–86	Oxford U	7	4
1986–87		18	3
1987–88		—	—
1987–88	*Shrewsbury T*	6	3
1988–89	Oxford U	12	1
1989–90	Reading	28	7
1990–91		10	—

LIGHTFOOT, Chris

Born Wimwick 1.4.70.   Ht 6 1   Wt 12 00
Midfield. From Trainee.

1987–88	Chester C	16	1
1988–89		36	7
1989–90		40	1
1990–91		37	2

LILLIS, Jason

Born Chatham 1.10.69.   Ht 5 11
Wt 11 10
Midfield. From Trainee.

1987–88	Gillingham	7	—
1988–89		22	3
1989–90	Maidstone U	33	14
1990–91		19	—
1990–91	*Carlisle U*	4	1

LILLIS, Mark

Born Manchester 17.1.60.   Ht 6 0
Wt 13 06
Forward. Local.

1978–79	Huddersfield T	12	—
1979–80		—	—
1980–81		34	7
1981–82		42	5
1982–83		46	20
1983–84		37	11
1984–85		35	13
1985–86	Manchester C	39	11
1986–87	Derby Co	14	1

1987–88	....	1	—
1987–88	Aston Villa..................	29	4
1988–89	....	2	—
1989–90	....	—	—
1989–90	Scunthorpe U	29	13
1990–91	....	39	10

LIM, Harvey

Born Halesworth 30.8.67.   Ht 6 0
Wt 13 07
Goalkeeper. From Apprentice.

1984–85	Norwich C	—	—
1985–86	....	—	—
1985–86	*Plymouth Arg*	—	—
1986–87	Norwich C	—	—
1987–88	....	—	—
From Sweden			
1989–90	Gillingham	4	—
1990–91	....	39	—

LIMBER, Nicholas

Born Doncaster 23.1.74.
Midfield. From Trainee.

| 1990–91 | Doncaster R................ | 1 | — |

LIMPAR, Anders

Born Sweden 24.9.65.
Forward. From Cremonese. Sweden full caps.

| 1990–91 | Arsenal....................... | 34 | 11 |

LINACRE, Phil

Born Middlesbrough 17.5.62.   Ht 6 0
Wt 11 00
Forward. From Apprentice.

1979–80	Coventry C	—	—
1980–81	Hartlepool U	1	—
1981–82	....	32	4
1982–83	....	30	6
From Whitby T,			
Bishop Auckland			
1983–84	Hartlepool U	19	7

From Newcastle Blue Star

| 1989–90 | Darlington .... | 2 | — |
| 1990–91 | .... | 8 | 3 |

LINEKER, Gary

Born Leicester 30.11.60.   Ht 5 9
Wt 11 10
Forward. From Apprentice. England B, 68 full caps.

1978–79	Leicester C.................	7	1
1979–80	....	19	3
1980–81	....	9	2
1981–82	....	39	17
1982–83	....	40	26
1983–84	....	39	22
1984–85	....	41	24
1985–86	Everton	41	30
1986–87	Barcelona....................	37	22
1987–88	....	36	16
1988–89	....	26	6
1989–90	Tottenham H	38	24
1990–91	....	32	15

LING, Martin

Born West Ham 15.7.66.   Ht 5 7   Wt 9 12
Forward. From Apprentice.

1983–84	Exeter C......................	29	—
1984–85	....	42	6
1985–86	....	45	8
1986–87	Swindon T	2	—
1986–87	Southend U.................	24	8
1987–88	....	42	7
1988–89	....	44	6
1989–90	....	25	10
1990–91	....	3	—
1990–91	*Mansfield T*	3	—
1990–91	*Swindon T*	1	—

LINIGHAN, Andy

Born Hartlepool 18.6.62.   Ht 6 3
Wt 13 07
Defender. From Smiths BC. England B.

| 1980–81 | Hartlepool U .... | 6 | — |
| 1981–82 | .... | 17 | — |

Season	Club	Apps	Goals
1982–83	....	45	3
1983–84	....	42	1
1984–85	Leeds U	42	2
1985–86	....	24	1
1985–86	Oldham Ath.........	15	1
1986–87	....	40	3
1987–88	....	32	2
1987–88	Norwich C	12	2
1988–89	....	37	4
1989–90	....	37	2
1990–91	Arsenal.............	10	—

LINIGHAN, David

Born Hartlepool 9.1.65.   Ht 6 1   Wt 13 03
Defender. Local.

Season	Club	Apps	Goals
1981–82	Hartlepool U	6	—
1982–83	....	6	1
1983–84	....	23	1
1984–85	....	17	2
1984–85	*Leeds* U............	—	—
1985–86	Hartlepool U	39	1
1986–87	Derby Co............	—	—
1986–87	Shrewsbury T.........	24	—
1987–88	....	41	1
1988–89	Ipswich T............	41	2
1989–90	....	41	—
1990–91	....	45	3

LINTON, Des

Born Birmingham 5.9.71.   Ht 6 1
Wt 11 13
Defender. From Trainee.

Season	Club	Apps	Goals
1989–90	Leicester C...........	2	—
1990–91	....	8	—

LISTER, Steve

Born Doncaster 18.11.61.   Ht 6 1
Wt 12 07
Midfield. From Apprentice.

Season	Club	Apps	Goals
1978–79	Doncaster R...........	9	—
1979–80	....	40	12
1980–81	....	39	3
1981–82	....	41	7
1982–83	....	41	4

Season	Club	Apps	Goals
1983–84	....	31	2
1984–85	....	36	2
1985–86	Scunthorpe U	37	2
1986–87	....	40	11
1987–88	....	39	6
1988–89	....	34	9
1989–90	....	6	1
1990–91	....	7	—
1990–91	*York C*	4	1

LITCHFIELD, Peter

Born Manchester 27.7.56.   Ht 6 1
Wt 13 07
Goalkeeper. From Manchester C and Droylsden.

Season	Club	Apps	Goals
1978–79	Preston NE................	—	—
1979–80	....	—	—
1980–81	....	3	—
1981–82	....	18	—
1982–83	....	23	—
1983–84	....	45	—
1984–85	....	18	—
1985–86	Bradford C...........	42	—
1986–87	....	39	—
1987–88	....	2	—
1988–89	....	5	—
1988–89	*Oldham Ath*............	3	—
1989–90	Scunthorpe U	17	—
1990–91	....	8	—

LITTLEJOHN, Adrian

Born Wolverhampton 26.9.70.   Ht 5 9
Wt 10 05
Forward. From WBA Trainee.

Season	Club	Apps	Goals
1989–90	Walsall	11	—
1990–91	....	33	1

LIVETT, Simon

Born Newham 8.1.69.   Ht 5 10   Wt 12 02
Forward. From Trainee.

Season	Club	Apps	Goals
1986–87	West Ham U	—	—
1987–88	....	—	—
1988–89	....	—	—
1989–90	....	—	—

1990–91 .... 1 —

LIVINGSTONE, Steve

Born Middlesbrough 8.9.69.   Ht 6 1
Wt 12 07
Forward. From Trainee.

1986–87	Coventry C	3	—
1987–88		4	—
1988–89		1	—
1989–90		13	3
1990–91		10	2
1990–91	Blackburn R	18	9

LLEWELLYN, Andy

Born Bristol 26.2.66.   Ht 5 7   Wt 11 00
Defender. From Apprentice. England
Youth.

1983–84	Bristol C	—	—
1984–85		22	—
1985–86		38	1
1986–87		31	—
1987–88		42	1
1988–89		16	1
1989–90		46	—
1990–91		42	—

LLOYD, Philip

Born Hemsworth 26.12.64.   Ht 5 11
Wt 11 11
Defender. From Apprentice.

1982–83	Middlesbrough	—	—
1983–84	Barnsley	—	—
1983–84	Darlington	14	—
1984–85		41	2
1985–86		29	—
1986–87		43	1
1987–88	Torquay U	46	2
1988–89		46	4
1989–90		46	1
1990–91		19	—

LOCKE, Adam

Born Croydon 20.8.70   Ht 5 10   Wt 11 10
Midfield. From Trainee.

1988–89	Crystal Palace	—	—
1989–90		—	—
1990–91	Southend U	28	4

LOCKETT, Phil

Born Stockport 6.9.72.   Ht 5 8   Wt 11 00
Forward. From Oldham Ath Schoolboy
and Rochdale Trainee.

| 1989–90 | Rochdale | 1 | — |
| 1990–91 | | 2 | — |

LOGAN, David

Born Middlesbrough 5.12.63.   Ht 5 9
Wt 10 11
Defender. From Whitby.

1984–85	Mansfield T	17	—
1985–86		24	1
1986–87		26	—
1986–87	Northampton T	15	1
1987–88		26	—
1988–89	Halifax T	3	—
1988–89	Stockport Co	35	—
1989–90		25	4
1990–91	Scarborough	34	1

LOGAN, Stephen

Born Glasgow 2.9.61   Ht 5 9   Wt 10 7
Forward. From Irvine Meadow

1982–83	Stranraer	1	—
1983–84		26	1
1984–85		29	7
1985–86		39	2
1986–87	Clyde	39	3
1987–88	Meadowbank T	34	5
1988–89		39	3
1989–90		9	—
1989–90	Falkirk	21	1
1990–91		1	—
1990–91	Meadowbank T	33	2

LONGDEN, Paul

Born Wakefield 28.9.62.   Ht 5 9
Wt 11 00
Defender. From Apprentice.

Season	Club	Appearances	Goals
1981–82	Barnsley	4	—
1982–83		1	—
1983–84	Scunthorpe U	43	—
1984–85		14	—
1985–86		31	—
1986–87		42	—
1987–88		44	—
1988–89		41	—
1989–90		46	—
1990–91		46	—

LONGHURST, David
(Deceased)

Born Northampton 15.1.65.   Ht 5 8
Wt 10 12
Forward. From Apprentice.

Season	Club	Appearances	Goals
1982–83	Nottingham F	—	—
1983–84		—	—
1984–85		—	—
1985–86	Halifax T	44	14
1986–87		41	10
1987–88	Northampton T	35	7
1988–89		2	—
1988–89	Peterborough U	37	7
1989–90		21	—
1989–90	York C	4	2
1990–91		2	—

LORAM, Mike

Born Brixham 13.8.67.   Ht 6 0   Wt 12 00
Forward. From Brixham.

Season	Club	Appearances	Goals
1984–85	Torquay U	14	2
1985–86		38	6
1985–86	QPR	—	—
1986–87	QPR	—	—
1986–87	Torquay U	13	4
1987–88	Torquay U	45	8
1988–89		37	4
1989–90		42	12
1990–91		41	7

LORENZO, Nestor

Born Argentina 28.2.66.   Ht 5 10
Wt 12 08
Defender. From Bari. Argentina full caps.

Season	Club	Appearances	Goals
1990–91	Swindon T	20	2

LORMOR, Tony

Born Ashington 29.10.70   Ht 6 1
Wt 12 03
Forward. From Trainee.

Season	Club	Appearances	Goals
1987–88	Newcastle U	5	2
1988–89		3	1
1988–89	Norwich C	—	—
1989–90	Newcastle U	—	—
1989–90	Lincoln C	21	8
1990–91		34	12

LOUGHLAN, Anthony

Born Surrey 19.1.70   Ht 6 0   Wt 12 03
Midfield. From Leicester U

Season	Club	Appearances	Goals
1989–90	Nottingham F	—	—
1990–91		2	1

LOVELL, Steve

Born Swansea 16.7.60.   Ht 5 10   Wt 11 10
Forward. From Apprentice. Wales 6 full caps.

Season	Club	Appearances	Goals
1977–78	Crystal Palace	—	—
1978–79		—	—
1979–80		—	—
1979–80	Stockport Co	12	—
1980–81	Crystal Palace	25	2
1981–82		30	1
1982–83		19	—
1982–83	Millwall	17	1
1983–84		46	7
1984–85		41	22
1985–86		42	14
1986–87		—	—
1986–87	Swansea C	2	1
1986–87	Gillingham	6	1
1987–88		46	25
1988–89		39	14
1989–90		41	16
1990–91		46	19

LOVELL, Stuart

Born Sydney 9.1.72.   Ht 5 10   Wt 10 06
Midfield. From Trainee.

Season	Club	App	Goals
1990–91	Reading	30	2

LOWE, David

Born Liverpool 30.8.65. Ht 5 11
Wt 11 02
Forward. From Apprentice. England
Youth, Under-21.

Season	Club	App	Goals
1982–83	Wigan Ath	28	6
1983–84		40	8
1984–85		29	5
1985–86		46	5
1986–87		45	16
1987–88	Ipswich T	41	17
1988–89		32	6
1989–90		34	13
1990–91		13	—

LOWERY, Tony

Born Wallsend 6.7.61. Ht 5 9 Wt 10 06
Midfield. From Ashington.

Season	Club	App	Goals
1980–81	WBA	—	—
1981–82		1	—
1981–82	*Walsall*	6	1
1982–83		—	—
1982–83	Mansfield T	1	—
1983–84		45	6
1984–85		45	3
1985–86		40	5
1986–87		44	5
1987–88		44	—
1988–89		12	—
1989–90		14	—
1990–91		7	—
1990–91	*Walsall*	6	—

LOWNDES, Steve

Born Cwmbran 17.6.60. Ht 5 10
Wt 10 06
Forward. From Amateur. Wales Under-21,
10 full caps.

Season	Club	App	Goals
1977–78	Newport Co	5	—
1978–79		43	8
1979–80		46	7
1980–81		40	9

Season	Club	App	Goals
1981–82		31	3
1982–83		43	12
1983–84	Millwall	20	3
1984–85		37	7
1985–86		39	6
1986–87	Barnsley	15	1
1987–88		44	9
1988–89		33	6
1989–90		24	4
1990–91		—	—
1990–91	Hereford U	17	1

LUCAS, Richard

Born Sheffield 22.9.70. Ht 5 10 Wt 11 04
Midfield. From Trainee.

Season	Club	App	Goals
1989–90	Sheffield U	—	—
1990–91		9	—

LUKE, Noel

Born Birmingham 28.12.64. Ht 5 10
Wt 12 05
Midfield. From school.

Season	Club	App	Goals
1981–82	WBA	—	—
1982–83		1	—
1983–84		8	1
1984–85	Mansfield T	36	6
1985–86		14	3
1986–87	Peterborough U	30	10
1987–88		43	7
1988–89		45	3
1989–90		43	5
1990–91		45	2

LUKIC, John

Born Chesterfield 11.12.60. Ht 6 4
Wt 13 13
Goalkeeper. From Apprentice. England
Youth, B, Under-21.

Season	Club	App	Goals
1978–79	Leeds U	—	—
1979–80		33	—
1980–81		42	—
1981–82		42	—
1982–83		29	—
1983–84	Arsenal	4	—

1984–85	....	27	—	
1985–86	....	40	—	
1986–87	....	36	—	
1987–88	....	40	—	
1988–89	....	38	—	
1989–90	....	38	—	
1990–91	Leeds U	38	—	

LUND, Gary

Born Grimsby 13.9.64   Ht 5 11   Wt 11 00
Forward. From school. England Youth.
Under-21.

1983–84	Grimsby T	7	4
1984–85	....	24	12
1985–86	....	29	8
1986–87	Lincoln C....................	44	13
1987–88	Notts Co.....................	40	20
1988–89	....	42	8
1989–90	....	40	9
1990–91	....	16	3

LUNDON, Sean

Born Liverpool 7.3.69.   Ht 5 10   Wt 10 10
Defender. From Apprentice.

1986–87	Chester C....................	12	—
1987–88	....	22	2
1988–89	....	6	—
1989–90	....	11	2
1990–91	....	5	—

LUNT, Robert

Born Widnes 11.12.73.   Ht 5 7   Wt 10 10
Midfield. From Trainee.

1990–91	Wrexham	8	—

LYNCH, Tommy

Born Limerick 10.10.64   Ht 6 0   Wt 12 06
Midfield. From Limerick.

1988–89	Sunderland.................	4	—
1989–90	....	—	—
1989–90	Shrewsbury T..............	22	—
1990–91	....	39	2

LYNE, Neil

Born Leicester 4.4.70.   Ht 6 1   Wt 12 04
Forward. From Leicester U

1989–90	Nottingham F.............	—	—
1989–90	*Walsall*	7	—
1990–91	Nottingham F.............	—	—
1990–91	*Shrewsbury T*	16	6

MABBUTT, Gary

Born Bristol 23.8.61. Ht 5 9 Wt 10 10
Defender . From Apprentice. England
Youth, Under-21, B, 13 full caps.

Season	Club	App	Goals
1978–79	Bristol R	11	—
1979–80		33	—
1980–81		42	5
1981–82		45	5
1982–83	Tottenham H	38	10
1983–84		21	2
1984–85		25	2
1985–86		32	3
1986–87		37	1
1987–88		37	2
1988–89		38	1
1989–90		36	—
1990–91		35	2

McADAM, Tom

Born Glasgow 9.4.54. Ht 6 0 Wt 12 9
Defender. From Glasgow Schools.

Season	Club	App	Goals
1971–72	Dumbarton	—	—
1972–73		17	9
1973–74		19	5
1974–75		33	11
1975–76		6	4
1975–76	Dundee U	26	12
1976–77		33	9
1977–78		2	—
1977–78	Celtic	33	8
1978–79		28	7
1979–80		34	8
1980–81		35	4
1981–82		34	5
1982–83		35	3
1983–84		28	1
1984–85		26	—
1985–86		5	—
1986–87	*Stockport Co*	5	1
1986–87	Hamilton A	3	—
1986–87	Motherwell	31	1
1987–88		34	1
1988–89		28	1
1989–90		6	—
1989–90	Airdrieonians	15	1

1990–91		9	—

McALLISTER, Brian

Born Glasgow 30.11.70 Ht 5 11
Wt 12 05
Defender. From Trainee.

Season	Club	App	Goals
1988–89	Wimbledon	—	—
1989–90		3	—
1990–91		—	—
1990–91	*Plymouth Arg*	8	—

McALLISTER, Gary

Born Motherwell 25.12.64. Ht 6 1
Wt 10 11
Midfield. From Fir Park BC. Scotland B,
Under-21, 8 full caps.

Season	Club	App	Goals
1981–82	Motherwell	1	—
1982–83		1	—
1983–84		21	—
1984–85		35	6
1985–86		1	—
1985–86	Leicester C	31	7
1986–87		39	10
1987–88		42	9
1988–89		46	11
1989–90		43	10
1990–91	Leeds U	38	2

McALLISTER, Kevin

Born Falkirk 8.11.62. Ht 5 5 Wt 11 0
Forward.

Season	Club	App	Goals
1983–84	Falkirk	35	11
1984–85		29	7
1985–86	Chelsea	20	—
1986–87		8	—
1987–88		5	—
1987–88	*Falkirk*	6	3
1988–89	Chelsea	36	6
1989–90		24	1
1990–91		13	—

McALLISTER, Pat

Born Belfast 3.2.72 Ht 5 11 Wt 10 11
Midfield. From Cliftonville

1990–91 Dunfermline Ath .... 1 —

McAVENNIE, Frank

Born Glasgow 22.11.59. Ht 5 9 Wt 11 0
Forward. From Johnstone Borough and
Partick T trialist. Scotland Under-21, 5
full caps.

1981–82	St Mirren	31	13
1982–83		36	9
1983–84		34	12
1984–85		34	16
1985–86	West Ham U	41	26
1986–87		36	7
1987–88		8	—
1987–88	Celtic	32	15
1988–89		23	12
1988–89	West Ham U	9	—
1989–90		5	—
1990–91		34	10

McCALL, Ian

Born Dumfries 13.9.64 Ht 5 10 Wt 11 07
Forward. From Motherwell Tech.

1983–84	Queen's Park	3	1
1984–85		28	—
1985–86		35	8
1986–87	Dunfermline Ath	43	8
1987–88		4	—
1987–88	Rangers	12	1
1988–89		5	1
1989–90		4	—
1989–90	Bradford C	12	1
1990–91	Dunfermline Ath	29	4

McCALL, Steve

Born Carlisle 15.10.60. Ht 5 11 Wt 12 06
Midfield. From Apprentice.England
Youth, Under-21, B, 11 full caps.

1978–79	Ipswich T	—	—
1979–80		10	—
1980–81		31	1
1981–82		42	1
1982–83		42	4
1983–84		42	1

1984–85		31	—
1985–86		33	—
1986–87		26	—
1987–88	Sheffield W	5	—
1988–89		2	—
1989–90		3	—
1989–90	*Carlisle U*	6	—
1990–91	Sheffield W	19	2

McCALL, Stuart

Born Leeds 10.6.64. Ht 5 6 Wt 10 01
Midfield. From Apprentice. Scotland
Under-21, 8 full caps.

1982–83	Bradford C	28	4
1983–84		46	5
1984–85		46	8
1985–86		38	4
1986–87		36	7
1987–88		44	9
1988–89	Everton	33	—
1989–90		37	3
1990–91		33	3

McCARRICK, Mark

Born Liverpool 4.2.62. Ht 5 8 Wt 10 08
Defender. From Witton Albion.

1983–84	Birmingham C	15	—
1984–85	Lincoln C	30	—
1985–86		14	—
1985–86	Crewe Alex	11	—
From Koparit, Runcorn			
1987–88	Tranmere R	40	5
1988–89		42	3
1989–90		32	4
1990–91		11	2

McCARRISON, Dugald

Born Lanark 22.12.69 Ht 5 11 Wt 10 7
Forward. From Celtic BC

1987–88	Celtic	—	—
1988–89		1	—
1989–90		—	—
1990–91		1	—
1990–91	*Ipswich T*	—	—

McCART, Chris

Born Motherwell 17.4.67. Ht 5 9
Wt 10 05
Midfield. From Fir Park BC.

Season	Club		
1984–85	Motherwell	—	—
1985–86		13	—
1986–87		—	—
1987–88		1	—
1988–89		26	—
1989–90		34	1
1990–91		36	—

McCARTHY, Alan

Born London 11.1.72. Ht 5 11 Wt 12 10
Defender. From Trainee.

Season	Club		
1989–90	QPR	—	—
1990–91		2	—

McCARTHY, Jon

Born Middlesbrough 18.8.70. Ht 5 9
Wt 11 05
Forward.

Season	Club		
1987–88	Hartlepool U	1	—
From Shepshed			
1990–91	York C	27	2

McCARTHY, Mick

Born Barnsley 7.2.59. Ht 6 1 Wt 13 3
Defender. From Apprentice. Eire 51 full caps.

Season	Club		
1977–78	Barnsley	46	1
1978–79		46	2
1979–80		44	1
1980–81		43	1
1981–82		42	1
1982–83		39	1
1983–84		12	—
1983–84	Manchester C	24	1
1984–85		39	—
1985–86		38	—
1986–87		39	1
1987–88	Celtic	22	—
1988–89		26	—

From Lyon.

Season	Club		
1989–90	Millwall	6	—
1990–91		12	—

McCARTHY, Paul

Born Cork 4.8.71. Ht 6 0 Wt 13 06
Defender. From Trainee. Eire Under-21.

Season	Club		
1989–90	Brighton	3	—
1990–91		21	—

McCARTHY, Sean

Born Bridgend 12.9.67 Ht 6 0 Wt 12 05
Forward. From Bridgend. Wales B.

Season	Club		
1985–86	Swansea C	22	3
1986–87		44	14
1987–88		25	8
1988–89	Plymouth Arg	38	8
1989–90		32	11
1990–91	Bradford C	42	13

McCATHIE, Norrie

Born Edinburgh 23.3.61. Ht 6 0
Wt 12 00
Midfield. From Edina Hibs.

Season	Club		
1980–81	Cowdenbeath	11	—
1981–82	Dunfermline Ath	19	4
1982–83		24	3
1983–84		38	5
1984–85		37	8
1985–86		37	8
1986–87		44	6
1987–88		39	1
1988–89		20	1
1988–89	*Ayr U*	2	—
1989–90	Dunfermline Ath	36	—
1990–91		36	1

McCLAIR, Brian

Born Bellshill 8.12.63. Ht 5 9 Wt 12 00
Forward. From Apprentice. Scotland
Youth, B, Under-21, 17 full caps.

Season	Club		
1980–81	Aston Villa	—	—

Season	Club	App	Goals
1981–82	Motherwell	11	4
1982–83		28	11
1983–84	Celtic	35	23
1984–85		32	19
1985–86		34	22
1986–87		44	35
1987–88	Manchester U	40	24
1988–89		38	10
1989–90		37	5
1990–91		36	13

McCLAREN, Steve

Born Fulford 3.5.61. Ht 5 7 Wt 9 04
Midfield. From Apprentice.

Season	Club	App	Goals
1978–79	Hull C	—	—
1979–80		1	—
1980–81		20	1
1981–82		37	4
1982–83		40	4
1983–84		40	3
1984–85		40	4
1985–86	Derby Co	23	—
1986–87		—	—
1986–87	*Lincoln C*	8	—
1987–88	Derby Co	2	—
1987–88	Bristol C	16	1
1988–89		45	1
1989–90		—	—
1989–90	Oxford U	22	—
1990–91		7	—

McCLEAN, Christian

Born Colchester 17.10.63. Ht 6 4
Wt 14 00
Forward. From Colchester U, Clacton,
Chelmsford C.

Season	Club	App	Goals
1987–88	Bristol R	6	—
1988–89		28	2
1989–90		15	4
1990–91		2	—

McCLELLAND, John

Born Belfast 7.12.55. Ht 6 2 Wt 13 02
Defender. From Portadown. Northern
Ireland 53 full caps. Football League.

Season	Club	App	Goals
1973–74	Cardiff C	—	—
1974–75		4	1
From Bangor			
1978–79	Mansfield T	36	1
1979–80		43	1
1980–81		46	6
1981–82	Rangers	14	—
1982–83		35	2
1983–84		36	2
1984–85		11	—
1984–85	Watford	29	1
1985–86		31	1
1986–87		41	1
1987–88		40	—
1988–89		43	—
1989–90	Leeds U	3	—
1989–90	*Watford*	1	—
1990–91	Leeds U	3	—

McCOIST, Ally

Born Bellshill 24.9.62. Ht 5 10 Wt 12 00
Forward. From Fir Park BC. Scotland
Youth, Under-21, 31 full caps.

Season	Club	App	Goals
1978–79	St Johnstone	4	—
1979–80		15	—
1980–81		38	22
1981–82	Sunderland	28	2
1982–83		28	6
1983–84	Rangers	30	9
1984–85		25	12
1985–86		33	24
1986–87		44	33
1987–88		40	31
1988–89		19	9
1989–90		34	14
1990–91		26	11

McCORD, Brian

Born Derby 24.8.68. Ht 5 10 Wt 11 06
Midfield. From Apprentice.

Season	Club	App	Goals
1987–88	Derby Co	1	—
1988–89		—	—
1989–90		4	—
1989–90	Barnsley	16	1
1990–91		24	1

McCOY, Gerard

Born Glasgow 24.12.60 Ht 5 9 Wt 10 5
Forward.

1979–80	Queen's Park	16	3
1980–81		37	17
1981–82	Hearts	21	9
1982–83		4	—
1982–83	Berwick R	3	—
1982–83	Hearts	2	—
1983–84	Partick T	7	—
1984–85	Falkirk	33	22
1985–86	Dumbarton	32	13
1986–87		39	21
1987–88		30	8
1988–89	Partick T	34	20
1989–90		8	3
1989–90	Falkirk	19	4
1990–91		1	—
1990–91	Clyde	19	4

McCREERY, David

Born Belfast 16.9.57. Ht 5 6 Wt 9 07
Midfield. From Apprentice. Northern
Ireland Schools. Youth Under-21, 67 full
caps.

1974–75	Manchester U	2	—
1975–76		28	4
1976–77		25	2
1977–78		17	1
1978–79		15	—
1979–80	QPR	42	4
1980–81		15	—
From Tulsa R			
1982–83	Newcastle U	26	—
1983–84		40	—
1984–85		35	1
1985–86		41	—
1986–87		30	—
1987–88		35	1
1988–89		36	—
1989–90	Hearts	22	—
1990–91		7	—

McDERMOTT, Brian

Born Slough 8.4.61. Ht 5 8 Wt 11 04
Forward. From Apprentice. England
Youth.

1978–79	Arsenal	2	—
1979–80		1	—
1980–81		23	5
1981–82		13	1
1982–83		9	4
1982–83	*Fulham*	3	—
1983–84	Arsenal	13	2
1984–85	Oxford U	18	2
1985–86		4	—
1986–87		2	—
1986–87	Huddersfield T	4	1
1987–88	Cardiff C	45	7
1988–89		6	1
1988–89	Exeter C	19	1
1989–90		41	3
1990–91		8	—

McDERMOTT, John

Born Middlesbrough 3.2.69. Ht 5 7
Wt 10 07
Defender.

1986–87	Grimsby T	13	—
1987–88		28	—
1988–89		38	1
1989–90		39	—
1990–91		43	—

McDONALD, Alan

Born Belfast 12.10.63. Ht 6 2 Wt 12 07
Defender. From Apprentice. Northern
Ireland Youth, 29 full caps.

1981–82	QPR	—	—
1982–83		—	—
1982–83	*Charlton Ath*	9	—
1983–84	QPR	5	—
1984–85		16	1
1985–86		42	—
1986–87		39	4
1987–88		36	3
1988–89		30	—
1989–90		34	—

Season	Club	Apps	Goals
1990–91		17	—

McDONALD, David

Born Dublin 2.1.71. Ht 5 10 Wt 11 00
Defender. From Trainee. Eire Youth,
Under-21.

Season	Club	Apps	Goals
1989–90	Tottenham H	—	—
1990–91		—	—
1990–91	*Gillingham*	10	—

MACDONALD, Gary

Born Middlesbrough 26.3.62. Ht 6 0
Wt 12 01
Forward. From Apprentice.

Season	Club	Apps	Goals
1979–80	Middlesbrough	—	—
1980–81		7	—
1981–82		8	1
1982–83		9	1
1983–84		29	3
1984–85	Carlisle U	9	—
1984–85	Darlington	33	4
1985–86		36	16
1986–87		10	3
1987–88		42	7
1988–89		41	5
1989–90	Stockport Co	1	—
1989–90	Hartlepool U	16	1
1990–91		2	—

MacDONALD, Innes

Born Aberdeen 19.10.62 Ht 5 10
Wt 11 3
Forward. From Keith

Season	Club	Apps	Goals
1986–87	Montrose	41	2
1987–88		11	2
1987–88	Airdrieonians	31	—
1988–89		36	3
1989–90		37	4
1990–91		12	—

MacDONALD, John

Born Glasgow 15.4.61. Ht 5 9 Wt 10 05
Forward. From Clydebank Strollers.
Scotland Schools, Youth, Under-21.

Season	Club	Apps	Goals
1978–79	Rangers	2	—
1979–80		26	5
1980–81		30	11
1981–82		34	14
1982–83		30	10
1983–84		18	1
1984–85		18	3
1985–86		2	—
1986–87	Charlton Ath	2	—
1986–87	Barnsley	25	7
1987–88		33	7
1988–89		32	5
1989–90		4	1
1989–90	Scarborough	29	5
1990–91		11	1
1990–91	Airdrieonians	14	3

MACDONALD, Ken

Born Dundee 9.3.61 Ht 5 9 Wt 11 0
Midfield. From Broughty Ath

Season	Club	Apps	Goals
1981–82	St Johnstone	9	2
1982–83		1	—
1982–83	Forfar Ath	25	16
1983–84		26	13
1984–85		31	14
Form Happy Valley			
1986–87	Forfar Ath	42	17
1987–88		43	20
1988–89	Airdrieonians	36	22
1989–90		8	5
1989–90	Raith R	26	10
1990–91		11	2
1990–91	St Johnstone	11	—

MACDONALD, Kevin

Born Inverness 22.12.60. Ht 6 1
Wt 12 01
Midfield. From Inverness Caley.

Season	Club	Apps	Goals
1980–81	Leicester C	20	2
1981–82		25	1
1982–83		42	4
1983–84		38	1
1984–85		13	—
1984–85	Liverpool	13	—
1985–86		17	1
1986–87		6	—

Season	Club	App	Goals
1987–88	....	1	—
1987–88	*Leicester C*	3	—
1988–89	Liverpool	3	—
1988–89	*Rangers*	3	—
1989–90	Coventry C	22	—
1990–91	....	9	—
1990–91	*Cardiff C*	8	—

McDONALD, Neil

Born Wallsend 2.11.65. Ht 5 11 Wt 11 4
Midfield. From Wallsend BC. England
Schools, Youth, Under-21.

Season	Club	App	Goals
1982–83	Newcastle U	24	4
1983–84	....	12	—
1984–85	....	36	6
1985–86	....	28	4
1986–87	....	40	7
1987–88	....	40	3
1988–89	Everton	25	1
1989–90	....	31	1
1990–91	....	29	2

McDONALD, Rod

Born London 20.3.67.
Forward. From South Liverpool, Colne
Dynamoes.

Season	Club	App	Goals
1990–91	Walsall	36	5

McDONOUGH, Darron

Born Antwerp 7.11.62. Ht 5 11 Wt 12 12
Defender. From Apprentice.

Season	Club	App	Goals
1979–80	Oldham Ath	—	—
1980–81	....	15	3
1981–82	....	36	1
1982–83	....	38	10
1983–84	....	38	—
1984–85	....	32	—
1985–86	....	20	—
1986–87	....	4	—
1986–87	Luton T	18	1
1987–88	....	27	4
1988–89	....	10	—
1989–90	....	15	—
1990–91	....	26	—

McDOWALL, Kenny

Born Glasgow 29.7.63. Ht 5 10 Wt 10 03
Forward. From Drumchapel Amateurs.

Season	Club	App	Goals
1980–81	Partick T	—	—
1981–82	....	1	—
1982–83	....	24	5
1983–84	....	36	13
1984–85	....	6	1
1984–85	St Mirren	23	3
1985–86	....	12	1
1986–87	....	19	1
1987–88	....	27	3
1988–89	....	9	—
1989–90	....	23	3
1990–91	....	23	4

McELHINNEY, Gerry

Born Londonderry 19.9.56 Ht 6 1
Wt 13 10
Defender. From Distillery. Northern
Ireland 6 full caps.

Season	Club	App	Goals
1980–81	Bolton W	17	—
1981–82	....	19	1
1982–83	....	16	—
1982–83	*Rochdale*	20	1
1983–84	Bolton W	43	1
1984–85	....	14	—
1984–85	Plymouth Arg	21	—
1985–86	....	44	2
1986–87	....	20	—
1987–88	....	6	—
1988–89	Peterborough U	33	1
1989–90	....	34	—
1990–91	....	20	—

McEWAN, Alexander

Born Glasgow 15.5.70. Ht 5 9 Wt 11 3
Defender. From Rangers S form.

Season	Club	App	Goals
1989–90	St. Mirren	2	—
1990–91	....	1	1

McGARVEY, Scott

Born Glasgow 22.4.63. Ht 5 11 Wt 12 04
Forward. From Apprentice. Scotland
Under-21.

Season	Club	App	Goals
1979–80	Manchester U	—	—
1980–81		2	—
1981–82		16	2
1982–83		7	1
1983–84		—	—
1983–84	*Wolverhampton W*	13	2
1984–85	Portsmouth	18	5
1985–86		5	1
1985–86	*Carlisle U*	10	3
1986–87	Carlisle U	25	8
1986–87	Grimsby T	11	1
1987–88		39	6
1988–89		—	—
1988–89	Bristol C	26	9
1989–90	Oldham Ath	4	1
1989–90	*Wigan Ath*	3	—

To Mazda, Japan

McGEE, Owen

Born Teesside 29.4.70   Ht 5 5   Wt 10 08
Defender. From Trainee.

Season	Club	App	Goals
1988–89	Middlesbrough	—	—
1989–90		13	—
1990–91		8	1

McGEE, Paul

Born Dublin 17.5.68   Ht 5 6   Wt 9 10
Forward. From Bohemians. Eire
Under-21.

Season	Club	App	Goals
1988–89	Colchester U	3	—
1988–89	Wimbledon	1	1
1989–90		13	—
1990–91		27	6

McGHEE, Mark

Born Glasgow 25.5.57.   Ht 5 10   Wt 12 00
Forward. From Apprentice. Scotland
Under-21, 4 full caps.

Season	Club	App	Goals
1974–75	Bristol C	—	—
1975–76	Morton	5	1
1976–77		39	20
1977–78		20	16
1977–78	Newcastle U	18	3
1978–79		10	2

Season	Club	App	Goals
1978–79	Aberdeen	11	4
1979–80		21	6
1980–81		36	13
1981–82		31	8
1982–83		32	16
1983–84		33	16
1984–85	SV Hamburg	26	6
1985–86		4	1
1985–86	Celtic	18	4
1986–87		17	1
1987–88		24	6
1988–89		29	16
1989–90	Newcastle U	46	19
1990–91		21	5

McGILL, Daniel

Born Paisley 7.7.71.   Ht 5 8   Wt 10 09
Midfield. From Gleniffer Th.

Season	Club	App	Goals
1989–90	St Mirren	2	—
1990–91		3	—

McGINLAY, John

Born Inverness 8.4.64   Ht 5 9   Wt 11 06
Forward. From Elgin C.

Season	Club	App	Goals
1988–89	Shrewsbury T	16	5
1989–90		44	22
1990–91	Bury	25	9
1990–91	Millwall	2	—

McGINLAY, Pat

Born Glasgow 30.5.67.   Ht 5 10   Wt 10 10
Midfield. Scottish Junior.

Season	Club	App	Goals
1985–86	Blackpool	—	—
1986–87		12	1
1987–88	Hibernian	—	—
1988–89		2	—
1989–90		28	3
1990–91		32	1

McGINNIS, Gary

Born Dundee 21.10.63.   Ht 5 11
Wt 10 03
Defender. From Dundee BC. Scotland
Schools, Youth, Under-21.

Season	Club	App	Goals
1981–82	Dundee U	—	—
1982–83		—	—
1983–84		4	—
1984–85		10	—
1985–86		4	—
1986–87		20	—
1987–88		11	—
1988–89		11	—
1989–90		7	—
1989–90	St Johnstone	11	—
1990–91		32	—

McGIVERN, Sam

Born Kilwinning 9.10.63 Ht 5 9 Wt 10 7
Midfield. From Glenfield

Season	Club	App	Goals
1981–82	Kilmarnock	28	2
1982–83		34	3
1983–84		37	7
1984–85		32	5
1985–86		36	11
1986–87		19	2
1986–87	Falkirk	16	3
1987–88		10	1
1988–89		34	8
1989–90		16	2
1990–91		30	15

McGLASHAN, John

Born Dundee 3.6.67. Ht 6 1 Wt 12 00
Forward. From Dundee Violet.

Season	Club	App	Goals
1988–89	Montrose	35	2
1989–90		33	9
1990–91	Millwall	8	—

McGOLDRICK, Eddie

Born London 30.4.65. Ht 5 10 Wt 11 07
Midfield. From Nuneaton, Kettering T.

Season	Club	App	Goals
1986–87	Northampton T	39	5
1987–88		46	2
1988–89		22	2
1988–89	Crystal Palace	21	—
1989–90		22	—
1990–91		26	—

McGOWNE, Kevin

Born Kilmarnock 16.12.69. Ht 6 0
Wt 11 4
Defender. From Hurlford U.

Season	Club	App	Goals
1989–90	St Mirren	2	—
1990–91		10	—

McGRATH, Derek

Born Dublin 21.1.72. Ht 5 5 Wt 10 01
Midfield. From Apprentice.

Season	Club	App	Goals
1989–90	Brighton	1	—
1990–91		5	—

McGRATH, Lloyd

Born Birmingham 24.2.65. Ht 5 5
Wt 11 6
Midfield. From Apprentice. England
Youth, Under-21.

Season	Club	App	Goals
1982–83	Coventry C	—	—
1983–84		1	—
1984–85		23	—
1985–86		32	—
1986–87		30	3
1987–88		17	—
1988–89		8	—
1989–90		13	—
1990–91		14	—

McGRATH, Paul

Born Greenford 4.12.59. Ht 6 0
Wt 13 09
Defender. From St Patrick's Ath. Eire 47
full caps. Football League.

Season	Club	App	Goals
1981–82	Manchester U	—	—
1982–83		14	3
1983–84		9	1
1984–85		23	—
1985–86		40	3
1986–87		35	2
1987–88		22	2
1988–89		20	1
1989–90	Aston Villa	35	1
1990–91		35	—

McGRAW, Mark

Born Rutherglen 5.1.71   Ht 5 11   Wt 10 7
Forward. From Port Glasgow R

1988–89	Morton	1	—
1989–90		11	3
1990–91	Hibernian	13	—

McGRILLEN, Paul

Born Glasgow 19.8.71   Ht 5 8   Wt 10 5
Forward. From Motherwell BC

1990–91	Motherwell	2	—

McGUGAN, Paul

Born Glasgow 17.7.64.   Ht 6 3   Wt 13 07
Defender. From Eastercraigs.

1980–81	Celtic	—	—
1981–82		—	—
1982–83		—	—
1983–84		1	—
1984–85		3	—
1985–86		21	2
1986–87		22	—
1987–88		2	—
1987–88	Barnsley	29	1
1988–89		20	1
1989–90		—	—
1990–91		—	—
1990–91	Chesterfield	22	1

McHUGH, Michael

Born Donegal 3.4.71.   Ht 5 11   Wt 11 00
Forward.

1989–90	Bradford C	—	—
1990–91		1	—

McILHARGEY, Steve

Born Ferryhill 28.8.63.   Ht 6 0   Wt 11 07
Goalkeeper. From Blantyre Celtic.
Scotland Schools

1987–88	Walsall	—	—
1988–89		—	—
1989–90	Blackpool	22	—
1990–91		44	—

McINALLY, Alan

Born Ayr 10.2.63.   Ht 6 1   Wt 13 03
Forward. From Ayr U BC. Scotland 8 full
caps.

1980–81	Ayr U	6	—
1981–82		17	9
1982–83		35	7
1983–84		35	16
1984–85	Celtic	11	1
1985–86		16	1
1986–87		38	15
1987–88	Aston Villa	25	4
1988–89		33	14

To Bayern Munich.

McINALLY, Jim

Born Glasgow 19.2.64.   Ht 6 0   Wt 12 00
Midfield. From Celtic BC. Scottish Youth,
Under-21. 5 full caps.

1982–83	Celtic	1	—
1983–84		—	—
1984–85	Nottingham F	24	—
1985–86		12	—
1985–86	Coventry C	5	—
1986–87	Dundee U	32	1
1987–88		36	2
1988–89		29	1
1989–90		35	3
1990–91		33	1

McINERNEY, Ian

Born Liverpool 26.1.64   Ht 5 10
Wt 11 08
Forward. From Blue Star.

1988–89	Huddersfield T	10	1
1989–90	Stockport Co	40	8
1990–91		2	—
1990–91	Rochdale	4	1

McINTOSH, Martin

Born East Kilbride 19.3.71   Ht 6 2
Wt 12 00
Defender. From Tottenham H apprentice.

Season	Club	Apps	Goals
1988–89	St Mirren	2	—
1989–90		2	—
1990–91		—	—
1990–91	*Sheffield U*	—	—

McINTYRE, Paul

Born Girvan 18.1.67
Midfield. From Maybole J

1990–91	St Mirren	4	1

McINTYRE, Tom

Born Bellshill 26.12.63 Ht 6 0 Wt 10 10
Defender. From Fir Park BC

1983–84	Aberdeen	10	—
1984–85		—	—
1985–86		5	—
1986–87		4	—
1986–87	Hibernian	15	—
1987–88		25	—
1988–89		17	2
1989–90		—	—
1990–91		9	—

MACKAY, Gary

Born Edinburgh 23.1.64. Ht 5 9
Wt 10 05
Midfield. From Salvesan BC. Scotland
Schools, Youth, 4 full caps.

1980–81	Hearts	12	—
1981–82		17	2
1982–83		34	6
1983–84		31	4
1984–85		17	2
1985–86		32	4
1986–87		37	7
1987–88		41	5
1988–89		29	2
1989–90		33	1
1990–91		30	3

McJANNET, Les

Born Cumnock 2.8.61. Ht 5 10 Wt 10 04
Defender.

1979–80	Mansfield T	2	—
1980–81		34	—
1981–82		38	—

From King's Lynn, Matlock T, Burton
Alb

1987–88	Scarborough	31	—
1988–89		3	—
1988–89	Darlington	26	1
1989–90		*40*	*1*
1990–91		39	4

McKEARNEY, David

Born Crosby 20.6.68. Ht 5 10 Wt 11 02
Forward.

1987–88	Bolton W	—	—
1988–89		—	—
1989–90	Crewe Alex	17	1
1990–91		31	1

McKENNA, Brian

Born Dublin 30.1.72. Ht 6 0 Wt 13 12
Goalkeeper. From Home Farm.

1989–90	Brighton	—	—
1990–91		1	—

MACKENZIE, Steve

Born Romford 23.11.61. Ht 5 11
Wt 12 05
Midfield. From Apprentice. England
Youth, Under-21, B.

1979–80	Crystal Palace	—	—
1979–80	Manchester C	19	2
1980–81		39	6
1981–82	WBA	37	5
1982–83		1	—
1983–84		19	4
1984–85		38	8
1985–86		31	4
1986–87		22	2
1987–88	Charlton Ath	32	2
1988–89		36	3
1989–90		17	1
1990–91		15	1
1990–91	Sheffield W	12	2

McKEOWN, Gary

Born Oxford 19.10.70 Ht 5 10 Wt 11 07
Midfield. From Trainee. FA Schools,
England Youth

1988–89	Arsenal	—	—
1989–90		—	—
1990–91		—	—

McKERNON, Craig

Born Gloucester 23.2.68. Ht 5 8
Wt 10 02
Midfield. From Apprentice.

1984–85	Mansfield T	2	—
1985–86		11	—
1986–87		18	—
1987–88		14	—
1988–89		42	—
1989–90		7	—
1989–90	Arsenal	—	—
1990–91		—	—

McKIMMIE, Stuart

Born Aberdeen 27.10.62. Ht 5 8
Wt 10 07
Defender. From Banks o'Dee. Scotland
Under-21, 10 full caps.

1980–81	Dundee	17	—
1981–82		16	—
1982–83		31	—
1983–84		16	—
1983–84	Aberdeen	18	1
1984–85		34	3
1985–86		34	3
1986–87		37	—
1987–88		42	—
1988–89		35	—
1989–90		33	—
1990–91		26	1

McKINLAY, Billy

Born Glasgow 22.4.69. Ht 5 9 Wt 9 13
Midfield. From Hamilton T. Scotland B,
Under-21.

1986–87	Dundee U	3	—
1988–89		30	1
1989–90		13	—
1990–91		34	2

McKINLAY, Tosh

Born Glasgow 3.12.64. Ht 5 7 Wt 10 03
Defender. From Celtic BC. Scotland
Youth, Under-21.

1981–82	Dundee	—	—
1982–83		1	—
1983–84		36	3
1984–85		34	3
1985–86		22	—
1986–87		32	2
1987–88		19	—
1988–89		18	—
1988–89	Hearts	17	1
1989–90		29	1
1990–91		33	2

McKINNON, Colin

Born Glasgow 29.8.69 Ht 6 0 Wt 11 7
Midfield. From Bellhaven Ath

1990–91	Falkirk	4	—
1990–91	East Stirling	9	—

McKINNON, Ray

Born Dundee 5.8.70 Ht 5 8 Wt 9 11
Defender. From S form. Scotland
Under-21.

1987–88	Dundee U	—	—
1988–89		1	—
1989–90		10	—
1990–91		17	2

McKINNON, Rob

Born Glasgow 31.7.66. Ht 5 11 Wt 11 01
Defender. From Rutherglen Glencairn.
Scotland Under-21.

1984–85	Newcastle U	—	—
1985–86		1	—

Season	Club		
1986–87	Hartlepool U	45	—
1987–88	....	42	2
1988–89	....	46	2
1989–90	....	46	1
1990–91	....	45	1
1990–91	*Manchester U*..............	—	—

McKNIGHT, Allen

Born Antrim 27.1.64   Ht 6 1   Wt 13 07
Goalkeeper. From Distillery. Northern
Ireland Under-23, 10 full caps.

Season	Club		
1986–87	Celtic..............................	—	—
1986–87	*Albion R*......................	36	—
1987–88	Celtic..............................	12	—
1988–89	West Ham U	23	—
1989–90	....	—	—
1990–91	....	—	—

McLAREN, Alan

Born Edinburgh 4.1.71.   Ht 5 11
Wt 11 06
Defender. From Cavalry Bank. Scotland
Under-21.

Season	Club		
1987–88	Hearts	1	—
1988–89	....	12	1
1989–90	....	27	1
1990–91	....	23	1

MacLAREN, Ross

Born Edinburgh 14.4.62.   Ht 5 10
Wt 12 12
Midfield. From Glasgow Rangers.

Season	Club		
1980–81	Shrewsbury T..............	4	—
1981–82	....	35	—
1982–83	....	40	5
1983–84	....	40	7
1984–85	....	42	6
1985–86	Derby Co......................	46	4
1986–87	....	42	—
1987–88	....	34	—
1988–89	Swindon T	37	4
1989–90	....	46	3
1990–91	....	45	1

McLAUGHLIN, Joe

Born Greenock 2.6.60.   Ht 6 1   Wt 12 00
Defender. From school. Scotland
Under-21.

Season	Club		
1977–78	Morton	—	—
1978–79	....	—	—
1979–80	....	30	2
1980–81	....	34	1
1981–82	....	36	—
1982–83	....	34	—
1983–84	Chelsea	41	—
1984–85	....	36	1
1985–86	....	40	1
1986–87	....	36	2
1987–88	....	36	1
1988–89	....	31	—
1989–90	Charlton Ath	31	—
1990–91	Watford	24	1

McLAUGHLIN, Paul

Born Johnstone 9.12.65   Ht 5 11   Wt 11 9
Defender. From Anniesland U

Season	Club		
1983–84	Queen's Park..............	—	—
1984–85	....	33	—
1985–86	....	23	1
1986–87	....	30	—
1987–88	....	33	2
1988–89	....	34	1
1989–90	Celtic..............................	—	—
1990–91	....	3	—

McLEAN, Paul

Born Johnstone 25.7.64.   Ht 5 10
Wt 12 00
Midfield. From Glenburn Am.

Season	Club		
1983–84	Queen's Park..............	5	—
1984–85	....	1	—
1985–86	....	13	2
1986–87	....	19	—
1987–88	....	39	3
1988–89	....	39	2
1989–90	Motherwell..................	2	—
1990–91	....	1	—

McLEARY, Alan

Born London 6.10.64. Ht 5 11 Wt 11 02
Defender. From Apprentice. England
Youth, B, Under-21.

Season	Club		
1981–82	Millwall	—	—
1982–83		3	1
1983–84		30	—
1984–85		21	—
1985–86		35	3
1986–87		42	—
1987–88		31	—
1988–89		38	1
1989–90		31	—
1990–91		42	—

McLEISH, Alex

Born Glasgow 21.1.59. Ht 6 1 Wt 12 04
Defender. From Glasgow United. Scotland
Under-21, 76 full caps.

Season	Club		
1977–78	Aberdeen	1	—
1978–79		19	1
1979–80		35	2
1980–81		32	3
1981–82		32	5
1982–83		34	2
1983–84		32	2
1984–85		30	1
1985–86		34	3
1986–87		40	3
1987–88		36	1
1988–89		34	—
1989–90		32	2
1990–91		33	—

MacLEOD, Joe

Born Edinburgh 30.12.67. Ht 5 7
Wt 9 11
Midfield. From Hutchison Vale BC.

Season	Club		
1984–85	Dundee U	—	—
1985–86		—	—
1986–87	*Dumbarton*	5	—
1986–87	Dundee U	2	—
1987–88		10	1
1988–89		3	—
1989–90		2	—

| 1990–91 | Motherwell | 22 | 1 |

MacLEOD, Murdo

Born Glasgow 24.9.58 Ht 5 8 Wt 12 00
Midfield. From Glasgow Amateurs.
Scotland Under-21, 20 full caps.

Season	Club		
1974–75	Dumbarton	—	—
1975–76		7	—
1976–77		27	7
1977–78		39	1
1978–79		14	1
1978–79	Celtic	23	3
1979–80		36	7
1980–81		18	8
1981–82		36	10
1982–83		35	11
1983–84		34	7
1984–85		31	3
1985–86		30	3
1986–87		38	4
From Borussia Dortmund			
1990–91	Hibernian	25	2

McLOUGHLIN, Alan

Born Manchester 20.4.67. Ht 5 8
Wt 10 00
Midfield. From Local. Eire B, 7 full caps.

Season	Club		
1984–85	Manchester U	—	—
1985–86		—	—
1986–87	Swindon T	9	—
1986–87	Torquay U	16	1
1987–88		8	3
1987–88	Swindon T	8	—
1988–89		26	3
1989–90		46	12
1990–91		17	4
1990–91	Southampton	22	1

McLOUGHLIN, Paul

Born Bristol 23.12.63. Ht 5 10 Wt 10 07
Forward. From Bristol C and Gisborne C.

Season	Club		
1984–85	Cardiff C	17	—
1985–86		32	4
From Gisborne C			

Season	Club	Apps	Goals
1987–88	Hereford U	29	1
1988–89		45	13
1989–90	Wolverhampton W	19	4
1990–91		6	—

McMAHON, Steve

Born Liverpool 20.8.61. Ht 5 9 Wt 11 08
Midfield. From Apprentice. England Under-21, B, 17 full caps.

Season	Club	Apps	Goals
1979–80	Everton	—	—
1980–81		34	5
1981–82		32	2
1982–83		34	4
1983–84	Aston Villa	37	5
1984–85		35	2
1985–86		3	—
1985–86	Liverpool	23	6
1986–87		37	5
1987–88		40	9
1988–89		29	3
1989–90		38	5
1990–91		22	—

McMANAMAN, Steven

Born Liverpool 11.2.72. Ht 5 11 Wt 10 02
Forward. From School. England Youth, Under-21.

Season	Club	Apps	Goals
1989–90	Liverpool	—	—
1990–91		2	—

McMILLAN, Andy

Born Bloemfontein 22.6.68. Ht 5 10 Wt 10 13
Defender.

Season	Club	Apps	Goals
1987–88	York C	22	—
1988–89		2	—
1989–90		25	—
1990–91		45	1

McMINN, Ted

Born Castle Douglas 28.9.62. Ht 5 11 Wt 11 02
Forward. From Glenafton Athletic.

Season	Club	Apps	Goals
1982–83	Queen of the S	22	1
1983–84		32	3
1984–85		8	1
1984–85	Rangers	20	1
1985–86		28	2
1986–87		15	1
From SevilleH			
1987–88	Derby Co	7	1
1988–89		32	4
1989–90		15	—
1990–91		13	—

McNAB, Neil

Born Greenock 4.6.57. Ht 5 7 Wt 11 00
Midfield. Scotland Schools. Under-21.

Season	Club	Apps	Goals
1972–73	Morton	3	—
1973–74		11	—
1973–74	Tottenham H	1	—
1974–75		2	—
1975–76		15	—
1976–77		10	—
1977–78		42	3
1978–79		2	—
1978–79	Bolton W	23	3
1979–80		12	1
1979–80	Brighton	16	—
1980–81		33	1
1981–82		40	3
1982–83		14	—
1982–83	*Leeds U*	5	—
1982–83	*Portsmouth*	—	—
1983–84	Manchester C	33	1
1984–85		18	—
1985–86		37	4
1986–87		42	4
1987–88		37	2
1988–89		42	5
1989–90		12	—
1989–90	Tranmere R	22	1
1990–91		40	3

McNALLY, Bernard

Born Shrewsbury 17.2.63. Ht 5 7 Wt 10 12
Midfield. From Apprentice. Northern Ireland 5 full caps.

Season	Club	League Appearances/Goals	
1980–81	Shrewsbury T	1	—
1981–82		33	1
1982–83		25	1
1983–84		41	4
1984–85		42	2
1985–86		35	6
1986–87		40	5
1987–88		43	2
1988–89		22	2
1989–90	WBA	41	5
1990–91		25	1

McNALLY, Mark

Born Bellshill 10.3.71   Ht 5 9   Wt 10 7
Midfield. From Celtic BC. Scotland Youth

Season	Club	League Appearances/Goals	
1987–88	Celtic	—	—
1988–89		—	—
1989–90		—	—
1990–91		19	—

McNEILL, William

Born Toronto 12.3.67   Ht 5 9   Wt 11 0
Forward. From Musselburgh Ath

Season	Club	League Appearances/Goals	
1987–88	East Stirling	13	3
1988–89		36	16
1989–90		27	4
1990–91	Falkirk	4	—

McNICHOL, Jim

Born Glasgow 9.6.58.   Ht 6 0   Wt 12 10
Defender. From Ipswich T Apprentice.
Scotland Under-21.

Season	Club	League Appearances/Goals	
1976–77	Luton T	2	—
1977–78		12	—
1978–79		1	—
1978–79	Brentford	32	4
1979–80		31	8
1980–81		14	—
1981–82		26	3
1982–83		32	3
1983–84		20	4
1984–85	Exeter C	42	5
1985–86		45	5
1986–87	Torquay U	42	3

Season	Club	League Appearances/Goals	
1987–88		46	6
1988–89		36	4
1989–90	Exeter C	33	8
1990–91		9	—

McPARLAND, Ian

Born Edinburgh 4.10.61.   Ht 5 8
Wt 10 08
Forward. From Ormiston Primrose.

Season	Club	League Appearances/Goals	
1980–81	Notts Co	2	—
1981–82		12	—
1982–83		11	1
1983–84		21	2
1984–85		20	—
1985–86		44	15
1986–87		45	24
1987–88		43	21
1988–89		23	6
1988–89	Hull C	11	1
1989–90		20	5
1990–91		16	1
1990–91	Walsall	11	6

MacPHAIL, John

Born Dundee 7.12.55.   Ht 6 0   Wt 12 03
Defender. From St. Columba's.

Season	Club	League Appearances/Goals	
1975–76	Dundee	6	—
1976–77		25	—
1977–78		34	—
1978–79		3	—
1978–79	Sheffield U	15	1
1979–80		44	5
1980–81		39	—
1981–82		26	1
1982–83		11	—
1982–83	York C	12	2
1983–84		46	10
1984–85		42	5
1985–86		42	7
1986–87	Bristol C	26	1
1987–88	Sunderland	46	16
1988–89		45	4
1989–90		38	2
1990–91		1	—
1990–91	Hartlepool U	42	1

McPHEE, Ian

Born Perth 31.1.61 Ht 5 8 Wt 10 10
Midfield. From Perth Schools

Season	Club	Apps	Goals
1977–78	Celtic	—	—
1978–79	Forfar Ath	12	1
1979–80		39	6
1980–81		35	1
1981–82		31	4
1982–83		39	6
1983–84		39	5
1984–85		39	3
1985–86		36	2
1986–87		41	4
1987–88		1	—
1987–88	Dundee U	10	1
1988–89		2	1
1988–89	Airdrieonians	27	3
1989–90		19	1
1990–91		36	1

McPHERSON, Angus

Born Glasgow 11.10.68 Ht 5 11
Wt 10 04
Defender. From S Form.

Season	Club	Apps	Goals
1986–87	Rangers	—	—
1987–88		—	—
1988–89		—	—
1989–90		—	—
1989–90	Exeter C	11	1
1990–91	Rangers	—	—

McPHERSON, David

Born Paisley 28.1.64. Ht 6 3 Wt 11 11
Defender. From Gartcosh United.
Scotland Youth, B, Under-21, 12 full caps.

Season	Club	Apps	Goals
1980–81	Rangers	—	—
1981–82		—	—
1982–83		18	1
1983–84		36	2
1984–85		31	—
1985–86		34	5
1986–87		42	7
1987–88		44	4
1988–89	Hearts	32	4
1989–90		35	4
1990–91		34	2

McPHERSON, Keith

Born Greenwich 11.9.63. Ht 5 11
Wt 10 11
Defender. From Apprentice.

Season	Club	Apps	Goals
1981–82	West Ham U	—	—
1982–83		—	—
1983–84		—	—
1984–85		1	—
1985–86		—	—
1985–86	Cambridge U	11	1
1985–86	Northampton T	20	—
1986–87		46	5
1987–88		32	—
1988–89		41	2
1989–90		43	1
1990–91	Reading	46	3

McPHILLIPS, Terry

Born Manchester 1.10.68. Ht 5 10
Wt 11 00
Forward. From Liverpool Trainee.

Season	Club	Apps	Goals
1987–88	Halifax T	25	3
1988–89		41	22
1989–90		22	3
1989–90	Northampton T	1	—
1990–91	Halifax T	5	—

McQUEEN, Tommy

Born Bellshill 1.4.63. Ht 5 11 Wt 11 00
Defender. From Gartcosh United.

Season	Club	Apps	Goals
1981–82	Clyde	39	—
1982–83		35	—
1983–84		38	1
1984–85	Aberdeen	35	3
1985–86		17	1
1986–87		1	—
1986–87	West Ham U	9	—
1987–88		12	—
1988–89		2	—
1989–90		7	—
1990–91		—	—
1990–91	Falkirk	32	2

McSTAY, Paul

Born Hamilton 22.10.64. Ht 5 10
Wt 10 07
Midfield. From Celtic BC. Scotland
Schools, Youth, Under-21, 51 full caps.

Season	Club		
1981–82	Celtic	10	1
1982–83		36	6
1983–84		34	3
1984–85		32	4
1985–86		34	8
1986–87		43	3
1987–88		44	5
1988–89		33	5
1989–90		35	3
1990–91		30	2

McSWEGAN, Gary

Born Glasgow 24.9.70 Ht 5 7 Wt 10 9
Forward. From Rangers Amateur BC

Season	Club		
1986–87	Rangers	—	—
1987–88		1	—
1988–89		1	—
1989–90		—	—
1990–91		3	—

McVICAR, Don

Born Perth 6.11.62. Ht 5 9 Wt 11 06
Defender. From Blairgowrie Jun.

Season	Club		
1981–82	St Johnstone	13	—
1982–83		26	—
1983–84		21	—
1984–85		26	1
1985–86	Tranmere R	7	—
1985–86	Montrose	12	—
1986–87	St Johnstone	23	2
1987–88		38	1
1988–89		28	3
1989–90		35	3
1990–91		23	1

McWALTER, Mark

Born Arbroath 20.6.68. Ht 5 11
Wt 10 09
Forward. From Arbroath Lads Club.

Season	Club		
1984–85	Arbroath	14	2
1985–86		37	14
1986–87		19	4
1987–88	St Mirren	4	—
1988–89		31	5
1989–90		22	—
1990–91		22	3

McWHIRTER, Norman

Born Johnstone 4.9.69. Ht 5 9 Wt 9 06
Defender. From Linwood Rangers BC.
Scotland Under-21.

Season	Club		
1986–87	St Mirren	5	—
1987–88		24	1
1988–89		4	—
1989–90		21	—
1990–91		25	—

McWILLIAMS, Derek

Born Broxburn 16.1.66 Ht 5 10 Wt 11 7
Forward. From Broxburn J

Season	Club		
1984–85	Dundee	16	2
1985–86		11	1
1986–87		1	—
1986–87	*Stirling Albion*	4	—
1986–87	Dundee	5	—
1987–88	Falkirk	31	4
1988–89		28	11
1989–90		33	17
1990–91		29	10

MADDEN, David

Born London 6.1.63. Ht 6 0 Wt 11 03
Defender. From Apprentice.

Season	Club		
1980–81	Southampton	—	—
1981–82		—	—
1982–83		—	—
1982–83	*Bournemouth*	5	—
1983–84	Arsenal	2	—
1984–85	Charlton Ath	20	1
1985–86		—	—
1986–87		—	—
1987–88	Reading	9	1
1988–89	Crystal Palace	19	5

1989–90	....	8	—
1989–90	*Birmingham C*............	5	1
1990–91	Maidstone U..............	10	—

MADDEN, Lawrie

Born London 28.9.55. Ht 6 0 Wt 13 07
Defender. From Arsenal Amateur.

1974–75	Mansfield T................	7	—
1975–76	....	3	—
From Manchester Univ			
1977–78	Charlton Ath..............	4	—
1978–79	....	38	3
1979–80	....	36	1
1980–81	....	28	1
1981–82	....	7	2
1981–82	Millwall......................	10	—
1982–83	....	37	2
1983–84	Sheffield W................	38	1
1984–85	....	19	—
1985–86	....	25	—
1986–87	....	35	1
1987–88	....	38	—
1988–89	....	27	—
1989–90	....	25	—
1990–91	....	5	—
1990–91	*Leicester C*................	3	—

MADDISON, Neil

Born Darlington 2.10.69. Ht 5 9
Wt 11 08
Midfield. From Trainee.

1987–88	Southampton..............	—	—
1988–89	....	5	2
1989–90	....	2	—
1990–91	....	4	—

MADDIX, Danny

Born Ashford 11.10.67. Ht 5 10
Wt 11 07
Defender. From Apprentice.

1985–86	Tottenham H..............	—	—
1986–87	....	—	—
1986–87	*Southend U*................	2	—
1987–88	QPR............................	9	—

1988–89	....	33	2
1989–90	....	32	3
1990–91	....	32	1

MAGILTON, John

Born Belfast 6.5.69. Ht 5 10 Wt 12 07
Midfield. From Apprentice. Northern
Ireland Under-23, 3 full caps.

1986–87	Liverpool....................	—	—
1987–88	....	—	—
1988–89	....	—	—
1989–90	....	—	—
1990–91	....	—	—
1990–91	Oxford U....................	37	6

MAGUIRE, Gavin

Born Hammersmith 24.11.67. Ht 5 10
Wt 11 08
Midfield. From Apprentice. Wales B, 5 full
caps.

1985–86	QPR............................	—	—
1986–87	....	14	—
1987–88	....	18	—
1988–89	....	8	—
1988–89	Portsmouth.................	18	—
1989–90	....	29	—
1990–91	....	23	—

MAGUIRE, Peter

Born Holmfirth 11.9.69. Ht 5 10
Wt 11 00
Forward. From Trainee.

1987–88	Leeds U......................	2	—
1988–89	....	—	—
1989–90	....	—	—
1989–90	Huddersfield T............	3	—
1990–91	....	4	1
1990–91	*Stockport Co*..............	2	—

MAIL, David

Born Bristol 12.9.62. Ht 5 11 Wt 12 00
Defender. From Apprentice.

| 1980–81 | Aston Villa................. | — | — |

Season	Club	Apps	Goals
1981–82	Blackburn R	—	—
1982–83		34	—
1983–84		11	1
1984–85		4	—
1985–86		18	1
1986–87		38	—
1987–88		36	—
1988–89		40	—
1989–90		25	2
1990–91	Hull C	36	1

MAIN, Alan

Born Elgin 5.12.67.   Ht 5 11   Wt 12 03
Goalkeeper. From Elgin C. Scotland
Under-21.

Season	Club	Apps	Goals
1986–87	Dundee U	2	—
1987–88		8	—
1988–89		—	—
1988–89	*Cowdenbeath*	3	—
1988–89	*East Stirling*	2	—
1989–90	Dundee U	27	—
1990–91		31	—

MAIORANA, Giuliano

Born Cambridge 18.4.69   Ht 5 9
Wt 11 08
Forward. From Histon.

Season	Club	Apps	Goals
1988–89	Manchester U	6	—
1989–90		1	—
1990–91		—	—

MAIR, Gordon

Born Bothwell 18.12.58   Ht 5 11
Wt 10 03
Midfield. From Apprentice. Scotland
schools.

Season	Club	Apps	Goals
1976–77	Notts Co	5	—
1977–78		—	—
1978–79		4	1
1979–80		42	5
1980–81		4	—
1981–82		34	9
1982–83		25	4
1983–84		17	—

Season	Club	Apps	Goals
1984–85	Lincoln C	31	—
1985–86		26	3
1986–87	Motherwell	29	1
1987–88		21	1
1988–89		12	—
1989–90		9	—
1990–91		2	—

MAKEL, Lee

Born Sunderland 11.1.73.   Ht 5 10
Wt 9 10
Midfield. From Trainee.

Season	Club	Apps	Goals
1990–91	Newcastle U	3	—

MALKIN, Chris

Born Bebington 4.6.67.   Ht 6 0   Wt 10 12
Forward. From Stork, Overpool.

Season	Club	Apps	Goals
1987–88	Tranmere R	5	—
1988–89		20	4
1989–90		40	18
1990–91		25	4

MALPAS, Maurice

Born Dunfermline 3.8.62.   Ht 5 8
Wt 10 11
Defender. 'S' Form. Scotland Schools,
Youth, Under-21, 42 full caps.

Season	Club	Apps	Goals
1979–80	Dundee U	—	—
1980–81		—	—
1981–82		19	—
1982–83		34	1
1983–84		34	2
1984–85		35	2
1985–86		36	2
1986–87		36	—
1987–88		44	—
1988–89		36	1
1989–90		30	2
1990–91		36	1

MANLEY, Roddy

Born Glasgow 23.7.65.   Ht 5 11   Wt 11 4
Defender. From Knightswood Jun.

Season	Club	Apps	Goals
1984–85	Falkirk	11	—
1985–86		31	—
1986–87		39	—
1987–88		43	1
1988–89		35	1
1989–90	St Mirren	30	—
1990–91		19	—

MANUEL, Billy

Born Hackney 28.6.69.   Ht 5 5   Wt 10 00
Defender. From Apprentice.

Season	Club	Apps	Goals
1987–88	Tottenham H	—	—
1988–89		—	—
1988–89	Gillingham	17	1
1989–90		32	4
1990–91		38	—

MARDENBOROUGH, Steve

Born Birmingham 11.9.64.   Ht 5 8
Wt 11 09
Forward. From Apprentice.

Season	Club	Apps	Goals
1982–83	Coventry C	—	—
1983–84	Wolverhampton W	9	1
1983–84	*Cambridge U*	6	—
1984–85	Swansea C	36	7
1985–86	Newport Co	39	7
1986–87		25	4
1986–87	Cardiff C	11	1
1987–88		21	—
1988–89	Hereford U	27	—
1989–90	*Darlington*	*17*	*1*
1990–91		35	1

MARDON, Paul

Born Bristol 14.9.69.   Ht 6 0   Wt 11 10
Defender. From Trainee.

Season	Club	Apps	Goals
1987–88	Bristol C	8	—
1988–89		20	—
1989–90		7	—
1990–91		7	—
1990–91	*Doncaster R*	3	—

MARGETSON, Martyn

Born West Glamorgan 8.9.71.
Goalkeeper. From Trainee.

Season	Club	Apps	Goals
1990–91	Manchester C	2	—

MARKER, Nick

Born Exeter 3.5.65.   Ht 6 1   Wt 13 00
Defender. From Apprentice.

Season	Club	Apps	Goals
1981–82	Exeter C	14	1
1982–83		18	1
1983–84		31	—
1984–85		45	—
1985–86		40	—
1986–87		43	1
1987–88		11	—
1987–88	Plymouth Arg	26	1
1988–89		43	6
1989–90		43	1
1990–91		39	2

MARPLES, Chris

Born Chesterfield 3.8.64.   Ht 5 11
Wt 11 12
Goalkeeper. From Sutton T and Goole

Season	Club	Apps	Goals
1984–85	Chesterfield	38	—
1985–86		32	—
1986–87		14	—
1986–87	Stockport Co	13	—
1987–88		44	—
1988–89	York C	45	—
1989–90		46	—
1990–91		29	—

MARRIOTT, Andrew

Born Nottingham 11.10.70   Ht 6 0
Wt 12 07
Goalkeeper. From Trainee. FA Schools,
England Youth.

Season	Club	Apps	Goals
1988–89	Arsenal	—	—
1989–90	Nottingham F	—	—
1989–90	*WBA*	3	—
1989–90	*Blackburn R*	2	—
1989–90	*Colchester U*	10	—

1990–91 Nottingham F............ — —

MARSDEN, Chris

Born Sheffield 3.1.69. Ht 5 11 Wt 10 12
Midfield. From Trainee.

1986–87	Sheffield U	—	—
1987–88		16	1
1988–89	Huddersfield T	14	1
1989–90		32	2
1990–91		43	5

MARSH, Chris

Born Dudley 14.1.70. Ht 5 11 Wt 12 10
Midfield. From Trainee.

1987–88	Walsall	3	—
1988–89		13	—
1989–90		9	—
1990–91		23	2

MARSH, Mike

Born Liverpool 21.7.69 Ht 5 8 Wt 11 00
Forward. From Kirkby T.

1987–88	Liverpool	—	—
1988–89		1	—
1989–90		2	—
1990–91		2	—

MARSHALL, Colin

Born Glasgow 1.11.69. Ht 5 5 Wt 9 05
Midfield. From Trainee.

1987–88	Barnsley	—	—
1988–89		1	—
1989–90		2	—
1990–91		1	—

MARSHALL, Gary

Born Bristol 20.4.64. Ht 5 11 Wt 10 10
Forward. From Shepton Mallet.

| 1983–84 | Bristol C | 1 | — |
| 1984–85 | | 5 | 2 |

1984–85	*Torquay U*	7	1
1985–86	Bristol C	19	2
1986–87		24	2
1987–88		19	1
1988–89	Carlisle U	21	2
1989–90	Scunthorpe U	34	3
1990–91		7	—
1990–91	Exeter C	32	3

MARSHALL, Gordon

Born Edinburgh 19.4.64 Ht 6 2 Wt 12 0
Goalkeeper. From Schools

1982–83	East Stirling	15	—
1982–83	East Fife	10	—
1983–84		34	—
1984–85		39	—
1985–86		39	—
1986–87		36	—
1986–87	Falkirk	10	—
1987–88		44	—
1988–89		39	—
1989–90		39	—
1990–91		39	—

MARSHALL, Ian

Born Oxford 20.3.66. Ht 6 1 Wt 12 12
Forward. From Apprentice.

1983–84	Everton	—	—
1984–85		—	—
1985–86		9	—
1986–87		2	1
1987–88		4	—
1987–88	Oldham Ath	10	—
1988–89		41	4
1989–90		25	3
1990–91		26	17

MARSHALL, John

Born Surrey 18.8.64 Ht 5 10 Wt 12 01
Defender. From Apprentice.

1982–83	Fulham	—	—
1983–84		25	—
1984–85		32	1
1985–86		42	3

Season	Club	App	Goals
1986–87	....	29	4
1987–88	....	25	2
1988–89	....	41	7
1989–90	....	36	4
1990–91	....	35	2

MARTIN, Alvin

Born Bootle 29.7.58.   Ht 6 1   Wt 13 07
Defender. From Apprentice. England
Youth, B, 17 full caps.

Season	Club	App	Goals
1976–77	West Ham U	—	—
1977–78	....	7	1
1978–79	....	22	1
1979–80	....	40	2
1980–81	....	41	1
1981–82	....	28	4
1982–83	....	38	3
1983–84	....	29	3
1984–85	....	40	1
1985–86	....	40	4
1986–87	....	16	2
1987–88	....	15	—
1988–89	....	27	1
1989–90	....	31	—
1990–91	....	20	1

MARTIN, Brian

Born Bellshill 24.2.63.   Ht 6 0   Wt 13 00
Defender. From Shotts Bon Accord.

Season	Club	App	Goals
1985–86	Falkirk	25	1
1986–87	....	34	1
1986–87	Hamilton A.................	7	—
1987–88	....	23	—
1987–88	St Mirren	12	1
1988–89	....	34	2
1989–90	....	35	2
1990–91	....	31	2

MARTIN, David

Born East Ham 25.4.63.   Ht 6 0
Wt 12 01
Defender. From Apprentice. England
Youth.

Season	Club	App	Goals
1979–80	Millwall.......................	3	—

Season	Club	App	Goals
1980–81	....	33	1
1981–82	....	38	1
1982–83	....	33	1
1983–84	....	31	3
1984–85	....	2	—
1984–85	Wimbledon	20	2
1985–86	....	15	1
1986–87	Southend U.................	32	2
1987–88	....	41	—
1988–89	....	37	1
1989–90	....	39	3
1990–91	....	41	11

MARTIN, Dean

Born Halifax 9.9.67.   Ht 5 10   Wt 10 02
Midfield. From Local.

Season	Club	App	Goals
1984–85	Halifax T	—	—
1985–86	....	—	—
1986–87	....	16	1
1987–88	....	40	3
1988–89	....	32	2
1989–90	....	37	—
1990–91	....	28	1

MARTIN, John

Born Edinburgh 27.10.58   Ht 6 1
Wt 12 0
Goalkeeper. From Tranent J

Season	Club	App	Goals
1980–81	Airdrieonians	22	—
1981–82	....	27	—
1982–83	....	39	1
1983–84	....	39	—
1984–85	....	36	—
1985–86	....	36	—
1986–87	....	44	—
1987–88	....	44	—
1988–89	....	36	—
1989–90	....	39	—
1990–91	....	38	—

MARTIN, Lee

Born Huddersfield 9.9.68.   Ht 5 11
Wt 11 08
Goalkeeper. From Trainee. England
Schools.

1987–88	Huddersfield T	18	—
1988–89		—	—
1989–90		25	—
1990–91		4	—

MARTIN, Lee

Born Hyde 5.2.68. Ht 5 11 Wt 11 05
Defender. England Under-21.

1986–87	Manchester U	—	—
1987–88		1	—
1988–89		24	1
1989–90		32	—
1990–91		14	—

MARTINDALE, Dave

Born Liverpool 9.4.64. Ht 5 11 Wt 11 10
Midfield. From Liverpool Apprentice,
Southport, Caernarfon.

1987–88	Tranmere R	34	4
1988–89		32	1
1989–90		19	2
1990–91		11	—

MARTYN, Nigel

Born St Austell 11.8.66. Ht 6 2 Wt 14 00
Goalkeeper. From St Blazey. England B,
Under-21.

1987–88	Bristol R	39	—
1988–89		46	—
1989–90		16	—
1989–90	Crystal Palace	25	—
1990–91		38	—

MARWOOD, Brian

Born Seaham Harbour 5.2.60. Ht 5 7
Wt 11 06
Midfield. From Apprentice. England 1 full
cap.

1977–78	Hull C	—	—
1978–79		—	—
1979–80		6	—
1980–81		31	4
1981–82		42	12

1982–83		40	19
1983–84		39	16
1984–85	Sheffield W	41	7
1985–86		37	13
1986–87		32	5
1987–88		18	2
1987–88	Arsenal	4	1
1988–89		31	9
1989–90		17	6
1990–91		—	—
1990–91	Sheffield U	17	2

MASKELL, Craig

Born Aldershot 10.4.68. Ht 5 10
Wt 11 04
Forward. From Apprentice.

1985–86	Southampton	2	1
1986–87		4	—
1986–87	*Swindon T*	—	—
1987–88	Southampton	—	—
1988–89	Huddersfield T	46	28
1989–90		41	15
1990–91	Reading	38	10

MASKREY, Steve

Born Edinburgh 16.8.62. Ht 5 6
Wt 10 00
Forward. From Strathbrock Jun.

1984–85	East Stirling	37	12
1985–86		21	12
1985–86	Queen of the S	12	2
1986–87		31	2
1987–88	St Johnstone	33	5
1988–89		31	12
1989–90		29	11
1990–91		34	7

MASON, Paul

Born Liverpool 3.9.63 Ht 5 8 Wt 11 09
Midfield. From Groningen.

1988–89	Aberdeen	28	4
1989–90		34	9
1990–91		26	3

MATHIE, Alexander

Born Bathgate 22.12.68   Ht 5 10
Wt 10 07
Forward. From Celtic BC.

Season	Club		
1987–88	Celtic	—	—
1988–89		1	—
1989–90		6	—
1990–91		4	—

MATTHEW, Damian

Born Islington, London 23.9.70.   Ht 5 11
Wt 10 10
Midfield. From Trainee. England
Under-21.

Season	Club		
1989–90	Chelsea	2	—
1990–91		8	—

MATTHEWS, Mike

Born Hull 25.9.60.   Ht 5 9   Wt 11 03
Midfield. From Apprentice.

Season	Club		
1978–79	Wolverhampton W	—	—
1979–80		—	—
1980–81		1	—
1981–82		32	2
1982–83		40	5
1983–84		3	—
1983–84	Scunthorpe U	25	1
1984–85		22	3
1985–86		11	1
1986–87	Halifax T	39	4
1987–88		45	3
1988–89		15	1
1988–89	Scarborough	7	1
1988–89	Stockport Co	19	1
1989–90		16	2
1989–90	Scarborough	21	3
1990–91		45	—

MATTHEWS, Neil

Born Grimsby 19.9.66.   Ht 5 11   Wt 12 00
Forward.

Season	Club		
1984–85	Grimsby T	4	1
1985–86		4	—
1985–86	Scunthorpe U	1	—
1986–87	Grimsby T	3	—
1986–87	Halifax T	9	2
1986–87	Bolton W	1	—
1987–88	Halifax T	32	10
1988–89		34	7
1989–90		39	12
1990–91	Stockport Co	29	14

MATTHEWS, Neil

Born Manchester 3.12.67.   Ht 6 0
Wt 11 07
Defender. From Apprentice.

Season	Club		
1985–86	Blackpool	1	—
1986–87		22	—
1987–88		27	—
1988–89		14	1
1989–90		12	—
1990–91	Cardiff C	37	1

MATTHEWSON, Trevor

Born Sheffield 12.2.63.   Ht 6 1   Wt 12 05
Defender. From Apprentice.

Season	Club		
1980–81	Sheffield W	1	—
1981–82		1	—
1982–83		1	—
1983–84		—	—
1983–84	Newport Co	32	—
1984–85		43	—
1985–86	Stockport Co	35	—
1986–87		45	—
1987–88	Lincoln C	40	6
1988–89		43	2
1989–90	Birmingham C	46	1
1990–91		46	3

MAUCHLEN, Ally

Born Kilwinning 29.6.60.   Ht 5 8
Wt 13 07
Midfield. From Irvine Meadow.

Season	Club		
1978–79	Kilmarnock	20	—
1979–80		30	2
1980–81		31	3
1981–82		37	4

1982–83	....	2	1
1982–83	Motherwell..................	25	3
1983–84	....	20	—
1984–85	....	30	1
1985–86	....	1	—
1985–86	Leicester C	37	2
1986–87	....	30	1
1987–88	....	36	2
1988–89	....	38	3
1989–90	....	38	1
1990–91	....	40	1

MAUGE, Ron

Born Islington 10.3.69　Ht 5 8　Wt 10 06
Defender. From Trainee.

1987–88	Charlton Ath	—	—
1988–89	Fulham	13	—
1989–90	....	37	2
1990–91	Bury	29	6

MAXWELL, Alistair

Born Hamilton 29.6.60.　Ht 5 7　Wt 10 05
Goalkeeper. From Fir Park BC.

1981–82	Motherwell..................	—	—
1982–83	....	—	—
1983–84	....	4	—
1984–85	....	15	—
1985–86	....	4	—
1986–87	....	21	—
1987–88	....	1	—
1987–88	*Clydebank*	1	—
1988–89	Motherwell..................	17	—
1989–90	....	36	—
1990–91	....	36	—

MAY, Andy

Born Bury 26.2.64.　Ht 5 8　Wt 11 01
Midfield. From Apprentice. England
Under-21.

1980–81	Manchester C	1	—
1981–82	....	6	—
1982–83	....	8	—
1983–84	....	42	5
1984–85	....	39	3

1985–86	....	37	—
1986–87	....	17	—
1987–88	Huddersfield T	28	3
1987–88	*Bolton W*......................	10	2
1988–89	Huddersfield T............	45	2
1989–90	....	41	—
1990–91	Bristol C	45	3

MAY, David

Born Oldham 24.6.70　Ht 6 0　Wt 11 07
Defender. From Trainee.

1988–89	Blackburn R	1	—
1989–90	....	17	—
1990–91	....	19	1

MAY, Edward

Born Edinburgh 30.8.67　Ht 5 7
Wt 10 03
Forward. From Hutchison Vale BC.
Scotland Youth, Under-21.

1983–84	Dundee U	—	—
1984–85	....	—	—
1984–85	Hibernian..................	—	—
1985–86	....	19	1
1986–87	....	30	5
1987–88	....	35	2
1988–89	....	25	2
1989–90	Brentford	30	8
1990–91	....	17	2

MEADE, Raphael

Born Islington 22.11.62.　Ht 5 10
Wt 11 09
Forward. From Apprentice.

1980–81	Arsenal......................	—	—
1981–82	....	16	4
1982–83	....	4	2
1983–84	....	13	5
1984–85	....	8	3
From Sporting Lisbon			
1988–89	Dundee U	11	4
1988–89	Luton T	4	—
1989–90	....	—	—
1989–90	Ipswich T....................	1	—

From Odense

1990–91	Plymouth Arg	5	—

MEAKER, Michael

Born Greenford 18.8.71. Ht 5 11
Wt 11 05
Midfield. From Trainee.

1989–90	QPR	—	—
1990–91		8	—

MEASHAM, Ian

Born Barnsley 14.12.64. Ht 5 11
Wt 11 08
Defender. From Apprentice.

1982–83	Huddersfield T	—	—
1983–84		—	—
1984–85		17	—
1985–86		—	—
1985–86	*Lincoln C*	6	—
1985–86	*Rochdale*	12	—
1986–87	Cambridge U	46	—
1987–88		—	—
1988–89		—	—
1988–89	Burnley	30	1
1989–90		35	—
1990–91		45	—

MEGSON, Gary

Born Manchester 2.5.59. Ht 5 10
Wt 12 00
Midfield. From Apprentice.

1977–78	Plymouth Arg	24	2
1978–79		42	8
1979–80		12	—
1979–80	Everton	12	1
1980–81		10	1
1981–82	Sheffield W	40	5
1982–83		41	4
1983–84		42	4
1984–85	Nottingham F	—	—
1984–85	Newcastle U	20	1
1985–86		4	—
1985–86	Sheffield W	20	3
1986–87		35	6

1987–88		37	2
1988–89		18	1
1988–89	Manchester C	22	1
1989–90		19	—
1990–91		19	1

MEGSON, Kevin

Born Halifax 1.7.71. Ht 5 11   Wt 11 00
Forward. From Trainee.

1989–90	Bradford C	23	—
1990–91		4	—
1990–91	Halifax T	5	—

MEHEW, David

Born Camberley 29.10.67. Ht 5 11
Wt 12 06
Forward.

1984–85	Leeds U	—	—
1985–86	Bristol R	4	—
1986–87		21	10
1987–88		18	8
1988–89		31	7
1989–90		46	18
1990–91		41	8

MELLON, Michael

Born Paisley 18.3.72. Ht 5 8   Wt 11 03
Midfield. From Trainee.

1989–90	Bristol C	9	—
1990–91		—	—

MELVILLE, Andy

Born Swansea 29.11.68. Ht 6 0   Wt 12 00
Defender. From school. Wales B, Under-21, 7 full caps.

1985–86	Swansea C	5	—
1986–87		42	3
1987–88		37	4
1988–89		45	10
1989–90		46	5
1990–91	Oxford U	46	3

MELVIN, Martin

Born Glasgow 7.8.69. Ht 5 11   Wt 11 6
Defender.

Season	Club	Apps	Goals
1988–89	Falkirk	1	—
1989–90		15	—
1990–91		10	—

MENDONCA, Clive

Born Tullington 9.9.68. Ht 5 10
Wt 11 07
Forward. From Apprentice.

Season	Club	Apps	Goals
1986–87	Sheffield U	2	—
1987–88		11	4
1987–88	*Doncaster R*	2	—
1987–88	Rotherham U	8	2
1988–89		10	1
1989–90		32	14
1990–91		34	10

MEOLA, Tony

Born Belleville 21.2.69. Ht 6 0 Wt 14 07
Goalkeeper. From United States Soccer
Federation. USSR full caps.

Season	Club	Apps	Goals
1990–91	Brighton	1	—
1990–91	Watford	—	—

MERCER, William

Born Liverpool 22.5.69. Ht 6 1 Wt 11 00
Goalkeeper. From Trainee.

Season	Club	Apps	Goals
1987–88	Liverpool	—	—
1988–89		—	—
1988–89	Rotherham U	—	—
1989–90		2	—
1990–91		13	—

MERSON, Paul

Born London 20.3.68. Ht 5 10 Wt 11 08
Forward. From Apprentice. England
Youth, Under-21.

Season	Club	Apps	Goals
1985–86	Arsenal	—	—
1986–87		7	3
1986–87	*Brentford*	7	—
1987–88	Arsenal	15	5
1988–89		37	10
1989–90		29	7

Season	Club	Apps	Goals
1990–91		37	13

METGOD, Johnny

Born Amsterdam 27.2.58. Ht 6 4
Wt 13 6
Midfield. From DWS, Haarlem, AZ'67
and Real Madrid. Holland full caps.

Season	Club	Apps	Goals
1984–85	Nottingham F	40	6
1985–86		39	6
1986–87		37	3
1987–88	Tottenham H	12	—
To Feyenoord			

METHVEN, Colin

Born India 10.12.55. Ht 6 2 Wt 12 06
Defender. From Leven Royals.

Season	Club	Apps	Goals
1974–75	East Fife	1	—
1975–76		26	1
1976–77		39	—
1977–78		39	2
1978–79		39	11
1979–80	Wigan Ath	35	2
1980–81		46	2
1981–82		46	9
1982–83		44	1
1983–84		39	—
1984–85		43	—
1985–86		43	7
1986–87	Blackpool	46	5
1987–88		40	2
1988–89		42	1
1989–90		45	3
1990–91		—	—
1990–91	*Carlisle U*	12	—
1990–91	Walsall	32	1

MEYER, Adrian

Born Bristol 22.9.70. Ht 6 0 Wt 14 00
Defender. From Trainee.

Season	Club	Apps	Goals
1989–90	Scarborough	18	2
1990–91		17	1

MICKLEWHITE, Gary

Born Southwark 21.3.61. Ht 5 7
Wt 10 04
Forward. From Apprentice.

Season	Club	League Appearances/Goals	
1977–78	Manchester U	—	—
1978–79		—	—
1979–80	QPR	—	—
1980–81		1	—
1981–82		26	2
1982–83		34	6
1983–84		30	2
1984–85		15	1
1984–85	Derby Co	19	4
1985–86		46	11
1986–87		42	6
1987–88		16	1
1988–89		26	3
1989–90		18	2
1990–91		35	2

MIDDLETON, Craig

Born Nuneaton 10.9.70.   Ht 5 9
Wt 11 00
Forward. From Trainee.

Season	Club	League Appearances/Goals	
1989–90	Coventry C	1	—
1990–91		—	—

MIKLOSKO, Ludek

Born Ostrava 9.12.61.   Ht 6 5   Wt 14 00
Goalkeeper. From Banik Ostrava.
Czechoslovakia full caps.

Season	Club	League Appearances/Goals	
1989–90	West Ham U	18	—
1990–91		46	—

MILLAR, John

Born Lanark 8.12.66.   Ht 5 10   Wt 10 00
Defender.

Season	Club	League Appearances/Goals	
1984–85	Chelsea	—	—
1985–86		7	—
1986–87		4	—
1986–87	Hamilton A	10	—
1986–87	Northampton T	1	—
1987–88	Blackburn R	15	—
1988–89		38	—
1989–90		39	1
1990–91		34	—

MILLAR, Paul

Born Belfast 16.11.66.   Ht 6 2   Wt 12 07
Forward. From Portadown. Northern
Ireland Under-23.

Season	Club	League Appearances/Goals	
1988–89	Port Vale	—	—
1989–90		23	4
1990–91		17	1
1990–91	Hereford U	5	2

MILLEN, Keith

Born Croydon 26.9.66.   Ht 6 2   Wt 12 04
Defender. From Juniors.

Season	Club	League Appearances/Goals	
1984–85	Brentford	17	—
1985–86		32	2
1986–87		39	2
1987–88		40	3
1988–89		36	3
1989–90		32	—
1990–91		32	2

MILLER, Allan

Born Epping 29.3.70.   Ht 6 2   Wt 13 08
Goalkeeper. From Trainee. FA Schools,
England Under-21.

Season	Club	League Appearances/Goals	
1987–88	Arsenal	—	—
1988–89		—	—
1988–89	Plymouth Arg	13	—
1989–90	Arsenal	—	—
1990–91		—	—

MILLER, David

Born Burnley 8.1.64.   Ht 5 11   Wt 11 12
Midfield. From Apprentice.

Season	Club	League Appearances/Goals	
1981–82	Burnley	—	—
1982–83		1	—
1982–83	Crewe Alex	3	—
1983–84	Burnley	17	2
1984–85		14	1
1985–86	Tranmere R	29	1
1986–87	Preston NE	15	—
1987–88		28	2
1988–89		12	—
1988–89	Burnley	4	—

Season	Club	App	Goals
1989–90	Preston NE	3	—
1989–90	Carlisle U	42	3
1990–91		41	4

MILLER, Ian

Born Perth 13.5.55. Ht 5 9 Wt 11 12
Forward.

Season	Club	App	Goals
1973–74	Bury	15	—
1974–75		—	—
1974–75	Nottingham F	—	—
1975–76	Doncaster R	43	9
1976–77		46	5
1977–78		35	—
1978–79	Swindon T	44	3
1979–80		40	2
1980–81		43	4
1981–82	Blackburn R	42	3
1982–83		32	4
1983–84		36	3
1984–85		38	4
1985–86		38	1
1986–87		28	—
1987–88		23	—
1988–89		31	1
1989–90	Port Vale	21	1
1990–91	Scunthorpe U	12	—

MILLER, Joe

Born Glasgow 8.12.67. Ht 5 8 Wt 9 12
Forward. 'S' Form. Scotland Schools,
Youth, Under-21.

Season	Club	App	Goals
1984–85	Aberdeen	1	—
1985–86		18	3
1986–87		27	6
1987–88		14	4
1987–88	Celtic	27	3
1988–89		22	8
1989–90		24	5
1990–91		30	8

MILLER, Kevin

Born Falmouth 15.3.69 Ht 6 1 Wt 12 10
Goalkeeper. From Newquay.

Season	Club	App	Goals
1988–89	Exeter C	3	—

Season	Club	App	Goals
1989–90		28	—
1990–91		46	—

MILLER, Paul

Born Bisley 31.1.68. Ht 6 0 Wt 11 00
Forward. From Trainee.

Season	Club	App	Goals
1987–88	Wimbledon	5	—
1987–88	Newport Co	6	2
1988–89	Wimbledon	18	5
1989–90		15	2
1989–90	Bristol C	3	—
1990–91	Wimbledon	1	—

MILLER, Paul

Born London 11.10.59. Ht 6 1 Wt 13 02
Defender. From Apprentice.

Season	Club	App	Goals
1977–78	Tottenham H	—	—
1978–79		7	—
1979–80		27	2
1980–81		25	2
1981–82		35	—
1982–83		23	1
1983–84		21	—
1984–85		39	—
1985–86		29	2
1986–87		2	—
1986–87	Charlton Ath	14	1
1987–88		23	1
1988–89		5	—
1988–89	Watford	20	—
1989–90	Bournemouth	31	—
1989–90	Brentford	3	—
1990–91	Bournemouth	16	1
1990–91	Swansea C	12	—

MILLER, William

Born Edinburgh 1.11.69. Ht 5 8 Wt 10 6
Defender. From Edina Hibs BC. Scotland
Under-21.

Season	Club	App	Goals
1989–90	Hibernian	11	—
1990–91		25	1

MILLIGAN, Mike

Born Manchester 20.2.67. Ht 5 8
Wt 11 00
Midfield. Eire B.

Season	Club	App	Goals
1984–85	Oldham Ath	—	—
1985–86		5	1
1986–87		38	2
1987–88		39	1
1988–89		39	6
1989–90		41	7
1990–91	Everton	17	1

MILLS, Brian

Born Swynnerton 26.12.71. Ht 5 9
Wt 10 10
Forward. From Trainee.

Season	Club	App	Goals
1989–90	Port Vale	—	—
1990–91		2	2

MILLS, Gary

Born Northampton 11.11.61. Ht 5 8
Wt 11 05
Forward. From Apprentice. England
Schools, Youth, Under-21.

Season	Club	App	Goals
1978–79	Nottingham F	4	1
1979–80		13	1
1980–81		27	5
1981–82		14	1
From Seattle S			
1982–83	Derby Co	18	1
From Seattle S			
1983–84	Nottingham F	7	—
1984–85		26	4
1985–86		14	—
1986–87		32	—
1987–88	Notts Co	46	5
1988–89		29	3
1988–89	Leicester C	13	—
1989–90		29	4
1990–91		45	5

MILLS, Simon

Born Sheffield 16.8.64. Ht 5 8 Wt 11 04
Defender. From Apprentice. England
Youth.

Season	Club	App	Goals
1982–83	Sheffield W	1	—
1983–84		2	—
1984–85		2	—

Season	Club	App	Goals
1985–86	York C	36	2
1986–87		45	1
1987–88		18	2
1987–88	Port Vale	19	5
1988–89		43	—
1989–90		45	1
1990–91		41	—

MILNE, Callum

Born Edinburgh 27.8.65. Ht 5 8
Wt 10 07
Defender. From Salvesen BC.

Season	Club	App	Goals
1983–84	Hibernian	—	—
1984–85		1	—
1985–86		7	—
1986–87		2	—
1987–88		3	—
1988–89		19	—
1989–90		3	—
1990–91		21	—

MILNE, Ralph

Born Dundee 13.5.61. Ht 5 9 Wt 12 00
Forward. 'S' Form. Scotland Youth,
Under-21.

Season	Club	App	Goals
1977–78	Dundee U	—	—
1978–79		—	—
1979–80		13	2
1980–81		21	7
1981–82		35	8
1982–83		34	16
1983–84		25	5
1984–85		19	4
1985–86		18	1
1986–87		14	1
1986–87	Charlton Ath	12	—
1987–88		10	—
1987–88	Bristol C	19	4
1988–89		11	2
1988–89	Manchester U	22	3
1989–90		1	—
1989–90	*West Ham U*	—	—
1990–91	Manchester U	—	—

MILNER, Andy

Born Kendal 10.2.67. Ht 5 11 Wt 11 07
Forward. From Netherfield.

Season	Club		
1988–89	Manchester C	—	—
1989–90		—	—
1989–90	Rochdale	16	4
1990–91		35	5

MILTON, Simon

Born London 23.8.63. Ht 5 9 Wt 11 09
Midfield. From Bury St Edmunds.

Season	Club		
1987–88	Ipswich T	8	1
1987–88	*Exeter C*	2	3
1987–88	*Torquay U*	4	1
1988–89	Ipswich T	35	10
1989–90		41	10
1990–91		31	6

MILTON, Steve

Born Fulham 13.4.63. Ht 6 0 Wt 12 07
Forward. From Apprentice.

Season	Club		
1981–82	West Ham U	—	—
From Whyteleafe.			
1989–90	Fulham	34	9
1990–91		23	—

MIMMS, Bobby

Born York 12.10.63. Ht 6 2 Wt 12 13
Goalkeeper. From Halifax T Apprentice.
England Under-21.

Season	Club		
1981–82	Rotherham U	2	—
1982–83		13	—
1983–84		22	—
1984–85		46	—
1985–86	Everton	10	—
1985–86	*Notts Co*	2	—
1986–87	Everton	11	—
1986–87	*Sunderland*	4	—
1986–87	*Blackburn R*	6	—
1987–88	Everton	8	—
1987–88	*Manchester C*	3	—
1987–88	Tottenham H	13	—
1988–89		20	—

Season	Club		
1989–90		4	—
1989–90	*Aberdeen*	6	—
1990–91	Tottenham H	—	—
1990–91	Blackburn R	22	—

MINETT, Jason

Born Peterborough 12.8.71. Ht 5 10
Wt 10 02
Midfield. From Trainee.

Season	Club		
1989–90	Norwich C	—	—
1990–91		2	—

MINTO, Scott

Born Cheshire 6.8.71 Ht 5 10 Wt 10 00
Defender. From Trainee. England Youth,
Under-21.

Season	Club		
1988–89	Charlton Ath	3	—
1989–90		23	2
1990–91		43	1

MITCHELL, Brian

Born Stonehaven 16.7.63. Ht 6 1
Wt 13 1
Defender. From King St. Scotland
Schools.

Season	Club		
1981–82	Aberdeen	1	—
1982–83		1	—
1983–84		9	—
1984–85		14	1
1985–86		23	—
1986–87		17	—
1986–87	Bradford C	16	—
1987–88		42	6
1988–89		45	1
1989–90		35	2
1990–91		20	—

MITCHELL, David

Born Glasgow 13.6.62 Ht 6 1 Wt 12 07
Forward. Australia full caps.

Season	Club		
1983–84	Rangers	12	2
1984–85		14	4

From Feyenoord

Season	Club		
1988–89	Chelsea	6	—
1989–90		—	—
1990–91		1	—
1990–91	*Newcastle U*	2	1

MITCHELL, Graham

Born Glasgow 2.11.62. Ht 5 10 Wt 11 08
Midfield. From Auchengill BC.

Season	Club		
1980–81	Hamilton A	4	—
1981–82		37	—
1982–83		32	1
1983–84		21	1
1984–85		30	—
1985–86		32	6
1986–87		23	1
1986–87	Hibernian	17	1
1987–88		41	1
1988–89		20	—
1989–90		31	—
1990–91		28	—

MITCHELL, Graham

Born Shipley 16.2.68. Ht 6 0 Wt 11 05
Defender. From Apprentice.

Season	Club		
1986–87	Huddersfield T	17	—
1987–88		29	1
1988–89		34	—
1989–90		37	1
1990–91		46	—

MITCHELL, Ian

Born Tredegar 1.10.71.
Forward. From Merthyr.

Season	Club		
1990–91	Hereford U	3	—

MITCHELL, Paul

Born Bournemouth 20.10.71. Ht 5 11
Wt 11 13
Defender. From Trainee

Season	Club		
1990–91	Bournemouth	2	—

MOCKLER, Andrew

Born Stockton 18.11.70 Ht 5 11
Wt 11 13
Midfield. From Trainee.

Season	Club		
1988–89	Arsenal	—	—
1989–90		—	—
1990–91	Scarborough	34	5

MOHAN, Nicky

Born Middlesbrough 6.10.70. Ht 6 2
Wt 12 00
Defender. From Trainee.

Season	Club		
1987–88	Middlesbrough	—	—
1988–89		6	—
1989–90		22	—
1990–91		—	—

MOLBY, Jan

Born Kolding 4.7.63. Ht 6 1 Wt 14 7
Midfield. From Kolding, Ajax. Denmark
Youth, Under-21, full caps.

Season	Club		
1984–85	Liverpool	22	1
1985–86		39	14
1986–87		34	7
1987–88		7	—
1988–89		13	2
1989–90		17	1
1990–91		25	9

MONCUR, John

Born Stepney 22.9.66. Ht 5 7 Wt 9 10
Midfield. From Apprentice.

Season	Club		
1984–85	Tottenham H	—	—
1985–86		—	—
1986–87		1	—
1986–87	*Cambridge U*	4	—
1986–87	*Doncaster R*	4	—
1987–88	Tottenham H	5	—
1988–89		1	—
1988–89	*Portsmouth*	7	—
1989–90	Tottenham H	5	1
1989–90	*Brentford*	5	1
1990–91	Tottenham H	9	—

MONEY, Campbell

Born Maybole 31.8.60.   Ht 5 11
Wt 12 03
Goalkeeper. From Dailly Ams. Scotland
Youth, B, Under–21.

Season	Club	App	Goals
1978–79	St Mirren	—	—
1979–80		—	—
1980–81		—	—
1981–82		1	—
1982–83		1	—
1983–84		6	—
1984–85		30	—
1985–86		33	—
1986–87		42	—
1987–88		41	—
1988–89		21	—
1989–90		28	—
1990–91		25	—

MONINGTON, Mark

Born Bilsthorpe 21.10.70   Ht 6 1
Wt 13 00
Midfield. From schoolboy.

Season	Club	App	Goals
1988–89	Burnley	8	1
1989–90		13	—
1990–91		—	—

MONKOU, Kenneth

Born Surinam 29.11.64   Ht 6 0   Wt 12 00
Defender. From Feyenoord. Holland
Under–21.

Season	Club	App	Goals
1988–89	Chelsea	2	—
1989–90		34	1
1990–91		27	1

MOONEY, Brian

Born Dublin 2.2.66.   Ht 5 10   Wt 11 02
Midfield. From Home Farm. Eire Youth,
B, Under–23.

Season	Club	App	Goals
1983–84	Liverpool	—	—
1984–85		—	—
1985–86		—	—
1985–86	*Wrexham*	9	2
1986–87	Liverpool	—	—
1987–88		—	—
1987–88	Preston NE	34	3
1988–89		40	6
1989–90		45	9
1990–91	*Sheffield W*	—	—
1990–91	Preston NE	9	2
1990–91	Sunderland	6	—

MOONEY, Martin

Born Alexandria 25.9.70   Ht 5 8   Wt 9 11
Midfield. From Duntocher BC

Season	Club	App	Goals
1988–89	Falkirk	6	—
1989–90		15	2
1990–91		4	—

MOONEY, Tommy

Born Teesside North 11.8.71.   Ht 5 10
Wt 12 05
Forward. From Trainee.

Season	Club	App	Goals
1989–90	Aston Villa	—	—
1990–91	Scarborough	27	13

MOORE, Allan

Born Glasgow 23.12.64.   Ht 5 6   Wt 9 10
Forward. From Possil YM.

Season	Club	App	Goals
1983–84	Dumbarton	4	—
1984–85		4	—
1985–86		33	4
1986–87		18	3
1986–87	Hearts	10	—
1987–88		7	1
1988–89		12	2
1989–90	St Johnstone	33	13
1990–91		31	5

MOORE, Gary

Born Greenwich 29.12.68.
Forward.

Season	Club	App	Goals
1990–91	Maidstone U	5	1

MOORE, John

Born Consett 1.10.66.   Ht 6 0   Wt 12 10
Forward. From Apprentice.

Season	Club	App	Goals
1984–85	Sunderland	4	1
From St Patrick's Ath			
1985–86	Sunderland	—	—
1985–86	*Newport Co*	2	—
1986–87	Sunderland	3	—
1986–87	*Darlington*	2	1
1986–87	*Mansfield T*	5	1
1987–88	Sunderland	9	—
1987–88	*Rochdale*	10	2
1988–89	Hull C	14	1
1988–89	*Sheffield U*	5	—
From Utrecht			
1990–91	Shrewsbury T	8	1
1990–91	Crewe Alex	1	—

MOORE, Kevin

Born Grimsby 29.4.58.   Ht 5 11   Wt 12 12
Defender. Local. England Schools.

Season	Club	App	Goals
1976–77	Grimsby T	28	—
1977–78		42	—
1978–79		46	6
1979–80		41	4
1980–81		41	1
1981–82		36	4
1982–83		38	—
1983–84		41	1
1984–85		31	4
1985–86		31	2
1986–87		25	5
1986–87	Oldham Ath	13	1
1987–88	Southampton	35	3
1988–89		25	3
1989–90		21	1
1990–91		19	1

MORAN, Kevin

Born Dublin 29.4.56.   Ht 5 11   Wt 12 09
Defender. From Pegasus-Eire Gaelic
Football. Eire 60 full caps.

Season	Club	App	Goals
1977–78	Manchester U	—	—
1978–79		1	—
1979–80		9	1
1980–81		32	—
1981–82		30	7
1982–83		29	2
1983–84		38	7

Season	Club	App	Goals
1984–85		19	4
1985–86		19	—
1986–87		33	—
1987–88		21	—
From Sporting Gijon			
1989–90	Blackburn R	19	2
1990–91		32	1

MORAN, Paul

Born Enfield 22.5.68.   Ht 5 10   Wt 11 00
Forward. From Trainee.

Season	Club	App	Goals
1984–85	Tottenham H	—	—
1985–86		—	—
1986–87		1	—
1987–88		13	1
1988–89		8	—
1988–89	*Portsmouth*	3	—
1989–90	Tottenham H	5	1
1989–90	*Leicester C*	10	1
1990–91	Totteham H	1	—
1990–91	*Newcastle U*	1	—
1990–91	*Southend U*	1	—

MORAN, Richie

Born Maidstone 9.9.63.
Forward. From Fujita.

Season	Club	App	Goals
1990–91	Birmingham C	8	1

MORAN, Steve

Born Croydon 10.1.61.   Ht 5 8   Wt 11 03
Forward. From Amateur. England
Under-21.

Season	Club	App	Goals
1979–80	Southampton	1	1
1980–81		31	18
1981–82		18	9
1982–83		36	10
1983–84		34	21
1984–85		32	11
1985–86		28	8
1986–87		—	—
1986–87	Leicester C	27	9
1987–88		16	5
1987–88	Reading	28	7
1988–89		34	4

| 1989–90 | .... | 28 | 11 |
| 1990–91 | .... | 26 | 8 |

MORGAN, Darren

Born Camberwell 5.11.67. Ht 5 6
Wt 9 10
Defender. From Apprentice. Wales Youth,
B.

1985–86	Millwall......................	—	—
1986–87	....	21	1
1987–88	....	4	—
1988–89	....	8	—
1989–90	....	2	1
1989–90	*Bradford C*...................	2	—
1990–91	Millwall......................	8	—
1990–91	*Peterborough U*...........	5	—

MORGAN, Jon

Born Cardiff 10.7.70 Ht 5 8 Wt 10 01
Midfield. From Trainee.

1988–89	Cardiff C.....................	19	—
1989–90	....	32	3
1990–91	....	4	—

MORGAN, Nicky

Born East Ham 30.10.59. Ht 5 10
Wt 13 10
Forward. From Apprentice.

1977–78	West Ham U	—	—
1978–79	....	2	—
1979–80	....	6	1
1980–81	....	6	1
1981–82	....	—	—
1982–83	....	7	—
1982–83	Portsmouth	6	1
1983–84	....	25	9
1984–85	....	30	8
1985–86	....	30	14
1986–87	....	4	—
1986–87	Stoke C.......................	29	10
1987–88	....	28	5
1988–89	....	18	5
1989–90	....	13	1
1989–90	Bristol C	7	4

| 1990–91 | .... | 44 | 13 |

MORGAN, Simon

Born Birmingham 5.9.66. Ht 5 10
Wt 11 00
Defender. England Under-21.

1984–85	Leicester C.................	—	—
1985–86	....	30	—
1986–87	....	41	1
1987–88	....	40	—
1988–89	....	32	—
1989–90	....	17	2
1990–91	....	—	—
1990–91	Fulham	32	—

MORGAN, Steve

Born Wrexham 28.12.70. Ht 5 9
Wt 11 05
Midfield. From Trainee.

1987–88	Oldham Ath...............	1	—
1988–89	....	1	—
1989–90	....	—	—
1989–90	*Wrexham*.....................	7	1
1990–91	Oldham Ath...............	—	—
1990–91	Rochdale....................	11	3

MORGAN, Steve

Born Oldham 19.9.68. Ht 5 11 Wt 13 00
Defender. From Apprentice. England
Youth.

1985–86	Blackpool...................	5	—
1986–87	....	11	—
1987–88	....	46	6
1988–89	....	44	3
1989–90	....	38	1
1990–91	Plymouth Arg............	40	3

MORGAN, Trevor

Born Forest Gate 30.9.56 Ht 6 2
Wt 13 04
Forward. From Leytonstone and Ilford.

| 1980–81 | Bournemouth.............. | 42 | 10 |

Season	Club	Apps	Goals
1981–82	....	11	3
1981–82	Mansfield T..............	12	6
1981–82	Bournemouth.............	14	4
1982–83	....	45	16
1983–84	....	29	13
1983–84	Bristol C	15	5
1984–85	....	17	3
1984–85	Exeter C...............	26	9
1985–86	....	4	—
1985–86	Bristol R	36	16
1986–87	....	19	8
1986–87	Bristol C	19	8
1987–88	Bolton W	38	7
1988–89	....	39	10
1989–90	....	—	—
1989–90	Colchester U.............	32	12
1990–91	....	—	—
1990–91	Exeter C...............	17	3

MORLEY, Trevor

Born Nottingham 20.3.61. Ht 5 11
Wt 12 01
Forward. From Derby Co, Corby T,
Nuneaton.

Season	Club	Apps	Goals
1985–86	Northampton T	43	13
1986–87	....	37	16
1987–88	....	27	10
1987–88	Manchester C	15	4
1988–89	....	40	12
1989–90	....	17	2
1989–90	West Ham U	19	10
1990–91	....	38	12

MORRELL, Paul

Born Poole 23.3.61. Ht 5 11 Wt 13 05
Defender. From Poole, Bath &
Weymouth.

Season	Club	Apps	Goals
1983–84	Bournemouth.............	22	2
1984–85	....	44	1
1985–86	....	38	1
1986–87	....	45	2
1987–88	....	42	—
1988–89	....	44	—
1989–90	....	21	—
1990–91	....	42	1

MORRIS, Andy

Born Sheffield 17.11.67. Ht 6 5 Wt 15 07
Forward.

Season	Club	Apps	Goals
1984–85	Rotherham U	1	—
1985–86	....	—	—
1986–87	....	6	—
1987–88	....	—	—
1987–88	Chesterfield................	10	—
1988–89	....	42	9
1989–90	....	43	4
1990–91	....	15	4

MORRIS, Chris

Born Newquay 24.12.63. Ht 5 10
Wt 10 08
Defender. England Schools. Eire 27 full
caps.

Season	Club	Apps	Goals
1982–83	Sheffield W................	—	—
1983–84	....	13	1
1984–85	....	14	—
1985–86	....	30	—
1986–87	....	17	—
1987–88	Celtic................	44	3
1988–89	....	33	3
1989–90	....	32	1
1990–91	....	19	—

MORRIS, David

Born Plumstead 19.11.71. Ht 5 11
Wt 12 00
Midfield. From Trainee.

Season	Club	Apps	Goals
1990–91	Bournemouth.............	1	—

MORRIS, Mark

Born Morden 26.9.62. Ht 6 1 Wt 13 08
Defender. From Apprentice.

Season	Club	Apps	Goals
1980–81	Wimbledon	—	—
1981–82	....	33	1
1982–83	....	26	3
1983–84	....	39	3
1984–85	....	29	1
1985–86	....	20	1
1985–86	*Aldershot*.....................	14	—

1986–87	Wimbledon	21	—
1987–88	Watford	39	1
1988–89		2	—
1989–90	Sheffield U	42	3
1990–91		14	—

MORRIS, Mark

Born Chester 1.8.68.   Ht 6 0   Wt 13 00
Goalkeeper.

1985–86	Wrexham	3	—
1986–87		—	—
1987–88		6	—
1988–89		3	—
1989–90		3	—
1990–91		40	—

MORRISON, Andy

Born Inverness 30.7.70   Ht 5 11   Wt 12 00
Midfield. From Trainee.

1987–88	Plymouth Arg	1	—
1988–89		2	—
1989–90		19	1
1990–91		32	2

MORRISSEY, John

Born Liverpool 8.3.65.   Ht 5 8   Wt 11 09
Midfield. From Apprentice. England
Youth.

1982–83	Everton	—	—
1983–84		—	—
1984–85		1	—
1985–86	Wolverhampton W	10	1
1985–86	Tranmere R	32	5
1986–87		38	7
1987–88		39	4
1988–89		42	4
1989–90		27	4
1990–91		40	9

MORROW, Grant

Born Glasgow 4.10.70.   Ht 5 10   Wt 11 07
Forward. From Rowntree Mackintosh.

1989–90	Doncaster R	7	2

1990–91		14	1

MORROW, Steve

Born Belfast 2.7.70.   Ht 6 0   Wt 11 03
Defender. From Bangor, Arsenal Trainee.
Northern Ireland Youth, Under-23, 4 full
caps.

1987–88	Arsenal	—	—
1988–89		—	—
1989–90		—	—
1990–91	Reading	10	—

MORTENSEN, Henrik

Born Odder (Denmark) 12.2.68.   Ht 5 10
Wt 11 07
Forward. From Aarhus. Denmark
Under-21.

1989–90	Norwich C	15	—
1990–91		3	—

MORTIMER, Paul

Born London 8.5.68.   Ht 5 11   Wt 11 03
Midfield. From Fulham Apprentice.
England Under-21.

1987–88	Charlton Ath	12	—
1988–89		33	5
1989–90		36	5
1990–91		32	7

MORTON, Neil

Born Congleton 21.12.68.   Ht 5 9
Wt 10 07
Forward. From Trainee.

1986–87	Crewe Alex	2	—
1987–88		24	1
1988–89		5	—
From Northwich Vic			
1990–91	Chester C	34	7

MOULDEN, Paul

Born Farnworth 6.9.67.   Ht 5 8   Wt 11 03
Forward. From Apprentice. England
Youth.

1984–85	Manchester C	—	—
1985–86		2	—
1986–87		20	5
1987–88		6	—
1988–89		36	13
1989–90	Bournemouth	32	13
1989–90	Oldham Ath	8	—
1990–91		24	3

MOUNTFIELD, Derek

Born Liverpool 2.11.62. Ht 6 1 Wt 12 07
Defender. From Apprentice. England B,
Under-21.

1980–81	Tranmere R	5	—
1981–82		21	1
1982–83	Everton	1	—
1983–84		31	3
1984–85		37	10
1985–86		15	3
1986–87		13	3
1987–88		9	—
1988–89	Aston Villa	24	1
1989–90		32	4
1990–91		32	4

MOWBRAY, Tony

Born Saltburn 22.11.63. Ht 6 1 Wt 13 00
Defender. From Apprentice. England B.

1981–82	Middlesbrough	—	—
1982–83		26	—
1983–84		35	1
1984–85		40	2
1985–86		35	4
1986–87		46	7
1987–88		44	3
1988–89		37	3
1989–90		28	2
1990–91		40	3

MOWER, Ken

Born Walsall 1.12.60 Ht 6 1 Wt 12 04
Defender. From Apprentice.

| 1978–79 | Walsall | 1 | — |
| 1979–80 | | 44 | 1 |

1980–81		33	2
1981–82		34	—
1982–83		45	1
1983–84		44	1
1984–85		41	1
1985–86		43	1
1986–87		28	1
1987–88		26	—
1988–89		29	—
1989–90		30	—
1990–91		17	—

MOYES, David

Born Blythswood 25.4.63. Ht 6 1
Wt 11 08
Defender. From Drumchapel A

1980–81	Celtic	—	—
1981–82		19	—
1982–83		5	—
1983–84		—	—
1983–84	Cambridge U	30	—
1984–85		40	1
1985–86		9	—
1985–86	Bristol C	27	2
1986–87		41	3
1987–88		15	1
1987–88	Shrewsbury T	17	2
1988–89		33	1
1989–90		46	8
1990–91	Dunfermline Ath	35	7

MUDD, Paul

Born Hull 13.11.70
Defender. From Trainee.

1988–89	Hull C	1	—
1989–90		—	—
1990–91	Scarborough	24	—

MUGGLETON, Carl

Born Leicester 13.9.68. Ht 6 1 Wt 11 13
Goalkeeper. From Apprentice. England
Under-21.

| 1986–87 | Leicester C | — | — |
| 1987–88 | | — | — |

1987–88	*Chesterfield*	17	—
1987–88	*Blackpool*	2	—
1988–89	Leicester C	3	—
1988–89	*Hartlepool U*	8	—
1989–90	Leicester C	—	—
1989–90	*Stockport Co*	4	—
1990–91	Leicester C	22	—
1990–91	*Liverpool*	—	—

MUIR, Ian

Born Coventry 5.5.63. Ht 5 8 Wt 11 00
Forward. From Apprentice. England
Youth.

1980–81	QPR	2	2
1981–82		—	—
1982–83		—	—
1982–83	*Burnley*	2	1
1983–84	Birmingham C	1	—
1983–84	Brighton	2	—
1984–85		2	—
1984–85	*Swindon T*	2	—
1985–86	Tranmere R	32	14
1986–87		46	20
1987–88		43	27
1988–89		46	21
1989–90		46	23
1990–91		35	13

MUIR, John

Born Sedgley 26.4.63. Ht 6 2 Wt 14 06
Forward. From Dudley T.

| 1989–90 | Doncaster R | 16 | 4 |
| 1990–91 | | 39 | 13 |

MUMBY, Peter

Born Bradford 22.2.69. Ht 5 9 Wt 11 05
Forward. From Trainee.

1987–88	Leeds U	5	—
1988–89		1	—
1988–89	*Shamrock R*	—	—
1989–90	Burnley	25	4
1990–91		20	5

MUNDEE, Denny

Born Swindon 10.10.68 Ht 5 10
Wt 11 00
Forward. From Apprentice.

1986–87	QPR	—	—
1986–87	Swindon T	—	—
1987–88	Bournemouth	—	—
1988–89		2	—
1989–90		10	—
1989–90	*Torquay U*	9	—
1990–91	Bournemouth	21	2

MUNGALL, Steve

Born Bellshill 22.5.58. Ht 5 8 Wt 11 05
Defender.

1976–77	Motherwell	3	—
1977–78		13	—
1978–79		4	—
1979–80	Tranmere R	24	—
1980–81		38	3
1981–82		44	1
1982–83		31	1
1983–84		26	—
1984–85		23	—
1985–86		46	1
1986–87		46	—
1987–88		45	—
1988–89		42	1
1989–90		17	1
1990–91		33	1

MUNRO, Stuart

Born Falkirk 15.9.62. Ht 5 8 Wt 10 05
Defender. From Bo'ness United. Scotland
B.

1980–81	St Mirren	1	—
1981–82		—	—
1982–83	Alloa	39	5
1983–84		21	1
1983–84	Rangers	5	—
1984–85		13	—
1985–86		29	—
1986–87		43	—
1987–88		17	—
1988–89		22	2

Season	Club	Apps	Goals
1989–90	....	36	1
1990–91	....	14	—

MURPHY, Aidan

Born Manchester 17.9.67. Ht 5 10
Wt 11 03
Midfield. From Apprentice. England
Schools, Youth.

Season	Club	Apps	Goals
1984–85	Manchester U	—	—
1985–86	....	—	—
1986–87	....	—	—
1986–87	*Lincoln C*	2	—
1986–87	*Oldham Ath*................	—	—
1987–88	Crewe Alex	20	2
1988–89	....	35	5
1989–90	....	35	3
1990–91	....	16	2

MURPHY, James

Born Islington 17.11.71.
Forward. From Leyton Orient Trainee.

Season	Club	Apps	Goals
1990–91	Aldershot	3	—

MURRAY, Edwin

Born Redbridge 31.8.73.
Midfield. From Trainee.

Season	Club	Apps	Goals
1990–91	Swindon T	1	—

MURRAY, Joey

Born Liverpool 5.11.71. Ht 5 8 Wt 10 11
Midfield. From Liverpool Trainee.

Season	Club	Apps	Goals
1990–91	Wrexham	11	—

MURRAY, Malcolm

Born Buckie 26.7.64. Ht 5 11 Wt 11 12
Defender. From Buckie Thistle.

Season	Club	Apps	Goals
1983–84	Hearts	1	—
1984–85	....	4	—
1985–86	....	—	—
1986–87	....	7	—

Season	Club	Apps	Goals
1987–88	....	7	—
1988–89	....	8	—
1988–89	Hull C........................	8	—
1989–90	....	3	—
1989–90	Mansfield T................	28	—
1990–91	....	30	—

MURRAY, Shaun

Born Newcastle 7.2.70. Ht 5 8 Wt 11 02
Forward. From Trainee. England Youth.

Season	Club	Apps	Goals
1987–88	Tottenham H	—	—
1988–89	....	—	—
1989–90	Portsmouth	—	—
1990–91	....	25	1

MUSKER, Russell

Born Liverpool 10.7.62.
From Apprentice.

Season	Club	Apps	Goals
1979–80	Bristol C	—	—
1980–81	....	4	—
1981–82	....	33	—
1982–83	....	6	1
1983–84	....	3	—
1983–84	Exeter C......................	6	—
1983–84	Gillingham	27	5
1984–85	....	28	1
1985–86	....	9	1
1986–87	Torquay U..................	24	—
Retired			
1990–91	Torquay U..................	21	1

MUSSELWHITE, Paul

Born Portsmouth 22.12.68. Ht 6 2
Wt 12 07
Goalkeeper.

Season	Club	Apps	Goals
1987–88	Portsmouth	—	—
1988–89	Scunthorpe U	41	—
1989–90	....	29	—
1990–91	....	38	—

MUSTOE, Robbie

Born Oxford 28.8.68. Ht 5 10 Wt 10 08
Midfield.

Season	Club	Apps	Goals
1986–87	Oxford U	3	—
1987–88		17	—
1988–89		33	3
1989–90		38	7
1990–91	Middlesbrough	41	4

MUTCH, Andy

Born Liverpool 28.12.63. Ht 5 10
Wt 11 00
Forward. From Southport. England B,
Under-21.

Season	Club	Apps	Goals
1985–86	Wolverhampton W	15	7
1986–87		41	12
1987–88		46	19
1988–89		45	21
1989–90		37	11
1990–91		29	8

MYERS, Andy

Born Hounslow 3.11.73.
Midfield. From Trainee. England Youth.

Season	Club	Apps	Goals
1990–91	Chelsea	3	—

MYERS, Chris

Born Yeovil 1.4.69. Ht 5 10   Wt 11 10
Midfield. From Apprentice.

Season	Club	Apps	Goals
1986–87	Torquay U	9	—
From Local			
1990–91	Torquay U	29	2

NARBETT, Jon

Born Birmingham 21.11.68. Ht 5 10
Wt 10 08
Midfield. From Apprentice.

Season	Club	Apps	Goals
1986–87	Shrewsbury T	1	—
1987–88		25	3
1988–89		—	—
1988–89	Hereford U	36	7
1989–90		36	5
1990–91		44	11

NAREY, David

Born Dundee 21.6.56. Ht 6 0   Wt 12 06
Defender. 'S' Form. Scotland Youth,
Under-21, Under-23, 35 full caps.

Season	Club	Apps	Goals
1973–74	Dundee U	12	—
1974–75		31	6
1975–76		33	—
1976–77		32	2
1977–78		35	—
1978–79		36	5
1979–80		35	1
1980–81		32	—
1981–82		34	1
1982–83		36	5
1983–84		34	1
1984–85		29	1
1985–86		35	—
1986–87		33	—
1987–88		39	—
1988–89		33	—
1989–90		31	—
1990–91		4	—

NAUGHTON, Willie

Born Catrine 20.3.62. Ht 6 0   Wt 12 08
Forward. From Apprentice.

Season	Club	Apps	Goals
1979–80	Preston NE	3	—
1980–81		10	2
1981–82		33	3
1982–83		41	1
1983–84		42	3
1984–85		33	1

Season	Club	Apps	Goals
1984–85	Walsall	13	—
1985–86		39	5
1986–87		23	1
1987–88		41	3
1988–89		35	7
1989–90	Shrewsbury T.	43	3
1990–91		6	1
1990–91	Walsall	16	1

NAYIM (Mohamed Ali Amar)

Born Morocco 5.11.66   Ht 5 8   Wt 11 04
Midfield. From Barcelona. Spain Youth, Under-21.

Season	Club	Apps	Goals
1988–89	Tottenham H	11	2
1989–90		19	—
1990–91		33	5

NAYLOR, Glenn

Born York 11.8.72.   Ht 5 9   Wt 11 10
Forward. From Trainee.

Season	Club	Apps	Goals
1989–90	York C	1	—
1990–91		20	5

NAYLOR, Stuart

Born Wetherby 6.12.62.   Ht 6 4   Wt 12 02
Goalkeeper. From Yorkshire A. England Youth, B.

Season	Club	Apps	Goals
1980–81	Lincoln C	—	—
1981–82		3	—
1982–83		1	—
1982–83	Peterborough U	8	—
1983–84	Lincoln C	—	—
1983–84	Crewe Alex	38	—
1984–85	Crewe Alex	17	—
1984–85	Lincoln C	25	—
1985–86		20	—
1985–86	WBA	12	—
1986–87		42	—
1987–88		35	—
1988–89		44	—
1989–90		39	—
1990–91		28	—

NAYLOR, Tony

Born Manchester 29.3.67.   Ht 5 8
Wt 10 08
Forward. From Droylsden.

Season	Club	Apps	Goals
1989–90	Crewe Alex	2	—
1990–91		14	1

NEBBELING, Gavin

Born Johannesburg 15.5.63.   Ht 6 0
Wt 12 10
Defender. From Arcadia Shepherds.

Season	Club	Apps	Goals
1981–82	Crystal Palace	1	—
1982–83		28	1
1983–84		16	—
1984–85		16	—
1985–86		14	—
1985–86	Northampton T	11	—
1986–87	Crystal Palace	23	—
1987–88		39	6
1988–89		14	1
1989–90	Fulham	36	—
1990–91		6	—

NEILL, Warren

Born Acton 21.11.62.   Ht 5 9   Wt 11 05
Defender. From Apprentice. England Schools.

Season	Club	Apps	Goals
1980–81	QPR	4	—
1981–82		11	—
1982–83		39	2
1983–84		41	1
1984–85		18	—
1985–86		16	—
1986–87		29	—
1987–88		23	—
1988–89	Portsmouth	43	—
1989–90		37	—
1990–91		30	—

NEILSON, Alan

Born Wegburg 26.9.72.   Ht 5 11
Wt 11 07
Defender. From Trainee.

1990–91 Newcastle U............. 3 —

NELSON, Garry

Born Braintree 16.1.61. Ht 5 10
Wt 11 07
Forward. From Amateur.

Season	Club	Apps	Goals
1979–80	Southend U...............	22	2
1980–81	....	22	3
1981–82	....	40	4
1982–83	....	45	8
1983–84	Swindon T	36	4
1984–85	....	43	3
1985–86	Plymouth Arg...........	42	13
1986–87	....	32	7
1987–88	Brighton...............	42	22
1988–89	....	46	15
1989–90	....	33	5
1990–91	....	23	5
1990–91	*Notts Co.*...................	2	—

NESBITT, Mark

Born Doncaster 11.1.72.
Midfield. From Trainee.

Season	Club	Apps	Goals
1989–90	Middlesbrough...........	—	—
1990–91	....	—	—
1990–91	Hartlepool U	1	—

NEVILLE, Steve

Born Walthamstow 18.9.57. Ht 5 7
Wt 11 04
Forward. From Apprentice

Season	Club	Apps	Goals
1975–76	Southampton	—	—
1976–77	....	—	—
1977–78	....	5	1
1978–79	....	—	—
1978–79	Exeter C.................	36	9
1979–80	....	43	8
1980–81	....	14	5
1980–81	Sheffield U	19	2
1981–82	....	30	4
1982–83	*Exeter C*.................	33	17
1983–84	Exeter C.................	43	9
1984–85	....	16	1
1984–85	Bristol C	28	8

Season	Club	Apps	Goals
1985–86	....	46	19
1986–87	....	20	8
1987–88	....	40	5
1988–89	Exeter C.................	38	14
1989–90	....	42	14
1990–91	....	40	11

NEVIN, Pat

Born Glasgow 6.9.63. Ht 5 6 Wt 10 00
Forward. From Gartcosh U. Scotland,
Youth, Under-21, B, 11 full caps.

Season	Club	Apps	Goals
1981–82	Clyde...........	34	12
1982–83	....	39	5
1983–84	Chelsea...............	38	14
1984–85	....	41	4
1985–86	....	40	7
1986–87	....	37	5
1987–88	....	37	6
1988–89	Everton	25	2
1989–90	....	30	4
1990–91	....	37	8

NEWELL, Mike

Born Liverpool 27.1.65. Ht 6 1 Wt 11 00
Forward. From Liverpool Amateur.
England, B, Under-21.

Season	Club	Apps	Goals
1983–84	Crewe Alex	3	—
1983–84	Wigan Ath	9	—
1984–85	....	39	9
1985–86	....	24	16
1985–86	Luton T	16	6
1986–87	....	42	12
1987–88	....	5	—
1987–88	Leicester C................	36	8
1988–89	....	45	13
1989–90	Everton	26	7
1990–91	....	29	7

NEWELL, Paul

Born Greenwich 23.2.69. Ht 6 1
Wt 11 05
Goalkeeper. From Trainee.

Season	Club	Apps	Goals
1987–88	Southend U...............	13	—
1988–89	....	2	—

Season	Club	App	Goals
1989–90	....	—	—
1990–91	Leyton Orient	8	—

NEWHOUSE, Aidan

Born Wallasey 23.5.72. Ht 6 2 Wt 13 05
Midfield. From Schoolboy, Trainee.
England Youth.

Season	Club	App	Goals
1987–88	Chester C	1	—
1988–89	....	25	2
1989–90	....	18	4
1989–90	Wimbledon	2	—
1990–91	....	8	1

NEWMAN, Rob

Born Bradford-on-Avon 13.12.63.
Ht 6 0 Wt 13 00
Defender. From Apprentice.

Season	Club	App	Goals
1981–82	Bristol C	21	3
1982–83	....	43	3
1983–84	....	30	1
1984–85	....	34	3
1985–86	....	39	3
1986–87	....	45	6
1987–88	....	44	11
1988–89	....	46	6
1989–90	....	46	8
1990–91	....	46	8

NEWSOME, Jon

Born Sheffield 6.9.70. Ht 6 2 Wt 13 11
Defender. From Trainee.

Season	Club	App	Goals
1989–90	Sheffield W	6	—
1990–91	....	1	—

NEWSON, Mark

Born Stepney 7.12.60. Ht 5 10 Wt 12 06
Defender. From Apprentice.

Season	Club	App	Goals
1979–80	Charlton Ath	—	—
	From Maidstone U		
1985–86	Bournemouth	46	5
1986–87	....	46	7
1987–88	....	29	3

Season	Club	App	Goals
1988–89	....	40	7
1989–90	....	16	1
1989–90	Fulham	16	—
1990–91	....	31	1

NGATA, Herry

Born New Zealand 24.8.71.
Midfield.

Season	Club	App	Goals
1989–90	Hull C	4	—
1990–91	....	10	—

NICHOLAS, Charlie

Born Glasgow 30.12.61. Ht 5 10
Wt 11 00
Forward. From Celtic BC. Scotland
Youth. Under-21, 20 full caps.

Season	Club	App	Goals
1980–81	Celtic	29	16
1981–82	....	10	3
1982–83	....	35	29
1983–84	Arsenal	41	11
1984–85	....	38	9
1985–86	....	41	10
1986–87	....	28	4
1987–88	....	3	—
1987–88	Aberdeen	16	3
1988–89	....	29	16
1989–90	....	33	11
1990–91	Celtic	14	6

NICHOLAS, Peter

Born Newport 10.11.59. Ht 5 8
Wt 11 08
Midfield. From Apprentice. Wales Under-
21, 72 full caps.

Season	Club	App	Goals
1976–77	Crystal Palace	—	—
1977–78	....	23	1
1978–79	....	37	3
1979–80	....	39	2
1980–81	....	28	1
1980–81	Arsenal	8	1
1981–82	....	31	—
1982–83	....	21	—
1983–84	....	—	—
1983–84	*Crystal Palace*	25	3

Season	Club	Apps	Goals
1984–85	Crystal Palace	22	4
1984–85	Luton T	19	—
1985–86		41	—
1986–87		42	1
1987–88	Aberdeen	39	3
1988–89	Chelsea	39	1
1989–90		29	—
1990–91		12	1
1990–91	Watford	15	—

NICHOLL, Jimmy

Born Canada 28.2.56. Ht 5 9 Wt 11 08
Defender. From Apprentice. Northern
Ireland Under-21, 73 full caps.

Season	Club	Apps	Goals
1973–74	Manchester U	—	—
1974–75		1	—
1975–76		20	—
1976–77		30	—
1977–78		37	2
1978–79		21	—
1979–80		42	—
1980–81		36	1
1981–82		1	—
1981–82	Sunderland	3	—
From Toronto B.			
1982–83	Sunderland	29	—
From Toronto B.			
1983–84	Rangers	17	—
1984–85	WBA	27	—
1985–86		29	—
1986–87	Rangers	42	—
1987–88		22	—
1988–89		1	—
1989–90	Dunfermline Ath	17	—
1990–91		7	—

NICHOLLS, David

Born Bellshill 5.4.72 Ht 5 8 Wt 10 0
Defender. From Ferguslie U

Season	Club	Apps	Goals
1989–90	Hibernian	—	—
1990–91		1	—

NICHOLSON, Max

Born Leeds 3.10.71.
Forward. From Trainee.

Season	Club	Apps	Goals
1989–90	Doncaster R	2	—
1990–91		1	—

NICHOLSON, Shane

Born Newark 3.6.70 Ht 5 10 Wt 11 00
Defender. From Trainee.

Season	Club	Apps	Goals
1986–87	Lincoln C	7	—
1987–88		*33*	*1*
1988–89		34	1
1989–90		23	—
1990–91		40	4

NICOL, Andrew

Born Falkirk 3.12.60 Ht 5 9 Wt 10 2
Defender. From Gairdoch BC

Season	Club	Apps	Goals
1978–79	Falkirk	2	—
1979–80		—	—
1980–81		15	—
1981–82		39	—
1982–83		39	—
1983–84		39	—
1984–85		34	2
1985–86		35	—
1986–87		24	—
1987–88		31	—
1988–89		38	—
1989–90		—	—
1990–91		11	—

NICOL, Steve

Born Irvine 11.12.61. Ht 5 10 Wt 12 00
Midfield. From Ayr U. BC. Scotland
Under-21, 26 full caps.

Season	Club	Apps	Goals
1979–80	Ayr U	20	2
1980–81		39	3
1981–82		11	2
1981–82	Liverpool	—	—
1982–83		4	—
1983–84		23	5
1984–85		31	5
1985–86		34	4
1986–87		14	3
1987–88		40	6
1988–89		38	2

1989–90	....	23	6	
1990–91	....	35	3	

NICOLSON, Keith

Born Perth 16.7.68. Ht 6 1   Wt 12 09
Defender. From East Craigie.

1988–89	St Johnstone	3	—
1989–90	....	1	—
1990–91	....	5	—

NIELSEN, Kent

Born Frederiksberg 28.12.61. Ht 6 2
Wt 14 01
Defender. From Brondby (Denmark).
Denmark full caps.

1989–90	Aston Villa..................	36	2
1990–91	....	37	2

NIJHOLT, Luc

Born Zaandam 29.7.61   Ht 5 11   Wt 12 1
Midfield. From BSC Old Boys Basel

1990–91	Motherwell..................	23	—

NILSSON, Roland

Born Helsingborg 27.11.63. Ht 6 0
Wt 11 06
Defender. From IFK Gothenburg. Sweden
full caps.

1989–90	Sheffield W..................	20	—
1990–91	....	22	—

NISBET, Scott

Born Edinburgh 30.1.68.   Ht 6 1
Wt 11 08
Defender. From Salvesen BC. Scotland
Schools, Youth, Under-21.

1985–86	Rangers	5	—
1986–87	....	1	—
1986–87	*East Fife*......................	6	—
1987–88	Rangers......................	25	—

1988–89	....	7	1
1989–90	....	7	—
1990–91	....	15	—

NIXON, Eric

Born Manchester 4.10.62.   Ht 6 2
Wt 14 03
Goalkeeper. From Curzon Ashton.

1983–84	Manchester C	—	—
1984–85	....	—	—
1985–86	....	28	—
1986–87	....	5	—
1986–87	*Wolverhampton W*.......	16	—
1986–87	*Bradford C*.................	3	—
1986–87	*Southampton*	4	—
1986–87	*Carlisle U*...................	16	—
1987–88	Manchester C	25	—
1987–88	*Tranmere R*.................	8	—
1988–89	Tranmere R	45	—
1989–90	....	46	—
1990–91	....	43	—

NIXON, Paul

Born Seaham 23.9.63   Ht 5 10   Wt 11 03
Forward. From New Zealand.

1988–89	Bristol R	1	—
1989–90	....	27	5
1990–91	....	16	1

NOBBS, Keith

Born Bishop Auckland 19.9.61.   Ht 5 10
Wt 11 10
Defender. From Apprentice.

1979–80	Middlesbrough............	—	—
1980–81	....	1	—
1981–82	....	—	—
1982–83	Halifax T	46	1
1983–84	....	41	—
From Bishop Auckland			
1985–86	Hartlepool U	39	1
1986–87	....	40	—
1987–88	....	43	—
1988–89	....	18	—
1989–90	....	32	—

| 1990–91 | | 40 | — |

NOBLE, Daniel

Born Cardiff 2.9.70. Ht 5 11 Wt 12 09
Goalkeeper. From Trainee.

| 1989–90 | Stoke C | 1 | — |
| 1990–91 | | 2 | — |

NOGAN, Kurt

Born Cardiff 9.9.70. Ht 5 10 Wt 11 01
Forward. From Trainee. Wales Under-21.

| 1989–90 | Luton T | 10 | 2 |
| 1990–91 | | 9 | — |

NOGAN, Lee

Born Cardiff 21.5.69. Ht 5 10 Wt 11 00
Forward. From Apprentice. Wales B,
Under-21.

1986–87	Oxford U	—	—
1986–87	*Brentford*	11	2
1987–88	Oxford U	3	—
1987–88	*Southend U*	6	1
1988–89	Oxford U	3	—
1989–90		4	—
1990–91		32	5

NORMAN, Tony

Born Mancot 24.2.58. Ht 6 2 Wt 13 10
Goalkeeper. From Amateur. Wales B, 5
full caps.

1976–77	Burnley	—	—
1977–78		—	—
1978–79		—	—
1979–80		—	—
1979–80	Hull C	17	—
1980–81		42	—
1981–82		36	—
1982–83		36	—
1983–84		46	—
1984–85		46	—
1985–86		42	—
1986–87		42	—

1987–88		44	—
1988–89		21	—
1988–89	Sunderland	24	—
1989–90		28	—
1990–91		37	—

NORRIS, Steve

Born Coventry 22.9.61 Ht 5 9 Wt 10 09
Forward. From Telford.

1988–89	Scarborough	31	9
1989–90		14	4
1989–90	*Notts Co*	1	—
1989–90	Carlisle U	24	3
1990–91		5	2
1990–91	Halifax T	39	30

NORTH, Marc

Born Ware 29.5.66. Ht 5 11 Wt 11 00
Forward. From Apprentice.

1983–84	Luton T	—	—
1984–85		—	—
1984–85	*Lincoln C*	4	—
1985–86	Luton T	13	3
1986–87		5	—
1986–87	*Scunthorpe U*	5	2
1986–87	*Birmingham C*	5	1
1987–88	Grimsby T	38	11
1988–89		29	6
1988–89	Leicester C	8	1
1989–90		24	6
1990–91		39	2

NORTH, Stacey

Born Luton 25.11.64. Ht 6 2 Wt 12 08
Defender. From Apprentice. England
Youth.

1982–83	Luton T	—	—
1983–84		1	—
1984–85		7	—
1985–86		2	—
1985–86	*Wolverhampton W*	3	—
1986–87	Luton T	14	—
1987–88		1	—
1987–88	WBA	18	—

1988–89	....	46	—
1989–90	....	34	—
1990–91	....	—	—
1990–91	Fulham	38	—

NORTON, David

Born Cannock 3.3.65.   Ht 5 7   Wt 11 03
Midfield. From Apprentice. England
Youth.

1982–83	Aston Villa..................	—	—
1983–84	....	—	—
1984–85	....	2	—
1985–86	....	20	2
1986–87	....	20	—
1987–88	....	2	—
1988–89	Notts Co	8	—
1989–90	....	15	1
1990–91	....	4	—
1990–91	*Rochdale*......................	9	—
1990–91	*Hull C*	15	—

NOTEMAN, Kevin

Born Preston 15.10.69.   Ht 5 10   Wt 10 09
Forward. From Trainee.

1987–88	Leeds U	1	—
1988–89	....	—	—
1989–90	....	—	—
1989–90	Doncaster R.................	30	3
1990–91	....	42	7

NTAMARK, Charlie

Born Cameroon 22.7.64.   Ht 5 8
Wt 11 12
Midfield. Cameroon full caps.

1990–91	Walsall	42	3

NUGENT, Kevin

Born Edmonton 10.4.69.   Ht 6 1
Wt 12 04
Forward. From Trainee.

1987–88	Leyton Orient	11	3
1988–89	....	3	—

1988–89	*Cork C*	—	—
1989–90	Leyton Orient	11	—
1990–91	....	33	5

NUGENT, Stephen

Born Wigan 7.5.73.
Forward. From Trainee.

1989–90	Wigan Ath..................	1	—
1990–91	....	1	—

OAKES, Keith

Born Bedworth 3.7.56.   Ht 6 1   Wt 12 13
Defender. From Apprentice.

Season	Club	Apps	Goals
1972–73	Peterborough	4	—
1973–74		4	—
1974–75		12	—
1975–76		9	1
1976–77		23	1
1977–78		10	—
1978–79		—	—
1978–79	Newport Co	34	5
1979–80		45	11
1980–81		43	8
1981–82		45	1
1982–83		28	1
1983–84		37	1
1984–85	Gillingham	45	5
1985–86		40	2
1986–87		1	—
1986–87	Fulham	41	3
1987–88		35	—
1988–89	Peterborough U	41	5
1989–90		29	1
1990–91		27	3

OAKES, Scott

Born Leicester 5.8.72.   Ht 5 10   Wt 9 12
Midfield. From Trainee.

Season	Club	Apps	Goals
1989–90	Leicester C	2	—
1990–91		—	—

O'BOYLE, George

Born Belfast 14.12.67.   Ht 5 7   Wt 10 2
Forward. From Linfield.

Season	Club	Apps	Goals
1989–90	Dunfermline Ath	28	3
1990–91		16	6

O'BRIEN, Liam

Born Dublin 5.9.64.   Ht 6 1   Wt 13 03
Midfield. From Shamrock R. Eire 8 full
caps.

Season	Club	Apps	Goals
1986–87	Manchester U	11	—

Season	Club	Apps	Goals
1987–88		17	2
1988–89		3	—
1988–89	Newcastle U	20	4
1989–90		19	2
1990–91		33	3

O'BRIEN, Michael

Born Dublin 28.11.70.   Ht 5 10   Wt 11 04
Midfield. From Trainee. Eire Youth.

Season	Club	Apps	Goals
1988–89	Luton T	—	—
1989–90		—	—
1990–91		—	—

O'BRIEN, Paul

Born Glasgow 3.12.65   Ht 5 4   Wt 10 0
Forward. From Hillwood Strollers

Season	Club	Apps	Goals
1986–87	Queen's Park	37	11
1987–88		38	17
1988–89		31	4
1989–90		39	9
1990–91	Dunfermline Ath	2	—

O'CALLAGHAN, Kevin

Born London 19.10.61.   Ht 5 8   Wt 11 07
Forward. From Apprentice. Eire Youth,
Under-21, 20 full caps.

Season	Club	Apps	Goals
1978–79	Millwall	10	—
1979–80		10	3
1979–80	Ipswich T	4	—
1980–81		24	—
1981–82		19	1
1982–83		28	—
1983–84		25	2
1984–85		15	—
1984–85	Portsmouth	15	2
1985–86		39	11
1986–87		33	3
1987–88	Millwall	22	7
1988–89		34	5
1989–90		—	—
1990–91		20	2

O'CONNELL, Brendan

Born London 12.11.66.   Ht 5 10
Wt 10 09
Forward.

Season	Club	App	Goals
1984–85	Portsmouth	—	—
1985–86			
1986–87	Exeter C	42	8
1987–88		39	11
1988–89	Burnley	43	13
1989–90		21	4
1989–90	*Huddersfield T*	11	1
1989–90	Barnsley	11	2
1990–91		45	9

O'CONNOR, Mark

Born Rochdale 10.3.63.   Ht 5 7   Wt 10 02
Midfield. From Apprentice. Eire Under-21.

Season	Club	App	Goals
1980–81	QPR	—	—
1981–82		1	—
1982–83		2	—
1983–84		—	—
1983–84	*Exeter C*	38	1
1984–85	Bristol R	46	8
1985–86		34	2
1985–86	Bournemouth	9	1
1986–87		43	7
1987–88		37	2
1988–89		33	2
1989–90		6	—
1989–90	Gillingham	15	1
1990–91		41	3

O'DOHERTY, Ken

Born Dublin 30.3.63.   Ht 6 0   Wt 12 00
Defender. From UCD. Eire Under-21.

Season	Club	App	Goals
1984–85	Crystal Palace	—	—
1985–86		13	—
1986–87		12	—
1987–88		17	—
1988–89	Huddersfield T	37	1
1989–90		18	—
1990–91		8	—

O'DONNELL, Phillip

Born Bellshill 25.3.72   Ht 5 10   Wt 10 5
Midfield. From X Form

Season	Club	App	Goals
1990–91	Motherwell	12	—

O'DRISCOLL, Sean

Born Wolverhampton 1.7.57.   Ht 5 8
Wt 11 03
Midfield. From Alvechurch. Eire 3 full
caps.

Season	Club	App	Goals
1979–80	Fulham	10	1
1980–81		42	2
1981–82		42	7
1982–83		42	3
1983–84		12	—
1983–84	*Bournemouth*	19	1
1984–85	Bournemouth	44	1
1985–86		46	5
1986–87		46	5
1987–88		39	4
1988–89		41	—
1989–90		39	—
1990–91		45	2

OGHANI, George

Born Manchester 2.9.60.   Ht 5 11
Wt 12 03
Forward. From Hyde.

Season	Club	App	Goals
1983–84	Bolton W	3	—
1984–85		41	16
1985–86		36	7
1986–87		19	4
1986–87	*Wrexham*	7	—
1987–88	Burnley	37	14
1988–89		37	7
1989–90	Stockport Co	8	2
1989–90	Hereford U	8	2
1989–90	Scarborough	14	4
1990–91		36	14

OGLEY, Mark

Born Barnsley 10.3.67.   Ht 5 10   Wt 11 07
Defender. From Apprentice.

Season	Club	App	Goals
1984–85	Barnsley	—	—
1985–86		2	—
1986–87		17	—
1987–88		—	—
1987–88	*Aldershot*	8	—
1987–88	Carlisle U	3	—
1988–89		26	—

Season	Club	Apps	Goals
1989–90	....	4	1
1989–90	Aldershot	28	—
1990–91	....	34	—

O'GORMAN, Dave

Born Chester 20.6.72. Ht 5 8 Wt 11 12
Forward. From School.

Season	Club	Apps	Goals
1990–91	Wrexham	17	—

OGRIZOVIC, Steve

Born Mansfield 12.9.57. Ht 6 5 Wt 15 00
Goalkeeper. From ONRYC.

Season	Club	Apps	Goals
1977–78	Chesterfield	16	—
1977–78	Liverpool	2	—
1978–79	....	—	—
1979–80	....	1	—
1980–81	....	1	—
1981–82	....	—	—
1982–83	Shrewsbury T.............	42	—
1983–84	....	42	—
1984–85	Coventry C	42	—
1985–86	....	42	—
1986–87	....	42	1
1987–88	....	40	—
1988–89	....	38	—
1989–90	....	37	—
1990–91	....	37	—

O'HANLON, Kelham

Born Saltburn 16.5.62. Ht 6 1 Wt 13 01
Goalkeeper. From Apprentice. Eire
Under-21, 1 full cap.

Season	Club	Apps	Goals
1980–81	Middlesbrough............	—	—
1981–82	....	—	—
1982–83	....	19	—
1983–84	....	30	—
1984–85	....	38	—
1985–86	Rotherham U	46	—
1986–87	....	40	—
1987–88	....	40	—
1988–89	....	46	—
1989–90	....	43	—
1990–91	....	33	—

O'HARA, Steve

Born Lanark 21.2.71. Ht 6 1 Wt 12 02
Defender. From Trainee.

Season	Club	Apps	Goals
1989–90	Walsall	18	—
1990–91	....	20	—

O'KEEFE, Vince

Born Birmingham 2.4.57. Ht 6 2
Wt 13 00
Goalkeeper. Local

Season	Club	Apps	Goals
1975–76	Birmingham C............	—	—
1975–76	*Peterborough U*..........	—	—
1976–77	Walsall	—	—
From AP LeamingtonH			
1978–79	Exeter C.....................	33	—
1979–80	....	20	—
1979–80	Torquay U.................	16	—
1980–81	....	46	—
1981–82	....	46	—
1982–83	Blackburn R	9	—
1983–84	....	12	—
1983–84	*Bury*	2	—
1984–85	Blackburn R	5	—
1985–86	....	10	—
1986–87	....	25	—
1986–87	*Blackpool*	1	—
1987–88	Blackburn R	5	—
1988–89	....	2	—
1988–89	*Blackpool*	6	—
1989–90	Wrexham	43	—
1990–91	....	6	—

OLDFIELD, David

Born Perth, Australia 30.5.68. Ht 6 0
Wt 12 02
Forward. From Apprentice. England
Under-21.

Season	Club	Apps	Goals
1986–87	Luton T	—	—
1987–88	....	8	3
1988–89	....	21	1
1988–89	Manchester C	11	3
1989–90	....	15	3
1989–90	Leicester C.................	20	5
1990–91	....	42	7

O'LEARY, David

Born London 2.5.58. Ht 6 1   Wt 13 02
Defender. From Apprentice. Eire, 57 full
caps.

Season	Club	App	Goals
1975–76	Arsenal	27	—
1976–77		33	2
1977–78		41	1
1978–79		37	2
1979–80		34	1
1980–81		24	1
1981–82		40	1
1982–83		36	1
1983–84		36	—
1984–85		36	—
1985–86		35	—
1986–87		39	—
1987–88		23	—
1988–89		26	—
1989–90		34	—
1990–91		21	1

OLIVER, Gavin

Born Felling 6.9.62. Ht 6 0   Wt 12 10
Defender. From Apprentice.

Season	Club	App	Goals
1980–81	Sheffield W	2	—
1981–82		—	—
1982–83		2	—
1982–83	*Tranmere R*	17	1
1983–84	Sheffield W	6	—
1984–85		10	—
1985–86		—	—
1985–86	*Brighton*	16	—
1985–86	Bradford C	27	1
1986–87		40	—
1987–88		43	—
1988–89		39	1
1989–90		22	—
1990–91		46	5

OLIVER, Neil

Born Berwick 11.4.67. Ht 5 11   Wt 11 10
Defender. From Coldstream.

Season	Club	App	Goals
1985–86	Berwick R	5	—
1986–87		37	—
1987–88		12	—
1988–89		39	—

Season	Club	App	Goals
1989–90	Blackburn R	3	—
1990–91		3	—

OLNEY, Ian

Born Luton 17.12.69. Ht 6 1   Wt 11 00
Forward. From Trainee. England
Under-21.

Season	Club	App	Goals
1988–89	Aston Villa	15	2
1989–90		35	9
1990–91		18	3

OLSEN, Jesper

Born Fakse 20.3.61. Ht 5 6   Wt 9 9
Forward. From Naestved and Ajax.
Denmark full caps.

Season	Club	App	Goals
1984–85	Manchester U	36	5
1985–86		28	11
1986–87		28	3
1987–88		37	2
1988–89		10	—

To Bordeaux

OLSSON, Paul

Born Hull 24.12.65. Ht 5 8   Wt 10 11
Midfield. From Apprentice.

Season	Club	App	Goals
1983–84	Hull C	—	—
1984–85		—	—
1985–86		—	—
1986–87		—	—
1986–87	*Exeter C*	8	—
1987–88	Exeter C	35	2
1988–89	Scarborough	32	4
1989–90		16	1
1989–90	Hartlepool U	23	2
1990–91		31	1

O'NEIL, John

Born Bellshill 6.7.71. Ht 5 7   Wt 10 02
Midfield. From Fir Park BC. Scotland
Under-21.

Season	Club	App	Goals
1988–89	Dundee U	1	—
1989–90		10	—

1990–91		15	—

O'NEILL, Colin

Born Belfast 14.6.63   Ht 5 8   Wt 10 09
Midfield. From Portadown. Northern
Ireland 3 full caps.

1988–89	Motherwell	19	2
1989–90		24	1
1990–91		21	1

O'NEILL, Michael

Born Portadown 5.7.69.   Ht 5 11
Wt 10 10
Forward. From Coleraine. Northern
Ireland 13 full caps.

1987–88	Newcastle U	21	12
1988–89		27	3
1989–90	Dundee U	18	5
1990–91		13	—

ONUORA, Iffy

Born Glasgow 28.7.67.   Ht 5 10   Wt 11 10
Forward. From British Universities

1989–90	Huddersfield T	20	3
1990–91		43	7

ONWERE, Udo

Born Hammersmith 9.11.71.   Ht 6 0
Wt 11 03
Midfield. From Trainee.

1990–91	Fulham	7	1

ORD, Richard

Born Easington 3.3.70.   Ht 6 2   Wt 12 08
Defender. From Trainee. England
Under-21.

1987–88	Sunderland	8	—
1988–89		34	1
1989–90		7	1
1989–90	*York C*	3	—

1990–91	Sunderland	14	—

O'REGAN, Kieran

Born Cork 9.11.63.   Ht 5 8   Wt 10 12
Midfield. From Tramore Ath. Eire Under-
21, 4 full caps.

1982–83	Brighton	1	—
1983–84		31	1
1984–85		15	—
1985–86		15	1
1986–87		24	—
1987–88	Swindon T	26	1
1988–89	Huddersfield T	36	2
1989–90		37	3
1990–91		46	11

O'REILLY, Gary

Born Isleworth 21.3.61.   Ht 5 11
Wt 13 05
Defender. From Amateur. Eire Youth.

1979–80	Tottenham H	—	—
1980–81		2	—
1981–82		5	—
1982–83		26	—
1983–84		12	—
1984–85	Brighton	36	3
1985–86		35	—
1986–87		8	—
1986–87	Crystal Palace	13	—
1987–88		4	—
1988–89		32	2
1989–90		21	—
1990–91		—	—
1990–91	*Birmingham C*	1	—

O'RIORDAN, Don

Born Dublin 14.5.57.   Ht 6 0   Wt 11 12
Midfield. From Apprentice. Eire Under-21.

1975–76	Derby Co	—	—
1976–77		1	—
1977–78		5	1
1977–78	*Doncaster R*	2	—
From Tulsa			
1978–79	Preston NE	32	—

Season	Club		
1979–80		18	—
1980–81		21	—
1981–82		46	4
1982–83		41	4
1983–84	Carlisle U	42	8
1984–85		42	10
1985–86	Middlesbrough	41	2
1986–87	Grimsby T	40	6
1987–88		46	8
1988–89	Notts Co	43	3
1989–90		17	—
1989–90	*Mansfield T*	6	—
1990–91	Notts Co	31	1

ORLYGSSON, Thorvaldur

Born Odense 2.8.66. Ht 5 11 Wt 10 08
Midfield. From FC Akureyri. Iceland full
caps.

1989–90	Nottingham F	12	1
1990–91		—	—

ORMONDROYD, Ian

Born Bradford 22.9.64. Ht 6 4 Wt 13 07
Forward. From Thackley.

1985–86	Bradford C	12	3
1986–87		13	4
1986–87	*Oldham Ath*	10	1
1987–88	Bradford C	37	9
1988–89		25	4
1988–89	Aston Villa	12	1
1989–90		25	4
1990–91		18	1

ORMSBY, Brendan

Born Birmingham 1.10.60. Ht 5 11
Wt 11 12
Defender. From Apprentice. England
Schools, Youth.

1978–79	Aston Villa	2	—
1979–80		23	—
1980–81		—	—
1981–82		12	—
1982–83		—	—
1983–84		34	2

1984–85		32	2
1985–86		14	—
1985–86	Leeds U	12	1
1986–87		33	4
1987–88		—	—
1988–89		1	—
1989–90		—	—
1989–90	*Shrewsbury T*	1	—
1990–91	Doncaster R	43	5

ORR, Neil

Born Airdrie 13.5.59. Ht 5 10 Wt 12 02
Defender. Scotland Under-21.

1975–76	Morton	4	—
1976–77		24	—
1977–78		39	—
1978–79		35	—
1979–80		35	1
1980–81		33	—
1981–82		16	—
1981–82	West Ham U	24	1
1982–83		14	—
1983–84		29	—
1984–85		20	—
1985–86		36	2
1986–87		22	1
1987–88		1	—
1987–88	Hibernian	38	1
1988–89		33	—
1989–90		29	1
1990–91		17	—

OSBORN, Simon

Born New Addington 19.1.72. Ht 5 10
Wt 11 04
Midfield. From Apprentice.

1989–90	Crystal Palace	—	—
1990–91		4	—

OSBORNE, Lawrence

Born London 20.10.67. Ht 5 11
Wt 12 07
Forward. From Apprentice.

1985–86	Arsenal	—	—

Season	Club	Apps	Goals
1986–87	....	—	—
1987–88	Newport Co	15	—
From Redbridge Forest			
1990–91	Maidstone U	37	4

OSBORNE, Steve

Born Middlesbrough 3.3.69   Ht 5 10
Wt 11 11
Forward. From South Bank.

Season	Club	Apps	Goals
1988–89	Peterborough U	9	1
1989–90	....	32	5
1990–91	....	19	1

O'SHAUGHNESSY, Steve

Born Wrexham 13.10.67.   Ht 6 2
Wt 13 00
Defender. Wales Youth.

Season	Club	Apps	Goals
1984–85	Leeds U	—	—
1985–86	....	—	—
1985–86	Bradford C	—	—
1986–87	....	—	—
1987–88	....	1	—
1988–89	Rochdale.....................	41	6
1989–90	....	30	8
1990–91	....	38	2

O'SHEA, Danny

Born Kennington 26.3.63.   Ht 6 0
Wt 12 02
Defender. From Apprentice.

Season	Club	Apps	Goals
1980–81	Arsenal........................	—	—
1981–82	....	—	—
1982–83	....	6	—
1983–84	....	—	—
1983–84	*Charlton Ath*	9	—
1984–85	Exeter C......................	45	2
1985–86	Southend U.................	35	9
1986–87	....	41	2
1987–88	....	22	—
1988–89	....	20	1
1989–90	Cambridge U	26	—
1990–91	....	40	—

O'SHEA, Tim

Born London 12.11.66.   Ht 5 11   Wt 11 4
Defender. From Arsenal Schoolboy. Eire Youth.

Season	Club	Apps	Goals
1984–85	Tottenham H	—	—
1985–86	....	—	—
1986–87	....	2	—
1986–87	*Newport Co*	10	—
1987–88	Tottenham H	1	—
1988–89	Leyton Orient	9	1
1988–89	Gillingham..................	17	—
1989–90	....	36	2
1990–91	....	29	—

OSMAN, Russell

Born Repton 14.2.59.   Ht 5 11   Wt 12 01
Defender. From Apprentice. England Under-21, B, 11 full caps.

Season	Club	Apps	Goals
1975–76	Ipswich........................	—	—
1976–77	....	—	—
1977–78	....	28	—
1978–79	....	39	2
1979–80	....	42	2
1980–81	....	42	1
1981–82	....	39	2
1982–83	....	38	4
1983–84	....	37	3
1984–85	....	29	3
1985–86	Leicester C..................	40	—
1986–87	....	31	3
1987–88	....	37	5
1988–89	Southampton	36	—
1989–90	....	35	5
1990–91	....	20	1

O'TOOLE, Pat

Born Dublin 2.1.65.   Ht 5 7   Wt 11 00
Midfield. From Shelbourne.

Season	Club	Apps	Goals
1989–90	Leicester C..................	—	—
1990–91	....	—	—
1990–91	*Exeter C*	6	—
1990–91	Shrewsbury T..............	11	—

OTTO, Ricky

Born London 9.11.67.
Midfield. From Dartford.

| 1990–91 | Leyton Orient | 1 | — |

OVERSON, Vince

Born Kettering 15.5.62.   Ht 6 0   Wt 13 00
Defender. From Apprentice.

1979–80	Burnley	22	—
1980–81		39	1
1981–82		36	4
1982–83		6	—
1983–84		38	—
1984–85		42	1
1985–86		28	—
1986–87	Birmingham C	34	1
1987–88		37	—
1988–89		41	—
1989–90		30	—
1990–91		40	2

OWEN, Gareth

Born Chester 21.10.71.   Ht 5 9   Wt 11 04
Midfield. From Trainee. Wales Under-21

| 1989–90 | Wrexham | 13 | — |
| 1990–91 | | 27 | 2 |

OWEN, Gordon

Born Barnsley 14.6.59.   Ht 5 8   Wt 10 09
Forward. From Amateur.

1976–77	Sheffield W	1	—
1977–78		2	—
1978–79		22	3
1979–80		4	1
1979–80	Rotherham U	9	—
1980–81	Sheffield W	6	—
1981–82		6	—
1982–83		7	1
1982–83	Doncaster R	9	—
1982–83	Chesterfield	6	2
1983–84	Cardiff C	39	14
1984–85	Barnsley	36	14
1985–86		32	11

1986–87	Bristol C	35	5
1987–88		18	6
1987–88	Hull C	3	—
1987–88	Mansfield T	17	3
1988–89		41	5
1989–90	Blackpool	28	4
1990–91		1	—
1990–91	Carlisle U	5	—
1990–91	Exeter C	4	—

OWERS, Adrian

Born Banbury 26.2.65.   Ht 5 8   Wt 10 02
Midfield. From Apprentice.

1982–83	Southend U	14	—
1983–84		1	—
1984–85		12	—
From Chelmsford C			
1987–88	Brighton	9	2
1988–89		24	2
1989–90		4	—
1990–91		3	—
1990–91	Gillingham	10	—

OWERS, Gary

Born Newcastle 3.10.68.   Ht 5 10
Wt 11 10
Midfield. From Apprentice.

1986–87	Sunderland	—	—
1987–88		37	4
1988–89		38	3
1989–90		43	9
1990–91		38	1

OXBROW, Darren

Born Ipswich 1.9.69   Ht 6 1   Wt 12 06
Defender. From Trainee.

1988–89	Ipswich T	—	—
1989–90	Maidstone U	24	—
1990–91		30	1

PAATELAINEN, Mixu

Born Helsinki 3.2.67. Ht 6 0 Wt 13 11
Forward. From Valkeakosken Haka.
Finland full caps.

1987–88	Dundee U	19	9
1988–89		33	10
1989–90		31	7
1990–91		20	1

PAGE, Don

Born Manchester 18.1.64 Ht 5 11
Wt 11 00
Forward. From Runcorn.

1988–89	Wigan Ath	15	2
1989–90		25	—
1990–91		34	13

PAINTER, Robert

Born Ince 26.1.71. Ht 5 11 Wt 11 00
Midfield. From Trainee.

1987–88	Chester C	2	—
1988–89		8	1
1989–90		32	4
1990–91		42	3

PALADINO, Giuseppe

Born Whiston 29.8.65.
Goalkeeper. From St Helens.

| 1990–91 | Wigan Ath | 7 | — |

PALIN, Leigh

Born Worcester 12.9.65. Ht 5 9
Wt 11 07
Midfield. From Apprentice. England
Youth.

1983–84	Aston Villa	—	—
1984–85		—	—
1984–85	*Shrewsbury T*	2	—
1985–86	Aston Villa	—	—
1985–86	Nottingham F	—	—

1986–87		—	—
1986–87	Bradford C	21	3
1987–88		20	3
1988–89		30	4
1989–90		—	—
1989–90	Stoke C	19	3
1989–90	Hull C	9	1
1990–91		35	5

PALLISTER, Gary

Born Ramsgate 30.6.65. Ht 6 4 Wt 13 04
Defender. England B, 4 full caps

1984–85	Middlesbrough	—	—
1985–86		28	—
1985–86	*Darlington*	7	—
1986–87	Middlesbrough	44	1
1987–88		44	3
1988–89		37	1
1989–90		3	—
1989–90	Manchester U	35	3
1990–91		36	—

PALMER, Carlton

Born West Bromwich 5.12.65. Ht 6 2
Wt 12 04
Defender. From Trainee. England B,
Under-21.

1984–85	WBA	—	—
1985–86		20	—
1986–87		37	1
1987–88		38	3
1988–89		26	—
1988–89	Sheffield W	13	1
1989–90		34	—
1990–91		45	2

PALMER, Charlie

Born Aylesbury 10.7.63. Ht 5 11
Wt 13 00
Defender. From Apprentice.

1981–82	Watford	—	—
1982–83		—	—
1983–84		10	1
1984–85	Derby Co	33	2

Season	Club	App	Goals
1985–86	....	18	—
1986–87	....	—	—
1986–87	Hull C	17	—
1987–88	....	35	—
1988–89	....	18	1
1988–89	Notts Co	11	—
1989–90	....	37	5
1990–91	....	40	1

PALMER, Lee

Born Gillingham 19.9.70   Ht 6 0
Wt 12 04
Defender. From Trainee.

Season	Club	App	Goals
1987–88	Gillingham	1	—
1988–89	....	—	—
1989–90	....	39	3
1990–91	....	21	1

PALMER, Les

Born Birmingham 5.9.71.   Ht 5 10
Wt 10 10
Forward. From Trainee.

Season	Club	App	Goals
1990–91	WBA	7	1

PALMER, Roger

Born Manchester 30.1.59.   Ht 5 10
Wt 11 00
Forward. From Apprentice.

Season	Club	App	Goals
1976–77	Manchester C	—	—
1977–78	....	5	3
1978–79	....	14	4
1979–80	....	7	1
1980–81	....	5	1
1980–81	Oldham Ath	21	6
1981–82	....	37	7
1982–83	....	42	15
1983–84	....	42	13
1984–85	....	36	9
1985–86	....	41	15
1986–87	....	42	16
1987–88	....	42	17
1988–89	....	46	15
1989–90	....	42	16
1990–91	....	29	9

PALMER, Steve

Born Brighton 31.3.68   Ht 6 1   Wt 12 07
Midfield. From Cambridge University.

Season	Club	App	Goals
1989–90	Ipswich T	5	—
1990–91	....	23	1

PARDEW, Alan

Born Wimbledon 18.7.61.   Ht 5 10
Wt 11 00
Midfield. From Yeovil.

Season	Club	App	Goals
1986–87	Crystal Palace	—	—
1987–88	....	20	—
1988–89	....	45	1
1989–90	....	36	6
1990–91	....	19	1

PARIS, Alan

Born Slough 15.8.64.   Ht 6 0   Wt 11 10
Defender. From Slough T.

Season	Club	App	Goals
1982–83	Watford	—	—
1983–84	....	—	—
1984–85	....	—	—
1985–86	Peterborough U	46	—
1986–87	....	45	—
1987–88	....	46	2
1988–89	Leicester C	37	1
1989–90	....	38	2
1990–91	....	13	—
1990–91	Notts Co	15	1

PARKER, Garry

Born Oxford 7.9.65.   Ht 5 10   Wt 12 06
Midfield. From Apprentice. England
Youth, B, Under-21.

Season	Club	App	Goals
1982–83	Luton T	1	—
1983–84	....	13	2
1984–85	....	20	1
1985–86	....	8	—
1985–86	Hull C	12	—
1986–87	....	38	—
1987–88	....	34	8
1987–88	Nottingham F	2	—
1988–89	....	22	7

| 1989–90 | | 37 | 6 |
| 1990–91 | | 36 | 3 |

PARKER, Paul

Born Essex 4.4.64.   Ht 5 7   Wt 10 13
Defender. From Apprentice. England
Youth, B, Under-21, 16 full caps.

1980–81	Fulham	1	—
1981–82		5	—
1982–83		16	—
1983–84		34	—
1984–85		36	—
1985–86		30	—
1986–87		31	2
1987–88	QPR	40	—
1988–89		36	—
1989–90		32	—
1990–91		17	1

PARKES, Phil

Born Sedgeley 8.8.50.   Ht 6 3   Wt 15 12
Goalkeeper. From Amateur. England
Under-21, Under-23, B, 1 full cap.

1967–68	Walsall	—	—
1968–69		8	—
1969–70		44	—
1970–71	QPR	41	—
1971–72		42	—
1972–73		41	—
1973–74		42	—
1974–75		41	—
1975–76		42	—
1976–77		40	—
1977–78		31	—
1978–79		24	—
1978–79	West Ham U	18	—
1979–80		40	—
1980–81		42	—
1981–82		39	—
1982–83		42	—
1983–84		42	—
1984–85		10	—
1985–86		42	—
1986–87		33	—
1987–88		1	—
1988–89		13	—

| 1989–90 | | 22 | — |
| 1990–91 | Ipswich T | 3 | — |

PARKIN, Brian

Born Birkenhead 12.10.65.   Ht 6 1
Wt 12 0
Goalkeeper. Local.

1982–83	Oldham Ath	—	—
1983–84		5	—
1984–85		1	—
1984–85	*Crewe Alex*	12	—
1985–86	Crewe Alex	39	—
1986–87		44	—
1987–88		3	—
1987–88	*Crystal Palace*	—	—
1988–89	Crystal Palace	19	—
1989–90		1	—
1989–90	Bristol R	30	—
1990–91		39	—

PARKIN, Steve

Born Mansfield 7.11.65.   Ht 5 6   Wt 11 00
Defender. From Apprentice. England
Schools, Youth, Under-21.

1982–83	Stoke C	2	—
1983–84		1	—
1984–85		13	1
1985–86		12	1
1986–87		38	—
1987–88		43	3
1988–89		4	—
1989–90	WBA	14	1
1990–91		25	1

PARKIN, Tim

Born Penrith 31.12.57.   Ht 6 2   Wt 13 02
Defender. From Apprentice.

1976–77	Blackburn R	1	—
1977–78		—	—
1978–79		12	—
1979–80		—	—
From Malmo and Almondsbury Greenway			
1981–82	Bristol R	40	2
1982–83		41	3

Season	Club	Apps	Goals
1983–84		39	2
1984–85		43	3
1985–86		43	2
1986–87	Swindon T	32	2
1987–88		40	2
1988–89		32	1
1989–90		6	1
1989–90	Port Vale	12	1
1990–91		29	—

PARKINSON, Gary

Born Middlesbrough 10.1.68. Ht 5 11 Wt 12 05
Defender. From Everton Amateur.

Season	Club	Apps	Goals
1985–86	Middlesbrough	—	—
1986–87		46	—
1987–88		38	—
1988–89		36	2
1989–90		41	2
1990–91		10	1

PARKINSON, Joe

Born Eccles 11.6.71 Ht 5 11 Wt 12 02
Midfield. From Trainee.

Season	Club	Apps	Goals
1988–89	Wigan Ath	12	1
1989–90		33	2
1990–91		25	—

PARKINSON, Philip

Born Chorley 1.12.67. Ht 6 0 Wt 11 06
Midfield. From Apprentice.

Season	Club	Apps	Goals
1985–86	Southampton	—	—
1986–87		—	—
1987–88		—	—
1987–88	Bury	8	1
1988–89		39	—
1989–90		22	2
1990–91		44	2

PARKS, Tony

Born Hackney 26.1.63. Ht 5 11 Wt 10 08
Goalkeeper. From Apprentice.

Season	Club	Apps	Goals
1980–81	Tottenham H	—	—
1981–82		2	—
1982–83		1	—
1983–84		16	—
1984–85		—	—
1985–86		—	—
1986–87		2	—
1986–87	*Oxford U*	5	—
1987–88	Tottenham H	16	—
1987–88	*Gillingham*	2	—
1988–89	Brentford	33	—
1989–90		37	—
1990–91		1	—
1990–91	*QPR*	—	—
1990–91	Fulham	2	—

PARRIS, George

Born Ilford 11.9.64. Ht 5 9 Wt 13 00
Defender. From Apprentice. England Schools.

Season	Club	Apps	Goals
1982–83	West Ham U	—	—
1983–84		—	—
1984–85		1	—
1985–86		26	1
1986–87		36	2
1987–88		30	1
1988–89		27	1
1989–90		38	2
1990–91		44	5

PARRISH, Sean

Born Wrexham 14.3.72. Ht 5 9 Wt 10 00
Midfield. From Trainee.

Season	Club	Apps	Goals
1989–90	Shrewsbury T	2	—
1990–91		1	—

PARROTT, Mark

Born Cheltenham 14.3.71. Ht 5 11 Wt 11 00
Forward. From Trainee. England schools, Youth.

Season	Club	Apps	Goals
1989–90	Aston Villa	—	—
1990–91		—	—

PARSLEY, Neil

Born Liverpool 25.4.66   Ht 5 10
Wt 10 11
Defender. From Witton Alb.

1988–89	Leeds U	—	—
1989–90		—	—
1989–90	*Chester C*	6	—
1990–91	Huddersfield T	8	—
1990–91	*Doncaster R*	3	—

PASCOE, Colin

Born Port Talbot 9.4.65.   Ht 5 9
Wt 10 00
Forward. From Apprentice. Wales Youth,
Under-21, 9 full caps.

1982–83	Swansea C	7	1
1983–84		32	2
1984–85		41	9
1985–86		19	3
1986–87		41	11
1987–88		34	13
1987–88	Sunderland	9	4
1988–89		39	10
1989–90		33	1
1990–91		25	5

PASKIN, John

Born Capetown 1.2.62   Ht 5 10   Wt 11 10
Forward. From Seiko.

1988–89	WBA	25	5
1989–90	Wolverhampton W	17	2
1990–91		15	1

PATERSON, Craig

Born South Queensferry 2.10.59.   Ht 6 2
Wt 12 12
Defender. From Bonnyrigg Rose. Scotland
Under-21.

1978–79	Hibernian	—	—
1979–80		30	—
1980–81		38	3
1981–82		36	1
1982–83	Rangers	20	—

1983–84		21	1
1984–85		22	2
1985–86		18	1
1986–87		2	—
1986–87	Motherwell	16	—
1987–88		44	2
1988–89		33	1
1989–90		33	3
1990–91		32	2

PATERSON, Jamie

Born Dumfries 26.4.73.
Forward. From Trainee.

| 1990–91 | Halifax T | 6 | 1 |

PATES, Colin

Born Mitcham 10.8.61.   Ht 5 11
Wt 11 00
Defender. From Apprentice. England
Youth.

1979–80	Chelsea	16	—
1980–81		15	—
1981–82		42	1
1982–83		35	4
1983–84		42	—
1984–85		36	1
1985–86		35	1
1986–87		33	2
1987–88		17	—
1988–89		10	1
1988–89	Charlton Ath	21	—
1989–90		17	—
1989–90	Arsenal	2	—
1990–91		1	—
1990–91	Brighton	17	—

PATTERSON, Darren

Born Belfast 15.10.69   Ht 6 2   Wt 11 10
Defender. From Trainee.

1988–89	WBA	—	—
1989–90	Wigan Ath	29	1
1990–91		28	4

PATTERSON, Mark

Born Darwen 24.5.65.   Ht 5 6   Wt 10 10
Forward. From Apprentice.

Season	Club	Apps	Goals
1983–84	Blackburn R	29	7
1984–85		9	—
1985–86		26	10
1986–87		24	1
1987–88		13	2
1988–89	Preston NE	42	15
1989–90		13	4
1989–90	Bury	20	4
1990–91		22	6
1990–91	Bolton W	19	2

PATTERSON, Mark

Born Leeds 13.9.68 Ht 5 10 Wt 11 05
Defender. From Trainee.

Season	Club	Apps	Goals
1986–87	Carlisle U	6	—
1987–88		16	—
1987–88	Derby Co	—	—
1988–89		1	—
1989–90		9	—
1990–91		11	1

PAYNE, Lee

Born Luton 12.12.66 Ht 5 10 Wt 11 05
Forward. From Barnet.

Season	Club	Apps	Goals
1988–89	Newcastle U	7	—
1988–89	Reading	15	3
1989–90		12	—

To Veendam

PAYNE, Mark

Born Cheltenham 3.8.60 Ht 5 9
Wt 11 09
Forward. From Cambuur.

Season	Club	Apps	Goals
1988–89	Stockport Co	22	1
1989–90		34	6
1990–91		31	9

PAYTON, Andy

Born Burnley 23.10.66. Ht 5 9 Wt 10 06
Midfield. From Apprentice.

Season	Club	Apps	Goals
1985–86	Hull C	—	—
1986–87		2	—

Season	Club	Apps	Goals
1987–88		22	2
1988–89		28	4
1989–90		39	17
1990–91		43	25

PEACOCK, Darren

Born Bristol 3.2.68 Ht 6 2 Wt 12 06
Defender. From Apprentice.

Season	Club	Apps	Goals
1984–85	Newport Co	—	—
1985–86		18	—
1986–87		5	—
1987–88		5	—
1988–89	Hereford U	8	—
1989–90		36	3
1990–91		15	1
1990–91	QPR	19	—

PEACOCK, Gavin

Born Kent 18.11.67. Ht 5 8 Wt 11 08
Midfield. England School, Youth.

Season	Club	Apps	Goals
1984–85	QPR	—	—
1985–86		—	—
1986–87		12	1
1987–88		5	—
1987–88	Gillingham	26	2
1988–89		44	9
1989–90	Bournemouth	41	4
1990–91		15	4
1990–91	Newcastle U	27	7

PEAKE, Andy

Born Market Harborough 1.11.61.
Ht 5 10 Wt 12 00
Midfield. From Apprentice. England
Youth, Under-21.

Season	Club	Apps	Goals
1978–79	Leicester C	18	2
1979–80		25	3
1980–81		24	1
1981–82		31	2
1982–83		4	—
1983–84		24	4
1984–85		21	1
1985–86	Grimsby T	36	4
1986–87		3	—

Season	Club	App	Goals
1986–87	Charlton Ath	29	—
1987–88		16	—
1988–89		31	1
1989–90		36	—
1990–91		45	4

PEAKE, Jason

Born Leicester 29.9.71.   Ht 5 9   Wt 11 05
Midfield. From Trainee. England Youth.

Season	Club	App	Goals
1989–90	Leicester C	—	—
1990–91		8	1

PEAKE, Trevor

Born Nuneaton 10.2.57.   Ht 6 0   Wt 12 9
Defender. From Nuneaton Bor.

Season	Club	App	Goals
1979–80	Lincoln C	45	1
1980–81		43	1
1981–82		37	4
1982–83		46	1
1983–84	Coventry C	33	3
1984–85		35	1
1985–86		37	1
1986–87		39	—
1987–88		31	—
1988–89		32	—
1989–90		33	—
1990–91		36	1

PEARCE, Andy

Born Bradford 20.4.66.   Ht 6 4   Wt 13 00
Defender. From Halesowen

Season	Club	App	Goals
1990–91	Coventry C	11	1

PEARCE, Chris

Born Newport 7.8.61.   Ht 6 0   Wt 11 04
Goalkeeper. From Wolverhampton W.
Apprentice. Wales Schools, Youth.

Season	Club	App	Goals
1979–80	Blackburn R	—	—
1980–81	*Rochdale*	5	—
1981–82	*Barnsley*	—	—
1982–83	Rochdale	36	—
1983–84	Port Vale	7	—

Season	Club	App	Goals
1984–85		36	—
1985–86		5	—
1986–87	Wrexham	25	—
1987–88	Burnley	46	—
1988–89		39	—
1989–90		39	—
1990–91		43	—

PEARCE, Ian

Born Bury St Edmunds 7.5.74.
Defender. From Schoolboy.

Season	Club	App	Goals
1990–91	Chelsea	1	—

PEARCE, Stuart

Born London 24.4.62.   Ht 5 10   Wt 12 08
Defender. From Wealdstone. England
Under-21, 41 full caps.

Season	Club	App	Goals
1983–84	Coventry C	23	—
1984–85		28	4
1985–86	Nottingham F	30	1
1986–87		39	6
1987–88		34	5
1988–89		36	6
1989–90		34	5
1990–91		33	11

PEARCEY, Jason

Born Leamington Spa 2.7.71   Ht 6 1
Wt 13 05
Goalkeeper. From Trainee.

Season	Club	App	Goals
1988–89	Mansfield T	1	—
1989–90		5	—
1990–91		4	—

PEARS, Steve

Born Brandon 22.1.62.   Ht 6 0   Wt 12 11
Goalkeeper. From Apprentice.

Season	Club	App	Goals
1978–79	Manchester U	—	—
1979–80		—	—
1980–81		—	—
1981–82		—	—
1982–83		—	—

1983–84	....	—	—
1983–84	*Middlesbrough*............	12	—
1984–85	Manchester U	4	—
1985–86	Middlesbrough............	38	—
1986–87	....	46	—
1987–88	....	43	—
1988–89	....	26	—
1989–90	....	25	—
1990–91	....	27	—

PEARSON, John

Born Sheffield 1.9.63.   Ht 6 3   Wt 13 00
Forward. From Apprentice. England
Youth.

1980–81	Sheffield W..................	15	4
1981–82	....	24	7
1982–83	....	30	7
1983–84	....	27	4
1984–85	....	9	2
1985–86	Charlton Ath	42	14
1986–87	....	19	1
1986–87	Leeds U	18	4
1987–88	....	28	6
1988–89	....	33	1
1989–90	....	7	—
1990–91	....	13	1
1990–91	Rotherham U	11	5

PEARSON, Nigel

Born Nottingham 21.8.63.   Ht 6 1
Wt 13 03
Defender. From Heanor T.

1981–82	Shrewsbury T..............	—	—
1982–83	....	39	1
1983–84	....	26	—
1984–85	....	—	—
1985–86	....	35	1
1986–87	....	42	3
1987–88	....	11	—
1987–88	Sheffield W.................	19	2
1988–89	....	37	2
1989–90	....	33	1
1990–91	....	39	6

PEEL, Nathan

Born Blackburn 17.5.72.
Forward. From Trainee.

1990–91	Preston NE	10	1

PEER, Dean

Born Dudley 8.8.69.   Ht 6 2   Wt 12 00
Midfield. From Trainee.

1986–87	Birmingham C	2	—
1987–88	....	—	—
1988–89	....	17	1
1989–90	....	27	3
1990–91	....	40	2

PEJIC, Mel

Born Chesterton 27.4.59.   Ht 5 9
Wt 10 08
Defender. Local.

1977–78	Stoke C......................	—	—
1978–79	....	—	—
1979–80	....	1	—
1980–81	Hereford U	13	—
1981–82	....	27	—
1982–83	....	45	1
1983–84	....	44	—
1984–85	....	46	1
1985–86	....	45	1
1986–87	....	31	—
1987–88	....	44	1
1988–89	....	18	3
1989–90	....	38	5
1990–91	....	46	1

PEMBERTON, John

Born Oldham 18.11.64.   Ht 5 11
Wt 12 03
Defender. From Chadderton.

1984–85	Rochdale....................	1	—
1984–85	Crewe Alex	6	—
1985–86	....	41	—
1986–87	....	43	—
1987–88	....	31	1
1987–88	Crystal Palace.............	2	—

Season	Club			
1988–89	....	42	1
1989–90	....	34	1
1990–91	Sheffield U	21	—

PEMBRIDGE, Mark

Born Methyr Tydfil 29.11.70. Ht 5 7
Wt 11 01
Midfield. From Trainee. Wales B,
Under-21.

1989–90	Luton T	—	—
1990–91	....	18	1

PENDER, John

Born Luton 19.11.63. Ht 6 0 Wt 12 03
Defender. From Apprentice. Eire Youth,
Under-21.

1981–82	Wolverhampton W	8	—
1982–83	....	39	1
1983–84	....	34	1
1984–85	....	36	1
1985–86	Charlton Ath	38	—
1986–87	....	1	—
1987–88	....	2	—
1987–88	Bristol C	28	2
1988–89	....	45	1
1989–90	....	10	—
1990–91	....	—	—
1990–91	Burnley	40	—

PENNEY, David

Born Wakefield 17.8.64. Ht 5 8 Wt 10 7
Forward. From Pontefract.

1985–86	Derby Co	—	—
1986–87	....	1	—
1987–88	....	9	—
1988–89	....	9	—
1989–90	Oxford U	29	2
1990–91	....	9	1
1990–91	Swansea C	12	3

PENNEY, Steve

Born Ballymena 16.1.64. Ht 5 8
Wt 10 07
Midfield. From Ballymena U. Northern
Ireland 17 full caps.

1983–84	Brighton	25	1
1984–85	....	26	4
1985–86	....	37	3
1986–87	....	27	3
1987–88	....	13	3
1988–89	....	10	1
1989–90	....	—	—
1990–91	....	—	—

PENNOCK, Adrian

Born Ipswich 27.3.71. Ht 6 0 Wt 12 04
Defender. From Trainee.

1989–90	Norwich C	1	—
1990–91	....	—	—

PENNOCK, Tony

Born Swansea 10.4.71. Ht 5 11 Wt 10 09
Goalkeeper. From School.

1990–91	Stockport Co	—	—
1990–91	Wigan Ath	2	—

PENNYFATHER, Glenn

Born Billericay 11.2.63. Ht 5 8 Wt 11 08
Midfield. From Apprentice.

1980–81	Southend U	1	—
1981–82	....	33	4
1982–83	....	34	1
1983–84	....	33	4
1984–85	....	41	7
1985–86	....	41	7
1986–87	....	38	10
1987–88	....	17	3
1987–88	Crystal Palace	19	1
1988–89	....	15	—
1989–90	....	—	—
1989–90	Ipswich T	8	1
1990–91	....	—	—

PENRICE, Gary

Born Bristol 23.3.64. Ht 5 8 Wt 10 06
Forward. From Bristol C. Apprentice.

1984–85	Bristol R	5	1

1985–86	....	39	5
1986–87	....	43	7
1987–88	....	46	18
1988–89	....	43	20
1989–90	....	12	3
1989–90	Watford	29	13
1990–91	....	14	5
1990–91	Aston Villa...............	12	—

PEPPER, Nigel

Born Rotherham 25.4.68. Ht 5 10
Wt 11 05
Midfield. From Apprentice.

1985–86	Rotherham U	7	—
1986–87	....	2	—
1987–88	....	15	—
1988–89	....	2	—
1989–90	....	19	1
1990–91	York C......................	39	3

PERDOMO, Jose

Born Uruguay 6.1.65.
Midfield. From Penarol, Genoa. Uruguay
full caps.

| 1990–91 | Coventry C .... | 4 | — |

PERKS, Steve

Born Bridgnorth 19.4.63. Ht 6 0
Wt 12 02
Goalkeeper. From Apprentice.

1980–81	Shrewsbury T..............	—	—
1981–82	....	—	—
1982–83	....	—	—
1983–84	....	—	—
1984–85	....	23	—
1985–86	....	42	—
1986–87	....	36	—
1987–88	....	42	—
1988–89	....	22	—
1989–90	....	46	—
1990–91	....	10	—

PERRY, Jason

Born Newport 2.4.70. Ht 5 11 Wt 10 04
Defender. Wales B, Under-21.

1986–87	Cardiff C....................	1	—
1987–88	....	3	—
1988–89	....	—	—
1989–90	....	36	—
1990–91	....	43	—

PETERS, Rob

Born Kensington 18.5.71. Ht 5 8
Wt 11 02
Defender. From Trainee.

| 1989–90 | Brentford .... | 2 | — |
| 1990–91 | .... | 6 | 1 |

PEYTON, Gerry

Born Birmingham 20.5.56. Ht 6 2
Wt 13 09
Goalkeeper. From Atherstone T. Eire 29
full caps.

1975–76	Burnley	20	—
1976–77	....	10	—
1976–77	Fulham	23	—
1977–78	....	42	—
1978–79	....	40	—
1979–80	....	31	—
1980–81	....	28	—
1981–82	....	44	—
1982–83	....	42	—
1983–84	....	27	—
1983–84	*Southend U*	10	—
1984–85	Fulham	32	—
1985–86	....	36	—
1986–87	Bournemouth..............	46	—
1987–88	....	42	—
1988–89	....	39	—
1989–90	....	39	—
1990–91	....	36	—

PHELAN, Mike

Born Nelson 24.9.62. Ht 5 11 Wt 11 01
Defender. From Apprentice. England
Youth, 1 full cap.

1980–81	Burnley	16	2
1981–82	....	23	1
1982–83	....	42	3

Season	Club	App	Goals
1983–84		44	2
1984–85		43	1
1985–86	Norwich C	42	3
1986–87		40	4
1987–88		37	—
1988–89		37	2
1989–90	Manchester U	38	1
1990–91		33	1

PHELAN, Terry

Born Manchester 16.3.67.   Ht 5 8
Wt 10 00
Defender. Eire Youth, B, Under-21,
Under-23.

Season	Club	App	Goals
1984–85	Leeds U	—	—
1985–86		14	—
1986–87	Swansea C	45	—
1987–88	Wimbledon	30	—
1988–89		29	—
1989–90		34	—
1990–91		29	—

PHILLIBEN, John

Born Stirling 14.3.64.   Ht 5 10   Wt 11 00
Defender. From Gairdoch U. Scotland
Youth.

Season	Club	App	Goals
1980–81	Stirling A	15	—
1981–82		37	1
1982–83		34	—
1983–84		23	—
1983–84	Doncaster R	12	—
1984–85		36	1
1985–86		22	—
1985–86	*Cambridge U*	6	—
1986–87	Doncaster R	1	—
1986–87	Motherwell	37	—
1987–88		35	2
1988–89		19	—
1989–90		24	—
1990–91		11	1

PHILLIPS, David

Born Wegberg 29.7.63.   Ht 5 10
Wt 11 02
Midfield. From Apprentice. Wales Under-
21, 32 full caps.

Season	Club	App	Goals
1981–82	Plymouth Arg	8	1
1982–83		23	8
1983–84		42	6
1984–85	Manchester C	42	12
1985–86		39	1
1986–87	Coventry C	39	4
1987–88		35	2
1988–89		26	2
1989–90	Norwich C	38	4
1990–91		38	4

PHILLIPS, Jimmy

Born Bolton 8.2.66.   Ht 6 0   Wt 12 0
Defender. From Apprentice.

Season	Club	App	Goals
1983–84	Bolton W	1	—
1984–85		40	1
1985–86		33	1
1986–87		34	—
1986–87	Rangers	6	—
1987–88		19	—
1988–89	Oxford U	45	5
1989–90		34	3
1989–90	Middlesbrough	12	—
1990–91		44	2

PHILLIPS, Justin

Born Derby 17.12.71.   Ht 6 3   Wt 14 07
Defender. From Trainee. England Youth.

Season	Club	App	Goals
1990–91	Derby Co	3	1

PHILLIPS, Les

Born Lambeth 7.1.63.   Ht 5 8   Wt 10 06
Midfield. From Apprentice.

Season	Club	App	Goals
1980–81	Birmingham C	—	—
1981–82		11	1
1982–83		13	2
1983–84		20	—
1983–84	Oxford U	6	—
1984–85		3	—
1985–86		28	2
1986–87		35	—
1987–88		30	4
1988–89		26	2
1989–90		8	—

1990–91	....	25	1

PHILLIPS, Stewart

Born Halifax 30.12.61. Ht 6 0 Wt 11 07
Forward. From Amateur.

1977–78	Hereford U	1	—
1978–79	....	8	—
1979–80	....	11	2
1980–81	....	8	1
1981–82	....	43	12
1982–83	....	41	13
1983–84	....	46	17
1984–85	....	46	19
1985–86	....	20	5
1986–87	....	39	11
1987–88	....	30	3
1987–88	WBA	10	2
1988–89	....	5	2
1988–89	Swansea C	6	—
1989–90	....	14	1
1990–91	Hereford U	37	10

PHILLIPS, Wayne

Born Bangor 15.12.70. Ht 5 10 Wt 11 00
Defender. From Trainee.

1989–90	Wrexham	5	—
1990–91	....	28	—

PHILLISKIRK, Tony

Born Sunderland 10.2.65. Ht 6 1
Wt 12 02
Forward. From Amateur. England
Schools.

1983–84	Sheffield U	21	8
1984–85	....	23	2
1985–86	....	4	—
1986–87	....	6	1
1986–87	*Rotherham U*	6	1
1987–88	Sheffield U	26	9
1988–89	Oldham Ath	10	1
1988–89	Preston NE	14	6
1989–90	Bolton W	45	18
1990–91	....	43	19

PHILPOTT, Lee

Born Barnet 21.2.70 Ht 5 9 Wt 10 06
Midfield. From Trainee.

1987–88	Peterborough U	1	—
1988–89	....	3	—
1989–90	Cambridge U	42	5
1990–91	....	45	5

PICKARD, Owen

Born Barnstaple 18.11.69 Ht 5 10
Wt 11 03
Forward. From Trainee.

1988–89	Plymouth Arg	2	—
1989–90	....	5	—
1990–91	....	7	1

PICKERING, Ally

Born Manchester 22.6.67. Ht 5 9
Wt 10 08
Defender. From Buxton

1989–90	Rotherham U	10	—
1990–91	....	1	—

PICKERING, Nick

Born Newcastle 4.8.63. Ht 6 0 Wt 11 10
Midfield. From Apprentice. England
Youth, Under-21, 1 full cap.

1981–82	Sunderland	37	3
1982–83	....	39	7
1983–84	....	42	1
1984–85	....	37	2
1985–86	....	24	5
1985–86	Coventry C	15	4
1986–87	....	36	5
1987–88	....	27	—
1988–89	Derby Co	8	—
1989–90	....	23	3
1990–91	....	13	—

PIKE, Chris

Born Cardiff 19.10.61. Ht 6 2 Wt 13 07
Forward. From Barry T.

Season	Club		
1984–85	Fulham	—	—
1985–86		26	4
1986–87		13	—
1986–87	*Cardiff C*	6	2
1987–88	Fulham	3	—
1988–89		—	—
1989–90	Cardiff C	41	18
1990–91		39	14

PIKE, Geoff

Born Clapton 28.9.56. Ht 5 6   Wt 11 04
Midfield. From Apprentice.

Season	Club		
1975–76	West Ham U	3	—
1976–77		20	6
1977–78		28	2
1978–79		14	2
1979–80		31	4
1980–81		42	6
1981–82		34	2
1982–83		40	6
1983–84		28	2
1984–85		30	2
1985–86		10	—
1986–87		11	—
1987–88	Notts Co	46	14
1988–89		36	3
1989–90		—	—
1989–90	Leyton Orient	14	—
1990–91		30	1

PIKE, Martin

Born South Shields 21.10.64.   Ht 5 11
Wt 11 07
Defender. From Apprentice.

Season	Club		
1982–83	WBA	—	—
1983–84	Peterborough U	35	2
1984–85		45	4
1985–86		46	2
1986–87	Sheffield U	42	—
1987–88		39	—
1988–89		45	5
1989–90		3	—
1989–90	*Tranmere R*	2	—
1989–90	*Bolton W*	5	1
1989–90	Fulham	20	2
1990–91		46	3

PILLING, Andy

Born Wigan 30.6.69.   Ht 5 10   Wt 11 04
Midfield. From Trainee.

Season	Club		
1985–86	Preston NE	1	—
1986–87		—	—
1987–88	Wigan Ath	20	3
1988–89		39	2
1989–90		26	6
1990–91		13	3

PITCHER, Darren

Born London 12.10.69.   Ht 5 9   Wt 12 02
Defender. From Trainee.

Season	Club		
1987–88	Charlton Ath	—	—
1988–89		—	—
1988–89	*Galway*	—	—
1989–90	Charlton Ath	—	—
1990–91		44	3

PLACE, Mark

Born Mansfield 16.11.69   Ht 5 11
Wt 10 06
Defender. From Trainee.

Season	Club		
1988–89	Mansfield T	14	—
1989–90		1	—
1990–91	Doncaster R	1	—

PLATNAUER, Nicky

Born Leicester 10.6.61.   Ht 5 11
Wt 12 06
Defender. From Northampton T Amateur
and Bedford T.

Season	Club		
1982–83	Bristol R	24	7
1983–84	Coventry C	34	6
1984–85		10	—
1984–85	Birmingham C	11	1
1985–86		17	1
1985–86	*Reading*	7	—
1986–87	Cardiff C	38	3
1987–88		38	1
1988–89		39	2
1989–90	Notts Co	44	—
1990–91		13	1

1990–91	*Port Vale*	14	—

PLATT, David

Born Chadderton 10.6.66. Ht 5 10
Wt 11 12
Forward. From Chadderton. England B,
Under-21, 22 full caps.

1984–85	Manchester U	—	—
1984–85	Crewe Alex	22	5
1985–86		43	8
1986–87		43	23
1987–88		26	19
1987–88	Aston Villa	11	5
1988–89		38	7
1989–90		37	19
1990–91		35	19

PLUMMER, Calvin

Born Nottingham 14.2.63. Ht 5 8
Wt 11 03
Forward. From Apprentice.

1980–81	Nottingham F	—	—
1981–82		9	2
1982–83		3	—
1982–83	Chesterfield	28	7
1983–84	Derby Co	27	3
1983–84	Barnsley	2	1
1984–85		26	2
1985–86		23	3
1986–87		3	—
1986–87	Nottingham F	—	—
1987–88		8	2
1987–88	*Derry C*	—	—
1988–89	Nottingham F	—	—
1988–89	Plymouth Arg	23	1
1989–90	Chesterfield	44	8
1990–91		27	4

POINTON, Neil

Born Church Warsop 28.11.64. Ht 5 10
Wt 11 00
Defender. From Apprentice.

1981–82	Scunthorpe U	5	—
1982–83		46	1

1983–84		45	1
1984–85		46	—
1985–86		17	—
1985–86	Everton	15	—
1986–87		12	1
1987–88		33	3
1988–89		23	—
1989–90		19	1
1990–91	Manchester C	35	1

POLLOCK, Jamie

Born Stockton 16.2.74.
Midfield. From Trainee.

1990–91	Middlesbrough	1	—

POLSTON, Andy

Born Walthamstow 26.7.70. Ht 5 10
Wt 11 00
Defender. From Trainee.

1988–89	Tottenham H	—	—
1989–90		1	—
1989–90	*Cambridge U*	3	—
1990–91	Tottenham H	—	—

POLSTON, John

Born London 10.6.68. Ht 5 11 Wt 11 03
Defender. From Apprentice. England
Youth.

1985–86	Tottenham H	—	—
1986–87		6	—
1987–88		2	—
1988–89		3	—
1989–90		13	1
1990–91	Norwich C	27	4

POOLE, Kevin

Born Bromsgrove 21.7.63. Ht 5 10
Wt 11 10
Goalkeeper. From Apprentice.

1981–82	Aston Villa	—	—
1982–83		—	—
1983–84		—	—

1984–85	....	7	—
1984–85	*Northampton T*............	3	—
1985–86	Aston Villa..................	11	—
1986–87	....	10	—
1987–88	Middlesbrough.............	1	—
1988–89	....	12	—
1989–90	....	21	—
1990–91	....	—	—
1990–91	*Hartlepool U*	12	—

POPE, Neil

Born Ashton 9.10.72.
Midfield. From Cambridge U Trainee.

| 1990–91 | Peterborough U.......... | 2 | — |

PORTER, Andy

Born Manchester 17.9.68.   Ht 5 9
Wt 11 02
Midfield. From Trainee.

1986–87	Port Vale....................	1	—
1987–88	....	6	—
1988–89	....	14	1
1989–90	....	36	1
1990–91	....	40	—

PORTER, Gary

Born Sunderland 6.3.66.   Ht 5 6
Wt 10 01
Midfield. From Apprentice. England
Youth, Under-21.

1983–84	Watford	2	—
1984–85	....	9	—
1985–86	....	8	1
1986–87	....	26	4
1987–88	....	40	3
1988–89	....	42	10
1989–90	....	32	4
1990–91	....	45	4

POTTS, Steven

Born Hartford (USA) 7.5.67.   Ht 5 7
Wt 10 11
Defender. From Apprentice. England
Youth.

1984–85	West Ham U	1	—
1985–86	....	1	—
1986–87	....	8	—
1987–88	....	8	—
1988–89	....	28	—
1989–90	....	32	—
1990–91	....	37	1

POUNDER, Tony

Born Yeovil 11.3.66.   Ht 5 8   Wt 11 00
Forward. From Westland Sports and
Weymouth.

| 1990–91 | Bristol R .... | 45 | 3 |

POWELL, Chris

Born Lambeth 8.9.69.   Ht 5 8   Wt 10 08
Defender.

1987–88	Crystal Palace............	—	—
1988–89	....	3	—
1989–90	....	—	—
1989–90	*Aldershot*	11	—
1990–91	Southend U.................	45	1

POWELL, Cliff

Born Watford 21.2.68.   Ht 6 0   Wt 12 00
Defender. From Apprentice.

1985–86	Watford	—	—
1986–87	....	—	—
1987–88	....	—	—
1987–88	*Hereford U*..................	7	—
1987–88	Sheffield U	6	—
1988–89	....	4	—
1988–89	Doncaster R................	4	—
1989–90	Sheffield U	—	—
1989–90	*Cardiff C*....................	1	—
1990–91	Sheffield U	—	—

POWELL, Darryl

Born Lambeth 15.1.71   Ht 6 0   Wt 12 03
Forward. From Trainee.

| 1988–89 | Portsmouth .... | 3 | — |
| 1989–90 | .... | — | — |

1990–91		8 —

POWELL, Gary

Born Holylake 2.4.69.   Ht 5 10   Wt 10 02
Forward. From Trainee.

1987–88	Everton	— —
1988–89		— —
1989–90		— —
1990–91		— —
1990–91	*Lincoln C*	11 —
1990–91	*Scunthorpe U*	4 1
1990–91	*Wigan Ath*	14 4

POWER, Lee

Born Lewisham 30.6.72.   Ht 5 11
Wt 11 02
Forward. From Trainee. Eire Under-21.

1989–90	Norwich C	1 —
1990–91		16 3

PREECE, Andy

Born Evesham 27.3.67   Ht 6 1   Wt 12 00
Midfield.

1988–89	Northampton T	1 —
From Worcester C.		
1989–90	Wrexham	7 1
1990–91		34 4

PREECE, David

Born Bridgnorth 28.5.63.   Ht 5 5
Wt 11 07
Midfield. From Apprentice. England B.

1980–81	Walsall	8 —
1981–82		8 —
1982–83		42 2
1983–84		41 3
1984–85		12 —
1984–85	Luton T	21 2
1985–86		41 2
1986–87		14 —
1987–88		13 —
1988–89		26 —

1989–90		32 1
1990–91		37 1

PREECE, Roger

Born Much Wenlock 9.6.69.   Ht 5 9
Wt 10 12
Midfield. From Coventry C Apprentice.

1986–87	Wrexham	7 2
1987–88		40 4
1988–89		31 5
1989–90		32 1
1990–91	Chester C	35 —

PRESSMAN, Kevin

Born Fareham 6.11.67.   Ht 6 1   Wt 14 02
Goalkeeper. From Apprentice. England
Schools, Youth, Under-21.

1985–86	Sheffield W	— —
1986–87		— —
1987–88		11 —
1988–89		9 —
1989–90		15 —
1990–91		23 —

PRESTON, Allan

Born Edinburgh 16.8.68.   Ht 5 10
Wt 10 01
Midfield. From Hutchison Vale BC.

1985–86	Dundee U	— —
1986–87		— —
1987–88		2 —
1988–89		9 1
1989–90		8 —
1990–91		3 —

PRICE, Chris

Born Hereford 30.3.60.   Ht 5 7   Wt 10 02
Defender. From Apprentice. England
Youth.

1976–77	Hereford U	2 —
1977–78		13 —
1978–79		29 —

Season	Club	League Appearances/Goals	
1979–80		42	—
1980–81		42	2
1981–82		41	10
1982–83		42	5
1983–84		37	1
1984–85		41	5
1985–86		41	4
1986–87	Blackburn R	40	1
1987–88		43	10
1988–89	Aston Villa	36	—
1989–90		34	1
1990–91		38	1

PRICE, Gareth

Born Swindon 21.2.70   Ht 5 9   Wt 10 02
Defender. From Trainee.

Season	Club		
1988–89	Mansfield T	—	—
1989–90	Bury	1	—
1990–91		3	—

PRIESTLEY, Jason

Born Leeds 25.10.70.   Ht 5 11   Wt 12 02
Goalkeeper. From Trainee.

Season	Club		
1989–90	Carlisle U	—	—
1989–90	*Hartlepool U*	16	—
1990–91	Carlisle U	22	—

PRINDIVILLE, Steve

Born Harlow 26.12.68   Ht 5 8   Wt 10 11
Defender. From Apprentice.

Season	Club		
1986–87	Leicester C	—	—
1987–88		1	—
1988–89	Chesterfield	43	1
1989–90	Mansfield T	22	—
1990–91		6	—

PRIOR, Spencer

Born Rochford 22.4.71   Ht 6 3   Wt 12 10
Defender. From Trainee.

Season	Club		
1988–89	Southend U	14	1
1989–90		15	1
1990–91		19	—

PRITCHARD, Howard

Born Cardiff 18.10.58.   Ht 5 10   Wt 12 00
Forward. From Apprentice. Wales Youth,
1 full cap.

Season	Club		
1976–77	Bristol C	—	—
1977–78		—	—
1978–79		1	—
1979–80		16	—
1980–81		21	2
1981–82	Swindon T	28	1
1982–83		37	10
1983–84	Bristol C	46	10
1984–85		39	6
1985–86		34	6
1986–87	Gillingham	46	12
1987–88		42	8
1988–89	Walsall	41	6
1989–90		4	1
1989–90	Maidstone U	24	4
1990–91		9	2

PROCTOR, Mark

Born Middlesbrough 30.1.61.   Ht 5 10
Wt 11 13
Midfield. From Apprentice. England
Youth, Under-21.

Season	Club		
1978–79	Middlesbrough	33	9
1979–80		38	2
1980–81		38	1
1981–82	Nottingham F	37	1
1982–83		27	4
1982–83	*Sunderland*	5	—
1983–84	Sunderland	41	2
1984–85		17	2
1985–86		19	7
1986–87		31	8
1987–88		4	—
1987–88	Sheffield W	35	2
1988–89		24	2
1988–89	Middlesbrough	10	—
1989–90		45	4
1990–91		18	—

PROUDLOCK, Paul

Born Hartlepool 25.10.65   Ht 5 9
Wt 11 09
Forward. From Local.

Season	Club		
1984–85	Hartlepool U	14	—
1985–86		1	—
1986–87	Middlesbrough	3	1
1987–88		1	—
1988–89		1	—
1988–89	Carlisle U	10	3
1989–90		40	6
1990–91		45	7

PRUDHOE, Mark

Born Washington 8.11.63.   Ht 6 0
Wt 13 00
Goalkeeper. From Apprentice.

Season	Club		
1981–82	Sunderland	—	—
1982–83		7	—
1983–84		—	—
1983–84	*Hartlepool U*	3	—
1984–85	Sunderland	—	—
1984–85	Birmingham C	1	—
1985–86	Walsall	16	—
1986–87		10	—
1986–87	*Doncaster R*	5	—
1986–87	*Sheffield W*	—	—
1986–87	*Grimsby T*	8	—
1987–88	Walsall	—	—
1987–88	*Hartlepool U*	13	—
1987–88	*Bristol C*	3	—
1987–88	Carlisle U	22	—
1988–89		12	—
1988–89	Darlington	12	—
1989–90		*34*	—
1990–91		46	—

PUCKETT, David

Born Southampton 29.10.60.   Ht 5 7
Wt 10 4
Forward. From Apprentice.

Season	Club		
1978–79	Southampton	—	—
1979–80		—	—
1980–81		7	—
1981–82		17	3

Season	Club		
1982–83		25	3
1983–84		18	3
1983–84	*Nottingham F*	—	—
1984–85	Southampton	13	1
1985–86		15	4
1986–87	Bournemouth	19	10
1987–88		12	4
1987–88	*Stoke C*	7	—
1988–89	Bournemouth	4	—
1988–89	*Swansea C*	8	3
1988–89	Aldershot	21	11
1989–90		46	18
1990–91		46	21

PUGH, David

Born Liverpool 19.9.64.   Ht 5 10
Wt 11 02
Midfield. From Runcorn.

Season	Club		
1989–90	Chester C	35	3
1990–91		37	3

PULIS, Tony

Born Newport 16.1.58.   Ht 5 10
Wt 11 08
Midfield. From Apprentice.

Season	Club		
1975–76	Bristol R	4	—
1976–77		9	—
1977–78		23	—
1978–79		7	—
1979–80		34	3
1980–81		8	—
From Happy Valley, Hong Kong			
1982–83	Bristol R	17	—
1983–84		28	2
1984–85	Newport C	37	—
1985–86		40	—
1986–87	Bournemouth	35	—
1987–88		29	3
1988–89		10	—
1989–90	Gillingham	16	—
1990–91	Bournemouth	15	1

PULLAN, Chris

Born Durham 14.12.67.   Ht 5 8   Wt 10 12
Midfield.

Season	Club		
1986–87	Watford	1	—
1987–88		4	—
1988–89		1	—
1988–89	*Halifax T*	5	1
1989–90	Watford	4	—
1990–91		2	—
1990–91	Maidstone U	1	—

PURNELL, Philip

Born Bristol 16.9.64.   Ht 5 6   Wt 9 08
Forward.

Season	Club		
1985–86	Bristol R	11	2
1986–87		21	3
1987–88		41	8
1988–89		37	7
1989–90		22	2
1990–91		9	—

PUTNEY, Trevor

Born Harold Hill 11.2.61.   Ht 5 7
Wt 10 11
Midfield. From Brentwood & W.

Season	Club		
1980–81	Ipswich T	—	—
1981–82		—	—
1982–83		20	3
1983–84		35	2
1984–85		27	2
1985–86		21	1
1986–87	Norwich C	23	4
1987–88		26	1
1988–89		33	4
1989–90	Middlesbrough	25	—
1990–91		23	1

PUTTNAM, David

Born Leicester 3.2.67   Ht 5 10   Wt 11 09
Midfield. From Leicester U.

Season	Club		
1988–89	Leicester C	3	—
1989–90		4	—
1989–90	Lincoln C	23	1
1990–91		43	6

QUAMINA, Mark

Born St Helier 25.11.69   Ht 5 10
Wt 11 07
Midfield. From Trainee.

Season	Club		
1988–89	Wimbledon	1	—
1989–90		—	—
1990–91		—	—

QUINLAN, Paul

Born Madrid 17.4.71.
Forward. From Trainee.

Season	Club		
1989–90	Everton	—	—
1990–91		—	—
1990–91	*Huddersfield T*	8	2

QUINN, Jimmy

Born Belfast 18.11.59.   Ht 6 0   Wt 12 07
Forward. From Oswestry T. Northern
Ireland 28 full caps.

Season	Club		
1981–82	Swindon T	4	—
1982–83		13	3
1983–84		32	7
1984–85	Blackburn R	25	10
1985–86		31	4
1986–87		15	3
1986–87	Swindon T	22	9
1987–88		42	21
1988–89	Leicester C	31	6
1988–89	Bradford C	12	8
1989–90		23	6
1989–90	West Ham U	21	12
1990–91		26	6

QUINN, Mick

Born Liverpool 2.5.62.   Ht 5 10   Wt 13 04
Forward. From Derby Co Apprentice.

Season	Club		
1979–80	Wigan Ath	4	1
1980–81		36	14
1981–82		29	4
1982–83	Stockport Co	39	24
1983–84		24	15

Season	Club	League Appearances/Goals	
1983–84	Oldham Ath	14	5
1984–85		40	18
1985–86		26	11
1985–86	Portsmouth	11	6
1986–87		39	22
1987–88		32	8
1988–89		39	18
1989–90	Newcastle U	45	32
1990–91		43	18

QUINN, Niall

Born Dublin 6.10.66.   Ht 6 3   Wt 13 10
Forward. From Eire Youth, B, Under-21,
Under-23, 24 full caps.

Season	Club	League Appearances/Goals	
1983–84	Arsenal	—	—
1984–85		—	—
1985–86		12	1
1986–87		35	8
1987–88		11	2
1988–89		3	1
1989–90		6	2
1989–90	Manchester C	9	4
1990–91		38	20

QUOW, Trevor

Born Peterborough 28.9.60.   Ht 5 8
Wt 11 07
Midfield. From Apprentice.

Season	Club	League Appearances/Goals	
1978–79	Peterborough U	8	—
1979–80		29	3
1980–81		44	4
1981–82		10	1
1982–83		18	1
1983–84		28	4
1984–85		36	1
1985–86		30	3
1986–87	Gillingham	19	1
1987–88		40	1
1988–89		20	1
1988–89	Northampton T	18	1
1989–90		30	1
1990–91		13	—

RAE, Alex

Born Glasgow 30.9.69.   Ht 5 9   Wt 11 00
Forward. From Bishopbriggs. Scotland
Under-21.

Season	Club	League Appearances/Goals	
1987–88	Falkirk	12	—
1988–89		37	12
1989–90		34	8
1990–91	Millwall	39	10

RAFFERTY, Stuart

Born Port Glasgow 6.3.61.   Ht 5 10
Wt 11 00
Midfield. From Port Glasgow. Scotland
Youth.

Season	Club	League Appearances/Goals	
1978–79	Motherwell	5	—
1979–80		7	2
1980–81		5	2
1981–82		13	5
1982–83		33	4
1983–84		26	4
1984–85	Dundee	36	4
1985–86		29	3
1986–87		36	4
1987–88		30	4
1988–89		32	1
1989–90	Dunfermline Ath	32	1
1990–91		14	—

RAMAGE, Craig

Born Derby 30.3.70   Ht 5 9   Wt 11 08
Forward. From Trainee. England
Under-21.

Season	Club	League Appearances/Goals	
1988–89	Derby Co	—	—
1988–89	*Wigan Ath*	10	2
1989–90	Derby Co	12	1
1990–91		17	1

RAMMELL, Andy

Born Nuneaton 10.2.67.   Ht 5 10
Wt 11 07
Forward. From Atherstone U.

Season	Club	League Appearances/Goals	
1989–90	Manchester U	—	—

1990–91 Barnsley 40 12

RAMSEY, Paul

Born Londonderry 3.9.62. Ht 5 11
Wt 13 00
Defender. From Apprentice. Northern
Ireland 14 full caps.

1970–80	Leicester C	—	—
1980–81		3	—
1981–82		10	—
1982–83		40	1
1983–84		33	1
1984–85		39	—
1985–86		13	1
1986–87		29	6
1987–88		42	1
1988–89		22	—
1989–90		35	3
1990–91		24	—

RANDALL, Adrian

Born Amesbury 10.11.68. Ht 5 11
Wt 10 11
Forward. From Apprentice. England
Youth.

1985–86	Bournemouth	2	—
1986–87		—	—
1987–88		1	—
1988–89		—	—
1988–89	Aldershot	37	2
1989–90		34	2
1990–91		36	8

RANKINE, Mark

Born Doncaster 30.9.69   Ht 5 10
Wt 11 08
Midfield. From Trainee.

1987–88	Doncaster R	18	2
1988–89		46	11
1989–90		36	2
1990–91		40	2

RANSON, Ray

Born St. Helens 12.6.60. Ht 5 9
Wt 11 12
Defender. From Apprentice. England
Schools, Youth, Under-21.

1978–79	Manchester C	8	—
1979–80		40	—
1980–81		33	1
1981–82		36	—
1982–83		40	—
1983–84		26	—
1984–85		—	—
1984–85	Birmingham C	28	—
1985–86		37	—
1986–87		17	—
1987–88		38	—
1988–89		17	—
1988–89	Newcastle U	14	1
1989–90		33	—
1990–91		27	—

RATCLIFFE, Kevin

Born Mancot 12.11.60. Ht 5 11
Wt 12 07
Defender. From Apprentice. Wales
Schools, Youth, Under-21, 56 full caps.

1978–79	Everton	—	—
1979–80		2	—
1980–81		21	—
1981–82		25	—
1982–83		29	1
1983–84		38	—
1984–85		40	—
1985–86		39	1
1986–87		42	—
1987–88		24	—
1988–89		30	—
1989–90		24	—
1990–91		36	—

RATCLIFFE, Simon

Born Davyhulme 8.2.67. Ht 5 11
Wt 11 09
Defender. From Apprentice. England
Schools, Youth.

1984–85	Manchester U	— —
1985–86		— —
1986–87		— —
1987–88	Norwich C	9 —
1988–89		— —
1988–89	Brentford	9 1
1989–90		35 2
1990–91		38 2

RATHBONE, Mike

Born Birmingham 6.11.58. Ht 5 10
Wt 11 12
Defender. From Apprentice. England
Youth.

1976–77	Birmingham C	16 —
1977–78		2 —
1978–79		2 —
1978–79	Blackburn R	15 —
1979–80		28 1
1980–81		27 —
1981–82		41 1
1982–83		42 —
1983–84		11 —
1984–85		42 —
1985–86		42 —
1986–87		25 —
1987–88	Preston NE	36 1
1988–89		34 2
1989–90		8 —
1990–91		13 1

RAVEN, Paul

Born Salisbury 28.7.70   Ht 6 0   Wt 12 03
Defender. From School. England Schools,
Youth.

1987–88	Doncaster R	17 3
1988–89		35 1
1988–89	WBA	3 —
1989–90		7 —
1990–91		13 —

RAWCLIFFE, Peter

Born Cleethorpes 8.12.63.
Midfield. From Louth U.

| 1986–87 | Grimsby T | 20 2 |

1987–88		2 —
From King's Lynn		
1990–91	Lincoln C	1 —

RAYNOR, Paul

Born Nottingham 29.4.66.   Ht 5 11
Wt 11 12
Forward. From Apprentice.

1983–84	Nottingham F	— —
1984–85		3 —
1984–85	*Bristol R*	8 —
1985–86	Huddersfield T	30 5
1986–87		20 4
1986–87	Swansea C	12 1
1987–88		44 8
1988–89		26 5
1988–89	*Wrexham*	6 —
1989–90	Swansea C	40 6
1990–91		43 5

RECK, Sean

Born Oxford 5.5.67.   Ht 5 10   Wt 12 07
Midfield. From Apprentice.

1984–85	Oxford U	— —
1985–86		— —
1985–86	*Newport Co*	15 —
1985–86	*Reading*	1 —
1986–87	Oxford U	6 —
1987–88		2 —
1988–89		6 —
1989–90	Wrexham	32 1
1990–91		13 1

REDDISH, Shane

Born Bolsover 5.5.71.   Ht 5 10   Wt 11 10
Midfield. From Mansfield T Trainee and
Doncaster R Trainee.

| 1989–90 | Doncaster R | 1 — |
| 1990–91 | | 11 — |

REDFEARN, Neil

Born Dewsbury 20.6.65.   Ht 5 10
Wt 12 09
Midfield. From Nottingham F Apprentice.

Season	Club		
1982–83	Bolton W	10	—
1983–84		25	1
1983–84	*Lincoln C*	10	1
1984–85	Lincoln C	45	4
1985–86		45	8
1986–87	Doncaster R	46	14
1987–88	Crystal Palace	42	8
1988–89		15	2
1988–89	Watford	12	2
1989–90		12	1
1989–90	Oldham Ath	17	2
1990–91		45	14

REDFERN, David

Born Sheffield 8.11.62. Ht 6 2 Wt 13 12
Goalkeeper. From School.

Season	Club		
1981–82	Sheffield W	—	—
1982–83		—	—
1983–84		—	—
1984–85		—	—
1984–85	*Doncaster R*	—	—
1984–85	*Rochdale*	19	—
1985–86	Rochdale	46	—
1986–87		22	—
1987–88		—	—
From Gainsborough T.			
1989–90	Stockport Co	11	—
1990–91		24	—

REDFORD, Ian

Born Perth 5.4.60. Ht 5 11 Wt 11 10
Midfield. From Errol Rovers. Scotland
Youth, Under-21.

Season	Club		
1976–77	Dundee	1	—
1977–78		34	10
1978–79		37	15
1979–80		13	9
1979–80	Rangers	13	—
1980–81		35	9
1981–82		32	2
1982–83		34	3
1983–84		32	4
1984–85		26	5
1985–86	Dundee U	30	4
1986–87		37	8
1987–88		25	6

Season	Club		
1988–89		9	2
1988–89	Ipswich T	24	2
1989–90		18	2
1990–91		26	4

REDKNAPP, Jamie

Born Barton on Sea 25.6.73. Ht 5 11
Wt 11 08
Midfield. From Tottenham H Schoolboy,
Bournemouth Trainee. England Youth.

Season	Club		
1989–90	Bournemouth	4	—
1990–91		9	—
1990–91	Liverpool	—	—

REDMOND, Steven

Born Liverpool 2.11.67. Ht 5 11
Wt 12 13
Defender. From Apprentice. England
Youth, Under-21.

Season	Club		
1984–85	Manchester C	—	—
1985–86		9	—
1986–87		30	2
1987–88		44	—
1988–89		46	1
1989–90		38	—
1990–91		37	3

REECE, Andy

Born Shrewsbury 5.9.62. Ht 5 11
Wt 12 04
Midfield. From Walsall, Worcester C,
Willenhall.

Season	Club		
1987–88	Bristol R	40	1
1988–89		42	7
1989–90		43	2
1990–91		46	1

REECE, Paul

Born Nottingham 16.7.68 Ht 5 11
Wt 12 07
Goalkeeper. From Kettering.

Season	Club		
1988–89	Grimsby T	14	—

Season	Club	Appearances	Goals
1989–90		15	—
1990–91		—	—

REED, John

Born Rotherham 27.8.72. Ht 5 6
Wt 8 11
Forward. From Trainee.

Season	Club	Appearances	Goals
1990–91	Sheffield U	—	—
1990–91	*Scarborough*	14	5

REES, Jason

Born Pontypridd 22.12.69. Ht 5 5
Wt 9 08
Midfield. From Trainee. Wales Schools,
Youth, B, Under-21.

Season	Club	Appearances	Goals
1988–89	Luton T	—	—
1989–90		14	—
1990–91		21	—

REES, Mel

Born Cardiff 25.1.67. Ht 6 3   Wt 13 05
Goalkeeper. From Plymouth Arg
Schoolboy and Trainee. Wales Youth.

Season	Club	Appearances	Goals
1984–85	Cardiff C	1	—
1985–86		9	—
1986–87		21	—
1987–88	Watford	3	—
1988–89		—	—
1989–90		—	—
1989–90	*Crewe Alex*	6	—
1989–90	*Southampton*	—	—
1989–90	*Leyton Orient*	9	—
1990–91	Watford	—	—
1990–91	WBA	18	—

REES, Tony

Born Merthyr Tydfil 1.8.64. Ht 5 9
Wt 11 08
Forward. From Apprentice. Wales Youth,
Under-21, 1 full cap.

Season	Club	Appearances	Goals
1982–83	Aston Villa	—	—
1983–84	Birmingham C	25	2

Season	Club	Appearances	Goals
1984–85		9	2
1985–86		8	—
1985–86	*Peterborough U*	5	2
1985–86	*Shrewsbury T*	2	—
1986–87	Birmingham C	30	4
1987–88		23	4
1987–88	Barnsley	14	2
1988–89		17	1
1989–90	Grimsby T	35	13
1990–91		36	10

REEVES, Alan

Born Birkenhead 19.11.67   Ht 6 0
Wt 12 00
Defender.

Season	Club	Appearances	Goals
1988–89	Norwich C	—	—
1988–89	*Gillingham*	18	—
1989–90	Chester C	30	2
1990–91		10	—

REEVES, David

Born Birkenhead 19.11.67. Ht 6 0
Wt 11 05
Forward. From Heswall.

Season	Club	Appearances	Goals
1986–87	Sheffield W	—	—
1986–87	*Scunthorpe U*	4	2
1987–88	Sheffield W	—	—
1987–88	*Scunthorpe U*	6	4
1987–88	*Burnley*	16	8
1988–89	Sheffield W	17	2
1989–90	Bolton W	41	10
1990–91		44	10

REGIS, Cyrille

Born French Guyana 9.2.58. Ht 6 0
Wt 13 5
Forward. From Moseley, Hayes. England
Under-21, B, 5 full caps.

Season	Club	Appearances	Goals
1977–78	WBA	34	10
1978–79		39	13
1979–80		26	8
1980–81		38	14
1981–82		37	17
1982–83		26	9

Season	Club	Apps	Goals
1983–84		30	10
1984–85		7	1
1984–85	Coventry C	31	5
1985–86		34	5
1986–87		40	12
1987–88		31	10
1988–89		34	7
1989–90		34	4
1990–91		34	4

REGIS, Dave

Born Paddington 3.3.64. Ht 6 3
Wt 13 00
Forward. From Barnet.

Season	Club	Apps	Goals
1990–91	Notts Co	37	15

REHN, Stefan

Born Stockholm 22.9.66. Ht 5 10
Wt 10 10
Midfield. From Djurgaarden. Sweden full
caps.

Season	Club	Apps	Goals
1989–90	Everton	4	—

To IFK Gothenburg.

REID, Brian

Born Paisley 15.6.70 Ht 6 2 Wt 11 12
Defender. From Refrew Waverley

Season	Club	Apps	Goals
1988–89	Morton	2	—
1989–90		36	1
1990–91		19	—
1990–91	Rangers	3	—

REID, Chris

Born Edinburgh 4.11.71. Ht 5 11
Wt 11 06
Goalkeeper. From Hutcheson Vale BC.

Season	Club	Apps	Goals
1989–90	Hibernian	2	—
1990–91		1	—

REID, Mark

Born Kilwinning 15.9.61. Ht 5 8 Wt 11 5
Defender. From Celtic BC. Scotland
Youth, Under-21.

Season	Club	Apps	Goals
1980–81	Celtic	22	—
1981–82		36	2
1982–83		26	1
1983–84		24	2
1984–85		16	—
1985–86	Charlton Ath	42	8
1986–87		42	—
1987–88		36	4
1988–89		36	1
1989–90		31	—
1990–91		24	2

REID, Nicky

Born Ormston 30.10.60. Ht 5 10
Wt 12 00
Defender. From Apprentice. England
Under-21.

Season	Club	Apps	Goals
1978–79	Manchester C	8	—
1979–80		23	—
1980–81		37	—
1981–82		36	—
1982–83		25	—
1983–84		19	2
1984–85		32	—
1985–86		30	—
1986–87		7	—
1987–88	Blackburn R	44	1
1988–89		37	1
1989–90		42	4
1990–91		30	2

REID, Paul

Born Warley 19.1.68. Ht 5 8 Wt 10 08
Forward. From Apprentice.

Season	Club	Apps	Goals
1985–86	Leicester C	—	—
1986–87		6	—
1987–88		26	5
1988–89		45	6
1989–90		40	8
1990–91		33	2

REID, Peter

Born Huyton 20.6.56. Ht 5 8 Wt 10 07
Midfield. From Apprentice. England
Under-21, 13 full caps.

Season	Club	App	Goals
1974–75	Bolton W	27	—
1975–76		42	2
1976–77		42	5
1977–78		38	9
1978–79		14	—
1979–80		17	3
1980–81		18	2
1981–82		12	1
1982–83		15	1
1982–83	Everton	7	—
1983–84		35	2
1984–85		36	2
1985–86		15	1
1986–87		16	1
1987–88		32	1
1988–89		18	1
1988–89	QPR	14	1
1989–90		15	—
1989–90	Manchester C	18	1
1990–91		30	—

REID, Shaun

Born Huyton 13.10.65.   Ht 5 8   Wt 11 10
Midfield. Local.

Season	Club	App	Goals
1983–84	Rochdale	17	—
1984–85		21	1
1985–86		8	—
1985–86	*Preston NE*	3	—
1986–87	Rochdale	41	1
1987–88		28	—
1988–89		18	2
1988–89	York C	24	2
1989–90		25	4
1990–91		29	—

REID, Wesley

Born Lewisham 10.9.68.   Ht 5 8
Wt 11 03
Midfield. From Trainee.

Season	Club	App	Goals
1986–87	Arsenal	—	—
1987–88	Millwall	—	—
1988–89		1	—
1989–90		5	—
1990–91		—	—
1990–91	Bradford C	16	—

REINELT, Robert

Born Epping 11.3.74.
Forward. From Trainee.

Season	Club	App	Goals
1990–91	Aldershot	5	—

RENNIE, David

Born Edinburgh 29.8.64.   Ht 5 11
Wt 12 00
Defender. From Apprentice. Scotland
Youth.

Season	Club	App	Goals
1982–83	Leicester C	—	—
1983–84		15	—
1984–85		3	1
1985–86		3	—
1985–86	Leeds U	16	2
1986–87		24	—
1987–88		28	2
1988–89		33	1
1989–90	Bristol C	45	4
1990–91		32	2

RENNIE, Paul

Born Nantwich 26.10.71.   Ht 5 9
Wt 11 07
Defender. From Trainee.

Season	Club	App	Goals
1989–90	Crewe Alex	2	—
1990–91	Stoke C	3	—

RHODES, Andy

Born Doncaster 23.8.64.   Ht 6 1
Wt 13 06
Goalkeeper. From Apprentice.

Season	Club	App	Goals
1982–83	Barnsley	—	—
1983–84		31	—
1984–85		5	—
1985–86		—	—
1985–86	Doncaster R	30	—
1986–87		41	—
1987–88		35	—
1987–88	Oldham Ath	11	—
1988–89		27	—
1989–90		31	—
1990–91	Dunfermline Ath	35	—

RICE, Brian

Born Glasgow 11.10.63.   Ht 6 0   Wt 12 04
Midfield. From Whitburn Central.
Scotland Youth, Under-21.

Season	Club		
1980–81	Hibernian	1	—
1981–82		1	—
1982–83		22	2
1983–84		25	5
1984–85		35	4
1985–86	Nottingham F	19	3
1986–87		3	1
1986–87	*Grimsby T*	4	—
1987–88		30	2
1988–89		20	1
1988–89	*WBA*	3	—
1989–90	Nottingham F	18	2
1990–91		1	—
1990–91	*Stoke C*	18	—

RICHARDS, Carl

Born Jamaica 12.1.60.   Ht 6 0   Wt 13 00
Forward. Dulwich H, Enfield.

Season	Club		
1986–87	Bournemouth	43	11
1987–88		20	4
1988–89		8	—
1988–89	Birmingham C	19	2
1989–90	Peterborough U	20	5
1989–90	Blackpool	16	4
1990–91		22	4

RICHARDS, Steve

Born Dundee 24.10.61.   Ht 6 1   Wt 12 05
Defender. From Apprentice.

Season	Club		
1979–80	Hull C	1	—
1980–81		25	1
1981–82		29	1
1982–83		3	—
From Gainsborough T.			
1984–85	York C	7	—
1985–86	Lincoln C	21	—
1985–86	Cambridge U	4	2
1986–87	Scarborough	—	—
1987–88		42	5
1988–89		42	1
1989–90		35	4

Season	Club		
1990–91		45	3

RICHARDSON, Barry

Born Willington Key 5.8.69.   Ht 6 0
Wt 12 00
Goalkeeper. From Trainee.

Season	Club		
1987–88	Sunderland	—	—
1988–89	Scunthorpe U	—	—
1989–90	Scarborough	24	—
1990–91		6	—

RICHARDSON, Kevin

Born Newcastle 4.12.62.   Ht 5 9
Wt 11 02
Midfield. From Apprentice.

Season	Club		
1980–81	Everton	—	—
1981–82		18	2
1982–83		29	3
1983–84		28	4
1984–85		15	4
1985–86		18	3
1986–87		1	—
1986–87	Watford	39	2
1987–88	Arsenal	29	4
1988–89		34	1
1989–90		33	—
To Real Sociedad			

RICHARDSON, Lee

Born Halifax 12.3.69.   Ht 5 11   Wt 11 00
Midfield.

Season	Club		
1986–87	Halifax T	1	—
1987–88		30	1
1988–89		25	1
1988–89	Watford	9	—
1989–90		32	1
1990–91	Blackburn R	38	2

RICHARDSON, Neil

Born Sunderland 3.3.68.   Ht 5 10
Wt 13 05
Defender. From Brandon U.

Season	Club		
1989–90	Rotherham U	2	—

1990–91	....	16	2

RICHARDSON, Nick

Born Halifax 11.4.67   Ht 6 0   Wt 12 07
Midfield. Local.

Season	Club	App	Goals
1988–89	Halifax T	7	—
1989–90	....	27	6
1990–91	....	26	3

RICHARDSON, Steve

Born Slough 11.2.62.   Ht 5 5   Wt 10 03
Defender. From Apprentice.

Season	Club	App	Goals
1979–80	Southampton	—	—
1980–81	....	—	—
1981–82	....	—	—
1982–83	Reading.......................	40	1
1983–84	....	34	—
1984–85	....	43	—
1985–86	....	32	—
1986–87	....	37	1
1987–88	....	27	—
1988–89	....	39	—
1989–90	....	43	—
1990–91	....	32	—

RIDEOUT, Paul

Born Bournemouth 14.8.64.   Ht 5 11
Wt 12 01
Forward. From Apprentice. England
Schools, Youth, Under-21.

Season	Club	App	Goals
1980–81	Swindon T	16	4
1981–82	....	35	14
1982–83	....	44	20
1983–84	Aston Villa..................	25	5
1984–85	....	29	14
1985–86	Bari	28	6
1986–87	....	34	10
1987–88	....	37	7
1988–89	Southampton	24	6
1989–90	....	31	7
1990–91	....	16	6
1990–91	Swindon T	9	1

RILEY, David

Born Northampton 8.12.60.   Ht 5 7
Wt 10 10
Forward. From Keyworth U.

Season	Club	App	Goals
1983–84	Nottingham F.............	1	—
1984–85	....	10	2
1985–86	....	—	—
1986–87	....	1	—
1986–87	*Darlington*	6	2
1987–88	Nottingham F.............	—	—
1987–88	*Peterborough U*	12	2
1987–88	Port Vale....................	34	8
1988–89	....	40	3
1989–90	....	2	—
1989–90	Peterborough U	15	5
1990–91	....	41	7

RIMMER, Neill

Born Liverpool 13.11.67.   Ht 5 6
Wt 10 03
Midfield. From Apprentice. England
Schools, Youth.

Season	Club	App	Goals
1984–85	Everton	1	—
1985–86	Ipswich T	2	—
1986–87	....	1	—
1987–88	....	19	3
1988–89	Wigan Ath	25	3
1989–90	....	38	1
1990–91	....	34	2

RIMMER, Stuart

Born Southport 12.10.64.   Ht 5 8
Wt 11 00
Forward. From Apprentice. England
Youth.

Season	Club	App	Goals
1981–82	Everton	2	—
1982–83	....	—	—
1983–84	....	1	—
1984–85	....	—	—
1984–85	Chester C....................	24	14
1985–86	....	18	16
1986–87	....	38	13
1987–88	....	34	24
1987–88	Watford	9	1
1988–89	....	1	—

Season	Club	Apps	Goals
1988–89	Notts Co	4	2
1988–89	Walsall	20	8
1989–90		41	10
1990–91		27	13
1990–91	Barnsley	15	1

RIPLEY, Stuart

Born Middlesbrough 20.11.67.   Ht 5 11
Wt 12 05
Forward. From Apprentice. England
Youth, Under-21.

Season	Club	Apps	Goals
1984–85	Middlesbrough	1	—
1985–86		8	—
1985–86	*Bolton W*	5	1
1986–87	Middlesbrough	44	4
1987–88		43	8
1988–89		36	4
1989–90		39	1
1990–91		39	6

RITCHIE, Andy

Born Manchester 28.11.60.   Ht 5 10
Wt 11 11
Forward. From Apprentice. England
Schools, Youth, Under-21.

Season	Club	Apps	Goals
1977–78	Manchester U	4	—
1978–79		17	10
1979–80		8	3
1980–81		4	—
1980–81	Brighton	26	5
1981–82		39	13
1982–83		24	5
1982–83	Leeds U	10	3
1983–84		38	7
1984–85		28	12
1985–86		29	11
1986–87		31	7
1987–88	Oldham Ath	36	19
1988–89		31	14
1989–90		38	15
1990–91		31	15

RIX, Graham

Born Doncaster 23.10.57.   Ht 5 9
Wt 11 0
Midfield. From Apprentice. England
Under-21, 17 full caps.

Season	Club	Apps	Goals
1974–75	Arsenal	—	—
1975–76		—	—
1976–77		7	1
1977–78		39	2
1978–79		39	3
1979–80		38	4
1980–81		35	5
1981–82		39	9
1982–83		36	6
1983–84		34	4
1984–85		18	2
1985–86		38	3
1986–87		18	2
1987–88		10	—
1987–88	*Brentford*	6	—

To Caen

ROAST, Jesse

Born Barking 16.3.64.   Ht 6 1   Wt 12 07
Defender. From Walthamstow Avenue,
Hornchurch, Dagenham, Brighton,
Barking (1987)

Season	Club	Apps	Goals
1989–90	Maidstone U	16	—
1990–91		16	—

ROBERTS, Brian

Born Manchester 6.11.55.   Ht 5 8
Wt 11 07
Defender. From Apprentice.

Season	Club	Apps	Goals
1974–75	Coventry C	—	—
1974–75	*Hereford U*	5	—
1975–76	Coventry C	2	—
1976–77		12	—
1977–78		26	—
1978–79		17	—
1979–80		14	—
1980–81		42	—
1981–82		34	—
1982–83		38	1
1983–84		30	—

1983–84	Birmingham C	11	—
1984–85		41	—
1985–86		33	—
1986–87		24	—
1987–88		27	—
1988–89		41	—
1989–90		10	—
1990–91	Wolverhampton W	21	—

ROBERTS, Garreth

Born Hull 15.11.60. Ht 5 5 Wt 10 10
Midfield. From Apprentice. Wales
Under-21.

1978–79	Hull C	19	3
1979–80		44	2
1980–81		20	3
1981–82		29	6
1982–83		44	6
1983–84		38	9
1984–85		29	3
1985–86		33	4
1986–87		35	5
1987–88		44	3
1988–89		35	3
1989–90		36	—
1990–91		8	—

ROBERTS, Graham

Born Southampton 3.7.59. Ht 5 10
Wt 12 12
Defender. From Southampton, Sholing,
Bournemouth, Portsmouth, Dorchester T
and Weymouth. England B, 6 full caps.

1980–81	Tottenham H	24	—
1981–82		37	6
1982–83		24	2
1983–84		35	6
1984–85		40	7
1985–86		32	1
1986–87		17	1
1986–87	Rangers	18	2
1987–88		37	1
1988–89	Chelsea	46	15
1989–90		24	3
1990–91		—	—
1990–91	WBA	27	4

ROBERTS, Iwan

Born Bangor 26.6.68. Ht 6 3 Wt 12 06
Forward. Wales Youth, 1 full cap.

1985–86	Watford	4	—
1986–87		3	1
1987–88		25	2
1988–89		22	6
1989–90		9	—
1990–91	Huddersfield T	44	13

ROBERTS, Tony

Born Bangor 4.8.69. Ht 6 0
Goalkeeper. From Trainee. Wales
Under-21.

1987–88	QPR	1	—
1988–89		—	—
1989–90		5	—
1990–91		12	—

ROBERTSON, Alexander

Born Edinburgh 26.4.71 Ht 5 9
Wt 10 07
Midfield. From S Form. Scotland
Under-21.

1987–88	Rangers	—	—
1988–89		2	—
1989–90		1	—
1990–91		15	1

ROBERTSON, Craig

Born Dunfermline 22.4.63. Ht 5 9
Wt 11 02
Midfield. From 'S' Form.

1979–80	Hearts	—	—
1980–81	Raith R	—	—
1981–82		11	—
1982–83		22	—
1983–84		38	3
1984–85		39	11
1985–86		25	2
1986–87		35	3
1987–88	Dunfermline Ath	42	13
1988–89		13	5

1988–89	Aberdeen	4	1
1989–90		22	2
1990–91		8	1

ROBERTSON, David

Born Aberdeen 17.10.68. Ht 5 11
Wt 11 00
Defender. From Deeside BC. Scotland
Under-21.

1986–87	Aberdeen	34	—
1987–88		23	—
1988–89		23	—
1989–90		20	1
1990–91		35	1

ROBERTSON, Ian

Born Inverness 14.10.66. Ht 5 9
Wt 10 10
Midfield. 'S' Form. Scotland Youth.

1983–84	Aberdeen	—	—
1984–85		—	—
1985–86		4	—
1986–87		4	—
1987–88		—	—
1988–89		7	—
1989–90		5	—
1990–91		1	—

ROBERTSON, Jimmy

Born Gateshead 24.11.69 Ht 5 7
Wt 10 08
Defender. From Trainee.

1987–88	Carlisle U	5	—
1988–89		7	—
1989–90		1	—
1990–91	Falkirk	7	—

ROBERTSON, John

Born Edinburgh 2.10.64. Ht 5 7
Wt 11 06
Forward. From Edina Hibs. Scotland B,
Under-21, 4 full caps.

| 1980–81 | Hearts | — | — |

1981–82		1	—
1982–83		23	19
1983–84		35	15
1984–85		33	8
1985–86		35	20
1986–87		37	16
1987–88		39	26
1987–88	Newcastle U	—	—
1988–89		12	—
1988–89	Hearts	15	4
1989–90		32	17
1990–91		31	12

ROBERTSON, Paul

Born Stockport 5.2.72. Ht 5 7 Wt 11 06
Defender. From York C Trainee.

| 1989–90 | Stockport Co | 9 | — |
| 1990–91 | | 1 | — |

ROBINS, Mark

Born Ashton-under-Lyme. 22.12.69.
Ht 5 7 Wt 10 01
Forward. From Apprentice. England
Under-21.

1986–87	Manchester U	—	—
1987–88		—	—
1988–89		10	—
1989–90		17	7
1990–91		19	4

ROBINSON, Colin

Born Birmingham 15.5.60. Ht 5 10
Wt 10 12
Forward. From Mile Oak Rovers.

1982–83	Shrewsbury T	12	3
1983–84		30	4
1984–85		42	14
1985–86		42	10
1986–87		41	9
1987–88		27	1
1987–88	Birmingham C	4	1
1988–89		33	5
1989–90	Hereford U	29	4
1990–91		35	2

ROBINSON, David

Born Newcastle 27.11.69   Ht 6 0
Wt 13 02
Forward. From Trainee.

Season	Club		
1988–89	Newcastle U	1	—
1989–90		1	—
1990–91		3	—
1990–91	*Peterborough U*	7	3

ROBINSON, David

Born Cleveland 14.1.65.   Ht 6 0   Wt 12 03
Defender.

Season	Club		
1983–84	Hartlepool U	7	—
1984–85		38	—
1985–86		21	1
1986–87	Halifax T	10	—
1987–88		32	—
1988–89		30	1
1989–90	Peterborough U	45	4
1990–91		6	2

ROBINSON, John

Born Bulawayo, Rhodesia 29.8.71.
Ht 5 10   Wt 11 02
Midfield. From Apprentice.

Season	Club		
1989–90	Brighton	5	—
1990–91		15	—

ROBINSON, Les

Born Mansfield 1.3.67.   Ht 5 8   Wt 11 1
Defender. From Local.

Season	Club		
1984–85	Mansfield T	6	—
1985–86		7	—
1986–87		2	—
1986–87	Stockport Co	30	1
1987–88		37	2
1987–88	Doncaster R	7	1
1988–89		43	3
1989–90		32	8
1989–90	Oxford U	1	—
1990–91		43	—

ROBINSON, Liam

Born Bradford 29.12.65.   Ht 5 7
Wt 11 05
Forward. From Nottingham F schoolboy.

Season	Club		
1983–84	Huddersfield T	5	1
1984–85		15	1
1985–86		1	—
1985–86	*Tranmere R*	4	3
1986–87	Bury	33	13
1987–88		43	19
1988–89		43	20
1989–90		45	17
1990–91		43	4

ROBINSON, Mark

Born Manchester 21.11.68.   Ht 5 9
Wt 11 08
Midfield. From Trainee.

Season	Club		
1985–86	WBA	1	—
1986–87		1	—
1987–88	Barnsley	3	—
1988–89		18	2
1989–90		24	—
1990–91		22	1

ROBINSON, Michael

Born Leicester 12.7.58.   Ht 6 0   Wt 13 04
Forward. From Apprentice. Eire, 23 full
caps.

Season	Club		
1975–76	Preston NE	2	—
1976–77		—	—
1977–78		10	2
1978–79		36	13
1979–80	Manchester C	30	8
1980–81	Brighton	42	19
1981–82		35	11
1982–83		36	7
1983–84	Liverpool	24	6
1984–85		6	—
1984–85	QPR	11	1
1985–86		26	5
1986–87		11	—
To Osasuna			

ROBINSON, Paul

Born Nottingham 21.2.71. Ht 6 4
Wt 14 07
Forward. From Notts Co & Bury Trainee.

1989–90	Scarborough	20	3
1990–91	Plymouth Arg	11	3

ROBINSON, Philip

Born Stafford 6.1.67. Ht 5 9 Wt 10 10
Defender. From Apprentice.

1984–85	Aston Villa	—	—
1985–86		—	—
1986–87		3	1
1987–88	Wolverhampton W	41	5
1988–89		30	3
1989–90	Notts Co	46	2
1990–91		19	3
1990–91	Birmingham C	9	—

ROBINSON, Ronnie

Born Sunderland 22.10.66. Ht 5 9
Wt 11 05
Defender.

1984–85	Ipswich T	—	—
From Vaux Breweries			
1985–86	Leeds U	16	—
1986–87		11	—
1986–87	Doncaster R	12	—
1987–88		37	1
1988–89		29	4
1988–89	WBA	1	—
1989–90	Rotherham U	43	1
1990–91		38	—

ROBSON, Bryan

Born Chester-le-Street 11.1.57. Ht 5 10
Wt 11 11
Midfield. From Apprentice. England
Schools, Youth, Under-21, B, 89 full caps.

1974–75	WBA	3	2
1975–76		16	1
1976–77		23	8
1977–78		35	3

1978–79		41	7
1979–80		34	8
1980–81		40	10
1981–82		5	—
1981–82	Manchester U	32	5
1982–83		33	10
1983–84		33	12
1984–85		33	9
1985–86		21	7
1986–87		30	7
1987–88		36	11
1988–89		34	4
1989–90		20	2
1990–91		17	1

ROBSON, Gary

Born Durham 6.7.65. Ht 5 7 Wt 10 12
Midfield. From Apprentice.

1982–83	WBA	2	—
1983–84		7	—
1984–85		11	—
1985–86		14	—
1986–87		5	1
1987–88		31	1
1988–89		38	8
1989–90		25	5
1990–91		31	2

ROBSON, Mark

Born Newham 22.5.69. Ht 5 7 Wt 10 05
Forward. From Trainee.

1986–87	Exeter C	26	7
1987–88	Tottenham H	—	—
1987–88	*Reading*	7	—
1988–89	Tottenham H	5	—
1989–90		3	—
1989–90	*Watford*	1	—
1989–90	*Plymouth Arg*	7	—
1990–91	Tottenham H	—	—

ROBSON, Stewart

Born Billericay 6.11.64. Ht 5 11
Wt 12 04
Midfield. From Apprentice. England
Youth, Under-21.

Season	Club	League Appearances/Goals	
1981–82	Arsenal	20	2
1982–83		31	2
1983–84		28	6
1984–85		40	2
1985–86		27	4
1986–87		5	—
1986–87	West Ham U	18	1
1987–88		37	2
1988–89		6	—
1989–90		7	1
1990–91		1	—
1990–91	*Coventry C*	4	—

ROCASTLE, David

Born Lewisham 2.5.67. Ht 5 9 Wt 11 12
Forward. From Apprentice. England
Under-21, 11 full caps.

Season	Club	League Appearances/Goals	
1984–85	Arsenal	—	—
1985–86		16	1
1986–87		36	2
1987–88		40	7
1988–89		38	6
1989–90		33	2
1990–91		16	2

ROCHE, David

Born Newcastle 13.12.70 Ht 5 11
Wt 12 01
Defender. From Trainee.

Season	Club	League Appearances/Goals	
1988–89	Newcastle U	2	—
1989–90		—	—
1990–91		8	—

RODGER, Graham

Born Glasgow 1.4.67. Ht 6 2 Wt 11 11
Defender. From Apprentice. England
Under-21.

Season	Club	League Appearances/Goals	
1983–84	Wolverhampton W	1	—
1984–85	Coventry C	—	—
1985–86		10	—
1986–87		6	—
1987–88		12	1
1988–89		8	1
1989–90	Luton T	2	—

Season	Club	League Appearances/Goals	
1990–91		14	2

RODGERSON, Ian

Born Hereford 9.4.66. Ht 5 10 Wt 10 07
Midfield. From Pegasus Juniors.

Season	Club	League Appearances/Goals	
1984–85	Hereford U	—	—
1985–86		19	2
1986–87		44	1
1987–88		37	3
1988–89	Cardiff C	40	—
1989–90		45	4
1990–91		14	—
1990–91	Birmingham C	25	2

RODWELL, Tony

Born Southport 26.8.62. Ht 5 11
Wt 11 02
Forward. From Colne Dynamoes.

Season	Club	League Appearances/Goals	
1990–91	Blackpool	45	7

ROEDER, Glenn

Born Woodford 13.12.55. Ht 6 0
Wt 12 13
Defender. From Apprentice. England B.

Season	Club	League Appearances/Goals	
1974–75	Orient	6	—
1975–76		25	2
1976–77		42	2
1977–78		42	—
1978–79	QPR	27	4
1979–80		40	9
1980–81		39	2
1981–82		41	2
1982–83		9	—
1983–84		1	—
1983–84	*Notts Co*	4	—
1983–84	Newcastle U	23	—
1984–85		36	—
1985–86		42	6
1986–87		37	1
1987–88		37	1
1988–89		18	—
1989–90	Watford	45	1
1990–91		33	1

ROGAN, Anton

Born Belfast 25.3.66.   Ht 5 11   Wt 12 06
Defender. From Distillery. Northern
Ireland, 16 full caps.

1986–87	Celtic	10	1
1987–88		33	1
1988–89		34	1
1989–90		18	—
1990–91		27	1

ROGERS, Darren

Born Birmingham 9.4.71   Ht 5 10
Wt 11 02
Defender. From Trainee.

1988–89	WBA	—	—
1989–90		—	—
1990–91		4	—

ROGERS, Lee

Born Bristol 8.4.67.   Ht 5 11   Wt 12 08
Defender. From Apprentice.

1984–85	Bristol C	6	—
1985–86		21	—
1986–87		3	—
1986–87	*Hereford U*	13	—
1987–88	Bristol C	—	—
1987–88	*York C*	7	—
1988–89	Exeter C	45	—
1989–90		16	—
1990–91		17	—

ROGERS, Lee

Born Doncaster 21.10.66.   Ht 5 10
Wt 12 00
Defender. From Doncaster R.

1986–87	Chesterfield	36	—
1987–88		43	—
1988–89		24	—
1989–90		32	—
1990–91		34	—

ROGERSON, Lee

Born Darwen 21.3.67.   Ht 6 0   Wt 12 00
Midfield. From Clitheroe.

1989–90	Wigan Ath	3	—
1990–91		1	—

ROLPH, Andy

Born Birmingham 28.10.69   Ht 5 6
Wt 10 00
Forward. From Birmingham C Trainee.

1988–89	Chesterfield	12	1
1989–90		9	—
1990–91		15	—

ROSARIO, Robert

Born Hammersmith 4.3.66.   Ht 6 3
Wt 12 01
Forward. From Hillingdon Bor. England
Youth.

1983–84	Norwich C	8	1
1984–85		4	1
1985–86		8	2
1985–86	*Wolverhampton W*	2	1
1986–87	Norwich C	25	3
1987–88		14	2
1988–89		27	4
1989–90		31	5
1990–91		9	—
1990–91	Coventry C	2	—

ROSE, Colin

Born Winsford 22.1.72.   Ht 5 8   Wt 10 09
Midfield. From Trainee.

1990–91	Crewe Alex	17	1

ROSE, Kevin

Born Evesham 23.11.60.   Ht 6 1
Wt 13 03
Goalkeeper. From Ledbury T.

1979–80	Lincoln C	—	—
1980–81		—	—
From Ledbury T			
1982–83	Hereford U	15	—
1983–84		46	—
1984–85		46	—

1985–86	....	46	—
1986–87	....	46	—
1987–88	....	46	—
1988–89	....	23	—
1989–90	Bolton W	6	—
1989–90	*Halifax T*	—	—
1989–90	*Carlisle U*	11	—
1990–91	Bolton W	—	—
1990–91	*Rochdale*	3	—

ROSENIOR, Leroy

Born London 24.3.64.   Ht 6 1   Wt 11 10
Forward. From school. England Schools.

1982–83	Fulham	1	—
1983–84	....	23	8
1984–85	....	30	8
1985–86	QPR	18	3
1986–87	....	20	4
1987–88	Fulham	34	20
1987–88	West Ham U	9	5
1988–89	....	28	7
1989–90	....	5	2
1990–91	....	2	—
1990–91	*Fulham*	11	3

ROSENTHAL, Ronny

Born Haifa 11.10.63.   Ht 5 11   Wt 12 00
Forward. From Maccabi Haifa, FC
Brugge, Standard Liege. Israel full caps.

1989–90	*Luton T*	—	—
1989–90	*Liverpool*	8	7
1990–91	Liverpool	16	5

ROSS, Mike

Born Southampton 2.9.71.   Ht 5 6
Wt 9 13
Forward.

1988–89	Portsmouth	1	—
1989–90	....	—	—
1990–91	....	—	—

ROSTRON, Wilf

Born Sunderland 29.9.56.   Ht 5 6
Wt 11 01
From Apprentice. England Schools.

1973–74	Arsenal........................	—	—
1974–75	....	6	2
1975–76	....	5	—
1976–77	....	6	—
1977–78	Sunderland	34	6
1978–79	....	34	11
1979–80	....	8	—
1979–80	Watford	31	3
1980–81	....	27	1
1981–82	....	27	2
1982–83	....	42	3
1983–84	....	39	4
1984–85	....	38	3
1985–86	....	30	5
1986–87	....	39	1
1987–88	....	37	—
1988–89	....	7	—
1988–89	Sheffield W................	7	—
1989–90	Sheffield U	26	3
1990–91	....	10	—
1990–91	Brentford	22	2

ROWBOTHAM, Darren

Born Cardiff 22.10.66.   Ht 5 10   Wt 11 05
Midfield. From Trainee.

1984–85	Plymouth Arg	7	—
1985–86	....	14	1
1986–87	....	16	1
1987–88	....	9	—
1987–88	Exeter C......................	23	2
1988–89	....	45	20
1989–90	....	32	21
1990–91	....	13	3

ROWE, Ben

Born Hull 1.10.70.   Ht 5 7   Wt 10 07
Midfield. From Bristol C.

1989–90	Exeter C......................	10	2
1990–91	....	2	—

ROWE, Brian

Born Sunderland 24.10.71.
Midfield. From Trainee.

1990–91	Doncaster R................	4	—

ROWLAND, Andy

Born Taunton 1.10.65. Ht 6 3 Wt 13 08
Forward. From Weymouth.

Season	Club	Apps	Goals
1989–90	Southampton	—	—
1990–91		—	—
1990–91	Torquay U	9	—

RUDDOCK, Neil

Born London 9.5.68. Ht 6 2 Wt 12 6
Defender. From Apprentice. England
Youth, Under-21.

Season	Club	Apps	Goals
1985–86	Millwall	—	—
1985–86	Tottenham H	—	—
1986–87		4	—
1987–88		5	—
1988–89	Millwall	2	1
1988–89	Southampton	13	3
1989–90		29	3
1990–91		35	3

RUMBLE, Paul

Born Hemel Hempstead 14.3.69.
Ht 5 11 Wt 11 05
Defender. From Trainee.

Season	Club	Apps	Goals
1986–87	Watford	—	—
1987–88		—	—
1988–89		—	—
1988–89	*Scunthorpe U*	8	1
1989–90	Maidstone U	23	2
1990–91		27	1

RUSH, David

Born Sunderland 15.5.71. Ht 5 11
Wt 10 10
Forward. From Trainee.

Season	Club	Apps	Goals
1989–90	Sunderland	—	—
1990–91		11	2

RUSH, Ian

Born St. Asaph 20.10.61. Ht 6 0
Wt 12 06
Forward. From Apprentice. Wales
Schools, Under-21, 51 full caps.

Season	Club	Apps	Goals
1978–79	Chester	1	—
1979–80		33	14
1979–80	Liverpool	—	—
1980–81		7	—
1981–82		32	17
1982–83		34	24
1983–84		41	32
1984–85		28	14
1985–86		40	22
1986–87		42	30
1987–88	Juventus	29	7
1988–89	Liverpool	24	7
1989–90		36	18
1990–91		37	16

RUSH, Matthew

Born Dalston 6.8.71. Ht 5 11 Wt 12 10
Midfield. From Trainee.

Season	Club	Apps	Goals
1990–91	West Ham U	5	—

RUSSELL, Billy

Born Glasgow 14.9.59. Ht 5 10 Wt 11 03
Defender. From Apprentice. Scotland
Youth.

Season	Club	Apps	Goals
1977–78	Everton	—	—
From Glasgow Celtic			
1979–80	Doncaster R	42	—
1980–81		46	1
1981–82		37	3
1982–83		40	5
1983–84		41	6
1984–85		38	—
1985–86	Scunthorpe U	42	—
1986–87		41	3
1987–88		34	4
1988–89	Rotherham U	44	2
1989–90		29	—
1990–91		25	—

RUSSELL, Bobby

Born Glasgow 11.2.57. Ht 5 8 Wt 10 03
Midfield. From Shettleston. Scotland
Under-21.

Season	Club	Apps	Goals
1976–77	Rangers	—	—

Season	Club	League Appearances/Goals	
1977–78	....	33	3
1978–79	....	36	4
1979–80	....	23	7
1980–81	....	28	6
1981–82	....	32	6
1982–83	....	21	4
1983–84	....	31	4
1984–85	....	18	—
1985–86	....	27	—
1986–87	....	1	—
1987–88	Motherwell..................	32	3
1988–89	....	31	5
1989–90	....	33	3
1990–91	....	19	2

RUSSELL, Kevin

Born Portsmouth 6.12.66. Ht 5 8
Wt 10 10
Forward. From Brighton Apprentice.
England Youth.

Season	Club		
1984–85	Portsmouth	—	—
1985–86	....	1	—
1986–87	....	3	1
1987–88	Wrexham	38	21
1988–89	....	46	22
1989–90	Leicester C..................	10	—
1990–91	....	13	5
1990–91	*Peterborough U*...........	7	3
1990–91	*Cardiff C*.....................	3	—

RUSSELL, Lee

Born Southampton 3.9.69 Ht 5 11
Wt 11 04
Defender. From Trainee.

Season	Club		
1988–89	Portsmouth	2	—
1989–90	....	3	—
1990–91	....	19	1

RUSSELL, Martin

Born Dublin 27.4.67. Ht 5 11 Wt 11 00
Midfield. From Apprentice. Eire Youth,
Under-21, Under-23.

Season	Club		
1984–85	Manchester U.............	—	—
1985–86	....	—	—

Season	Club		
1986–87	....	—	—
1986–87	*Birmingham C*............	5	—
1986–87	*Norwich C*...................	—	—
1986–87	Leicester C..................	5	—
1987–88	....	5	—
1988–89	....	10	—
1988–89	Scarborough...............	20	2
1989–90	....	31	7
1989–90	Middlesbrough............	—	—
1990–91	....	11	2

RUTHERFORD, Mark

Born Birmingham 25.3.72. Ht 5 11
Wt 11 00
Forward. From Trainee.

Season	Club		
1989–90	Birmingham C............	2	—
1990–91	....	3	—

RUTHERFORD, Michael

Born Greenwich 6.6.72. Ht 5 9 Wt 11 10
Forward. From Trainee.

Season	Club		
1989–90	QPR...........................	2	—
1990–91	....	—	—

RUTHERFORD, Paul

Born Sunderland 23.2.67 Ht 5 9 Wt 11 0
Forward. Newcastle U app.

Season	Club		
1987–88	Alloa	31	14
1988–89	....	7	1
1988–89	Falkirk	28	9
1989–90	....	28	7
1990–91	....	6	3

RYAN, Darren

Born Oswestry 3.7.72.
Midfield. From Trainee.

Season	Club		
1990–91	Shrewsbury T.............	2	—

RYAN, John

Born Ashton 18.2.62. Ht 5 10 Wt 11 07
Defender. From Apprentice. England
Under-21.

Season	Club	App	Goals
1979–80	Oldham Ath	—	—
1980–81		—	—
1981–82		37	—
1982–83		40	8
1983–84	Newcastle U	22	1
1984–85		6	—
1984–85	Sheffield W	8	1
1985–86	Oldham Ath	22	—
1986–87		1	—
1987–88		—	—
1987–88	Mansfield T	32	1
1988–89		30	—
1989–90	Chesterfield	43	4
1990–91		39	2

RYAN, Vaughan

Born Westminster 2.9.68.   Ht 5 8
Wt 10 12
Midfield.

Season	Club	App	Goals
1986–87	Wimbledon	1	—
1987–88		22	1
1988–89		5	—
1988–89	*Sheffield U*	3	—
1989–90	Wimbledon	31	—
1990–91		2	—

SAGE, Mel

Born Gillingham 24.3.64.   Ht 5 8
Wt 10 04
Defender. From Apprentice.

Season	Club	App	Goals
1981–82	Gillingham	1	—
1982–83		9	—
1983–84		40	2
1984–85		36	1
1985–86		46	2
1986–87	Derby Co	26	2
1987–88		13	—
1988–89		16	1
1989–90		34	—
1990–91		34	1

SALAKO, Andy

Born Nigeria 8.11.72.
Defender. From Trainee.

Season	Club	App	Goals
1990–91	Charlton Ath	1	—

SALAKO, John

Born Nigeria, 11.2.69.   Ht 5 10   Wt 11 00
Forward. From Trainee. England 4 full
caps.

Season	Club	App	Goals
1986–87	Crystal Palace	4	—
1987–88		31	—
1988–89		28	—
1989–90		17	2
1989–90	*Swansea C*	13	3
1990–91	Crystal Palace	35	6

SALMAN, Danis

Born Cyprus 12.3.60.   Ht 5 10   Wt 11 13
Defender. From Apprentice. England
Youth.

Season	Club	App	Goals
1975–76	Brentford	6	—
1976–77		18	1
1977–78		37	—
1978–79		40	1
1979–80		41	3
1980–81		38	—
1981–82		40	—

Season	Club		
1982–83		1	—
1983–84		21	—
1984–85		43	3
1985–86		40	—
1986–87	Millwall	31	2
1987–88		36	1
1988–89		19	1
1989–90		7	—
1989–90	Plymouth Arg	11	—
1990–91		35	3

SALMON, Mike   —

Born Leyland 14.7.64.   Ht 6 2   Wt 12 12
Goalkeeper. Local.

Season	Club		
1981–82	Blackburn R	1	—
1982–83		—	—
1982–83	*Chester C*	16	—
1983–84	Stockport Co	46	—
1984–85		46	—
1985–86		26	—
1986–87	Bolton W	26	—
1986–87	*Wrexham*	17	—
1987–88	Wrexham	40	—
1988–89		43	—
1989–90	Charlton Ath	—	—
1990–91		7	—

SALTON, Darren

Born Edinburgh 16.3.72.   Ht 6 1
Wt 13 08
Forward. From Trainee. Scotland Schools,
Youth.

Season	Club		
1988–89	Luton T	—	—
1989–90		—	—
1990–91		—	—

SAMWAYS, Mark

Born Doncaster 11.11.68.   Ht 6 0
Wt 11 12
Goalkeeper. From Trainee.

Season	Club		
1987–88	Doncaster R	11	—
1988–89		12	—
1989–90		46	—
1990–91		26	—

SAMWAYS, Vinny

Born Bethnal Green 27.10.68.   Ht 5 8
Wt 9 00
Midfield. From Apprentice. England
Youth, Under-21.

Season	Club		
1985–86	Tottenham H	—	—
1986–87		2	—
1987–88		26	—
1988–89		19	3
1989–90		23	3
1990–91		23	1

SANCHEZ, Lawrie

Born Lambeth 22.10.59.   Ht 5 11
Wt 12 00
Midfield. From Thatcham. Northern
Ireland 3 caps.

Season	Club		
1977–78	Reading	8	1
1978–79		39	4
1979–80		46	5
1980–81		37	2
1981–82		35	3
1982–83		37	1
1983–84		45	10
1984–85		15	2
1984–85	Wimbledon	20	5
1985–86		42	9
1986–87		29	—
1987–88		38	4
1988–89		36	5
1989–90		18	1
1990–91		29	—

SANDEMAN, Bradley

Born Northampton 24.2.70   Ht 5 10
Wt 10 08
Midfield. From Trainee.

Season	Club		
1987–88	Northampton T	2	—
1988–89		22	2
1989–90		29	1
1990–91		5	—
1990–91	Maidstone U	20	1

SANDFORD, Lee

Born Basingstoke 22.4.68. Ht 6 01
Wt 12 00
Defender. From Apprentice. England
Youth.

1985–86	Portsmouth	7	—
1986–87		—	—
1987–88		21	1
1988–89		31	—
1989–90		13	—
1989–90	Stoke C	23	2
1990–91		32	2

SANDISON, James

Born Edinburgh 22.6.65. Ht 6 0
Wt 11 02
Midfield. From Edinburgh Emmet.

1983–84	Hearts	—	—
1984–85		3	—
1985–86		3	—
1986–87		13	—
1987–88		2	—
1988–89		14	—
1989–90		12	2
1990–91		25	1

SANSOM, Kenny

Born Camberwell 26.9.58. Ht 5 7
Wt 10 04
Defender. From Apprentice. England
Schools, Youth, Under-21, B, 86 full caps.
Football League.

1974–75	Crystal Palace	1	—
1975–76		6	—
1976–77		46	—
1977–78		41	2
1978–79		42	—
1979–80		36	1
1980–81	Arsenal	42	3
1981–82		42	—
1982–83		40	—
1983–84		40	1
1984–85		39	1
1985–86		42	—
1986–87		35	—

1987–88		34	1
1988–89		—	—
1988–89	Newcastle U	20	—
1989–90	QPR	36	—
1990–91		28	—
1990–91	Coventry C	9	—

SANSOME, Paul

Born N. Addington 6.10.61. Ht 5 11
Wt 12 00
Goalkeeper. From Crystal Palace
Apprentice.

1979–80	Millwall	—	—
1980–81		—	—
1981–82		8	—
1982–83		24	—
1983–84		31	—
1984–85		46	—
1985–86		36	—
1986–87		10	—
1987–88		1	—
1987–88	Southend U	6	—
1988–89		44	—
1989–90		46	—
1990–91		46	—

SAUNDERS, Carl

Born Marston Green 26.11.64. Ht 5 8
Wt 11 02
Forward. Local.

1982–83	Stoke C	1	—
1983–84		—	—
1984–85		23	2
1985–86		37	2
1986–87		31	13
1987–88		17	3
1988–89		33	2
1989–90		22	1
1989–90	Bristol R	20	5
1990–91		38	16

SAUNDERS, Dean

Born Swansea 21.6.64. Ht 5 8   Wt 10 06
Forward. From Apprentice. Wales 27 full
caps.

Season	Club		App	Goals
1982–83	Swansea C		—	—
1983–84			19	3
1984–85			30	9
1984–85	*Cardiff C*		4	—
1985–86	Brighton		42	15
1986–87			30	6
1986–87	Oxford U		12	6
1987–88			37	12
1988–89			10	4
1988–89	Derby Co		30	14
1989–90			38	11
1990–91			38	17

SAUNDERS, Wes

Born Sunderland 23.2.63.   Ht 6 0
Wt 11 11
Defender. From school.

Season	Club		App	Goals
1981–82	Newcastle U		29	—
1982–83			13	—
1983–84			16	—
1984–85			21	—
1984–85	*Bradford C*		4	—
1985–86	Carlisle U		35	3
1986–87			37	3
1987–88			25	5
1987–88	Dundee		11	—
1988–89			30	1
1989–90			9	1
1990–91	Torquay U		37	3

SAVILLE, Andrew

Born Hull 12.12.64.   Ht 6 0   Wt 12 06
Forward. From local.

Season	Club		App	Goals
1983–84	Hull C		1	—
1984–85			4	1
1985–86			9	1
1986–87			35	9
1987–88			31	6
1988–89			20	1
1988–89	Walsall		12	4
1989–90			26	1
1989–90	Barnsley		15	3
1990–91			45	12

SAYER, Andy

Born Brent 6.6.66   Ht 5 9   Wt 10 12
Forward. From Apprentice.

Season	Club		App	Goals
1983–84	Wimbledon		2	—
1984–85			20	8
1985–86			7	—
1986–87			20	7
1987–88			9	—
1987–88	*Cambridge U*		5	—
1988–89	Fulham		28	10
1989–90			25	5
1989–90	Leyton Orient		10	1
1990–91			11	2
1990–91	*Sheffield U*		3	—

SCALES, John

Born Harrogate 4.7.66.   Ht 6 2   Wt 12 07
Defender.

Season	Club		App	Goals
1984–85	Leeds U		—	—
1985–86	Bristol R		29	1
1986–87			43	1
1987–88	Wimbledon		25	1
1988–89			38	5
1989–90			28	2
1990–91			36	2

SCHOFIELD, Jon

Born Barnsley 16.5.65   Ht 5 11   Wt 11 03
Midfield. From Gainsborough T.

Season	Club		App	Goals
1988–89	Lincoln C		29	2
1989–90			29	2
1990–91			42	3

SCOPE, David

Born Newcastle 10.5.67.   Ht 5 8
Wt 10 12
Forward. From Blyth Spartans.

Season	Club		App	Goals
1989–90	Northampton T		7	—
1990–91			7	—

SCOTT, Colin

Born Glasgow 19.5.70.   Ht 6 1   Wt 12 04
Goalkeeper. From Dalry Thistle.

Season	Club	App	Goals
1987–88	Rangers	—	—
1988–89		—	—
1989–90		—	—
1989–90	*Brentford*	6	—
1990–91	Rangers	—	—

SCOTT, Colin

Born Glasgow 19.5.70   Ht 6 1   Wt 12 4
Goalkeeper. From Dalry Thistle

Season	Club	App	Goals
1987–88	Rangers	—	—
1988–89		—	—
1989–90		—	—
1990–91		—	—
1990–91	Airdrieonians	1	—

SCOTT, Ian

Born Radcliffe 20.9.67.   Ht 5 9   Wt 11 04
Forward. From Apprentice. England
Schools.

Season	Club	App	Goals
1985–86	Manchester C	—	—
1986–87		—	—
1987–88		23	3
1988–89		1	—
1989–90	Stoke C	19	1
1990–91		2	—
1990–91	*Crewe Alex*	12	1

SCOTT, Keith

Born London 10.6.67.   Ht 6 3   Wt 12 00
Forward. From Leicester U.

Season	Club	App	Goals
1989–90	Lincoln C	10	2
1990–91		6	—

SCOTT, Kevin

Born Easington 17.12.66.   Ht 6 2
Wt 11 06
Defender.

Season	Club	App	Goals
1984–85	Newcastle U	—	—
1985–86		—	—
1986–87		3	1
1987–88		4	1
1988–89		29	—

Season	Club	App	Goals
1989–90		42	3
1990–91		42	—

SCOTT, Martin

Born Sheffield 7.1.68.   Ht 5 8   Wt 10 10
Midfield. From Apprentice.

Season	Club	App	Goals
1984–85	Rotherham U	3	—
1985–86		—	—
1986–87		12	—
1987–88		19	—
1987–88	*Nottingham F.*	—	—
1988–89	Rotherham U	19	1
1989–90		28	1
1990–91		13	1
1990–91	Bristol C	27	1

SCOTT, Morrys

Born Swansea 17.12.70.   Ht 6 3   Wt 12 06
Forward. From Swansea C Trainee and
Cardiff C Trainee.

Season	Club	App	Goals
1989–90	Cardiff C	9	—
	From Colchester U		
1990–91	Southend U	—	—

SCOTT, Peter

Born London 1.10.63.   Ht 5 9   Wt 11 12
Midfield. From Apprentice.

Season	Club	App	Goals
1981–82	Fulham	1	—
1982–83		—	—
1983–84		32	4
1984–85		19	1
1985–86		32	5
1986–87		30	6
1987–88		23	2
1988–89		37	3
1989–90		41	3
1990–91		23	2

SCULLY, Pat

Born Dublin 23.6.70.   Ht 6 1   Wt 12 07
Defender. Eire Schools, B, Under-21,
Under-23, 1 full cap.

Season	Club	App	Goals
1987–88	Arsenal	—	—

1988–89	....	—	—
1989–90	....	—	—
1989–90	*Preston NE*	13	1
1990–91	Arsenal........................	—	—
1990–91	*Northampton T*...........	15	—
1990–91	Southend U.................	21	—

SEAGRAVES, Mark

Born Bootle 22.10.66. Ht 6 1 Wt 12 10
Defender. From England Schools, Youth.

1983–84	Liverpool	—	—
1984–85	....	—	—
1985–86	....	—	—
1986–87	....	—	—
1986–87	*Norwich C*...................	3	—
1987–88	Liverpool	—	—
1987–88	Manchester C	17	—
1988–89	....	23	—
1989–90	....	2	—
1990–91	Bolton W	32	—

SEALEY, Les

Born Bethnal Green 29.9.57. Ht 6 1
Wt 13 06
Goalkeeper. From Apprentice.

1975–76	Coventry C	—	—
1976–77	....	11	—
1977–78	....	2	—
1978–79	....	36	—
1979–80	....	20	—
1980–81	....	35	—
1981–82	....	15	—
1982–83	....	39	—
1983–84	Luton T	42	—
1984–85	....	26	—
1984–85	*Plymouth Arg*.............	6	—
1985–86	Luton T	35	—
1986–87	....	41	—
1987–88	....	31	—
1988–89	....	32	—
1989–90	....	—	—
1989–90	*Manchester U*..............	2	—
1990–91	Manchester U	31	—

SEALY, Tony

Born London 7.5.59 Ht 5 8 Wt 11 08
Forward. From Apprentice.

1977–78	Southampton	2	—
1978–79	....	5	—
1978–79	Crystal Palace	5	—
1979–80	....	—	—
1979–80	*Port Vale*....................	17	6
1980–81	Crystal Palace	19	5
1980–81	QPR	8	2
1981–82	....	7	—
1981–82	*Port Vale*....................	6	4
1982–83	QPR	40	16
1983–84	....	8	—
1983–84	*Fulham*	5	1
1984–85	QPR	—	—
1984–85	Fulham	13	6
1985–86	....	7	3
1985–86	Leicester C..................	21	6
1986–87	....	18	1
1986–87	*Bournemouth*	13	2
From Braga			
1988–89	Brentford	12	4
1989–90	Swindon T	—	—
1989–90	Bristol R	19	3
1990–91	....	18	4

SEAMAN, David

Born Rotherham 19.9.63. Ht 6 3
Wt 13 00
Goalkeeper. From Apprentice. England B,
Under-21, 7 full caps.

1981–82	Leeds U	—	—
1982–83	Peterborough U	38	—
1983–84	....	45	—
1984–85	....	8	—
1984–85	Birmingham C	33	—
1985–86	....	42	—
1986–87	QPR	41	—
1987–88	....	32	—
1988–89	....	35	—
1989–90	....	33	—
1990–91	Arsenal........................	38	—

SEARLE, Damon

Born Cardiff 26.10.71.   Ht 5 11   Wt 10 04
Defender. From Trainee. Wales Youth,
Under-21.

1990–91	Cardiff C	35	—

SEDGLEY, Steve

Born Enfield 26.5.68.   Ht 6 1   Wt 12 06
Midfield. From Apprentice. England
Under-21.

1986–87	Coventry C	26	—
1987–88		27	2
1988–89		31	1
1989–90	Tottenham H	32	—
1990–91		34	—

SEGERS, Hans

Born Eindhoven 30.10.61.   Ht 5 11
Wt 12 12
Goalkeeper. From PSV Eindhoven.

1984–85	Nottingham F	28	—
1985–86		11	—
1986–87		14	—
1986–87	*Stoke C*	1	—
1987–88	Nottingham F	5	—
1987–88	*Sheffield U*	10	—
1987–88	*Dunfermline Ath*	4	—
1988–89	Nottingham F	—	—
1988–89	Wimbledon	33	—
1989–90		38	—
1990–91		37	—

SELLARS, Scott

Born Sheffield 27.11.65   Ht 5 7   Wt 9 10
Midfield. From Apprentice. England
Under-21.

1982–83	Leeds U	1	—
1983–84		19	3
1984–85		39	7
1985–86		17	2
1986–87	Blackburn R	32	4
1987–88		42	7
1988–89		46	2

1989–90		43	14
1990–91		9	1

SENDALL, Richard

Born Stamford 10.7.67.   Ht 5 10
Wt 11 06
Forward. From Watford Apprentice.

1985–86	Blackpool	8	—
1986–87		3	—
1987–88		—	—
1988–89	Carlisle U	29	6
1989–90		19	4
1989–90	*Cardiff C*	4	—
1990–91	Carlisle U	25	2

SENIOR, Steve

Born Sheffield 15.5.63.   Ht 5 8   Wt 12 07
Defender. From Apprentice.

1980–81	York C	3	—
1981–82		17	1
1982–83		10	1
1983–84		39	1
1984–85		28	—
1984–85	*Darlington*	5	—
1985–86	York C	34	3
1986–87		37	—
1987–88	Northampton T	4	—
1987–88	Wigan Ath	22	1
1988–89		44	2
1989–90		43	—
1990–91	Preston NE	38	2

SENIOR, Trevor

Born Dorchester 28.11.61.   Ht 6 1
Wt 13 07
Forward. From Dorchester T.

1981–82	Portsmouth	9	2
1982–83		2	—
1982–83	*Aldershot*	10	7
1983–84	Reading	45	36
1984–85		31	22
1985–86		46	27
1986–87		42	17
1987–88	Watford	24	1

1987–88	Middlesbrough	6	2
1988–89		4	—
1988–89	Reading	37	16
1989–90		35	14
1990–91		40	15

SERTORI, Mark

Born Manchester 1.9.67. Ht 6 3
Wt 13 04
Defender.

1986–87	Stockport Co	3	—
1987–88		1	—
1987–88	Lincoln C	*28*	*6*
1988–89		26	4
1989–90		24	5
1989–90	Wrexham	18	2
1990–91		29	—

SEYMOUR, Chris

Born Reading 14.9.71. Ht 5 10 Wt 11 00
Defender. From Trainee.

1990–91	Reading	9	—

SHAKESPEARE, Craig

Born Birmingham 26.10.63. Ht 5 10
Wt 12 05
Midfield. From Apprentice.

1981–82	Walsall	—	—
1982–83		31	4
1983–84		46	6
1984–85		41	9
1985–86		32	4
1986–87		44	11
1987–88		45	8
1988–89		45	3
1989–90	Sheffield W	17	—
1989–90	WBA	18	1
1990–91		36	1

SHANLEY, Kevin

Born Ireland 8.9.70. Ht 5 11 Wt 11 11
Defender. From Trainee.

1989–90	Luton T	—	—

1990–91		—	—

SHARP, Graeme

Born Glasgow 16.10.60. Ht 6 1 Wt 11 09
Forward. From Eastercraigs. Scotland
Under-21, 12 full caps.

1978–79	Dumbarton	6	1
1979–80		34	16
1979–80	Everton	2	—
1980–81		4	—
1981–82		29	15
1982–83		41	15
1983–84		28	7
1984–85		36	21
1985–86		37	19
1986–87		27	5
1987–88		32	13
1988–89		26	7
1989–90		33	6
1990–91		27	3

SHARP, Raymond

Born Stirling 16.11.69. Ht 5 6 Wt 9 04
Defender. From Gairdoch U. Scotland
Under-21.

1986–87	Dunfermline Ath	—	—
1987–88		—	—
1988–89	*Stenhousemuir*	5	—
1988–89	Dunfermline Ath	9	—
1989–90		27	—
1990–91		31	—

SHARPE, Lee

Born Halesowen 25.7.71 Ht 5 11
Wt 11 04
Midfield. From Trainee. England Under-
21. 1 full cap.

1987–88	Torquay U	14	3
1988–89	Manchester U	22	—
1989–90		18	1
1990–91		23	2

SHAW, Adrian

Born Easington 13.4.66. Ht 5 9
Wt 11 03
Forward. From Apprentice.

Season	Club	App	Goals
1983–84	Nottingham F	—	—
1984–85	Halifax T	21	1
1985–86		34	—
1986–87		21	—
1987–88		24	—
1988–89	York C	5	—
1988–89	Chesterfield	25	1
1989–90		24	2
1990–91		1	—

SHAW, Gary

Born Birmingham 21.1.61. Ht 5 10
Wt 11 13
Forward. From Apprentice. England
Under-21.

Season	Club	App	Goals
1978–79	Aston Villa	3	—
1979–80		28	9
1980–81		40	18
1981–82		26	9
1982–83		39	17
1983–84		12	5
1984–85		—	—
1985–86		12	1
1986–87		1	—
1987–88		4	—
1987–88	*Blackpool*	6	—
From Klagenfurt.			
1989–90	Walsall	9	3
1990–91	Shrewsbury T	22	5

SHAW, George

Born Glasgow 10.2.69. Ht 5 7 Wt 9 02
Forward. From Ayresome N.

Season	Club	App	Goals
1987–88	St Mirren	2	—
1988–89		10	1
1989–90		23	2
1990–91		33	1

SHAW, Graham

Born Stoke 7.6.67. Ht 5 8 Wt 10 05
Forward. From Apprentice.

Season	Club	App	Goals
1985–86	Stoke C	20	5
1986–87		18	2
1987–88		33	6

Season	Club	App	Goals
1988–89		28	5
1989–90	Preston NE	31	5
1990–91		44	10

SHAW, Richard

Born Brentford 11.9.68. Ht 5 9 Wt 11 08
Defender. From Apprentice.

Season	Club	App	Goals
1986–87	Crystal Palace	—	—
1987–88		3	—
1988–89		14	—
1989–90		21	—
1989–90	*Hull C*	4	—
1990–91	Crystal Palace	36	1

SHEARER, Alan

Born Newcastle 13.8.70. Ht 5 11
Wt 11 03
Forward. From Trainee. England Youth,
Under-21.

Season	Club	App	Goals
1987–88	Southampton	5	3
1988–89		10	—
1989–90		26	3
1990–91		36	4

SHEARER, Duncan

Born Fort William 28.8.62. Ht 5 10
Wt 10 09
Forward. From Inverness Clach.

Season	Club	App	Goals
1983–84	Chelsea	—	—
1984–85		—	—
1985–86		2	1
1985–86	Huddersfield T	8	7
1986–87		42	21
1987–88		33	10
1988–89	Swindon T	36	14
1989–90		42	20
1990–91		44	22

SHEARER, Peter

Born Birmingham 4.2.67. Ht 6 0
Wt 11 06
Forward. From Apprentice.

Season	Club	App	Goals
1984–85	Birmingham C	4	—

Season	Club	App	Goals
1985–86	....	—	—
1986–87	Rochdale......................	1	—
From Cheltenham T			
1988–89	Bournemouth..............	4	1
1989–90	....	34	4
1990–91	....	5	—

SHEEDY, Kevin

Born Builth Wells 21.10.59.   Ht 5 9
Wt 10 11
Midfield. From Apprentice. Eire Youth,
Under-21, 37 full caps.

Season	Club	App	Goals
1975–76	Hereford U	1	—
1976–77	....	16	1
1977–78	....	34	3
1978–79	Liverpool	—	—
1979–80	....	—	—
1980–81	....	1	—
1981–82	....	2	—
1982–83	Everton	40	11
1983–84	....	28	4
1984–85	....	29	11
1985–86	....	31	5
1986–87	....	28	13
1987–88	....	17	1
1988–89	....	26	8
1989–90	....	37	9
1990–91	....	22	4

SHEFFIELD, Jon

Born Bedworth 1.2.69.   Ht 5 11   Wt 11 07
Goalkeeper.

Season	Club	App	Goals
1986–87	Norwich C	—	—
1987–88	....	—	—
1988–89	....	1	—
1989–90	....	—	—
1989–90	*Aldershot*	11	—
1989–90	*Ipswich T*	—	—
1990–91	Norwich C	—	—
1990–91	*Aldershot*	15	—
1990–91	*Cambridge U*	2	—

SHELTON, Gary

Born Nottingham 21.3.58.   Ht 5 7
Wt 10 12
Midfield. From Apprentice. England
Under-21.

Season	Club	App	Goals
1975–76	Walsall	2	—
1976–77	....	10	—
1977–78	....	12	—
1977–78	Aston Villa.................	—	—
1978–79	....	19	7
1979–80	....	4	—
1979–80	*Notts Co*......................	8	—
1980–81	Aston Villa.................	—	—
1981–82	....	1	—
1981–82	Sheffield W.................	9	1
1982–83	....	40	4
1983–84	....	40	5
1984–85	....	41	4
1985–86	....	31	1
1986–87	....	37	3
1987–88	Oxford U	32	—
1988–89	....	33	1
1989–90	Bristol C	43	9
1990–91	....	43	8

SHEPHERD, Tony

Born Glasgow 16.11.66.   Ht 5 9   Wt 10 07
Midfield. From Celtic BC. Scotland
Schools, Youth.

Season	Club	App	Goals
1983–84	Celtic	—	—
1984–85	....	—	—
1985–86	....	1	—
1986–87	....	21	2
1987–88	....	6	1
1988–89	....	—	—
1988–89	*Bristol C*......................	3	—
1989–90	Carlisle U..................	31	2
1990–91	....	44	6

SHEPSTONE, Paul

Born Coventry 8.11.70.   Ht 5 8   Wt 10 06
Midfield. FA Schools.

Season	Club	App	Goals
1987–88	Coventry C	—	—
1988–89	....	—	—
1989–90	Birmingham C	—	—

From Atherstone U

Season	Club		
1989–90	Blackburn R	—	—
1990–91		25	1

SHERIDAN, John

Born Manchester 1.10.64.   Ht 5 9
Wt 10 08
Midfield. Local. Eire Youth, Under-21,
Under-23, 13 full caps.

Season	Club		
1981–82	Leeds U	—	—
1982–83		27	2
1983–84		11	1
1984–85		42	6
1985–86		32	4
1986–87		40	15
1987–88		38	12
1988–89		40	7
1989–90	Nottingham F	—	—
1989–90	Sheffield W	27	2
1990–91		46	10

SHERINGHAM, Teddy

Born Highams Park 2.4.66.   Ht 6 0
Wt 12 05
Forward. From Apprentice. England
Youth.

Season	Club		
1983–84	Millwall	7	1
1984–85		—	—
1984–85	Aldershot	5	—
1985–86	Millwall	18	4
1986–87		42	13
1987–88		43	22
1988–89		33	11
1989–90		31	9
1990–91		46	33

SHERON, Mike

Born Liverpool 11.1.72.
Midfield. From Trainee.

Season	Club		
1990–91	Manchester C	—	—
1990–91	Bury	5	1

SHERWOOD, Steve

Born Selby 10.12.53.   Ht 6 4   Wt 14 07
Goalkeeper. From Apprentice.

Season	Club		
1970–71	Chelsea	—	—
1971–72		1	—
1972–73		3	—
1973–74		—	—
1973–74	Brighton	—	—
1973–74	Millwall	1	—
1973–74	Brentford	16	—
1974–75	Chelsea	—	—
1974–75	Brentford	46	—
1975–76	Chelsea	12	—
1976–77		—	—
1976–77	Watford	8	—
1977–78		16	—
1978–79		16	—
1979–80		4	—
1980–81		22	—
1981–82		41	—
1982–83		42	—
1983–84		40	1
1984–85		9	—
1985–86		2	—
1986–87		11	—
1987–88	Grimsby T	46	—
1988–89		32	—
1989–90		31	—
1990–91		46	—

SHERWOOD, Tim

Born St Albans 6.2.69.   Ht 6 1   Wt 11 04
Midfield. From Trainee. England
Under-21.

Season	Club		
1986–87	Watford	—	—
1987–88		13	—
1988–89		19	2
1989–90	Norwich C	27	3
1990–91		37	7

SHILTON, Peter

Born Leicester 18.9.49.   Ht 6 0   Wt 14 00
Goalkeeper. From Apprentice. England
Schools, Youth, Under-23, 125 full caps.
Football League.

Season	Club		
1965–66	Leicester C	1	—
1966–67		4	—
1967–68		35	1
1968–69		42	—

Season	Club	League Appearances/Goals	
1969–70	....	39	—
1970–71		40	—
1971–72		37	—
1972–73		41	—
1973–74		42	—
1974–75		5	—
1974–75	Stoke C......................	25	—
1975–76		42	—
1976–77		40	—
1977–78		3	—
1977–78	Nottingham F............	37	—
1978–79		42	—
1979–80		42	—
1980–81		40	—
1981–82		41	—
1982–83	Southampton	39	—
1983–84		42	—
1984–85		41	—
1985–86		37	—
1986–87		29	—
1987–88	Derby Co....................	40	—
1988–89		38	—
1989–90		35	—
1990–91		31	—

SHIRTLIFF, Peter

Born Barnsley 6.4.61.   Ht 5 11   Wt 12 2
Defender. From Apprentice.

1978–79	Sheffield W.................	26	1
1979–80		3	—
1980–81		28	—
1981–82		31	2
1982–83		8	—
1983–84		36	1
1984–85		35	—
1985–86		21	—
1986–87	Charlton Ath	33	3
1987–88		36	2
1988–89		34	2
1989–90	Sheffield W.................	33	2
1990–91		39	2

SHORT, Chris

Born Munster 9.5.70   Ht 5 10   Wt 12 02
Defender.

1988–89	Scarborough................	2	—

1989–90	....	41	1
1990–91		—	—
1990–91	*Manchester U*............	—	—
1990–91	Notts Co......................	15	1

SHORT, Craig

Born Bridlington 25.6.68.   Ht 6 0
Wt 11 04
Defender. From Pickering T. England
Schools.

1987–88	Scarborough...............	21	2
1988–89		42	5
1989–90	Notts Co.....................	44	2
1990–91		43	—

SHOTTON, John

Born Hartlepool 17.8.71.
Forward. From Manchester U Trainee.

1990–91	Hartlepool U	1	—

SHOTTON, Malcolm

Born Newcastle 16.2.57.   Ht 6 3
Wt 13 12
Defender. From Apprentice.

1974–75	Leicester C..................	—	—
1975–76		—	—
From Nuneaton Bor			
1980–81	Oxford U....................	38	5
1981–82		40	4
1982–83		46	1
1983–84		43	1
1984–85		42	1
1985–86		42	—
1986–87		11	—
1987–88		1	—
1987–88	Portsmouth	10	—
1987–88	Huddersfield T............	14	—
1988–89		2	1
1988–89	Barnsley	37	5
1989–90		29	1
1989–90	Hull C........................	16	2
1990–91		26	—

SHUTT, Carl

Born Sheffield 10.10.61. Ht 5 10
Wt 11 13
Forward. From Spalding U.

1984–85	Sheffield W	—	—
1985–86		19	9
1986–87		20	7
1987–88		1	—
1987–88	Bristol C	22	9
1988–89		24	1
1988–89	Leeds U	3	4
1989–90		20	2
1990–91		28	10

SIDDALL, Barry

Born Ellesmere Port 12.9.54. Ht 6 1
Wt 14 02
Goalkeeper. From Apprentice. England
Youth.

1971–72	Bolton W	—	—
1972–73		4	—
1973–74		42	—
1974–75		42	—
1975–76		42	—
1976–77		7	—
1976–77	Sunderland	34	—
1977–78		42	—
1978–79		41	—
1979–80		12	—
1980–81		15	—
1980–81	*Darlington*	8	—
1981–82	Sunderland	23	—
1982–83	Port Vale	33	—
1983–84		39	—
1983–84	*Blackpool*	7	—
1984–85	Port Vale	9	—
1984–85	Stoke C	15	—
1985–86		5	—
1985–86	*Tranmere R*	12	—
1985–86	*Manchester C*	6	—
1986–87	Blackpool	37	—
1987–88		38	—
1988–89		35	—
1989–90	Stockport Co	21	—
1989–90	Hartlepool U	11	—
1990–91	WBA	—	—

| 1990–91 | Carlisle U | 24 | — |

SIMPSON, Fitzroy

Born Trowbridge 26.2.70 Ht 5 8
Wt 10 07
Midfield. From Trainee.

1988–89	Swindon T	7	—
1989–90		30	2
1990–91		38	3

SIMPSON, Neil

Born London 15.11.61. Ht 5 10
Wt 11 06
Midfield. From Middlefield Wasps.
Scotland Youth, Under-21, 4 full caps.

1978–79	Aberdeen	—	—
1979–80		—	—
1980–81		16	2
1981–82		29	4
1982–83		33	5
1983–84		24	2
1984–85		33	4
1985–86		22	1
1986–87		9	—
1987–88		15	1
1988–89		16	—
1989–90		9	—
1990–91	Newcastle U	4	—

SIMPSON, Paul

Born Carlisle 26.7.66. Ht 5 7 Wt 11 04
Forward. From Apprentice. England
Youth, Under-21.

1983–84	Manchester C	—	—
1984–85		10	6
1985–86		37	8
1986–87		32	3
1987–88		38	1
1988–89		1	—
1988–89	Oxford U	25	8
1989–90		42	9
1990–91		46	17

SIMS, Steve

Born Lincoln 2.7.57. Ht 6 1 Wt 14 04
Defender. From Apprentice. England
Youth, Under-21 B.

Season	Club	App	Goals
1974–75	Leicester C	—	—
1975–76		10	—
1976–77		32	1
1977–78		29	2
1978–79		8	—
1978–79	Watford	14	1
1979–80		34	2
1980–81		37	1
1981–82		17	—
1982–83		28	—
1983–84		22	—
1984–85		—	—
1984–85	Notts Co	34	2
1985–86		41	—
1986–87		10	3
1986–87	Watford	19	1
1987–88	Aston Villa	29	—
1988–89		12	—
1989–90		—	—
1990–91	Lincoln C	5	—

SINCLAIR, Chris

Born Sheffield 11.11.70. Ht 5 9 Wt 10 05
Midfield. From Sauchie Ath.

Season	Club	App	Goals
1989–90	Dunfermline Ath	1	—
1990–91		3	—

SINCLAIR, Frank

Born Lambeth 3.12.71.
Defender. From Trainee.

Season	Club	App	Goals
1989–90	Chelsea	—	—
1990–91		4	—

SINCLAIR, Ron

Born Stirling 19.11.64. Ht 5 9 Wt 11 13
Goalkeeper. From Apprentice. Scotland
Schools, Youth.

Season	Club	App	Goals
1982–83	Nottingham F	—	—
1983–84		—	—

Season	Club	App	Goals
1983–84	Wrexham	11	—
1984–85	Nottingham F	—	—
1984–85	Derby Co	—	—
1985–86	Nottingham F	—	—
1985–86	Sheffield U	—	—
1985–86	Leeds U	—	—
1986–87	Leeds U	8	—
1986–87	Halifax T	4	—
1987–88	Leeds U	—	—
1988–89		—	—
1988–89	Halifax T	10	—
1989–90	Leeds U	—	—
1989–90	Bristol C	27	—
1990–91		17	—

SINCLAIR, Trevor

Born Dulwich 2.3.73.
Midfield. From Trainee.

Season	Club	App	Goals
1989–90	Blackpool	9	—
1990–91		31	1

SINGLETON, Martin

Born Banbury 2.8.63. Ht 5 10 Wt 11 00
Midfield. From Apprentice. England
Youth.

Season	Club	App	Goals
1980–81	Coventry C	—	—
1981–82		3	1
1982–83		5	—
1983–84		13	—
1984–85		2	—
1984–85	Bradford C	17	—
1985–86		36	2
1986–87		18	1
1986–87	WBA	7	—
1987–88		12	1
1987–88	Northampton T	29	3
1988–89		11	1
1989–90		10	—
1990–91	Walsall	28	1

SINNOTT, Lee

Born Pelsall 12.7.65. Ht 6 1 Wt 12 07
Defender. From Apprentice. England
Youth, Under-21.

Season	Club	App	Goals
1981–82	Walsall	4	—

Season	Club	App	Goals
1982–83	....	32	2
1983–84	....	4	—
1983–84	Watford	20	—
1984–85	....	30	—
1985–86	....	18	2
1986–87	....	10	—
1987–88	Bradford C	42	1
1988–89	....	42	2
1989–90	....	45	2
1990–91	....	44	1

SINTON, Andy

Born Newcastle. 19.3.66.   Ht 5 8
Wt 10 10
Midfield. From Apprentice. England
Schools, B.

Season	Club	App	Goals
1982–83	Cambridge U	13	5
1983–84	....	34	6
1984–85	....	26	2
1985–86	....	20	—
1985–86	Brentford	26	3
1986–87	....	46	5
1987–88	....	46	11
1988–89	....	31	9
1988–89	QPR	10	3
1989–90	....	38	6
1990–91	....	38	3

SITTON, John

Born Hackney 21.10.59.   Ht 5 11
Wt 12 04
Defender. From Apprentice.

Season	Club	App	Goals
1978–79	Chelsea	12	—
1979–80	....	1	—
1979–80	Millwall	13	1
1980–81	....	32	—
1981–82	....	—	—
1981–82	Gillingham	30	2
1982–83	....	30	—
1983–84	....	42	3
1984–85	....	5	—
1985–86	Orient	39	—
1986–87	....	13	—
1987–88	....	20	1
1988–89	....	37	4
1989–90	....	37	2

| 1990–91 | .... | 24 | — |

SKINNER, Craig

Born Bury 21.10.70.   Ht 5 10   Wt 11 00
Forward. From Trainee.

Season	Club	App	Goals
1989–90	Blackburn R	—	—
1990–91	....	7	—

SKINNER, Justin

Born London 30.1.69.   Ht 6 0   Wt 11 03
Midfield. From Apprentice.

Season	Club	App	Goals
1986–87	Fulham	3	—
1987–88	....	32	6
1988–89	....	38	8
1989–90	....	30	4
1990–91	....	32	5

SKIPPER, Peter

Born Hull 11.4.58.   Ht 6 0   Wt 13 08
Defender. Local.

Season	Club	App	Goals
1978–79	Hull C	17	2
1979–80	....	6	—
1979–80	*Scunthorpe U*	1	—
1980–81	Darlington	46	2
1981–82	....	45	2
1982–83	Hull C	46	4
1983–84	....	46	1
1984–85	....	46	5
1985–86	....	40	1
1986–87	....	41	4
1987–88	....	43	2
1988–89	....	3	—
1988–89	Oldham Ath	27	1
1989–90	Walsall	40	1
1990–91	....	41	1

SLATER, Stuart

Born Sudbury 27.3.69.   Ht 5 9   Wt 10 04
Forward. From Apprentice. England B,
Under-21.

Season	Club	App	Goals
1986–87	West Ham U	—	—
1987–88	....	2	—

1988–89	....	18	1
1989–90	....	40	7
1990–91	....	40	3

SLAVEN, Bernie

Born Paisley 13.11.60.   Ht 5 11   Wt 12 00
Forward. Eire 6 full caps.

1981–82	Morton	13	1
1982–83	....	9	—
1983–84	Airdrie...........................	2	—
1983–84	Queen of the South	2	—
1983–84	Albion R......................	3	—
1984–85	....	39	27
1985–86	Middlesbrough............	32	8
1986–87	....	46	17
1987–88	....	44	21
1988–89	....	37	15
1989–90	....	46	21
1990–91	....	46	16

SLEEUWENHOEK, Kris

Born Oldham 2.10.71   Ht 5 7   Wt 10 00
Forward. From Wolverhampton W
schoolboys.

1988–89	Derby Co	—	—
1989–90	....	—	—
1990–91	....	—	—

SLOAN, Scott

Born Wallsend 14.12.67.
Forward. From Ponteland.

1988–89	Berwick R	26	4
1989–90	....	35	16
1990–91	Newcastle U................	16	1

SMALL, Mike

Born Birmingham 2.3.62.   Ht 6 0
Wt 13 05
Forward.

1980–81	Luton T	—	—
1981–82	....	3	—
1982–83	....	—	—

1982–83	Peterborough U..........	4	1
From Go Ahead Eagles, Twente, Standard		
Liege, PAOK Salonika		
1990–91	Brighton......................	39	15

SMALLEY, Mark

Born Newark 2.1.65.   Ht 5 11   Wt 11 06
Defender. From Apprentice. England
Youth.

1982–83	Nottingham F............	1	—
1983–84	....	1	—
1984–85	....	1	—
1985–86	....	—	—
1985–86	*Birmingham C*	7	—
1986–87	Orient...........................	22	1
1986–87	Nottingham F............	—	—
1986–87	*Bristol R*......................	10	—
1987–88	Leyton Orient	35	3
1988–89	....	4	—
1989–90	....	3	—
1989–90	Mansfield T................	28	1
1990–91	....	21	1

SMALLEY, Paul

Born Nottingham 17.11.66.   Ht 5 11
Wt 11 0
Defender. From Apprentice. England
Youth.

1984–85	Notts Co	—	—
1985–86	....	26	—
1986–87	....	46	—
1987–88	....	46	—
1988–89	....	—	—
1988–89	Scunthorpe U	39	1
1989–90	....	44	—
1990–91	....	3	—
1990–91	*Blackpool*	6	—
1990–91	Leeds U	—	—
1990–91	Doncaster R................	14	—

SMART, Gary

Born Totnes 29.4.64   Ht 5 9   Wt 11 03
Defender. From Wokingham.

1988–89	Oxford U	17	—

Season	Club	Appearances	Goals
1989–90	....	40	—
1990–91	....	15	—

SMART, Jason

Born Rochdale 15.2.69.   Ht 6 0   Wt 12 10
Defender. From Trainee.

Season	Club	Appearances	Goals
1985–86	Rochdale....................	1	—
1986–87	....	38	1
1987–88	....	36	3
1988–89	....	42	—
1989–90	Crewe Alex	41	2
1990–91	....	37	—

SMILLIE, Neil

Born Barnsley 19.7.58.   Ht 5 6   Wt 10 07
Forward. From Apprentice.

Season	Club	Appearances	Goals
1975–76	Crystal Palace	—	—
1976–77	....	1	—
1976–77	*Brentford*....................	3	—
1977–78	Crystal Palace	1	—
1978–79	....	8	1
1979–80	....	8	1
1980–81	....	24	2
1981–82	....	41	3
1982–83	Brighton	25	—
1983–84	....	26	2
1984–85	....	24	—
1985–86	Watford	16	3
1986–87	....	—	—
1986–87	Reading....................	16	—
1987–88	....	23	—
1988–89	Brentford	28	2
1989–90	....	43	5
1990–91	....	36	3

SMITH, Alan

Born Birmingham 21.11.62.   Ht 6 3
Wt 12 08
Forward. From Alvechurch. England B, 7
full caps. Football League.

Season	Club	Appearances	Goals
1982–83	Leicester C....................	39	13
1983–84	....	40	15
1984–85	....	39	12
1985–86	....	40	19
1986–87	....	33	14
1986–87	*Leicester C*....................	9	3
1987–88	Arsenal....................	39	11
1988–89	....	36	23
1989–90	....	38	10
1990–91	....	37	23

SMITH, Andrew

Born Aberdeen 22.11.68   Ht 6 1   Wt 12 7
Forward. From Peterhead

Season	Club	Appearances	Goals
1990–91	Airdrieonians	28	3

SMITH, Anthony

Born Sunderland 21.9.71.
Defender. From Trainee. England Youth.

Season	Club	Appearances	Goals
1990–91	Sunderland	9	—

SMITH, Brian

Born Sheffield 27.10.66.   Ht 5 10
Wt 11 06
Defender. Local.

Season	Club	Appearances	Goals
1984–85	Sheffield U	6	—
1985–86	....	8	—
1986–87	....	12	—
1986–87	*Scunthorpe U*	6	1
1987–88	Sheffield U	23	—
1988–89	....	35	—
1989–90	....	—	—
1990–91	....	—	—

SMITH, David

Born Liverpool 26.12.70.   Ht 5 9
Wt 11 12
Midfield. From Trainee.

Season	Club	Appearances	Goals
1989–90	Norwich C	1	—
1990–91	....	3	—

SMITH, David

Born Sidcup 25.6.61.   Ht 6 0   Wt 11 00
Forward. From Welling U.

Season	Club	Appearances	Goals
1986–87	Gillingham	27	1

1987–88	....	35	7
1988–89	....	42	2
1989–90	Bristol C	45	4
1990–91	....	34	5

SMITH, David

Born Gloucester 29.3.68.   Ht 5 8
Wt 10 02
Midfield. England Under-21.

1986–87	Coventry C	—	—
1987–88	....	16	4
1988–89	....	35	3
1989–90	....	37	6
1990–91	....	36	1

SMITH, Dean

Born West Bromwich 19.3.71   Ht 6 1
Wt 12 00
Defender. From Trainee.

1988–89	Walsall	15	—
1989–90	....	7	—
1990–91	....	33	—

SMITH, Gary

Born Glasgow 25.3.71   Ht 6 0   Wt 10 4
Midfield. From Duntocher BC

1988–89	Falkirk	3	—
1989–90	....	36	—
1990–91	....	31	—

SMITH, Henry

Born Lanark 10.3.56.   Ht 6 2   Wt 12 00
Goalkeeper. From school. Scotland
Under-21.

1978–79	Leeds U	—	—
1979–80	....	—	—
1980–81	....	—	—
1981–82	Hearts	33	—
1982–83	....	39	—
1983–84	....	36	—
1984–85	....	36	—
1985–86	....	36	—

1986–87	....	43	—
1987–88	....	44	—
1988–89	....	36	—
1989–90	....	36	—
1990–91	....	23	—

SMITH, Jim

Born Elderslie 14.5.61.   Ht 6 1   Wt 11 04
Defender. From Greenock Juniors

1980–81	Dundee.........................	—	—
1981–82	....	17	1
1982–83	....	36	—
1983–84	....	34	—
1984–85	....	23	1
1985–86	....	32	—
1986–87	....	39	—
1987–88	....	40	2
1988–89	....	7	—
1989–90	....	4	—
1990–91	Airdrieonians	28	1

SMITH, Kevan

Born Eaglescliffe 13.12.59.   Ht 6 3
Wt 11 09
Defender. From Stockton

1979–80	Darlington	35	1
1980–81	....	39	2
1981–82	....	45	1
1982–83	....	46	3
1983–84	....	44	2
1984–85	....	36	2
1985–86	Rotherham U	43	3
1986–87	....	16	1
1986–87	Coventry C	—	—
1987–88	....	6	—
1987–88	York C.........................	—	—
1988–89	....	31	5
1989–90	Darlington	*39*	*3*
1990–91	....	46	4

SMITH, Mark

Born Bell Hill 16.12.64.   Ht 5 9   Wt 10 01
Forward. From St Mirren BC.

1983–84	Queen's Park...............	15	2

Season	Club	Apps	Goals
1984–85	....	36	2
1985–86	....	31	3
1986–87	Celtic..................................	6	1
1987–88	Dunfermline Ath	30	5
1988–89	....	23	1
1989–90	....	—	—
1989–90	*Stoke C*	2	—
1989–90	Nottingham F.............	—	—
1990–91	....	—	—
1990–91	*Mansfield T*.................	7	—

SMITH, Mark

Born Sheffield 21.3.60.   Ht 6 0   Wt 11 11
Defender. From Apprentice. England
Under-21.

Season	Club	Apps	Goals
1977–78	Sheffield W..................	2	—
1978–79	....	21	—
1979–80	....	44	9
1980–81	....	41	1
1981–82	....	41	—
1982–83	....	41	2
1983–84	....	27	2
1984–85	....	36	2
1985–86	....	13	—
1986–87	....	16	—
1987–88	Plymouth Arg.............	41	6
1988–89	....	35	—
1989–90	....	6	—
1989–90	Barnsley	25	3
1990–91	....	37	6

SMITH, Mark

Born Sheffield 19.12.61.   Ht 5 9   Wt 12 0
Forward.

Season	Club	Apps	Goals
1979–80	Sheffield U	—	—
1980–81	....	—	—
1981–82	....	—	—
From Worksop, Gainsborough T.			
1985–86	Scunthorpe U	1	—
From Kettering			
1988–89	Rochdale......................	27	7
1988–89	Huddersfield T............	20	2
1989–90	....	44	7
1990–91	....	32	2
1990–91	Grimsby T	11	—

SMITH, Mark

Born Bellshill 16.12.64.   Ht 5 9   Wt 10 04
Midfield. From St Mirren BC.

Season	Club	Apps	Goals
1983–84	Queen's Park...............	15	2
1984–85	....	36	2
1985–86	....	31	3
1986–87	Celtic..................................	6	1
1987–88	Dunfermline Ath	30	5
1988–89	....	23	1
1989–90	*Stoke C*	2	—
1989–90	Nottingham F.............	—	—
1990–91	....	—	—
1990–91	*Reading*	3	—

SMITH, Michael

Born Hull 19.12.68.   Ht 5 8   Wt 12 03
Forward.

Season	Club	Apps	Goals
1987–88	Hull C..................................	—	—
1988–89	....	12	1
1989–90	....	1	—
1990–91	....	6	—

SMITH, Mick

Born Sunderland 28.10.58.   Ht 6 0
Wt 11 09
Defender. Lambton St BC.

Season	Club	Apps	Goals
1977–78	Lincoln C....................	5	—
1978–79	....	20	—
1979–80	....	—	—
1979–80	Wimbledon	20	—
1980–81	....	45	2
1981–82	....	39	2
1982–83	....	24	4
1983–84	....	24	3
1984–85	....	23	—
1984–85	*Aldershot*	7	—
1985–86	Wimbledon	24	3
1986–87	....	6	—
1987–88	....	—	—
From Seaham Red Star.			
1989–90	Hartlepool U	35	5
1990–91	....	12	1

SMITH, Neil

Born Warley 10.2.70. Ht 5 11 Wt 12 00
Midfield. From Trainee.

Season	Club	Apps	Goals
1988–89	Shrewsbury T	1	—
From Reddich			
1989–90	Lincoln C	4	—
1990–91		12	—

SMITH, Nigel

Born Leeds 21.12.69. Ht 5 7 Wt 10 04
Midfield. From Leeds U.

Season	Club	Apps	Goals
1989–90	Burnley	11	—
1990–91		2	—

SMITH, Paul

Born Currie 2.11.62 Ht 5 11 Wt 11 04
Forward. From Edinburgh BC.

Season	Club	Apps	Goals
1980–81	Dundee	—	—
1981–82		—	—
1982–83	Dundee U	—	—
1982–83	Raith R	16	2
1983–84		38	8
1984–85		38	19
1985–86		35	21
1986–87	Motherwell	44	9
1987–88		30	4
1988–89		4	—
1988–89	Dunfermline Ath	35	5
1989–90		33	4
1990–91		31	2

SMITH, Paul

Born Rotherham 9.11.64. Ht 5 10
Wt 10 09
Forward. From Apprentice.

Season	Club	Apps	Goals
1982–83	Sheffield U	7	—
1983–84		3	—
1984–85		8	1
1985–86		18	—
1985–86	*Stockport Co*	7	5
1986–87	Port Vale	42	7
1987–88		2	—
1987–88	Lincoln C	*33*	*8*

Season	Club	Apps	Goals
1988–89		28	10
1989–90		33	5
1990–91		46	6

SMITH, Paul

Born London 5.10.67. Ht 5 8 Wt 9 09
Forward. From Apprentice.

Season	Club	Apps	Goals
1985–86	Arsenal	—	—
1986–87		—	—
1987–88	Brentford	17	1
1988–89	Bristol R	16	1
1988–89	Torquay U	11	1
1989–90		33	6
1990–91		29	5

SMITH, Paul

Born Lenham 18.9.71. Ht 5 11 Wt 12 00
Forward. From Trainee.

Season	Club	Apps	Goals
1989–90	Southend U	10	1
1990–91		2	—

SMITH, Richard

Born Leicester 3.10.70.
Defender. From Trainee.

Season	Club	Apps	Goals
1988–89	Leicester C	—	—
1989–90		4	—
1989–90	*Cambridge U*	4	—
1990–91	Leicester C	4	—

SNEDDON, Alan

Born Baillieston 12.3.58. Ht 5 11
Wt 12 03
Defender. From Larkhall Thistle. Scotland
Under-21.

Season	Club	Apps	Goals
1977–78	Celtic	15	—
1978–79		4	—
1979–80		32	1
1980–81		15	—
1980–81	Hibernian	14	—
1981–82		36	—
1982–83		36	—
1983–84		35	1

Season	Club	League Appearances/Goals		
1984–85		....	36	2
1985–86		....	31	2
1986–87		....	26	—
1987–88		....	32	—
1988–89		....	26	—
1989–90		....	29	2
1990–91		....	6	—

SNELDERS, Theo

Born Westervoort 7.12.63 Ht 6 2
Wt 14 02
Goalkeeper. From Twente. Holland full
caps.

1988–89	Aberdeen	....	36	—
1989–90		....	23	—
1990–91		....	21	—

SNODIN, Glynn

Born Rotherham 14.2.60. Ht 5 6
Wt 9 05
Midfield. From Apprentice.

1976–77	Doncaster R	....	4	—
1977–78		....	22	2
1978–79		....	34	3
1979–80		....	41	1
1980–81		....	44	3
1981–82		....	40	7
1982–83		....	38	14
1983–84		....	43	13
1984–85		....	43	18
1985–86	Sheffield W	....	28	1
1986–87		....	31	—
1987–88	Leeds U	....	35	7
1988–89		....	35	3
1989–90		....	4	—
1990–91		....	20	—

SNODIN, Ian

Born Rotherham 15.8.63. Ht 5 7
Wt 8 11
Midfield. From Apprentice. England
Youth, Under-21.

1979–80	Doncaster R	....	9	1
1980–81		....	32	2

Season	Club	League Appearances/Goals		
1981–82		....	33	2
1982–83		....	34	3
1983–84		....	39	9
1984–85		....	41	8
1985–86	Leeds U	....	37	5
1986–87		....	14	1
1986–87	Everton	....	16	—
1987–88		....	31	2
1988–89		....	23	—
1989–90		....	25	—
1990–91		....	1	—

SOLOMAN, Jason

Born Welwyn 6.10.70. Ht 6 1 Wt 11 09
Defender. From Trainee. England Youth.

1988–89	Watford	....	—	—
1989–90		....	—	—
1990–91		....	8	—

SONNER, Danny

Born Wigan 9.1.72.
Forward. From Wigan Ath.

1990–91	Burnley	....	2	—

SORRELL, Tony

Born London 17.10.66. Ht 5 10
Wt 12 04
Midfield. From Barking and Bishop's
Stortford (1988).

1989–90	Maidstone U	....	28	3
1990–91		....	27	5

SOUTHALL, Neville

Born Llandudno 16.9.58. Ht 6 1
Wt 12 02
Goalkeeper. From Winsford. Wales
Under-21, 52 full caps.

1980–81	Bury	....	39	—
1981–82	Everton	....	26	—
1982–83		....	17	—
1982–83	*Port Vale*	....	9	—
1983–84	Everton	....	35	—

1984–85	....	42	—
1985–86	....	32	—
1986–87	....	31	—
1987–88	....	32	—
1988–89	....	38	—
1989–90	....	38	—
1990–91	....	38	—

SOUTHGATE, Gareth

Born Watford 3.9.70.   Ht 5 10   Wt 11 12
Defender. From Trainee.

1988–89	Crystal Palace	—	—
1989–90	....	—	—
1990–91	....	1	—

SPACKMAN, Nigel

Born Romsey 2.12.60.   Ht 6 1   Wt 13 02
Midfield. From Andover.

1980–81	Bournemouth	44	3
1981–82	....	35	3
1982–83	....	40	4
1983–84	Chelsea	40	3
1984–85	....	42	1
1985–86	....	39	7
1986–87	....	20	1
1986–87	Liverpool	12	—
1987–88	....	27	—
1988–89	....	12	—
1988–89	QPR	16	1
1989–90	....	13	—
1989–90	Rangers	21	1
1990–91	....	35	—

SPEARING, Tony

Born Romford 7.10.64.   Ht 5 9   Wt 10 12
Defender. From Apprentice. England
Youth.

1982–83	Norwich C	—	—
1983–84	....	4	—
1984–85	....	—	—
1984–85	*Stoke C*	9	—
1984–85	*Oxford U*	5	—
1985–86	Norwich C	8	—
1986–87	....	39	—

1987–88	....	18	—
1988–89	Leicester C	36	—
1989–90	....	20	1
1990–91	....	17	—

SPEED, Gary

Born Hawarden 8.9.69   Ht 5 9   Wt 10 06
Midfield. From Trainee. Wales Under-21,
6 full caps.

1988–89	Leeds U	1	—
1989–90	....	25	3
1990–91	....	38	7

SPEEDIE, David

Born Glenrothes 20.2.60.   Ht 5 7
Wt 11 00
Forward. From Amateur. Scotland Under-
21, 10 full caps.

1978–79	Barnsley	10	—
1979–80	....	13	—
1980–81	Darlington	44	4
1981–82	....	44	17
1982–83	Chelsea	34	7
1983–84	....	37	13
1984–85	....	35	10
1985–86	....	34	14
1986–87	....	22	3
1987–88	Coventry C	36	6
1988–89	....	36	14
1989–90	....	32	8
1990–91	....	18	3
1990–91	Liverpool	12	6

SPENCER, John

Born Glasgow 11.9.70   Ht 5 7   Wt 9 10
Forward. From Rangers Am BC. Scotland
Under-21.

1986–87	Rangers	—	—
1987–88	....	—	—
1988–89	....	—	—
1988–89	*Morton*	4	1
From Lisburg, HK			
1990–91	Rangers	5	1

SPINK, Dean

Born Birmingham 22.1.67.   Ht 5 11
Wt 13 08
Forward. From Halesowen.

Season	Club		
1989–90	Aston Villa	—	—
1989–90	*Scarborough*	3	2
1989–90	*Bury*	6	1
1989–90	Shrewsbury T	13	5
1990–91		43	6

SPINK, Nigel

Born Chelmsford 8.8.58.   Ht 6 1
Wt 14 10
Goalkeeper. From Chelmsford C. England
B, 1 full cap.

Season	Club		
1976–77	Aston Villa	—	—
1977–78		—	—
1978–79		—	—
1979–80		1	—
1980–81		—	—
1981–82		—	—
1982–83		22	—
1983–84		28	—
1984–85		19	—
1985–86		31	—
1986–87		32	—
1987–88		44	—
1988–89		34	—
1989–90		38	—
1990–91		34	—

SPOONER, Steve

Born London 25.1.61.   Ht 5 10   Wt 12 00
Midfield. From Apprentice.

Season	Club		
1978–79	Derby Co	1	—
1979–80		1	—
1980–81		2	—
1981–82		4	—
1981–82	Halifax T	29	—
1982–83		43	11
1983–84	Chesterfield	20	3
1984–85		41	6
1985–86		32	5
1986–87	Hereford U	42	11
1987–88		42	8

Season	Club		
1988–89	York C	31	5
1989–90		41	6
1990–91	Rotherham U	19	1
1990–91	Mansfield T	12	—

SRNICEK, Pavel

Born Ostrava 10.3.68.   Ht 6 2   Wt 14 09
Goalkeeper. From Banik Ostrava.
Czechoslovakia full caps.

Season	Club		
1990–91	Newcastle U	7	—

STAINROD, Simon

Born Sheffield 1.2.59.   Ht 5 10   Wt 12 9
Forward. From Apprentice. England
Youth.

Season	Club		
1975–76	Sheffield U	7	2
1976–77		21	3
1977–78		25	6
1978–79		14	3
1978–79	Oldham Ath	14	5
1979–80		37	11
1980–81		18	5
1980–81	QPR	15	4
1981–82		39	17
1982–83		31	9
1983–84		41	13
1984–85		19	5
1984–85	Sheffield W	9	1
1985–86		6	1
1985–86	Aston Villa	30	10
1986–87		29	6
1987–88		4	—
1987–88	Stoke C	12	2
1988–89		16	4
From Strasbourg			
1990–91	Falkirk	37	16

STANCLIFFE, Paul

Born Sheffield 5.5.58.   Ht 6 2   Wt 13 03
Defender. From Apprentice.

Season	Club		
1975–76	Rotherham U	42	2
1976–77		46	—
1977–78		32	3
1978–79		33	—

Season	Club	League Appearances/Goals	
1979–80	....	33	1
1980–81	....	44	—
1981–82	....	42	2
1982–83	....	13	—
1983–84	Sheffield U	43	1
1984–85	....	33	1
1985–86	....	40	1
1986–87	....	36	2
1987–88	....	41	3
1988–89	....	42	3
1989–90	....	40	1
1990–91	....	3	—
1990–91	*Rotherham U*	5	—
1990–91	Wolverhampton W	17	—

STANISLAUS, Roger

Born Hammersmith 2.11.68.   Ht 5 9
Wt 12 11
Defender. From Trainee.

1986–87	Arsenal........................	—	—
1987–88	Brentford	37	2
1988–89	....	43	1
1989–90	....	31	1
1990–91	Bury	44	2

STANNARD, Jim

Born London 6.10.62.   Ht 6 0   Wt 13 02
Goalkeeper. Local.

1980–81	Fulham	17	—
1981–82	....	2	—
1982–83	....	—	—
1983–84	....	15	—
1984–85	....	7	—
1984–85	*Charlton Ath*	1	—
1984–85	*Southend U*	17	—
1985–86	Southend U.................	46	—
1986–87	....	46	—
1987–88	Fulham	46	—
1988–89	....	45	—
1989–90	....	44	1
1990–91	....	42	—

STANT, Phil

Born Bolton 13.10.62.   Ht 6 1   Wt 12 07
Forward. From Camberley.

1982–83	Reading.......................	4	2
From Army			
1986–87	Hereford U	9	1
1987–88	....	39	9
1988–89	....	41	28
1989–90	Notts Co.....................	22	6
1990–91	....	—	—
1990–91	*Blackpool*	12	5
1990–91	*Lincoln C*	4	—
1990–91	*Huddersfield T*.............	5	1
1990–91	Fulham	19	5

STAPLETON, Frank

Born Dublin 10.7.56.   Ht 6 0   Wt 13 01
Forward. From Apprentice. Eire Youth,
70 full caps.

1973–74	Arsenal........................	—	—
1974–75	....	1	—
1975–76	....	25	4
1976–77	....	40	13
1977–78	....	39	13
1978–79	....	41	17
1979–80	....	39	14
1980–81	....	40	14
1981–82	Manchester U	41	13
1982–83	....	41	14
1983–84	....	42	13
1984–85	....	24	6
1985–86	....	41	7
1986–87	....	34	7
1987–88	Ajax	4	—
1987–88	Derby Co.....................	10	1
From Le Havre			
1989–90	Blackburn R	43	3
1990–91	....	38	10

STARBUCK, Philip

Born Nottingham 24.11.68.   Ht 5 10
Wt 10 13
Forward. From Apprentice.

1986–87	Nottingham F.............	5	2
1987–88	....	10	—
1987–88	*Birmingham C*.............	3	—
1988–89	Nottingham F.............	7	—
1989–90	....	2	—
1989–90	*Hereford U*..................	6	—

Season	Club	App	Goals
1990–91	Nottingham F	12	—
1990–91	*Blackburn R*	6	1

STATHAM, Brian

Born Zimbabwe 21.5.69.   Ht 5 11
Wt 11 00
Defender. From Apprentice. England
Youth, Under-21.

Season	Club	App	Goals
1987–88	Tottenham H	18	—
1988–89		6	—
1989–90		—	—
1990–91		—	—
1990–91	*Reading*	8	—

STATHAM, Derek

Born Wolverhampton 24.3.59.   Ht 5 5
Wt 11 10
Defender. From Apprentice. England
Youth, Under-21, B, 3 full caps.

Season	Club	App	Goals
1976–77	WBA	16	1
1977–78		40	—
1978–79		39	1
1979–80		16	—
1980–81		31	—
1981–82		35	—
1982–83		32	2
1983–84		16	—
1984–85		30	4
1985–86		37	—
1986–87		6	—
1987–88		1	—
1987–88	Southampton	38	—
1988–89		26	2
1989–90	Stoke C	19	—
1990–91		22	1

STAUNTON, Steve

Born Drogheda 19.1.69.   Ht 5 11
Wt 11 02
Defender. From Dundalk. Eire Under-21,
26 full caps.

Season	Club	App	Goals
1986–87	Liverpool	—	—
1987–88		—	—
1987–88	*Bradford C*	8	—

Season	Club	App	Goals
1988–89	Liverpool	21	—
1989–90		20	—
1990–91		24	—

STEBBING, Gary

Born Croydon 11.8.65.   Ht 5 9   Wt 11 06
Defender. From Apprentice. England
Youth.

Season	Club	App	Goals
1982–83	Crystal Palace	—	—
1983–84		31	2
1984–85		24	1
1985–86		3	—
1985–86	*Southend U*	5	—
1986–87	Crystal Palace	23	—
1987–88		21	—
From KV Ostend.			
1989–90	Maidstone U	6	—
1990–91		33	1

STEEL, Jim

Born Dumfries 4.12.59.   Ht 6 3   Wt 14 00
Forward. From Apprentice.

Season	Club	App	Goals
1978–79	Oldham Ath	7	4
1979–80		33	10
1980–81		24	3
1981–82		37	7
1982–83		7	—
1982–83	*Wigan Ath*	2	2
1982–83	*Wrexham*	9	6
1982–83	Port Vale	13	3
1983–84		15	3
1983–84	Wrexham	21	—
1984–85		45	14
1985–86		43	14
1986–87		37	17
1987–88		18	6
1987–88	Tranmere R	29	7
1988–89		44	7
1989–90		36	5
1990–91		44	6

STEELE, Tim

Born Coventry 1.2.67.   Ht 5 9   Wt 10 10
Forward. From Apprentice.

Season	Club	App	Goals
1985–86	Shrewsbury T	2	—

1986–87	....	11	1
1987–88	....	33	3
1988–89	....	15	1
1988–89	Wolverhampton W	11	1
1989–90	....	15	1
1990–91	....	28	2

STEIN, Brian

Born S. Africa 19.10.57.   Ht 5 10
Wt 11 08
Forward. From Edgware T. England
Under-21, 1 full cap.

1977–78	Luton T	24	3
1978–79	....	34	10
1979–80	....	42	8
1980–81	....	42	18
1981–82	....	42	21
1982–83	....	21	15
1983–84	....	42	9
1984–85	....	42	9
1985–86	....	33	14
1986–87	....	38	12
1987–88	....	28	9
To Caen			

STEIN, Mark

Born S. Africa 28.1.66.   Ht 5 5   Wt 11 04
Forward. England Youth.

1983–84	Luton T	1	—
1984–85	....	1	—
1985–86	....	6	—
1985–86	*Aldershot*	2	1
1986–87	Luton T	21	8
1987–88	....	25	11
1988–89	QPR	31	4
1989–90	....	2	—
1989–90	Oxford U	41	9
1990–91	....	34	8

STEINMANN, Gijfrertus

Born Utrecht 2.4.61.
Defender. From Utrecht.

| 1990–91 | Dundee U .... | 14 | 1 |

STEJSKAL, Jan

Born Czechoslovakia 15.1.62.   Ht 6 3
Wt 12 00
Goalkeeper. From Sparta Prague.
Czechoslovakia full caps.

| 1990–91 | QPR .... | 26 | — |

STEMP, Wayne

Born Epsom 9.9.70.   Ht 5 11   Wt 11 02
Defender. From Trainee.

1988–89	Brighton	—	—
1989–90	....	2	—
1990–91	....	2	—

STEPHENS, Lee

Born Cardiff 30.9.71.   Ht 5 7   Wt 10 03
Midfield. From Trainee.

| 1990–91 | Cardiff C .... | 3 | — |

STEPHENSON, Geoff

Born Tynemouth 28.4.70   Ht 5 7
Wt 11 00
Defender. From Trainee.

1987–88	Grimsby T	—	—
1988–89	....	14	—
1989–90	....	7	—
1990–91	....	—	—

STEPHENSON, Paul

Born Wallsend 2.1.68.   Ht 5 10   Wt 10 9
Forward. From Apprentice. England
Youth.

1985–86	Newcastle U	22	1
1986–87	....	24	—
1987–88	....	7	—
1988–89	....	8	—
1989–90	Millwall	12	1
1989–90	....	23	2
1990–91	....	30	1

STERLAND, Mel

Born Sheffield 1.10.61.   Ht 6 0   Wt 13 05
Defender. From Apprentice. England
Under-21, B, 1 full cap. Football League.

Season	Club	Apps	Goals
1978–79	Sheffield W	2	1
1979–80		2	—
1980–81		22	2
1981–82		27	—
1982–83		35	—
1983–84		39	8
1984–85		24	2
1985–86		38	8
1986–87		30	2
1987–88		38	8
1988–89		22	6
1988–89	Rangers	9	3
1989–90	Leeds U	42	5
1990–91		38	5

STERLING, Worrell

Born Bethnal Green 8.6.65.   Ht 5 7
Wt 10 11
Midfield. From Apprentice.

Season	Club	Apps	Goals
1982–83	Watford	3	—
1983–84		10	1
1984–85		15	4
1985–86		24	3
1986–87		18	4
1987–88		21	2
1988–89		3	—
1988–89	Peterborough U	12	3
1989–90		46	5
1990–91		46	9

STEVEN, Trevor

Born Berwick 21.9.63.   Ht 5 8   Wt 10 09
Midfield. From Apprentice. England
Under-21, 30 full caps.

Season	Club	Apps	Goals
1980–81	Burnley	1	—
1981–82		36	3
1982–83		39	8
1983–84	Everton	27	1
1984–85		40	12
1985–86		41	9
1986–87		41	14
1987–88		36	6
1988–89		29	6
1989–90	Rangers	34	3
1990–91		19	2

STEVENS, Gary

Born Hillingdon 30.3.62.   Ht 6 0
Wt 12 00
Defender. From Apprentice. England
Under-21, 7 full caps.

Season	Club	Apps	Goals
1979–80	Brighton	26	1
1980–81		34	1
1981–82		32	—
1982–83		41	—
1983–84	Tottenham H	40	4
1984–85		28	—
1985–86		29	2
1986–87		20	—
1987–88		18	—
1988–89		5	—
1989–90		7	—
1989–90	Portsmouth	21	1
1990–91		31	2

STEVENS, Gary

Born Barrow 27.3.63.   Ht 5 11   Wt 10 11
Defender. From Apprentice. England 42
full caps.

Season	Club	Apps	Goals
1980–81	Everton	—	—
1981–82		19	1
1982–83		28	—
1983–84		27	1
1984–85		37	3
1985–86		41	1
1986–87		25	2
1987–88		31	—
1988–89	Rangers	35	1
1989–90		35	1
1990–91		36	4

STEVENS, Ian

Born Malta 21.10.66.   Ht 5 9   Wt 12 00
Forward. From Trainee.

Season	Club	Apps	Goals
1984–85	Preston NE	4	1
1985–86		7	1
1986–87	Stockport Co	2	—
From Lancaster C			
1986–87	Bolton W	8	2
1987–88		9	—
1988–89		21	5

Season	Club	Apps	Goals
1989–90		4	—
1990–91		5	—

STEVENS, Keith

Born Merton 21.6.64. Ht 6 0 Wt 12 12
Defender. From Apprentice.

Season	Club	Apps	Goals
1980–81	Millwall	1	—
1981–82		7	—
1982–83		26	—
1983–84		17	—
1984–85		41	—
1985–86		33	1
1986–87		35	1
1987–88		35	1
1988–89		23	—
1989–90		28	—
1990–91		42	1

STEVENSON, Andy

Born Scunthorpe 29.9.67. Ht 6 0
Wt 12 03
Midfield. From school.

Season	Club	Apps	Goals
1985–86	Scunthorpe U	2	—
1986–87		7	—
1987–88		8	—
1988–89		26	—
1989–90		24	1
1990–91		9	—

STEWART, Billy

Born Liverpool 1.1.65. Ht 5 11 Wt 11 07
Goalkeeper. From Apprentice.

Season	Club	Apps	Goals
1982–83	Liverpool	—	—
1983–84		—	—
1984–85	Wigan Ath	6	—
1985–86		8	—
1986–87	Chester C	29	—
1987–88		27	—
1988–89		46	—
1989–90		46	—
1990–91		38	—

STEWART, Ian

Born Belfast 10.9.61. Ht 5 7 Wt 10 9
Forward. From juniors. Northern Ireland
Schools Youth, 31 full caps.

Season	Club	Apps	Goals
1980–81	QPR	1	—
1981–82		3	—
1982–83		19	—
1982–83	*Millwall*	11	3
1983–84	QPR	31	2
1984–85		13	—
1985–86	Newcastle U	28	2
1986–87		14	1
1987–88	Portsmouth	1	—
1987–88	*Brentford*	7	—
1988–89	Portsmouth	—	—
1988–89	Aldershot	22	—
1989–90		43	—
1990–91		36	—

STEWART, Paul

Born Manchester 7.10.64. Ht 5 11
Wt 11 03
Forward. From Apprentice. England
Youth, B, Under-21.

Season	Club	Apps	Goals
1981–82	Blackpool	14	3
1982–83		38	7
1983–84		44	10
1984–85		31	7
1985–86		42	8
1986–87		32	21
1986–87	Manchester C	11	2
1987–88		40	24
1988–89	Tottenham H	30	12
1989–90		28	8
1990–91		35	3

STEWART, Ray

Born Perth 7.9.59. Ht 5 11 Wt 11 13
Defender. From Errol Rovers. Scotland
Schools, Under-21, 10 full caps.

Season	Club	Apps	Goals
1975–76	Dundee U	—	—
1976–77		1	—
1977–78		6	1
1978–79		34	4
1979–80		3	—
1979–80	West Ham U	38	10
1980–81		41	5
1981–82		42	10
1982–83		39	8
1983–84		42	7

Season	Club	League Appearances/Goals	
1984–85		37	6
1985–86		39	6
1986–87		23	4
1987–88		33	4
1988–89		6	2
1989–90		—	—
1990–91		5	—

STEWART, Sandy

Born Bellshill 14.10.65   Ht 5 9   Wt 10 10
Midfield. From Pollok J

Season	Club	League Appearances/Goals	
1987–88	Hearts	—	—
1988–89		—	—
1988–89	Kilmarnock	7	1
1989–90	Airdrieonians	8	3
1990–91		25	—

STICKROTH, Thomas

Born Stuttgart 13.4.65.
Midfield. From Bayer Uerdingen.

Season	Club	League Appearances/Goals	
1989–90	St Mirren	7	—
1990–91		31	1

STILES, John

Born Manchester 6.5.64.   Ht 5 9
Wt 11 08
Midfield. From Vancouver W.

Season	Club	League Appearances/Goals	
1984–85	Leeds U	1	—
1985–86		12	1
1986–87		29	—
1987–88		13	1
1988–89		10	—
1989–90	Doncaster R	42	2
1990–91		37	—

STIMSON, Mark

Born Plaistow 27.12.67.   Ht 5 11
Wt 11 00
Defender. From Trainee.

Season	Club	League Appearances/Goals	
1984–85	Tottenham H	—	—
1985–86		—	—
1986–87		1	—
1987–88		—	—
1987–88	*Leyton Orient*	10	—
1988–89	Tottenham H	1	—
1988–89	*Gillingham*	18	—
1989–90	Newcastle U	37	1
1990–91		23	1

STOCKWELL, Mike

Born Chelmsford 14.2.65.   Ht 5 6
Wt 10 2
Midfield. From Apprentice.

Season	Club	League Appearances/Goals	
1982–83	Ipswich T	—	—
1983–84		—	—
1984–85		—	—
1985–86		8	—
1986–87		21	1
1987–88		43	1
1988–89		23	2
1989–90		34	3
1990–91		44	6

STORER, Stuart

Born Harborough 16.1.67.   Ht 5 11
Wt 11 08
Forward. Local.

Season	Club	League Appearances/Goals	
1983–84	Mansfield T	1	—
1984–85	Birmingham C	—	—
1985–86		2	—
1986–87		6	—
1986–87	Everton	—	—
1987–88		—	—
1987–88	*Wigan Ath*	12	—
1987–88	Bolton W	15	1
1988–89		23	2
1989–90		38	4
1990–91		35	5

STOUTT, Stephen

Born Halifax 5.4.64.   Ht 5 8   Wt 11 06
Defender. Local.

Season	Club	League Appearances/Goals	
1983–84	Huddersfield T	3	—
1984–85		3	—
1984–85	Wolverhampton W	—	—
1985–86		28	—

Season	Club	App	Goals
1986–87	....	44	4
1987–88	....	22	1
1988–89	Grimsby T	2	1
1989–90	....	1	—
1989–90	Lincoln C..................	21	—
1990–91	....	25	1

STOWELL, Mike

Born Preston 19.4.65. Ht 6 2 Wt 11 10
Goalkeeper. From Leyland Motors.

Season	Club	App	Goals
1984–85	Preston NE..................	—	—
1985–86	....	—	—
1985–86	Everton	—	—
1986–87	....	—	—
1987–88	*Chester C*..................	14	—
1987–88	*York C*....................	6	—
1987–88	*Manchester C*.............	14	—
1988–89	Everton	—	—
1988–89	*Port Vale*..................	7	—
1988–89	*Wolverhampton W*.......	7	—
1989–90	Everton	—	—
1989–90	*Preston NE*	2	—
1990–91	Wolverhampton W	39	—

STRACHAN, Gordon

Born Edinburgh 9.2.57. Ht 5 6 Wt 10 06
Midfield. Scotland Youth, Under-21, 46
full caps.

Season	Club	App	Goals
1974–75	Dundee..................	1	—
1975–76	....	23	6
1976–77	....	36	7
1977–78	Aberdeen..................	12	2
1978–79	....	31	5
1979–80	....	33	10
1980–81	....	20	6
1981–82	....	30	7
1982–83	....	32	12
1983–84	....	25	13
1984–85	Manchester U	41	15
1985–86	....	28	5
1986–87	....	34	4
1987–88	....	36	8
1988–89	....	21	1
1988–89	Leeds U	11	3
1989–90	....	46	16
1990–91	....	34	7

STREETE, Floyd

Born W. Indies 5.5.59. Ht 5 11 Wt 14 00
Defender. From Rivet Sports.

Season	Club	App	Goals
1976–77	Cambridge U	3	1
1977–78	....	21	3
1978–79	....	13	1
1979–80	....	21	1
1980–81	....	22	4
1981–82	....	31	5
1982–83	....	14	4
From Utrecht and SC Cambuur.			
1984–85	Derby Co..................	30	—
1985–86	....	5	—
1985–86	Wolverhampton W	25	1
1986–87	....	35	—
1987–88	....	44	—
1988–89	....	38	5
1989–90	....	17	—
1990–91	Reading..................	4	—

STRINGFELLOW, Ian

Born Nottingham 8.5.69. Ht 5 9
Wt 10 03
Forward. From Apprentice.

Season	Club	App	Goals
1985–86	Mansfield T................	3	—
1986–87	....	22	4
1987–88	....	30	8
1988–89	....	8	1
1989–90	....	19	3
1990–91	....	24	2

STRODDER, Gary

Born Leeds 1.4.65. Ht 6 1 Wt 12 06
Defender. From Apprentice.

Season	Club	App	Goals
1982–83	Lincoln C..................	8	—
1983–84	....	22	1
1984–85	....	26	2
1985–86	....	43	1
1986–87	....	33	2
1986–87	West Ham U	12	—
1987–88	....	30	1
1988–89	....	7	—
1989–90	....	16	1
1990–91	WBA..................	34	1

STUART, Graham

Born Tooting, London 24.10.70. Ht 5 8
Wt 11 06
Forward. From Trainee. FA Schools.
England Under-21.

1989–90	Chelsea	2	1
1990–91		19	4

STUART, Mark

Born Hammersmith 15.12.66. Ht 5 10
Wt 11 03
Forward. From QPR Schoolboy.

1984–85	Charlton Ath	6	1
1985–86		30	12
1986–87		36	9
1987–88		31	6
1988–89		4	—
1988–89	Plymouth Arg	32	5
1989–90		25	6
1989–90	*Ipswich T.*	5	2
1990–91	Bradford C	13	2

STUBBS, Alan

Born Kirkby 6.10.71. Ht 6 2 Wt 12 12
Defender. From Trainee.

1990–91	Bolton W	23	—

STURRIDGE, Simon

Born Birmingham 9.12.69 Ht 5 5
Wt 10 07
Forward. From Trainee.

1988–89	Birmingham C	21	3
1989–90		31	10
1990–91		38	6

SUCKLING, Perry

Born Leyton 12.10.65. Ht 6 1 Wt 11 02
Goalkeeper. From Apprentice. England
Youth, Under-21.

1982–83	Coventry C	3	—
1983–84		24	—
1984–85		—	—
1985–86		—	—
1986–87	Manchester C	37	—
1987–88		2	—
1987–88	Crystal Palace	17	—
1988–89		27	—
1989–90		12	—
1989–90	*West Ham U*	6	—
1990–91	Crystal Palace	—	—

SULLEY, Chris

Born Camberwell 3.12.59. Ht 5 8
Wt 10 00
Defender. From Apprentice.

1978–79	Chelsea	—	—
1979–80		—	—
1980–81		—	—
1980–81	Bournemouth	8	—
1981–82		46	—
1982–83		46	1
1983–84		46	2
1984–85		23	—
1985–86		37	—
1986–87	Dundee U	7	—
1986–87	Blackburn R	13	—
1987–88		34	—
1988–89		19	—
1989–90		36	—
1990–91		25	3

SULLIVAN, Neil

Born Sutton 24.2.70 Ht 6 0 Wt 12 01
Goalkeeper. From Trainee.

1988–89	Wimbledon	—	—
1989–90		—	—
1990–91		1	—

SUMMERBEE, Nicky

Born Altrincham 26.8.71. Ht 5 11
Wt 11 08
Forward. From Trainee.

1989–90	Swindon T	1	—
1990–91		7	—

SUMMERFIELD, Kevin

Born Walsall 7.1.59.   Ht 5 11   Wt 11 00
Midfield. From Apprentice.

Season	Club		
1976–77	WBA	—	—
1977–78		—	—
1978–79		2	1
1979–80		3	1
1980–81		—	—
1981–82		4	2
1982–83	Birmingham C	5	1
1982–83	Walsall	21	9
1983–84		33	8
1984–85	Cardiff C	10	1
1984–85	Plymouth Arg	17	2
1985–86		26	7
1986–87		28	9
1987–88		37	5
1988–89		20	2
1989–90		10	1
1989–90	*Exeter C*	4	—
1990–91	Plymouth Arg	1	—
1990–91	Shrewsbury T	32	5

SUMMERS, Chris

Born Cardiff 6.1.72.   Ht 5 11   Wt 11 02
Forward. From Trainee.

Season	Club		
1990–91	Cardiff C	3	—

SUSSEX, Andy

Born Enfield 23.11.64.   Ht 6 0   Wt 11 06
Forward. From Apprentice.

Season	Club		
1981–82	Orient	8	1
1982–83		24	2
1983–84		29	6
1984–85		19	2
1985–86		36	4
1986–87		20	1
1987–88		8	1
1988–89	Crewe Alex	25	4
1989–90		33	9
1990–91		44	11

SUTCH, Daryl

Born Lowestoft 11.9.71.   Ht 6 0
Wt 12 00
Midfield. From Trainee. England Youth.

Season	Club		
1989–90	Norwich C	—	—
1990–91		4	—

SUTTON, Chris

Born Nottingham 10.3.73.
Forward. From Trainee.

Season	Club		
1990–91	Norwich C	2	—

SUTTON, Steve

Born Hartington 16.4.61.   Ht 6 1
Wt 13 07
Goalkeeper. From Apprentice.

Season	Club		
1980–81	Nottingham F	1	—
1980–81	*Mansfield T*	8	—
1981–82	Nottingham F	1	—
1982–83		17	—
1983–84		6	—
1984–85		14	—
1984–85	*Derby Co*	14	—
1985–86	Nottingham F	31	—
1986–87		28	—
1987–88		35	—
1988–89		36	—
1989–90		30	—
1990–91		—	—
1990–91	*Coventry C*	1	—

SWAILES, Chris

Born Gateshead 19.10.70.   Ht 6 1
Wt 12 11
Defender. From Trainee.

Season	Club		
1989–90	Ipswich T	—	—
1990–91		—	—
1990–91	Peterborough U	—	—

SWAIN, Kenny

Born Birkenhead 28.1.52.   Ht 5 9
Wt 11 07
Defender. From Wycombe W.

Season	Club	League Appearances/Goals	
1973–74	Chelsea	7	1
1974–75		—	—
1975–76		25	4
1976–77		36	13
1977–78		36	4
1978–79		15	4
1978–79	Aston Villa	24	2
1979–80		41	—
1980–81		42	—
1981–82		39	—
1982–83		2	—
1982–83	Nottingham F	32	1
1983–84		41	1
1984–85		39	—
1985–86	Portsmouth	39	—
1986–87		42	—
1987–88		32	—
1987–88	*WBA*	7	1
1988–89	Crewe Alex	41	—
1989–90		43	1
1990–91		41	—

SWAN, Peter

Born Leeds 29.9.66. Ht 6 0 Wt 12 00
Forward. Local.

Season	Club	League Appearances/Goals	
1984–85	Leeds U	—	—
1985–86		16	3
1986–87		7	—
1987–88		25	8
1988–89		1	—
1988–89	Hull C	11	1
1989–90		31	11
1990–91		38	12

SWANN, Gary

Born York 11.4.62. Ht 5 9 Wt 11 12
Midfield. From Apprentice.

Season	Club	League Appearances/Goals	
1980–81	Hull C	20	2
1981–82		20	—
1982–83		25	—
1983–84		41	2
1984–85		32	3
1985–86		39	2
1986–87		9	—
1986–87	Preston NE	30	5
1987–88		46	12

Season	Club	League Appearances/Goals	
1988–89		18	2
1989–90		46	8
1990–91		30	5

SWEENEY, Paul

Born Glasgow 10.1.65 Ht 5 8 Wt 11 05
Midfield. From St Kentigerns Acad.

Season	Club	League Appearances/Goals	
1981–82	Raith R	—	—
1982–83		2	—
1983–84		29	1
1984–85		32	—
1985–86		37	3
1986–87		38	—
1987–88		39	2
1988–89		28	2
1988–89	Newcastle U	8	—
1989–90		19	—
1990–91		9	—
1990–91	St Johnstone	8	—

SYMONS, Kit

Born Basingstoke 8.3.71 Ht 6 1
Wt 10 10
Defender. From Trainee. Wales Under-21.

Season	Club	League Appearances/Goals	
1988–89	Portsmouth	2	—
1989–90		1	—
1990–91		1	—

TAGGART, Gerry

Born Belfast 18.10.70 Ht 6 1 Wt 12 03
Defender. From Trainee. Northern Ireland
Under-23, 7 full caps.

Season	Club	Apps	Goals
1988–89	Manchester C	11	1
1989–90		1	—
1989–90	Barnsley	21	2
1990–91		30	2

TAIT, Mick

Born Wallsend 30.9.56. Ht 5 11
Wt 12 05
Midfield. From Apprentice.

Season	Club	Apps	Goals
1974–75	Oxford U	4	—
1975–76		37	12
1976–77		23	11
1976–77	Carlisle U	13	3
1977–78		43	10
1978–79		46	7
1979–80		4	—
1979–80	Hull C	33	3
1980–81	Portsmouth	38	8
1981–82		35	9
1982–83		44	6
1983–84		36	3
1984–85		33	1
1985–86		26	2
1986–87		28	1
1987–88		—	—
1987–88	Reading	35	2
1988–89		36	4
1989–90		28	3
1990–91	Darlington	45	2

TAIT, Paul

Born Sutton Coldfield 31.1.71. Ht 6 1
Wt 10 00
Midfield. From Trainee.

Season	Club	Apps	Goals
1987–88	Birmingham C	1	—
1988–89		10	—
1989–90		14	2
1990–91		17	3

TALBOT, Brian

Born Ipswich 21.7.53. Ht 5 10 Wt 12 00
Midfield. From Apprentice. England
Under-21, B, 6 full caps.

Season	Club	Apps	Goals
1972–73	Ipswich T	—	—
1973–74		15	3
1974–75		40	8
1975–76		19	2
1976–77		42	5
1977–78		40	4
1978–79		21	3
1978–79	Arsenal	20	—
1979–80		42	1
1980–81		40	7
1981–82		42	7
1982–83		42	9
1983–84		27	6
1984–85		41	10
1985–86	Watford	41	7
1986–87		7	1
1986–87	Stoke C	32	3
1987–88		22	2
1987–88	WBA	15	2
1988–89		39	2
1989–90		20	1
1990–91	Fulham	5	1
1990–91	Aldershot	10	—

TALLON, Darren

Born Glasgow 1.6.72.
Defender. From Trainee.

Season	Club	Apps	Goals
1990–91	Plymouth Arg	1	—

TANKARD, Allen

Born Fleet 21.5.69. Ht 5 10 Wt 11 07
Defender. From Trainee. England Youth.

Season	Club	Apps	Goals
1985–86	Southampton	3	—
1986–87		2	—
1987–88		—	—
1988–89	Wigan Ath	33	1
1989–90		45	1
1990–91		46	1

TANNER, Nick

Born Bristol 24.5.65. Ht 6 2 Wt 13 07
Defender. From Mangotsfield.

Season	Club		
1984–85	Bristol R	—	—
1985–86		37	2
1986–87		44	1
1987–88		26	—
1988–89	Liverpool	—	—
1989–90		4	—
1989–90	*Norwich C*	6	—
1990–91	Liverpool	—	—
1990–91	*Swindon T*	7	—

TAYLOR, Alex

Born Baillieston 13.6.62 Ht 5 7 Wt 10 11
Midfield. From Blantyre St. J.

Season	Club		
1982–83	Dundee U	3	—
1983–84		9	1
1984–85		21	5
1985–86		—	—
1986–87	Hamilton A	25	1
1987–88		41	4
1988–89	Walsall	13	3
1989–90		32	3
1990–91		—	—
1990–91	Falkirk	29	2

TAYLOR, Andrew

Born Rawmarsh 19.1.73.
Defender. From Trainee.

Season	Club		
1990–91	Rotherham U	5	—

TAYLOR, Bob

Born Horden 3.2.67. Ht 5 10 Wt 11 09
Forward. From Horden CW.

Season	Club		
1985–86	Leeds U	2	—
1986–87		2	—
1987–88		32	9
1988–89		6	—
1988–89	Bristol C	12	8
1989–90		37	27
1990–91		39	11

TAYLOR, Colin

Born Liverpool 25.12.71. Ht 6 0
Wt 12 07
Forward. From Trainee. England Youth.

Season	Club		
1989–90	Wolverhampton W	—	—
1990–91		15	2

TAYLOR, John

Born Norwich 24.10.64 Ht 6 2 Wt 11 12
Forward. Local.

Season	Club		
1982–83	Colchester U	—	—
1983–84		—	—
1984–85		—	—
From Sudbury			
1988–89	Cambridge U	40	12
1989–90		45	15
1990–91		40	14

TAYLOR, Kevin

Born Wakefield 22.1.61. Ht 5 9
Wt 11 01
Midfield. From Apprentice.

Season	Club		
1978–79	Sheffield W	5	—
1979–80		21	6
1980–81		30	5
1981–82		35	7
1982–83		29	3
1983–84		5	—
1984–85	Derby Co	22	2
1984–85	Crystal Palace	13	—
1985–86		31	6
1986–87		41	8
1987–88		2	—
1987–88	Scunthorpe U	35	5
1988–89		41	8
1989–90		39	8
1990–91		42	4

TAYLOR, Mark

Born Hartlepool 20.11.64. Ht 5 7
Wt 10 00
Midfield. Local.

Season	Club		
1982–83	Hartlepool U	—	—

Season	Club	League Appearances/Goals
1983–84		6 —
1984–85		36 4
1985–86		5 —
1985–86	*Crewe Alex*	3 —
1986–87	Blackpool	40 14
1987–88		41 21
1988–89		9 3
1989–90		— —
1990–91		19 3
1990–91	*Cardiff C*	6 3

TAYLOR, Mark

Born Walsall 22.2.66. Ht 5 8 Wt 11 08
Midfield. Local.

Season	Club	League Appearances/Goals
1984–85	Walsall	4 —
1985–86		18 2
1986–87		17 —
1987–88		40 1
1988–89		34 1
1989–90	Sheffield W	9 —
1990–91		— —
1990–91	*Shrewsbury T*	19 2

TAYLOR, Martin

Born Tamworth 9.12.66. Ht 5 11
Wt 12 04
Goalkeeper. From Mile Oak R.

Season	Club	League Appearances/Goals
1986–87	Derby Co	— —
1987–88		— —
1987–88	*Carlisle U*	10 —
1987–88	*Scunthorpe U*	8 —
1988–89	Derby Co	— —
1989–90		3 —
1990–91		7 —

TAYLOR, Robert

Born Norwich 30.4.71. Ht 6 0 Wt 11 07
Forward. From Trainee.

Season	Club	League Appearances/Goals
1989–90	Norwich C	— —
1990–91		— —
1990–91	*Leyton Orient*	3 1

TAYLOR, Scott

Born Portsmouth 23.11.70 Ht 5 9
Wt 11 00
Midfield. From Trainee.

Season	Club	League Appearances/Goals
1988–89	Reading	3 —
1989–90		29 2
1990–91		32 1

TAYLOR, Shaun

Born Plymouth 26.3.63. Ht 6 1 Wt 13 00
Defender. From Bideford.

Season	Club	League Appearances/Goals
1986–87	Exeter C	23 —
1987–88		41 1
1988–89		46 6
1989–90		45 5
1990–91		45 4

TEALE, Shaun

Born Southport 10.3.64 Ht 6 0 Wt 13 07
Defender. From Southport, Northwich
Vics, Weymouth.

Season	Club	League Appearances/Goals
1988–89	Bournemouth	20 —
1989–90		34 —
1990–91		46 4

TELFER, Paul

Born Edinburgh 21.10.71. Ht 5 9
Wt 10 02
Midfield. From Trainee.

Season	Club	League Appearances/Goals
1988–89	Luton T	— —
1989–90		— —
1990–91		1 —

TERRY, Peter

Born Enfield 11.9.72.
Midfield. From Trainee.

Season	Club	League Appearances/Goals
1990–91	Aldershot	1 —

TERRY, Steve

Born Clapton 14.6.62. Ht 6 1 Wt 13 05
Defender. From Apprentice.

Season	Club	League Appearances/Goals
1979–80	Watford	2 —
1980–81		5 —
1981–82		26 2

Season	Club	League Appearances/Goals	
1982–83		7	1
1983–84		17	1
1984–85		38	4
1985–86		41	4
1986–87		18	2
1987–88		6	—
1988–89	Hull C	33	1
1989–90		29	3
1989–90	Northampton T	17	2
1990–91		46	6

TESTER, Paul

Born Stroud 10.3.59. Ht 5 8 Wt 10 12
Forward. From Cheltenham T.

Season	Club	League Appearances/Goals	
1983–84	Shrewsbury T	8	—
1984–85		23	5
1984–85	*Hereford U*	4	—
1985–86	Shrewsbury T	9	1
1986–87		29	5
1987–88		29	1
1988–89	Hereford U	44	6
1989–90		26	5
1990–91		44	3

THACKERAY, Andy

Born Huddersfield 13.2.68. Ht 5 9
Wt 11 00
Midfield.

Season	Club	League Appearances/Goals	
1985–86	Manchester C	—	—
1986–87	Huddersfield T	2	—
1986–87	Newport Co	11	3
1987–88		43	1
1988–89	Wrexham	35	2
1989–90		34	7
1990–91		41	2

THIELE, Gunter

Season	Club	League Appearances/Goals	
1990–91	St Mirren	1	—

THOMAS, Andy

Born Oxford 16.12.62. Ht 6 0 Wt 10 10
Forward. From Apprentice.

Season	Club	League Appearances/Goals	
1980–81	Oxford U	9	1

Season	Club	League Appearances/Goals	
1981–82		39	14
1982–83		24	7
1982–83	*Fulham*	4	2
1982–83	*Derby Co*	1	—
1983–84	Oxford U	23	7
1984–85		4	1
1985–86		17	2
1986–87		—	—
1986–87	Newcastle U	27	6
1987–88		4	—
1988–89	Bradford C	23	5
1989–90	Plymouth Arg	36	12
1990–91		14	6

THOMAS, Dean

Born Bedworth 19.12.61 Ht 5 9
Wt 11 08
Defender. From Nuneaton Borough.

Season	Club	League Appearances/Goals	
1981–82	Wimbledon	18	—
1982–83		24	5
1983–84		15	3
From Fortuna DusseldorfH			
1988–89	Northampton T	43	9
1989–90		31	2
1989–90	Notts Co	10	1
1990–91		44	3

THOMAS, Geoff

Born Manchester 5.8.64. Ht 5 10
Wt 12 04
Midfield. Local. England B, 7 full caps.

Season	Club	League Appearances/Goals	
1981–82	Rochdale	—	—
1982–83		1	—
1983–84		10	1
1983–84	Crewe Alex	8	1
1984–85		40	4
1985–86		37	6
1986–87		40	9
1987–88	Crystal Palace	41	6
1988–89		22	5
1989–90		35	1
1990–91		38	6

THOMAS, Glen

Born Hackney 6.10.67. Ht 6 1 Wt 12 02
Defender. From Apprentice.

Season	Club	Apps	Goals
1985–86	Fulham	—	—
1986–87		1	—
1987–88		27	—
1988–89		40	1
1989–90		17	1
1990–91		34	1

THOMAS, Gwyn

Born Swansea 26.9.57. Ht 5 8   Wt 11 00
Midfield. From Apprentice. Wales
Under-21.

Season	Club	Apps	Goals
1974–75	Leeds U	1	—
1975–76		—	—
1976–77		7	1
1977–78		3	1
1978–79		2	—
1979–80		3	—
1980–81		2	—
1981–82		15	—
1982–83		39	1
1983–84		17	—
1983–84	Barnsley	13	—
1984–85		40	1
1985–86		39	5
1986–87		40	5
1987–88		42	4
1988–89		24	2
1989–90		3	—
1989–90	Hull C	11	—
1990–91		11	—

THOMAS, John

Born Wednesbury 5.8.58. Ht 5 8
Wt 11 03
Forward.

Season	Club	Apps	Goals
1978–79	Everton	—	—
1978–79	*Tranmere R*	11	2
1979–80	Everton	—	—
1979–80	*Halifax T*	5	—
1980–81	Bolton W	17	5
1981–82		5	1
1982–83	Chester	44	20
1983–84	Lincoln C	37	15
1984–85		30	5
1985–86	Preston NE	40	17
1986–87		38	21

Season	Club	Apps	Goals
1987–88	Bolton W	44	22
1988–89		29	9
1989–90	WBA	18	1
1989–90	Preston NE	11	3
1990–91		5	1

THOMAS, Martin

Born Caerphilly 28.11.59. Ht 6 1
Wt 13 00
Goalkeeper. From Apprentice. Wales
Under-21, 1 full cap.

Season	Club	Apps	Goals
1976–77	Bristol R	1	—
1977–78		37	—
1978–79		42	—
1979–80		38	—
1980–81		25	—
1981–82		19	—
1982–83	*Cardiff C*	15	—
1982–83	*Tottenham H*	—	—
1982–83	*Southend U*	6	—
1982–83	*Newcastle U*	3	—
1983–84	Newcastle U	23	—
1984–85		18	—
1984–85	*Middlesbrough*	4	—
1985–86	Newcastle U	32	—
1986–87		39	—
1987–88		3	—
1988–89		—	—
1988–89	Birmingham C	36	—
1989–90		42	—
1990–91		45	—

THOMAS, Michael

Born Lambeth 24.8.67. Ht 5 10
Wt 12 02
Midfield. From Apprentice. England
Schools, Youth, B, Under-21, 2 full caps.

Season	Club	Apps	Goals
1985–86	Arsenal	—	—
1986–87		12	—
1986–87	*Portsmouth*	3	—
1987–88	Arsenal	37	9
1988–89		37	7
1989–90		36	5
1990–91		31	2

THOMAS, Mickey

Born Mochdre 7.7.54.   Ht 5 6   Wt 10 07
Midfield. From Amateur. Wales Under-23,
51 full caps.

1971–72	Wrexham	20	3
1972–73		26	—
1973–74		19	4
1974–75		31	5
1975–76		30	2
1976–77		45	6
1977–78		43	7
1978–79		16	6
1978–79	Manchester U	25	1
1979–80		35	8
1980–81		30	2
1981–82	Everton	10	—
1981–82	Brighton	20	—
1982–83	Stoke C	41	11
1983–84		16	3
1983–84	Chelsea	17	4
1984–85		27	5
1985–86		—	—
1985–86	WBA	20	—
1985–86	*Derby Co*	9	—
From Wichita W			
1988–89	Shrewsbury T	40	1
1989–90	Leeds U	3	—
1989–90	*Stoke C*	5	—
1990–91	Stoke C	38	7

THOMAS, Mitchell

Born Luton 2.10.64   Ht 6 0   Wt 12 00
Defender. From Apprentice. England
Youth, B, Under-21.

1982–83	Luton T	4	—
1983–84		26	—
1984–85		36	—
1985–86		41	1
1986–87	Tottenham H	39	4
1987–88		36	—
1988–89		25	1
1989–90		26	1
1990–91		31	—

THOMAS, Rod

Born London 10.10.70.   Ht 5 6   Wt 10 03
Forward. From Trainee. England Youth,
Under-21.

1987–88	Watford	4	—
1988–89		18	2
1989–90		32	6
1990–91		24	1

THOMAS, Tony

Born Liverpool 12.7.71   Ht 5 11
Wt 12 05
Defender. From Trainee.

1988–89	Tranmere R	9	2
1989–90		42	2
1990–91		33	3

THOMPSON, Andy

Born Carnock 9.11.67.   Ht 5 4   Wt 10 06
Midfield. From Apprentice.

1985–86	WBA	15	1
1986–87		9	—
1986–87	Wolverhampton W	29	8
1987–88		42	2
1988–89		46	6
1989–90		33	4
1990–91		44	3

THOMPSON, Chris

Born Walsall 24.1.60.   Ht 5 11   Wt 12 04
Forward. From Apprentice. England
Youth.

1977–78	Bolton W	—	—
1978–79		—	—
1979–80		15	1
1980–81		6	1
1981–82		36	12
1982–83		16	4
1982–83	*Lincoln C*	6	—
1983–84	Blackburn R	33	8
1984–85		35	15
1985–86		17	1
1986–87	Wigan Ath	43	9

1987–88	....	31	5
1988–89	Blackpool..................	36	8
1989–90	....	3	—
1989–90	Cardiff C..................	2	—
1990–91	Walsall	3	—

THOMPSON, David

Born Manchester 27.5.62.   Ht 5 11
Wt 12 10
Forward. Local.

1981–82	Rochdale....................	2	—
1982–83	....	46	5
1983–84	....	40	4
1984–85	....	40	2
1985–86	....	27	2
1985–86	*Manchester U.............*	—	—
1986–87	Notts Co....................	46	7
1987–88	....	9	1
1987–88	Wigan Ath	27	2
1988–89	....	42	7
1989–90	....	39	5
1990–91	Preston NE	21	2

THOMPSON, David

Born Ashington 20.11.68.   Ht 6 3
Wt 12 07
Defender. From Trainee.

1986–87	Millwall......................	—	—
1987–88	....	5	—
1988–89	....	15	1
1989–90	....	27	2
1990–91	....	17	3

THOMPSON, Garry

Born Birmingham 7.10.59.   Ht 6 1
Wt 14 00
Forward. From Apprentice. England
Under-21.

1977–78	Coventry C	6	2
1978–79	....	20	8
1979–80	....	17	6
1980–81	....	35	8
1981–82	....	36	10
1982–83	....	20	4

1982–83	WBA	12	7
1983–84	....	37	13
1984–85	....	42	19
1985–86	Sheffield W..................	36	7
1986–87	Aston Villa..................	31	6
1987–88	....	24	11
1988–89	....	5	—
1988–89	Watford	21	7
1989–90	....	13	1
1989–90	Crystal Palace	9	2
1990–91	....	11	1

THOMPSON, Keith

Born Birmingham 24.4.65.   Ht 5 9
Wt 11 2
Forward. From Apprentice. England
Youth.

1982–83	Coventry C	5	—
1983–84	....	6	—
1983–84	*Wimbledon ....*	3	—
1984–85	Coventry C	1	—
1984–85	*Northampton T............*	10	1
1985–86	Coventry C	—	—
From Oviedo			
1988–89	Coventry C	9	1
1989–90	....	1	—
1990–91	....	1	—

THOMPSON, Les

Born Cleethorpes 23.9.68.   Ht 5 10
Wt 11 00
Forward.

1986–87	Hull C........................	—	—
1987–88	....	7	2
1988–89	....	7	—
1988–89	*Scarborough ....*	3	1
1989–90	Hull C........................	1	—
1990–91	....	20	2

THOMPSON, Neil

Born Beverley 2.10.63.   Ht 6 0   Wt 13 07
Defender. From Nottingham F
Apprentice.

| 1981–82 | Hull C........................ | 23 | — |

Season	Club	App	Goals
1982–83	....	8	—
To Scarborough			
1987–88	Scarborough................	41	6
1988–89		46	9
1989–90	Ipswich T....................	45	3
1990–91		38	6

THOMPSON, Simon

Born Sheffield 27.2.70 Ht 5 9 Wt 10 06
Forward. From Trainee.

Season	Club	App	Goals
1988–89	Rotherham U	1	—
1989–90		11	—
1990–91		16	—

THOMPSON, Steve

Born Oldham 2.11.64. Ht 5 11 Wt 11 12
Midfield. From Apprentice.

Season	Club	App	Goals
1982–83	Bolton W	3	—
1983–84		40	3
1984–85		34	4
1985–86		35	8
1986–87		44	7
1987–88		44	7
1988–89		43	9
1989–90		45	6
1990–91		45	5

THOMPSTONE, Ian

Born Manchester 17.1.71. Ht 6 0
Wt 11 03
Midfield. From Trainee.

Season	Club	App	Goals
1987–88	Manchester C	1	1
1988–89		—	—
1989–90		—	—
1990–91	Oldham Ath...............	—	—

THOMSON, Billy

Born Linwood 10.2.58. Ht 6 2 Wt 12 03
Goalkeeper. From Glasgow United.
Scotland Under-21, 7 full caps.

Season	Club	App	Goals
1975–76	Partick T....................	—	—
1976–77		—	—
1977–78		—	—
1978–79	St Mirren	34	—
1979–80		36	—
1980–81		36	—
1981–82		35	—
1982–83		35	—
1983–84		30	—
1984–85	Dundee U	11	—
1985–86		28	—
1986–87		42	—
1987–88		36	—
1988–89		36	—
1989–90		7	—
1990–91		5	—

THOMSON, Scott

Born Edinburgh 8.11.66. Ht 6 0
Wt 11 04
Goalkeeper. From Hutcheson Vale BC.

Season	Club	App	Goals
1984–85	Dundee U	—	—
1985–86		—	—
1986–87		—	—
1987–88		—	—
1988–89		1	—
1989–90		2	—
1990–91		—	—
1990–91	*Barnsley*	—	—

THORN, Andy

Born Carshalton 12.11.66. Ht 6 0
Wt 11 05
Defender. From Apprentice. England
Under-21.

Season	Club	App	Goals
1984–85	Wimbledon	10	—
1985–86		28	—
1986–87		34	2
1987–88		35	—
1988–89	Newcastle U...............	26	1
1989–90		10	1
1989–90	Crystal Palace............	17	1
1990–91		34	1

THORNBER, Stephen

Born Dewsbury 11.10.65. Ht 5 10
Wt 11 02
Midfield. Local.

1983–84	Halifax T	4	1
1984–85		31	3
1985–86		18	—
1986–87		16	—
1987–88		35	—
1988–89	Swansea C	31	—
1989–90		34	1
1990–91		19	—

THORPE, Adrian

Born Chesterfield 20.11.63. Ht 5 7
Wt 11 06
Forward. From Heanor T.

1984–85	Bradford C	—	—
1985–86		10	1
1986–87		5	—
1986–87	*Tranmere R*	5	3
1987–88	Bradford C	2	—
1987–88	Notts Co	23	5
1988–89		36	4
1989–90	Walsall	27	1
1989–90	Northampton T	13	3
1990–91		27	1

THORPE, Andy

Born Stockport 15.9.60. Ht 5 11
Wt 12 02
Defender. From Amateur.

1977–78	Stockport Co	4	—
1978–79		38	—
1979–80		36	1
1980–81		38	1
1981–82		46	—
1982–83		46	—
1983–84		45	1
1984–85		31	—
1985–86		30	—
1986–87	Tranmere R	39	—
1987–88		14	—
1987–88	Stockport Co	20	—
1988–89		41	—
1989–90		40	—
1990–91		40	—

THORPE, Jeffrey

Born Whitehaven 17.11.72.
Midfield. From Trainee.

1990–91	Carlisle U	13	—

THORSTVEDT, Erik

Born Stavanger 28.10.62. Ht 6 0
Wt 12 01
Goalkeeper. From IFK Gothenburg.
Norway full caps.

1988–89	Tottenham H	18	—
1989–90		34	—
1990–91		37	—

TIGHE, Aaron

Born Banbury 11.7.69. Ht 5 9   Wt 10 09
Midfield. From Apprentice. Eire Schools
Youth, Under-21.

1986–87	Luton T	—	—
1987–88		—	—
1988–89		—	—
1989–90	*Leicester C*	—	—
1990–91	Luton T	—	—

TILER, Carl

Born Sheffield 11.2.70. Ht 6 2   Wt 13 00
Defender. From Trainee. England
Under-21.

1987–88	Barnsley	1	—
1988–89		4	—
1989–90		21	1
1990–91		45	2

TILLSON, Andy

Born Huntingdon 30.6.66. Ht 6 2
Wt 12 07
Defender. From Kettering.

1988–89	Grimsby T	45	2
1989–90		42	3
1990–91		18	—
1990–91	QPR	19	2

TILSON, Steve

Born Essex 27.7.66 Ht 5 11 Wt 11 10
Forward. From Burnham.

Season	Club		
1988–89	Southend U	16	2
1989–90		16	—
1990–91		38	8

TINKLER, John

Born Trimdon 24.8.68. Ht 5 8 Wt 11 07
Midfield.

Season	Club		
1986–87	Hartlepool U	2	—
1987–88		20	—
1988–89		38	3
1989–90		45	2
1990–91		26	2

TINNION, Brian

Born Stanley 23.2.68. Ht 5 11 Wt 11 05
Defender. From Apprentice.

Season	Club		
1985–86	Newcastle U	—	—
1986–87		3	—
1987–88		16	1
1988–89		13	1
1988–89	Bradford C	14	1
1989–90		37	5
1990–91		41	5

TITTERTON, David

Born Hatton 25.9.71. Ht 5 11 Wt 10 09
Midfield. From Trainee. England Youth.

Season	Club		
1989–90	Coventry C	1	—
1990–91		1	—

TODD, Lee

Born Hartlepool 7.3.72. Ht 5 5 Wt 10 03
Forward. From Hartlepool U Trainee.

Season	Club		
1990–91	Stockport Co	14	—

TODD, Mark

Born Belfast 4.12.67. Ht 5 7 Wt 10 00
Midfield. From Trainee. Northern Ireland
Under-23.

Season	Club		
1985–86	Manchester U	—	—
1986–87		—	—
1987–88	Sheffield U	12	—
1988–89		39	4
1989–90		16	1
1990–91		3	—
1990–91	*Wolverhampton W*	7	

TOMAN, Andy

Born Northallerton 7.3.62. Ht 5 10
Wt 11 09
Midfield. From Bishop Auckland.

Season	Club		
1985–86	Lincoln C	24	4
1986–87	Hartlepool U	21	5
1987–88		46	17
1988–89		45	6
1989–90	Darlington	*40*	7
1990–91		43	5

TOMLINSON, Michael

Born Lambeth 15.9.72.
Forward. From Trainee.

Season	Club		
1990–91	Leyton Orient	1	1

TOMLINSON, Paul

Born Brierley Hill 22.2.64. Ht 6 2
Wt 13 12
Goalkeeper. From Middlewood R.

Season	Club		
1983–84	Sheffield U	30	—
1984–85		2	—
1985–86		—	—
1986–87		5	—
1986–87	*Birmingham C*	11	—
1987–88	Bradford C	42	—
1988–89		38	—
1989–90		41	—
1990–91		43	—

TORFASON, Gudmundor

Born Westann Isles 13.12.61. Ht 6 1
Wt 13 02
Forward. From RSC Genk. Iceland full
caps.

Season	Club	App	Goals
1989–90	St Mirren	29	12
1990–91		18	4

TORPEY, Stephen

Born Islington 8.12.70 Ht 6 2 Wt 12 11
Forward. From Trainee.

Season	Club	App	Goals
1988–89	Millwall	—	—
1989–90		7	—
1990–91		—	—
1990–91	Bradford C	29	7

TORTOLANO, Joe

Born Stirling 6.4.66. Ht 5 8 Wt 11 02
Forward. From Apprentice. Scotland
Under-21.

Season	Club	App	Goals
1983–84	WBA	—	—
1984–85		—	—
1985–86	Hibernian	20	3
1986–87		33	—
1987–88		21	4
1988–89		25	—
1989–90		7	—
1990–91		18	1

TOSHACK, Cameron

Born Cardiff 7.3.70 Ht 6 2 Wt 12 00
Forward. From Trainee.

Season	Club	App	Goals
1988–89	Swansea C	—	—
1989–90	Bristol C	—	—
1990–91		—	—
1990–91	Cardiff C	4	—

TOWNSEND, Andy

Born Maidstone 23.7.63. Ht 5 11
Wt 12 13
Midfield. From Welling and Weymouth.
Eire 25 full caps.

Season	Club	App	Goals
1984–85	Southampton	5	—
1985–86		27	1
1986–87		14	1
1987–88		37	3
1988–89	Norwich C	36	5

Season	Club	App	Goals
1989–90		35	3
1990–91	Chelsea	34	2

TRACEY, Simon

Born Woolwich 9.12.67. Ht 6 0
Wt 12 00
Goalkeeper. From Apprentice.

Season	Club	App	Goals
1985–86	Wimbledon	—	—
1986–87		—	—
1987–88		—	—
1988–89		1	—
1988–89	Sheffield U	7	—
1989–90		46	—
1990–91		31	—

TREACY, Darren

Born Lambeth 6.9.70 Ht 5 10 Wt 12 09
Forward. From Trainee.

Season	Club	App	Goals
1988–89	Millwall	3	—
1989–90		4	—
1990–91		—	—
1990–91	Bradford C	16	2

TREANOR, Mark

Born Glasgow 1.4.63. Ht 6 0 Wt 11 00
Defender. From Eastercraigs.

Season	Club	App	Goals
1979–80	Clydebank	1	—
1980–81		16	—
1981–82		35	—
1982–83		36	3
1983–84		18	1
1984–85		38	1
1985–86		32	—
1986–87		33	—
1987–88		37	3
1988–89		27	5
1988–89	St Johnstone	3	—
1989–90		30	4
1990–91		30	4

TREVITT, Simon

Born Dewsbury 20.12.67. Ht 5 11
Wt 11 02
Defender. From Apprentice.

Season	Club	Appearances	Goals
1986–87	Huddersfield T	11	—
1987–88		37	1
1988–89		39	—
1989–90		7	—
1990–91		38	—

TRICK, Des

Born Swansea 7.11.69   Ht 5 11   Wt 12 00
Defender. From Trainee.

Season	Club	Appearances	Goals
1988–89	Swansea C	—	—
1989–90		14	—
1990–91		15	—

TROLLOPE, Paul

Born Swindon 3.6.72.   Ht 6 0   Wt 12 02
Midfield. From Trainee.

Season	Club	Appearances	Goals
1989–90	Swindon T	—	—
1990–91		—	—

TROTTER, Michael

Born Hartlepool 27.10.69.   Ht 6 3
Wt 12 02
Defender. From Trainee.

Season	Club	Appearances	Goals
1987–88	Middlesbrough	—	—
1988–89		—	—
1988–89	*Doncaster R*	3	—
1989–90	Middlesbrough	—	—
1990–91	Darlington	24	2

TRUSSON, Mike

Born Northolt 26.5.59.   Ht 6 0   Wt 12 04
Forward. From Apprentice.

Season	Club	Appearances	Goals
1976–77	Plymouth Arg	4	—
1977–78		15	2
1978–79		27	5
1978–79	*Stoke C*	—	—
1979–80	Plymouth Arg	27	8
1980–81	Sheffield U	39	8
1981–82		44	11
1982–83		32	9
1983–84		11	3
1983–84	Rotherham U	25	2

Season	Club	Appearances	Goals
1984–85		45	7
1985–86		37	6
1986–87		17	4
1987–88	Brighton	15	2
1988–89		22	—
1989–90		—	—
1989–90	Gillingham	25	2
1990–91		39	4

TUCKER, Jason

Born Isleworth 3.2.73.
Defender. From Trainee.

Season	Club	Appearances	Goals
1990–91	Aldershot	1	—

TUPLING, Steve

Born Wensleydale 11.7.64.   Ht 6 0
Wt 11 03
Midfield. From Apprentice.

Season	Club	Appearances	Goals
1982–83	Middlesbrough	—	—
1983–84		—	—
1984–85	*Carlisle U*	1	—
1984–85	Darlington	39	4
1985–86		40	4
1986–87		32	—
1987–88	Newport Co	33	2
1988–89	Cardiff C	4	—
1988–89	*Torquay U*	3	—
1988–89	*Exeter C*	9	1
1989–90	Cardiff C	1	—
1989–90	Hartlepool U	26	1
1990–91		42	2

TURNBULL, Lee

Born Teesside 27.9.67.   Ht 6 0   Wt 11 09
Midfield. Local.

Season	Club	Appearances	Goals
1985–86	Middlesbrough	2	—
1986–87		14	4
1987–88		—	—
1987–88	Aston Villa	—	—
1987–88	Doncaster R	30	1
1988–89		32	4
1989–90		42	10
1990–91		19	6
1990–91	Chesterfield	19	9

TURNER, Chris

Born Sheffield 15.9.58. Ht 5 11 Wt 11 12
Goalkeeper. From Apprentice. England
Youth.

Season	Club		
1976–77	Sheffield W	45	—
1977–78		23	—
1978–79		23	—
1978–79	*Lincoln C*	5	—
1979–80	Sunderland	30	—
1980–81		27	—
1981–82		19	—
1982–83		35	—
1983–84		42	—
1984–85		42	—
1985–86	Manchester U	17	—
1986–87		23	—
1987–88		24	—
1988–89		—	—
1988–89	Sheffield W	29	—
1989–90		23	—
1989–90	*Leeds U*	2	—
1990–91	Sheffield W	23	—

TURNER, Phil

Born Sheffield 12.2.62. Ht 5 8 Wt 10 07
Midfield. From Apprentice.

Season	Club		
1979–80	Lincoln C	14	1
1980–81		38	4
1981–82		28	1
1982–83		40	3
1983–84		42	3
1984–85		36	3
1985–86		43	4
1986–87	Grimsby T	34	3
1987–88		28	5
1987–88	Leicester C	8	—
1988–89		16	2
1988–89	Notts Co	16	2
1989–90		44	6
1990–91		38	1

TURNER, Robert

Born Durham 18.9.66. Ht 6 3 Wt 14 00
Forward. From Apprentice.

Season	Club		
1984–85	Huddersfield T	1	—

Season	Club		
1985–86	Cardiff C	34	7
1986–87		5	1
1986–87	*Hartlepool U*	7	1
1986–87	Bristol R	17	1
1987–88		9	1
1987–88	Wimbledon	4	—
1988–89		6	—
1988–89	Bristol C	19	6
1989–90		33	6
1990–91	Plymouth Arg	39	14

TURNER, Tommy

Born Johnstone 11.10.63. Ht 5 9 Wt 10 7
Midfield. From Glentyan Thistle

Season	Club		
1983–84	Morton	—	—
1984–85		13	1
1985–86		34	7
1986–87		38	4
1987–88		29	1
1988–89		31	10
1989–90		30	6
1990–91	St Johnstone	28	3

TUTILL, Steve

Born Derwent 1.10.69. Ht 6 0 Wt 11 10
Defender. From Trainee. England Schools.

Season	Club		
1987–88	York C	21	—
1988–89		22	1
1989–90		42	—
1990–91		42	—

TUTTLE, David

Born Reading 6.2.72. Ht 6 1 Wt 12 10
Defender. From Trainee. England Youth.

Season	Club		
1989–90	Tottenham H	—	—
1990–91		6	—

TWENTYMAN, Geoff

Born Liverpool 10.3.59. Ht 6 1 Wt 13 02
Defender. From Southport, Maghull,
Formby and Chorley.

Season	Club		
1983–84	Preston NE	28	2

Season	Club	Apps	Goals
1984–85		44	2
1985–86		26	—
1986–87	Bristol R	43	—
1987–88		38	1
1988–89		46	1
1989–90		46	3
1990–91		46	—

TYNAN, Tommy

Born Liverpool 17.11.55.   Ht 5 10
Wt 11 11
Forward. From Apprentice.

Season	Club	Apps	Goals
1972–73	Liverpool	—	—
1973–74		—	—
1974–75		—	—
1975–76		—	—
1975–76	*Swansea C*	6	2
1976–77	Liverpool	—	—
1976–77	Sheffield W	39	14
1977–78		44	16
1978–79		8	1
1978–79	Lincoln C	9	1
1978–79	Newport Co	20	7
1979–80		34	8
1980–81		45	13
1981–82		38	13
1982–83		46	25
1983–84	Plymouth Arg	35	12
1984–85		45	31
1985–86	Rotherham U	30	13
1985–86	*Plymouth Arg*	9	10
1986–87	Rotherham U	2	—
1986–87	Plymouth Arg	40	18
1987–88		43	17
1988–89		46	24
1989–90		44	15
1990–91	Torquay U	35	13

ULLATHORNE, Robert

Born Wakefield 11.10.71.   Ht 5 8
Wt 10 00
Defender. From Trainee.

Season	Club	Apps	Goals
1989–90	Norwich C	—	—
1990–91		2	—

UNSWORTH, Jamie

Born Bury 1.5.73.
Midfield. From Trainee.

Season	Club	Apps	Goals
1990–91	Cardiff C	1	—

UZZELL, John

Born Plymouth 31.3.59.   Ht 5 10
Wt 11 03
Defender. From Apprentice.

Season	Club	Apps	Goals
1976–77	Plymouth Arg	—	—
1977–78		44	1
1978–79		21	—
1979–80		1	—
1980–81		16	—
1981–82		35	2
1982–83		42	1
1983–84		42	—
1984–85		29	1
1985–86		8	—
1986–87		21	—
1987–88		10	1
1988–89		33	—
1989–90	Torquay U	36	2
1990–91		46	—

VALENTINE, Peter

Born Huddersfield 16.6.63.   Ht 5 11
Wt 12 00
Defender. From Apprentice.

Season	Club	League Appearances	Goals
1980–81	Huddersfield T	—	—
1981–82		14	1
1982–83		5	—
1983–84	Bolton W	42	1
1984–85		26	—
1985–86	Bury	46	3
1986–87		46	2
1987–88		42	2
1988–89		30	1
1989–90		38	—
1990–91		42	2

VAN DE VEN, Peter

Born Hunsel 8.1.61   Ht 6 1   Wt 13 5
Forward. From Willem II

Season	Club	League Appearances	Goals
1990–91	Aberdeen	23	9

VAN DEN HAUWE, Pat

Born Dendermonde 16.12.60.   Ht 6 0
Wt 10 08
Defender. From Apprentice. Wales 13 full caps.

Season	Club	League Appearances	Goals
1978–79	Birmingham C	8	—
1979–80		1	—
1980–81		4	—
1981–82		31	—
1982–83		31	1
1983–84		42	—
1984–85		6	—
1984–85	Everton	31	—
1985–86		40	1
1986–87		11	1
1987–88		28	—
1988–89		25	—
1989–90		—	—
1989–90	Tottenham H	31	—
1990–91		32	—

VAN DER ARK, Willem

Born Groningen 13.11.63.   Ht 6 5
Wt 13 06
Forward. From Willem II

Season	Club	League Appearances	Goals
1988–89	Aberdeen	8	2
1989–90		26	7
1990–91		11	4

VAN DER HOORN, Freddy

Born Den Bosch 12.10.63.   Ht 6 0
Wt 12 06
Defender. From BVV Den Bosch.

Season	Club	League Appearances	Goals
1989–90	Dundee U	31	2
1990–91		32	1

VAN DER LAAN, Robin

Born Schiedam 5.9.68.   Ht 5 11   Wt 12 05
Forward. From Wageningen.

Season	Club	League Appearances	Goals
1990–91	Port Vale	18	4

VARADI, Imre

Born Paddington 8.7.59.   Ht 5 8
Wt 12 09
Forward. From Letchworth G.C.

Season	Club	League Appearances	Goals
1977–78	Sheffield U	—	—
1978–79		10	4
1978–79	Everton	—	—
1979–80		4	—
1980–81		22	6
1981–82	Newcastle U	42	18
1982–83		39	21
1983–84	Sheffield W	38	17
1984–85		38	16
1985–86	WBA	32	9
1986–87		—	—
1986–87	Manchester C	30	9
1987–88		32	17
1988–89		3	—
1988–89	Sheffield W	20	3
1989–90		2	—
1989–90	Leeds U	13	2

1990–91	....	6	2

VAUGHAN, John

Born Isleworth 26.6.64. Ht 5 10
Wt 13 01
Goalkeeper. From Apprentice.

1981–82	West Ham U	—	—
1982–83	....	—	—
1983–84	....	—	—
1984–85	....	—	—
1984–85	*Charlton Ath*	6	—
1985–86	....	—	—
1985–86	*Bristol R*	6	—
1985–86	*Wrexham*	4	—
1985–86	*Bristol C*	2	—
1986–87	Fulham	44	—
1987–88	....	—	—
1987–88	*Bristol C*	3	—
1988–89	Cambridge U	29	—
1989–90	....	46	—
1990–91	....	43	—

VAUGHAN, Nigel

Born Caerleon 20.5.59. Ht 5 5 Wt 8 10
Midfield. From Apprentice. Wales Under-21, 10 full caps.

1976–77	Newport Co	1	—
1977–78	....	11	—
1978–79	....	27	4
1979–80	....	46	12
1980–81	....	45	1
1981–82	....	44	3
1982–83	....	43	7
1983–84	....	7	5
1983–84	Cardiff C	36	8
1984–85	....	38	16
1985–86	....	43	12
1986–87	....	32	6
1986–87	*Reading*	5	1
1987–88	Wolverhampton W	36	6
1988–89	....	32	4
1989–90	....	25	—
1990–91	Hereford U	1	—

VENISON, Barry

Born Consett 16.8.64. Ht 5 9 Wt 11 09
Defender. From Apprentice. England
Youth, Under-21.

1981–82	Sunderland	20	1
1982–83	....	37	—
1983–84	....	41	—
1984–85	....	39	1
1985–86	....	36	—
1986–87	Liverpool	33	—
1987–88	....	18	—
1988–89	....	15	—
1989–90	....	25	—
1990–91	....	6	—

VENUS, Mark

Born Hartlepool 6.4.67. Ht 6 0 Wt 11 08
Defender.

1984–85	Hartlepool U	4	—
1985–86	Leicester C	1	—
1986–87	....	39	—
1987–88	....	21	1
1987–88	Wolverhampton W	4	—
1988–89	....	35	—
1989–90	....	44	2
1990–91	....	6	—

VERTANNES, Des

Born Hounslow 25.4.72.
Midfield. From Chelsea and Fulham
Trainee.

1989–90	Fulham	2	—
1990–91	Aldershot	—	—

VEYSEY, Ken

Born Hackney 8.6.67. Ht 5 11 Wt 11 08
Goalkeeper. From Arsenal Apprentice.

1987–88	Torquay U	—	—
1988–89	....	25	—
1989–90	....	46	—
1990–91	....	1	—
1990–91	Oxford U	25	—

VICKERS, Steve

Born Bishop Auckland 13.10.67. Ht 6 2
Wt 12 00
Defender. From Spennymoor U.

Season	Club	Apps	Goals
1985–86	Tranmere R	3	—
1986–87		36	2
1987–88		46	1
1988–89		46	3
1989–90		42	3
1990–91		42	1

VICTOR (MUNOZ)

Born Zaragoza 15.3.57
Midfield. From Sampdoria

Season	Club	Apps	Goals
1990–91	St Mirren	18	1

VINNICOMBE, Chris

Born Exeter 20.10.70 Ht 5 9 Wt 10 04
Midfield. England Under-21.

Season	Club	Apps	Goals
1988–89	Exeter C	25	—
1989–90		14	1
1989–90	Rangers	7	—
1990–91		10	1

VIVEASH, Adrian

Born Swindon 30.9.69 Ht 6 1 Wt 11 12
Forward. From Trainee.

Season	Club	Apps	Goals
1988–89	Swindon T	—	—
1989–90		—	—
1990–91		25	1

WADDLE, Chris

Born Hepworth 14.12.60. Ht 6 0
Wt 11 05
Forward. From Tow Law T. England
Under-21, 61 full caps. Football League.

Season	Club	Apps	Goals
1980–81	Newcastle U	13	1
1981–82		42	7
1982–83		37	7
1983–84		42	18
1984–85		36	13
1985–86	Tottenham H	39	11
1986–87		39	6
1987–88		22	2
1988–89		38	14
To Marseille			

WADDOCK, Gary

Born Alperton 17.3.62. Ht 5 10
Wt 11 12
Midfield. From Apprentice. Eire B, Under-
21, Under-23, 20 full caps.

Season	Club	Apps	Goals
1979–80	QPR	16	1
1980–81		33	3
1981–82		35	—
1982–83		33	—
1983–84		36	3
1984–85		31	1
1985–86		15	—
1986–87		4	—
1987–88		—	—
From Charleroi			
1989–90	Millwall	18	—
1990–91		40	2

WADE, Bryan

Born Bath 25.6.63. Ht 5 8 Wt 11 05
Forward. From Trowbridge T.

Season	Club	Apps	Goals
1985–86	Swindon T	34	10
1986–87		23	9
1987–88		3	—
1988–89	Swansea C	25	4
1989–90		11	1
From Haverfordwest			

1990–91	Brighton	11	6

WAITES, Paul

Born Hull 24.1.71. Ht 5 10 Wt 12 08
Defender. From Trainee.

1989–90	Hull C	1	—
1990–91		10	—

WALKER, Alan

Born Mossley 17.12.59. Ht 6 2 Wt 12 04
Defender. From Stockport Co and Telford U.

1983–84	Lincoln C	33	2
1984–85		42	2
1985–86	Millwall	26	3
1986–87		40	1
1987–88		26	4
1987–88	Gillingham	7	—
1988–89		22	1
1989–90		38	1
1990–91		44	4

WALKER, Andy

Born Glasgow 6.4.65. Ht 5 8 Wt 10 07
Forward. From Baillieston Juniors.
Scotland, Under-21, 1 full cap.

1984–85	Motherwell	11	3
1985–86		22	4
1986–87		43	10
1987–88	Celtic	42	16
1988–89		22	8
1989–90		32	6
1990–91		11	—

WALKER, Clive

Born Oxford 26.5.57. Ht 5 7 Wt 11 09
Forward. From Apprentice. England
Schools.

1974–75	Chelsea	—	—
1975–76		—	—
1976–77		1	—
1977–78		23	7

1978–79		30	4
1979–80		36	13
1980–81		37	11
1981–82		36	16
1982–83		29	6
1983–84		6	3
1984–85	Sunderland	38	10
1985–86		12	—
1985–86	QPR	5	1
1986–87		16	—
1987–88		—	—
1987–88	Fulham	26	8
1988–89		38	8
1989–90		45	13
1990–91	Brighton	45	3

WALKER, Des

Born Hackney 26.11.65. Ht 5 10
Wt 11 05
Defender. From Apprentice. England
Under-21, 36 full caps

1983–84	Nottingham F	4	—
1984–85		3	—
1985–86		39	—
1986–87		41	—
1987–88		35	—
1988–89		34	—
1989–90		38	—
1990–91		37	—

WALKER, Ian

Born Watford 31.10.71. Ht 6 1 Wt 11 09
Goalkeeper. From Trainee. England
Youth. Under-21.

1989–90	Tottenham H	—	—
1990–91		1	—
1990–91	*Oxford U*	2	—
1990–91	*Ipswich T*	—	—

WALKER, Keith

Born Edinburgh 17.4.66. Ht 6 0
Wt 11 09
Midfield. From ICI Juveniles

1984–85	Stirling Albion	38	6

Season	Club	Apps	Goals
1985–86		32	5
1986–87		21	6
1987–88	St Mirren	19	3
1988–89		14	1
1989–90		10	2
1989–90	Swansea C	13	—
1990–91		24	—

WALKER, Nicky

Born Aberdeen 29.9.62. Ht 6 2 Wt 11 12
Goalkeeper. From Elgin C. Scotland
Youth.

Season	Club	Apps	Goals
1980–81	Leicester C	—	—
1981–82		6	—
1982–83	Motherwell	16	—
1983–84		15	—
1983–84	Rangers	8	—
1984–85		14	—
1985–86		34	—
1986–87		2	—
1987–88		5	—
1987–88	*Dunfermline Ath*	1	—
1988–89	Rangers	12	—
1989–90	Hearts	—	—
1990–91		13	—

WALKER, Ray

Born North Shields 28.9.63. Ht 5 10
Wt 11 12
Midfield. From Apprentice. England
Youth.

Season	Club	Apps	Goals
1981–82	Aston Villa	—	—
1982–83		1	—
1983–84		8	—
1984–85		7	—
1984–85	*Port Vale*	15	1
1985–86	Aston Villa	7	—
1986–87	Port Vale	45	4
1987–88		42	6
1988–89		43	5
1989–90		40	—
1990–91		45	6

WALLACE, Danny

Born London 21.1.64. Ht 5 4 Wt 10 04
Forward. From Apprentice. England
Youth, Under-21, 1 full cap.

Season	Club	Apps	Goals
1980–81	Southampton	2	—
1981–82		7	—
1982–83		35	12
1983–84		41	11
1984–85		35	7
1985–86		35	8
1986–87		31	8
1987–88		33	11
1988–89		31	5
1989–90		5	2
1989–90	Manchester U	26	3
1990–91		19	3

WALLACE, Ray

Born Lewisham 2.10.69. Ht 5 6
Wt 10 02
Defender. From Trainee, England
Under-21.

Season	Club	Apps	Goals
1987–88	Southampton	—	—
1988–89		26	—
1989–90		9	—
1990–91		—	—

WALLACE, Rodney

Born Lewisham 2.10.69. Ht 5 7
Wt 10 01
Forward. From Trainee. England B,
Under-21

Season	Club	Apps	Goals
1987–88	Southampton	15	1
1988–89		38	12
1989–90		38	18
1990–91		37	14

WALLER, David

Born Urmston 20.12.63. Ht 5 10
Wt 12 10
Forward. Local.

Season	Club	Apps	Goals
1981–82	Crewe Alex	1	—
1982–83		37	17

Season	Club	League Appearances/Goals	
1983–84		42	10
1984–85		44	15
1985–86		44	13
1986–87	Shrewsbury T	11	3
1986–87	Chesterfield	—	—
1987–88		40	19
1988–89		36	18
1989–90		43	16
1990–91		—	—

WALLINGTON, Mark

Born Sleaford 17.9.52. Ht 6 1 Wt 14 11
Goalkeeper. England Youth, Under-23.

1971–72	Walsall	11	—
1971–72	Leicester C	5	—
1972–73		1	—
1973–74		—	—
1974–75		30	—
1975–76		42	—
1976–77		42	—
1977–78		42	—
1978–79		42	—
1979–80		42	—
1980–81		42	—
1981–82		36	—
1982–83		42	—
1983–84		35	—
1984–85		11	—
1985–86	Derby Co	33	—
1986–87		34	—
1987–88		—	—
1988–89	Lincoln C	38	—
1989–90		26	—
1990–91		23	—

WALMSLEY, David

Born Hull 23.11.72.
Forward. From Trainee.

1990–91	Hull C	1	1

WALSH, Colin

Born Hamilton 22.7.62. Ht 5 10
Wt 12 02
Midfield. From Apprentice. Scotland
Youth, Under-21.

1979–80	Nottingham F	—	—
1980–81		16	4
1981–82		15	3
1982–83		37	5
1983–84		38	13
1984–85		13	1
1985–86		20	6
1986–87		—	—
1986–87	Charlton Ath	33	6
1987–88		11	3
1988–89		5	—
1988–89	*Peterborough U*	5	1
1989–90	Charlton Ath	27	2
1990–91		13	—
1990–91	*Middlesbrough*	13	1

WALSH, Derek

Born Hamilton 24.10.67. Ht 5 7
Wt 10 01
Midfield. From Apprentice.

1984–85	Everton	1	—
1985–86		—	—
1986–87		—	—
1987–88	Hamilton A	2	—
1988–89	Carlisle U	35	3
1989–90		28	3
1990–91		19	—

WALSH, Gary

Born Wigan 21.3.68. Ht 6 1 Wt 13 01
Goalkeeper. England Under-21.

1984–85	Manchester U	—	—
1985–86		—	—
1986–87		14	—
1987–88		16	—
1988–89		—	—
1988–89	*Airdrie*	3	—
1989–90	Manchester U	—	—
1990–91		5	—

WALSH, Paul

Born Plumstead 1.10.62. Ht 5 7
Wt 10 08
Forward. From Apprentice. England
Youth, Under-21, 3 full caps.

Season	Club	App	Goals
1979–80	Charlton Ath	9	—
1980–81		40	11
1981–82		38	13
1982–83	Luton T	41	13
1983–84		39	11
1984–85	Liverpool	26	8
1985–86		20	11
1986–87		23	6
1987–88		8	—
1987–88	Tottenham H	11	1
1988–89		33	6
1989–90		26	2
1990–91		29	7

WALSH, Ray

Born Duntocher 4.6.67 Ht 5 10 Wt 11 2
Defender. From Campsie Black Watch

Season	Club	App	Goals
1989–90	Airdrieonians	4	—
1990–91		2	—

WALSH, Steve

Born Fulwood 3.11.64. Ht 6 3 Wt 13 08
Defender. Local.

Season	Club	App	Goals
1982–83	Wigan Ath	31	—
1983–84		42	1
1984–85		40	2
1985–86		13	1
1986–87	Leicester C	21	—
1987–88		32	7
1988–89		30	2
1989–90		34	3
1990–91		35	3

WALTER, David

Born Barnstaple 3.9.64 Ht 6 3 Wt 13 03
Goalkeeper. From Bideford T.

Season	Club	App	Goals
1988–89	Exeter C	26	—
1989–90		18	—
1989–90	*Plymouth Arg*	—	—
1990–91	Plymouth Arg	10	—

WALTERS, Mark

Born Birmingham 12.1.61. Ht 5 9
Wt 10 12
Forward. From Apprentice. England
Youth, B, Under-21, 1 full cap.

Season	Club	App	Goals
1981–82	Aston Villa	1	—
1982–83		22	1
1983–84		37	8
1984–85		36	10
1985–86		40	10
1986–87		21	3
1987–88		24	7
1987–88	Rangers	18	7
1988–89		31	8
1989–90		27	5
1990–91		30	12

WALTERS, Steve

Born Plymouth 9.1.72 Ht 5 10 Wt 11 08
Forward. From Schoolboy, Trainee. FA
Schools.

Season	Club	App	Goals
1987–88	Crewe Alex	1	—
1988–89		22	1
1989–90		30	1
1990–91		4	—

WALTON, Mark

Born Merthyr 1.6.69. Ht 6 2 Wt 13 13
Goalkeeper. From Swansea C. Wales
Under-21.

Season	Club	App	Goals
1986–87	Luton T	—	—
1987–88		—	—
1987–88	Colchester U	17	—
1988–89		23	—
1989–90	Norwich C	1	—
1990–91		4	—

WALWYN, Keith

Born W Indies 17.2.56. Ht 6 1 Wt 13 04
Forward. From Winterton.

Season	Club	App	Goals
1979–80	Chesterfield	—	—
1980–81		3	2
1981–82	York C	44	23
1982–83		41	21
1983–84		45	25
1984–85		27	9
1985–86		46	22
1986–87		42	19
1987–88	Blackpool	39	13

Season	Club	Apps	Goals
1988–89	....	30	3
1989–90	Carlisle U....................	40	11
1990–91	....	22	4

WARBURTON, Ray

Born Rotherham 7.10.67.   Ht 6 0
Wt 12 00
Defender. From Apprentice.

Season	Club	Apps	Goals
1984–85	Rotherham U	1	—
1985–86	....	—	—
1986–87	....	3	—
1987–88	....	—	—
1988–89	....	—	—
1989–90	York C........................	43	2
1990–91	....	22	4

WARD, Ashley

Born Manchester 24.11.70.   Ht 6 1
Wt 11 07
Forward. From Trainee.

Season	Club	Apps	Goals
1989–90	Manchester C	1	—
1990–91	....	—	—
1990–91	*Wrexham*......................	4	2

WARD, Gavin

Born Sutton Coldfield 30.6.70   Ht 6 2
Wt 12 12
Goalkeeper. From Aston Villa Trainee.

Season	Club	Apps	Goals
1988–89	Shrewsbury T..............	—	—
1989–90	WBA............................	—	—
1989–90	Cardiff C....................	2	—
1990–91	....	1	—

WARD, Kenny

Born Blairhall 16.8.63.   Ht 5 8   Wt 9 07
Forward. From Oakley U.

Season	Club	Apps	Goals
1983–84	Cowdenbeath..............	31	5
1984–85	....	36	16
1985–86	....	16	8
1985–86	Forfar Ath..................	16	1
1986–87	....	33	4
1987–88	....	37	7

Season	Club	Apps	Goals
1988–89	....	35	12
1989–90	....	2	—
1989–90	St Johnstone	18	4
1990–91	....	10	1

WARD, Mark

Born Prescot 10.10.62.   Ht 5 6   Wt 10 12
Midfield. From Everton Apprentice and
Northwich Vic.

Season	Club	Apps	Goals
1983–84	Oldham Ath................	42	6
1984–85	....	42	6
1985–86	West Ham U	42	3
1986–87	....	37	1
1987–88	....	37	1
1988–89	....	30	2
1989–90	....	19	5
1989–90	Manchester C	19	3
1990–91	....	36	11

WARD, Mitch

Born Sheffield 18.6.71.   Ht 5 8   Wt 10 07
Defender. From Trainee

Season	Club	Apps	Goals
1989–90	Sheffield U	—	—
1990–91	....	4	—
1990–91	*Crewe Alex*.................	4	1

WARD, Paul

Born Sedgefield 15.9.63.   Ht 5 11
Wt 12 05
Midfield. From Apprentice.

Season	Club	Apps	Goals
1981–82	Chelsea........................	—	—
1982–83	Middlesbrough............	15	—
1983–84	....	28	1
1984–85	....	30	—
1985–86	....	3	—
1985–86	Darlington	35	2
1986–87	....	44	1
1987–88	....	45	6
1988–89	Leyton Orient	28	1
1989–90	....	3	—
1989–90	Scunthorpe U	25	4
1990–91	....	30	2
1990–91	Lincoln C....................	9	—

WARD, Peter

Born Durham 15.10.64. Ht 6 0 Wt 11 10
Forward. From Chester-le-Street.

Season	Club		
1986–87	Huddersfield T	7	—
1987–88		26	2
1988–89		4	—
1989–90	Rochdale	40	5
1990–91		44	5

WARE, Paul

Born Congleton 7.11.70. Ht 5 8
Wt 11 02
Midfield. From Trainee.

Season	Club		
1987–88	Stoke C	1	—
1988–89		11	1
1989–90		16	—
1990–91		34	2

WARHURST, Paul

Born Stockport 26.9.69. Ht 6 1 Wt 14 00
Defender. From Trainee. England
Under-21.

Season	Club		
1987–88	Manchester C	—	—
1988–89	Oldham Ath	4	—
1989–90		30	1
1990–91		33	1

WARK, John

Born Glasgow 4.8.57. Ht 5 11 Wt 12 12
Midfield. From Apprentice. Scotland
Under-21, 29 full caps.

Season	Club		
1974–75	Ipswich T	3	—
1975–76		3	—
1976–77		33	10
1977–78		18	5
1978–79		42	6
1979–80		41	12
1980–81		40	18
1981–82		42	18
1982–83		42	20
1983–84		32	5
1983–84	Liverpool	9	2
1984–85		40	18

Season	Club		
1985–86		9	3
1986–87		11	5
1987–88		1	—
1987–88	Ipswich T	7	—
1988–89		41	13
1989–90		41	10
1990–91	Middlesbrough	32	2

WARREN, Lee

Born Manchester 28.2.69. Ht 6 0
Wt 11 10
Midfield. From Trainee.

Season	Club		
1987–88	Leeds U	—	—
1987–88	Rochdale	31	1
1988–89	Hull C	28	—
1989–90		10	—
1990–91		15	—
1990–91	*Lincoln C*	3	1

WARZYCHA, Robert

Born Poland 20.6.63.
Forward. From Gornik Zabrze. Poland
full caps.

Season	Club		
1990–91	Everton	8	2

WASSALL, Darren

Born Edgbaston 27.6.68. Ht 5 11
Wt 11 09
Defender.

Season	Club		
1987–88	Nottingham F	3	—
1987–88	*Hereford U*	5	—
1988–89	Nottingham F	—	—
1988–89	*Bury*	7	1
1989–90	Nottingham F	3	—
1990–91		7	—

WATKIN, Steve

Born Wrexham 16.6.71. Ht 5 10
Wt 11 00
Forward. From School.

Season	Club		
1989–90	Wrexham	—	—
1990–91		9	1

WATKINS, Dale

Born Peterborough 4.11.71.
Forward. From Sheffield U, Grimsby T
and Peterborough U Trainee.

1989–90	Peterborough U	1	—
1990–91		9	—

WATSON, Alex

Born Liverpool 5.4.68. Ht 5 11   Wt 11 09
Defender. From Apprentice. England
Youth.

1984–85	Liverpool	—	—
1985–86		—	—
1986–87		—	—
1987–88		2	—
1988–89		2	—
1989–90		—	—
1990–91		—	—
1990–91	*Derby Co*	5	—
1990–91	Bournemouth	23	3

WATSON, Andy

Born Huddersfield 1.4.67.   Ht 5 9
Wt 11 02
Defender. From Harrogate T

1988–89	Halifax T	45	5
1989–90		38	10
1990–91	Swansea C	14	1

WATSON, Dave

Born Liverpool 20.11.61.   Ht 6 0
Wt 11 12
Defender. From Amateur. England Under-
21, 12 full caps.

1979–80	Liverpool	—	—
1980–81		—	—
1980–81	Norwich C	18	3
1981–82		38	3
1982–83		35	1
1983–84		40	1
1984–85		39	—
1985–86		42	3
1986–87	Everton	35	4

1987–88		37	4
1988–89		32	3
1989–90		29	1
1990–91		32	2

WATSON, Gordon

Born Kent 20.3.71.   Ht 6 0   Wt 12 00
Forward. From Trainee. England
Under-21.

1988–89	Charlton Ath	—	—
1989–90		9	—
1990–91		22	7
1990–91	Sheffield W	5	—

WATSON, Gregg

Born Glasgow 21.9.70.   Ht 5 9   Wt 10 09
Midfield. From Aberdeen Lads. Scotland
Youth.

1987–88	Aberdeen	—	—
1988–89		4	—
1989–90		4	—
1990–91		7	—

WATSON, John

Born Edinburgh 13.2.59.   Ht 6 0
Wt 12 06
Forward. From Hong Kong R.

1983–84	Dunfermline Ath	21	3
1984–85		37	15
1985–86		37	24
1986–87		40	13
1987–88		25	3
1988–89		35	14
1989–90	Fulham	14	—
1989–90	Airdrie	11	1
1990–91		30	4

WATSON, John

Born South Shields 14.4.74.   Ht 5 9
Wt 10 10
Midfield. From Trainee.

1990–91	Newcastle U	1	—

WATSON, Steve

Born North Shields 1.4.74. Ht 6 0
Wt 12 07
Defender. From Trainee. England Youth.

| 1990–91 Newcastle U | 24 | — |

WATSON, Tommy

Born Liverpool 29.9.69 Ht 5 8 Wt 10 10
Midfield. From Trainee.

1987–88 Grimsby T	19	—
1988–89	21	4
1989–90	16	1
1990–91	41	9

WATT, Michael

Born Aberdeen 27.11.70. Ht 6 1
Wt 11 10
Goalkeeper. From Cove R. Scotland
Under-21.

| 1989–90 Aberdeen | 7 | — |
| 1990–91 | 10 | — |

WATTS, Julian

Born Sheffield 17.3.71. Ht 6 3 Wt 12 01
Defender.

| 1990–91 Rotherham U | 10 | — |

WAUGH, Keith

Born Sunderland 27.10.56. Ht 6 1
Wt 13 00
Goalkeeper. From Apprentice.

1974–75 Sunderland	—	—
1975–76	—	—
1976–77 Peterborough U	32	—
1977–78	26	—
1978–79	46	—
1979–80	46	—
1980–81	45	—
1981–82 Sheffield U	45	—
1982–83	28	—
1983–84	16	—

1984–85	10	—
1984–85 *Bristol C*	3	—
1984–85 *Cambridge U*	4	—
1985–86 Bristol C	44	—
1986–87	46	—
1987–88	40	—
1988–89	37	—
1989–90 Coventry C	1	—
1990–91	—	—
1990–91 *Watford*	—	—

WDOWCZYK, Dariusz

Born Warsaw 21.9.62.
Defender. From Legia Warsaw. Poland
full caps.

| 1989–90 Celtic | 23 | 1 |
| 1990–91 | 24 | — |

WEATHERHEAD, Shaun

Born Halifax 3.9.70. Ht 5 11 Wt 12 03
Defender. From Trainee.

| 1989–90 Huddersfield T | — | — |
| 1990–91 York C | 8 | — |

WEBB, Alan

Born Wellington 1.1.63. Ht 5 10
Wt 12 00
Defender. From Apprentice.

1979–80 WBA	—	—
1980–81	—	—
1981–82	6	—
1982–83	13	—
1983–84	5	—
1983–84 *Lincoln C*	11	—
1984–85 Port Vale	46	—
1985–86	39	1
1986–87	21	1
1987–88	26	—
1988–89	37	—
1989–90	14	—
1990–91	4	—

WEBB, Neil

Born Reading 30.7.63. Ht 6 0 Wt 13 03
Midfield. From Apprentice. England
Youth, B, Under-21, 20 full caps. Football
League.

1979–80	Reading	5	—
1980–81		27	7
1981–82		40	15
1982–83	Portsmouth	42	8
1983–84		40	10
1984–85		41	16
1985–86	Nottingham F	38	14
1986–87		32	14
1987–88		40	13
1988–89		36	6
1989–90	Manchester U	11	2
1990–91		32	3

WEBSTER, Simon

Born Earl Shilton 20.1.64. Ht 6 0
Wt 11 07
Defender. From Apprentice.

1981–82	Tottenham H	—	—
1982–83		2	—
1983–84		1	—
1983–84	*Exeter C*	26	—
1984–85	Tottenham H	—	—
1984–85	*Norwich C*	—	—
1984–85	Huddersfield T	16	1
1985–86		41	2
1986–87		39	1
1987–88		22	—
1987–88	Sheffield U	5	1
1988–89		12	2
1989–90		20	—
1990–91	Charlton Ath	40	—

WEGERLE, Roy

Born South Africa 19.3.64. Ht 5 11
Wt 11 00
Forward. From Tampa Bay R.

1986–87	Chelsea	12	2
1987–88		11	1
1987–88	*Swindon T*	7	1
1988–89	Luton T	30	8
1989–90		15	2
1989–90	QPR	19	6
1990–91		35	18

WEIR, Billy

Born Baillieston 11.4.68. Ht 5 5 Wt 9 12
Forward. From Baillieston Juniors.

1989–90	Shrewsbury T	9	—
1990–91		8	1

WEIR, Michael

Born Edinburgh 16.1.66. Ht 5 4 Wt 9 02
Midfield. From Portobello Thistle.

1982–83	Hibernian	—	—
1983–84		—	—
1984–85		12	—
1985–86		7	—
1986–87		24	4
1987–88		5	1
1987–88	Luton T	8	—
1987–88	Hibernian	13	2
1988–89		7	—
1989–90		18	3
1990–91		20	1

WELCH, Keith

Born Bolton 3.10.68. Ht 6 0 Wt 12 0
Goalkeeper. From Trainee.

1986–87	Bolton W	—	—
1986–87	Rochdale	24	—
1987–88		46	—
1988–89		46	—
1989–90		46	—
1990–91		43	—

WELSH, Brian

Born Edinburgh 23.2.69 Ht 6 2
Wt 12 01
Defender. From Tynecastle BC.

1986–87	Dundee U	1	—
1987–88		1	1
1988–89		1	—

Season	Club	Apps	Goals
1989–90		5	—
1990–91		17	—

WELSH, Steve

Born Glasgow 19.4.68.   Ht 6 0   Wt 12 03
Defender. From Army.

Season	Club	Apps	Goals
1989–90	Cambridge U	—	—
1990–91		1	—

WEST, Colin

Born Wallsend 13.11.62.   Ht 6 0
Wt 13 11
Forward. From Apprentice.

Season	Club	Apps	Goals
1980–81	Sunderland	—	—
1981–82		18	6
1982–83		23	3
1983–84		38	9
1984–85		23	3
1984–85	Watford	12	7
1985–86		33	13
1986–87	Rangers	9	2
1987–88		1	—
1987–88	Sheffield W	25	7
1988–89		20	1
1988–89	WBA	17	8
1989–90		21	4
1990–91		28	8

WEST, Dean

Born Wakefield 5.12.72.
Defender. From Leeds U Schoolboy.

Season	Club	Apps	Goals
1990–91	Lincoln C	1	1

WEST, Gary

Born Scunthorpe 25.8.64.   Ht 6 2
Wt 13 02
Defender. From Apprentice. England Youth.

Season	Club	Apps	Goals
1982–83	Sheffield U	26	1
1983–84		24	—
1984–85		25	—
1985–86	Lincoln C	38	2

Season	Club	Apps	Goals
1986–87		45	2
1987–88	Gillingham	42	2
1988–89		10	1
1988–89	Port Vale	14	1
1989–90		3	—
1990–91		—	—
1990–91	*Lincoln C*	3	—
1990–91	*Gillingham*	1	—

WESTLEY, Shane

Born Canterbury 16.6.65.   Ht 6 2
Wt 13 08
Defender. From Apprentice.

Season	Club	Apps	Goals
1983–84	Charlton Ath	8	—
1984–85		—	—
1984–85	Southend U	12	—
1985–86		36	5
1986–87		32	—
1986–87	*Norwich C*	—	—
1987–88	Southend U	36	5
1988–89		28	—
1989–90	Wolverhampton W	37	—
1990–91		5	1

WESTWATER, Ian

Born Loughborough 8.11.63.   Ht 6 0
Wt 13 00
Goalkeeper. From Salvesen BC.

Season	Club	Apps	Goals
1980–81	Hearts	2	—
1981–82		—	—
1982–83		—	—
1983–84		—	—
1984–85		—	—
1984–85	Dunfermline Ath	8	—
1985–86		38	—
1986–87		42	—
1987–88		28	—
1988–89		39	—
1989–90		36	—
1990–91		1	—

WETHERALL, David

Born Sheffield 14.3.71.   Ht 6 3   Wt 12 00
Defender. From School.

Season	Club	Apps	Goals
1989–90	Sheffield W	—	—

Season	Club	App	Goals
1990–91		—	—

WHEELER, Paul

Born Caerphilly 3.1.65. Ht 5 9 Wt 11 00
Forward. From Apprentice.

Season	Club	App	Goals
1982–83	Bristol R	—	—
1983–84		—	—
From Aberaman			
1985–86	Cardiff C	21	2
1986–87		37	7
1987–88		16	—
1988–89		27	1
1989–90			
1989–90	Hull C	5	—
1989–90	Hereford U	21	8
1990–91		33	4

WHELAN, Ronnie

Born Dublin 25.9.61. Ht 5 9 Wt 10 13
Midfield. From Home Farm. Eire Schools,
Youth, Under-21, 41 full caps.

Season	Club	App	Goals
1979–80	Liverpool	—	—
1980–81		1	1
1981–82		32	10
1982–83		28	2
1983–84		23	4
1984–85		37	7
1985–86		39	10
1986–87		39	3
1987–88		28	1
1988–89		37	4
1989–90		34	1
1990–91		14	1

WHELAN, Spencer

Born Liverpool 17.9.71. Ht 6 1 Wt 11 13
Defender. From Liverpool.

Season	Club	App	Goals
1990–91	Chester C	11	—

WHISTON, Peter

Born Widnes 4.1.68. Ht 6 0 Wt 11 06
Forward.

Season	Club	App	Goals
1987–88	Plymouth Arg	—	—

Season	Club	App	Goals
1988–89		2	—
1989–90		8	—
1989–90	*Torquay U*	8	1
1990–91	Torquay U	28	—

WHITBREAD, Adrian

Born Epping 22.10.71. Ht 6 2 Wt 11 13
Defender. From Trainee

Season	Club	App	Goals
1989–90	Leyton Orient	8	—
1990–91		38	—

WHITE, David

Born Manchester 30.10.67. Ht 6 1
Wt 12 09
Forward. England Youth, B, Under-21.

Season	Club	App	Goals
1985–86	Manchester C	—	—
1986–87		24	1
1987–88		44	13
1988–89		45	6
1989–90		37	8
1990–91		38	16

WHITE, Devon

Born Nottingham 2.3.64. Ht 6 3
Wt 14 00
Forward. From Arnold T.

Season	Club	App	Goals
1984–85	Lincoln C	7	1
1985–86		22	3
1986–87		—	—
From Boston U			
1987–88	Bristol R	39	15
1988–89		40	5
1989–90		43	12
1990–91		45	11

WHITE, Steve

Born Chipping Sodbury 2.1.59. Ht 5 10
Wt 11 04
Forward. From Mangotsfield U.

Season	Club	App	Goals
1977–78	Bristol R	8	4
1978–79		27	10
1979–80		15	6

Season	Club	App	Goals
1979–80	Luton T	9	—
1980–81		21	7
1981–82		42	18
1982–83	Charlton Ath	29	12
1982–83	*Lincoln C*	3	—
1982–83	*Luton T*	4	—
1983–84	Bristol R	43	9
1984–85		18	3
1985–86		40	12
1986–87	Swindon T	35	15
1987–88		25	11
1988–89		43	13
1989–90		43	18
1990–91		35	9

WHITE, Winston

Born Leicester 26.10.58. Ht 5 10
Wt 10 12
Midfield. From Apprentice.

Season	Club	App	Goals
1976–77	Leicester C	4	—
1977–78		6	1
1978–79		2	—
1978–79	Hereford U	15	3
1979–80		34	2
1980–81		43	5
1981–82		46	8
1982–83		37	3
1983–84	Chesterfield	1	—
1983–84	Port Vale	1	—
1983–84	Stockport Co	4	—
1983–84	Bury	29	1
1984–85		46	4
1985–86		43	5
1986–87		7	1
1986–87	*Rochdale*	4	—
1986–87	Colchester U	14	1
1987–88		41	7
1988–89		10	—
1988–89	Burnley	35	5
1989–90		40	7
1990–91		29	2
1990–91	WBA	6	1

WHITEHEAD, Clive

Born Birmingham 24.11.55. Ht 5 10
Wt 12 03
Defender. From Northfield J.

Season	Club	App	Goals
1973–74	Bristol C	12	2
1974–75		14	—
1975–76		22	4
1976–77		41	—
1977–78		33	2
1978–79		30	2
1979–80		40	—
1980–81		31	—
1981–82		6	—
1981–82	WBA	8	1
1982–83		36	1
1983–84		34	1
1984–85		32	—
1985–86		24	—
1985–86	*Wolverhampton W*	2	—
1986–87	WBA	34	3
1987–88	Portsmouth	33	2
1988–89		32	—
1989–90	Exeter C	38	5
1990–91		8	—

WHITEHEAD, Philip

Born Halifax 17.12.69 Ht 6 3   Wt 13 07
Goalkeeper. From Trainee.

Season	Club	App	Goals
1986–87	Halifax T	12	—
1987–88		—	—
1988–89		11	—
1989–90		19	—
1989–90	Barnsley	—	—
1990–91		—	—
1990–91	*Halifax T*	9	—

WHITEHOUSE, Dane

Born Sheffield 14.10.70. Ht 5 8   Wt 10 12
Midfield. From Trainee.

Season	Club	App	Goals
1988–89	Sheffield U	5	—
1989–90		12	1
1990–91		4	—

WHITEHOUSE, Phil

Born Wolverhampton 23.3.71. Ht 5 6
Wt 10 09
Defender. From Trainee.

Season	Club	App	Goals
1989–90	WBA	—	—

Season	Club	Apps	Goals
1989–90	Walsall	9	—
1990–91		3	—

WHITEHURST, Billy

Born Thurnscoe 10.6.59. Ht 6 0
Wt 14 09
Forward. From Mexborough.

Season	Club	Apps	Goals
1980–81	Hull C	26	1
1981–82		36	6
1982–83		36	3
1983–84		37	10
1984–85		40	20
1985–86		18	7
1985–86	Newcastle U	20	7
1986–87		8	—
1986–87	Oxford U	20	2
1987–88		20	2
1987–88	Reading	15	6
1988–89		2	2
1988–89	Sunderland	17	3
1988–89	Hull C	21	5
1989–90		15	—
1989–90	Sheffield U	14	2
1990–91		8	—
1990–91	*Stoke C*	3	—
1990–91	Doncaster R	13	1

WHITESIDE, Norman

Born Belfast 7.5.65. Ht 6 0 Wt 12 11
Forward. From Apprentice. Northern
Ireland Schools, Youth, 38 full caps.

Season	Club	Apps	Goals
1981–82	Manchester U	2	1
1982–83		39	8
1983–84		37	10
1984–85		27	9
1985–86		37	4
1986–87		31	8
1987–88		27	7
1988–89		6	—
1989–90	Everton	27	9
1990–91		2	—

WHITLOCK, Mark

Born Portsmouth 14.3.61. Ht 6 0
Wt 12 02
Defender. From Apprentice.

Season	Club	Apps	Goals
1978–79	Southampton	—	—
1979–80		—	—
1980–81		—	—
1981–82		9	1
1982–83	*Grimsby T*	8	—
1982–83	*Aldershot*	14	—
1983–84	Southampton	16	—
1984–85		22	—
1985–86		14	—
1986–87	Bournemouth	45	1
1987–88		41	—
1988–89		13	—
1988–89	Reading	17	—
1989–90		10	—
1990–91	Aldershot	29	2

WHITLOW, Mike

Born Northwich 13.1.68. Ht 5 11
Wt 12 01
Midfield. From Witton Alb.

Season	Club	Apps	Goals
1988–89	Leeds U	20	1
1989–90		29	1
1990–91		18	1

WHITTAKER, Brian

Born Glasgow 23.9.56. Ht 6 0 Wt 11 09
Defender. From Sighthill Amateurs.

Season	Club	Apps	Goals
1974–75	Partick T	1	—
1975–76		1	—
1976–77		36	1
1977–78		35	—
1978–79		36	—
1979–80		35	1
1980–81		34	1
1981–82		28	—
1982–83		35	1
1983–84	Celtic	10	2
1984–85	Hearts	28	1
1985–86		25	—
1986–87		37	—
1987–88		42	—
1988–89		24	—
1989–90		6	—
1990–91	Falkirk	25	1

WHITTINGHAM, Guy

Born Evesham 10.11.64.   Ht 5 10
Wt 11 12
Forward. From Yeovil and Army.

Season	Club	Apps	Goals
1989–90	Portsmouth	42	23
1990–91		37	12

WHITTON, Steve

Born East Ham 4.12.60.   Ht 6 0
Wt 12 07
Forward. From Apprentice.

Season	Club	Apps	Goals
1978–79	Coventry C	—	—
1979–80		7	—
1980–81		1	—
1981–82		28	9
1982–83		38	12
1983–84	West Ham U	22	5
1984–85		17	1
1985–86		—	—
1985–86	*Birmingham C*	8	2
1986–87	Birmingham C	39	9
1987–88		33	14
1988–89		23	5
1988–89	Sheffield W	12	3
1989–90		19	1
1990–91		1	—
1990–91	Ipswich T	10	2

WHITWORTH, Neil

Born Ince 12.4.72.
Defender. From Trainee. England Youth.

Season	Club	Apps	Goals
1989–90	Wigan Ath	2	—
1990–91	Manchester U	1	—

WHYTE, Chris

Born London 2.9.61.   Ht 6 1   Wt 11 10
Defender. From Amateur. England
Under-21.

Season	Club	Apps	Goals
1979–80	Arsenal	—	—
1980–81		—	—
1981–82		32	2
1982–83		36	3
1983–84		15	2
1984–85		—	—
1984–85	*Crystal Palace*	13	—
1985–86	Arsenal	7	1
From Los Angeles R			
1988–89	WBA	40	3
1989–90		44	4
1990–91	Leeds U	38	3

WHYTE, Derek

Born Glasgow 31.8.68.   Ht 5 11   Wt 11 05
Defender. From Celtic BC. Scotland
Schools, Youth, B, Under-21, 3 full caps.

Season	Club	Apps	Goals
1985–86	Celtic	11	—
1986–87		42	—
1987–88		41	3
1988–89		22	—
1989–90		35	1
1990–91		24	2

WIGLEY, Steve

Born Ashton 15.10.61.   Ht 5 9   Wt 10 05
Forward. From Curzon Ashton.

Season	Club	Apps	Goals
1980–81	Nottingham F	—	—
1981–82		—	—
1982–83		4	—
1983–84		35	1
1984–85		35	1
1985–86		8	—
1985–86	Sheffield U	10	1
1986–87		18	—
1986–87	Birmingham C	11	1
1987–88		43	2
1988–89		33	1
1988–89	Portsmouth	11	—
1989–90		45	4
1990–91		41	5

WIGNALL, Steve

Born Liverpool 17.9.54.   Ht 5 11
Wt 11 11
Defender. From Liverpool Amateur.

Season	Club	Apps	Goals
1971–72	Doncaster R	—	—
1972–73		23	—
1973–74		38	—

Season	Club	Apps	Goals
1974–75	....	35	1
1975–76	....	23	—
1976–77	....	11	—
1976–77	*Nottingham F*	—	—
1977–78	Doncaster R	—	—
1977–78	Colchester U	34	2
1978–79	....	42	4
1979–80	....	40	3
1980–81	....	42	1
1981–82	....	43	—
1982–83	....	44	4
1983–84	....	36	8
1984–85	Brentford	36	—
1985–86	....	28	2
1986–87	....	3	—
1986–87	Aldershot	40	1
1987–88	....	37	1
1988–89	....	32	1
1989–90	....	38	1
1990–91	....	14	—

WILCOX, Jason

Born Bolton 15.7.71. Ht 5 10   Wt 11 06
Forward. From Trainee

Season	Club	Apps	Goals
1989–90	Blackburn R	1	—
1990–91	....	18	—

WILCOX, Russell

Born Hemsworth 25.3.64.   Ht 6 0
Wt 11 10
Defender. From Apprentice.

Season	Club	Apps	Goals
1980–81	Doncaster R	1	—
From Cambridge U, Frickley Ath.			
1986–87	Northampton T	35	1
1987–88	....	46	4
1988–89	....	11	1
1989–90	....	46	3
1990–91	Hull C	31	1

WILDER, Chris

Born Wortley 23.9.67   Ht 5 11   Wt 10 10
Defender. From Apprentice.

Season	Club	Apps	Goals
1985–86	Southampton	—	—
1986–87	Sheffield U	11	—

Season	Club	Apps	Goals
1987–88	....	25	—
1988–89	....	29	1
1989–90	....	8	—
1989–90	*Walsall*	4	—
1990–91	Sheffield U	16	—
1990–91	*Charlton Ath*	1	—

WILKES, David

Born Barnsley 10.3.64.   Ht 5 8   Wt 10 02
Midfield. From Apprentice.

Season	Club	Apps	Goals
1981–82	Barnsley	2	—
1982–83	....	4	—
1982–83	*Halifax T*	4	—
1983–84	Barnsley	11	2
From Hong Kong			
1986–87	Stockport Co	8	—
From Hong Kong			
1990–91	Carlisle U	1	—

WILKIN, Kevin

Born Cambridge 1.10.67.
Forward. From Cambridge C.

Season	Club	Apps	Goals
1990–91	Northampton T	9	2

WILKINS, Dean

Born Hillingdon 12.7.62.   Ht 5 8
Wt 11 08
Midfield. From Apprentice.

Season	Club	Apps	Goals
1980–81	QPR	2	—
1981–82	....	1	—
1982–83	....	3	—
1983–84	Brighton	2	—
1983–84	*Orient*	10	—
From PEC Zwolle			
1987–88	Brighton	44	3
1988–89	....	43	1
1989–90	....	46	6
1990–91	....	46	7

WILKINS, Ray

Born Hillingdon 14.9.56.   Ht 5 8
Wt 11 02
Midfield. From Apprentice. England
Under-21, Under-23, 84 full caps. Football
League.

Season	Club	Apps	Goals
1973–74	Chelsea	6	—
1974–75		21	2
1975–76		42	11
1976–77		42	7
1977–78		33	7
1978–79		35	3
1979–80	Manchester U	37	2
1980–81		13	—
1981–82		42	1
1982–83		26	1
1983–84		42	3
1984–85	AC Milan	28	—
1985–86		29	2
1986–87		16	—
From Paris St Germain			
1987–88	Rangers	24	1
1988–89		31	1
1989–90		15	—
1989–90	QPR	23	1
1990–91		38	2

WILKINS, Richard

Born London 28.5.65. Ht 6 0 Wt 12 00
Midfield. From Haverhill R.

Season	Club	Apps	Goals
1986–87	Colchester U	23	2
1987–88		46	9
1988–89		40	7
1989–90		43	4
1990–91	Cambridge U	41	3

WILKINSON, Paul

Born Louth 30.10.64. Ht 6 0 Wt 11 09
Forward. From Apprentice. England
Under-21.

Season	Club	Apps	Goals
1982–83	Grimsby T	4	1
1983–84		37	12
1984–85		30	14
1984–85	Everton	5	2
1985–86		4	1
1986–87		22	4
1986–87	Nottingham F	8	—
1987–88		26	5
1988–89	Watford	45	19
1989–90		43	15
1990–91		46	18

WILKINSON, Steve

Born Lincoln 1.9.68. Ht 6 0 Wt 10 12
Forward. From Apprentice.

Season	Club	Apps	Goals
1986–87	Leicester C	1	—
1987–88		5	1
1988–89		1	—
1988–89	*Rochdale*	—	—
1988–89	*Crewe Alex*	5	2
1989–90	Leicester C	2	—
1989–90	Mansfield T	37	15
1990–91		39	11

WILLIAMS, Adrian

Born Reading 16.8.71 Ht 5 10 Wt 11 00
Defender. From Trainee.

Season	Club	Apps	Goals
1988–89	Reading	8	—
1989–90		16	2
1990–91		7	—

WILLIAMS, Andy

Born Birmingham 29.7.62. Ht 6 2
Wt 12 00
Midfield. From Dudley and Solihull B.

Season	Club	Apps	Goals
1985–86	Coventry C	8	—
1986–87		1	—
1986–87	Rotherham U	36	4
1987–88		36	6
1988–89		15	3
1988–89	Leeds U	18	1
1989–90		16	2
1990–91		12	—

WILLIAMS, Bill

Born Rochdale 7.10.60. Ht 5 10
Wt 12 11
Defender. Local.

Season	Club	Apps	Goals
1981–82	Rochdale	6	—
1982–83		37	—
1983–84		27	2
1984–85		25	—
1985–86	Stockport Co	22	—
1986–87		30	—
1987–88		45	1

Season	Club	App	Goals
1988–89	....	7	—
1988–89	Manchester C	1	—
1988–89	Stockport Co	28	2
1989–90	....	37	—
1990–91	....	18	1

WILLIAMS, Brett

Born Dudley 19.3.68. Ht 5 10   Wt 11 12
Defender. From Apprentice.

Season	Club	App	Goals
1985–86	Nottingham F.............	11	—
1986–87	....	3	—
1986–87	*Stockport Co*	2	—
1987–88	Nottingham F.............	4	—
1987–88	*Northampton T*	4	—
1988–89	Nottingham F.............	2	—
1989–90	....	1	—
1989–90	*Hereford U*	14	—
1990–91	Nottingham F.............	4	—

WILLIAMS, Darren

Born Birmingham 15.12.68. Ht 5 10
Wt 10 05
Midfield. From Trainee.

Season	Club	App	Goals
1986–87	Leicester C	—	—
1987–88	....	—	—
1988–89	....	6	1
1989–90	....	4	1
1989–90	*Lincoln C*	9	—
1990–91	Leicester C	—	—
1990–91	*Chesterfield*	5	1

WILLIAMS, David

Born Liverpool 18.9.68. Ht 6 0   Wt 12 00
Goalkeeper. From Trainee.

Season	Club	App	Goals
1987–88	Oldham Ath...............	—	—
1987–88	Burnley	—	—
1988–89	....	7	—
1989–90	....	7	—
1990–91	....	3	—

WILLIAMS, Dean

Born Lichfield 5.1.72. Ht 6 0   Wt 11 07
Goalkeeper. From Trainee.

Season	Club	App	Goals
1989–90	Birmingham C	3	—
1990–91	....	1	—

WILLIAMS, Gareth

Born Isle of Wight 12.3.67. Ht 5 10
Wt 11 08
Forward. From Gosport Borough.

Season	Club	App	Goals
1987–88	Aston Villa................	1	—
1988–89	....	1	—
1989–90	....	10	—
1990–91	....	—	—

WILLIAMS, Gary

Born Wolverhampton 17.6.60. Ht 5 9
Wt 11 12
Defender. From Apprentice.

Season	Club	App	Goals
1978–79	Aston Villa................	23	—
1979–80	....	2	—
1979–80	*Walsall*	9	—
1980–81	Aston Villa................	22	—
1981–82	....	28	—
1982–83	....	36	—
1983–84	....	40	—
1984–85	....	38	—
1985–86	....	25	—
1986–87	....	26	—
1987–88	Leeds U	31	3
1988–89	....	8	—
1989–90	....	—	—
1989–90	Watford	18	—
1990–91	....	24	—

WILLIAMS, Gary

Born Bristol 8.6.63. Ht 5 8   Wt 10 11
Midfield. From Apprentice.

Season	Club	App	Goals
1980–81	Bristol C	1	—
1981–82	....	33	1
1982–83	....	36	—
1983–84	....	30	—
1984–85	Portsmouth	—	—
1984–85	Swansea C..................	6	—
1984–85	Bristol R	—	—
1985–86	Oldham Ath...............	9	1
1986–87	....	32	9

Season	Club	League Appearances/Goals	
1987–88		9	1
1988–89		6	1
1989–90		3	—
1990–91		2	—

WILLIAMS, Geraint

Born Treorchy 5.1.62. Ht 5 7 Wt 10 6
Midfield. From Apprentice. Wales Youth,
Under-21, 11 full caps.

Season	Club		
1979–80	Bristol R	—	—
1980–81		28	1
1981–82		16	—
1982–83		35	3
1983–84		34	4
1984–85		28	—
1984–85	Derby Co	12	—
1985–86		40	4
1986–87		40	1
1987–88		40	1
1988–89		37	1
1989–90		38	—
1990–91		31	—

WILLIAMS, Jeremy

Born Didcot 24.3.60. Ht 5 11 Wt 11 10
Midfield. From Apprentice.

Season	Club		
1976–77	Reading	5	—
1977–78		13	2
1978–79		1	—
1979–80		15	2
1980–81		27	3
1981–82		45	—
1982–83		41	2
1983–84		38	—
1984–85		38	1
1985–86		31	4
1986–87		34	2
1987–88		21	1
1988–89	Gillingham	13	—
1989–90	Aldershot	28	1
1990–91		39	6

WILLIAMS, John

Born Liverpool 3.10.60. Ht 6 1 Wt 13 12
Defender. From Amateur.

Season	Club		
1978–79	Tranmere R	1	—
1979–80		3	—
1980–81		27	2
1981–82		44	6
1982–83		35	—
1983–84		20	1
1984–85		43	4
1985–86	Port Vale	36	2
1986–87		14	—
1986–87	Bournemouth	26	3
1987–88		38	2
1988–89		37	2
1989–90		16	2
1990–91		—	—

WILLIAMS, Mike

Born Mancot 6.2.65. Ht 5 10 Wt 11 00
Midfield. From Apprentice. Wales Youth.

Season	Club		
1981–82	Chester	2	—
1982–83		12	2
1983–84		20	2
1984–85	Wrexham	27	—
1985–86		27	—
1986–87		42	1
1987–88		42	2
1988–89		27	—
1989–90		13	—
1990–91		—	—

WILLIAMS, Neil

Born Waltham Abbey 23.10.64. Ht 5 11
Wt 11 04
Midfield. From Apprentice. England
Youth.

Season	Club		
1982–83	Watford	—	—
1983–84		—	—
1984–85	Hull C	17	3
1985–86		19	3
1986–87		30	2
1987–88		25	2
1988–89	Preston NE	41	2
1989–90		41	3
1990–91		13	—

WILLIAMS, Paul

Born Liverpool 25.9.70. Ht 6 0 Wt 12 02
Midfield. From Trainee.

1988–89	Sunderland	1	—
1989–90		1	—
1990–91		1	—
1990–91	*Swansea C*	12	—

WILLIAMS, Paul

Born Leicester 11.9.69. Ht 5 7 Wt 10 00
Forward. From Trainee

1988–89	Leicester C	—	—
1989–90	Stockport Co	7	—
1990–91		24	2

WILLIAMS, Paul

Born Burton 26.3.71. Ht 5 11 Wt 12 00
Midfield. From Trainee. England
Under-21.

1989–90	Derby Co	10	1
1989–90	*Lincoln C*	3	—
1990–91	Derby Co	19	4

WILLIAMS, Paul

Born London 16.8.65. Ht 5 7 Wt 10 03
Forward. From Woodford T. England B,
Under-21.

1986–87	Charlton Ath	—	—
1987–88		12	—
1987–88	*Brentford*	7	3
1988–89	Charlton Ath	32	13
1989–90		38	10
1990–91	Sheffield W	46	15

WILLIAMS, Paul

Born Sheffield 8.9.63 Ht 6 3 Wt 14 06
Forward. From Distillery, Leeds U,
Grenaker R, Nuneaton. Northern Ireland
1 full cap.

| 1986–87 | Preston NE | 1 | — |
| 1987–88 | Newport Co | 26 | 3 |

1987–88	Sheffield U	6	—
1988–89		2	—
1989–90	Hartlepool U	8	—
1990–91	Stockport Co	24	14
1990–91	WBA	10	—

WILLIAMS, Steve

Born London 12.7.58. Ht 5 9 Wt 11 04
Midfield. From Apprentice. England
Under-21, B, 6 full caps.

1974–75	Southampton	—	—
1975–76		1	—
1976–77		33	—
1977–78		39	5
1978–79		39	—
1979–80		32	2
1980–81		33	4
1981–82		21	—
1982–83		39	3
1983–84		27	3
1984–85		14	1
1984–85	Arsenal	15	1
1985–86		17	—
1986–87		34	2
1987–88		29	1
1988–89	Luton T	10	—
1989–90		14	1
1990–91		16	—

WILLIAMS, Steven

Born Mansfield 18.7.70 Ht 5 11
Wt 10 06
Midfield. From Trainee.

1986–87	Mansfield T	4	—
1987–88		4	—
1988–89		3	—
1989–90	Chesterfield	11	1
1990–91		25	4

WILLIAMS, Wayne

Born Delford 17.11.63. Ht 5 11
Wt 11 09
Defender. From Apprentice.

| 1981–82 | Shrewsbury T | — | — |

Season	Club	Apps	Goals
1982–83	....	42	4
1983–84	....	40	—
1984–85	....	28	—
1985–86	....	30	1
1986–87	....	40	—
1987–88	....	31	2
1988–89	....	10	—
1988–89	Northampton T	26	1
1989–90	....	15	—
1990–91	....	14	—

WILLIAMSON, Andy

Born Kirkcaldy 4.9.69. Ht 6 0 Wt 11 00
Midfield. From Glenrothes Strollers.

Season	Club	Apps	Goals
1987–88	Dunfermline Ath	2	—
1988–89	....	6	—
1989–90	....	1	—
1990–91	....	5	—

WILLIAMSON, Bobby

Born Glasgow 13.8.61. Ht 5 10 Wt 11 00
Forward. From Auchengill BC.

Season	Club	Apps	Goals
1980–81	Clydebank	2	—
1981–82	....	12	1
1982–83	....	39	23
1983–84	....	17	4
1983–84	Rangers	17	6
1984–85	....	1	—
1985–86	....	23	6
1986–87	WBA	31	8
1987–88	....	22	3
1988–89	Rotherham U	42	27
1989–90	....	42	19
1990–91	....	9	3
1990–91	Kilmarnock	23	14

WILLIS, Jimmy

Born Liverpool 12.7.68. Ht 6 2 Wt 12 04
Defender. From Blackburn R.

Season	Club	Apps	Goals
1986–87	Halifax T	—	—
1987–88	Stockport Co	10	—
1987–88	Darlington	9	—
1988–89	....	41	2
1989–90	....	38	2

Season	Club	Apps	Goals
1990–91	....	28	2

WILLMOTT, Ian

Born Bristol 10.7.68 Ht 5 10 Wt 12 07
Defender. From Weston-super-Mare.

Season	Club	Apps	Goals
1988–89	Bristol R	—	—
1989–90	....	17	—
1990–91	....	3	—

WILMOT, Rhys

Born Newport 21.2.62. Ht 6 1 Wt 12 00
Goalkeeper. From Apprentice. Wales
Youth, Under-21.

Season	Club	Apps	Goals
1979–80	Arsenal	—	—
1980–81	....	—	—
1981–82	....	—	—
1982–83	....	—	—
1982–83	*Hereford U*	9	—
1983–84	Arsenal	—	—
1984–85	*Orient*	46	—
1985–86	Arsenal	2	—
1986–87	....	6	—
1987–88	....	—	—
1988–89	....	—	—
1988–89	*Swansea C*	16	—
1988–89	*Plymouth Arg*	17	—
1989–90	Plymouth Arg	46	—
1990–91	....	36	—

WILSON, Clive

Born Manchester 13.11.61. Ht 5 7
Wt 10 00
Midfield. From Local.

Season	Club	Apps	Goals
1979–80	Manchester C	—	—
1980–81	....	—	—
1981–82	....	4	—
1982–83	....	—	—
1982–83	*Chester*	21	2
1983–84	Manchester C	11	—
1984–85	....	27	4
1985–86	....	25	5
1986–87	....	31	—
1986–87	Chelsea	—	—
1986–87	*Manchester C*	11	—

Season	Club	App	Goals
1987–88	Chelsea	31	2
1988–89		32	3
1989–90		18	—
1990–91	QPR	13	1

WILSON, Danny

Born Wigan 1.1.60. Ht 5 6 Wt 11 00
Midfield. From Wigan Ath. Northern
Ireland 22 full caps.

Season	Club	App	Goals
1977–78	Bury	12	1
1978–79		46	7
1979–80		32	—
1980–81	Chesterfield	33	3
1981–82		43	3
1982–83		24	7
1982–83	Nottingham F	10	1
1983–84	*Scunthorpe U*	6	3
1983–84	Brighton	26	10
1984–85		38	5
1985–86		33	11
1986–87		38	7
1987–88	Luton T	38	8
1988–89		37	9
1989–90		35	7
1990–91	Sheffield W	36	6

WILSON, David

Born Burnley 20.3.69. Ht 5 9 Wt 10 10
Midfield. From Apprentice.

Season	Club	App	Goals
1986–87	Manchester U	—	—
1987–88		—	—
1988–89		4	—
1989–90		—	—
1990–91		—	—
1990–91	*Charlton Ath*	7	2
1990–91	*Lincoln C*	3	—

WILSON, Ian

Born Aberdeen 27.3.58. Ht 5 7 Wt 10 10
Midfield. From Elgin C. Scotland 5 full
caps.

Season	Club	App	Goals
1978–79	Leicester C	—	—
1979–80		24	2
1980–81		40	1

Season	Club	App	Goals
1981–82		35	—
1982–83		36	8
1983–84		41	—
1984–85		39	1
1985–86		25	2
1986–87		37	1
1987–88		8	2
1987–88	Everton	16	—
1988–89		18	1
From Besiktas			
1990–91	Derby Co	11	—

WILSON, Kevin

Born Banbury 18.4.61. Ht 5 8 Wt 11 06
Forward. From Banbury U. Northern
Ireland 21 full caps.

Season	Club	App	Goals
1979–80	Derby Co	4	—
1980–81		27	7
1981–82		24	9
1982–83		22	4
1983–84		32	2
1984–85		13	8
1984–85	Ipswich T	17	7
1985–86		39	7
1986–87		42	20
1987–88	Chelsea	25	5
1988–89		46	13
1989–90		37	14
1990–91		22	7

WILSON, Paul

Born Bradford 2.8.68 Ht 5 10 Wt 13 00
Defender. From Trainee.

Season	Club	App	Goals
1985–86	Huddersfield T	7	—
1986–87		8	—
1987–88	Norwich C	—	—
1987–88	Northampton T	15	1
1988–89		39	1
1989–90		27	—
1990–91		44	3

WILSON, Phil

Born Hemsworth 16.10.60. Ht 5 6
Wt 11 13
Midfield. From Apprentice.

Season	Club	Apps	Goals
1978–79	Bolton W	—	—
1979–80		17	1
1980–81		22	3
1981–82	Huddersfield T	34	2
1982–83		45	6
1983–84		41	3
1984–85		40	3
1985–86		35	1
1986–87		38	1
1987–88	York C	36	1
1988–89		10	1
From Macclesfield			
1989–90	Scarborough	24	1
1990–91		19	1

WILSON, Robert

Born Kensington 5.6.61. Ht 5 10
Wt 12 00
Midfield. From Apprentice. Eire Under-21.

Season	Club	Apps	Goals
1979–80	Fulham	2	—
1980–81		35	4
1981–82		43	5
1982–83		40	11
1983–84		16	3
1984–85		39	11
1985–86	Millwall	28	12
1986–87	Luton T	21	1
1987–88		3	—
1987–88	Fulham	20	3
1988–89		27	1
1989–90	Huddersfield T	28	6
1990–91		29	2

WILSON, Steve

Born Hull 24.4.74.
Goalkeeper. From Trainee.

Season	Club	Apps	Goals
1990–91	Hull C	2	—

WILSON, Terry

Born Broxburn 8.2.69. Ht 6 0 Wt 10 10
Midfield. From Apprentice. Scotland
Under-21.

Season	Club	Apps	Goals
1986–87	Nottingham F	—	—
1987–88		36	5

Season	Club	Apps	Goals
1988–89		27	1
1989–90		21	—
1990–91		15	3

WILSON, Tommy

Born Paisley 2.8.61. Ht 5 8 Wt 9 07
Defender. From School. Scotland
Under-21.

Season	Club	Apps	Goals
1979–80	Queens Park	1	—
1980–81		1	—
1981–82		30	—
1982–83	St Mirren	36	—
1983–84		1	—
1984–85		35	—
1985–86		27	—
1986–87		25	1
1987–88		35	—
1988–89		31	—
1989–90		9	—
1989–90	Dunfermline Ath	15	—
1990–91		28	—

WIMBLETON, Paul

Born Havant 13.11.64. Ht 5 8 Wt 10 12
Midfield. From Apprentice. England
Schools, Youth.

Season	Club	Apps	Goals
1981–82	Portsmouth	8	—
1982–83		—	—
1983–84		2	—
1984–85		—	—
1985–86		—	—
1986–87	Cardiff C	46	8
1987–88		37	9
1988–89		36	—
1989–90	Bristol C	16	2
1989–90	Shrewsbury T	16	—
1990–91		18	1
1990–91	*Maidstone U*	2	1

WINNIE, David

Born Glasgow 26.10.66. Ht 5 1 Wt 10 07
Defender. S Form. Scotland Schools,
Youth, Under-21.

Season	Club	Apps	Goals
1983–84	St Mirren	8	—

Season	Club	App	Goals
1984–85		30	3
1985–86		20	1
1986–87		14	—
1987–88		26	2
1988–89		30	—
1989–90		17	—
1990–91		1	—

WINSTANLEY, Mark

Born St. Helens 22.1.68. Ht 6 1
Wt 12 04
Defender. From Trainee.

Season	Club	App	Goals
1984–85	Bolton W	—	—
1985–86		3	—
1986–87		13	—
1987–88		8	1
1988–89		44	—
1989–90		43	1
1990–91		32	—

WINTER, Julian

Born Huddersfield 6.9.65. Ht 6 0
Wt 11 10
Midfield. Local.

Season	Club	App	Goals
1983–84	Huddersfield T	—	—
1984–85		16	2
1985–86		4	—
1986–87		31	1
1987–88		7	—
1988–89		35	2
1988–89	*Scunthorpe U*	4	—
1989–90	Sheffield U	—	—
1990–91		—	—

WINTERBURN, Nigel

Born Nuneaton 11.12.63. Ht 5 10
Wt 10 09
Defender. Local. England Youth, B,
Under-21, 1 full cap.

Season	Club	App	Goals
1981–82	Birmingham C	—	—
1982–83		—	—
1983–84	Oxford U	—	—
1983–84	Wimbledon	43	1
1984–85		41	4

Season	Club	App	Goals
1985–86		39	1
1986–87		42	2
1987–88	Arsenal	17	—
1988–89		38	3
1989–90		36	—
1990–91		38	—

WISE, Dennis

Born Kensington 15.12.66. Ht 5 6
Wt 9 05
Forward. From Southampton Apprentice.
England B, Under-21, 5 full caps.

Season	Club	App	Goals
1984–85	Wimbledon	1	—
1985–86		4	—
1986–87		28	4
1987–88		30	10
1988–89		37	5
1989–90		35	8
1990–91	Chelsea	33	10

WISHART, Fraser

Born Johnstone 1.3.65. Ht 5 8 Wt 10 00
Defender. From Pollok.

Season	Club	App	Goals
1983–84	Motherwell	6	—
1984–85		—	—
1985–86		26	—
1986–87		44	3
1987–88		43	1
1988–89		35	1
1989–90	St Mirren	20	—
1990–91		22	—

WITHE, Chris

Born Liverpool 25.9.62. Ht 5 10
Wt 11 02
Defender. From Apprentice.

Season	Club	App	Goals
1980–81	Newcastle U	2	—
1981–82		—	—
1982–83		—	—
1983–84	Bradford C	45	1
1984–85		45	—
1985–86		33	—
1986–87		18	1
1987–88		2	—

Season	Club	App	Goals
1987–88	Notts Co	35	2
1988–89		45	1
1989–90	Bury	31	1
1990–91		—	—
1990–91	*Chester C*	2	—
1990–91	*Mansfield T*	11	—
1990–91	Mansfield T	10	—

WOAN, Ian

Born Wirrall 14.12.67   Ht 5 10   Wt 11 09
Midfield. From Runcorn.

Season	Club	App	Goals
1989–90	Nottingham F	—	—
1990–91		12	3

WOOD, Darren

Born Scarborough 9.6.64.   Ht 5 10
Wt 11 00
Defender. From Apprentice. England
Schools.

Season	Club	App	Goals
1981–82	Middlesbrough	11	1
1982–83		42	3
1983–84		42	2
1984–85		6	—
1984–85	Chelsea	19	1
1985–86		28	—
1986–87		41	—
1987–88		34	1
1988–89		22	1
1988–89	Sheffield W	8	—
1989–90		3	—
1990–91		—	—

WOOD, Darren

Born Derby 22.10.68.   Ht 6 1   Wt 12 08
Defender. From Trainee.

Season	Club	App	Goals
1986–87	Chesterfield	10	1
1987–88		35	1
1988–89		22	1
1989–90	Reading	32	2
1990–91	Northampton T	2	1

WOOD, George

Born Douglas 26.9.52.   Ht 6 3   Wt 14 00
Goalkeeper. From East Stirling. Scotland
4 full caps.

Season	Club	App	Goals
1970–71	East Stirling	23	1
1971–72		21	—
1971–72	Blackpool	4	—
1972–73		20	—
1973–74		12	—
1974–75		4	—
1975–76		35	—
1976–77		42	—
1977–78	Everton	42	—
1978–79		42	—
1979–80		19	—
1980–81	Arsenal	11	—
1981–82		26	—
1982–83		23	—
1983–84	Crystal Palace	42	—
1984–85		42	—
1985–86		39	—
1986–87		42	—
1987–88		27	—
1987–88	Cardiff C	13	—
1988–89		45	—
1989–90		9	—
1989–90	*Blackpool*	15	—
1990–91	Hereford U	41	—

WOOD, Mark

Born Scarborough 27.6.72.   Ht 5 7
Wt 9 12
Midfield. From Trainee.

Season	Club	App	Goals
1990–91	York C	1	—

WOOD, Paul

Born Middlesbrough 1.11.64.   Ht 5 9
Wt 10 04
Forward. From Apprentice.

Season	Club	App	Goals
1982–83	Portsmouth	—	—
1983–84		8	1
1984–85		6	1
1985–86		25	4
1986–87		8	—
1987–88		—	—
1987–88	Brighton	31	4
1988–89		35	1
1989–90		26	3
1989–90	Sheffield U	17	3
1990–91		7	—

1990–91	*Bournemouth*	21 —

WOOD, Steve

Born Bracknell 2.2.63. Ht 6 1   Wt 12 02
Defender. From Apprentice.

Season	Club	App	Goals
1979–80	Reading	2	—
1980–81		6	—
1981–82		32	—
1982–83		18	—
1983–84		37	3
1984–85		46	1
1985–86		46	4
1986–87		32	1
1987–88	Millwall	22	—
1988–89		35	—
1989–90		21	—
1990–91		25	—

WOOD, Trevor

Born Jersey 3.11.68 Ht 5 11   Wt 13 00
Goalkeeper. From Apprentice.

Season	Club	App	Goals
1986–87	Brighton	—	—
1987–88		—	—
1988–89	Port Vale	2	—
1989–90		3	—
1990–91		32	—

WOODMAN, Andy

Born Denmark Hill 11.8.71.   Ht 6 1
Wt 12 04
Goalkeeper. From Apprentice.

Season	Club	App	Goals
1989–90	Crystal Palace	—	—
1990–91		—	—

WOODS, Chris

Born Boston 14.11.59.   Ht 6 2   Wt 12 08
Goalkeeper. From Apprentice. England
B,Under-21, 24 full caps.

Season	Club	App	Goals
1976–77	Nottingham F	—	—
1977–78		—	—
1978–79		—	—
1979–80	QPR	41	—

Season	Club	App	Goals
1980–81		22	—
1980–81	*Norwich C*	10	—
1981–82	Norwich C	42	—
1982–83		42	—
1983–84		42	—
1984–85		38	—
1985–86		42	—
1986–87	Rangers	42	—
1987–88		39	—
1988–89		24	—
1989–90		32	—
1990–91		36	—

WOODS, Neil

Born York 30.7.66.   Ht 6 1   Wt 12 12
Forward. From Apprentice.

Season	Club	App	Goals
1982–83	Doncaster R	4	—
1983–84		7	1
1984–85		6	2
1985–86		30	7
1986–87		18	6
1986–87	Rangers	3	—
1987–88	Ipswich T	19	4
1988–89		1	—
1989–90		7	1
1989–90	Bradford C	14	2
1990–91		—	—
1990–91	Grimsby T	44	12

WOODS, Ray

Born Birkenhead 7.6.65   Ht 5 11
Wt 10 00
Forward. From Apprentice.

Season	Club	App	Goals
1982–83	Tranmere R	1	—
1983–84		6	2
From Colne D.			
1988–89	Wigan Ath	8	—
1989–90		—	—
1990–91		20	3
1990–91	Coventry C	12	1

WOODTHORPE, Colin

Born Ellesmere Pt 13.1.69.   Ht 5 11
Wt 11 08
Defender. From Apprentice.

1986–87	Chester C	30	2
1987–88		35	—
1988–89		44	3
1989–90		46	1
1990–91	Norwich C	1	—

WORSLEY, Graeme

Born Liverpool 4.1.69   Ht 5 10   Wt 11 02
Defender. From Bootle.

1988–89	Shrewsbury T	6	—
1989–90		15	—
1990–91		31	1

WORTHINGTON, Gary

Born Cleethorpes 10.11.66.   Ht 5 10
Wt 10 05
Forward. From Apprentice. England
Youth.

1984–85	Manchester U	—	—
1985–86		—	—
1986–87	Huddersfield T	—	—
1987–88	Darlington	9	3
1988–89		31	12
1989–90	Wrexham	42	12
1990–91		30	6
1990–91	Wigan Ath	12	5

WORTHINGTON, Nigel

Born Ballymena 4.11.61.   Ht 5 11
Wt 12 05
Defender. From Ballymena U. Northern
Ireland Youth, 32 full caps.

1981–82	Notts Co	2	—
1982–83		41	3
1983–84		24	1
1983–84	Sheffield W	14	1
1984–85		38	1
1985–86		15	—
1986–87		35	—
1987–88		38	—
1988–89		28	—
1989–90		32	2
1990–91		33	1

WRATTEN, Paul

Born Middlesbrough 29.11.70   Ht 5 7
Wt 9 13
Midfield. From Trainee. England Youth.

1988–89	Manchester U	—	—
1989–90		—	—
1990–91		2	—

WRIGHT, Alan

Born Ashton-under-Lyme 28.9.71.
Ht 5 4   Wt 9 04
Midfield. From Schoolboy, Trainee.
England Schools, Youth.

1987–88	Blackpool	1	—
1988–89		16	—
1989–90		24	—
1990–91		45	—

WRIGHT, George

Born South Africa 22.12.69.   Ht 5 7
Wt 10 02
Defender. From Hutcheson Vale BC.

1987–88	Hearts	—	—
1988–89		—	—
1989–90		1	—
1990–91		17	2

WRIGHT, Ian

Born Lichfield 10.3.72.
Defender. From Trainee.

1989–90	Stoke C	1	—
1990–91		1	—

WRIGHT, Ian

Born Woolwich 3.11.63.   Ht 5 11
Wt 11 06
Forward. From Greenwich Bor. England
B. 4 full caps.

1985–86	Crystal Palace	32	9
1986–87		38	8
1987–88		41	20

1988–89	....	42	24
1989–90	....	26	8
1990–91	....	38	15

WRIGHT, Mark

Born Manchester 29.1.70 Ht 5 11
Wt 10 12
Defender. From Trainee.

1988–89	Everton	—	—
1989–90	....	1	—
1990–91	....	—	—
1990–91	*Blackpool*	3	—
1990–91	*Huddersfield T*	10	1

WRIGHT, Mark

Born Dorchester 1.8.63. Ht 6 3 Wt 12 01
Defender. From Amateur. England Under-21, 40 full caps.

1980–81	Oxford U	—	—
1981–82	....	10	—
1981–82	Southampton	3	—
1982–83	....	39	2
1983–84	....	29	1
1984–85	....	36	—
1985–86	....	33	3
1986–87	....	30	1
1987–88	....	—	—
1987–88	Derby Co	38	3
1988–89	....	33	1
1989–90	....	36	6
1990–91	....	37	—

WRIGHT, Paul

Born East Kilbride 17.8.67. Ht 5 8
Wt 10 08
Forward. S Form. Scotland Youth, Under-21.

1983–84	Aberdeen	1	—
1984–85	....	—	—
1985–86	....	10	2
1986–87	....	25	4
1987–88	....	9	4
1988–89	....	23	6
1989–90	QPR	15	5

| 1989–90 | Hibernian .... | 3 | 1 |
| 1990–91 | .... | 33 | 6 |

WRIGHT, Stephen

Born Bellshill 27.8.71. Ht 5 10 Wt 10 10
Defender. From Aberdeen Lads. Scotland Youth, Under-21.

1987–88	Aberdeen	—	—
1988–89	....	—	—
1989–90	....	1	—
1990–91	....	17	1

WRIGHT, Tommy

Born Belfast 29.8.63. Ht 6 1 Wt 13 05
Goalkeeper. From Linfield. Northern Ireland 4 full caps.

1987–88	Newcastle U	—	—
1988–89	....	9	—
1989–90	....	14	—
1990–91	....	—	—
1990–91	*Hull C*	6	—

WRIGHT, Tommy

Born Dunfermline 10.1.66. Ht 5 7
Wt 9 10
Forward. From Apprentice. Scotland Under-21.

1982–83	Leeds U	4	1
1983–84	....	25	8
1984–85	....	42	14
1985–86	....	10	1
1986–87	....	—	—
1986–87	Oldham Ath	28	7
1987–88	....	41	9
1988–89	....	43	7
1989–90	Leicester C	41	3
1990–91	....	44	7

WRIGHTSON, Jeff

Born Newcastle 18.5.68. Ht 5 11
Wt 11 00
Defender. From Apprentice.

| 1986–87 | Newcastle U .... | 4 | — |

Season	Club	League Appearances/Goals	
1987–88	Preston NE	25	—
1988–89		38	—
1989–90		26	—
1990–91		40	3

YALLOP, Frank

Born Watford 4.4.64. Ht 5 11   Wt 11 04
Defender. From Apprentice. England
Youth, Canada full caps.

Season	Club	League Appearances/Goals	
1981–82	Ipswich T	—	—
1982–83		—	—
1983–84		6	—
1984–85		10	—
1985–86		34	—
1986–87		31	—
1987–88		41	2
1988–89		40	2
1989–90		31	—
1990–91		45	—

YANUSHEVSKI, Viktor

Born Minsk 23.1.60.
Defender. From CSKA Moscow. USSR
full caps.

Season	Club	League Appearances/Goals	
1990–91	Aldershot	6	1

YATES, Dean

Born Leicester 26.10.67.   Ht 6 1
Wt 10 04
Defender. From Apprentice. England
Under-21.

Season	Club	League Appearances/Goals	
1984–85	Notts Co	8	—
1985–86		44	4
1986–87		42	9
1987–88		46	2
1988–89		41	6
1989–90		45	6
1990–91		41	4

YATES, Mark

Born Birmingham 24.1.70.   Ht 5 11
Wt 11 09
Midfield. From Trainee.

Season	Club	League Appearances/Goals	
1987–88	Birmingham C	3	—
1988–89		20	3
1989–90		20	2
1990–91		9	1

YATES, Steve

Born Bristol 29.1.70. Ht 5 11 Wt 11 00
Defender. From Trainee.

1986–87	Bristol R	2	—
1987–88		—	—
1988–89		35	—
1989–90		42	—
1990–91		34	—

YORKE, Dwight

Born Tobago 3.12.71. Ht 5 10 Wt 11 12
Forward. From St Clair's Coaching
School, Tobago.

1989–90	Aston Villa	2	—
1990–91		18	2

YOUDS, Edward

Born Liverpool 3.5.70 Ht 6 0 Wt 10 00
Defender. From Trainee.

1988–89	Everton	—	—
1989–90		—	—
1989–90	*Cardiff C*	1	—
1989–90	*Wrexham*	20	2
1990–91	Everton	8	—

YOUNG, Eric

Born Singapore 25.3.60. Ht 6 3
Wt 12 06
Defender. From Slough Town. Wales 6
full caps.

1982–83	Brighton	—	—
1983–84		30	4
1984–85		35	3
1985–86		32	2
1986–87		29	1
1987–88	Wimbledon	29	3
1988–89		35	1
1989–90		35	5
1990–91	Crystal Palace	34	3

YOUNG, Richard

Born Nottingham 31.12.68 Ht 6 3
Wt 13 07
Forward. From Apprentice.

1986–87	Notts Co	35	5
1987–88	Southend U	7	—
1988–89		2	—
1988–89	*Wimbledon*	—	—
1988–89	Exeter C	14	4
1989–90		28	6
1990–91		7	—

ZONDERVAN, Romeo

Born Surinam 4.3.59.   Ht 5 11   Wt 10 10
Midfield. From Den Haag and Twente.
Holland Schools, Under-21, full caps.

Season	Club		
1981–82	WBA	14	—
1982–83		41	2
1983–84		29	3
1983–84	Ipswich T	8	2
1984–85		41	1
1985–86		28	2
1986–87		39	1
1987–88		29	4
1988–89		37	3
1989–90		30	—
1990–91		34	—

ZORICICH, Chris

Born New Zealand 3.5.69.   Ht 5 11
Wt 11 10
Defender.

Season	Club		
1989–90	Leyton Orient	—	—
1990–91		28	—